THE VICT

OWEN CHADWICK

THE VICTORIAN CHURCH

PART I

1829–1859

SCM PRESS LTD

British Library Cataloguing in Publication Data

Chadwick, Owen
The Victorian church.——3rd ed.
Part 1 : 1829–1859
1. Great Britain——Church history——19th
century
I. Title
274.1′081   BR759
ISBN 0–334–02409–9

First published 1966 by A. & C. Black
Third edition 1971
This paperback edition first published 1987 by
SCM Press Ltd
26–30 Tottenham Road London N1 4BZ

Printed in Great Britain by
Redwood Burn Ltd
Trowbridge, Wilts

PREFACE

CERTAIN parts of the early chapters have already appeared before the public: the section on church rates is based upon the Albrecht Stumpff Memorial Lecture at Queen's College, Birmingham, delivered on 29 May 1961; parts of chapters I and II formed the Sir D. Owen Evans Lectures at University College, Aberystwyth, in December 1963; parts of chapters IV and V formed the Edward Cadbury Lectures at the University of Birmingham in March 1964; parts of chapter VIII the Zabriskie Lectures at the Protestant Episcopal Theological Seminary in Virginia, 1966.

The work would hardly have been possible without generous access to unpublished material.

I have to acknowledge the gracious permission of Her Majesty the Queen to make use of material in the Royal Archives.

The Cardinal Prefect of the Sacred Congregation of Propaganda and Mgr. Kowalsky; the Trustees of the Broadlands Archives; Mr. A. Ll. Armitage, President of Queens' College, Cambridge; the librarians of Lambeth Palace, the Archdiocese of Westminster, Rugby School, Trinity College at Cambridge, Wadham College, Oriel College, Keble College, Pusey House; the Norwich City Library; the Fathers of the Oratory at Birmingham; the Dean and Chapter of Durham; the Oblates of St Charles at Bayswater; Mrs. J. R. H. Moorman; Canon J. Norwood; and the incumbents of several parishes—have kindly allowed me access to their papers.

I owe thanks for information and suggestions and criticism to Mr. Robert Mackworth Young, Professor John Roach, Father Stephen Dessain, Dr. John Kent, Dr. G. F. A. Best, Mr. Roger Fulford, Dr. Derek Beales, Mr. David Newsome, Miss M. L. Burn, Mr. E. H. Milligan, Mrs. Georgina Battiscombe, Mrs. Kathleen Lamb, Mr. Hugh Mead, Mr. Geoffrey Rowell, Mr. G. A. K. Howes, Dr. B. E. Hardman, Mr. Martin Chadwick, Mr. A. S. Bell, Dr. G. V. Bennett, and Miss Edith Baker.

CONTENTS

INTRODUCTION

VICTORIAN England was religious. Its churches thrived and multiplied, its best minds brooded over divine metaphysic and argued about moral principle, its authors and painters and architects and poets seldom forgot that art and literature shadowed eternal truth or beauty, its legislators professed outward and often accepted inward allegiance to divine law, its men of empire ascribed national greatness to the providence of God and Protestant faith. The Victorians changed the face of the world because they were assured. Untroubled by doubt whether Europe's civilisation and politics were suited to Africa or Asia, they saw vast opportunities open to energy and enterprise, and identified progress with the spread of English intelligence and English industry. They confidently used the word English to describe Scots and Welsh and Irish. Part of their confidence was money, a people of increasing wealth and prosperity, an ocean of retreating horizons. And part was of the soul. God is; and we are his servants, and under his care, and will do our duty.

The Victorian age continued till the war of 1914. But boom and strike and slump, and the new power of the worker, had already weakened the assurance of money, the stability of a merchant standing serene in his counting-house. And earlier still the Victorian soul found itself trembling upon the edge of chasms. Public law and private morals, mental philosophy and social convention—the life of the nation was rooted in age-long conviction of Christian truth. And mid-Victorian England asked itself the question, for the first time in popular understanding, is Christian faith true?

The question had been asked before; by medieval schoolmen as an exercise of the lecture-room, by Hobbes and Hume, by Voltaire and Rousseau. Among English aristocrats of 1750 were plenty of well-bred sceptics. Such had not vanished from Victorian England. The queen's first prime minister hardly ever went to church and stretched his well-read mind pleasantly upon hard religious questions. But the morals of the people depended upon Christian truth. The most sceptical of lords did not want the faith of the poor shaken. It was observed or believed that robbery and fornication and extravagance and drunkenness went with laxity in religion, that God-fearing families were sober, honest, self-respecting. The French Revolution confirmed among English people a desire to be Christian. They saw the end of Christianity to mean the end of public morals.

Dreary was the typical Victorian epithet to describe atheism. Early Victorians expected hopelessness of a man who scorns providence and fixes his eyes upon this world. It seemed deliberate and unnecessary rejection of the noblest in human aspiration. Because atheism sometimes accompanied moral failure, and reeked of guillotine or anarchy, the Victorians strove earnestly to make Christianity alive to their children. And still the question nagged, is atheism true? This was torment to the later Victorian soul, that a philosophy which nearly everyone confessed to be dangerous might nevertheless be found probable.

Posterity has seen *The Origin of Species*, published by Charles Darwin in 1859, as symbol of this loss of assurance. The reality, as we shall see, was not simple. But I take date and book to represent an important fact of English history. Doubt was growing before 1860 in the Victorian soul. But until that year it scarcely touched the national life, the assumptions of legislators, the convictions of moralists. We can study early Victorian England and its churches as though doubt was almost as rare and academic as a century before. After 1859 that is not possible.

Darwin was only a sign of a movement bigger than Darwin, bigger than biological science, bigger than intellectual enquiry. In 1886 a professed atheist was permitted to take a seat in the House of Commons. This event occurred when the churches of England flourished as almost never before. It had a little to do with the question in the Victorian soul. It had more to do with the development of the English constitution. For a second question pressed upon England: how democratic shall the constitution be and if democratic or representative, must not all religions be equal before the law?

The second great question therefore was the alliance of church and state. Everyone confessed England to be Christian and nearly everyone wanted to keep the country Christian or make it more Christian. Since the English formed a people out of Saxon tribes, their Christianity had been displayed by an established church. The church in England was earlier than the state and helped to mould tribes into nation.

In the age of the Reformation the English grew articulate about their nationality. Through political turmoil and foreign menace and civil war, the governing classes came to identify Roman Catholic with disloyalty to England and Protestant dissenter with disloyalty to the king. By the reign of Charles II the reformed Church of England as by law established had become inseparable from national consciousness. How inseparable was proved by the exile of a Roman Catholic sovereign in the revolution of 1688. Since that revolution every sovereign and every spouse of the sovereign must by law be a member of the Church of England. After 1673 every member of a municipal corporation and every other senior officer of state must assent to the established church.

Political facts seldom correspond to political theory. There was anomaly in Scotland, where the church established by the same state differed in doctrine and organisation from the Church of England; anomaly in Ireland, where seven-eighths of the people refused to belong to the church established by law; anomaly in Wales, where more than half the people refused to belong to the same church; anomaly in the handful of Protestant dissenters who sat in the House of Commons, and in dissenters who were members of municipal corporations. The old world disregarded majorities. The world after the French Revolution hankered for representation, extension of the vote, equality before the law. In 1828 the old test and corporation acts, which would have excluded dissenters from municipal corporations but for the annual acts of indemnity, were almost casually repealed.

And therefore the great question of constitution in church and state affected every town and village in the country, embittered relations, bred enmity between church and chapel, governed the utterance and programme of political candidates, entered class-room and guildhall. Except in Ireland and Wales and among Independents or Quakers, the question was not usually framed, ought there to be an established church? England continued to believe in a church as by law established, which in many eyes was part of Englishness as well as wise Christianity. The question was framed, how is an established church compatible with equality before the law? Or, does equality before the law include religious equality?

The Victorians plagued themselves over the subject. It was not agony in the soul like doubts about Christian truth. But it made immediate difference to a man's practical thinking and his vote if he had a vote. Establishment in Ireland was worst till Gladstone settled it; establishment in Scotland was for a few years almost as tiresome to Whitehall; establishment in Wales was smouldering ash, hardly noticed till Queen Victoria was a mature widow, but then blown into flames by Welsh eloquence; establishment troubled some English villages and all English towns, the right of burial or of education, the duty of repairing the church; establishment in the great cities, where slums of heathen masses were believed to need religion and morals and education, impossible to provide without assistance from the state, and how shall the state provide without breaking a rule of religious equality?

Not only was the problem for the law. It spoilt friendliness of Christian bodies, raised barriers between denominations, and encouraged questions about religious authority and the truths of doctrine. Scientist and historian asked quietly and prudently, *what is truth?* The same question was asked less quietly in a babel of competing sects. The world moved out of an age of toleration, where a single church dominated, into an age of equality where speakers and writers sought to capture the public mind. The change coincided with the new power of the press. We are so familiar with a free market of religious or philosophical ideas that we find it hard to realise the discomfort of early Victorians when religious argument came out of lecture-room or back street and stood on a box at Marble Arch. The press made religious strife more strident, aggressive, and continuous. It had the merit of making everyone more exercised about the debate, the demerit of breaking tables of Sinai in the dust.

Free competition in religion is so repellent to religious instinct that we shrink from an evident truth of history, that the age of religious equality encouraged every Christian body to strive; if not to be more devout, at least to be better organised, more liberal, more popular, and open-minded. A placard of *All welcome* outside church or chapel is an offspring of that age. Chapels came out of the back streets and occupied prominent and elaborate buildings in the market square. A Roman Catholic prelate returned from Rome as cardinal in flaming cloak. Wayside pulpits began to remind the passer-by of great texts.

This new aggressiveness derived from a higher need than competition. About the beginning of Queen Victoria's reign, or a few years before, it was discovered with surprise that England, if a Christian country, contained multitudes of citizens who were not Christian. It dawned upon the public that England was no longer a country of villages and godly poor. By 1840 the idea of mission not only to heathen overseas but to heathen at home was established in Christian minds. They understood as yet little of the social consequences of modern industry. But they perfectly understood that the number of babies in England was outgrowing churches and schools, and that conditions of city life demanded radical attitudes of evangelism and pastoral care. Therefore they approached the manufacturing poor more loudly and insistently than was fitting to the establishment of squires a century before.

The Victorians inherited a great movement of the religious spirit, which we have agreed to name evangelical. Wesley discovered that unadorned gospel of atonement preached to labouring crowds converted on the instant. The efficacy or mode or nature of these conversions was controversial in Wesley's day and remained in perpetual doubt. But evangelicals had too potent an experience to hesitate. Throughout the mid-Victorian age the evangelical movement was the strongest religious force in British life. The direct descendants of Wesley formed the largest group outside the establishment. But evangelical fervour touched every denomination besides Methodists. Congregationalists and Baptists and Quakers were warmed by its fire. Within the established church was a small but growing group of evangelical clergymen, who attained their summit of influence as Queen Victoria was widowed. But outside the Anglican clergy who called themselves evangelical were high churchmen and converts to Rome whose mind and piety accepted typical insights of evangelical tradition. If we look at the Church of England alone, evangelicals often appear weak and despised. If we look at the religious map of all England, from Brompton Oratory among Roman Catholics to the simplest Quaker meetinghouse in Rochdale, we trace at unexpected points the evangelical mind. To many Victorians evangelical doctrine was the authentic voice and the scriptural piety of Protestant Reformation. It looked to be the sharpest arrow to pierce the soul of labouring heathen. In contemplating Victorian religion we need to remember the Salvation Army as well as Oxford University.

Across the seas evangelical mission was known contemptuously as Exeter hall, from that building in the Strand where missionary societies held each year their May meetings. Modern transport and emigration and expanding Europe invited missions to Buddhist and Hindu, Muslim and animist, and insisted that all churches should shepherd their emigrant settlers. Endeavour to care for new people at home was paralleled by extraordinary and romantic endeavour to care for new people overseas. The expansion of English Christianity into Africa and Asia elicited rare heroism and devotion. Just as political expansion helped British self-confidence, so missionary expansion helped Christian self-confidence. If they disregarded the hidden needle which pricked them with a tiny pain, whether they carried nothing but truth, the Victorian churches had a message for the world and knew it.

This volume treats only of England and will not enter English lands abroad. But the missions must not be forgotten in understanding Victorian piety.

The leading questions thus before the nation, in the succession by which they troubled England, were these:

First, whether representative government was compatible with an established church; that is, how religious inequality could be married to political equality.

Second, whether Christian churches, established or dissenting, could adjust themselves to industrial revolution, speedy growth of population, and empire overseas.

Third, whether the Christian church taught truth.

I turn to the constitutional revolution of 1829–32, which asked the first of these questions, not in a whisper.

CHAPTER I

CHURCH IN DANGER

I. CATHOLIC EMANCIPATION

THE third reading of the bill for the emancipation of the Roman Catholics from their civil disabilities was carried in the House of Lords on Friday, 13 April 1829. Even at this twelfth hour some ultras thought that King George IV might veto it. On Monday, 16 April, hating the bill and sobbing as his gouty hand signed, the king returned it approved. 'God bless us, and his church!' exclaimed Lord Eldon sadly and hopelessly.[1] The Duke of Norfolk, senior Roman Catholic peer, asked whether King George IV would be pleased with an address of thanks from the English Roman Catholics; and the Duke of Wellington as prime minister replied that it would be better not, since the act aimed to efface all distinctions among the king's subjects on the score of religion. Pope Pius VIII granted an audience to the English envoy in Rome, and told him that nothing could equal the gratitude which he felt to King George IV and the British government.[2]

Most Englishmen, Welshmen and Scotsmen were indifferent or hostile to the act. Historians have doubted whether a reformed House of Commons, a Parliament more representative, more submissive to popular opinion, more afraid of its constituents, could then have passed it. The Englishman knew himself to be Protestant. The memories or legends of his history, from fires of Smithfield to glorious revolution of 1688, were vague but powerful in his feeling that popery was un-English and ought legally to be discouraged. Gladstone, then an undergraduate at Christ Church, reported to his family that his college scout was troubled about the king breaking his coronation oath, that the bedmakers were in a great fright, and that the egg-woman wondered how Mr. Peel, always such a well-behaved man at

[1] Twiss, *Eldon*, iii, 87.
[2] Ellenborough, ii, 22; cf. J. F. Broderick, *The Holy See and the Irish Movement*, 1951, 70.

7

the university, could think of letting in the Roman Catholics. Some simple people attributed the bad weather of that summer to the passing of the bill.[1]

Illiterate citizens were confronted with pictures of Bloody Mary burning heretics, with large-lettered placards about murder and Judge Jeffreys, with the question whether they would have a Protestant or a Popish king. Even the king's brother, Duke Ernest of Cumberland, told the House of Lords that the question was whether the country was to be a Protestant country with a Protestant government or a Roman Catholic country with a Roman Catholic government. Colonel Wilson told the House of Commons that the ministers were deliberately asking the king to build a stepping-stone to the scaffold with his own hands—though a neighbouring member tried to pull him down by his coat-tails. If these opinions were evident in Parliament, they were still more evident among the people. Cartoonists showed the Tory ministers responsible for the bill, the Duke of Wellington and Mr. Peel, carrying rosaries and kissing the pope's toe.[2] The bill passed, not because a majority of Englishmen wanted it, but because the government expected civil war in Ireland if it refused to concede the Roman Catholic claims. Wellington afterwards confessed that his only reason for granting emancipation was that he could not help it.

Underlying the changing relation of church and state during this age was a fact more momentous than the single act of emancipation—the political union with Ireland, passed in 1800-1. Elsewhere in the history of Christianity it has been observed how a state, which by conquest or inheritance or accident acquires a new and large population practising a different religion from the religion of the old population, is forced to modify its religious policy if it wishes to survive as a state. Something of this sort happened to England by the act of union with Ireland. Though England and Ireland were politically united under the crown since the middle ages, it was only with the act of union that the Parliament at Westminster became directly responsible for Irish affairs. The government in London became aware of responsibility for seven million and more persons of whom about five and a half million were Roman Catholics. In those days, before the famine of

[1] Morley (1908 ed.), i, 40. Cf. the tenant at Kingston, and Lady Goderich's maid-servant, in Twiss, *Eldon*, iii, 95.

[2] Hansard, 19 and 26 February 1829, xx, 378; xx, 84; *Mirror of Parliament*, 26 February 1829; Gash, *Peel*, i, 558.

the 1840s and consequent flight or emigration, the population of Ireland was a big fraction of the population of Britain. In 1831 the number of the population returned as living in England and Wales was just over fourteen million. Therefore the government of Westminster acquired direct responsibility for the fate of a number of Roman Catholics equal to more than a third of the total population of England and Wales. To maintain the special disabilities of so large a number of Roman Catholic persons appears in the long view to have been impracticable and preposterous. Home rule was out of the question; and therefore the establishment of the Church of England and Ireland must be altered; and must be altered by a Parliament in which many members wanted strongly to maintain the established church. Either the establishment of the Church of England must be modified, or the union must be ended and home rule given to Ireland. In 1829 home rule was the dream of eccentrics in England and the aim of O'Connell and his agitators in Ireland.

A small majority in the House of Commons had steadily supported the Catholic claims over twenty years, despite the dominance of a Tory government committed to the union of church and state. Among the anti-Catholic minority in the House of Commons, and the majority in the House of Lords, not all were so prejudiced as the cartoonists and the Oxford bedmakers. To many sensible men the revolution of 1688, and the Jacobite rebellions, felt uncomfortably close. They saw the liberties and the greatness of Britain to depend upon a revolution which excluded a Catholic king and enacted a Protestant constitution. They had no desire to revive anti-Catholic penal laws and thought persecution of Catholics intolerable. Justice meant fair treatment before the courts, not political equality. They perceived power and stability in an established structure of historical institutions, and had been taught by the French Revolution to fear the irreverent hands of reformers with abstract principles. The history of England meant more to them than the logic of political theorists. Even Robert Peel, most sensible and moderate of men, resisted the Catholic claims until the summer of 1828, when the crisis in Ireland helped him to change his mind.

The divines of the Church of England were not all hostile to the bill.

Dr. J. B. Sumner had lately been made Bishop of Chester, and was known to be moderate about the Catholic question. In the House of

Lords Bishop Bathurst of Norwich, ancient in years, was the only bishop on the bench who was decisively for the Whigs and committed to Whig desire for emancipation. A few leading divines believed that relief should be given upon principle, and not merely upon grounds of Irish expediency. In 1829 Dr. Thomas Arnold, who the year before became the headmaster of Rugby School, published a booklet entitled *The Christian Duty of conceding the Roman Catholic claims*[1] wherein he maintained that every Englishman ought to support the claims of Irish Roman Catholics on grounds of natural justice; that it is a want of faith in God and an unholy zeal to think that God can be served by injustice. In the course of the arguments of 1828–9 a few more bishops and clergy were persuaded that the government was right, and that the claims must be conceded as expedient, provided that adequate safeguards could be found to secure the Church of England and Ireland. Even Dr. Phillpotts, most militant of Tory clergymen, was ready to accept the bill if stringent pledges were given to the Protestants. For the benefit of anxious churchmen, the Duke of Wellington declared that the passing of the bill would strengthen the Protestant and Anglican establishment. To settle Ireland, to remove a running sore of grievance, must help the stability of the existing constitution. In the House of Commons it was occasionally contended[2] that persecution is what keeps the Roman Catholic Church alive. Optimists expected that freedom in Ireland would remove the obstacle to Protestant advance. Remove the disabilities and you remove the sense of being persecuted. Remove the grievance and you open the mind to reason and light. Though it was predictable that a staunch Whig like Dr. Arnold would believe this, it was less predictable that the level-headed Bishop Lloyd of Oxford believed it enthusiastically. Bishop Sumner of Chester was more hesitant; 'the safety of the whole measure', he wrote to the Duke of Wellington, 'depends very much upon the presumption that the papal cause is a declining cause, and will become so more and more.'[3] Without this act of faith it was possible for good bishops to argue that the constitution was safer if the complaint were settled, and that it was impossible to be secure

---

[1] *Misc. Works*, 5ff.

[2] e.g. Butler Clarke, Hansard, 1828, xix, 666.

[3] Bishop J. B. Sumner of Chester to Wellington, 22 December 1828, Wellington's *Despatches*, v. 350. Besides J. B. Sumner his brother C. R. Sumner of Winchester (to the king's horror, for he was a favourite bishop) was convinced; Bishop Lloyd of Oxford; Bishop Copleston of Llandaff. Cf. Wellington, *Despatches*, v, 324–5; Arnold, *Misc. Works*, 32; Hansard, xx, 92, 1561.

unless the ground of agitation were removed. Ten bishops voted for the second and third readings in the House of Lords, and in the circumstances that was a triumph for the government.

But the nineteen bishops who voted against the second reading, and raised their number to twenty against the third, were more representative of the English church and people. They rejoiced in a weight of seniority, the Archbishops of Canterbury and York, the Bishops of London and Durham. They all dissented from the argument that the constitution would be preserved by settling the grievance, for they believed that this mode of settlement overturned the constitution. Otherwise they varied in their antagonisms. Van Mildert of Durham would have voted against any bill which emancipated the Roman Catholics. Others, like Archbishop Vernon (Harcourt) of York, objected not to any bill but to this bill, on the plea that it failed to provide sufficient safeguards for the Protestant constitution and the established Church of Ireland. Some were not afraid of sad consequences for the Church of England and only feared disestablishment of the Church of Ireland. Others believed that the insecurity of the Church of Ireland must lead afterwards to insecurity of the Church of England, when the voices of Irish Roman Catholic members of Parliament, pledged by their religion to be hostile to Protestantism, were added to the votes of dissenting and radical critics already found at Westminster. Bishop Lloyd of Oxford replied to these anxieties that he had no fear for the Church of England; and as for the Church of Ireland, it was hardly possible for an establishment to be more insecure than that church at the moment. He did not deny danger to the Church of Ireland, but argued that the danger from emancipation was less imminent than the danger from civil war.[1]

Archbishop Howley of Canterbury swayed several votes among the bishops. They liked and respected him. No one could be less liable to popular prejudice. Among politicians he had a reputation for weakness, and some thought him so timid that he could be treated as not present. In truth he was a man of strong principle and quiet courage, who had once been the regius professor of divinity at Oxford and formed a habit of looking at both sides of a question. His stature was small, his countenance benevolent and emaciated, his manner courteous and deferential, his nature retiring and unassuming, his voice peculiar; men claimed that he had never been young. It is evidently

[1] Hansard, xxi, 79ff.

true, but appears incredible, that when a boy at Winchester he knocked down Sydney Smith with a chess board.[1] But what appeared as weakness to the public was not so much timidity as the hesitancy of the theorist. When he made up his mind everyone knew that he decided painfully and reluctantly; and his prudence and tranquillity of mind exerted a quiet influence over his colleagues. He was a classical scholar with a retentive memory, a command of wide information, and fluency in German Italian and Spanish. Unfortunately for his causes he was a lamentable speaker. Though eloquence would have been out of keeping with his character and countenance, he could rarely make a point with decision, his delivery was not only dull but embarrassing, his critics said that he drivelled. He perpetually lost the right words and visibly groped for the wrong, contrived to make a long speech sound interminable, and threw his hearers into a nervous fever. Making a speech at a girls' school, he could not think how to address the girls. 'My dear young friends—my dear girls—my dear young catechumens—my dear Christian friends—my dear young female women.'[2] While Bishop of London he made himself the laughing-stock of the coarse when, snatching vainly for words in the House of Lords, he seemed to suggest that King George IV could do no wrong, even if he misbehaved to his wife. 'It can scarcely be said', reported the *Times* unkindly after his death, 'that what fell from his lips ever deserved to be called a speech.' Governments were to find that this stumbling apologist had clearer principles than he could easily express.[3]

The king preferred bishops who opposed Catholic claims. He refused to allow eminent divines to be considered for bishoprics if

[1] Sydney Smith, *Letter I to Singleton, Works*, 621.

[2] Ellenborough, ii, 3; Romilly's *Diary*, 6 May 1835; *Journals of Caroline Fox*, i, 214. Good study of Howley's character in B. Harrison, *Charge to the Clergy of Maidstone*, 1848; T, 12 February 1848; F. W. Newman, *Phases of Faith* (1850), 2, 18; N. S. Wheaton, *Journal* (1830), 43–44.

[3] Ellenborough, who was a critic of the speech, once admitted that Howley was very effective on the reform bill. Cf. Aspinall, *Three Early Nineteenth Century Diaries*, 144. The story of 'the king can do no wrong' grew in the telling. At its richest DNB declared Howley to assert with much emphasis that the king could do no wrong either morally *or physically*. This is a misreading of the *Times* (12 February 1848), which made him say that the king can do no wrong either morally or politically. The report of his actual words on the bill of pains and penalties upon the queen reads (Hansard, N.S., iii, 1820, 1711): 'It was a maxim of the constitution . . . that the king could do no wrong. . . . This principle, if carried to the full length, would seem to remove all ground for recrimination, all enquiry into the conduct of His Majesty in his conjugal relations. He did not however mean to argue it on such a principle. . . .'

their opinions were not clear against the Catholics. Dr. Copleston was not sanctioned for the see of Llandaff until he satisfied the king that though he could give no pledge to vote against Catholic emancipation in all circumstances he believed it to be inexpedient at the moment. Even when the bill was in the House of Lords the king wrote to at least one of his episcopal protégés, C. R. Sumner of Winchester, demanding that he should not vote for the bill. The king could have no such complaint against Dr. Howley. In 1827 he used Howley as a means of conveying to the public, at a banquet of clergy, that his opinions of the Catholic question, and of his obligations under the coronation oath, were as firm as ever.[1] He was glad to have an archbishop whose opinions coincided with his own.

Howley was translated to the see of Canterbury in July 1828. The Duke of Wellington was already prime minister and engaged upon the path towards emancipation. He would have preferred to nominate to Canterbury someone less celebrated for hostility to Catholic relief. But the few bishops friendly to relief were either antique and Whiggish, like Bathurst, or new arrivals on the Bench. When he took office and formed a cabinet, he formed it on the principle that the cabinet was neutral on the Catholic question, and that the patronage of the crown would be exercised without regard to that question, but would promote men on the sole ground of merit and service. King George IV tried to exempt the higher dignitaries of the Church of England from this principle. Wellington was angry at the idea of refusing to promote men to bishoprics because they were friendly to Catholic claims, and even threatened resignation.[2] He carried his point. Therefore he could hardly object to Dr. Howley, whose personal and scholarly merits everyone applauded, on the sole ground that he agreed with the king about the Catholics. Wellington may have thought that if he was bound to have an archbishop opposed to Catholic emancipation, it was best to have one who looked so easy to frighten.

In order to placate the fears of the archbishop and most churchmen, of the king, and of many moderate Tories, the provisions of the emancipation act must make safe, or appear to make less unsafe, the establishment of the Church of England and Ireland.

[1] Aspinall, *Letters of George IV*, iii, 294–5, 333, 335, 232–3; Wellington, *Despatches*, iv, 273.
[2] Aspinall, *Letters of King George IV*, iii, 399–400. The second name considered for Canterbury in 1828 was van Mildert of Durham. Wellington, *Despatches* iv, 549.

Since the years of the French Revolution the debate over Roman Catholic relief turned upon the nature of the safeguards, or 'securities', which would be be demanded from Roman Catholics in return for the full rights of citizens. Neither Wellington nor Peel questioned that securities were necessary to preserve the Protestant constitution of the state and the establishment of the United Church of England and Ireland. The question was never whether there should be securities or not, but what securities the government must demand from Roman Catholics in exchange for emancipation. They owed, it was said, allegiance to a foreign sovereign, and must afford pledges of their loyalty to a Protestant crown; and their loyalty to a Protestant crown must include pledges to secure the Protestant constitution of the country.

For the king of England must be Protestant and married to a Protestant. At his coronation he must swear a solemn oath to maintain the church as by law established. He was the supreme governor of the Church of England. In the eyes of the pope he was as heretical as Queen Elizabeth. And popes had released Catholics from the duty of allegiance to a heretical sovereign. To demand guarantees of loyalty from Catholics was part of every plan for Catholic emancipation.

Tories saw the coronation oath as a security. Not inclined by tradition to underestimate royal power, they believed in the duty of the king to veto any measure which weakened the established church. It had been no matter of form when George III refused to countenance Catholic relief despite pressure from Pitt. It was no matter of form in 1828 and 1829 when Wellington spent wearisome hours softening George IV before bringing in his bill. Some supposed that in the new Britain, where Roman Catholics would exercise parliamentary power, the king could still preserve the establishment. If Catholic votes passed a bill to diminish the privileges of the Church of England, the king could and must protect the Church of England with his veto.

But the passing of Catholic emancipation proved the vanity of relying on the coronation oath. Ultra Tories said that it was impossible for the king not to veto the bill, and pressed the petulant sorely tried king in that sense. Moderates said that the king must have an eye to the strength of the established church, and if amid all the balancing circumstances the church would be less weakened by concession than by rigidity, the king was right to sanction the law. Whigs or radicals argued that the oath was nothing to do with the king's part in making laws, but only with his executive authority as guardian of whatever laws Parliament approved; or that the oath was taken to the people of England and the people could release the sovereign from his obligation; or that the king had no personal duty under the oath, but must interpret it with the advice of his cabinet. No sovereign who took the oath conscientiously could rest content with these laxer modes of dispensing with its obligations.

But the argument was academic. The king's government must be carried on. The coronation oath faded into the background as a security for the Protestant constitution, because it was part of the royal veto. By 1828 the prime minister's threat of resignation was so compelling that a king could only dare to veto a measure if he could find a reasonable cabinet elsewhere. In 1829 he could find no other cabinet.

Thus the coronation oath sank, not into insignificance, but into the background, because the royal veto fell into the background. The king was important because he possessed a distant threat of veto, not because he was able to use it; and by possessing the threat was able to influence ministers and cabinets. In every crisis of church and state the oath was proclaimed by Tory defenders of the church in danger. In every crisis the king ended by accepting the verdict of the parliamentary majority that the bill was not contrary to his oath. King William IV, who possessed a more delicate conscience than his elder brother, suffered twinges about the oath when he resented the church programme of his Whig ministers. In 1835, tormented by severe scruples about a measure which might harm the Church of Ireland, he suggested that the case be submitted to fifteen judges to advise his conscience. In the face of objections he waived the fifteen judges, and demanded to put the case to the lord chancellor. When the lord chancellor refused to give an opinion the king waived the scruples.[1]

Intelligent Tories lost faith in the oath as a political security. Peel, most intelligent and moderate of Tories, was a man naturally inclined to take a liberal view of the oath because he was one of the progenitors of Catholic emancipation. He still thought that the king ought to reject a measure—preferably by refusing leave for its introduction and not by veto of a passed bill—which endangered the maintenance or essential rights of the church, but that it was ridiculous to suppose the oath to

[1] William IV to Lord Melbourne, 15 April 1835; ibid., 16 April 1835. *Melbourne Papers*, Box 7.

entail the duty of vetoing any measure which diminished a privilege of the established church.[1]

Between 1828 and 1840, therefore, the obligation of the coronation oath changed its character. From being understood as an oath to veto any bill which diminished the security of the established church, it became a small additional reason why the sovereign should privately dissuade ministers from measures which affected the office of supreme governor in the established church, and why ministers should be chary of advising the crown to a manifest act against the oath.

The Protestant obligation of the crown was therefore not enough. When Wellington first reconciled himself to the idea that relief must be granted, he dallied over a series of securities which needed something like a concordat with the pope. He suggested the payment of Irish (but not English) Catholic priests by the state, their licensing by government, a veto upon the appointment of Irish bishops or at least upon the exercise of their rights. To put it crudely, the establishment of the Protestant Church of England and Ireland could only be safe if the Roman Catholic Church in Ireland was also established. His advisers ransacked the concordats of other European countries to find good precedent to justify a government, even a Protestant government, insisting upon these measures of control. The Roman Catholic Archbishop of Armagh expressed himself willing to accept a veto by government upon the temporalities of Irish Catholic bishops.[2] Roman Catholic bishops were familiar for thirty years with proposals of this kind, and unlike the Archbishop of Armagh most of them disliked and feared the prospect.

Wellington's advisers were decisive against anything resembling control by concordat. Peel, who for all his moderation was a deep-dyed Protestant, disliked the prospect of a Protestant government recognising the Roman Catholic religion by establishing official relations of stipend and licence and veto. Henry Phillpotts, that stout churchman who was permitted to bombard Wellington with memoranda on the subject, believed that the proposed veto upon bishops would be irritating without being truly effective,[3] and in company

---

[1] Cf., e.g., Hurrell Froude, *Remarks on State Interference in Matters Spiritual*, in *Remains*, iii, 212. Contrast AR, 1833, 99; Parker, *Peel*, ii, 218–20. At the time of the Maynooth question in 1845 Prince Albert asked Peel for papers on the matter; cf. *Add. MSS.* 40441, 158. Cf. also Hansard debate of 6 May 1833.

[2] Dr. Curtis to Wellington, 4 December 1828, Wellington's *Despatches*, v. 308–9.

[3] Wellington, *Despatches*, v. 397 and 444; memoranda of January 1829; for Howley's attitude cf. *Wellington and his Friends* (ed. the Duke of Wellington 1965), 84–85.

with nearly all Tory churchmen prophesied that grants of money to Roman Catholic priests would be very unpopular in England. In February 1829 the government abandoned all idea of safeguards in the form of a concordat. There was to be no security by a quasi-establishment of the Roman Catholic Church in Ireland.

If the Irish were henceforth permitted to elect Roman Catholic members of Parliament, they would introduce a solid new party into the House of Commons. Since the franchise in Ireland was more widely extended than in England, the Irish electors might send to Westminster a large number of radical and Catholic members, reckoned in one estimate at sixty. One of the securities proposed was to limit the number of Roman Catholic members. This was achieved for the time by reducing the number of Irish voters. An act took the vote away from the Irish 40s. freeholders, raising the qualification from 40s. to £10. By removing the popular vote, this was an important political safeguard for the Protestant ascendancy in Ireland. The election of 1830 returned only eight Irish Catholic members to Westminster.

The emancipation act contained other securities for the constitution and the established church. But when the idea of a concordat was abandoned on principle, hard-headed politicians recognised that any other securities would be trivial, and must be trivial if the object of the act was to be achieved. Roman Catholics must not be left with a feeling of political disability. Some members of the cabinet wanted no securities at all, and thought of these provisions more as a sop to secure the passage of the bill through the House of Lords, and as a comfort to the tortured mind of King George IV, than as a buttress to the Protestant constitution. While the cabinet was publicly declaring its proposed securities to be sufficient, at least two of its members privately thought that the effect of the measure must be the establishment within twenty years of the Roman Catholic Church in Ireland.[1] Wellington himself was inclined to doubt the value of these securities. But others of his colleagues conceived the little securities as a genuine safeguard and not simply as a harmless device for passing the bill. Determined to preserve the establishment in something like its existing form, they believed that they would succeed.

The law already provided that a Roman Catholic could not be sovereign. The emancipation act now provided that the same bar

[1] Ellenborough, *Diary*, i, 356–7; Hansard, xx, 1425.

should apply to other offices—regent, lord chancellor, lord chancellor of Ireland, lord lieutenant of Ireland, high commissioner to the general assembly of the Church of Scotland. The lord chancellor possessed the duty or privilege of exercising the patronage of the crown in presenting to a large number of the benefices of the Church of England. If on this ground the lord chancellor might not be a Roman Catholic, what of the prime minister, who exercised patronage more momentous in the nomination of bishops and deans? At first Wellington suggested to the cabinet that no Roman Catholic should become prime minister, and in discussion widened the exclusion to home secretary, foreign secretary and colonial secretary, all of whom must advise the crown on high matters of policy. But Peel feared that these exclusions, and even the sole exclusion from the office of prime minister, would be regarded by Roman Catholics as a disability grave enough to warrant grievance. Roman Catholics must be awarded sufficient equality not to feel oppressed and sufficient inequality to prevent attacks upon the established Church of England and Ireland. Bishop J. B. Sumner of Chester agreed with the view that the ban against a Roman Catholic prime minister would be an irritant, and recommended that the ecclesiastical functions be put into commission if the office were held by a Roman Catholic. The cabinet hesitantly accepted this view. In committee on 24 March 1829, Chandos moved[1] that the bill be amended to prevent the prime minister from being a Roman Catholic. Peel resisted the amendment, partly on the specious plea that the *theory* of the constitution recognised no such person as prime minister. But the act provided that no Roman Catholic might advise the crown in ecclesiastical matters. If a Roman Catholic became prime minister—sensible men in 1829 thought the supposition to be incredible—he was excluded from all part in the nomination of bishops or other ecclesiastical offices, and the duty lapsed to the Archbishop of Canterbury.

The act provided that no Roman Catholic bishop or dean should take the title used by a bishop or dean of the established church. Thus, on the most obvious interpretation of the clauses, it became legal for a Roman Catholic to become Dean of London or Bishop of Westminster, but illegal if he became Bishop of London or Dean of Westminster, since these places were the titles of the Anglican dignitaries. Peel privately disliked the proviso, and Wellington admitted in

[1] Wellington, *Despatches*, v, 350, 476; Hansard, xx, 1425.

the debate that this was no security; but it gave satisfaction, and later helped to lessen friction.

The government believed it necessary to prevent Roman Catholics from performing their rites in public. No civil officer, judge or mayor, for example, might attend public worship in his robes of office or with insignia; no monk might appear in his habit, no procession might walk the streets, no funerals might be conducted at the grave. The most bizarre of these lesser securities provided for the slow death of Jesuit houses and all male religious orders. Though nuns were left undisturbed, every member of a male religious order must register with a clerk of the peace, notifying his name, age, order, place of residence and superior. No religious community shall admit a new member. Anyone becoming a Jesuit or member of a religious order shall be banished and, if he returns, shall be liable to transportation for life. Peel suggested this clause and the cabinet passed it because it would capture many votes.

Archbishop Howley could not believe that this proviso was intended to be anything but a dead letter and sought to be reassured.[1] The cynicism of some members of the cabinet was never more evident than in their welcome for this clause. Though the other securities in the act were in some measure effective, this clause had no chance from the beginning. A return of 1830 showed 117 Jesuits in England and 1 in Wales; 51 Benedictines, 7 Dominicans, 5 Franciscans, 1 Carmelite, 1 Cistercian, and 1 of an order not given on the return, and a more numerous return for Ireland. In 1831 only the counties of Cornwall and Somerset bothered to make a return; in 1832 only Somerset, which returned 1 Cistercian; in 1836 not a single county of England and Wales made a return, except that Flint repeated two old registrations of 1829.[2] The last year in which these returns were printed among the parliamentary papers was in 1863, when there was a nil return. It is a surprise to find that these curious clauses were not repealed until 1926; in which year the clause making it illegal to perform ceremonies or wear a habit in public was also repealed.

Of all these securities, the most important was the oath to be exacted

---

[1] Ellenborough, i, 308; Hansard, xxi, 66.

[2] PP, 1830, xxx, 177; 1831–2, xxx, 53; 1833, xxvii, 561; 1836, xl, 7. The Wiltshire County Record Office at Trowbridge contains a bundle of papers on the registration of 1829 with appended letters. Britain was by no means unique. In Switzerland an ordinance of 1848 against Jesuits was made more stringent in 1874, and they are still (1965) excluded from the country. Compare the existing French laws against religious.

from Roman Catholics who entered Parliament. An oath of this kind appeared in all such negotiations. An oath was provided for English Roman Catholics by an act of 1791, and for Irish Roman Catholics by an act of 1793, which they might take for the purpose of exempting themselves from certain disabilities. The oath of 1791 swore allegiance to the Protestant Succession of the House of Hanover, but in terms which resounded with memories of Guy Fawkes and with popular notions of the history of England. The Catholic promised to defend the king against all conspiracies, to make known all treason, and to renounce all allegiance to Stuart pretenders.

No one doubted that Catholic members of Parliament must take an oath. Protestant members must take the oaths of supremacy, adjuration and allegiance, and these oaths contained Protestant clauses which could not be taken by conscientious Roman Catholics. Should the existing Protestant oaths be altered to enable Catholics to take them, or should Catholics be permitted to take a peculiar oath? Lord Grey, leader of the Whig opposition, disliked the idea of two distinct oaths, and one or two members of Wellington's cabinet agreed that it would be better to draft a new oath for everyone. But past negotiations expected separate oaths; the cabinet was doubtful of pushing a revision of the Protestant oath through Parliament and even more doubtful of pushing it past the king. They decided upon a separate oath for Catholics, based upon the oath of 1791, and newly drafted by Peel.[1]

The momentous clause in the oath was a pledge not to subvert the present church establishment in England or Ireland.

Here the fears of the king and Tory churchmen were most painful. They would never allow emancipation unless they were assured that Roman Catholic members of Parliament would not use their votes to destroy the established church. At first there was talk of disqualifying Catholic members from voting on questions directly or indirectly relating to the established church. Wilmot Horton proposed this plan in the debates, and it was widely expected that some such provision would be made. But it was an intolerable disadvantage if some members could not vote on certain subjects, and it was impossible to determine which subjects affected the established church either directly or indirectly.[2] The fear must be met, not by debarring votes by law,

[1] Ellenborough, *Diary*, i, 311, 386.
[2] Cf. Hansard, xx, 757. For opinions of Wilmot Horton's lack of sense, cf. L. C. Sanders, *Lord Melbourne's Papers*, 376; Ellenborough, *Diary*, i, 123. For the wide expectation of Horton's plan, see Greville, 5 February 1829; Greville thought it

but by relying on the consciences of Catholic members, and demanding from them an oath to preserve the established church.

Accordingly the oath contained a clause which was to be the subject of painful dispute. It had been suggested that the Catholic must pledge himself to maintain the established church. The cabinet considered that no Catholic could reasonably be asked for a promise to *maintain* a Protestant church and that he could only be required not to overthrow; but the clause which became law was stringent:

I do hereby disclaim, disavow, and solemnly abjure any intention to subvert the present church establishment as settled by law within within this realm; and do solemnly swear, that I never will exercise any privilege to which I am, or may become entitled, to disturb or weaken the Protestant religion or Protestant government in the United Kingdom.[1]

Catholics hesitated whether they could take the oath. Some at once did so. When Parliament reassembled on 28 April 1829 three Catholic

---

absurd and impracticable. Lord Harrowby wanted it, and Bunsen, who probably understood little about it, approved the plan; cf. Greville, 4 June 1830.

[1] The whole oath now read:

'I AB do sincerely promise and swear that I will be faithful and bear true allegiance to H.M. King George IV, and will defend him to the utmost of my power against all conspiracies and attempts whatever which shall be made against His Person, Crown, or Dignity. And I will do my utmost endeavour to disclose and make known to H.M., his Heirs and Successors, all treasons and traitorous conspiracies which may be formed against him or them; and I do faithfully promise to maintain, support, and defend, to the utmost of my power, the succession of the Crown, which succession, by an Act, entitled *An Act for the further Limitation of the Crown and better securing the Rights and Liberties of the Subject* is and stands limited to the Princess Sophia, Electress of Hanover, and the Heirs of her body, being Protestants; hereby utterly renouncing and abjuring any obedience or allegiance unto any other person claiming or pretending a right to the Crown of this Realm; and I do further declare, that it is not an article of my faith, and that I do renounce, reject and abjure the opinion, that Princes excommunicated and deprived by the Pope or any other authority of the see of Rome, may be deposed or murdered by their subjects, or by any Person whatsoever; and I do declare, that I do not believe that the Pope of Rome, or any other foreign Prince, Prelate, Person, State or Potentate, hath or ought to have any Temporal or Civil Jurisdiction, Power, Superiority, or Pre-eminence, directly or indirectly within this Realm. I do swear, that I will defend to the utmost of my power the settlement of Property within this Realm, as established by the Laws; and I do hereby disclaim, disavow, and solemnly abjure any Intention to subvert the present Church Establishment as settled by Law within this Realm; and do solemnly swear, That I never will exercise any Privilege to which I am, or may become entitled, to disturb or weaken the Protestant Religion or Protestant Government in the United Kingdom; and I do solemnly, in the presence of God, profess, testify and declare, That I do make this declaration, and every part thereof in the plain and ordinary sense of the words of this oath, without any evasion, equivocation, or mental reservation whatsoever. So help me God.'

peers, led by the Duke of Norfolk, took the prescribed oaths and their seats. On 15 May the first Catholic member took his seat in the Commons—Lord Surrey, from the borough of Horsham, where the Duke of Norfolk had influence.[1] But doubt existed, especially among priests, whether members who took their seats were right in the eyes of their church.

On 4 May 1829 Bishop Baines, Catholic vicar-apostolic for the western district of England, had a long interview with Pope Pius VIII upon the lawfulness of taking the oath. The English vicars-apostolic would have liked a decision from Rome. But the pope said that the oath contained gross imputations against the Catholic religion and could not be sanctioned by a declaration from Rome. He could not approve, but would not condemn, and left it to their decision. On 24 November 1829 the four English vicars-apostolic, and their two coadjutors, agreed that the oath might safely be taken by Catholics.[2]

Their subjects did not always agree. Mr. Andrews, printer and publisher in the City of London, drew up a petition against the 'soul-ensnaring oath', which he believed it immoral to take in order to qualify for civil rights.[3] An eccentric Yorkshire naturalist, Mr. Waterton, declared that Catholic emancipation had not enabled him to become a member of Parliament or magistrate, because no power on earth would make him take an oath binding him to abjure an intention of subverting an establishment church which he would do everything in his power, 'fairly and honourably as a gentleman', to upset.[4] A Catholic bishop in the British Empire caused alarm at home by refusing to take the oath. When a council was established at Malta the Bishop of Malta found that he must take the oath, and said that he must consult the Pope. He sent a copy of the oath to Rome, which replied that it could not sanction the oath.

But most English and Irish Catholics, though disliking the language of the oath, felt no difficulty about taking it. They all confessed that

[1] But the phrasing of the act excluded Roman Catholic members of the House of Commons until the next election. Daniel O'Connell, elected for County Clare before the passing of the act, had been unable to take his seat, and after all was still unable to take his seat. On 18 May he came to the bar of the House and pleaded his right of admission. But the argument was hopeless, the by-election was ordered, and O'Connell took his seat unopposed at the next session. Walpole, *Hist.*, ii, 520–5.

[2] Baines to Lord Shrewsbury, 28 April 1838; Hansard, xlii, 968. Consultators at Rome had been asked to express opinions on the form of the oath in the winter of 1828–9; cf. *PA Scritture Riferite: Anglia* VIII/530ff.

[3] *Catholic Magazine*, ii, 731, November 1832.

[4] Letter of 6 March 1835 from Wakefield; Hansard, xli, 300.

they were bound to abstain from voting on certain subjects. It was certain, the *Catholic Magazine* declared in November 1833, that the oath was lawful, but only if Catholics in Parliament observed its limitations with scrupulous care. What were these limitations, and how far did they extend? On which subjects ought they to abstain? It was understood, by scrupulous Catholics as by adherents of the Protestant constitution, that Catholics would abstain from questions concerning the church. Which questions concerned the church?

English Catholic members of Parliament were not easily elected unless they had strong local influence, and were therefore aristocrats and conservatives. The reform of constituencies in 1832, by abolishing members who were nominated by a great patron, made it more difficult for a Catholic to be elected from an English constituency to the House of Commons. Mr. Petre, M.P. for Ilchester in 1832, took a stringent view of his obligations under the oath. English and Irish Catholic peers shared the same scruples.

But Daniel O'Connell and his Irish radical members were not able, and would not have been allowed by their constituents, to take so scrupulous a view of the oath. They represented the popular drive of the Irish people against English and Protestant ascendancy. A fortress of that ascendancy was the established Church of Ireland which members were pledged not to subvert. O'Connell, backed hesitantly by some Catholic moral theologians, sought to distinguish the church from the property of the church. O'Connell confessed that he would not vote on a motion to alter the Thirty-nine Articles or the number of dioceses; but over the property of the church he claimed to be as free as any other member. With this distinction he was prepared to vote for motions which proposed to confiscate some of the property of the Church of Ireland for the benefit of the Irish Catholic population. The Roman Catholics, he said, swore only not to subvert the established church, they did not swear to continue it. 'Surely religion is not a thing of pounds, shillings and pence? . . . Will the Protestant church be less an established church if deprived of its temporalities?'[1] He argued that though the king had been allowed or forced to interpret his coronation oath in a sense as wide as that suggested for the Catholic oath, no one accused the king of perjury.

---

[1] Hansard, xxii, 53, when O'Connell moved for a select committee to enquire into the oath; and *Morning Chronicle*, 2 April 1833; Hansard, xv, 426, 432; DR, 2 (1837), 563ff. (by Bagshawe); DR, 4 (1838), 485ff. (by Graves).

The contention did not please the more scrupulous among English Catholic peers. It encountered charges of perjury from stout controversialists of the ultra-Tory party, and was useful in elections against radical candidates. In 1836 Dr. Phillpotts, now Bishop of Exeter and still a warrior, delivered a charge to his clergy, accusing the Irish members of treachery aggravated by perjury, and continued in Parliament to accuse them of violating their oaths. The charge was renewed whenever debates over Irish church property waxed hot. The Catholic members, for the most part, continued to honour their pledge with scrupulous care; and leading Protestant parliamentarians—Lord Melbourne, Lord John Russell, Sir Robert Peel, Lord Campbell—defended those who thought it right to interpret the pledge broadly.[1] Even Dr. Phillpotts, who scoured the realm for perjured Catholics, once admitted that he trusted English Roman Catholics 'generally not universally', and from him this was praise.[2]

The social consequences of emancipation were immediate. The coronation of King William IV was the first since the Revolution which a Catholic bishop attended in his habit.[3]

2. THE REFORM ACT AND THE CHURCH

The emancipation act weakened the Tory party. The Tories had held office almost continuously since the early years of the French Revolution. Wellington and Peel, jettisoning a plank of the traditional Tory platform, divided the party. Peel was not re-elected for Oxford University and found a seat at Westbury, Wellington was regarded for a time as a traitor. The Tory party was not in ruins; but its right wing could not forgive. Some members of the party began to favour the Whig clamour for parliamentary reform, on the notion that a more representative Parliament would not have passed emancipation. A general election, made necessary by the death of George IV on 26 June 1830, lost the Tories about thirty seats. The government was too weak

---

[1] Hansard, xli, 316 (Lord Melbourne); lxxi, 733 (Lord Campbell); cii, 1199 (Peel).

[2] Hansard, xli, 1311. Serious attempts to alter the words of the oath were made in 1859 and 1865; in 1859 after the Protestant oath was altered to admit Jews to Parliament, and in 1865 when the question of disestablishing the Church of Ireland had come to the forefront of politics. The suggested revision omitted any pledge not to subvert the establishment, and the more lurid phrases at the end of the oath. PP, 1859, ii, 717, and 1865, iv, 375. In 1865 it passed the Commons, but was rejected by the Lords. Hansard, clxxx, 764ff. Cf. also Br. Mag., 1849, 2, 77–91. The change came in 1866.

[3] Br. Mag., 5, 1834, 353.

to meet the surge of popular opinion which followed the news of the French Revolution of 1830, and the fire was fed by the troubles of the English labourer. In November, Wellington made the notorious statement that the system of representation needed no reform. The government fell, and a Whig cabinet under Earl Grey, pledged to reform in state and church, came into office. Wellington's last act[1] as prime minister was a hasty filling of the ecclesiastical preferments. Dr. Phillpotts, who for thirty years would carry Tory principles of the extreme right into every aspect of affairs, was elevated to the see of Exeter.

Certainly the church looked more likely to run into danger from the Whigs.

The first reform bill passed its second reading in the Commons on 23 March 1831. On a defeat in committee King William IV agreed to a dissolution, and the general election gave the reformers a working majority. The new bill swept away the pocket or nomination boroughs, gave the new industrial cities an adequate number of representatives, and established a vote in the boroughs for every householder rated at £10, and a vote in the counties for £10 copyholders and £50 lease-holders. It passed the House of Commons in September 1831. Grey was not confident that the bill would pass the Lords and tried to sway the votes of the bishops to the Whig side. Except for Dr. Maltby of Chichester, whom Grey hurriedly[2] appointed, all the bishops had been nominated under Tory governments. Grey threatened them, telling them to put their house in order. The only prelate to speak in the debate was Archbishop Howley, and he against. On 8 October 1831 the House of Lords rejected the bill by forty-one votes. Two bishops, Maltby and (by proxy) the venerable Bathurst of Norwich, voted for the reform bill. The archbishop and twenty of his colleagues voted in the majority. Six bishops abstained; the Archbishop of York

---

[1] Greville, 17 November 1830. Phillpotts was nominated on 11 November: conse-crated 2 January 1831. The room was made by translating Bethell, who only six *months* before had been translated from Gloucester to Exeter, to Bangor (nominated 28 October).

[2] So hurriedly that it caused scandal. The vacancy was made by the death of the Bishop of Worcester. Carr of Chichester, who had been intimate with George IV and ministered to his death-bed, was translated to Worcester in fulfilment of a promise made by George IV, and so made room for Maltby at Chichester. The speed was such that the *congé d'élire* for Worcester arrived before the funeral of the dead bishop. Tory hacks rumoured that the speed was necessary to secure Maltby a £2,000 fine just about to fall in to the Bishop of Chichester. Grey had a more important motive. He needed Maltby's vote on the reform bill in the House of Lords.

because he was busy in Yorkshire, Bishop Blomfield of London who was in mourning for his father, Bishop Carr of Worcester because though a Tory he owed his translation to Lord Grey, and Sumner of Chester, Jenkinson of St. David's and Huntingford of Hereford for unknown reasons. The government had not expected so wholesale a defection of prelates.

The tide of popular rage poured itself against the House of Lords, the peers, the Tory leadership, and conspicuously upon the bishops. The press remarked that if the twenty-one bishops had voted in the opposite sense the bill would have passed. At crowded meetings on 10 October the mention of bishops was greeted with groans and yells and hisses. In Regent's Park the chairman, Joseph Hume, was handed a large placard inscribed 'Englishmen—remember it was the bishops, and the bishops only, whose vote decided the fate of the Reform Bill'. Whig and radical newspapers pilloried them as allies of borough-mongers, maintainers of graft and corruption and bribery, enemies of liberty and the civil rights of Englishmen. Throughout October and into November reforming orators denounced them, compared their wealth and state with apostolic simplicity, demanded that they be excluded from the House of Lords, asserted that they had no right to interfere in politics, but ought to be about their pastoral duties. They were charged with voting against reform because they owed their incomes to corruption and must defend corruption; with revelling in fashionable luxury at their palaces while they knew nothing of the labourer's cottage. They were paid £528,698 a year for keeping liberty from the people. Archbishop Howley was represented as Herod and Judas Iscariot, but orators needed to be unusually eloquent to succeed in blowing up that harmless divine into a Caliban.

The rhetoric spilt over into cries for the disestablishment of the church. Hatred of bishops was reflected in occasional horror of parsons. The vicar of Huddersfield was groaned at and hissed in his vicarage, the vicar of Sherborne had his windows broken and cellar sacked, it was not always comfortable to walk through London in a parson's dress, a curate near Bristol left a moving account of his expedition to baptise a dying child near Bristol, passing the abuse of a crowd outside a public house and afraid of assault.[1] But not all the clergy disliked the reform bill. Several appeared upon the platforms of reforming meetings. The Whig press gleefully reported a speech by

[1] *Br. Mag.*, 5, 1834, 397.

Sydney Smith at Taunton on 11 October, comparing the anti-reformers of the House of Lords to Mrs. Partington, working with her mop to repel the Atlantic.

For a few weeks it was harassing to be a bishop. While the Duke of Wellington's windows were broken, and the Marquis of Londonderry was rabbled, most peers could lie low. But bishops in their way of duty must appear in public. On 11 October a mob of 8,000 paraded through Carlisle and burnt the effigy of their bishop at the market cross. Bishop Ryder of Lichfield and Coventry received a threat that if he passed through Coventry he would be thrown in the pond. A dissenting minister was mistaken for a prelate and insulted in a London suburb.[1] A crowd at Bath heard that the Bishop of Cork was arriving in the stage-coach. They opened the door and, seeing a shovel hat, started to pull him out. Dr. Murphy, who was the Roman Catholic and not the Anglican Bishop of Cork, protested that he had nothing to do with the matter, but they did not believe him; and while they were arguing the coachman whipped up his horses and so rescued the inoffensive passenger. On 18 October Howley took the chair at the annual meeting of S.P.G. in Croydon Town Hall, and suffered heckling inside and a menacing crowd outside. On 23 October Bishop Blomfield was to preach at the reopening of St. Anne's church in Soho, but when the neighbourhood planned to walk out of church the churchwardens issued a notice that the bishop was unavoidably prevented. At a public house in Deansgate at Manchester, where the sign was a bishop, wags turned the bishop upside down and inscribed it *One bishop reformed*. Bishop Copleston of Llandaff was warned by friends to avoid the town of Abergavenny and kept a brown greatcoat and round hat in readiness lest it be necessary to escape from the back of his house across the fields in disguise. Van Mildert was grossly insulted in the streets of Durham.[2] On 24 October, while the Bishop of Bath and Wells was consecrating a new church at Bedminster, a crowd collected outside to waylay him, and stoned his carriage as he drove away. Many bishops postponed their public engagements into the new year. Mr. William Johnson, supplier of clerical hats in the Strand, sold off his shovel hats at 30s. a dozen. Handbills were distributed to inform the world in huge letters of the incomes of the bishops.

When Sir Charles Wetherell, the Tory recorder of Bristol, arrived

[1] Stoughton, ii, 4.   [2] EHR, 1941, 468.

there on 29 October, escorted by three troops of horse and a body of special constables, a mob attacked the Mansion House, and next midday appeared again. While the crowd threw bottles and stones, Christopher Davis stood by the railing under the window of the banqueting-room, encouraging the hooligans and shouting abuse at the corporation, the bishops and the parsons. He was heard saying: 'This is the end of your damned magistrates and bishops, and we'll send them all to hell.' Two hours later Davis was observed with the mob breaking open the new city gaol. As the gaol was burning Davis said that he hoped all the bishops would be hanged and the churches burnt. At 8 p.m. he was outside the bishop's palace, just as the doors were broken down, saying: 'The damned bishops have brought all this on', and what a shame it was that one bishop should have £40,000 a year and so many people starving. Thirty to forty men got into the palace; the bishop was out and his butler escaped over the wall at the back. Inside the palace they hardly knew what to do, and stood about; a few smashed furniture, china and glass, and set four beds on fire. Later the whole palace was on fire, and some of the mob climbed through the broken windows of the cathedral chapter-house near by to fetch old volumes for the flames.[1] Davis was only a tipsy old man waving his hat on an umbrella, but they hanged him with three others before a silent crowd.

Guy Fawkes day 1831 was the anxious time. Over the country the effigy of the local bishop replaced Guy Fawkes or the pope, and at Clerkenwell all twenty-one bishops were consumed in a holocaust. Archbishop Howley heard a rumour that the mob would attack Lambeth palace and asked the home secretary for an armed guard. Lord Melbourne replied, not comfortingly, that Lambeth was so near the Horse Guards that little damage could be done before succour arrived. He advised the archbishop to see that the servants of the palace were ready for an onslaught.[2] Guards were placed at the bishop's palace in Winchester,[3] Farnham castle was barricaded, twenty-five special constables drove away a mob from the bishop's palace at Worcester. Bishop Phillpotts of Exeter asked for protection. From 5 to 7 November the palace at Exeter was filled with men of the

---

[1] The bishop's mitre was among the casualties. It had not been replaced by the time of his death three years later and was not able to take its ceremonious place on his coffin. *Br. Mag.*, 6, 1834, 583.

[2] Melbourne to Howley, 5 November 1831, MP.

[3] *Journal of Mary Frampton*, 383.

7th Yeomanry cavalry, and the crowd only burnt a guy of Phillpotts, with hollow turnip as head and candle as nose, clad in mitre and lawn sleeves, in the cathedral yard outside his palace. An urchin successfully made the bishop jump by throwing a fire-cracker at his feet. At Crayford in Kent the procession changed the words of the old song:

> Remember, remember
> That God is the sender
> Of every good gift unto man;
> But the devil, to spite us
> Sent fellows with mitres
> Who rob us of all that they can.

The twenty-one bishops held different opinions about reform. Some of them, like Copleston of Llandaff and Kaye of Lincoln, believed in the necessity of a reform bill, but thought it imperative to throw out this reform bill, because a time of riot and mobs was no time to legislate upon such delicate machinery as the constitution. George Murray, Bishop of Rochester, descended of an ancient line of aristocrats, and with an uncomplicated dignity, wanted to follow his ancestors in making Britain safe for aristocrats. Van Mildert of Durham loathed the spirit of innovation and the desire to change institutions because they were ancient. Phillpotts of Exeter thought that pocket boroughs, though unseemly, were necessary to the harmony of the constitution and the restraint of democracy, and that they must be preserved until equivalent security was devised. When the bishops voted most of them were not defending a specially ecclesiastical order. They were defending the old constitution in the state, and therefore in the church as by law established.

No bishop voiced in Parliament the fear of disestablishment. That fear nevertheless lay on the surface. In the House of Lords, Lord Ellenborough expressed the crude alarm. Popular representation would mean that the Irish members of the House of Commons were elected by Roman Catholics, the Scottish members by Presbyterians, many English members by dissenters, and then where would the Church be?[1] Cool judgments admitted this argument to be clumsy. Few would assert the proposed £10 qualification to be so radical in its effect. But Phillpotts held that, whatever might be the consequences in England, the established church in Ireland must be ruined. The Irish Reform Bill would transfer the political power of Ireland

[1] Cf. Hansard, xii, 38, 9 April 1832.

from the Protestant to the Catholic, destroy the security whereby Wellington disfranchised the 40*s*. freeholders at the time of emancipation and end in Irish disestablishment, the loss of Protestant ascendancy, and at last the repeal of the union.

Lord Grey, seeking to win waverers among the peers, turned towards the bishops. Since it could not be in the interest of the church that bishops should be pilloried in market squares over the country, some of them were likely to choose reform as a lesser evil for the church. He addressed himself to convert the Archbishop of Canterbury.

Dr. Howley's hesitant and innocuous appearance took its usual paradoxical effect. Grey imagined Howley to be weak and indecisive. He nevertheless thought it exceedingly important to bring him round, and did not underestimate the difficulty of the manoeuvre.

On his way into London on 23 November 1831 Grey stopped at Fulham palace to see Bishop Blomfield. He was pleased with the interview. Blomfield was abused by Whig and Tory journals for sitting on the fence. It was made a jest that on the morning after he abstained from a vote on the reform bill, on the plea that his father was dead, he was sufficiently out of mourning to give a public address at the opening of King's College, London. The radical papers called him as bad as the bishops who voted against the bill, the Tory papers called him smooth-faced and shilly-shallying and asked whether he was weak or wicked or both.[1] Bishop Blomfield perceived the necessity of descending from his perch. He now told Lord Grey that he regretted the course which the bishops had taken, that he would vote for the new bill, and that he expected others to come over— perhaps the Bishops of Llandaff, Chester, Bath and Wells, and Gloucester. On the following day, 24 November, Grey saw Howley. It was not a satisfactory meeting. Howley confessed that he had not expected the bishops' vote so to trouble the country. But he was still doubtful, starting objections, alarmed. Grey could not gain him. Grey then tried to persuade the king to persuade the bishops; perhaps the archbishop, perhaps Carr of Worcester, who had been so friendly with the royal family. William IV, though wishing the bishops to come over, refused at first to exert any pressure either upon them or upon Tory peers.[2] A fortnight later he invited Howley to visit him at the

[1] JB, 27 May 1832.
[2] Grey to Sir H. Taylor, 25 November 1831; Taylor to Grey, 27 November. *Correspondence of Grey and King William IV*, i, 443–4.

Brighton pavilion. Even to the king Archbishop Howley was very mild and refused to give a decisive answer. His words gave no hope that he could be converted, his manner encouraged the king to think that he might not vote against the bill. He denied that he used his influence to persuade other bishops to follow his vote. Grey could not imagine the archbishop to be other than weak and inferred that he was dominated by the Tory leaders. He assailed him again in February 1832, but got no more than a confession that Howley was personally inclined to vote for the bill, but felt that he could not do so with consistency.[1]

Meanwhile the king and Grey were more successful with other bishops, especially the Archbishop of York and Bishop Carr of Worcester. When the second reading was finally carried in the House of Lords on 13 April 1832 twelve bishops voted for the bill in person or by proxy; those old faithfuls, Bathurst of Norwich and Maltby of Chichester; York, London and Worcester, whose votes had been secured by eminent encouragement; five moderates, Sumner of Chester, Ryder of Lichfield, Kaye of Lincoln, Copleston of Llandaff and Jenkinson of St. David's; and the Irishman Knox of Killaloe. Though Howley and fifteen others voted against the bill, Whigs thought the result respectable. 'The spiritual peers', said the *Morning Chronicle*, which had been vituperating them for six months, 'somewhat redeemed their character and their reputation with the nation.'

Neither reform bill nor bishops were yet beyond question. On 7 May 1832 the Lords carried an amendment postponing the vital clause for disfranchising the pocket boroughs. Three archbishops and thirteen bishops voted for the amendment. Grey was shocked to find the Archbishop of York, who later proved not to have understood what it was about, voting against him. On 8 May he asked the king to create peers to defeat the opposition, and resigned when the king refused.

Grey's resignation, and the vain attempt of Wellington to form a Tory government, revived the popular fury of the previous autumn and brought the country near to civil war. The death bells of Birmingham churches tolled all night. On the following Saturday the mob hissed and hooted the king and queen at Hounslow. Dr. Phillpotts of Exeter was mockingly recommended to preach at Windsor on the text of Ecclesiastes about 'an old and foolish king that will no more be

[1] *Corr.*, ii, 34, 240.

admonished'.[1] That Sunday Dr. Ryder, Bishop of Lichfield and Coventry, who voted for the amendment, came to St. Bride's church to preach a charity sermon before the lord mayor of London. Reformers distributed handbills calling for demonstration. They received Ryder's carriage with yells and hisses, rendered his sermon inaudible by massed groans and coughs; there was a fight between the sidesmen and the interrupters, a collection plate was upset and its contents scrambled, and Ryder's departing carriage galloped down Fleet Street with the mob in pursuit. He was billed to preach the same evening at St. Paul's church in Islington and reformers gathered. It was deemed prudent that he should not appear. On the next Wednesday evening a crowd in York, unaware that their archbishop did not understand what he was voting about, paraded the streets of the city with his effigy, marched to his palace at Bishopthorpe, smashed the fence, broke some windows, and burnt the effigy in front of the house.

On 15 May Wellington abandoned the hopeless task. Grey returned, the king gave the promise to create peers, and so the third reading passed the Lords on 4 June. Only twenty-two peers recorded dissent and not a bishop among them. But the public had not forgotten. On 7 August 1832 Archbishop Howley, looking as nervous as ever, arrived at Canterbury to hold his primary visitation and was met by a hissing crowd. Hats, caps, brickbats, cabbage stalks were flung at the carriage, breaking one of the windows, but not harming the archbishop.

To abuse the Church of England was not new. What was new was the amount of vituperation and the number of people who listened. In 1831 pamphleteers against the establishment commanded an unusually avid public.

To placard the incomes of the bishops in capital letters was the simplest form of attack. Why do the people pay so much to maintain prelates who are the enemies of the people? What use is an established church? Ought there to be any connexion between the clergy and politics? Why should farmers be burdened with the payment of tithe? The handful of Utilitarians and sceptics who thought Christianity untrue saw in all these payments a prodigious waste of national resources, inculcating superstitious notions and financing the performance of meaningless ceremonies, and thought that a reformed clergy would be

[1] MC, 16 May 1832.

more usefully employed in lecturing on ethics, botany or political economy,[1] or providing social meetings and decorous dances on Sundays.

The extreme dissenting pamphleteer wanted Christianity, but objected to bishops on principle and inherited a grievance against parsons from the long history of national intolerance. 'St. Bartholomew', wrote R. M. Beverley in a *Letter to the Archbishop of York* which ran through several editions, 'was pressed to take the see of Jericho, but he preferred holding the deanery of Naphtali, with the great living of Succoth, which last was of the clear yearly value of £8,000, and besides was encumbered with very little duty. . . .' The more moderate dissenters were not sorry to see the clergy under fire. But these complaints and cries of pain, utilitarian or dissenting, radical or self-critical, were mingled in the vaster national agonies of a society where the bonds were loosening, through agricultural oppression and wages near subsistence level, attack upon tithe, hatred of the machinery of government, and agitation whipped up by local factions. Without being so articulate as the radical orators, an industrial and farming people was told that the church was an engine for oppression and for a moment was inclined to believe it.

The most effective of the published attacks was that by John Wade, a Utilitarian journalist. He had published *The Black Book* in periodical numbers from 1820 to 1823, and by 1831 had sold 14,000 copies. Wade remodelled and rewrote the earlier numbers into *The Extraordinary Black Book*, published during the summer of 1831. It appeared again in 1832 and 1835, and altogether sold 50,000 copies. It was an attack, not only upon the church, but upon the Tory establishment in its widest sense: crown, civil list, aristocracy, Bank of England, East India company. But the first chapter was entitled Church of England, the second was entitled Church of Ireland. These were the fountains of corruption and graft, or the easiest to make ridiculous. No one could contrast the behaviour of the Bank of England with ideals of conduct which it was supposed to be propagating.

The Extraordinary Black Book was an adult and complicated version of the street placards, parading the incomes of the bishops. With a mass of imposing but erroneous statistics, Wade calculated the income of the English clergy to exceed the revenues of Austria or Prussia. He reckoned the total at just under 9½ million pounds and was confident

[1] Cf. the article by James Mill, *London Review*, 1835, 257.

that he understated it. The church was a monstrous overgrown Croesus in the state, the amount of its revenues incredible, unbearable. Who would rise to abate the colossal nuisance? Wade was not the only author who looked forward to the rapid abolition of the Church of England by act of Parliament, or at least the confiscation of its property.

The newspapers fastened upon the pluralities and the wealth. It was disclosed that nineteen bishops held a total of sixty-one pieces of preferment. Dr. Hodgson, the Dean of Carlisle, was the rector of St. George's in Hanover Square and of two other livings in different parts of the country. The *Times* (12 November 1832) printed a little poem upon St. Jerome, who returned to earth and tried to find Dr. Hodgson, vainly, because Dr. Hodgson was always in another of his residences. He went to see the Bishop of Durham—

> He found that pious soul van Mildert
> Much with his money-bags bewildered.

When the Canterbury clergy sent a loyal address to Archbishop Howley, deprecating hasty reform, the reporters soon discovered that the ringleaders of this 'scandalous address' were well-provided pluralists, headed by Richard Bagot, the Dean of Canterbury, who was also Bishop of Oxford and the rector of Blithfield in Staffordshire.[1]

Denying the prejudice and the overstatement, candid churchmen were forced to admit that much in their system needed remedy, though they were not agreed on the disease or the cure. All old institutions stood under criticism, law, medicine, prisons, civil service, army. The church was the oldest of institutions and the least easy to alter by act of Parliament. The church was of the land, its parochial system adapted to ministry in villages, its clergy gentlemen, its legal framework inflexible and unable to meet new circumstances. The machine was cumbersome and creaked. The clergy were learned, well connected, socially acceptable, influential as magistrates are influential. There was beginning to be a demand, because there was beginning to be a crying need, for pastoral and resident clergymen. In 1827, of 10,533 benefices returned, the incumbents of only 4,413 were resident; and though this understates the amount of residence, by excluding many clergymen living near their churches but outside the legal boundaries of the parish, it afforded a formidable stick to the critics.

[1] *Times*, 8 November 1832.

The pamphleteers claimed that from the ill-gotten goods of the church one bishop bequeathed £700,000, that an archbishop left more than a million, that Bishop Sparke of Ely so promoted his son and son-in-law in the diocese that between them they were drawing £31,000, that the Bishop of London would shortly receive an annual stipend of £100,000 and the Archbishop of Armagh £140,000. Though these allegations were inaccurate or false, something in the system prevented honest churchmen from brushing them off with contempt. The charge of the *Extraordinary Black Book*, that the Church of England and Ireland was the most unreformed church in Christendom, could be defended. By English conservatism the church came through the Reformation altered in doctrine and liturgy, but still medieval in its legal framework. Parson's freehold, ecclesiastical courts, sinecures, parishes *in commendam*, pluralities, wealthy livings with few parishioners, sale of advowsons, pocket boroughs of the church—it all smelt of the middle ages, an archaic order which encouraged the well placed and left the work to poor and ill-equipped curates at £80 a year. The days had not yet come for sentimental lingering over the box pew and the three-decker pulpit.

Everyone was touched by panic and found it difficult to see clearly. Churchmen were pardonably convinced that the country was near revolution, that the church faced disestablishment, that only drastic remedies could preserve it, that guillotines and temples of reason stood round the corner. They remembered how French revolutionaries identified priest with aristocrat and how Louis XVI entered Paris to mob cries of *Hang all the bishops on lamp-posts!* Peel guessed that the monarchy might last only five or six years; and if so practical a Tory as Peel feared this, theorists and regius professors and headmasters and remote country clergymen were likely to look into the future with fear.[1] Orators shouted that the bones of Tory parsons would soon be rotting with Tory peers and Tory squires. They talked again of the Commonwealth, and Cromwell, and the downfall of the old church, and when a speaker at Canterbury cried that the cathedral be used for stabling horses, the townsmen waved their grim applause. 'What is the church,' asked Sir Samuel Whalley of a meeting at the Globe, King's Cross, 'at present managed by ecclesiastics, but one unvaried system of fraud and robbery?'[2]

In a panic the Book of Revelation rose easily to the surface of

[1] Le Marchant, *Life of Althorp*, 255.   [2] T, 17 November 1832.

Christian minds. The French Revolution encouraged English evangelicals to study the signs of the times, and Catholic emancipation stirred again the apocalyptic mysteries. The best evangelicals had strange companions. From 1829 to 1833 a Scottish Presbyterian minister at Regent Square chapel in London, Edward Irving, published a paper called *The Morning Watch* to propagate the doctrine that Christ would shortly come to reign for 1,000 years. He was joined and in part financed by Henry Drummond, a wealthy banker, who made his seat at Albury Park into the headquarters of the movement. Evangelical leaders and magazines hammered at these enthusiasts. In 1830 reports came from Scotland of a girl at Gairloch speaking 'in an unknown tongue'. Irving hailed it as a pentecostal sign of the end and believed that his disciples had received the gift of tongues. On 16 October 1831 a woman in Irving's congregation broke out in unintelligible sounds during the service, and soon the unknown tongues became habitual. Irving was forced to leave his chapel in 1832, and in 1833 was deprived of his ministry by the Presbyterian authorities on a charge of heresy. Eight hundred of his great congregation followed him into a new chapel and there founded the Catholic Apostolic Church.[1]

In October 1831 cholera reached England from the continent. Not only fanatics saw it as a judgment of God upon the nation in this evil hour. There were cries to close theatres and ballrooms, to destroy card-tables, to remedy breaches in keeping the Sabbath, to end parsons who hunted. The spokesman of the exceeding devout in the House of Commons was Spencer Perceval, eldest son of that prime minister who was assassinated in 1812.[2]

[1] Best study in A. L. Drummond, *Edward Irving and his Circle*, 1938. The age produced another small, though not quite so small and much more separatist, English millennial denomination, the Plymouth Brethren. They began first as a little extreme evangelical group in Dublin from 1827 with the principle that anyone may celebrate the Lord's Supper or preach, and received the name when the strange powerful Irish ex-Anglican clergyman J. N. Darby went to Plymouth in 1830. In 1847–9 the Brethren divided, through Darby's rigidity, into Open Brethren and Exclusive Brethren, the latter holding no communion with the others. At the best-attended services on 30 March 1851 there were in England and Wales 7,272 Brethren and 3,077 members of the Catholic Apostolic Church. The Irvingites developed a high Anglican ritual and often remained worshippers with the Church of England.

[2] When Perceval first moved for a general fast, as an act of penitence for the state of the nation, many members did not understand what he meant, and cried 'General *what?*' Hansard, ii, 81, 23 December 1830. Two months later, when Mr. Hughes prayed the House to address the crown for the same purpose, Henry Hunt asked the promoters whether they were aware that one-third of the people of Britain fasted almost every day in the week. Hansard, ii, 204, 7 February 1831. In November 1831,

In January 1832 Perceval moved for a general fast in the House of Commons. The government gave way. King William issued a call to a national day of fasting and humiliation on 21 March 1832, on account of the cholera. In Parliament on the eve Spencer Perceval rose to a terrible fanaticism. While members stood in groups, uncertain what to do, muttering or tittering, punctuating the speech with cries of *Order* or *Adjourn* or *Oh!* Perceval took his Bible in his hand and for an hour and three-quarters denounced the nation and the Parliament in the name of Jehovah, prophesying that the land would be desolate, that pestilence would be loosed upon it, that the church should be laid low because she had corrupted the way before God, played harlot with the state, and forsaken the doctrines of the Lord.[1] One of the minor merits of the reformed franchise was the exclusion of Spencer Perceval from the House of Commons. He soon became an apostle of the Irvingite church.

Many country villages and some town churches kept the fast day with devotion and made collections to relieve the suffering and the poor. The new Whig Bishop of Chichester, Dr. Maltby, preached a good sermon in Westminster abbey to the House of Lords. Only twenty peers attended, but Archbishop Howley and ten other bishops and Earl Grey with some of the cabinet were there, and the abbey was crowded. The people had not expected the sombre penitential exclusion of choir and organ, and became talkative and restless, so that it was difficult to hear. In St. Margaret's church Dr. Allen preached a sermon to 100 members of the House of Commons in so thin and reedy a monotone that a member of the audience expressed anxiety lest he become a bishop (he became a bishop two and a half years later).[2] At St. Paul's cathedral the seats were half full, but the nave was crowded with persons standing because they refused or failed to tip the vergers. All the preachers spoke of the judgment of God, the need for national penitence, and the especial need to better the lot of

---

when the bishops were most hated, Archbishop Howley proposed it to Lord Grey. Grey welcomed it or professed to welcome it as an individual, but told Howley that it would give ground to scoffers. Howley to Grey, 19 November 1831; Grey to Howley, 21 November 1831, HP.

[1] Scene described in the diaries of Le Marchant and Littleton. Aspinall, *Three Diaries*, 212–13.

[2] Aspinall, *Three Diaries*, 212: T, 22 March 1832. The members of Parliament were not the only critics of Dr. Allen. When he became a bishop the *Morning Herald* remarked that he was one of the most inefficient preachers that ever ascended a pulpit. He had been tutor at Cambridge to Lord Althorp, chancellor of the exchequer.

the poor. At the Chapel Royal, to a thin congregation which included the Duchess of Kent and her daughter the Princess Victoria, aged 12, Bishop Blomfield of London denounced the morals of the upper classes, especially in the national sin of failing to observe the Sabbath.

Meanwhile the Political Union of London organised a parody which they called a Farce Day. Grim wits issued a counter-proclamation that they would celebrate the fast by distributing bread and *meat* to the lower orders at noon in Finsbury Square. Nearly 25,000 people, many of them destitute, assembled in Finsbury Square to find no bread nor meat and wounded several policemen in the ensuing riot. Two illuminés called Zion and Shiloh stuck posters ridiculing the fast and Christianity and clergy, and beat with an umbrella a parson found tearing the posters down.[1]

The connexion between public panic and religious enthusiasm was found elsewhere than among illuminés. No one could number among fanatics a headmaster who was changing the face of English education, or put Dr. Arnold of Rugby in the same category as Spencer Perceval. Arnold laboured under the sense of doom. When he heard of the death of someone dear to him he felt a sort of joy mingled with the sense of loss, joy that the dead one was safe from the evil to come.[2] In the month of October 1831 he was half inclined to believe that the gift of tongues in Irving's congregation was a sign of the coming of the day of the Lord, and whether the gift was an authentic charisma or not, the time was a day of the Lord in this sense, that an epoch of the human race was ending.[3]

The people demanded reform of the church. Candidates for Parliament declared that a reformed Parliament must undertake sweeping reform of church endowments, pluralities, non-residence, bishops, and political parsons. Churchmen accepted the view that reform was necessary. They were not behind the radicals and dissenters in bombarding the public with pamphlets on church reform. The bishops took counsel on the possibility of passing hasty bills to avert the worst abuses. In June 1831 Archbishop Howley introduced a bill to limit pluralities, of so modest a nature that the Whig press regarded its insufficiency as offensive. It would not be just to describe these proceedings as a mode of buying off the enemies of the church, a feint to

---

[1] AR, 1832 *Chron.*, 40, 104. For a description of the keeping of the fast at an evangelical church in the country, see *Christian Guardian*, 1832, 214.

[2] Stanley, *Life*, i, 273.

[3] Arnold to Blackstone, 25 October 1831, Stanley, *Life*, i, 273–5.

elude the whips of public scorn. The looming crisis gave a rare stimulus to moderate churchmen who had long been working to reform the ecclesiastical administration, and need no longer be hopeless about vested interests now slinking away under umbrellas.

Since heaped endowments were evident targets, it was better to unheap them where possible. In 1831 Archbishop Howley carried through Parliament another modest little bill, to enable ecclesiastical corporations to augment the poor livings (of less value than £350) with which they were connected. The reforming press found this to be as inadequate as the failed pluralities bill. But under it Bishop van Mildert of Durham unloaded about £1,000 a year from his vast resources, to help the poorer livings of his diocese; Sumner of Winchester, Ryder of Lichfield and other bishops used the act to the same end.[1]

Radicals regarded the leisured comfort of cathedral closes as waste of endowments. Among all cathedrals they found Durham to be uniquely scandalous. With rich lands and coal Durham attained preeminent abundance among ecclesiastical corporations. Each of the twelve canons received about £3,000 a year; but the Dean was Bishop of St. David's, and among the canons were Bishops Gray of Bristol, Sumner of Chester and Phillpotts of Exeter. Durham had not forgotten the eighth Earl of Bridgewater, who held a prebend for forty-nine years while he lived in Paris.

Hopeful pamphleteers defended rich canons by proclaiming their learning and benevolence, their dignity of deportment, their decorum at cathedral services, their refusal to attend the races, their amusements at all times more refined than exciting, their rational and superior conversation.[2] Practical men knew that this defence was not enough. If the endowments were not used hurriedly, they would be confiscated. Who first suggested a university is not known. The Dean of Durham heard that it was Howley's idea, but others offered advice to the chapter.[3] On 28 September 1831 the chapter resolved unanimously

[1] Pusey gave an account in *British Critic*, 1838, January–April, 535–6, of the amount of good done under the bill. Cf. *Br. Mag.*, 1833, 3, 190, 214.

[2] *Durham in 1831*, 1834.

[3] Dr. Durell, one of the prebendaries, wrote to Bishop van Mildert that Durham would be the first object of attack after the reform act. 'It has occurred to us that it will be prudent if possible to ward off the blow, and that no plan is so likely to take as making the public partakers of our income by annexing an establishment of enlarged education.' C. E. Whiting, 30, 33. Van Mildert was afraid of any plan which needed an act of Parliament and therefore discussion by Hume and O'Connell in the House of Commons. He wanted it not only as a peace-offering to reformers but as a good in itself.

but not enthusiastically to institute 'Durham College'. The chapter gave up property in South Shields to the capital value of £80,000, and van Mildert contributed several thousands in money and later Durham Castle. The necessary bill could not pass through Parliament without query. It was discovered that, like the degrees of Oxford and Cambridge, the degrees of the college would be open only to members of the Church of England. A meeting of dissenters in Newcastle petitioned against the religious test and in the Commons Hume applied for postponement. Van Mildert said that he would withdraw from the scheme if degrees were given to dissenters.[1] The Whig leaders thought it hard that a private endowment of this kind might not be directed to the object intended by the benefactors. Private endowment? This, said O'Connell, 'is Protestant property, and therefore public property.'[2] The opposition withdrew, the bill received royal assent on 4 July 1832, and a new university was founded. Van Mildert wrote to the bishops, asking whether they would accept Durham degrees to qualify men for holy orders. All but two said that they would. One of the two was Grey of Hereford, the other George Murray of Rochester, staunch aristocrat, who disapproved of encouraging the lower classes to aspire to stations for which there were already too many candidates from the classes immediately above them.[3] The two Whigs Bathurst of Norwich and Maltby of Chichester thought that it might be better than Oxford and Cambridge.

The main device for repelling confiscators of church property was a commission of enquiry. Orators and pamphleteers made wild statements about the oriental wealth of the church. They could not be refuted by figures, because figures were not available. When the radical Hume suggested an enquiry Tory churchmen were quick to see that they had everything to gain. Stiffer Tories thought that a commission was solely a method of finding the facts or disproving lies and should not lead to acts of reform. Moderate churchmen were not so happy with the existing system, and agreed with the Whigs that the commission ought to lead to reform. On 23 June 1832 Lord Grey issued the names of the commission.

Its members were almost all conservatives. It included the Archbishops of Canterbury and York, the Bishops of London, Durham, Lincoln and Bangor, Sir Robert Inglis, the stalwart churchman who replaced Peel as M.P. for Oxford University in the emancipation

---

[1] Hansard, xii, 1832, 1215.   [2] Hansard, xiii, 1053.   [3] Whiting, 54.

election of 1829. Lord Grey believed in the Church of England as by law established. He agreed with the clergy that the church ought to be reformed by churchmen and not by the rude hands of hostile critics. No hot-head was selected for the commission. The nearest to it was Stephen Lushington, an ecclesiastical lawyer and Whig of the left wing, who was not tepid against ecclesiastical abuses.

The commission was a low bulwark against hasty change. It was not difficult, but was a little more difficult, to reform the church while a government commission was discovering what needed reform.

Among the thirty or more schemes for church reform which well-meaning pamphleteers offered the public during 1832, one topped the rest by cubits, if the measuring-rod was sober practical sense; the plan of Lord Henley, who had married Peel's sister.

Lord Henley was a devout churchman with two axioms. First, the entanglement of the ecclesiastical system with politics and secular patronage generated graft, worldliness and corruption. Second, the cathedrals of England were useless except as parish churches, and should lose their endowments to benefit the parishes.

He therefore proposed to exclude bishops from the House of Lords; to prohibit their translation from see to see, except to archbishoprics, and to level the inequalities of income among the bishops, with the object of averting the scramble for places and diminishing the power of crown patronage which Henley abused as oil for greasing the wheels of government; to remove the effective appointment of bishops from the prime minister and give it to a commission of ten persons, five senior bishops and five lay churchmen chosen for their devotion to the Church of England; to diminish the rewards of patronage by associating all stipends with pastoral duties—abolishing sinecures, commendams, canonries at cathedrals, converting the cathedrals into parish churches, and instituting commissions to devote the money saved from equalised bishoprics and suppressed canonries to create new parishes and raise the income of poor livings; to revive Convocation, suppressed since 1717, as a mouthpiece for the church when its bishops departed from Parliament. He proposed two new bishoprics, one for the counties of Derby and Nottingham and one for the southern end of the diocese of Lincoln, which then reached to the Thames. He desired stiffer rules against pluralities, and retiring pensions for clergymen aged 70.

Even moderate Whigs would hardly have dared to propose so

drastic a reformation. Tories everywhere denounced Lord Henley and his plan. They described it as absurd, impracticable, mischievous. The regius professor of Hebrew in the University of Oxford, Dr. Edward Bouverie Pusey, fastened upon Lord Henley's contempt for learning and social influence, betrayed in his desire to dismantle the cathedrals.[1]

Only one of the numerous replies to Lord Henley splashed into the headlines of the national press. Dr. Arnold determined to answer Lord Henley. In the middle of January 1833 he published a pamphlet of eighty-eight pages, *The Principles of Church Reform*. The pamphlet had the momentous consequence that it destroyed Arnold's ecclesiastical prospects and career, and so disqualified him for future leadership in the Church of England.

Arnold's plan was wild; no wilder than various suggestions thrown among the darkness of country rectories or dissenting pulpits or radical hustings, but, written by a headmaster of Rugby School, a scholar and man of stature, solitary in its wildness.

With his essay of 1829 in favour of the Roman Catholics Arnold achieved notoriety with the Tory party. The Tory press scrutinised his college at Oxford, Oriel, and found a trio of Whigs with little to commend them. The reporters offered adverse comments upon Dr. Edward Hawkins, provost of Oriel, a moderate dull man denounced by hostile journalists for little better reason than his headship of a college alleged to house radical firebrands. Their principal target was Richard Whately, a philosopher of sufficient eminence to be reviving the study of logic in Oxford; more ingenious than profound, but the hardest head in the university; with rough manners and huge frame, eating vast helpings at high table, smoker of many pipes, wearing hairy untidy garments, utterly unclerical in appearance and caring nothing for convention. Whately never read books. He revolved his meditations round five or six favourite authors, and was a dialectician battling his ideas out of the rough and tumble of militant conversation. In Oxford he was known as the White Bear, and in the early morning could be seen walking the meadows with a white hat on the back of his head, a rough white coat and a great white dog,

---

[1] Pusey, *Remarks on the prospective and past benefits of Cathedral Institutions*, 1833. He meant to write an open letter to Lord Henley, but Newman suggested that a pamphlet would be better, and Pusey's pamphlets always swelled into books. He sent the manuscript to Newman just as Newman and Froude were starting on their long Mediterranean holiday; Newman returned the manuscript from Falmouth. He criticised Pusey for calling Calvin a 'saint' and Pusey changed the word into 'giant'.

not on the paths, but scrambling through hedges and ditches and swamps. He was known as the most acute clerical mind upon the Whig side, in emancipation, the affairs of Ireland, and the necessity for drastic reform of the church. Arnold qualified among the four or five men who penetrated beyond that formidable intelligence to perceive the inner heart which most men supposed not to exist. In 1830 a journalist described Arnold as Whately's bottle-holder. *John Bull* wrote a leader against these *noetics*, as the Oriel school was christened. It declared that Arnold and Hawkins were conspicuous in failing to observe the Lord's Day, published extracts from Arnold's sermons to prove that he cared nothing for the Church of England, urged parents to enquire diligently into the conduct of Rugby and Oriel, and saluted Richard Whately as the head of the Oriel group and a man who regarded all men as fools but himself.[1]

Whately was open to the charge of intellectual arrogance. He believed that the world wished to be instructed and was ready with interminable monologues or letters to satisfy that desire. Arnold's mind was humbler, more historical, more reverent. Whately dissected the truths of religion like an anatomist, Arnold retained and communicated a sense of awe. But not in political thought. A schoolmaster since he left Oxford, he imparted a didactic tone in his publications. He listened meekly to advice and reproaches, but would not let them alter his ideas. Busy with boys, he was more remote and secluded, understood less of the world even than Whately, but was as ready to pronounce magisterially upon issues engaging worldly men. With ethical passion rising quickly to the surface, and with far less humour than Whately, he made these pronouncements in a tone of burning moral vehemence. In a pulpit the effect was noble. Whately left no sermon which posterity cared to preserve, Arnold left volumes of the finest sermons of the century. Love of scholarship and breadth of mind worked in rare harmony with the ethical drive to make Christian faith and conduct supreme in school and nation. But in politics, secular or ecclesiastical, the one-sidedness and passion and energy made Arnold no guide. Everything he wrote was written in haste, in moments snatched from his school.

In the autumn and winter of 1832–3 Arnold laboured under his

---

[1] JB, 2 and 9 May 1830. Arnold contemplated suing *John Bull* for libel, but was dissuaded by the lawyers and Provost Hawkins and Bishop Blomfield of London. Stanley, i, 242.

apocalyptic sense of doom. Troubled by two intimate bereavements, he was sorely touched by an incident of December where he was solely to blame. *John Bull* had urged the public to eye the conduct of Rugby School. In a towering passion at what he believed to be lying, Arnold flogged a boy who a few days later was proved innocent. The press was not friendly.

Arnold called his pamphlet *The Principles of Church Reform*, but omitted most of the principles which would have made the plan less unintelligible. For several years he considered whether to write a big work on church and state; but lack of time, seclusion and cast of mind prevented the plan from getting beyond a few fragments. Even the central ideas were never more than half formed in his head.

Henley's plan was a device of ecclesiastical machinery. Arnold wanted a national plan, and fastened upon the yawning gap in Henley's proposals; the omission of dissent. He believed the establishment to be doomed by alliance between radicals and dissenters, and yet thought an establishment necessary to the sound life of the nation. Therefore he declared the only hope to lie in opening the doors of the Church of England to dissenters, and so to establish a church broad enough to contain the great majority of the English people. Such a church must allow variety of opinion and of ceremony. Its dogmatic articles must be framed in conciliatory language and kept as few as possible—belief in God, in Christ as Saviour, in the scriptures as containing the revelation of God's will to man, in notions of right and wrong. He wanted to keep the liturgy in the parish churches on Sunday mornings and allow a varied or freer service at other times, conducted by ex-dissenting ministers, for 'the morning song of the lark is not the same with the evening song of the nightingale'.[1] He admitted that Roman Catholics and Unitarians and Quakers would not join this church. Against reformers who wanted to abolish bishops or diminish their numbers, Arnold proposed that the number of dioceses be increased until every large town had its bishop. He wanted the existing bishops in the House of Lords. He agreed with Henley in seeing no use in deans and would take their revenues to endow the new bishops, who should not sit in the House of Lords. Each bishop was given a council of clergy and laity with whom he must sit to administer the discipline of the church.

He confessed these practical arrangements of a comprehensive

---

[1] *Principles*, 68.

church to be tentative. But unless something like this is done, the establishment is gone, the noblest churches of the land will decay because the people refuse money to repair them, marriage will become a private ceremony, universities will cease to control religious education. If England is to be Christian, there must be an established church; and there cannot be, unless the established church houses the dissenters.

Half concealed beneath this astonishing plan lay two axioms. The first was the old latitudinarian theory of the previous century that re-union of all sects would be possible upon the basis of few fundamental doctrines. The word *latitudinarian* was then a term of abuse. Arnold pleaded not guilty and was convicted by every critic. The second was a foggy version of the old idea of a union between church and state. Middle Ages and Reformation identified church with nation, citizen with churchman. For a century and a half the theory was perforce modified and retained only the loyalties of old-fashioned Tories. Arnold, the unusual Whig, assumed it as an axiom. The church is not a corporation separate from the state but the state in its religious aspect. If citizen and churchman are still to be the same, the church must be extended and altered to include far more of the citizens than the contemporary members of the Church of England. The theory, of interest to an abstract theorist, was too sketchy to convince even sympathetic readers. To the unsympathetic majority, the practical consequences—that Parliament, a new popular Parliament, must alter or arrange the ritual and doctrines of the church—was worse than offensive.

The public received Arnold's plan with friendliness or contempt. It was dubbed clever, well meaning, strange, charitable, wrong-headed. But whether friend or foe, everyone agreed that, whatever the value of various suggestions, the plan was impracticable. *The Times*, politically disposed to befriend Arnold, thought that nothing was gained except a kind of ecclesiastical Noah's ark, and that it would win not a single proselyte nor influence a single reformer.[1] Even the friendliest of critics said that it would be difficult to discern why Christian unity would be better promoted by assembling in the same buildings at different hours than by assembling in different buildings

---

[1] T, 25–26 January 1833; MC, 21 January, 25 January. The Noah's ark phrase was taken up by Bishop Blomfield in a speech in the House of Lords. Hansard, xxxvi, 1837, 766.

at the same hour.[1] High churchmen replied with a confidence embarrassed by the feeling that nothing needed reply. They contemptuously described Arnold's hypothetical church as the new national omnibus.[2]

John Keble, once an intimate friend, would have no more to do with him. A preacher in the university pulpit at Oxford denounced him, though not by name, the sale of his sermons declined, and when that summer the boys of Rugby mutinied over a ban upon fishing the hostile newspapers turned the affair into a political occasion. He was sensitive, fiercely resented the critics, especially at his own Oxford, and was almost as pained by radicals who claimed him as an ally. He found more and more pleasure in holiday retirements to his haven at Fox How in the Lake District.

Impracticable ideas which become sensible over the next hundred years come only to the minds of great men. But the public of 1833, especially the religious public, was left aware that Arnold was a dreamer, probably a dangerous dreamer.

The campaign to elect members to the reformed Parliament occupied October and November of 1832. No one knew what the reformed franchise would bring. Whigs and Tories feared a radical government which might yet sweep away king and aristocrats and church. The bitterness of the hustings generated bitterness among the churches. Tory candidates observed dissenters joining radical candidates who shouted for the overthrow of the church, and condemned them with fury. Whigs observed forty-nine out of every fifty clergymen encouraging Tory candidates. The *Times* kept denouncing political parsons, but applauded the vicar of Thaxted when he rode to the polling booth at Saffron Walden at the head of 200 true reforming voters.[3] Many candidates put reform of the church into election addresses, calling for the end of tithe, church rate, pluralities, together with lower taxes or no flogging in the army or repeal of the corn laws or abolition of negro slavery. The most ominous sign, convincing even Dr. Arnold that his fears of doom were well founded, was the

---

[1] Dickinson (Whately's chaplain), *Observations on Ecclesiastical Legislature and Church Reform*, 1833, 40–41.

[2] A more contemptuous phrase then than now, because the noun was vulgar. Cf. CO, 1834, 167: 'When will an educated person be induced, except from necessity, to call a long-coach an omnibus?'

[3] T, 25 December 1832.

refusal by Birmingham of a church rate. The rate to repair a church must be voted at an annual Easter vestry. The Birmingham reformers made sure that they possessed a majority in the vestry, and postponed the grant of a rate from meeting to meeting, amid indescribable scenes of turmoil in St. Martin's church, until on 2 October 1832 they finally refused to pay. The 'establishment of the Church of England is now in serious peril', wrote the *Times* when it heard the news from Birmingham, 'and that peril becomes every hour more imminent'. If reform, wrote Sydney Smith, is effected by the present government, it will probably be sensible. If it comes into the hands of madmen and revolutionaries, 'it will be a scene of robbery, villainy and plunder'.[1] But whatever government attained power, most electors were convinced that the Church of England could not survive without drastic change. The people would no longer endure it.

'The church as it now stands', wrote Dr. Arnold, 'no human power can save.'

'I suppose', wrote John Keble, 'there can be no doubt that the die for a separation is now cast.'

'Whatever turn things take,' wrote Richard Whately, 'I can see nothing that bodes well to the church establishment; I fear its days are numbered.'[2]

3 . IRELAND

Ireland forced a Tory England to emancipate the Roman Catholics. Ireland was the sore which new Irish members in the House of Commons never allowed England to forget. The Irish Church, Protestant and established amidst so large a Catholic population, was the point where the most conservative of Whigs lost their conservatism. Because Whigs sympathised with radical demands in Ireland, some of them came to sympathise with radical demands in England.

The Irish peasants were poor or destitute. Their cottages were hovels, their clothes rags, their food was at or below the level of subsistence. Political and religious strife fostered their tradition of violence. In 1828 most of the British army camped in Ireland to help the police. The advocates of Catholic emancipation, seeing how religious strife embittered the people and kept alive hatred of England,

---

[1] T, 9 October and 8 November 1832.

[2] Stanley, i, 287; Burgon, *Lives of Twelve Good Men*, 78; *Life of Whately*, 1st ed., i, 159.

predicted that emancipation would heal the sore. Never was a prophecy more erroneous. The quarrel of Protestant and Catholic was part of a national and social resentment. If Roman Catholic emancipation is regarded not as act of justice but as political settlement, it was a total failure.[1] The Irish were heartened and encouraged by the knowledge that the English succumbed, not because they believed the Irish case to be just, but because they bowed before the threat of murder, violence, riot and civil war.

The disqualifications afflicting Roman Catholics were the least of the grievances of Irishmen. To remove them affected most of the Irish not at all. This grievance was the easiest grievance to remedy, partly because there was also a group of Roman Catholics in England, and partly because there existed a strong body of Englishmen who believed that the disqualifications were unjust and inexpedient. But the emancipation act helped the peasants of Ireland not at all, since they were not eligible for the high offices which the act opened. They were affected adversely, for a large number of Irishmen lost the vote in the act which accompanied emancipation and without which it would not have passed.

Although the peasantry was still destitute, the Catholic community was reviving in wealth, education and self-confidence. They were beginning to build cathedrals and schools and new monastic houses, to replace their thatched barns for worship with slated chapels. The college at Maynooth, founded in 1795 to train priests because during Napoleonic wars they could no longer seek their training on the continent of Europe, was growing in stature and public regard. Catholicism was resurgent. In its revival it encountered missionary Protestantism in a clash which exacerbated the social strife.

The established Church of Ireland was not minded to missionary endeavour. Rich in proportion to its population, it was quiet, reasonable, instructed, and expected that in time the Roman Catholics would be converted by reason and by education. Its old-fashioned members frowned on enthusiastic attempts to evangelise the Roman Catholics. Its merit was the encouragement of learning and social influence. Its power, as the Tory party justly observed, was the chain binding Ireland to England. But its lapses were blatant. Though not

---

[1] So Tories afterwards repented that they voted for it. C. R. Sumner, Bishop of Winchester, in his charge of 1845, 38–39 said that he would not have voted for it if he had foreseen what would happen.

so guilty of non-residence as the English, some 30 per cent of the incumbents were non-resident, 18 per cent of the parishes had not even a church, the twenty-two bishops received large stipends, and when non-resident they were spectacularly non-resident. Since there were 2,436 parishes, 1,252 benefices, and only 900 incumbents, pluralism was inevitable. We hear of one clergyman in the diocese of Cashel who was said to be under engagement to reside for six months on each of three livings in rotation.[1] But they usually resided, quiet, benevolent and friendly. They were praised as the best of the resident gentry of Ireland.[2]

In the same epoch that the Roman Catholic Church revived the evangelicals advanced into Ireland. The puritan tradition, strong in Irish Protestantism since the Reformation, reinforced by the plantation of Ulster and the immigrant Scotsmen, was kept alive by the barbarous Catholic multitude. In the years between 1800 and 1830 this movement become more missionary. Societies distributed Bibles and tracts among the people, founded Sunday schools to educate their children, and had no belief whatever in the gradual power of reason.[3] There was talk of a new Reformation in Ireland, promoted by the English and Irish Bible Societies. Evangelists toured the country, preaching sermons, proffering pamphlets, and making public attacks on the Roman Catholic creed and its ceremonies. Resurgent Catholicism met resurgent Protestantism on a battlefield where the people saw the argument less in religious than in social terms. At a race meeting there was riot when a horse named *Protestant Boy* beat a horse named *Daniel O'Connell*.

The Irish won the struggle for emancipation by agitating. A severe depression of agriculture made their plight desperate and loosened the bonds of society at the moment when in Westminster the fight over reform weakened central government and encouraged radical hopes. It needed only a small tinder-box to inflame Irish resistance to tithes.

Graigue is a little town on the border of the counties of Carlow and Kilkenny, and then contained 4,779 Catholics and 63 Protestants. Its ancient and non-resident rector, Dr. Alcock, maintained the common and courteous habit of not troubling the Catholic priest for his tithe. His resident curate, Mr. Macdonnell, was an ardent member of the New Reformation society. He collected tithes in person and

[1] *Catholic Mag.*, I, 1831, 523.   [2] PP, 1831–2, xxi, 12.
[3] Cf. R. B. McDowell, 30–33.

demanded tithes from Father Doyle. Father Doyle refused. Macdonnell took Doyle's horse. The peasants of Graigue then refused to pay tithes. To the arguments of a local magistrate they replied, 'Daniel O'Connell will get the tithes taken off us, as he got us emancipation.' Father Doyle was said to have denounced from the altar the payment of tithe.[1] After vain negotiation the resident magistrate collected a posse of 350 police and 250 soldiers from the 21st Fusiliers and the 1st Dragoon Guards, and on 1 March 1831 threw a cordon round Graigue, with the object of driving off the village cattle. The law forbade forcible entry or the removal of possessions under lock and key. The villagers collected the cattle at points round the village, and when police were observed a warning was given by blowing of horns and ringing of chapel bells and the cattle were driven inside cattle-folds. After two months at this hide-and-seek, Colonel Harvey's force succeeded in collecting one-third of the tithe.

The example of successful resistance was imitated in several parts of the country, especially in the counties of Kilkenny, Carlow, Wexford and Tipperary. At Newtownbarry a fight for some cattle became so ugly that the yeomanry fired, killing twelve peasants outright and mortally wounding twenty more. At the lane of Carrickshock, where the peasantry succeeded in surrounding the police, they almost annihilated the entire force, killing thirteen and wounding fourteen. In April 1832 a seized cow was sold for £12 under the protection of two pieces of artillery, sixty men of the 12th Lancers, five companies of the 92nd Highlanders, and a strong detachment of police. In September 1832 a force of police and troops, under the command of an admiral, two generals and three magistrates, attempted to collect the tithes of Wallstown. In the pitched affray which followed only four peasants were killed, but many on both sides were wounded. As late as 18 December 1834 there was a battle at Rathcormac where twelve peasants were killed outright, seven died of wounds, and forty-two others were wounded. The cattle were branded by the people with the word TITHE and could not be sold at local auctions. Catholic priests and Protestant incumbents tried to pacify. But meanwhile the tithe could not be collected, some Protestant incumbents were nearly destitute, and some were no longer safe in their vicarages. One clergyman was shot dead upon his lawn. The government began to fear that successful resistance to the law of tithe would breed

[1] PP, 1831–2, xxi, 46; cf. xxii, 131.

resistance to other legal dues. It was reported that at hurling matches an emblematic bull had been used, with *No tithes* on the one side and on the other *No taxes*. Mr. Burke, an Irish priest, was accused of declaring from his altar, 'Boys, the tottering fabric of the heretics is falling around us while the Catholic religion is rising in glory every day. Ireland was once Catholic, boys; it will and shall be Catholic again!' Mr. Burke, when charged, denied using the word *Boys*.

The unreformed Whig government was harassed into activity. They agreed to maintain the law, and to save the destitute clergy by a grant of public money, reimbursing the treasury by collecting the tithes for themselves; a measure which did not increase their popularity in Ireland. Tithe was still refused over wide areas. Nothing could establish order in Ireland, nothing could collect the tithe, except military law modifying the normal courts of justice. Martial law was repellent to the constitutional traditions of Westminster, repellent to Whigs as liberals, and anathema to radicals on the left wing of Parliament.

The lord lieutenant of Ireland was the Marquess of Anglesey, an eminent officer who commanded the cavalry and lost a leg at the battle of Waterloo. He believed that disorder could not be settled without disestablishment of the Church of Ireland. He suggested that the state should confiscate the revenues of the Irish church, pay priests or ministers according to need, and use the surplus to relieve the poor. An inarticulate soldier, less mighty with the pen than the sword, he met the difficulty that Earl Grey was not only reluctant to commit himself to so radical a plan, but thought that the Whig cabinet would collapse if he tried to implement it.

It was certain that the endowments of the Irish church must be the first duty of the new reformed government in 1833. It had been made the more certain by the Irish reform act which followed the English. English and Protestant power over the constituencies in Ireland was maintained before and after Catholic emancipation by the existence of pocket boroughs. By substituting numbers for influence the reform act decreased the political power of Protestants, increased that of Catholics, and destroyed some of the security for the church and constitution which Wellington thought to achieve by disfranchising the 40s. freeholders. On 27 August 1832 Sydney Smith wrote to the wife of the prime minister that one of the first acts of government must be to provide for the Catholic clergy out of the revenues of the Protestant clergy, that it could not be delayed and that the alternative was bloody war.[1] Everyone knew that Parliament must deal with the Irish church. Everyone feared or wanted disestablishment and disendowment.

Lord Grey was a Whig of conservative mind. Under the conditions which prevailed in favour of Tories over the last twenty years, only a Whig of sober complexion had a prospect of leading the opposition. An aristocrat who wished for conservative principles, who feared radicals and democrats, who loathed O'Connell, who regarded change more as a concession to popular feeling in the country than as a need in itself, clear-headed and honest, commanding universal respect, he was too cautious to satisfy the left wing of his followers. He had strenuously contended for the emancipation of the Roman Catholics; and once that was conceded, he believed in yielding sufficient reform to satisfy the people. He knew that he must allow relief to Irish and English dissenters. But he could not shake himself from the habit of regarding it more as something which could not be avoided than as something which he ought to want. His opinions on the reform of the English church were all that the middle Tories could have desired. He told the Tory Archbishop of York in January 1834 that the views of the cabinet upon this subject 'are purely of a conservative character and tend to the support of the church establishment by the removal of some causes of complaint'.[2] If there was to be revolution in church and state, it would be in spite of, not because of, the Whig prime minister.

In 1831 he had the opportunity of appointing bishops to two of the chief sees of Ireland, Derry the wealthiest and Dublin the most influential. The Whigs were short of able men in important departments, and in none more grievously than the law and the church. Most lawyers and nearly all clergymen voted against them. It cost Grey much anxiety to find a clergyman who would vote Whig and at the same time be big enough to prevent the government becoming contemptible by his appointment. The simplest method was old-fashioned nepotism. He knew his relatives to be worthy and was not shy of promoting them. Minor honours were showered upon his brothers, his son became an under-secretary, five other relatives held posts in the administration. When the see of Derry fell vacant he

---

[1] *Letters of Sydney Smith*, ed. Nowell Smith, 563.
[2] Grey to Archbishop Vernon Harcourt, 25 January 1834, HP. For the same sentiment, Grey to Archbishop Howley, 19 October 1832, HP.

nominated his brother-in-law, Dr. Ponsonby, on condition that if the government hereafter diminished the vast stipend Ponsonby should accept the new condition of service.[1] When the Bishop of Hereford died in college at Winchester, where he lived as warden, Grey advanced his brother Edward, to whom he had lately given the deanery of Hereford. Though the press smiled at this family loyalty and found it unusual in a bishop that Edward Grey should have been married three times, Tories were not dissatisfied. Ponsonby and Edward Grey were not eminent in their profession, but were believed at least to be reasonably conservative.

In August 1831 the Archbishop of Dublin died. Grey offered the see to that veteran Whig Henry Bathurst, Bishop of Norwich, already 87 years old and incapable of performing the duty of the diocese of Norwich. The shortage of Whig clergymen was desperate if Henry Bathurst must be offered Dublin. Bathurst refused with courtesy and vainly solicited the preferment for his son.[2]

Lord Chancellor Brougham suggested Dr. Arnold of Rugby or Dr. Whately of Oriel College and was surprised to find that Grey had never heard of Whately. Grey immediately accepted Whately. And so this rough militant philosopher, who once preached a sermon with one leg dangling out of the pulpit and shocked Bishop Bathurst by receiving him with feet on the table and looked like a Yorkshire ostler, became Archbishop of Dublin, the quickest punster in Ireland and the least episcopal bishop of the century.[3] 'Heaven save the mark,' exclaimed a journalist,'—HIS GRACE!'

Whately compared himself to a helmsman called to the rudder of a

[1] Greville, ii, 75; leader against his nepotism with illustrations, JB, 18 September 1831. Ponsonby was a good man. His successor was told by a Roman Catholic shopkeeper of Derry, 'Auld Ponsonby . . . was twenty years here and a better Christian we never saw. Sure no man ever heard a word of releegion out of him.' The word religion is here being used in its political sense. Cf. *Life of Alexander*, 83.

[2] Grey to Bathurst, 21 August 1831, HP; Bathurst to Grey, 22 August 1831, HP. The son, poor Archdeacon Bathurst, survived to plague Grey and then Melbourne with piteous and menacing and at last unbalanced letters for their failure to redeem a half-promise to his father. 'This', wrote the Tory Bishop of Rochester to Archdeacon Bathurst, 'is the way in which the Whigs serve their friends.'
There was a rumour that the only illegitimate son of King William IV to be in holy orders would succeed. JB, 11 September 1831.

[3] Aspinall, *Three Diaries*, 16, 363; JB, 29 December 1832. Whately was on a visit to Arnold at Rugby when the offer arrived. The letter arrived at breakfast. Whately put it in his pocket without remark and afterwards walked in the garden for an hour. He came back decided and told the family. Arnold thought at the time that he was right to accept. Later he was less sure. For his recantation in the matter cf. *Memorials of Bishop Hampden*, 63.

crazy ship in a storm. He conceived that in large districts of Ireland the established church was such as you might establish in China or Turkey with the aid of a map, with no place of worship, no congregation, no payment. Predicting that he would be the last Protestant Archbishop of Dublin, he expected and desired desperate remedies. He believed that Roman Catholic priests ought to be paid by the state, and perhaps that the money should come from the revenues of the established church. In accepting Grey's offer, he said that he wanted to devote a large part of the revenues of his see to purposes connected with religion.[1]

All the talk was beginning to be of seizing money from the Irish bishoprics. Ponsonby of Derry agreed to be diminished, Whately of Dublin asked to be diminished. On 22 November 1832 the *Times* wrote a leader against the excessive number of Irish bishops, four archbishops and eighteen bishops, for so small a Protestant population. If the property of the Church of Ireland were not to be confiscated as the radicals suggested, at least the Whigs might diminish these top-heavy mitres and use the annual income to benefit Roman Catholics. The diocese of Raphoe had twenty-five benefices, Killala twenty. The English diocese of Lincoln contained as many benefices as twenty-two Irish dioceses put together. Reforming newspapers suggested that one archbishop and four bishops would be ample for the Church of Ireland.

By 7 January 1833 it was known that the new Whig cabinet planned to reduce the Irish bishops. The elections had gone better than the Whigs feared, in that the new House of Commons was not so revolutionary as pessimists had predicted. They had gone worse than the more sanguine Tories hoped. The election produced only about 156 known Tory members; Ireland returned a strong force of Roman Catholics; Scotland, which was formerly a vast Tory pocket borough, returned a sweep of reforming members. The Tories reconciled themselves hopelessly to an infinite vista of exclusion from power. They determined to resist the coming reform of the Church of England and Ireland and do what they could to prevent it becoming destruction.

For confiscating the money of the Church of Ireland, the Whig cabinet was not a suitable body. It was an aristocratic cabinet.

In the country it was believed to be more revolutionary than it was. Any measure to pay Roman Catholic priests from the funds of the

---

[1] Whately to Grey, September 1831, HP; *Life of Whately*, i, 110–12.

Church of Ireland, any radical measure to confiscate the endowments of the Church of Ireland and apply them to the benefit of a Catholic peasantry, made some members of the Whig cabinet quake; and among them the prime minister. Lord Grey was not a man who enjoyed dividing the country. He was also aware of a House of Lords which he did not control. To secure' the passing of the reform act he had fought the House of Lords. But he was too much of a Whig lord to enjoy weakening that House and shrank from further quarrels between the Houses. He was aware that behind the House of Lords stood King William IV, who trusted Archbishop Howley of Canterbury to advise him on ecclesiastical affairs.

The complexion of government, though Whig, was conservative. The atmosphere of the House of Commons was heady, sweet air of representative government, sense of power at last to change, conviction that mountains needed but a push to fall. The immorality caused by London theatres and the failure of London to observe the Sabbath were as formidably attacked as flogging in the army or the East India company. Dissenting fervour united with radical liberty to pass the act of that summer which at last emancipated (from 1 August 1834) all slaves in the British Empire subject to an interim apprenticeship of not more than six years. But even in this great law, which posterity has seen as the supreme moral act of those reforming years, the provisions showed how conservative were Whig ministers. Radicals and dissenters and a few evangelicals like Fowell Buxton wanted immediate freedom for slaves without apprenticeship and without compensation to slave-owners. Guided by Edward Stanley, the government insisted on the apprenticeship as a reasonable transition, and on an ample compensation of twenty million pounds to the slave-owners.

The Whigs were numerous enough not to need radical votes for their power. But they suffered loss of reputation by their alliance with this left wing hostile not only to the Irish church but to the idea of establishment; and among their members were some who sat loose to the stricter obligations of churchmanship. In the eyes of Tory churchmen they were blackened with a suspicion of free-thinking or deism. They were alleged to feel no concern for the true interests of the church, and to have their laboratory in Holland House, notorious for the atheistic conversation of its librarian Allen. Yet they could not commend measures to a majority in Parliament or the country unless they presented the measures as strength to the established church by removing obstacles, corruptions, abuse. They must appear to promote reform for the good of the church. And some of them were not pretending. Grey was a staunch churchman. Lord Althorp, leader of the House of Commons, was devout for all his racy past. But the husting cries of extreme supporters clothed this claim with a seeming hypocrisy. John Keble wrote of 'the ruffian band come to reform, where ne'er they came to pray'.[1]

The inescapable fact was anarchy in Ireland and the first need of government was to govern. The necessity was a peace preservation bill, commonly called coercion bill, which gave stringent powers of curfew and court-martial to the Irish authorities. Such an act was foreign to the habits of the British constitution. The cabinet became aware that their bill to mend the Irish church must be radical, partly because only thus could they persuade the Irish of their benevolence, and partly because their supporters in Commons and country shouted as often for demolition as for repair.

The church temporalities (Ireland) bill appeared in the House of Commons on 12 February 1833, in chilly silence, and soon surprised everyone by its radical clauses. It abolished two (Cashel and Tuam) of the four Irish archbishoprics and eight of the bishoprics; or if the word *abolish* is a little strong, it amalgamated their dioceses with neighbouring dioceses at the next vacancy and removed the stipends. It reduced the revenues of the two wealthiest sees, Armagh and Derry; abolished church cess, the tax paid by parishioners to maintain a parish church in repair; ruled that when a benefice was so destitute of worshippers, and had become such a sinecure that no worship had been held in the parish for three years, the appointment to the benefice might be suspended and the money applied elsewhere; relieved the clergy of paying first-fruits on their benefices and in return instituted an income tax on livings worth £200 (in the final bill £300), on a gradually increasing scale from 5 per cent to 15 per cent. The tenants of bishops, who held leases with power to renew on payment of a fine at fixed intervals, were permitted to convert these leases into perpetual tenancies.

Here was the money of the Church of Ireland—money from two archbishoprics and eight bishoprics; money from suspended benefices, money from two great sees reduced, money from the sale of tenants' leases after compensating the bishops, and money from income tax

---

[1] *Lyra Apostolica* (1836), 142; March 1833.

on Irish benefices. This money, reckoned at about £150,000, the bill placed in trust with a new corporation called Ecclesiastical Commissioners, who should determine its disposal.

Much depended on the objects to which the money was allotted. Since church cess was abolished, part of the revenue must be directed to repairing churches and part to augment the stipends of poor clergy. Thereafter it was a question whether the remainder might be used to build Catholic or secular schools, or even to pay Roman Catholic priests. The bill was vague. 'The surplus of the said monies', it said, '. . . shall be applied to such purposes as Parliament shall hereafter appoint and decide.' Upon this clause, celebrated later as clause 147, the battle centred.[1]

When Lord Althorp explained the bill to the House of Commons on 12 February 1833 the first cold silence soon gave way to excitement. They gave him loud cheers when he abolished church cess and tumultuous applause when he abolished ten bishops. O'Connell himself cheered loudly. Radicals believed that the surplus money must be destined by clause 147 to pay stipends to Catholic priests. One Whig observer declared that he had never seen such joy in the House of Commons and could have wept for very pleasure.[2] The faces of Tory clergymen were black as their coats. A House of Commons which need not be Anglican was proposing to rob the Church of Ireland, and why not afterwards the Church of England? Far away, on holiday in Naples, John Henry Newman heard the news. He thought it atrocious and sacrilegious. 'Well done! my blind premier', he wrote savagely, 'confiscate and rob till, like Samson, you pull down the political structure on your own head!'[3]

[1] Much depended on the composition of the commission which should decide how to spend the money. For although the allocation of money to secular or Catholic purposes rested with Parliament alone and not with the commissioners, the decision of the commissioners would determine whether or not there was a surplus to spend; and if the commission consisted entirely of bishops, it was a prediction that there would be no surplus. The final bill determined the commissioners to be: six bishops, of whom the Archbishops of Armagh and Dublin must be two and four others to be appointed by the lord lieutenant; five other persons, all of whom must be members of the Church of Ireland, and two of whom were ex officio the lord chancellor of Ireland and the lord chief justice of Ireland (if the last was a member of the Church of Ireland). The last three need not be laymen, but might be salaried.

[2] Littleton's Diary, ap. Aspinall, Three Diaries, 301. There was a rumour that the government intended to suppress more than ten sees, but were dissuaded by an Irish prelate, perhaps Ponsonby. W. Palmer, Narrative, 1843, 3.

[3] LC i, 353, 372. On 3 June 1833 to everyone's surprise the Tory Lords defeated the government by twelve votes (including seven bishops) in a motion about neutrality in Portugal. The clubs were heavy with more talk of impending resignation. Grey and

Tories divided in resistance to the Irish church bill. Ultra-Tories under the Duke of Cumberland held that the state had no right to abolish a single bishopric in Ireland without leave of the Church. They said that the state had no right to interfere with the property of the church and that this interference was like robbing Peter because Paul asked for his purse. To confiscate the funds of the Church of Ireland appeared to them as tyrannical as confiscating the funds of Roman Catholics or dissenters. They therefore felt bound in conscience to vote against the bill and precipitate collision between the Houses of Parliament. The more moderate Tory lords under the Duke of Wellington wished to avert collision at almost all cost. They could not see what principle was transgressed in diminishing the number of bishoprics *provided the intention was the good of the church*. They did not mind the bill so far as it claimed to reform the Church of Ireland for the sake of the Church of Ireland. They therefore concentrated their fire upon the appropriation clause 147, the vital clause of the bill sanctioning confiscation. They were determined that the funds of the church, however rearranged, should be applied to the purposes of the church and not to pay Roman Catholic priests or build non-Anglican schools.

In the middle of June, Edward Stanley, chief author of both the Irish bills, went to see Archbishop Howley. Stanley had long been uneasy about clause 147 and probably inserted it as the only means of getting the coercion bill through Parliament and of satisfying the party. The coercion act was safely on the statute book. Stanley now saw that the Irish church bill must fail in the House of Lords if it contained clause 147, and that failure in the Lords would vastly increase the chance of disestablishment.[1] He persuaded the prime

---

Brougham went down to Windsor to see the king. He received them cordially and said that he would stand firm in their support. Aspinall, *Three Diaries*, 333. He probably told them that he would intervene to secure the passing of the Irish church bill, if necessary by creating peers. He perhaps told them that he would ask Archbishop Howley to stop the bishops from interfering in politics. The cabinet determined to continue. But everyone knew that the Irish church bill was driving the two houses of Parliament into another collision with an even more radical issue. On 6 June Dr. Phillpotts of Exeter marked the fighting spirit of the ultras with a tremendous warrior utterance about the king's duties under the coronation oath. The *Times* again switched on fury against bishops, clamouring for their exclusion from the House of Lords. The king wrote a letter to Archbishop Howley, urging the bishops, for the sake of their order and the church, not to meddle in politics.

[1] *Letters of Charles Arbuthnot*, 171–2.

minister that as the surplus of Irish church money appeared likely to be smaller than expected, clause 147 was not worth a fight. The prime minister was convinced and relieved. He went round the cabinet. He obtained the consent of Brougham, who was in a hurry and hardly listened, Holland, who did not like to oppose Grey, Althorp, who was poorly with gout but gave an impression of not caring, and Graham, who agreed with Stanley that the clause was bad. Lord John Russell said, 'We could not have a revolution once a year.' Some of the Whig lords were more anxious than Tories to avoid the collision which might destroy the powers of the House of Lords.[1]

With the cabinet squared, Grey went to the king to propose the dropping of clause 147. The king was delighted and said that under these conditions he could guarantee the safe passage of the bill. It was finally decided at 4 p.m. on 21 June; and an hour later Edward Stanley announced the decision to an electric House of Commons.[2]

O'Connell and the Irish members were embittered beyond measure. From the Irish church they demanded money for the Irish people and cheered clause 147 as the one little ray of hope. Now the money must go back into the Irish church, into repairs of roofs and increase of stipends. Instead of a national measure for Ireland, the bill became a tinkering with the established church. O'Connell, Hume and Sheil violently accused the Whigs of breaking faith. 'I repudiate it,' cried O'Connell, 'on the part of the people of Ireland.' They claimed that the coercion act had been passed on trust in promises which had now been broken. 'The pith, substance, the marrow and essence of the bill is plucked out of it, and the husk, the rind, the void and valueless shell, the shrivelled and empty skin, is left behind.'[3]

Eight months before the sky was cloudy with rumours of disestablishment and disendowment. For conservative churchmen the air was now lighter. If the Whig government could not or would not carry a small measure to take away funds from the Church of Ireland, it would not sensibly attempt to disestablish the Church of England. The fate of this first bill to take Irish church money was heavy with disaster for Whig reform. The Whigs were not finished with appropriation. The proposal to take the money of the Irish church survived for several years, to plague their politics, divide their counsels and

[1] Le Marchant and Ellenborough, Aspinall 338, 340.
[2] Peel was told that the decision to withdraw clause 147 was caused by a positive order from the king. Parker, *Peel*, ii, 222.
[3] Sheil in Hansard, xix, 1833, 268; O'Connell in Hansard xviii, 1077.

weaken their party. For the rest of his life Edward Stanley claimed that this bill which abolished ten bishops saved the establishment of the Church of Ireland.[1]

An acrimonious battle still developed in the Lords over the measure which had thus been stripped of the only proposal to content radicals. For the Whig cabinet it was a matter of prestige. They promised the nation an Irish measure and this was the measure promised. They secured the coercion act on this promise, felt like breakers of faith if they failed to pass it, regarded it as earnest of their endeavour to correct abuses in the church as in other institutions of the country. Though now a mouse of a measure it must be brought to birth. They therefore laboured under the difficulty that enemies could represent their plea of reforming the church to be hypocrisy, and their true motive to be the casting of a sop to the Irish Cerberus.

Though conservative members of the Church of England lost a little of their panic, they still felt painful anxiety about the coming parliamentary session of 1834. If it had been the turn of the Irish church in 1833 it would infallibly be the turn of the English church in 1834. And although Tory clergymen could be found to whisper behind locked doors that the Church of England needed reform, radical ideas of reform looked suspiciously like burglary. Their friends had stripped the Irish church act of its most offensive clause. But they hated the precedent. Without consulting church authorities a government which leaned on Catholic and dissenting votes abolished bishoprics and arranged endowments. What might such a government do to the Church of England? They awaited the parliament of 1834 with foreboding.

4. CHURCH AND DISSENT IN 1834

Clamour to disestablish the Church of England rose from dissenting throats. Dissenters of the Independent tradition held an established church to be unchristian. Their doctrine repudiated alliance between church and magistrate. Seeing the clergy of the Church of England abused by radical reformers, they found it tempting or proper to join the hunt. The new bear-garden of a House of Commons witnessed language shocking to conservative ears. As lay meetings of the Church of England evoked Tory rhetoric, dissenting meetings were inflamed

[1] Cf. his speech in the Lords, 18 June 1857. Hansard, cxlv, 1975.

with Whig and radical rhetoric. The claims of dissenters were spun into webs of acrimony, fabricated not only from the ills of dissenters but from farmers' vexation against tithe or radical abuse of aristocratic corruption. A sturdy Yorkshire chairman told a meeting of dissenters at Cleckheaton that a church raised on hay cocks and wheatsheaves would fall.[1] But tithe, however irritant, was not an authentic grievance of dissenters as dissenters. If large numbers of dissenters wished to remain quiet and not destroy the peace of their parish and village life, if reputable dissenting journals like the *Congregational Magazine* or the *Eclectic Review* would not touch the political campaign, the war of conservative and radical became partly identified with a war of churchman versus dissenter. In the House of Commons a dissenter named Faithfull denounced the Church of England as a harlot and Rippon secured sixty-seven votes for a motion to dismiss bishops from the House of Lords. A Carmarthen society of dissenters offered prizes for essays against the church. Occasional ministers inflamed the Tory public by statements like that of a pastor in Leeds, 'I do not want to reform the church; I want to pull it down.'[2] When dissenting members in the House of Commons allied themselves with O'Connell and Irish Roman Catholics in motions against the established church, their conduct and their language filled the breasts of high churchmen with intolerable anger.

During the early months of 1834 the discomfort between church and dissent thus reached a bitterness without precedent in English history.

The revolutionary demand, advocated by some dissenters and not by others, was adopted by the only body which could claim any sort of right to represent the dissenters. The Protestant dissenting deputies met regularly in London and had been meeting for more than a century. They consisted and still consist of two persons chosen from each congregation of the three denominations (Presbyterian, Independent, Baptist) within twelve miles of London, with the special purpose of protecting the civil rights of dissenters. As common subjects of disabilities which the state imposed upon dissenters from the established church, the three denominations had long been accustomed to work together. The Whig party, which alone offered them hopes of religious equality before the law, was their natural home. The

[1] *Br. Mag.*, 5, 1834, 393.
[2] *Br. Mag.*, 5, 1834, 223, 257.

deputies represented some hundred congregations.[1] Their watchdog committee of twenty-one met regularly at the King's Head tavern in the Poultry. Though an organ of the London congregations, they were widely recognised as speaking for dissenting bodies through the nation and possessed the privilege of presenting addresses to the crown. They were a respectable and sober body who took the best of legal advice and preferred private influence to public agitation. They had been powerful in securing the repeal in 1828 of the test and corporation acts.

Open to the pressure of dissenting opinion over the country, the deputies went further than the demand for relief from disabilities. A general meeting on 27 December 1833 declared the union of church and state to be unjust and unscriptural, however it might be modified. The deputies were instructed to prepare petitions in this sense. During February 1834 the united committee for dissenting grievances met almost daily and was often in consultation with friendly members of the Whig cabinet, Holland, Lansdowne, Lord John Russell. On 8 May 1834 400 delegates from over the country met with Edward Baines M.P., in the chair and demanded disestablishment, with only three votes against the motion.

They received no encouragement from Lord Grey. The prime minister was not a little displeased at the violent party among the dissenters. In the cabinet was talk of throwing dissenters off and letting them shift for themselves.[2] The government felt embarrassed and thought that dissenting clamour for disestablishment strengthened the Tory party.

The Tory parson toiled in a tangled state of mind. He believed in an established church and wanted to resist dissenters. He began to bristle towards dissent. So far as the phrase *high* churchman meant stiff for the Church of England against dissenters, the clergy of 1830 to 1834 grew higher and higher; until some of them grew so high that hardly any communication was possible with persons of normal stature. War in press and parliament was reflected in parish battles.

---

[1] The evidence for exact numbers in 1834 is lost. At the beginning of 1836 there were fourteen Presbyterian, 53 Independent and 36 Baptist, a total of 103 congregations. Eight Presbyterian congregations seceded in 1836. In a petition of 11 January 1843 the deputies claimed to represent nearly 100 congregations (B. L. Manning, 36, 78), and met once or twice a year.

[2] *Memoir of R. Aspland*, 534.

Even evangelicals who once worked against slavery or at Bible Society in happy alliance with dissenters, started declining to stand on the same platform. Zealots recommended an end to social intercourse with dissenters, if necessary the removal of custom from dissenting shops.[1] The curate of Milford in Yorkshire refused to read the burial service over the child of a Baptist ,because he was unbaptised. The little Unitarian congregation at Thorne buried an infant in the yard of their chapel because the parson declined to inter the child unless the parents would dispense him from reading the prayer book. The vicar of St. Mary the Virgin at Oxford, J. H. Newman, refused to marry in church the daughter of a Baptist pastrycook because she was unbaptised, and it was falsely alleged in the press, which dubbed him the Reverend Bigot, that he refused because she was a dissenter. Newman was troubled but not moved by the abuse. 'We must make a stand *somewhere*—things are rolling downhill so gradually that, wherever we make a stand, it will be said to be a harsh measure. . . . The church shall not crumble away without my doing in my place what I can to hinder it.'[2]

But the attitudes of Anglican clergymen were diverse. Bishop Maltby of Chichester shocked the world by inviting a Unitarian minister to a public dinner, graced by the presence of the Duke of Richmond; and Dr. Fullagar was no ordinary minister, but a prominent assailant of church rate and militant for disestablishment. Maltby scorned the uproar and invited to another public dinner Father Tierney, Roman Catholic chaplain to the Duke of Norfolk.[3]

Parsons found a perplexity in standing stiff for the Church of England. Most of them wished to keep establishment, could not imagine England without the Church of England, and kept their eyes from the distant view. But others saw further. Prepared to welcome the idea of an established church, they perceived suddenly that establishment is loss as well as profit. No government would dream of annihilating ten Roman Catholic bishoprics or introducing a bill to

[1] *Br. Mag.*, 7, 1835, 585–6.

[2] Newman to Bowden, 13 July 1834, OM; cf. LC, ii, 56. For Milford, etc., cf. *Br. Mag.*, 5, 1834, 176–7; *Unit. Mag.*, 1834, 191–2.

[3] JB, 31 August and 14 September 1834. At the end of 1834 Blanco White, who had become a resident chaplain in the household of Archbishop Whately, announced his conversion to the Unitarian faith and hastily left Dublin. Whately, though pained and abused, continued to pay him a pension and to treat him with affection; cf. *Life of Whately*, i, 248–89. Cf. the Newman-Whately social relationship in *Life of Whately*, i, 233–40; the letter in LC, ii, 68–69, also printed at the end of later editions of the *Apologia*; the J. H. Newman-Frank Newman relation in M. Trevor, i, 156.

confiscate the property of Baptist churches. Yet because the Church of England was established the government thought nothing of playing dominoes with prelates and mulcting ecclesiastical incomes. To some parsons the danger was neither dissenting clamour which they despised nor disestablishment which they could endure. They feared the state more than the dissenting deputies, a corrupt establishment more than disendowment. From the tortures of imagination rose misty spectres, half-atheist ministers nominating heretical bishops, destroying as useless the beauty and grandeur of English cathedrals, cutting doctrines from the prayer book to make it more palatable.

In the autumn of 1833 the political clubs spread rumours of this or that reform planned for or against the Church of England. The talk now was not only of reforming pluralities or redistributing incomes. There were demands that Parliament should cut passages from the liturgy, or revise the Thirty-nine Articles, or draft new forms of prayer. This last threat touched the deepest principles of conscience. Disobedience hung in the air. Clergymen debated the prospects of going out to a free Church of England, like non-jurors after the revolution of 1688. They turned their eyes with new interest to countries where the Book of Common Prayer was used by a church though not established, to the Episcopal Church of Scotland and the Protestant Episcopal Church of the United States of America. Do we, it was asked, owe any obedience to the House of Commons if its act is opposed to our religious duty and our ecclesiastical superiors?[1] The members of the House of Commons need no longer be members of the Church of England. For a few months it seemed unendurable that a Whig government, depending on Roman Catholic votes in Ireland and Presbyterian votes in Scotland and dissenting votes in England, should plan drastic change in the Church of England without asking the Church of England.

No one seemed to know whom or what, when you wished to ask the Church of England, you asked.

The first 'Tracts for the Times'

The swing towards high churchmanship, evident everywhere during these years, is plain in the history of John Henry Newman. Newman was elected Fellow of Oriel College in April 1822 and vicar of St. Mary the Virgin, university church at Oxford, in 1828. Son of

[1] Br. Mag., 4, 1833, 652.

an unsuccessful London banker and a devout mother of Huguenot descent, he was sensitive, shy and complicated, puritan in austerity, evangelical in inclination, somewhat introverted, aloof by reason of nervousness and not from sense of superiority. He wrote articles for the chief evangelical magazine, the *Christian Observer*, and interspersed his conversation with Biblical texts. Something in the family bred enthusiasm, for one brother Charles was soon planning to be atheist and socialist in a day when those professions were fanatical as well as wicked, and another brother Frank joined an expedition to convert the Persians to the doctrines of the Plymouth Brethren.

Richard Whately, discovering this fervent and shrinking fellow at high table, barked and monologued him out of his corner. He forced Newman to be interested in logic, made him his dialectical anvil and assistant, elicited the originality of his mind, badgered him into reading David Hume and Gibbon as though they had something important if erroneous to say, arranged for him to write articles for the *Encyclopaedia Metropolitana*. When Whately became principal of St. Alban hall in Oxford he made Newman for a short time his vice-principal. Whately declared that Newman had the clearest mind he knew. And though the praise is evidence chiefly that Newman was a good listener unlikely to interrupt, it shows him moving out of his evangelical phase into a more critical or academic mood. Newman later defined the process regretfully as beginning to prefer intellectual to moral excellence. Edward Hawkins, whom Newman helped to elect as provost of Oriel in the election of 1828, when John Keble was the rival candidate, guided him towards a more staid and traditional churchmanship. They argued whether the world could rightly be divided into sheep and goats, saints and sinners, and Hawkins prevailed. Newman's evangelical belief, though not his evangelical habits of mind and conduct, were fading away. He wrote in retrospect that Whately taught him to see with his own eyes and walk with his own feet.[1]

In 1827 Hurrell Froude became a junior tutor at Oriel and a year later Newman, now a senior tutor, began to know him intimately. Froude was the son of the Archdeacon of Totnes in Devonshire, an epitome of the old high churchmen of England; revering King Charles I, distrusting religious enthusiasm, stern Tories in politics, not quite able to reconcile themselves to the revolution of 1688,

[1] *Apologia*, 37.

strong for that church government by bishops which the enemies of Charles I tried to abolish, and stalwart for the rights and privileges of the Church of England. Hurrell Froude had bright eyes and a gay manner, was hard-riding and ironical, enjoyed extreme language and preferred to shock. He was sent as pupil to John Keble, fellow of Oriel and curate of Southrop, near Fairford, by whom the principles were lived not as a political platform but as a reverent and spiritual way of life. Froude learnt of Catholic authority, of apostolic succession, of modes of devotion far removed from the Roundhead and Calvinist tradition which he was educated to detest. He hated Milton and his poetry, adored (his word) King Charles and Archbishop Laud.[1]

In the intellectual solitude of Oriel, Froude turned for comfort and anchor to Keble. Froude maintained a steady correspondence, telling him that he was the shadow of a great rock in a weary land.[2] Under Keble's guidance he read over and over again the devotional classics of the high tradition, Law's Serious Call and Jeremy Taylor's Holy Living and Holy Dying. He once told Keble that after his mother died five and a half years before he felt as if he were 'without God in the world' and that Keble's letter had given him something more like happiness than he had known since her death. He revered Keble's saintliness and found it a check against bad language to imagine himself always in Keble's presence.[3] In the autumn after his election to a fellowship, though still laughing and amusing to the outside world, he began a 'sort of monastic' life, more austere than Keble approved, sleeping on the floor, fasting not by minor acts of self-denial but sometimes by going without food until the late evening and then only taking a little bread. He kept a journal of confession and self-examination, which Keble advised him to burn,[4] but which survived to be printed posthumously by the imprudence of Newman and Keble. When every allowance is made for the nature of the document, there was something immature as well as stern about this lonely and secret attempt to practise Catholic devotion in a college where the conversation pounded away at the traditional axioms on which it was based.

From 1819 Keble was writing verses on the Sundays of the English

[1] Remains, i, 177, 31 March 1825.
[2] Froude to Keble, April or May 1826, Remains, i, 197.
[3] Froude to Keble, 5 November 1826, Remains, i, 206: cf. i, 445.
[4] Remains, i, 60. Keble's letter was printed by Coleridge, Keble, i, 142–3. The journal ran from July 1826 for six months.

calendar. He had a modest opinion of their poetic quality, but believed them to be useful in devotion. By 1825 he completed a series of poems on all the Sundays of the prayer book and wondered whether to publish them. He sent them to a number of friends for advice.[1] Keble's father wanted them published and for Keble this was a final command. If he wanted to declare some statement true, it was enough to declare that it was what his father thought. In June 1827 Keble published the poems anonymously under the title *The Christian Year*. Keble had no high opinion of them. Perceiving their faults of style and finish, he rarely spoke of them without melancholy. When they became popular he thought them overrated. Froude was not sure that Keble was right to publish or that the poems were worthy of their author. It took him four months to find admiration first of loyalty and then of the heart. Newman, not yet intimate with Keble, leaped far more quickly into praise. He instantly thought the poems quite exquisite.[2]

Keble wrote in the preface that he aimed to establish 'a sober standard of feeling in matters of practical religion'. The high churchmen of the recent past had been sober in their religion, so sober that they were later known as the high and dry, for their sobriety consisted of a rational fear of emotional riots which they believed themselves able to discern among dissenters and English evangelicals. They so suspected feeling that they appeared at times to have no religious feelings. And yet the general reaction of the age against the alleged shallowness of the eighteenth century, the desire to afford a proper outlet for feeling, the emotional upsurge of romantic literature, the poetry of sentiment, caused religious expression to seek new forms outside the language of the evangelical party. The hymnody of dissenters and evangelicals taught English Christianity the worth of poetry as a kindling and satisfaction of devotional aspiration. In 1827 nearly all high churchmen still refused to allow hymns in their churches. Keble intended his verses not for the congregation but for the soul at his bedside; and therefore permitted himself phrases which, for all his professed aim of sobriety, an older generation would have feared as enthusiastic:

> Sun of my soul, thou Saviour dear,
> It is not night if thou be near

---

[1] e.g. Davison, J. T. Coleridge, Hurrell Froude.   [2] LC, i, 165.

The expressions of a romantic age here entered Christian devotion, and the evangelical love of hymnody began to pass into the affections of more traditional English churchmen. *The Christian Year* sold 108,000 copies by January 1854, 265,000 copies by April 1868. The devout among the Anglican middle classes came to value it as dissenters valued *Pilgrim's Progress*. Though the book was supposed to be still anonymous, Keble was elected (1831) professor of poetry at Oxford.

With his old evangelical heritage Newman responded to these verses. He still regarded Froude as a red-hot high churchman. Froude still regarded Newman as lax in his religious opinions, and regretted that he held advanced opinions about the damnatory clauses of the Athanasian creed.[1] In August 1828 Newman accepted an invitation from Keble to stay with him at Fairford. Keble was growing upon Newman's mind. At Fairford the verses of *The Christian Year* kept running in Newman's head as he watched the simple happiness of the Keble family. Froude afterwards claimed that he succeeded in bringing Keble and Newman together. When he was dying he said that if he were asked what good deed he had ever done he would say that he brought Keble and Newman to understand each other.[2] By September 1828 Froude was telling his friend Robert Wilberforce, son of the slave-emancipator, that Newman 'is a fellow that I like more, the more I think of him; only I would give a few odd pence if he were not a heretic'.[3] As late as March 1829 Newman allowed himself to be elected a secretary of the Oxford branch of the Church Missionary Society. As late as August 1829 Newman still called Froude *bigot* to his face, but now in affectionate jest. They fought shoulder to shoulder in the fight at Oxford over Catholic emancipation, to prevent Peel being re-elected as member for the university; and Whately and Hawkins (now called by Newman the meddling Hawkins) fought hard upon the other side. By the summer of 1829 Newman had left the dialectical stoa of Whately and entered the sacramental world of Froude and Keble. In religion as in politics his mind swung decisively towards the conservatives. On 14 November 1829 his sister Harriett wrote in alarm that she had been reading two of his sermons and found them very high church.[4] In February 1830 an ironical Fellow of St. John's

---

[1] Froude to Newman, 26 September 1831, *Remains*, i, 245.
[2] *Remains*, i, 438; LC, i, 190.
[3] Froude to Wilberforce, 7 September 1828, *Remains*, i, 232–3.
[4] LC, i, 215.

College told Bishop Murray of Rochester in hyperbole that, though once called evangelical, Newman was now as staunch a churchman as Addison's landlord, who, when he could not find time to go to church, headed mobs to pull down meeting-houses; that he drank church and king every day in a bumper after dinner, and every night after supper sang 'A health to old England, the king and the church'.[1] Newman wrote an anonymous pamphlet to purge the Oxford branch of the Church Missionary Society of its leaning to friendliness with dissenters, and was turned out of his secretaryship by a large public meeting. In June 1830 he resigned from the Oxford branch of the Bible Society. He marked the break from Whately by wondering whether to dedicate a book to him in the lapidary words, 'He had not only taught me to think, but to think for myself'. Whately took an individual and humorous revenge by inviting Newman to a dinner of the dons least intellectual and most addicted to port, and asking him if he was proud of his friends.[2] They were far from being enemies. When Whately was made Archbishop of Dublin Newman half expected that Whately would invite him to go, and that his conscience would tell him to accept. But no invitation came.

The struggle for the reform bill turned Newman into as decided a conservative high churchman as Froude. He admired the resistance of the bishops and longed that they should continue to do their duty. Where once he had written for the evangelical *Christian Observer*, he now wrote for the new *British Magazine*, founded in 1832 to be organ of resistance to Whig church reform. When in December 1832 he set out for a holiday in the Mediterranean with Froude and his father, the archdeacon, he conscientiously averted his gaze from a tricolour flying from a French ship in Algiers harbour. When he passed through Paris and was forced to stay for a day he refused to enjoy the city, but kept obstinately indoors.[3] This closing of the eyes was a symbol of inward refusal to contemplate the liberal cause triumphing across Europe. In the religious excitements of Malta, amid the processions of the madonna and the saints, he wrote home wistfully of the English church: 'How awful seems (to me here) the crime of demolition in England! All one can say of Whigs, radicals and the rest is, that they know not what they do.'[4]

The coughing, consumptive Froude lived almost solitary in Oriel

---

[1] LC, i, 224–5.   [2] *Apologia*, 37, 39.
[3] *Apologia*, 54.   [4] LC, i, 338.

during the long vacation of 1833.[1] In the common room he frequently met William Palmer of Worcester College and discussed with him the state of church and nation. Palmer was a dry and learned Irishman from Trinity College, Dublin, and felt the wrongs and ills of the Irish church, refusal of tithe and maltreatment of clergy, loss of ten bishoprics and weakening of Protestant ascendancy, more passionately than his cool restraint allowed to show.[2] In Oriel common room Palmer and Froude decided to form an association to defend the liberties and principles of the church. Froude was to enlist Keble, Palmer to enlist Hugh James Rose, the editor of the British Magazine. On 11 July Newman reached Oxford from France. Three days later he heard Keble use the assize sermon to denounce the government for its 'sacrilegious' conduct in Ireland and threw himself into the campaign which Froude and Palmer had agreed.[3]

Rose was vicar of Hadleigh in Suffolk and invited Froude and Palmer to a conference there of four days, 25-29 July 1833. Present also were Arthur Perceval, a royal chaplain and cousin to the enthusiast ex-M.P. Spencer Perceval, and Rose's curate, R. C. Trench.

The debates at Hadleigh decided nothing and disclosed a radical division of opinions. Froude later classified the two sides as apostolicals and conservatives or Xs and Zs. The Xs were high churchmen who now cared nothing for establishment and wanted to recover the spiritual authority of the church apart from the state. The Zs were conservatives who believed that no good could come of abandoning establishment or endowment, and that the only consequence would be harm to the Christianity of the country. Froude was inclined to regard the union of church and state as evil and to want a radical change in the mode of appointing bishops. Palmer and Rose could see no practicable mode of electing bishops which had more advantages, and thought that if the clergy were forced to depend on voluntary contributions

---

[1] Palmer, Narrative, 6.

[2] In 1832 Palmer published in two volumes Origines Liturgicae, a study of the primitive liturgies and of the antiquities underlying the English prayer book. It is not known whether Froude was first attracted by this original and solid piece of learning or by Palmer's reputation as the doughtiest pamphleteer against Arnold's plan of church reform.

[3] In reaction to the misunderstanding derived from Newman's Apologia that this assize sermon began the Oxford Movement, it has been maintained that it was altogether unimportant except to Newman's breast. This is almost but not quite true. Keble had it printed and sent off numerous copies; and nine years later A. P. Perceval referred to it as an important illustration of the mood of the time, A Collection, 1842,10. On the other hand, the pages of the copy which Keble sent to E. B. Pusey remained uncut till Pusey's death. Liddon, Life of Pusey, i, 276.

their independence would soon perish. Palmer and Rose wished to exercise political pressure to maintain the establishment, by memorials, committees, unions, protests. Froude cared nothing for committees and wanted to blow idealistic trumpets calling the church to resist a Whig state. Rose hoped for a new Tory government, the end of popular power, perhaps even a return of pocket boroughs. Froude had no use for this sort of Toryism and wanted the church to go to the people, to root itself in popular affection. Rose believed that the clergy must have proper pay and be respected in their walk of life. Froude thought this the *gentleman heresy* and associated it with the *stuff* about prizes in the church to tempt men of talent into taking orders. He returned gloomily to Oxford, wanting a public breach with Rose. Palmer returned gloomily to Oxford, thinking Froude ignorant and rash.

The conference at Hadleigh loomed large in the mind of posterity, because eight years later it came to be charged with concocting a secret plot to alter the doctrines and discipline of the Church of England. Froude liked to jest about the *conspiracy* in which they were engaged. In fact, the conference ended in amicable frustration. But they succeeded in agreeing thus far: that since the suppression of Irish bishops was intelligible only among a people ignorant of the nature and constitution of the church, they must first restore to the public mind the sense that the Christian ministry possessed a divine authority independent of the state and establishment. By annihilating ten bishoprics the Whig government invited the English clergy to open their eyes to the idea of apostolic succession and its connexion with the independent authority of the church.

Froude and Palmer returned to Oxford and found Newman and Keble. By 14 August 1833 they agreed the principles of their new movement, not without hesitation. First, they will proclaim the doctrine of apostolic succession. Second, it is sinful voluntarily to allow persons or bodies not members of the church to interfere in matters spiritual. Third, it is desirable to make the church more popular (Keble demurred to this proposition). Fourth, they will protest against all attempts to separate church from state, while they will steadily contemplate the possibility of disestablishment and begin to prepare for it. (Keble demurred to this, because he now thought the existing union of church and state to be sinful.)[1]

---

[1] When Perceval was sent the resolutions he agreed with Keble, *A Collection*, 12–13; Froude to Perceval, 14 August 1833. Newman fully explained their plans in a letter of 11 August to Golightly, in *Golightly Papers*, box 1.

The little group in Oxford continued to discuss these propositions through August into September and continued to divide. Palmer agreed with Rose that fierce talk of disestablishment would lose support and wished to water down the resolutions. Newman and Keble were for Irish disestablishment by encouraging the Irish clergy of an amalgamated diocese to resist their new bishop, or by persuading other Irish bishops to consecrate a new bishop for a see which the Whigs had just abolished. Keble always advocated principle without regard for worldly consequences, and declared his determination not to accept any curacy or other office, though he was not yet clear that he must resign what he occupied. Like Froude, he wanted to tell the government, 'Take every pound, shilling and penny, and the curse of sacrilege along with it; only let us make our own bishops, and be governed by our own laws.'[1] Of course, he added to Newman, 'If we could get our liberty at an easier price, so much the better.' Newman saw that they must not be prematurely violent or they would lose their influence when another crisis came. But he likewise believed the church to be corrupted by union with the state and was ready for disestablishment if the government committed any further 'tyrannical' acts.[2]

Both Keble and Newman wanted the campaign to be more religious and less political. By 6 September they agreed to circulate books and tracts to inculcate the doctrine of apostolic succession, to revive more frequent communion and daily common prayer, to resist all attempts by government to alter the Book of Common Prayer, and to instruct the people in misunderstood points of Anglican discipline and worship. 'If we leave our flocks in ignorance,' wrote Newman to Keble on 5 August,[3] '. . . will they not be surprised at a call to follow us *from* the establishment, should it come to that?'

In the last ten days of August they wrote to their friends among the country clergy persuading them to join the association. It was not encouraging. Newman's old pupil Golightly thought that they were not going far enough, and wanted disestablishment and Irish resistance to the bishoprics act as a firm part of the programme.[4] Others regarded them as wild ultras.

---

[1] Keble to Newman, 8 August 1833, LC, i, 442.
[2] LC, i, 440, 449.
[3] LC, i, 441; *A Collection*, 13–14, Newman to Perceval, 6 September 1833, largely using Keble's words.
[4] Golightly to Newman, 22 August 1833, LC, i, 445.

Bad lungs kept Froude from activity, and Palmer possessed none of the qualities of a journalist or pamphleteer. Newman, now inflamed, wrote within a few days three little tracts and a popular history of St. Ambrose for the *British Magazine*. These first tracts were dated 9 September 1833, but were written, printed and already circulated by the end of August. Newman, wrote a young friend on 20 September,[1] 'is now becoming perfectly ferocious for the cause, and proportionately sanguine of success. "We'll do them," he says, at least twenty times a day.'

For the following five months the unequal yoke-fellows worked uncomfortably together. Palmer toured the country trying to form a national association, or local associations, to defend the church. Newman sat in Oxford penning lively leaflets and persuading his friends to send him matter. Palmer wanted to gather all good men and true. Newman and Froude and Keble thought that a broad base meant a milk-and-water programme, that they must be extremists and enthusiasts, risking the establishment, restoring the sense of church authority. Newman disapproved of Palmer's association, Palmer of Newman's tracts. Palmer saw that lively and ultra tracts would shock moderate men of good will into suspecting the association. Newman saw that an association would become so broad that it would end in noble platitudes. 'We cannot afford', he told Palmer, 'to dilute . . .'[2] After the first four tracts of September 1833 (three by Newman and one by Keble) Palmer persuaded Newman to stop the series, which he thought violent and offensive, while the association was under discussion. Newman agreed to wait for five weeks and to make it public that the tracts were individual manifestoes for which Palmer's association was not responsible. Towards the end of October Palmer was reconciled to tracts, and a further six (five by Newman and one by Froude) appeared between 29 October and 11 November. Palmer heard enough criticism to make him ask again that the tracts should stop. Newman was trenchant. He told Palmer that although he disliked the association he would join it if Palmer wished; but his tracts he would not stop. He continued to have qualms whether he was ruining Palmer's game. On 2 December 1833 the evangelical newspaper the *Record* launched a sudden onslaught upon the tracts, quoted extracts about apostolic succession or the eucharistic sacrifice, and declared that its surprise was extreme and its sorrow poignant

[1] J. B. Mozley, *Letters*, 36.   [2] LC, 1, 465.

to read such literature from the pen of a Protestant minister. The chief evangelical organ the *Christian Observer* rebuked the extraordinary theological doctrines of the Oxford papers connected with the association. Numbers of clergymen refused to join the Oxford association because though they had not read the tracts they read what the *Record* said about the tracts. Newman was called a papist to his face[1] and was delighted by the publicity. During the middle of December Newman made the tracts more respectable by choosing graver authors—one by Palmer himself, two by Benjamin Harrison, who was chaplain to Archbishop Howley, and one on fasting by the most respectable of all, Professor Pusey. It was characteristic of Pusey that though the longest tract hitherto had been a leaflet of sixteen pages and the majority had been eight pages or less, Pusey's ran to twenty-eight pages. On 23 December some readers of the *Record* rejoiced that the original series of tracts was withdrawn. The optimism was premature. On the same day Newman printed the first of three more tracts written by himself. By the end of the year there were twenty tracts in all, fifty by the end of 1834, sixty-six by 25 July 1835, when the last tract of sixteen pages was published and the whole series altered its complexion by turning to a different and more informed public. In the spring of 1834 Newman found that the printer was incompetent and defaulting, and changed to an arrangement with Rivingtons. He failed to persuade the booksellers to stock them and they continued to be private sheets.

The earliest tracts were anonymous and ephemeral sheets of a few pages, privately circulated. Newman conceived them not as regular troops but as sharp-shooters. Is it fair to suffer the bishops to bear the brunt of the battle without doing our part? If the government disendows the church, will its ministers rest upon their social prestige, their birth or their wealth? Is it not our office to oppose the world? We have the authority of apostolic commission whether the world hears or refuses to hear. We declare that no one who has not the bishop's laying on of hands possesses this commission. A notion has gone abroad that they can take away your power because your power lies in church property and they can confiscate property. Are we content to be accounted the mere creation of the state, like schoolmasters or soldiers? Did the state make us? Can it unmake us? Would St. Paul have suffered the Roman government to appoint Timothy to be

[1] CO, 1833, 811; LC, ii, 10.

Bishop of Miletus as well as of Ephesus? We believe in a visible Catholic church, representative of Christ to the end of time, and we cannot countenance interference by the nation in its concerns. We must protest against the sacrilege in Ireland, show a bold front and prepare for the worst. We must resist attempts to alter the prayer book, knowing that the innovators are men of lax conversation and little personal religion. Let us restore the discipline of the church and the practice of excommunication. Why do we talk so much of establishment and so little of apostolic succession? Our church is the only church of this country which has a right to be sure that it has the Lord's Body to give to his people. The Church of England claims the allegiance of the English people not because it is recognised by the state but because it is the divinely authorised teacher of truth. The dissenters are wrong not because they refuse a state establishment but because they refuse constituted *Christian* authority.

In short, the first tracts wanted to make the old principles of high churchmen popular and applicable to Whig times. Though Newman bustled and agitated, their success was not remarkable. Privately printed sheets, circulated from hand to hand, were not likely to reach a public beyond the clerical right wing. Bishop Sumner of Winchester, who saw and blessed some of them, thought that they harped too much on the one subject of apostolic ministry and would be improved by more variety.[1] Pusey thought the subject of apostolic succession to be dry and was surprised to find that the tracts interested people. Even in December 1833 the prevailing impression was of torpor and apathy among the clergy, of failure to don their armour.

Addresses to archbishop and king

Meanwhile Palmer's association made headway in an unexpected direction. It was not clear what the association was to do. Rose suggested that it should formally address Archbishop Howley of Canterbury against alterations in the doctrine and discipline of the church. Newman passed the idea to Palmer, who embraced it. Each of the local associations would secure signatures from the clergy. The proposed declaration was intended by Newman and Hurrell Froude as a threat against what they both called 'extra-ecclesiastical interference'.

[1] LC, i, 477. Bishop C. R. Sumner had at this time a reputation with high churchmen. Late in 1833 even a reporter in the *British Magazine* called him 'this exemplary divine', cf. 1833, 707; Liddon, *Life of Pusey*, i, 279.

But some of Palmer's colleagues were not likely to append their names to menace against government. Therefore the drafting of the declaration became an affair of prolonged and embarrassing delicacy.

Froude's draft of the declaration has been preserved[1] and the contrast between it and the final version is ludicrous. Froude wanted the clergy to declare to Archbishop Howley that there was a great deal wrong with the Church of England, especially in not being faithful to the prayer book, and that they deprecated all parliamentary interference in reforming it. In the final version the clergy expressed their deep attachment to the apostolical doctrine and liturgy and polity of the Church of England, and declared that though they deprecated rash changes they were ready to co-operate with the bishops in carrying measures (minor-sounding by the phraseology) to reform the church 'should anything from the lapse of years or altered circumstances require renewal or correction',[2] *if* the bishops decided such reform to be necessary.

Froude was cross. He asked Newman whether he had not been a spoon to allow the petition to be milk-and-water, and said that he would have had no hand in printing it. He thought it had been waste of time, his father said that it had no meaning, Rose thought it imbecile. What was aimed as a threat against a cabinet was blunted into a compliment to an archbishop.

Newman was glad that they were addressing the archbishop, instead of petitioning king or Parliament, because the archbishop represented the authority of the church. If the leading bishops had been Whigs, the sentiments of high churchmen would have been more complex. They would have nothing more to do with Archbishop Whately of Dublin and distrusted every word of Bishop Blomfield of London. But most bishops were steady against innovation. The Archbishop of Canterbury had shown himself to be a consistent Tory and an unshakeable defender of the church. A rising wave of affection for Archbishop Howley swept over the country clergy of England. While these unknown perils of a future bill were under discussion they wanted to do something, to make a public protest.

---

[1] *Remains*, i, 330. Newman drafted an address moderate in his eyes and sent it to Palmer in London on 28 October 1833. Palmer removed some of the bite, Dr. Spry and other friends in London removed more, and returned it to Newman written in uncouth English. Newman polished the English and sent it back. It returned as uncouth as before. Newman amended it again and printed it. LC, i, 434.

[2] Palmer, *Narrative*, 11.

The Archbishop of Canterbury was pronounced to be a great man and the best hope of the church.[1] 'In the character of the Archbishop of Canterbury', declared *John Bull* warm-heartedly, after reading the declaration, 'there is none of that restless littleness, that fidgety desire for spurious popularity . . . Upon his Grace the people feel that they may rely for an earnest support of the church.' Newman wished the archbishop was not so cautious, not so apprehensive, not so pacific, not so unlike the warrior-prelates of the ancient church. He compared timorous-looking Howley with St. Ambrose and St. Athanasius, and sighed. But even Newman thought him a man of highest principle and willing to die as a martyr. They fancied meanwhile that they might get him elected chancellor of Oxford university.[2]

Some did not sign the declaration because the arrangements were not efficient and they were not canvassed. Some did not sign because they preferred to petition the king. Some believed it their duty to petition their bishop and thought that to petition the archbishop turned him into a pope. Some did not sign because they thought their bishop to disapprove and would not cast a slur upon him. Some refused to sign because the *Record* made them fear the tracts and therefore suspect the association. Some refused to sign because they wanted reform of the church and believed that the declaration was designed to strengthen Howley against reform. Several of the bishops were lukewarm, evangelical organs disapproved. But at last the declaration achieved 7,000 signatures of clergy and was presented in the library at Lambeth palace on 6 February 1834 by the Archdeacon of Canterbury at the head of nine other archdeacons, three deans, including Dr. Hodgson the celebrated pluralist of Carlisle, and nine other clergy, including John Keble, but neither Palmer nor Newman. (Froude had sailed for Barbados in a last attempt to recover his health.) The archbishop was moved and gave thanks in cautious and formal platitudes.

The advocates of apostolic succession toiled under the difficulty that the government which they hated could control the nomination of bishops in the apostolic line. The church needed an Ambrose or an Athanasius to anathematise Whigs, but would not receive such heroes as bishops under a Whig government. Instead they received Maltby or Whately and feared to receive worse. Newman thought

[1] JB, 1 December 1833.
[2] LC, i, 448, 493; ii, 27. Some evangelicals, while respecting the archbishop, thought the language of the declaration unfittingly humble and more appropriate in an address to the crown. CO, 1833, 811.

that the nominations of Dr. Arnold to a see would be an act of tyranny probably sufficient to justify disestablishment.[1] But Froude failed to persuade any of his group that the mode of appointing bishops needed altering. They agreed that it was bad. They could see no better.

Meanwhile the laity did not see why they should be left out. They demanded a declaration to sign. Palmer applied to Sir Robert Inglis, the ultra conservative and pious member for Oxford university, and to Sir William Heathcote. Inglis and Heathcote went to consult the vice-chancellor at Cambridge, and from the ensuing deliberations appeared the draft of an address by the laity to Archbishop Howley. The address was equally a platitude, though it differed from that of the clergy in declaring that to maintain the establishment was the hope and prayer of the laity—who avowed their 'firm determination to do all that in us lies . . . to uphold, unimpaired in its security and efficiency, that establishment . . .'.[2] This declaration also had its troubles. Some refused to sign because it was not fiercer in maintaining the privileges of the Church of England and yet was too fierce against reform. Inglis himself thought it important that an address to the archbishop should not become a list of prominent members of the Tory party. The Duke of Wellington was discouraging, but ended by signing the address. The management was not efficient, parcels of papers for signatures went astray, the committee confined the signatures to those who could write and to male heads of families, and was scrupulous in excluding names not well authenticated. It turned at last into an address not to the archbishop but to the king, and was presented to King William IV at a levée on 27 May 1834, with 230,000 signatures. But the archbishop could not be omitted. The committee waited ceremoniously upon the archbishop at Lambeth and craved his leave to deposit their sheaves of paper in his archives.

The declaration of the clergy and address of the laity were less important in themselves than as rediscovery to Tory churchmen that they had strength in the country and could afford to be militant. 'The fox and the monkey', it was said, 'have too long usurped the dominion of the forest. The lion is at length roused.'[3] In big towns all over the country, from Lostwithiel and Camelford to Liverpool and Newcastle, were held public meetings to declare unwavering attachment

[1] LC, i, 450.
[2] Palmer, *Narrative*, 15. According to Churton, *Joshua Watson*, 2nd ed., 208, Watson drafted the lay declaration.
[3] JB, 1834, 52.

to the established church. These meetings could hardly help being meetings of the Tory party. It had been difficult to keep the address of the clergy out of politics, although it was so vague that Whig and even radical clergymen were not afraid to express their loyalty to Archbishop Howley. It was impossible for large meetings of laymen. Dr. Bellamy at Plymouth asserted in his speech that the attacks upon the church were intended to separate church from state, that this was a mode of putting the monarchy in danger, by a set of downright republicans.[1] It was difficult not to say that they would teach dissenters a lesson and more decisive Tories took pains to say it. It was difficult for dissenters to avoid the attitude that the declaration was an aggressive act towards themselves, and in towns where dissent was powerful there were said to be cases of prominent dissenters abandoning the shops of tradesmen who signed the declaration.[2] Church meetings often ended with three cheers for *Church and King* and the old Tory toast of *Church and King* became more popular at public and private dinners. It was difficult not to drink the toast when proposed. In April 1835 speech day at Rugby School was ruined because a local Tory objected to Arnold's toast *The King* and proposed instead *Church and King*, raising a pandemonium in which one side shouted the toast and the other shouted *No insult to Dr. Arnold!*[3]

Dissenting grievances

The dissenters likewise held meetings and rallied their forces.

The largest body was the Wesleyan Methodist society, which refused to count itself as dissenting. Methodists remembered that John Wesley had not desired separation. They conceived themselves more as a society or 'connexion' than as a church, attended the services of the Church of England without qualm or protest, aimed at a peaceable spirit and distrusted political pastors as others distrusted political parsons. They were careful to dissociate themselves from the campaign against establishment. Their leading minister, especially after 1833, was Jabez Bunting, who controlled the financial administration in London and had no sympathy with radicals. During the early months of 1834 there was loose talk about reunion between the Church of England and the Methodists as a means of strengthening

---

[1] *Br. Mag.*, 5, 1834, 380.
[2] e.g. Chard, as reported in *Somersetshire Gazette*; *Br. Mag.*, 5, 1834, 638.
[3] Bamford, *Arnold*, 81–82.

the establishment in its peril. Some Methodists signed the lay declaration and Archbishop Howley publicly praised Methodists for
their restraint.[1]

Far to their left more vehement meetings of Methodists were as
hostile to the Church of England as any dissenter. In Lancashire a
radical minister, J. R. Stephens, joined a society to separate church
from state and was charged by the Methodist Conference with flagrant violation of the peaceable and anti-sectarian spirit of Wesleyan
Methodism.[2] They demanded a pledge that he would refrain. Stephens
refused the pledge and resigned. A number of Lancashire congregations followed Stephens and broke away from the main body, ending
in a legal suit with the Methodist Conference for the right to keep
their chapels. For all its power Conference could not quite control its
outlying members. The congregations at Newport in the Isle of Wight
and Chichester were among those willing to join the radical campaign.
There were complaints that two or three Methodist chapels were used
for political meetings.[3]

But other dissenters, who held establishment wrong on principle,
disliked the shouts of their colleagues. They had real grievances; and
believed it enough to campaign for the end of these grievances without raising a claim which many Englishmen regarded as revolution.
They were saddened that the violent language of their friends created
panic in Anglican breasts.

In pamphlets or meetings of 1833–4 they were in the habit of listing
grievances. In 1833 they formed a united committee on dissenting
grievances. In various forms and lists their surviving grievances were
reduced to five.

First: the state registered births only in the baptismal registers of
parish churches. Therefore some dissenters took their children to be
baptised in the parish church for civil reasons.

Second: since an act of 1753 a man and woman could be legally
married, unless Quakers or Jews, only in the parish church.

Third: the churchyard belonged to the Church of England, but
was grave of everyone. In big cities private companies ran cemeteries
neutral in religion, and little chapels had little graveyard-gardens. But

---

[1] Liddon, *Life of Pusey*, i, 286; Hansard, xxv, 860.
[2] *Minutes of Methodist Conferences*, 1834, 417.
[3] *Unitarian Mag.*, 1834, 87. Like the main body of Methodists, Lady Huntingdon's
Connexion was proud to disapprove the agitation.

often the dissenter must be buried in a cemetery either with rites which he disapproved or in total silence.

Fourth: every citizen (unless too poor) was liable to a local rate, not only to aid poor and maintain highways, but to repair the parish church. The dissenter was compelled by the state to subscribe to a religion which he rejected.

Fifth: the degrees of the two great universities of Oxford and Cambridge were confined to those who could subscribe the Thirty-nine Articles. The new college in Durham demanded the same subscription. University College was founded in Gower Street, London, in 1826, but had no right to grant degrees. No dissenter could acquire a university degree unless he crossed the border into Scotland.[1]

While 230,000 lay churchmen signed the declaration in favour of establishment, no fewer than 343,094 signatures were fixed to 1,094 public petitions for relief from dissenting disabilities.[2]

Church rate

Of the five grievances one was giant-sore: payment of tax to repair the parish church. More than any other cause this grievance kept the flames of bitterness flaring. Other disabilities, from marriage to universities, the dissenters could not help. They must suffer until a government thought it expedient or possible to remove them by act of Parliament. Alone among the grievances they had a chance of refusing church rate.

For the rate was a local tax and must be voted by the parish meeting in which every citizen had a vote. Ardent dissenters claimed to be the majority of the nation. If this claim were near true, they ought to be able to attend the Easter vestry meeting, secure a majority, and prevent money from being voted to repair the parish church. By law the parish was compelled to keep its church and its roads in repair. But if a majority of the parish refused money to repair the church, no one knew how to prosecute that majority. Here the divided parties of the nation were reflected in the sour hostilities of local partisans. Here religion and politics were inextricable. To vote the rate was at once defence of the established church and victory for the Tory party. To

---

[1] For list of grievances, cf., e.g., *The Case of Dissenters in a letter addressed to the Lord Chancellor*, 2nd ed., 1834; meeting at Leeds on 3 December 1833 reported MC, 4 and 10 December 1833.

[2] *Br. Mag. 6*, 34, 201.

refuse the rate was at once relief to dissenting scruples and triumph for radical politicians. If church and dissent came to blows as never before and never afterwards in the history of England, a main cause was the tea-cup parochial squabbles of church rate.

No one can accuse English taxation of being tidy. It is the pride of English illogicalities that they rest upon custom of immemorial antiquity, and so it is with rates. The village taxed itself, in labour if not in money, for its public services from a time beyond the written memory of Englishmen. From immemorial times the village regarded the repair of its parish church, with repair of highway or bridge or sea-wall, as a public service; and by the beginning of the fourteenth century at latest the custom was formal in ecclesiastical law. The rector—that is, whoever received the greater tithe—was legally responsible for repairing the chancel. The parishioners were legally responsible for repairing the nave and maintaining the churchyard. The rate levied for this purpose was probably not regularly levied, nor its nature codified, until after the Elizabethan poor rate acts. The poor rate became the standard form of rating and other rates were assimilated to it. With church rate, however, there was this important difference. If the parishioners refused poor rate, they were liable to penalty at common law before secular courts. If the parishioners refused church rate, they were liable to penalty at ecclesiastical law before ecclesiastical courts.

Until 1641—that is, so long as the courts of high commission and star chamber existed—the ecclesiastical courts were as effective as, more effective than, the secular courts in compelling recalcitrant parishioners to their duty. Afterwards the ecclesiastical courts were more cumbersome. Nevertheless, it is safe to say that until the year 1820 parishioners obeyed the law and voted money, either annually or whenever necessary, to repair the naves of their churches, to supply it with ornaments, and to maintain the churchyard and its walls or fences.

There were exceptions. In many parishes benevolent testators bequeathed money for the repair of churches. In a proportion of the parishes of England no church rates were levied. In some parishes the expenses were so small that they were usually paid out of the poor rate and no one bothered with a church rate. Within the city of London the churches were maintained from a general tax on city property and thus the parishioners were not liable to church rate. In wealthy churches of London, like St. George's, Hanover Square, or St. Mark's, North Audley Street, pew rents were sufficiently large to prevent any need for rates.[1]

Every Easter the churchwardens held a vestry meeting and presented to the parishioners their accounts and estimates for the coming year. These accounts or estimates could then be challenged; and though the rate was passed unhesitatingly in the vast majority of parishes, a lower rate could be passed if the parishioners were dissatisfied with the estimate, or the voting of the rate could be postponed for another year. All the parishioners had a legal right to attend the vestry and vote, even if they were dissenters or atheists (for all these arrangements dated from an epoch when dissenters and atheists were presumed not to exist). When the rate had been voted it was usually levied upon one form or paper with poor rate and highway rate and collected by the same officers. The church rate was technically a rate not upon owners but upon all occupiers of property, a rate not upon house or land but upon the person in respect of his occupation of house or land. Thus a non-resident property-owner was not liable, while a person who lived outside the parish but farmed fields within it was liable. When canals were dug or railway lines laid the canal or railway companies became liable for church rate for the land thus used in the parish. The assessment for rate customarily followed assessment to poor-rate. The poor were liable to pay rate, but churchwardens invariably exempted them from payment. It was not quite certain whether the churchwardens had valid grounds for so exempting poor persons, but the lawyers were sure that these exemptions, if challenged, would not invalidate a rate. For obvious reasons this was never tested in court.

The outcry against church rate began only with the struggle for the reform bill at the end of 1830. But objection on ground of conscience was long familiar to Englishmen, especially from members of the Society of Friends.

Just as Quakers objected on conscientious grounds to pay direct tax to support the army, they objected equally to pay for the support of steeple-houses. Unlike other citizens, unlike other dissenters, the Quakers were perpetually engaged in refusing church rate. An order was obtained from the justices of the peace, the agent entered the Quaker's home and seized property in accordance with what he

[1] PP, 1851, ix, 501. All royal land and all glebe land was exempt from the rate.

believed to be the approximate value equal to the rate plus the cost of seizing it. Accuracy in this collection was easier to achieve where the defaulter had money lying about, as in a shop. The agent entered the shop and removed the exact sum from the till, the Quaker protesting but not resisting.[1] When the defaulter was not a shopkeeper he was likely to lose more money than if he paid the rate, which some Quakers still called the steeple-house tax. Mr. John M. Knight lost twenty hairbrushes, 20 lb. pearl sago, nineteen packets of groats, three bottles of salad oil, nine bottles of fish sauce, and sixteen bottles of pickles, value £4 2s., in payment of a church rate of a guinea. Mr. Joseph Pryor of Exeter was distrained of thirty-five silk umbrellas and thirteen parasols, though he received a few shillings back from the sales. A lady lost two new tin boilers. We hear of other Quakers losing one or more of the following articles: clock ('in good going order'), wine, silver, stationery, bags of flour, sheep, carpet-bag, horse and harness, wheat, barley, hay, oats, sugar, tea, account-books, furniture, fire-irons, brass pestle and mortar, carpets, tablecloths, bolsters, coal-scuttles, looking-glass, cheese, chests of drawers, warming-pans, ham, bacon, candlesticks, tiles.[2] A minor but additional grievance was the automatic fee of 10s. costs in court, which usually went to the clerk of the court irrespective of the real costs of the case, a kind of minimum charge.

The tax to maintain churchyards and repair the naves of parish churches was no formality. It was the law. But those who carried their scruples of conscience to this length were not numerous. The grievance of a little and peaceable minority may for long go unnoticed.

The coming struggle was affected by a decision of Parliament in 1818. Observing the new industrial slums and their revolutionary menace, Parliament voted a million pounds to build churches (of course, of the established church). In 1824 it voted another half-million pounds.

To build churches was easier than to provide new parishes for those churches. The division of a big parish touched the rights of property.

---

[1] Not all distraint was received so passively. A dissenter of Tewkesbury invited the distraining officers to sit down, fetched a hive of bees from the garden and threw it into the room. AR, 1839, *Chron.*, 127. Richard Carlile was assessed for church rate soon after 1830. When his goods were distrained he retaliated by taking out the two front windows to exhibit effigies of a bishop and a distraining officer. After a time he added a devil, linked arm in arm with the bishop, DNB.

[2] Hodgkin's appendix to PP, 1851, ix, 639.

How shall glebe or tithe be divided? Should the incumbent of the old parish be compensated for loss of fees now that so many parishioners will go elsewhere to be married and buried? Will the patron of the old parish be compensated for the decline in value of his right to appoint the incumbent? And how will the old church be repaired? If the parishioners of the new parish are exempted from paying church rate to the old parish, a heavier rate will fall upon the surviving parishioners of the old parish.

The parochial system of the Church of England could hardly have been better designed to resist change. To create a new parish was less easy than to build a proprietary chapel, like the dissenters, and finance it out of pew rents and subscriptions. But proprietary chapels must attract worshippers who could afford to maintain them. They could not meet the needs of the slum districts, which the Tory government of 1818 wished to educate.

Struggling with vested interests and a belief in the sacred rights of property, Robert Peel and the drafters of the 1818 act hit upon a fatal answer. They provided that the repairs of the new or district church were to be paid by a church rate of the inhabitants after twenty years; and during that twenty years (to run from the date when the new church was consecrated) the inhabitants of the new district should continue to pay church rate to the old parish.

The issue of the enactment is plain. For twenty years the inhabitants of new parishes or districts were paying taxes to maintain a parish church in which they had no interest and no right, and in addition might be subscribing to maintain their own church. In a Tory world they might have come through the twenty years with little but rumbling and suppressed grievance. Their world was not to be Tory in that sense much longer. In some parishes, by a quirk of fortune depending on the application of local acts of Parliament, a dissenting ratepayer found himself legally compelled to pay rate to two churches—that of the district in which he lived, and that of a parish out of which the district was carved. At the new chapel at Goldenhill in the diocese of Lichfield the inhabitants of the district paid rate to maintain two churches (Wolstanton and Tunstall) neither of which was theirs. The moment agitation began, it found fruitful soil in the district parishes. To declare a rate successfully in Birmingham, where the dissenters were powerful, needed all the voting power which churchmen could command from the outlying districts. Yet churchmen in outlying districts were unwilling to vote a rate for a church not their own. They stayed away from the meeting.[1]

In the fight for the autumn election of 1832 the Birmingham refusal of a church rate contributed to the panic of Dr. Arnold and others that the establishment must shortly end. It was found that the state of the law encouraged such proceedings. Every kind of radical, whether he had any interest in religious matters or not, would assemble at the Easter meeting. Conscientious objectors among the dissenters might be present, but these would be far from the majority. The church-wardens might try to assemble their 'party'. But some of their supporters might live in newly created districts and felt no desire to vote for a rate which would fall upon themselves. Lukewarm churchmen were not discontented if the rate failed, for few men are discontented if rates are reduced by a few pence in the £, whatever the motives of the reduction. Other churchmen were not prepared to participate in the scenes of desecration which turned the church into hustings, struggles for the chair, cat-calls and blasphemous cries. All popular assemblies for taxing the members are unsatisfactory. Superimposed upon party division in this popular assembly was the genuine scruple of conscience among a minority of persons who had no desire for a cockfight, but felt impelled to take part because they truly believed it wrong to pay taxes to the established church. The assembly met in the church itself, and these public scenes of strife and passion were yearly enacted in the house of God.

In 1833 the Irish church temporalities act abolished church rate in Ireland. The act stimulated attempts to secure majorities against it in English cities. The news that the Whig cabinet was planning a measure for England further excited local strife. Many rural parishes were untouched by the struggle. But in all the big towns and many country towns the struggle became the centre of local politics. Among the most scandalous of many scandalous scenes were those enacted in

[1] One eminent Whig, Viscount Howick, Hansard, xxxvii, 1837, 333, was bold enough to declare that all the trouble over church rates stemmed from Peel, the Tories and their church building acts. It was an exaggeration, but had a partial truth.

Though it is true that the real attempt to abolish church rate began only in 1830 or 1831, we find ominous rumblings during the eighteen-twenties, especially in the cities of the north. In Sheffield there were scandalous scenes at the annual vestry between 1818 and 1822.

At Leeds in 1826 and 1827 the vestry refused to allow that part of the church-wardens' estimates which was directed towards the building or furnishing of district churches. At Bradford and Dewsbury rates for building new churches were successfully resisted, by what an anxious archdeacon called rabble vestries.

Bath abbey and in the collegiate church (now the cathedral) of Manchester. Where the result was in doubt at the meeting in church, either side could demand a poll, and then furies and drums and flags and bribery lasted for several days, perhaps with charges and counter-charges that the sides were using the same votes twice or bringing drunken men to the poll. When the church triumphed at Boston, the neighbouring villages rang peals of bells in honour of the victory.[1] This was the time when Philip Pusey, soon M.P. for Berkshire, and elder brother of Dr. Pusey, wrote a hymn which has passed into the national collections:

> See round thine ark the hungry billows curling;
> See how thy foes their banners are unfurling;
> Lord, while their darts envenomed they are hurling,
> Thou canst preserve us.[2]

The government of Lord Grey could not avoid church rates. They had abolished them in Ireland and were expected to abolish them in England. Whig lords laboured under a disadvantage of not comprehending the social status or predicament of dissenters. Lord Althorp dallied with a scheme for helping dissenting pastors by relieving them and clergymen of the tax on saddlehorses, until it was explained to him that hardly any dissenting pastors owned saddlehorses.[3] Whig lords resembled Tory lords thus far, that they believed establishment to consist in grants of public money. To the leader of the House of Commons, Lord Althorp, an establishment meant a church in which fabrics were repaired by the state. 'It is of the very essence of that union between church and state', declared Edward Stanley, 'that the state shall out of the public funds defray the expenses of the religion it establishes.'[4] The plea that it was wrong to exact money from members of one religion to repair the churches of another religion seemed to them beside the point. Taxpayers pay for the army. Citizens with pacifist scruples must nevertheless pay taxes which maintain the army. Whig leaders considered whether to exempt dissenters, on registering as dissenters, from the civic duty of paying church rate. They rejected the plan; partly because a national church

---

[1] *Br. Mag.*, 6, 1834, 230.
[2] Written in 1834, Liddon, *Life of E. B. Pusey*, i, 299. It is a paraphrase of a hymn by Löwenstern dating from the age of the Thirty Years War. Cf. *Historical Companion to Hymns Ancient and Modern* (1962), 282.
[3] Harriet Martineau, *Autobiography*, i, 264.
[4] Hansard, xxii, 1834, 1014, 1035.

ought to be maintained by the nation, and partly because the plan might increase the number of dissenters by tempting men to declare scruples for the sake of not paying church tax. The Whig cabinet was again in conflict with its radical supporters. Expected to abolish church rate, they were prepared to abolish it only if a better mode of repairing roofs was devised. They briefly considered whether parish churches could be maintained by voluntary subscription and decided not. Old fabrics in tiny and impoverished villages, they believed, would fall into ruin unless the nation kept them in repair.

When Lord Althorp introduced his heralded bill on church rates (21 April 1834) he was greeted with radical gloom and ejaculation. For he proposed that the rate be abolished and the repair of churches a charge upon the Treasury. The land tax of England and Wales should provide £250,000 a year to the Church Building Commission, and repairs of churches should be undertaken on certificates from the county surveyor. This money should repair chancel as well as nave and churchyard walls; and the old duty of the tithe-owner to repair the chancel should be transferred to the duty of providing the essentials of furniture—holy table and covering and rails, bread and wine, chalice, font, pulpit, seats, Bible, two prayer books (one for the minister and one for the clerk), table of ten commandments, bier, bell, chest for alms, chest for registers, and a surplice. (Archbishop Howley was shown this list beforehand. He crossed out surplice and wrote in the margin, two surplices.)[1] The bill made no provision for various objects which parishes had legally or illegally provided from time to time out of church rate—choir, organ, coal, prayer books for the people, chime of bells, laundry, beadles or vergers, stipend of minister, extermination of vermin, and the miscellany usually concealed in old accounts under the heading *Sundries*.

Radicals and dissenters denounced the assumption that a religious establishment was necessary to the nation and therefore that everyone in the nation ought to pay for it. 'You may as well propose', said a radical as final proof of the absurdity, 'a national medical establishment, and oblige everyone to pay for its support. Whether sick or well, all would then be called on to pay the state physician.'[2] The

---

[1] Add. MSS. 40404, 187. Howley also wanted Roman Catholics and dissenters legally prevented from becoming churchwardens, and thought it unjust to charge the rector with font, pulpit, seats. He wanted the parish to make good all these things before the change, or the rector would suffer for the past negligence of the parish.

[2] Hansard, xxii, 1834, 1022.

conscience of the dissenters was as scrupulous against a national tax as against local rates. The dissenter was to be compelled to pay money out of one pocket instead of the other. Since the money was now to be found from the national purse instead of the local rate, Ireland and Scotland were going to contribute indirectly to repair the churches of England and the number of persons with scruples would be increased. Why cannot this wealthy church take the cost of repairs out of its endowments? Why not abolish sinecures and remove the lands of cathedrals and with their funds repair the churches? Dissenters disliked national tax even more than local rate. For the rate could be fought. It was their opportunity, the only grievance which they could abolish by collecting votes. Convert it to a national tax and it was taken out of their power.

The motion was carried in the House of Commons by 256 votes to 140. It is pleasant to speculate what would have happened to the history of English churches if it had passed both Houses that summer and become law; if the nation had then accepted the burden of keeping parish churches in repair. The government intended to pass it that summer, could easily have done so, and only failed to do so because it petered out absurdly as a government. It was disturbed by petitions which flowed in from dissenters and from Scotland, and still more by the discovery at the division that it was supported, not only by the Tory leader Sir Robert Peel and his church-minded supporters but even by ultras like Sir Robert Inglis. To find 140 radicals and Whigs voting against it and extreme Tories voting in favour of it caused the cabinet to ponder. Dr. Lushington, eminent ecclesiastical lawyer and strong Whig, voted for the motion, but told Althorp privately afterwards that he would never be able to carry it, because it still violated the religious scruples of two million dissenters.[1] A further objection to the bill appeared on reflection, namely, that in thousands of parishes no rates were levied because they were not necessary, and therefore those parishes would now be contributing despite their endowments. The government still intended to carry it and could easily have carried it through both Houses. But Althorp was forced to pause. And while he paused Lord John Russell upset the cabinet's coach.

The Dissenters and the universities

To be excluded from universities was not the most pressing of the

[1] Hansard, xxxvii, 1837, 378.

five dissenting grievances. It was lifted to the front because in March 1834 sixty-three residents of Cambridge University petitioned that dissenters might be admitted. Lord Grey himself presented the petition to the House of Lords and was known to agree with its substance.

The universities of Oxford and Cambridge were institutions of England and of the Church of England, for England and the Church of England had been thought to be identical. Oxford was more severe, for every undergraduate who entered Oxford must subscribe to the Thirty-nine Articles when he matriculated. At Cambridge the undergraduate need make no such subscription and might not be a member of the Church of England. There is evidence that a few colleges exempted rare Roman Catholic undergraduates from attending chapel, and Trinity Hall even allowed a Mohammedan to reside. But the habit of colleges varied. A Jew exempted from chapel at Magdalene was compelled to attend chapel when he migrated to Trinity,[1] and the privilege of exemption was sparingly given. When a man took his degree at Cambridge he must declare himself a member of the established church, and in consequence the few dissenters went down without taking their degree. Some people agreed that this was no hardship, that the letters B.A. were worthless and what mattered was residence and education. Not all dissenters regarded the B.A. as so innocuous. The law of England compelled all persons to take the oath of supremacy on taking a degree, and the act of uniformity compelled all senior members of the university, whether professors or fellows, to conform to the liturgy of the Church of England. These restrictions had been founded to maintain the union of church and state. They were now defended, partly on the same grounds, partly because the colleges were religious foundations under religious trusts, and partly because Oxford and Cambridge were nurseries of the clergy of the Church of England. The proportion of future clergy among the undergraduates was high. The first boat race between Oxford and Cambridge was rowed at Henley in 1829. Eight members of the Oxford crew became one bishop, two deans, one prebendary and four other clergymen. Only four members of the Cambridge crew were afterwards ordained, one bishop, one dean, one rector, one curate.

Almost everyone agreed upon the axiom that education worth the name must be religious education. If religion is to be taught, a religion

[1] Winstanley, *Early Victorian Cambridge*, 83–85.

must be taught; there cannot be controversy in colleges and lecture-rooms. A wry picture was drawn of Cambridge in the year 1900, when preachers of the university sermon were forbidden to proclaim any doctrines, when colleges had changed their names to avoid offending the susceptibilities of dissenters, when Trinity had become Unity College and Christ's had been metamorphosed into Hope Hall.[1] If it were true, as churchmen contended, that Oxford and Cambridge were institutions of the Church of England, dissenters ought not to clamour for entry, but should found universities for themselves. Wellington and Peel believed that the Anglican constitution of the two universities was the strongest bond linking church with state.

The cry of dissenters to enter Oxford and Cambridge strengthened the conviction of some in both universities that at all costs dissenters must be kept out. The Duke of Wellington said in the House of Lords (21 March 1834) that he thought the union of church and state, possibly 'the existence of Christianity itself' might be endangered by giving way. But then the Duke of Wellington had recently been elected chancellor of Oxford University.

The attempt to modify the restrictions of the university was entangled with attacks upon the university as inefficient. Just as it was easier to modify the establishment by calling it reform, and sane Tories were weakened in resistance by recognising the need of reform, so it helped the university Whigs to place their desires in a context of general reform. Like the Church of England, the universities were ancient institutions. It could hardly be denied that the rust of time had not improved their efficiency as places of education. In November 1833 the notorious R. M. Beverley published *A Letter to H.R.H. the Duke of Gloucester on the present corrupt state of the University of Cambridge*, in which he portrayed the life of undergraduates as stained with wild debauches. Every responsible person knew that the pamphlet was vile slander. But many persons of sober judgment could not but confess that the university was an imperfect nursery for clergymen. Eminent public men remembered how in their undergraduate days they hurried unshaven or full of wine to their compulsory chapel and heard these pleas of a religious education with discomfort. At least there was a case for enquiry.

In the university of Cambridge existed a small but not contemptible minority of Whigs. The petition which Lord Grey presented to the

[1] *Standard*, 8 April 1834.

House of Lords on 21 March 1834 was signed by two heads of houses, nine professors, eleven tutors, sixty-three persons in all, of whom sixty-two were resident, and included such men as Professors Airy, Sedgwick, Musgrave and Lee, and tutors like the young historian Connop Thirlwall of Trinity College. The eminent signatures of the scientists Airy and Sedgwick enabled Tory papers to play a delightful game of mockery at this galaxy of astronomers, geologists, botanists, mineralogists, ornithologists and entomologists, assuming that the more eminent the scientist the less capable in politics. The counter-petition was signed by a far more numerous body, and included 258 names, eleven heads of colleges, seven professors, and thirty-one tutors. But this large number of signatures was achieved by inviting many non-residents to sign.

On 20 June 1834 the House of Commons gave the second reading to a bill introduced by G. W. Wood, a Unitarian. Cambridge Whigs regretted that the bill was introduced by a dissenter. They knew that they could achieve reasonable reform only if they gained the support of moderate churchmen, and saw that to associate reform with dissent would make Tory churchmen more resistant to change. They disliked the wording of Wood's bill. Wood provided that anyone may enter a university if he is of unexceptionable moral character and of competent knowledge, and is willing to conform to the discipline of his college or hall; while a Roman Catholic might enter on taking the relief oath of 1829. A revised bill, improved in committee, simply abolished subscription at entry or on taking any degree, but did not interfere with the right of colleges to exclude undergraduates who would not attend chapel. In this form it was carried through the House of Commons with substantial majorities, and thrown out by a majority of 102 in the House of Lords.

The failure of Wood's bill, though predictable by members of the cabinet, made the future more uneasy for Whig residents of Oxford and Cambridge universities. They laboured under a cloud in their societies. They not only encountered the suspicion of staunch churchmen, but the hostility of others who valued the independence of the university and thought that the Cambridge petition invited interference by government. At Trinity College in Cambridge, Connop Thirlwall wrote a pamphlet against the argument that the university was a sufficient nursery of clergymen, contended that the university would be strengthened by admitting dissenters, and attacked compulsory chapel for undergraduates. He was hastily dismissed from his tutorship by the Master of Trinity, Christopher Wordsworth, who divided the fellowship into bitter parties as a consequence and was pilloried in the radical press as a reverend tyrant.[1] The Master of Corpus Christi College, who would naturally have been elected the next vice-chancellor but one, was excluded from the succession.[2] The Master of Downing dismissed Mr. Dawes from his vice-mastership on the ground that he signed the petition to Parliament. The Whig Bishop of Ely, Dr. Allen, wrote to the prime minister that Whig principles were in danger of speedy extinction in Cambridge.[3]

If these were the consequences in slightly more liberal Cambridge, Oxford was less likely to be friendly to its few Whigs. For Oxford was the fortress of the Church of England.

But Oxford was not quite so Tory as the Tories preferred. There was no movement of strength equal to the reforming minority at Cambridge. But the course of debate showed the heads of Oxford colleges that the habit of demanding doctrinal subscription from schoolboys lay open to grave objection from the public and was not easily defensible. The Duke of Wellington suggested to them that change was advisable.[4] On 10 November 1834 the heads decided by a majority of one to abolish subscription, and possibly replace it with a declaration like that used in Cambridge. Scattered Whigs, hidden among the colleges at Oxford, began to raise their heads.

In November 1834, Dr. Hampden, principal of St. Mary Hall and since March professor of moral philosophy, published a pamphlet entitled *Observations on Religious Dissent*, which Newman later[5]

[1] It was widely thought in Cambridge that H. J. Rose pressed Christopher Wordsworth into the high-handed action. Julius Hare said that Rose, if guilty, ought never to be admitted to Trinity College again. There is no sufficient evidence to warrant the belief. Hare to Whewell 1 June 1834, Whewell Papers; Winstanley, 75.

[2] The constitutional situation over Dr. Lamb was not quite straightforward. The heads of colleges were elected vice-chancellor in rotation. The three senior heads were French (Jesus), Lamb (Corpus Christi) and Ainslie (Pembroke), in that order. The caput, which controlled the nominations, must put forward two names and always put forward the two senior names. On 4 November 1834, without warning, it put forward the names of French and Ainslie. Members of the university who thought this an illiberal act could only protest by voting for Ainslie instead of French. The voting was French 73, Ainslie 35. Cf. *Cambridge Chronicle*, 7 November 1834. The contest was renewed in November 1835, when Archdale of Emmanuel was put in front of Ainslie and the Whigs again registered a fruitless protest by voting for the second candidate. Romilly's *Diary*, 3-8 November 1835.

[3] Allen to Melbourne, 28 July 1836, MP. Thirlwall's pamphlet was entitled a *Letter to the Rev. Thomas Turton, D.D.* cf. Winstanley, 73ff.

[4] LC, ii, 78.   [5] LC, ii, 77.

described as the beginning of hostilities in Oxford. Hampden had no desire to summon Parliament to reform the universities. He contended for their independence. He did not deny that if dissenters came to Oxford they ought to conform to its discipline, even by worshipping in the college chapel. But why not? He wished all tests to be so removed that dissenters might come freely. And he argued for the university what Dr. Arnold argued for the nation, that the terms of communion were too narrow, that Anglicans and dissenters were agreed in all scriptural truths of moment, that they ought to be able to worship together. In the old latitudinarian tradition, he wanted to confine dogmas to the smallest area, and shocked some of his readers by refusing to deny the name of Christian to Unitarians, and indeed to anyone willing to call himself a Christian. He sent a copy to Newman, who acknowledged it frankly[1]—'The kindness which has led to your presenting me with your pamphlet encourages me to hope that you will forgive me, if I take the opportunity it affords to express to you my very sincere and deep regret that it has been published.'

The heads of houses rescinded their resolution. The proposal reappeared in the spring and was defeated in May 1835 by a big majority amid scenes of shouting and enthusiasm.[2]

In the same spring of 1834 which began the excitement over the claim of dissenters to enter Oxford and Cambridge, petitions were presented that University College in Gower Street might receive a charter as the University of London. Brougham tried vainly to get a charter as long ago as 1825. But the college had been founded by a mixture of dissenters and utilitarians and, despite dissenting dismay and later despite strong opposition from Dr. Arnold, agreed that it was prudent to offer no religious teaching whatever. By 1833 charters had been granted to King's College in the Strand, to Lampeter, and to Durham, but the opposition to University College was still powerful. University College wished to grant degrees. Oxford and Cambridge and the Royal College of Surgeons were determined that no one should trespass upon their monopoly of granting degrees with certain titles. The titles of bachelor of arts or master of arts were said to be a

[1] LC, ii, 77; 28 November 1834.
[2] Hurrell Froude, who had been vainly attempting to recover his health in the West Indies, appeared in Oxford for the vote, shocking his friends by the wasted look, but brilliant and ethereal, shouting with the rest at the *non-placet*. It was his last vote in Oxford before his premature death next year. LC, ii, 106. In 1835 Lord Radnor introduced a bill into the House of Lords to abolish subscriptions and failed to carry it. He failed again in 1837 with a motion for a commission of enquiry.

sign not only of a certain amount of classical and scientific and theological learning but also of the habits of a gentleman.[1] Councel for Oxford University was that Sir Charles Wetherell whose arrival at Bristol precipitated reform riots. At the hearing before the Privy Council, Wetherell argued that the government of a university is a matter ecclesiastical, and by the law of England a university is subject to the ecclesiastical visitation of the Archbishop of Canterbury. The degrees of Oxford were the indication of a religious profession, and of the habits, education and associations of a gentleman. The M.A. was a badge of a Christian education, and a Christian state must not, could not authorise a body without religion to award Christian titles, Church of England titles.[2] 'It does seem a little too bad', wrote Newman, 'that the dissenters are *to take our titles*. Why should they call themselves M.A., except to seem like us? Why not call themselves licentiates, etc?'

The defenders of Oxford and Cambridge did not mince their words. *John Bull* gave to University College the nickname of Stinkomalee, and the name was taken up by undergraduates of Oxford and groaned at commemoration in the Sheldonian theatre. Not until 28 November 1836 was the seal affixed to the charter of University College, and on the same day to the charter of the University of London as an examining body to which University College, King's College, and others to be approved thereafter, should belong. The existence and charter of University College helped to postpone for nearly twenty years the next sally of dissenters to carry the bastions at Oxford and Cambridge.

The new poor law

The Parliament of 1834 ended without the vaunted reform of the established church; nothing more done in Ireland, failure in England over church rates and universities. Anglican gloom lightened.

The one great act of the session reformed the poor law. A commission which was chaired by Bishop Blomfield of London and included Bishop J. B. Sumner of Chester collected valuable if slanted

[1] *Standard*, 14 April 1834.
[2] Greville, 25 April 1834; Hale Bellot, 233–40; LC ii, 29; Newman to Bowden, 14 March 1834. At the privy council it amused Greville to see among the audience Dr. Phillpotts of Exeter sitting next to Allen, the reputedly atheist librarian of Holland house. Bishops regarded an M.A. as a sufficient qualification for holy orders. Newman, who was inclined to expect the worst, was afraid that soon the bishops would be bullied into accepting London M.A.s as qualifying for holy orders.

evidence, and the government carried its main recommendations. Forms of relief which supplemented the wages of labourers, and therefore enabled employers to keep wages low, were restricted. Workhouses were built throughout the country to care for the poor while ensuring that their life was less agreeable than that of the independent labourer. The measure was not the panacea which its proponents supposed, but was medicinal. Wages were raised by necessity.

The evangelical *Christian Observer* and the Unitarian *Monthly Repository* approved warmly. Of the great London dailies only the *Morning Chronicle* approved, but it was bought by a wealthy Whig member for that purpose. The *Times* and most newspapers hated the act. Cobbett called it the Poor Man Robbery bill.[1]

Clergymen varied in their attitude to the new poor law. Many agreed with Bishops Blomfield and J. B. Sumner that the old system promoted immorality by encouraging idleness, and increased bastardy by child allowance. Some were so extreme as to contend that all forms of state relief were mistaken, and that its benevolence not only made the poor more improvident but restrained the compassion of the rich. They idealised charity and almsgiving. If they were romantics, pictures of medieval monasteries distributing dole floated upon their minds. Some observed no change whatever in the morals of their flocks after the act. Others claimed to see improvement. The labourer feared the workhouse and was anxious not to lose his job. He was therefore less insolent and more diligent. Since he worked longer hours instead of receiving a dole, he infested gin shops less. Keepers of beer shops and gin shops suffered from the act. Several clergymen testified to a marked change for the better in the behaviour of their people.[2]

Anglicans liked the provisions for religious instruction in workhouses. Divine service must be celebrated, the Bible and catechism taught, and a chaplain might be appointed.[3] The dissenters were pleased that their pastors might visit the workhouse to teach their own people. An assistant commissioner claimed that few persons outside universities had better opportunities for religious instruction than in-

---

[1] Webb, viii, 99.

[2] PP, 1836, xxix, i, 491–2; PP, 1835, xxxv, 278, 281.

[3] A good many parishes neglected or refused to appoint chaplains. The highest stipends of chaplains were £250 at Liverpool and £200 at Manchester. Most of them were at £30 to £50. Some local clergy were officially appointed chaplains, but gave their services free. For those unions which did not appoint, PP, 1844, xl, 171, 179; cf. 1840, xxxix, 463.

habitants of the new workhouses. 'Some of the paupers, I was assured, had complained that they had too much divine service.' It was also observed that under the old system nine-tenths of the paupers never entered a church, and therefore the new system was bringing them to worship.[1]

But many clergy and ministers disliked the rule that no one might attend in their parish church or chapel outside the workhouse. Strong pressure was exerted to make the poor law commissioners change their rule for Sundays. Their reasons betrayed the weakness of the system. Life in the workhouse must be made more unattractive than life outside. Since well-meaning endeavours found it impossible to lower diet and rooms to standards below those of surrounding labourers without starving the inhabitants of the workhouse, this comfort of living must be compensated by imprisonment. So long as a man was receiving relief he must be confined to the workhouse. The commissioners observed also that when paupers went out on Sundays their steps were drawn as by magnets towards beer shops instead of church. One of their assistants used the sad argument that paupers would crowd the parish church to excess, and that when they went to church at Eastry the clergyman complained of their presence as inconveniencing other worshippers.[2]

The trouble was an unseen contradiction in Blomfield's report. It was impossible to produce a general workhouse at once so uncomfortable as to discourage those who ought not to be there and so comfortable as to give proper care to those who ought. Yorkshiremen may be forgiven for calling the workhouse *Basty* (the Bastille).[3] And the result was *Oliver Twist* and years of abuse directed against the commissioners and their system. Hardships of old and sick paupers made the Whigs unpopular. The poor stoned a magistrate at Chesham, rioted at Eastbourne and Bradford and Todmorden, attended a meeting of guardians at Wilsby armed with bludgeons, committed arson in the workhouses of Bishop's Stortford and Saffron Walden. Relief by bread instead of money produced much anger. The poor of Okehampton believed the bread to contain poison.[4] Archdeacon Hare of Lewes, who was always formidable to his little rustic flock at Hurstmonceux, accepted a place on the local poor law board, and the village rumoured that at the school feast he intended to send all the

[1] PP, 1836, xxix, i, 450; Thomas Spencer, PP, 1836, xxix, i, 493-5.
[2] PP, 1836, xxix, i, 450.   [3] Webb, viii, 117.   [4] PP, 1836, xxix, i, 5-6.

children sailing in Pevensey Bay and to sink the boat with all hands. Some simple folk suspected a plan to remove useless mouths. Starving people were known to refuse the bread. The new system was better than the old; but countrymen and the poor were not quickly reconciled.

The fall of the Whig government

King William IV was an honest, undignified, open man. He liked Lord Grey and disliked his allies. Proposals to take the money of the Church of Ireland worried him. He was harassed about his coronation oath and genuinely attached to the established church. Whigs in alliance with O'Connell were abhorrent to him. He could not bear Lord John Russell, whom he conceived to lead the onslaught on the Irish church. At private or public occasions his feelings boiled up and made him say things which passed the bounds of decorum. On 28 May 1834 he suddenly spoke the fire in his heart, and almost caused a constitutional crisis.

It happened to be the day after a motion by H. G. Ward in the Commons to appropriate part of the church property of Ireland; the day after the king received the vast petition of lay churchmen in favour of the established church. A deputation of Irish bishops, led by their primate, Archbishop Beresford of Armagh, offered him a petition that no change should be made in the discipline and services of their church without consulting the church authorities. The king's usual answers to such deputations were drafted by a responsible minister and were formal. King William IV's answer was informal, from a full heart, and had not been drafted by any member of the Whig cabinet. He declared that he would be resolute in defence of the church; that he had allowed toleration to go to the utmost limit. The Protestant 'religion, and the church of England and Ireland, the prelates of which are now before me, it is my fixed purpose, determination, and resolution to maintain . . . If there are any of the inferior arrangements in the discipline of the church, which however I greatly doubt, that require amendment, I have no distrust of the readiness and ability of the prelates now before me to correct such things; and to you, I trust, they will be left to correct, with your authority unimpaired and unshackled. I trust it will not be supposed that I am speaking to you a speech which I have got by heart. . . .'

No one was likely to think that this was a speech got by heart.

Whigs believed it to be unconstitutional—a public declaration by the king that he would not tolerate the course on which his government was set. Conservative feeling in the country rose round the crown. Tory constituencies held banquets to thank His Majesty for his gracious and manly declaration. The king's speech was printed and circulated. Radical papers suggested that the report was a hoax and that the king made no such speech. At a luncheon in Macclesfield Bishop Sumner of Chester was received with deafening cheers when he declared that he heard the speech and could vouch for its accurate report.[1]

The cabinet divided over the money of the Irish church and whether a government was justified in taking part of it. Lord John Russell pressed for the money, ministers like Edward Stanley and Sir James Graham resigned office on the issue. When they met a clumsy contretemps over the renewal of martial law in the Irish coercion act, Lord Althorp, leading the House of Commons, could hold office no longer and resigned. Lord Grey resigned next day. And thus, un-looked for, a Whig lord whom few would have predicted, but who was to have much influence upon this history, became prime minister; Lord Melbourne. He insisted that Althorp be persuaded to come back, and this was achieved, partly by dropping the military clauses of the coercion act, and partly because the king and nearly every other responsible person worked to persuade him. The Whig government, though weaker in the public eye, was still in being. Its dissensions over the Irish church were patched but not mended.

Melbourne's first ministry lasted a short time. On 17 November 1834 Lord Althorp's father died, and so Althorp became Earl Spencer and went to the House of Lords. Melbourne must find a leader for the House of Commons, and the obvious leader was Lord John Russell. Russell had the disadvantage, first that the king could not bear him, and secondly that Melbourne was not sure of being able to hold the cabinet in being if Russell led Irish policy in the House of Commons. King William wanted an excuse to be rid of the Whigs and Mel-bourne was not sorry to be dismissed. Despite the Whig majority in Parliament, despite the evidence of Whig feeling in the country, the king believed that Tory feeling was rising and was afraid of further measures against the church. The king dismissed his minister on 14 November and sent for the Duke of Wellington. Wellington advised that only a minister in the Commons could lead the government in

[1] *Br. Mag.*, 6, 1834, 227.

these circumstances. And therefore Sir Robert Peel was fetched back from a Roman holiday to be prime minister.

This was the last time in English history that the crown dismissed a prime minister whose party possessed an overwhelming majority in the House of Commons.

Tories were uneasy to find themselves in power. They were not sure that it would do. If the king's gamble failed, the devil expelled would return with seven worse. But the king's judgment was proved almost correct. The election of December 1834 sent to Westminster a far more numerous body of Tory members; as numerous or almost as numerous as the Whigs. If the Whigs chose to ally with O'Connell or the radicals, the Tories would be outvoted. But this was a different Tory party from the battered huddle of 1833.

The cry of *Church in danger* seemed suddenly a balloon-bogey. Intangible threats which panicked an Arnold or steeled a Newman faded into the past. Tory churchmen were still afraid. Clear-sighted conservatives knew that the government of England had not finished with the reform which it promised the nation and never began. But henceforth reform looked as though it meant reform and was no longer a cynical word for robbery.

CHAPTER II

THE WHIG REFORM OF THE CHURCH

1. PEEL'S MINISTRY, JANUARY–APRIL 1835

SIR ROBERT PEEL was shy and solitary. Son of a rich Lancashire cotton-spinner, and retaining, despite Harrow and Oxford, his accent and gaucherie to the end of his life, he was never comfortable with the upper world of English society which still ruled Tory and Whig parties. Of all the prime ministers of the nineteenth century, Peel was least informative about his religion. As member of the middle class and representative of Lancashire industry, he believed in hard work, efficiency, practical business. His piety was genuine, but neither complex nor articulated. Despite the high honours which Oxford awarded, he was never an abstract theorist. Enemies accused him of lacking principle. He appears to have believed in a reasonable undogmatic faith. He regarded himself as a pillar of the Church of England and of the established constitution. The nation he conceived as a Christian society with its natural hierarchy of ranks, cemented socially by an honoured class of property-owners and morally by the religious teaching of the English clergy. He was endowed with little imagination and a powerful grasp of detail, was nearer to the administrator who governs by mastery of regulation than to the leader who moves society by appealing to ideals. He wanted the world to tick as efficiently and unemotionally as his own heart. A staunch conservative, he disapproved the right wing of his party and disliked the ultra views of Protestant Irish peers or of Oxford clergymen. The right wing of the party distrusted and disliked him. If he was indispensable, his part in Catholic emancipation was not forgotten.

The king had summoned a Tory minister because he wanted to protect the church, especially the Church of Ireland. A Tory minister who found himself in a minority in the House of Commons must attempt as his first duty to widen his support in House and country. Therefore he must persuade the right wing of the Whig party that he would promote moderate measures of reform which they wanted;

and must persuade the moderates of the country, especially the more moderate dissenters, that he was no enemy to their just claims for relief or their clamour for wise reform. Appointed to safeguard the church, he could safeguard it only by concession.

The first need was to dissolve Parliament and attempt to gain by a general election. The king was not wrong in thinking that Tory support had risen in the country. The election of December 1834 and January 1835 was a success for Peel. In that age the lines of party were not so clear nor the discipline of party so strict as they became later in the century. The electors sent to Westminster a far more numerous body of men who would be likely to support Peel.

In December 1834 he issued to his constituents at Tamworth the declaration known as the Tamworth manifesto.

He tried thus to capture moderate, Whig, and dissenting votes. The manifesto began by declaring that he would be no apostate from Tory principles. He affirmed that he considered the reform act of 1832 a final and irrevocable settlement of a great constitutional question; that he was no defender of abuse nor enemy of judicious reforms, was ready to review the civil or ecclesiastical institutions of the country, supported the principle of Althorp's bill to relieve the dissenters of church rates and of Lord John Russell's bill to relieve them of marriage disabilities; was bound to admit that he still opposed the dissenting claim to enter the universities, but wished to free dissenters from consequent disabilities in the professions of law and medicine. He could not consent to a plan for appropriating the money of the church to other than strictly ecclesiastical purposes. He favoured a plan for commuting tithe. But 'if, by an improved distribution of the revenues of the church, its just influence can be extended, and the true interests of the established religion promoted, all other considerations' (presumably meaning vested interests) must give way.

Peel thereby committed himself and his government to relieve the dissenters of two of their disabilities: marriage and church rate. He also committed himself to the view that even a Tory government could not avoid the reform of the church. 'The Trojans', wrote Sydney Smith, 'must put on the armour of the Greeks whom they have defeated.'[1]

The Tamworth manifesto was variously received. A meeting of dissenting deputies at Birmingham resolved that the manifesto was a

[1] Smith to Wilmot Horton, 15 January 1835; Nowell Smith, 602.

crafty manoeuvre to conciliate dissenters by promise of relief in a form so vague and Jesuitical that they must refuse his appeal for a fair trial. Peel replied that he could not believe this resolution to represent dissenting opinion, and he was partly right. Everywhere moderate men were surprised and pleased to find a Tory minister pursuing a moderate policy of reform. But only partly right. The dissenting *Christian Advocate* asked (5 January 1835) how a cabinet composed of the very garbage of Toryism could be expected to share the spirit of Peel's manifesto. In Oxford and Lambeth the manifesto was received uneasily and with lowered morale. They had been fighting change not because they believed the established church to be perfect but because any change must lead to more change, to unknown revolution. And now a Tory minister, from whom alone they could expect political defence, declared himself to favour reform. They were suspicious, and wrote letters to reassure each other. If Peel agreed to reform, reform must come.

The morale of high churchmen sank still lower when Peel appointed a commission to reform the church. For Peel wanted church reform. Tory friends like Croker thought that he should reform the church because he must lighten the Tory ship of this load, even cutting away the masts if necessary.[1] Peel was an astute politician and not blind to the political advantages and disadvantages of reforming the church. But he believed it a duty to reform the church, not only for the sake of the Tory party, but for the sake of the Church of England and its public influence.

On 4 January 1835 Peel had a long interview with Archbishop Howley and Bishop Blomfield of London. On 5 January he wrote to the king proposing a commission to review the state of crown patronage and bishops' patronage, to provide for the efficient discharge of the pastoral duties of the church.[2] He purposed—it was an axiom to Tory reform—that the plan for reform must come from churchmen. Whig measures were opposed by many bishops because they were forced on the church without consulting the bishops.[3] Reform must be proposed not by government but to government by a commission of responsible churchmen.

[1] Parker, *Peel*, 2, 284.
[2] Parker, *Peel*, 2, 276; approved by the king, 10 January, from Brighton.
[3] His chief advisers were Howley, Blomfield, and Goulburn, cf. Add MSS. 40333, 210ff. For the whole question of the commission, G. F. A. Best's *Temporal Pillars* (1963) is now fundamental.

The archbishop chose the clergy, Peel chose the laymen. On 4 February the names were published and afforded modest relief to anxious churchmen. They saw that Archbishop Howley consented to serve, were confident in his power of braking and wished that he looked a little fiercer. 'I dread the archbishop', wrote Newman to Hurrell Froude.[1] Archbishop Vernon Harcourt of York was for these purposes a nonentity. Bishop Blomfield of London was disliked and distrusted by high churchmen and had lately recommended, in a charge of 1834, that the chapters be partly disendowed for the sake of poor parishes. Some clergymen thought him a sarcastic time-server, and feared that his reforming zeal cast an eye upon promotion from a future government of Whigs. He shared in the odium of the new poor law. 'They tell me', wrote Croker to Peel, 'that the clergy have but a half confidence in the archbishop, and *worse than none* in the Bishop of London.'[2] Bishops Kaye of Lincoln and Monk of Gloucester would be likely to support Howley. The laymen were good conservative churchmen—Peel, Lord Chancellor Lyndhurst, Goulburn, home secretary, Wynn almost an ultra-Tory, Lord Harrowby, Sir Herbert Jenner, and Henry Hobhouse. Under the proper title of Ecclesiastical Duties and Revenues Commission it met for the first time at Peel's house on 9 February.

No one expected Archbishop Howley to drive. He was more fitted to delay than to advance reform. Peel himself drove the commission at alarming and imprudent speed. To it he devoted much of his time and energy as prime minister. He prodded his colleagues into publishing a first report on 17 March 1835; a plan, digested only in a month and a half, to begin remodelling the structure of the Church of England. The speed was made possible by statistics provided in that commission of enquiry into the revenues of the established church which had been elicited by legends of oriental wealth in the abuse of the reform crisis.

In view of rumours that even Peel might despoil the cathedrals, the first report ought to have eased the anxieties of conservative churchmen. It asserted the principle that the duties and stipends of bishops should be made more equal. To this end diocesan boundaries should be drastically altered; two new sees founded at Manchester and Ripon; two old sees suppressed to maintain the number of bishops as before—or, in the more polite language of Irish suppression, amalga-

---

[1] Newman to Froude, 18 January 1835, LC, ii, 86.   [2] Parker, *Peel*, 2, 284.

mated with neighbouring sees, St. Asaph with Bangor and Bristol with Llandaff. Northern Lancashire and Furness, now in the diocese of Chester, were to be in the diocese of Carlisle. The county of Dorset, which was most of the old diocese of Bristol but entirely cut off from the see-city by the diocese of Bath and Wells, was to be transferred to Salisbury. The counties of Huntingdon and Bedford, in the old diocese of Lincoln, were to be transferred to Ely. The counties of Essex and Hertford, in the old diocese of London, were to be transferred to Rochester . . . and so the reasonable but not revolutionary suggestions continued. Then it recommended that stipends of the bishops be made more equal; that Canterbury should no longer average £19,182 a year and Durham £19,066, Llandaff £924 and Rochester £1,459, but that most of the sees should be provided with £4,500 to £5,500, except the five most senior sees.

In calculating the benefit to the Tory party, Peel's friends were mistaken. The first report was hailed by many churchmen and even by the representative newspaper of the Tory party, the *Standard*, as a sensible move towards efficiency. But to genuine reformers, and to all anti-reformers, it was an earnest only of change to come. Rich endowments of the cathedrals were still locked away like unused chests of treasure. Radical critics fastened upon the triviality of the 'reform' and whipped Peel with its insignificance. They observed him *raising* the income of various bishoprics, and were caustic in their judgment. Though a minimum income of £4,500 a year for a bishop could no longer be pictured as oriental splendour, it could still be contrasted with primitive simplicity. The *Examiner* prophesied that the bishops would deal as tenderly with church abuses as Sancho Panza treated his body when he flogged himself.

Ultra churchmen were no more pleased. 'The battle', wrote Hugh James Rose, 'has been fought . . . and is lost.' The past is cut away, the threads are snapped, the ancient stream dried up, they must dig for new springs, the house of their fathers is to be reconstructed. *John Bull*, professing regret for its criticism because it respected Archbishop Howley, pronounced the plan to be so wild and extravagant that it threatened the ruin of the establishment.[1]

They were not alarmed because one bishop's stipend was to be moved from £1,000 to £5,000 and another's from £19,000 to £15,000. They were alarmed because they disliked parliamentary

[1] *Br. Mag.*, 7, 1835; Walpole, *Hist.*, v, 256; JB, 1835, 100, 29 March 1835.

interference with the internal polity of the Church of England, interference though the members of Parliament need no longer be members of the Church of England. They saw it as an ominous, a fatal precedent; for if these things were done in the green tree, what would be done in the dry, when the Whigs returned despite the king?

The first report of the church commission was signed on 17 March. Peel's fall was already near. An alliance of Irish radicals and Whigs agreed upon the single motion which could command their united votes: a motion by Lord John Russell that any 'surplus' from the money of the Church of Ireland ought to be applied to general education in Ireland. After three successive defeats Peel resigned on 8 April 1835 and the Whigs and Lord Melbourne were back. 'Everything', wrote a friend to Newman, 'humanly speaking, seems darkening round the church.'[1]

Peel achieved no legislation. But his short ministry of three months changed the history of the church. He showed that even Tories wanted reform and so made reform inevitable. He showed that even Tories were willing to consider the grievances of dissenters about marriage and so ensured that the next Whig government would carry relief. Above all he created in the commission an instrument for church reform. The Whigs vacillated in their understanding of the phrase church reform. Their leaders wanted a reasonable establishment and agreed with Peel that the government should reform the church for its good. Their anti-church supporters knew that to reform the church was to extend its influence; and by reform they often meant confiscation of endowments, end of tithes, destruction of influence. Peel succeeded in diverting the main stream of agitation into a channel of internal, beneficial, constructive reform. Admit change, alter everything discreditable, jettison the load of indefensible archaisms, fortify the inner life of the church by liberating the pastoral instincts, and the Church of England will rise like a giant shaking off withes and recapture its waning authority.

2. MELBOURNE

Melbourne was a man of quiet sense who preferred to wear the mask of a man of the world. He was charming, good-humoured, with a quaint manner, in conversation sparkling and pungent, and liked to give the impression of being lazy or nonchalant. The impression was

[1] Anthony Buller to Newman, 6 April 1835, LC, ii, 100.

altogether misleading if it referred to content of mind or carelessness over detail. His mind was full, he was widely read and equipped with extensive and rare information. But the nonchalance was not misleading if it referred to his parliamentary conduct. He was a Whig lord whose inmost heart had been hardened to cynicism by the tragedy of his wife and her infatuation for Lord Byron. He could not take the human race and its passions seriously. He was amused at mankind and could not sympathise with partisan feeling, or zeal, or earnestness. To him a parliamentary bill was never a matter of life and death, and even worse never appeared to be a matter of life and death; he usually confessed to his inmost circle that it was no such matter. Melbourne was the most moderate of Whigs. He never liked the reform bill, had no zeal to abolish slavery and thought the campaign for abolition a pack of nonsense,[1] had neither strength of conviction nor Whig feelings to make a strong prime minister, never identified himself with the backbenchers of his party. Yet he was responsible, conscientious, and full of common sense.

He had long been of the table at Holland House, that focus of free-thinking in religion. Allen, the atheist librarian at Holland House, claimed him for a free-thinker. The evidence rather suggests that he was a questing liberal, dissatisfied with orthodoxy but disliking enthusiasm in religion, even enthusiasm in irreligion, as much as he distrusted political zeal. He never liked dissenters, because they were enthusiasts. 'If we are to have a prevailing religion,' he wrote, 'let us have one that is cool, and indifferent, and such a one as we have got . . .'[2] He liked the establishment for reasons of the previous century which were obsolescent. In his older years he studied divinity and history, but never reached convinced faith. In so far as he fully shared Whig conviction, it was belief in toleration. He thought the Protestant establishment in Ireland really wrong, contrary to reason and common sense. He hated trouble. His object as prime minister seemed to be to keep a rickety concern together. He was not a faithful attender at the services of the Church of England. Queen Victoria once remarked mockingly to him that he always seemed to be ill or too busy at church time. Churchmen suspected him of moral laxity and indifference to religion.

[1] Whately's *Life*, ii, 452, cf. Sanders, 376.
[2] March 1800, *Melbourne Papers*, ed. Sanders, 29. He disliked the idea of civil marriage, thinking it repugnant to the habits and feelings of the people. M to Lord John Russell, 16 August 1834, Sanders, 209.

The reform of municipal corporations

The reforming impetus of a reformed House of Commons still carried the government.

Everyone knew that the reform act of 1832 must be followed by another act to reform the municipalities. The Scottish boroughs were reformed by an act of 1833 and for three years a radical-tinted commission gathered evidence about the English boroughs. Lord John Russell, whom the king accepted with disgust as leader of the House of Commons, introduced the bill to reform municipal corporations on 5 June 1835. Peel refused to oppose it in principle, and it became law on 9 September. The act provided that the local council should in all cases be elected by ratepayers resident for three years in the borough and abolished the old closed and oligarchic corporations, self-elected or dominated by an aristocratic patron, which formerly controlled local politics. The new representative councils proved to be less radical than the Tories feared; partly because the House of Lords insisted that the council should nominate members equal to one-third of its total membership, and partly because payment of rates for three years proved to be a stiff qualification. In Liverpool in 1859 fewer people possessed the municipal franchise than the parliamentary.[1]

This reform of the boroughs affected churchmen and dissenters.

Prophets threatened that the act would mean local government by dissenters. The prediction was sweeping. But the ban upon dissenters under test and corporation acts survived the repeal of those acts because oligarchic corporations continued to elect only members of the established church. At Wisbech, where the corporation was elected, the local elections became a campaign of dissent versus church, and the vicar used authority and beer at the vicarage to keep the corporation safe for the establishment. The battle was slowly lost; and by 1834 under a new and less political vicar, dissenters shared comfortably with churchmen in the local administration of Wisbech.[2] In many other corporations there was no semblance of popular election and dissenters continued to be excluded, even at populous boroughs like Northampton and Leicester. Therefore the prophets were right thus far. New elective constitutions must mean more dissenters exercising power in local government.

[1] B. D. White, *Liverpool 1835–1904*, 1951, 15.
[2] PP, 1835, xxvi, 2553, 2564.

The fact was admitted in Parliament. Most of the corporations inherited ecclesiastical patronage. In many parishes this was no more than a right to appoint the schoolmaster or nominate old men to an almshouse. But an important number of corporations controlled the choice of their vicar. Liverpool, Bristol and Norwich were exceptional in that their corporations nominated incumbents to several churches. The Bristol corporation possessed the advowsons of eight livings in the city, two country parishes in Somerset and one country parish in Gloucestershire. The corporation of Liverpool appointed the rector and seven other clergymen. The corporation of Norwich appointed eleven rural parsons in the diocese of Norwich. Bath, Penzance, Plymouth, Lincoln, Dartmouth, St. Albans, Ipswich, Thetford, Bedford, Boston and other towns appointed the incumbents of one or more livings.

Lord Melbourne and Lord John Russell could see no harm in an elected corporation continuing to appoint. In its first form the bill provided that the new corporations should exercise their rights like the old. The established church was the church of the nation. If the House of Commons, which contained dissenters, rightly possessed power over the national establishment, Russell could see no reason why local councils with dissenters should not possess power over their parishes. But the House of Lords refused to accept this view of the matter. Tory lords thought that to allow a corporation of dissenters to appoint a parson was as wrong as allowing the established church to appoint a dissenting minister. Bishop Blomfield made himself still more unpopular among dissenters by hinting that a dissenting corporation might deliberately appoint an incompetent vicar to prevent competition with the dissenting minister in the parish.[1]

Lord Lyndhurst proposed a clause that only the members of the established church on the corporation should exercise ecclesiastical patronage. To the majority of the House of Commons, Lyndhurst's clause seemed to revive religious tests abandoned in 1828.[2] A compromise was reached that all corporations must sell their church patronage, under the direction of the Ecclesiastical Duties and Revenues commission, and apply the proceeds to the common uses of the towns.

[1] Hansard, xxx, 971–2.
[2] Joseph Hume said that it was monstrous to exclude dissenters on corporations when everyone knew that a dissenter might purchase the advowson of a living at a public auction. Hansard, xxx, 1156. Accordingly Spring Rice, the chancellor of the exchequer, proposed the compromise.

Thus a large number of livings came to be offered upon the open market. Few saw objections to this proceeding. Amid the numerous cries for church reform, the auction of advowsons was not an abuse of which either party wished to be rid.

In the purchase of these livings wealthy men invested their money or their public spirit. Even in the middle twentieth century many of the old advowsons of corporations were still in the hands of private patrons or trustees. In Bath and Bristol and Plymouth members of the evangelical party bought to ensure the continuity of evangelical teaching. The doyen of evangelical clergy, old Charles Simeon, then within a few months of his death, bought the appointment to Bath Abbey for £6,330, which contemporaries thought an inflated price;[1] and to this day the advowson is owned by the Simeon trustees.

Forty years later the ecclesiastical patronage of Oxford and Cambridge colleges was left to them when dissenters were admitted to their governing bodies, and no harmful consequences ensued. But in 1835 the quarrel of church versus dissent was too vehement to allow this degree of trust. The established church gained little by the transfer of patronage into private hands. Corporations had sometimes appointed the son or relative of an alderman as their parson; and the exchange of corporation nepotism for private nepotism was little profit. The church suffered a loss of interest and sense of responsibility when the corporation was detached from ecclesiastical patronage.

But this detachment was inevitable and happened in other ways. The old corporations, especially in small boroughs, were content to support the Church of England. They administered charitable trusts for the established church and felt no more difficulty in paying money to the church than they found in nominating a vicar to a parish or an aged pauper to an almshouse. Sometimes they administered special trusts for the benefit of the church. The salary of the organist at St. Paul's, Bedford, had once been a charge upon corn tolls, and the Bedford corporation continued the payment and retained his appointment in their hands. In numerous boroughs the organist was paid in part or whole by the corporation; which might also pay bellringer, 'tunist and blower', singing boys, sexton, beadle, clerk, and sometimes make substantial contributions to repairs, thus preventing the need of a church rate. The Beccles corporation bought a new flag for the steeple

[1] About half the money was contributed by subscribers in Bath: cf. Br. Mag., 13, 1838, 107.

in 1830,[1] Oxford paid for coals to heat Carfax church, Lostwithiel paid for the sacramental bread and wine out of the harbour dues, the Norwich corporation paid a guinea to every preacher in the cathedral unless he were a dignitary of the cathedral or the Master of Corpus Christi College in Cambridge, the Totnes corporation allocated all the seats in the nave of the parish church, several corporations habitually granted money to repairs, and Liverpool made heavy grants to build churches as its population rose. The number and amount of these grants was small in relation to the national budget of the corporations.

The end of the system in 1835 meant a sudden effort by many parishes to replace what had vanished. The citizens of Helston in Cornwall made a strenuous and successful effort to find the stipend of their organist, formerly paid by the corporation. And wherever repairs had been open or concealed in the accounts of the old corporation, the community was confronted with the flaming controversy of raising a church rate in a town unaccustomed to that impost. The Church of England in the parishes became less national. It had taken a step towards the status of an independent denomination.

The prophecy of corporations ruled by dissenters was sometimes fulfilled. The appearance of Unitarians as mayors in Manchester and Liverpool was new to English history. The elections of 1835 inserted eminent dissenters into the corporations of Bury, Bristol, Boston, Cambridge, Chester, Colchester, Hull, Ipswich, Liverpool, Leicester, Leeds, Northampton, Saffron Walden and other towns.[2] Before the act every member of the Leicester corporation was Anglican, after the act the corporation contained sixteen Anglicans, twelve Unitarians, twelve Baptists, three Quakers, two Wesleyans and a few Independents.[3] The first seven mayors of Leicester after the act were all dissenters; and the nonconformist domination of towns like Birmingham and Leicester lasted all the century. In Liverpool the liberals won a sweeping victory at the local election and soon stopped the teaching of the prayer book in two schools inherited from the old régime, amid storms of opposition and with Bibles carried on poles at elections.[4] But in most boroughs churchmen and dissenters worked harmoniously.

[1] PP, 1835, xxvi, 2145.
[2] CM, 1836, 67.
[3] A. T. Patterson, *Radical Leicester*, 214.
[4] B. D. White, *Liverpool*, 22–23.

Municipal officers were accustomed by immemorial usage to attend church or cathedral on high days wearing robes of office and walking in procession headed by beadles and mace-bearers. Many dissenting officers cheerfully continued the custom. But the new corporation of Leicester said that they were not going to march up and down in tomfoolery and even auctioned a mace given to them in 1649. When the new mayor of Chester was asked to attend cathedral on the first Sunday after his election he replied that as a dissenter he had a duty to attend the chapel in Queen Street, and that as a Christian he regarded the customary pomp as profaning the Lord's Day. There was argument whether dissenting mayors should appoint dissenting chaplains. Two dissenting ministers, invited to be chaplains of a London sheriff, took scruples and refused.[1] But the absolute right of dissenting or Roman Catholic citizens to hold public office became everywhere established under Lord Melbourne's government. The government even dismissed the Duke of Newcastle from being lord lieutenant of Nottinghamshire because he refused to insert the names of dissenters in the commission of peace. The reform of the corporations opened some endowed schools to dissenters.

3. PROFESSOR HAMPDEN

Lord Melbourne needed Whig clergymen and found it not easy to find enough. At first he relied upon the advice of Archbishop Whately, who despised opponents as stupid, or upon Bishop Copleston of Llandaff, who had plenty of brains but not much sense. He was told that he must encourage the friends of his government at Oxford and Cambridge, that since the debates over dissenters the university Whigs were under a cloud, and that unless something were done there would be no Whigs left among the younger fellows of colleges.[2] The leaders of the Whigs at Cambridge received rewards in abundance. Professor Sedgwick was made a canon of Norwich. Dr. Bowstead of Corpus Christi was given the see of Sodor and Man. Dr. Lamb, who had been passed over for the vice-chancellorship, was given the deanery of Bristol. Dr. Musgrave of Trinity was given the see of

---

[1] CM, 1836, 96.
[2] Allen of Ely to Melbourne, 28 July 1836, MP.

Hereford. Connop Thirlwall of Trinity was given a good living in Yorkshire and later the see of St. David's.

Oxford Whigs were few. Two jutted out as clergymen richly deserving preferment: Dr. Arnold of Rugby and Dr. Hampden, principal of St. Mary Hall.

Arnold was aware that his name was mentioned for bishoprics.[1] Lord Melbourne greatly admired Arnold's sermons. He also thought his *Principles of Church Reform* to be overexcited, and did not easily forgive excitement. In the election of the winter 1834–5 Arnold, who had hitherto voted for a conservative Whig, travelled 200 miles from Westmorland to vote for a radical candidate who recommended the removal of bishops from the House of Lords; and in the early spring of 1835 the viler Tory press was presenting him as a heretic.[2] As late as December 1835 Melbourne wondered whether to make Arnold a bishop. He decided against the plan[3] and the verdict was prudent.

Dr. Hampden was an ugly, stolid, dull man with a heavy manner and a harsh voice. He had done much for the undergraduates of St. Mary Hall. He led the Oxford party which wished to substitute a declaration for subscription to the Thirty-nine Articles. In October 1835 Melbourne was almost determined to make Hampden a bishop.

But on 19 January 1836 Dr. Burton, the regius professor of divinity at Oxford, died suddenly. Archbishop Howley sent Melbourne a list of suitable persons, with Pusey at the head, then Shuttleworth, warden of New College, then Ogilvie, one of Howley's chaplains, Newman fourth, and Keble fifth. The archbishop quaintly supposed that Melbourne might dream of appointing Keble, Newman or Pusey, for he can hardly have been so naïve as to think that politics were not relevant to divinity. Even Newman was sanguine or visionary enough to imagine that Melbourne might name Keble, though he saw there was little chance, and wrote earnestly to Keble urging him not to decline an offer merely because it came from a Whig.[4] Newman was afraid that if Keble refused they might get

---

[1] *Life*, i, 357, 24 January 1835.

[2] By a violent wresting of his language in the appendix to vol. iii of the *Sermons* about the priesthood of the laity he was accused of teaching that his butler was as authorised to administer the sacrament as himself.

[3] Greville, iii, 267; vi. 9.

[4] LC, ii, 160. Hugh James Rose as Howley's chaplain knew the names on the list and told Newman that the names of Pusey and Keble and Newman were there. Whately commented the list for Melbourne, 27 January 1836, Broadlands Papers.

Hampden and that Keble would not be justified in risking such a calamity. Hampden's name was not on Howley's list. But Archbishop Whately pressed Hampden upon Melbourne, and Bishop Copleston of Llandaff supported.

On 7 February 1836 Melbourne wrote to Hampden offering him the professorship: 'the reputation which you enjoy of various and extended information, as well as of great theological knowledge, and also of a liberal spirit of enquiry, tempered by due caution . . . induce me . . .' Hampden accepted the offer by return of post. Now the king's consent must be obtained. On 9 February Melbourne wrote to the king at Brighton suggesting Hampden without comment. The king had never heard of Hampden and approved by return of post without comment.

Meanwhile the rumour leaked at Oxford. Sight of Melbourne's frank on the letter to Hampden inspired an official of the post office to an accurate guess. Hampden was taxed, and would neither deny nor affirm. Oxford men were convinced. The news spread through Oxford on 8 February, the day that Melbourne's letter arrived. Pusey gave a dinner party that same evening to consider what was to be done.[1]

These circumstances are important. If Oxford had been confronted with a *fait accompli*, with an appointment already approved by the king, the coming events would have been different. But Oxford was confronted with a well-based rumour, not yet made final, and therefore there might be time to appeal to the crown against it. When Melbourne and Hampden were afterwards bitter against the agitation, they ought to have remembered that the carelessness of one, perhaps of both, invited the university to agitate by offering the chance of successful agitation.

The wind blew up to such force that, for the first and only time in his administration of patronage, Melbourne hesitated about bowing before it, and by hesitating, allowed it time to rise into a gale. On 10 February a violent article against Hampden appeared in the *Standard*; and on the same day Melbourne wrote to Hampden that the difficulties were so great that it was doubtful whether it was advisable in the interests of the university to persevere. On 11 February he must have been privately relieved to receive the king's ignorant

---

[1] *Letters of J. B. Mozley*, 50–55. Keble, away at Cirencester, received a letter the next day from a friend in Oxford.

approval and have it safely in his pocket, but on 12 February he wrote again to Hampden that the question was by no means decided.[1]

Why the hesitation on the part of the prime minister? By 12 February it was inconceivable that he could pretend no offer to have been made, and therefore not to persist would be victory to his opponents and weakness to his party. It was inevitable that he must go through with it. Yet he paused again. Suspected by the Tory public of being indifferent to religion, he took pains to avoid appointments which could appear to justify this charge, and only a month before had refused to make a bishop out of Dr. Arnold, a bigger man than Hampden, because Arnold was not considered orthodox and his appointment would offend high churchmen. None of his advisers hinted to him that Hampden might be open to a charge of unorthodoxy. Yet this was now the charge lodged in Oxford, spread among members of Parliament, and carried down to Brighton for the king's ear.

This question of unorthodoxy was the weakness of the Oxford opponents. They distrusted Hampden for his conduct over the admission of dissenters in 1834–5. But they could not make this an objection to his appointment, except on the general ground that it is undesirable to make a regius professor of someone who commands no confidence among his colleagues. It was also a weakness that few had been attacking Hampden for heresy until this moment, and that in 1834 he had been elected without comment to the chair of moral philosophy. It was also a weakness that on all sides Hampden was admitted to be a virtuous man who did much for the undergraduates of St. Mary Hall.

The opposition therefore consisted of a few—high churchmen and evangelicals, Newman, Keble, Pusey, Golightly and others—who genuinely believed that Hampden was heretical and unfit to instruct the young of Oxford; a large number of Oxford men who resented the selection of one with Hampden's record over the dissenters; and a still larger number of others who perceived that the blunder was an excellent chance of harassing Lord Melbourne's government. The Tory press clamoured that this Whig minister, Gallio Melbourne, was now moving from an attack upon the property of the church to invade the citadel of faith, and intended to deluge the church with a torrent of scepticism and indifference to religious truth.

[1] Melbourne to Hampden, 12 February 1836, MP.

To prove Hampden unorthodox, it was necessary to prove that his pamphlet of 1834, *Observations on Religious Dissent*, stemmed logically from his theological principles. In 1832 Hampden delivered the Bampton Lectures, *The Scholastic Philosophy considered in its relation to Christian Theology*. These lectures were sober and dull. They distinguished an original, simple, and scriptural gospel from the various dogmatic formulas introduced by Greek philosophical influence and later by the schoolmen. They were a reasonable exposition of an old latitudinarian point of view. If Hampden was heretical, so were Bishop Watson, Archdeacon Paley, Professor Hey, Bishop Hoadly and a row of eighteenth-century divines. Strong Oxford churchmen would not have shrunk from the proposition that Bishops Watson and Hoadly had been heretics. Newman sat up all the night of 10 February[1] writing a pamphlet to disclose the logical consequences of Hampden's divinity; he called it *Elucidations of Dr Hampden's Theological Statements* and rushed it into print on 13 February. It was a one-sided interpretation of Hampden's statements, which were often vague and obscure.[2]

Meanwhile Oxford was at work raising petitions. On 10 February a meeting was held in the common room of Corpus Christi College, and thereafter a petition sent to Archbishop Howley, with seventy-three signatures, to be presented to the king. On the same day the archbishop went to see Melbourne, to be followed by the Archbishop of York. Pusey's brother, Philip Pusey, a member of Parliament, sent a message to Melbourne that if the government would abandon its intention he could get the petition dropped. Both archbishops made personal representations to the king. They found Melbourne brusque. He said: 'I know very little about Dr. Hampden's works, but I know infinitely more than the Right Reverend Prelates.'[3]

Melbourne received other advice, as well as petitions from Oxford. It was pointed out to him that the 'heresy' of Hampden was an excuse, and that the real ground was his attitude to subscription. He was told that the leaders of the opposition, Newman and Pusey, were disguised Roman Catholics; and that Newman was a violent and ultra bigot who had acquired notoriety by refusing to marry an Oxford

[1] LC, ii, 170.
[2] The principal of Brasenose sent a copy to Lord Melbourne, who found the topics treated in it 'very abstruse' and 'handled in a very abstruse style and manner'. Melbourne to A. T. Gilbert, 17 February 1836, MP.
[3] Queen Victoria's *Journal*, 28 December 1839, RA

girl because she was a Baptist.[1] Melbourne formed the impression that it was unreasonable clamour. He hardly needed the information about the alleged bigotry of Hampden's opponents, and by the evening of 13 February decided that the appointment must stand. He wrote to inform Hampden.

It would have been better for him if he could have gazetted it at once. The opposition had already five days to form a powerful party. But again he was forced to delay. The king at last acted.

Oxford had been hoping to make the king refuse the nomination of the prime minister. There is little doubt that they would have succeeded—but for the fact that the king, in ignorance of Hampden, had already sanctioned the appointment. Oxford was in despair that he failed to act, but they knew nothing of the letter which Melbourne had extracted.[2] There was little that the king could do now. On 14 February he wrote to Melbourne that he must withhold his sanction until Melbourne should further consult Archbishop Howley.

On 15 February Melbourne laid this letter before the cabinet and sent a respectful but indignant letter to the king. He said that the king had already approved; that his own honour, and that of his government, was a stake; that Dr. Hampden's honour was at stake, seeing he was accused of not believing the articles which he had signed and the creed which he professed. The question, he said 'seriously infringes upon the rights of private judgment and free enquiry which are the foundations of the Protestant faith; and it saps the great principle of toleration, the great glory of this age and of your Majesty's reign. Finally, it seriously endangers the real interests of the Church of England into which it introduces schism and division.' He told the king that he was very little disposed to yield to unreasonable agitation.[3] He had already heard the opinions of the two archbishops, and would see Archbishop Howley again in obedience to the king's command, but 'unless his Grace can produce something much more decisive and cogent than any of his previous arguments, your Majesty will perceive that it will be impossible that Viscount Melbourne

---

[1] Dr. Falconer to Macdonald, 13 February 1836, MP, forwarded to Melbourne perhaps by Morpeth, with an important postscript written by the forwarder.

[2] Public rumour, however, guessed that the king approved because Melbourne failed to tell the king enough. The story was circulated in an untrue form which made it appear that Melbourne deliberately withheld vital information. Cf., e.g., JB, 1836, 140, on Melbourne's 'bit of jockeyship'.

[3] Sanders, 498–9.

should alter an opinion which Viscount Melbourne conceives himself to have formed upon the soundest and most certain grounds'.

It could not alter the result, but he was still losing time. Later on the 15th he interviewed the archbishop again. On the 16th he felt obliged to travel all the way to Brighton to see the king, not without anxiety and desire to be inconspicuous. At Brighton the king remarked that he could hardly regard the representations of two archbishops as clamour, and accused him, no doubt unjustly, of keeping back vital information when he recommended Hampden. The appointment was at last gazetted on 17 February, Ash Wednesday. It was not public property until 20 February.[1]

Thanks to the blunder of Melbourne or Hampden on the first day, and then to Melbourne's two days of hesitation, and then to the action of the king, twelve days elapsed between the offer to Hampden and its publication; days during which all the church fear of Whigs rose and was harnessed to the chariots of Hampden's Oxford antagonists. Those twelve days meant that the storm could no longer be calmed by publishing the appointment. Newman saw the chance which Melbourne gave him. Shortly before he heard the official decision he was writing that whichever way the decision now went they would gain as well as lose. If Hampden were not appointed, they gained a victory, were safe from the annoyance and mischief of having Hampden as regius, and curbed the liberal propensities of anyone else who might succeed. If Hampden were appointed, Melbourne's ministry would be at war with the church, the archbishop would be roused and many Oxford waverers would join Newman's party.[2] The diagnosis was just. With the aid of Hampden and the opposition of the king, Melbourne had put himself into a situation where he could only lose.

All through March Oxford did what it could against Hampden. That was little. Pusey achieved a public declaration that Hampden was guilty of systematic teaching of rationalism.[3] Over England bodies of churchmen gathered together to petition the crown, sometimes appealing for security against the nomination of improper persons to high station in the church, at least without sanction of the

---

[1] *London Gazette*, 19 February 1836.

[2] LC, ii, 168; in the Selborne Papers vol. viii is an important series of letters on the Hampden case from a detached and unusual point of view.

[3] Liddon, *Life*, i, 373. On 12 March Pusey published a pamphlet with the same aim as Newman's *Elucidations*.

Archbishop of Canterbury. For the first time in English history there was angry criticism of the English mode of appointing bishops. On 17 March Hampden delivered a quietly orthodox inaugural lecture which did nothing to discourage his opponents. A statute was hesitantly proposed to the Oxford convocation by the heads of houses, declaring that since Hampden's theology failed to possess the confidence of the university, he should be deprived of his place on the syndicate for choosing select preachers, and that he should not be consulted when a sermon was called in question before the vicechancellor. Melbourne felt himself so touched by Hampden's troubles that he sent advice to give a series of practical and elementary lectures, to which no objection could be taken.

Bishop Phillpotts of Exeter, never backward in joining a fray, wrote to Exeter College to declare that he would dispense with certificates of attendance at lectures by the regius professor.[1]

The statute was brought forward on 22 March 1836 and vetoed by the proctors, amid immense shouts of *Placet* and some hissing of Pusey from Hampden's friends. In April those friends began a counterattack upon the teaching of the *Tracts* and of Newman's sermons, extracted and commented according to the model of the *Elucidations*. Various pamphlets accused the Oxford high churchmen of popery.[2] In the April number of the *Edinburgh Review* Arnold released a regrettable cry of pain against *The Oxford Malignants*,[3] whom he charged with conspiracy, fanaticism, wickedness, corrupt conscience. The article did more harm than good to Hampden's cause. But despite Arnold's fury the public was beginning to think that Hampden was being persecuted. Everyone admitted him to be a good man. Many of the few who took the trouble to enquire found him more orthodox in general intention than the extracts of loose language suggested. Even Rose confessed that on close examination he wondered whether

[1] Hampden to Melbourne, 6 March 1836, MP.
Sydney Smith on 25 March 1836, Nowell Smith, 641: 'A sad affair, this inaugural lecture of Hampden; instead of being like the worldly Hampden, martial and truculent, it is elegiac, precatory and hypocritical. I would have fetched blood at every sentence . . .'
[2] Dickinson, *A Pastoral Epistle from His Holiness the Pope*. Pusey published on 25 April *An Earnest Remonstrance to the author of the Pope's Pastoral Letter*, Liddon, *Life*, i, 380.
[3] This notorious title was added to the article by the editor and was not Arnold's. It sufficiently represents the contents of the article. It was known to Arnold, and had become public property that in private conversation Newman had asked dubiously whether Arnold was a Christian, LC, ii, 47.

Hampden was more bewildered than heretical.[1] The word *elucidate* began to be celebrated as a humorous synonym for *misrepresent*.

On 5 May with new proctors the statute was reintroduced to convocation. The undergraduates misbehaved at the earlier convocation and though generally hostile to Hampden were now excluded for the sake of good order. Some 700 or 800 of them gathered outside the theatre and were indignant. They punctuated the ritual with shouts, threw stones and broke the windows and at last interrupted the anti-Hampden Latin speeches of Miller and Keble by battering open the locked doors and rushing headlong to the gallery. When the senior proctor established order in the gallery the statute passed by 474 votes to 94. Hampden started legal proceedings over this statute, but in June the quarrel was so fierce that, on a hint from Melbourne, Hampden asked (8 June) to be removed from office to 'a higher post of professional usefulness', though two days later he said he was ready to persevere.[2] Dr. Gilbert, the principal of Brasenose, posted a notice in the hall forbidding his men to attend Hampden's lectures, and other Oxford tutors attempted to preserve the purity of their minds by the same method. It is often a mistake to forbid undergraduates to go somewhere, and this occasion was no exception.

This condemnation has often been mocked as a mouse of a penalty, unfitting to the mountain of travail which bore it. It must be remembered that, though the bolt was ostensibly aimed at Hampden, its real quarry was higher. The condemnation was a public declaration that the Whig prime minister was unfit to choose leaders in the Church of England, and a further mode of rallying staunch churchmen against his government. If Oxford was directly attacking Hampden, it was indirectly attacking the royal supremacy. And one of its aims was to frighten Melbourne into not making another appointment of the kind. 'We had to give the alarm', wrote Pusey, 'and to cry Fire!'[3] The agitation was not a failure. In May there was a rumour, said to originate with the assistant masters at Rugby School; the headmaster, it was said, received a letter from Melbourne regretting that the Hampden

---

[1] *Br. Mag.*, 11, 1837, 659–60.

[2] In December he received a legal opinion (by John Campbell the attorney-general, Stephen Lushington, and W. W. Hall, dated Middle Temple, 17 December 1836. Lushington alone had given a similar opinion in April, and this opinion was vainly waved at the vice-chancellor in the convocation of 5 May) that the statute was illegal, and Melbourne offered him money to fight the case. It seemed better on reflection to submit.

[3] Cf. J. F. Christie on Arnold, LC, ii, 185; Liddon, i, 388.

controversy prevented him from offering preferment, and disclosing (so it was improbably alleged) that twelve bishops were engaged to remonstrate.[1] The Tory press copied extracts from the *Oxford Malignants* article to show how unfitted was Arnold for one of the vacant sees. Melbourne's subsequent moderation in ecclesiastical appointments, and his steady refusal thereafter to make Hampden a bishop or Arnold either a bishop or a professor of divinity, his disregard of further advice from Whately or Copleston, may in part be attributed to the fate of Hampden.

But if the campaign was not a failure, it finally marked Pusey and Newman as suspect. Against the cry of rationalism, the cry of popery and of bigotry was shouted to the nation.

Melbourne's church patronage

That same spring three bishops died—van Mildert of Durham, Ryder of Lichfield, and Sparke of Ely—and everyone envied Melbourne's good fortune in being able to add three Whigs to the House of Lords. 'How fortunate the ministers are', it was said, 'to have such a mortality of bishops at such a crisis!'

Melbourne alone saw no cause for envy. Ecclesiastical appointments henceforth bothered him. He must find clergymen whose views on politics agreed with his own and who would yet command the respect of a Tory clergy. Such men were not easy to find. Melbourne was perfectly frank that he must have Whigs and took more trouble to discover the political views of the candidates than to learn their pastoral capacity. Charles Lushington once described Melbourne's enquiries thus—

'Is he a good man?'

'An excellent man; he is a most accomplished theologian, an exemplary clergyman, and is truly beloved throughout his district. . . .'

'Aye, aye, I understand all that; but is he a good man—is he a good Whig—will he vote for the Irish corporation bill?'[2]

Melbourne often wrote letters to candidates, telling them that he wanted to nominate them for high office in the church, and asking for their views on controverted questions of church policy, like the appropriation of money belonging to the Irish church. Without openly demanding, he really demanded a promise of political support before he would allow the name to go forward to the sovereign. Even

[1] JB, 1836, 157.   [2] Hansard, xxxv, 33.

so he was abused by more decisive supporters when bishops, nominated by himself, voted against the government or abstained in a division. He was not insistent upon rigid conditions on appointment; he could not afford to be rigid. Butler (Lichfield) and Longley (Ripon) were given leave to disagree on the Irish church. Melbourne declared to Longley that what he wanted was general agreement in political opinion and general disposition to support the measures of the present government, and could not wish to bind his support on every question.[1] But afterwards he was mortified when they took him at his word. He was aware that the government would suffer in repute unless the appointment commanded public respect; and one of the reasons why Melbourne's supporters kept pressing Arnold or Hampden upon him was the scarcity of Whig clergymen who would command regard on the bench. His life was further complicated by the custom whereby bishops should be chosen alternately from the graduates of the universities of Oxford and Cambridge, Oxford being the more difficult if regarded as a nursery of Whig divines. 'I have found some difficulty in selecting from the members of the university of Oxford', he told Archbishop Howley when nominating Denison to the see of Salisbury in March 1837.[2] It is easy to understand why Melbourne, to whom the accidents of death gave valuable patronage, made his weary cry, 'Damn it, another bishop dead!' when he received the news of a vacancy.[3] He slowly abandoned the custom of alternate appointments from Oxford and Cambridge.[4] The Archbishop of York once accused him of nominating a majority of Cambridge men. Melbourne thought that Cambridge produced ten able men to Oxford's five, and told the archbishop flatly that the old rule of alternative appointments was absurd and bad, because it compelled the prime minister to nominate inferior men. The grumble was certainly true of a Whig prime minister who needed all the liberty he could find.[5] 'I', he wrote plaintively to Bishop Longley, who promised to

[1] Melbourne to Longley, 10 April 1836, MP.
[2] Melbourne to Howley, 4 March 1837, MP. Denison was queried by Howley on the ground that he was hardly above the canonical age and this might carry dissatisfaction. Melbourne replied that his age was 37, and that more than one of the existing bishops must have been a bishop by that age.
[3] Sanders, 495.
[4] In February 1836 he thought it unwise to break the custom, M. to Butler, 28 February 1836, MP. But he ended by appointing four from Oxford and nine from Cambridge, Add. MSS. 54034, 244.
[5] Archbishop Vernon Harcourt to Melbourne, 29 August 1840; Melbourne to the archbishop, 31 August 1840, MP.

support him except on Ireland and then joined with other bishops in resisting a government bill for church rate, 'am continually subjected to the reproach of having disposed more ecclesiastical patronage than any other minister within so short a period, and of having so arranged it, as neither to secure one steady personal friend, nor one firm supporter of my own principles and opinions.'[1] He became melancholy and cross when his bishops failed him with their votes.

But after the row over Hampden he avoided the risk of unorthodox opinions. When Connop Thirlwall called on the prime minister after being nominated to the see of St. David's he found him sitting up in bed, surrounded with letters and newspapers; and Melbourne said, 'I only wish you to understand that I don't intend if I know it to make a heterodox bishop. I don't like heterodox bishops. As men they may be very good anywhere else, but I think they have no business on the bench.'[2] After the Hampden affair he avoided theologians. Some thought that Denison was made bishop in 1837 because though learned he never published books and was totally passive in theology.[3] 'I am most anxious', Melbourne wrote to Archbishop Howley, 'not to advance any man, whose doctrines are not in union with those of the established church, or even whose promotion would be disagreeable to the great body of the clergy.'[4] He steadily refused preferment to Arnold as bishop or divine. Under heavy fire from Arnold's friends he offered him the deanery of Manchester, which Arnold refused, and at last made him (1841) regius professor of modern history at Oxford. He no doubt consoled himself with the thought that history is not divinity and that as his government was expiring that week it could not matter if he were blamed. Arnold lived barely a year to enjoy this tardy preferment.

Melbourne troubled himself much over bishops. He might have acted more forthrightly for his political side. The warden of New College was a Whig, sardonic Shuttleworth, who wanted to be a bishop and whose want was well known to his friends. Melbourne's neglect of Shuttleworth caused remark. He was kind, learned, hospitable, and the wittiest don in Oxford. Whether because he was not

[1] Melbourne to Longley, 11 March 1837, MP.
[2] Torrens, ii, 330–20; *Letters of Thirlwall*, 160. The difficulty was Thirlwall's introduction to his translation of *A Critical Essay on the Gospel of St Luke, by F. D. E. Schleiermacher,* 1825.
[3] Blanco White to Hawkins; Oriel Coll. MSS., 2.111.
[4] Melbourne to Howley, 15 July 1840, MP.

decisive enough in Whiggery, for at one point in his career he was lampooned for trimming, or because he was sharp and unpopular with the undergraduates of New College, or because he was a little worldly, inventing a mahogany railway to carry decanters of port across the senior common room of his college—see after see passed him by. He had been tutor to Lord Holland's son and few in Oxford could understand it. Lord Holland was known to have Melbourne's ear and told Shuttleworth that he would soon be a bishop. King William IV was believed to have refused to have him.[1] When the king was near death Shuttleworth was assured on high authority that he would be Bishop of Salisbury, told his friends, and was mortified when the more conservative Denison was nominated. But even after Queen Victoria reigned and no sovereign resisted Melbourne's wishes, see after see continued to be filled with others. Shuttleworth vainly applied for the deanery of Exeter. At last in September 1840, after contemplating several other names and offering the see unsuccessfully to a half-brother of Lord John Russell, Melbourne came with the utmost reluctance to offer the see of Chichester to Shuttleworth. 'I know little of him myself,' Melbourne told Lord John Russell, 'and what I do know, I do not very much like.'[2] Archbishop Howley approved, and most of Oxford. But general approval in Oxford did not include Newman's men, whom Shuttleworth attacked. When Shuttleworth died at Chichester fifteen months later, as he was announced to deliver his primary charge, Dr. Pusey saw in his death a token of God's presence with the Church of England.[3] Shuttleworth as bishop had the single distinction of disregarding advice and appointing Henry Edward Manning as Archdeacon of Chichester.[4]

Though Melbourne grumbled that to find Whig bishops was difficult, the quality of his nominees was consistent. The analysed list, omitting poor George Davys, the queen's tutor, looks donnish: four recent fellows of Cambridge colleges, the head of an Oxford

[1] Tait MSS. 75, 51.

[2] Melbourne to Russell, 27 August 1840, MP. Among those considered were Dean Waddington of Durham and Julius Hare; the latter was rejected because too conservative. Lord Wriothesley Russell refused the see: it was not his first refusal, for he refused Lichfield in 1839; cf. R., 23 December 1839.

[3] Liddon, ii, 294.

[4] Cf. Manning Papers, *Divers*, ii, notes by H. Denvers Clarke. Shuttleworth went to a diocesan meeting in Brighton when Manning spoke with great power. When the bishop returned home the decayed archdeacon came to resign. Shuttleworth's mind was so full of Manning that he could think of no one else. He found that the Dean of Chichester agreed and so disregarded the warning.

college, the head of King's College in London, a fellow of Oriel College, the headmasters of Shrewsbury and Harrow, the rector of Bloomsbury who had earlier been censor of Christ Church, and two country vicars both of noble family. Melbourne's patronage was nothing if not respectable. This respectability had many political virtues and only caused him the corresponding lament that they did not all use their votes as he wished.

One of the two country parsons ran the risk which Melbourne sought to avoid: the nomination of Edward Stanley to the see of Norwich (1837) when Bathurst at last died in his ninety-fourth year. Stanley was decisively of the Arnold school and had spoken out for Roman Catholic emancipation and for reform. He was an admirable Whig pastor at Alderley in Cheshire, and except for a seagoing tang and charming breath of singularity, looked to be an excellent choice for the see of Norwich. Even King William IV much approved the choice, telling Melbourne that he attached great value to an exemplary discharge of the duty of parish priest, and that he rejoiced when a man like Stanley added to this virtue that of a good family, gentlemanly habits, and literary and scientific pursuits.[1]

Stanley turned out to be more outspoken than anyone expected. He began by inviting Dr. Arnold to preach the sermon at his consecration in the chapel of Lambeth palace. Howley refused to allow the preacher. He courteously expressed his respect for Arnold, but said that he could not allow him to preach, because it would be so very ill received by the clergy.[2] Stanley refused to choose anyone else and Howley appointed a chaplain to preach the sermon. Then Stanley must be installed in Norwich cathedral before the mayor and civic authority, and clergy of the diocese, and twelve hundred charity children placed on scaffolding before the altar, each school with a different flag. It happened to be the season of a general election, and various contenders against Melbourne had already accused Stanley of being a political adventurer.

Stanley preached a sermon declaring that conscientious dissent was neither sinful nor schismatic and advocating education even when not religious education. At the ensuing dinner the proposer of the bishop's health pointedly omitted to ask him to publish his sermon; the

[1] William IV to Melbourne, 13 April 1837, MP.
[2] Stanley, *Memoir of Edward and Catherine Stanley*, 80. Arnold warned Stanley that he might give offence if he accepted the invitation; cf. Arnold to Stanley, 19 April 1837, a letter in the possession of Mrs. J. R. H. Moorman.

omission was publicly rebuked, and uproar ensued which London newspapers enjoyed. There was talk of the heretical sermon of a liberal bishop.[1] Lord Melbourne got little credit among the clergy for his nomination of Edward Stanley. Yet the man was so courageous and engaging that he had a way of captivating even the enemy. And in her closet first at Windsor and then among the alien furnishings of the Brighton pavilion, the girl Queen Victoria read the installation sermon and thought it very good because it inculcated the feeling which all good Christians ought to have.[2] She invited him to preach two months later in the private chapel of Buckingham Palace.

4. ECCLESIASTICAL COMMISSION

The Ecclesiastical Commission was generated by Sir Robert Peel and bore the marks of Peel's personality; bureaucratic, capable and cold. Ask Whitehall to reform the Church of England and you get the commission. In many respects Whitehall improved the administration of the established church. But churches are awkward institutions to reform. They have functions which the principle of utility cannot easily test.

Bishop Blomfield claimed that the commission saved the Church of England.[3] He was complacent. The church was carried by currents deeper than the pools and eddies of decision at the commissioners' board. Saved from what? The threat of disestablishment in England evaporated just before the commission was first created. The commission did not touch the greater menace of disestablishment in Ireland. Saved from partial disendowment? If the Whigs failed to take the money of the Irish church, they would have failed to take the money of the Church of England. But they were Whigs, not radicals, and had no desire whatever to take the money of the Church of England, except so far as opening Anglican universities to dissenters was a small and partial disendowment. The nearest they came to such a motion was a plan of 1837 to nationalise church leaseholds in order

---

[1] *Memoir of Edward and Catherine Stanley*, 63–65; the dinner was an SPCK dinner. The Rev. Lord Bayning omitted the usual request. When Archdeacon Glover rebuked him Bayning confessed that he did not share the opinions of the sermon and was loudly applauded. The mayor of Norwich called a meeting of the corporation and agreed an address to the bishop asking that the sermon be printed. Cf. *Norwich Mercury* (which was strong for Stanley), 19 August, 26 August, 9 September 1837: JB, 27 August 1837.

[2] Queen Victoria's *Journal*, 5 October 1837, RA.   [3] *Memoir, 170.*

to pay repairs to church buildings. The collapse of that plan does not suggest that the commission preserved for the Church of England the money of the Church of England.

But there is a subtler meaning of *save*. The old parochial bottles were incapable of containing the new wine. The ancient parish system was rigid and rustic. England was becoming a country of cities and manufactures. In the race to shepherd urban masses the established church would have been hopelessly outdistanced unless it altered its system to one more flexible, directed less to the village and more to the slum. The commission was an instrument for adjusting ancient endowments to new needs. It was aimed to take money from places where it was less useful and spend that money where the needs shrieked.

No one doubted in 1860, and few will doubt now, that the clergy of 1860 were more zealous than the clergy of 1830, conducted worship more reverently, knew their people better, understood a little more theology, said more prayers, celebrated sacraments more frequently, studied more Bible, preached shorter sermons and worse. Reform of ministry was the momentous reform of the Victorian church. Little of this reform can be awarded to the commission. Public opinion, press, nonconformist rivalry and nonconformist conscience, moral fibre of the middle classes, evangelical gospel and Puseyite sacramentalism, alarm at French Revolution and English slums, the highest change was a change in public opinion, of which the commission was symptom and not cause. Perhaps the parish will be better shepherded if the curate is better paid. Pay will save the curate's time, extend his energy and raise his morale. But more than this was needed to make curates devout or self-sacrificing. And the curate illustrates the complexity of our problem. In some ways he did better before Whig reform than after. The Whigs forced incumbents to reside in their parishes. In 1838, 3,078 curates acted for non-resident incumbents. In 1864 only 955 curates acted for non-resident incumbents.[1] An admirable change. But the curate's difficulty in finding a sufficient stipend was thereby increased. Before reform the curate often obtained a sole charge quickly, lived free in the parsonage house, and was independent. After reform he competed for 7,000 adequate (over £200) livings with some 5,000 incumbents of inadequate livings and 5,000 other curates; and of the 7,000 adequate livings

[1] S. Wilberforce, *Essays*, 2, 103.

many were family perquisites and not open to most curates. In the Exeter diocese of 1866 sixty-eight clergymen remained assistant curates on an average income of £100, though all had served at least fifteen years, and sometimes up to fifty years.

It is good that vicars should reside. It is good that curates should be better paid. The commissioners were right to seek both these ends. And the ends were not wholly compatible.

The commissioners of the thirties and forties and fifties were pelted with abuse and criticism. Some of the abuse was aimed at change because it was change, some because it was Whiggish change. A Tory government passing similar laws would not so have suffered. Posterity disregards the vituperation partly because it was vituperation and partly because it was gunfire in the political duel. We want to reckon whether it was good for the Church of England and may overlook critics who denounced its badness because all under Melbourne was bad. Other critics were dreamers of the past, cocooned in canonries with a south aspect, ignorant of Salford and Birmingham, living in feudal forelock-touching respect. They adopted a stance squared against change because the church was in danger. When the church was no longer in danger the mist lifted and they were seen stuck in that posture. Dr. Corrie, later Master of Jesus College in Cambridge, was type of blindfold courtesy while the world passed.

But still other critics had reason. And little by little they succeeded in altering the constitution and work of the Ecclesiastical Commission.

On taking office again in April 1835, Lord Melbourne renewed the commission. Archbishop Howley was uneasy. If he had qualms at serving with Peel, he had worse qualms at serving with Melbourne. Melbourne was committed to taking, and Howley to preserving, the money of the Irish church. In May 1835 archbishop and prime minister negotiated warily.

Before Howley would serve he wanted to know what ecclesiastical measures Melbourne intended to introduce. He would not sit on a government commission if government was going to shoot at the Church of England. To this rule he confessed two exceptions. This government must attempt to take the money of the Irish church, for this was its reason for existence as government; and it must be free to abolish church rates in England. Melbourne agreed to promote no other bill about the church without approval of the bishops. So Howley consented, and the commission was reconstituted. The bargain over church rates was left too vague. Melbourne then expected to compensate the Church of England for loss of rate by national taxation along the lines of Althorp's old bill. Howley imagined the bargain to cover only a bill of this sort. When two years later Melbourne wanted abolition without compensation, Howley thought it a breach of faith and (temporarily) broke the Ecclesiastical Commission.

This bargain showed how the Whig river of reform was diverted into a canal which Peel dug. The money of the Irish church was insecure. English church rates were insecure. But provided that the commission reformed the church drastically enough to satisfy critics, the thunders of the mob were passing into history. 'No man' (in 1831–3), wrote Sydney Smith, 'could tell to what excesses the new power conferred upon the multitude would carry them; it was not safe for a clergyman to appear in the streets. I bought a blue coat, and did not despair in time of looking like a layman. All this is passed over. Men are returned to their senses upon the subject of the church . . .'[1]

The commissioners began with the advantage that the political commissioners were often absent. Melbourne, Lord Lansdowne, Lord Cottenham, Lord John Russell, and Spring Rice, the chancellor of the exchequer, replaced Peel and his minions. They had the vice of being Whigs, the virtue of rarely attending meetings. Unlike Peel, they were not interested and left the bishops to go their way. The Church of England would at least be reformed by bishops, and Howley's selection of bishops. Melbourne made no attempt to insert Whig bishops like Maltby into the commission. He sighed wearily, and told Whately that he had had no notion what a deal of trouble it was, reforming a church.[2]

But the commission laboured also under disadvantage. Its motives for reform were mixed. Three of its episcopal members thought that the existing arrangements of the establishment were exceedingly good, that the clergy of the Church of England were doing admirable work, and that if changes were made they ought to be small. They wished to amend, not to upheave. Something about Howley and Vernon Harcourt of York and Monk of Gloucester, something occasional about Kaye of Lincoln, gives the air of reforming because they must

---

[1] *Second letter to Archdeacon Singleton*, in *Works*, 625 (1850 ed.).
[2] Whately to Hawkins, 14 November 1853: Oriel Coll.

and not because they want. Out of their mitred carriage door they rolled the carcasses of canons to the wolves with melancholy push, thus saving the remainder of their crew. They believed in cathedrals and stalls and prebends.

They must increase the number of canons at St. Paul's cathedral from three to four. St. Paul's cathedral needed no fourth canon, had managed excellent well with three. But four it must have, lest hungry prowlers prove by this example that all canonries except three be abolished at every cathedral in England and Wales; for if St. Paul's were satisfied with three, why not all?[1]

Thus they were (in fact) tinkering to defend. And another motive, apart from the interest and principle of the established church, distorted their deliberations. They wanted money from the government and rearranged church money as a first step. Government would hardly give the gold of taxpayers to the church unless it knew that the church's silver was deployed at best utility. The new English cities needed new churches and schools. Educated Englishmen saw that machine and birth-rate and survival-rate and Irish immigration were manufacturing a proletariat which needed health, police, education, morality and religion. They dimly perceived an underworld of cellars and caves and alleys beyond the reach of squires or parsons or magistrates. The state must help, the state's money must provide; but it was wan hope that a Whig state would provide while the treasure-chests of English cathedrals littered the countryside, but not the cities, with decorous and well-paid clergymen. The cathedral of Barchester supported Canon Stanhope in leisured style and thereby propagated the social influence of the Church of England among the higher classes. The need of the Church of England seemed rather to be social influence among the lower classes whom Canon Stanhope never met. The case for switching endowments was unanswerable.

The second report of the Ecclesiastical Commission (4 March 1836) justified the proposal to take cathedral money. It cited four parishes on the banks of the Thames with enough room in the churches for 8,200 people and a population of 166,000. It might have quoted Birmingham with room in the churches for 24,000 and a population of 143,000, or Manchester and Salford with room for under 24,000 and a population of 182,000.

Under this stimulus everyone who cared for working people

[1] J. Kaye, *Letter to the Archbishop of Canterbury*, 1838; *Works*, vii, 208.

wanted new churches, new chapels, new parishes, better-paid ministers, more ministers. Churchmen in England and Scotland demanded that the nation pay. A church which received a million and a half sterling from the taxpayer only eleven years before was inclined to accept the old axiom that the nation ought to supply the physical supports of morality and religion. They regarded it not so much as a need of the church as a need of the nation and thought that the nation should settle the bill. In 1835 the leaders of the Church of Scotland, less familiar than Archbishop Howley with the hazards of Westminster, asked Lord Melbourne to provide small stipends for new churches built by subscription in the Glasgow slums. 'Gentlemen,' the Duke of Wellington told the deputation in his crisp staccato, 'you will get nothing. That is my opinion. I am sorry for it; but so you will find it.'[1] The English bishops made no formal request. But it was never far from their minds. Peel hinted at it in the king's speech of 1835. Clergymen attacking the Ecclesiastical Commissioners asked why the cathedrals should shoulder the nation's burden. Bishop Blomfield suggested in 1836 that a tax of 2d. a ton be placed on coal, the proceeds to build new churches in London. Archbishop Howley was confident to a meeting of the new Additional Curates Society that the state would soon acknowledge its duty to pay curates.[2] In 1839 Oxford university petitioned Parliament and did not doubt (they said) that the people at large would rejoice to see a portion of the national wealth devoted to the honour of him who gave it.[3]

The people at large did not rejoice. No plan could bring religion to town labourers without strengthening the established church. To strengthen the established church banged dissent and bolstered the Tory party. The numbers of people and of church sittings, used to prove the problem insoluble without state intervention, often made the mistake of representing the parish churches as the only churches where people could worship. In many towns the dissenters claimed to be offering more opportunity for worship than the churches of the establishment. But no one was foolish enough to believe that the problem could be solved by the united, or rather the disunited, forces of church and dissent.

No money ever came from the state. But Archbishop Howley

---

[1] Buchanan, Ten Years Conflict, i, 366–7.
[2] Report of the Society, 1838, in Webster, Joshua Watson, 74.
[3] Petition in Br. Mag., 15, 1839, 465.

sometimes felt sanguine that it might. And therefore he must deploy the resources of the Church of England in an order which a Whig cabinet would see as useful. Government must confess the church to do its utmost for the slum, and then might add its inexhaustible bounty.

Stop radicals from thinking that you can run a cathedral with fewer than four canons—and therefore add a canon to St. Paul's. Prove to government that you do everything for the slum—and therefore subtract a canon from Canterbury cathedral. Five bishops teetered to and fro along a footpath of which one end was a rickety Anglican structure and the other end a phantom-bank of national gold.

The commissioners were unpopular. They were unpopular because their task was giving the money of ancient trusts to other purposes; and the wisest of heads would have excited anger. Almost their only resource was the rich endowment of English cathedrals. Cathedral closes harboured the most educated and influential clergymen of their day; far more powerful in their connexions, and eloquent in their resistance, than abbots of English monasteries under Henry VIII. Archbishop Howley could not hang the Dean of Norwich on Mousehold Heath as Henry VIII hanged the Abbot of Glastonbury high on the Tor; and to do Howley justice, he would have offered to hang there instead. Gently and meekly they tampered with entrenched corporations; and such is human nature that they would have been hardly more unpopular if they had acted less gently.

When it is said that they were unpopular, they were unpopular with the clergymen who dominated the Church of England; canons, archdeacons, deans, bishops, Oxford dons. A future archdeacon (Manning of Chichester); a professor (Pusey of Oxford); a canon (Sydney Smith of St. Paul's)—these were the damaging assailants of the commission. Evidence was adduced to show that poor parsons and curates were not hostile. They, it was said, would profit by the money taken from canonries. Mr. Quiverful, who had no chance whatever of a canonry, was alleged not to mind the downfall of Canon Stanhope. But poor curates were seldom articulate in rejoicing. It was pointed out that if all the corporate estates of cathedral chapters were distributed among the benefices, everyone's stipend would rise by £5 12s. 6½d, which (said Sydney Smith) would not stop a hiatus in a cassock.[1] Even Mr. Quiverful might prefer the chance of a canonry to raising his pitiful stipend from £100 to £105. The evidence that poor

[1] *Third Letter to Archdeacon Singleton, Works*, 639–41; cf. 605–7, 624.

parsons liked the commission was neither plentiful to produce nor simple to value.

Everyone liked Archbishop Howley. Everyone bestowed upon him the highest respect; at once the revering faculty for his strength and the protective instinct for his weakness. He acted so firmly that they almost felt him to be a leader and looked so feeble that they wanted to rally and surround him with their shields. It was impossible for Howley to be unpopular. And since the commission was unpopular, cathedral intelligence quickly inferred that the whole affair could be blamed upon Bishop Blomfield of London. Even an episcopal commissioner was willing to shift odium to those capacious shoulders. 'Till Blomfield comes', the Archbishop of York described the business of the commission, 'we all sit and mend our pens, and talk about the weather.'

From childhood Blomfield wanted to be a bishop. He began as scholar-recluse, never missed morning chapel as an undergraduate, and read for twelve hours or more every day. Endowed with high practical talents he was all his life remote from practical men, never invited familiarity or possessed the common touch. Something of the eighteenth century hung about him. He made his name as Fellow of Trinity College for his editing of classical texts, had been a non-resident incumbent, tutored sons of aristocrats at high fees. Though Phillpotts of Exeter was more disliked among Whigs and Maltby of Chichester more disliked among Tories, and though none could rival the odium of Dr. Whately among Irish Protestants, no English bishop of 1835 could claim to be so generally unpopular as Blomfield. They said that he was high-handed, sarcastic, meddlesome, hasty, overbearing, that even when he smiled he smiled episcopally, that he was always conscious of dignity. It is not easy to distinguish criticism from abuse of a trimmer. His conduct on the reform bill was not forgiven by Tories or Whigs. In an age of partisans neither side could count on his support. A strong Sabbatarian who led the movement to legislate for Sunday observance, he became a target for every Sunday newspaper. An austere bishop who hated fox-hunting parsons, insisted on clerical dress and was strenuous against clergy in secular work, might well have been suspect even if he were not guilty of milk-and-water Whiggery. Under these handicaps any bishop might have been pilloried, and Blomfield commanded neither the art of charm nor the virtue of tact.

Though he came out of an older world, he was no rigid conservative. He was the first bishop not to wear a wig. He told King William
IV, one hot summer's day at Brighton, that 'at this tropical season I
find my episcopal wig a serious encumbrance'. The king sent a message, 'Tell the bishop that he is not to wear a wig on my account; I
dislike it as much as he does, and shall be glad to see the whole bench
wear their own hair.'[1]

In company Blomfield possessed an agreeable streak of caustic
humour and anecdote. At desk he was plain and sober, wanted the
church to be pastorally efficient, worked many hours a day, could
note the answers to thirty letters while travelling across London in a
carriage, talked about the church and the beauty of her holy usefulness. One enemy called him a Right Reverend utilitarian, another
called him an ecclesiastical Peel;[2] and though Peel was more capable
and less amusing they resembled each other in practical energy, and
remoteness from the common man. If the subject of a sermon or a
speech were not theoretical, Blomfield could achieve heights of oratory. Copleston of Llandaff, not likely to be a friendly critic, declared
Blomfield to be the best public speaker whom he had ever heard. He
mastered detail and liked quick decisions. In short, he bustled. 'The lay
commissioners who are members of the government', jested the unfriendly Sydney Smith, 'cannot and will not attend—the Archbishops
of York and Canterbury are quiet and amiable men, going fast down
in the vale of life—some of the members of the commission are exple-
tives—some must be absent in their dioceses—the Bishop of London
is passionately fond of labour, has certainly no aversion to power, is
of quick temper, great ability, thoroughly versant in ecclesiastical law,
and always in London. He will become the commission. . . .'[3]

Blomfield should not be judged by the sardonic mockery of a
partisan. His subsequent career proved him to possess more qualities

---

[1] Shute Barrington has a claim to be the first bishop to discard the wig, G, 67, 1176.
But when Blomfield persuaded Carr of Chichester to make the same request of George
IV in 1824, George IV refused to dispense with wigs, *Memoir of Blomfield*, 72–73.
Within the next few years most of the bishops copied Blomfield's humane venture.
Copleston of Llandaff, who abandoned his wig on 22 February 1832 (*Memoir of Copleston*,
151), noted that he was one of the last. Archbishop Howley wore his till death. The
last bishop to wear an episcopal wig outside church was George Murray of Rochester,
who died in 1860. In church Archbishop Sumner continued till his death in 1862.

[2] Churton, *Joshua Watson* 316; JB, 34, 301; *Memoir of Blomfield*, 90, 219. There is a
good and sympathetic study of Blomfield's activity in Olive Brose, *Church and Parliament*, 1959.

[3] *Works*, 617.

than his clergy supposed in the year 1836. But the proceedings of the commission exuded a restless air of haste. Perhaps Whig reform stirred expedition into scurry. Since no one could imagine Archbishop Howley running, the speed of decision was attributed to Blomfield. And very impulsive the clergy thought it. Important schemes were proposed and never executed. The see of Sodor and Man was to be united with the see of Carlisle. The idea was thrown out in a London board-room without consulting the parties interested. The clergy of Man, who stood to profit by an almost visible increase of stipend if their bishop were replaced by an archdeacon, preferred to keep a bishop; and after argument ranged over storms in the Irish sea, the history of the island, the absence of profane swearing among its inhabitants, the advanced age of the Bishop of Carlisle and his numerous progeny, the proposal was repealed.[1] The see of Bristol passed through the plan of being united with Llandaff, then with Bath and Wells, finally with Gloucester.

The union was not proposed on pastoral motives. New sees were needed in northern industry at Manchester and Ripon. Yet the number of bishops in the House of Lords could not be increased. Since they objected to a bishop not in the House of Lords (lest radicals be encouraged to demand the exclusion of all bishops from that House) two sees must be suppressed to keep the same number. Bristol was safely united with Gloucester and a see of Ripon safely carved from the archdiocese of York. But the plan to unite St. Asaph with Bangor met far more opposition than the destruction of Sodor and Man; and for years the union hung fire while Welshmen demanded their old bishop and Manchester dissenters declared a new bishop useless. A pluralities bill contained several vexatious clauses which shocked the clergy and were hastily abandoned. Many of the schemes were sensible and useful. The dioceses needed rearranging. But some of the changes were published too quickly, without enough consultation. The clergy of England, transported without their leave from diocese to diocese as boundaries were rationalised, experienced a mood of restlessness, not knowing what to expect. Their unsettlement of mind contributed to their dislike of the commission. They feared what was coming.

The commissioners knew that they were rearranging an ancient and complex institution and wanted chance to recant. They therefore

[1] Sanctioned in the established church act, 1836: repealed in 1838.

designed a novelty in the British constitution. They did not make these changes by defining the details in acts of Parliament. The established church act of 1836 cited the third report of the commissioners; and in constituting them a permanent corporation, gave them power to effect their schemes by presenting them to the king in council; and if approved they should have the force of law. By this means they were able to change their minds upon consideration. By the same means they aimed to prevent caustic radicals in the House of Commons from discussing clerical duties and stipends. This last plan failed. Caustic radicals had discussed clerical duties and stipends for six years and no commission was going to stop them amusing themselves and their constituents by baiting parsons.

The recommendations of the commissioners became law by three main acts of Parliament: established church act of 1836, pluralities act of 1838, dean and chapter act of 1840.

The established church act of 1836 abolished livings held *in commendam* with sees; equalised the stipends of bishops by raising the lowest and reducing the highest while leaving senior sees with substantial advantage;[1] authorised two new sees at Ripon and Manchester and the corresponding suppression of two sees by a union of Bristol to Gloucester and St. Asaph to Bangor; incorporated the Ecclesiastical Commissioners as a permanent body and compelled them to subscribe a declaration that they were members of the Church of England and Ireland. Subsidiary acts suspended appointments until the recommendations were in force, and separated the old secular jurisdictions from the sees of York, Durham and Ely, pompous and expensive ruins of medieval prince-bishoprics.

The pluralities act of 1838 limited the number of benefices held by one person to two, which must be within ten statute miles; neither of them to have a population of more than 3,000, the joint value not to be over £1,000 and the two held under a dispensation from the Archbishop of Canterbury. A clause forbade a clergyman to carry on trade or deal in goods or merchandise; replacing a stricter clause inherited from canon law, under which the courts had lately disallowed the

---

[1] Canterbury £15,000; York and London £10,000; Durham £8,000, etc., down to a minimum of £4,000. The mode of payment was the worst that could have been designed. (It was designed by Lord Harrowby). The commissioners were to fix an annual sum of money which the bishop must hand over. Episcopal incomes depended on rents and leases and varied from year to year. Hence many a trial to both sides. This system was reformed from 1848 onwards.

claim of a company to recover debts because two clergymen were shareholders.[1] Another clause gave a bishop authority to require two full services each Sunday, both services to include a sermon or lecture. The power of the bishop to enforce residence in the parish was strengthened.

The 1840 act suppressed all non-resident prebends (about 360), all sinecure rectories (68), and resident canonries above the number of four to each cathedral—with exceptions, Westminster abbey, Christ Church at Oxford, Durham, Ely, Canterbury (six each), Winchester, Exeter (five each)—and vested the money in the Ecclesiastical Commissioners. The separate estates of deans and canons (as opposed to the corporate estates of the dean and chapter) were vested in the commissioners on the expiry of the life-interest. The patronage of the dean and chapter as a corporate body was left, but the patronage attached to its separate members was transferred to the bishop. Deans should henceforth be appointed by the crown, canons in cathedrals of old foundation (except St. Paul's) by the bishop. Twenty-four non-stipendiary canons were to have stalls in each cathedral which did not already possess such prebends, so that the bishop might confer distinctions of honour upon deserving clergymen. Two canonries at Oxford were annexed to new professorships and two canonries at Ely attached to the Cambridge professorships of Hebrew and Greek. The saved money was to create a new canonry at St. Paul's and at Lincoln to bring the number from three to four. A clause permitted the number to rise from four to five if the commissioners wished to endow an archdeacon.

Five years of hard work in Parliament and in the commission, produced as cash result a future sum of perhaps £360,000 a year with which commissioners might supplement poor livings and assist new parishes in the great cities.[2] The Whig reform of the Church of England was not a revolution.

Besides the provision of money, the act enabled the bishop to be more of a bishop. He had received the patronage of a number of benefices, and most bishops would henceforth appoint all their canons.

[1] *Law Journal Reports*, 1838, xvi, 110. By clause 28 clergymen were permitted to farm up to 80 acres. In 1850 an act limited pluralities further; the livings must be within three miles and the annual value of one must not exceed £100. A pluralities measure of 1885 raised the distance to four miles and the annual value of one to £200; raised to £400 in 1930.

[2] During the sixties the net disposable surplus averaged in fact rather over half a million; cf. Best, *Temporal Pillars*, 553.

(When the act's effects were complete, the bishops chose 90 canons, the crown 27, the lord chancellor 12, and the universities or colleges 5). This increase of authority was unwelcome to some chapters, but was necessary to that Victorian development of diocesan life which was to be as marked as the development of parish life.

The original propounders of the Ecclesiastical Commission intended a temporary institution to meet a crisis. Adjust diocesan boundaries, equalise bishops, receive stipends of suppressed canonries, use existing institutions to spend the money on new parishes or poor livings, and vanish. But they quickly saw that an institution of but a few years would not do. For they agreed to respect existing interests. No stipend was reduced nor canonry suppressed until the death or departure of the occupant. Instead of pouring into their coffers in a stream, the money came in spurts. The commissioners were an impoverished body for twenty years after Parliament made them permanent. The work assigned to them was work for half a century. They slowed the process themselves by tenderness towards cathedrals or their defenders. The cathedrals must be curtailed softly and slowly, here a little and there a little. The act of 1840 provided a laborious mode of suppressing canonries. If two canonries in succession were suppressed, the next vacancy was filled though still above the ration of four canons. At Winchester cathedral, where seven canonries were to be suppressed, it took eleven successive vacancies to reach the number five.[1]

The commissioners soon saw that they must be permanent. And permanence had the merit that thus they could administer efficiently more and more of the property of the church. Without saying so openly, administrators were attracted to centralise; and heeded not the canon who said, 'This property was not given to the Church of England but to the church of Ely.'[2]

Critics protested that it was political danger, and unjust to local interests, to run the church by government commission. Nothing looked more erastian. It was argued that the Whig government of 1836 chose thirteen persons to run the property of the Church of England, which was to run the Church of England; of these thirteen only five were ecclesiastics, who could be outvoted by laymen appointed by the crown. Even if all thirteen had been ecclesiastics, the objection remained. Sticklers found it irrelevant that two archbishops and three bishops served. What mattered was their choice by govern-

[1] Best, *Temporal Pillars*, 351, n.5.   [2] W. Selwyn, in PP, 1863, vi, 155

ment. It was further grumbled that the two junior of these bishops could be removed at pleasure of the crown. Why should bishoprics and canonries be tumbled about, neither by the Convocations which were not allowed to meet, nor by all the bishops meeting together, but by five bishops selected by an act of Parliament or by the minister of the day and controlled at need by a majority of laymen? A young clergyman heard Blomfield speak on the dean and chapter bill and told his father that the Bishop of London was striding towards the popedom of England. 'A most magnificent speech it was for *power and resolution* . . . but parading more monstrous principles of church tyranny—I mean tyranny over the church—than I could have conceived.'[1]

The dean and chapter act of 1840 met these qualms and reproaches by changing the membership of the commission. It added all the bishops of England and Wales, the lord chief justice and five other judges, the deans of Canterbury, St. Paul's and Westminster, and six lay persons of whom the crown appointed four and the archbishop two. Henceforth the commission was open neither to the charge that its members could be removed at the pleasure of the minister of the day, nor to the question why these few bishops were selected from the whole number. The complaints against the constitution faded and were replaced by equally legitimate complaints that this vast body was too clumsy to direct property.[2] In 1850 they needed to add three Church Estates Commissioners (one unpaid) to administer the property. The Archbishop of Canterbury (Sumner) disliked the change of 1850 because it would again remove the real control from the bishops.[3] But since the institution existed, the bishops could not control it, and the change was inevitable and sensible.

Stalwart Tories like Sir Robert Inglis defended the sacred right of

---

[1] Charles Merivale to his father, 7 August 1840: *Autobiography and Letters of Dean Merivale*, 198.

[2] The nefarious activities of the first secretary, C. K. Murray, have been delightfully described in Best, *Temporal Pillars*, 382 ff.

[3] Sumner to Lord John Russell, May 1849, PRO 30/22/7F. The act provided that the estates be administered by the three estates commissioners plus two members (one a layman) appointed by the Ecclesiastical Commission. A quorum of three could act provided that two of the three were estates commissioners. The act gave the estates committee absolute control over the management of the property, and enabled the Ecclesiastical Commission to delegate any other of its powers to the estates committee. The Ecclesiastical Commission could henceforth do no business unless two members of the estates committee were present. Best, 396. Two of the estates commissioners were appointed by the crown, one by the Archbishop of Canterbury.

property so warmly that no money from Durham should be allocated to Merthyr Tydfil; for the donors and testators gave it to help Durham. The doctrine would have stopped all reform. The commissioners met these objections by allowing the demands of local interests. But underlying this ultra opinion was an argument of more weight. The aim of the commission, in essence, was to adjust ancient trusts so that money could be taken from cathedrals and given to parishes. Was it certain, was it unquestionable, that the church would gain by the transfer?

Nearly all the Protestant countries dismantled their cathedrals during the Reformation, turned them into parish churches and used the endowment elsewhere. Cromwell had done the same in England, to the temporary benefit of parish ministers. But the conservatism of the English Reformation preserved cathedrals and most of their funds. Howley and Blomfield were making a half-turn towards the place which Swiss and Dutch and Scots reached two and a half centuries before.

No one knew what cathedrals were for. By the beauty of their music and singing they set forth the glory of God; and yet it was confessed that if the choirs of Durham and Canterbury were models of decorum and of art, the choirs of some cathedrals, including St. Paul's and Westminster abbey, were renowned for slipshod irreverence. The evangelical *Christian Observer* and Dr. Pusey suggested that they should be schools of theological study. Pusey said that the theological equipment of the English clergyman was pitiful, that the great divines of English history were cathedral dignitaries, that the ancient church surrounded the bishop with his ordinands. This doctrine was widely accepted, and created two small seminaries in cathedral closes, Wells (1840) and Chichester (1839).[1]

These were arguments of the circumference. Cathedral endowments were means of higher pay to certain clergymen. They enabled Copleston, who was dean of St. Paul's, or Bagot, who was dean of Canterbury, to be Bishops of Llandaff and Oxford though the endowment of the bishoprics was inadequate. They rewarded aristo-

---

[1] To be followed later in the century by others; Lichfield 1857, Salisbury 1861, Exeter 1861, Gloucester 1868, Lincoln 1874, Ely 1876: in part Cuddesdon 1854. The plea by Pusey evoked a famous and much misunderstood retort by Lord Melbourne in the debate of 1840: 'The study of theology might be a very good thing but he did not think it was a thing which they wanted.' The context shows that he was using *want* to mean *lack*, not *wish*. Hansard lv, 987.

cratic blood, pastoral merit, political service, private influence and a certain quantity of learning. Their defenders contended that the church ought not to consist of two ranks, parsons in equalised livings and bishops; and that so far as the rewards of cathedral prebends were confined to learning and pastoral merit, they rendered an irreplaceable service to the church. What needed reform was not the cathedral but the exercise of patronage. To this defence a certain number of pluralities were necessary.

It will be observed that both the main positions abandoned the functions of cathedrals. Blomfield looked at the slums round St. Paul's crying for ministers and saw the splendid endowments of the cathedral wasted in pastoral idleness. The defence agreed that cathedral duties were light and inferred that the prebend was a sensible mode of rewarding clergymen by supplementary payment. No one supposed that cathedrals could absorb all the time of all canons. Even the commissioners recognised this truth when they attached professorships to canonries or recommended that a stall in each cathedral be reserved for the archdeacon.

The argument for rewards was difficult to put without seeming, as Sydney Smith said, mammonish. You want clergy who shall be educated and who shall hold their own with all classes of the people. Divide the money of the church into equal shares and no one will have enough. We shall have no clergymen, said Smith, but ignoramuses and fanatics. No one wishes great wealth for the clergy, but there must be sufficient to enable them to equal the professions. On the view which is taken of this debate posterity will judge what was done. The commissioners were devoted to raising small stipends and new stipends. The money available was not sufficient to lift poor clergymen or new clergymen out of comparative poverty. One side argued that the true way to minister to urban England was not to spread butter thinly but to concentrate. To help the church in poor parishes the commission lowered the social status of the clergy; and it was a question whether at the long view a lower status would help the church in poor parishes. The other side knew that the sacraments of poor curates were better than no sacraments. One of the first five bishop-commissioners, Kaye of Lincoln, looked upon heathen streets and said, 'When I saw so many sheep without a shepherd, I could not refuse my consent.'[1]

1 PP, 1863, vi, 152.

5. TITHE

A necessary act of 1836 commuted tithe. Peel proposed, Melbourne executed, most of the clergy approved or were reconciled.[1] Placards of reform beat the church with tithe. If all tithe went to ecclesiastical rectors of parishes, payment of tithe might have been insecure. But the tithe of many monastic houses passed to laymen, impropriators. To abolish tithe meant compensating lay landowners. The clergy found tithe a hazardous means of support. They were rarely able to collect all, were usually content with a fraction, must be generous in bad times, and imperilled their friendship with truculent farmers. A fixed money payment was more convenient and might be less vexatious. Gloomy realists believed that the clergy often received only half their due, and therefore that a legal commutation for two-thirds would increase real income. A few high churchmen denounced the measure as converting a demand which reposed upon the law of God into a demand which reposed only upon the law of Parliament. They deplored that the clergyman's income lost its sacred obligation.[2] Parishioners ought to satisfy not only a legal demand but divine command. But few clergy met to protest or petition. A tithe commutation act became law amid goodwill. The act arranged a money payment fixed on the average price over seven years of wheat, barley and oats; not more than 75 per cent nor less than 60 per cent of gross value of tithe. All subsequent improvements of the land were exempted from tithe. Three tithe commissioners were appointed to arrange commutations, a process which proceeded with reasonable tranquillity over sixteen years. So old tithe-barns collapsed in ruin or were sold to farmers. Curious little tithes in kind remained for many years. The last remaining tithe in kind—the right of the vicar of Cockerham to fish caught at certain tides in a trap at the mouth of the River Lune—was commuted in 1961.

6. DISABILITIES OF DISSENTERS

While the commission pursued the internal reform of the Church of England, the government proceeded with those reliefs of dissenting grievances to which Peel had promised Tory support. Peel had not committed the opposition to opening the universities, and further

---

[1] Views of most clergy stated in *Br. Mag.*, 9, 1836, 444.
[2] *Br. Mag.*, 9, 1836, 413.

attempts by private members failed. But at least he promised relief of the marriage disability. For many clergymen were as sore at being compelled to marry Unitarians with Trinitarian formulas as Unitarians were sore at being so married.

They found it not easy to discover a measure which would satisfy both lawyers and dissenters. The dissenters wanted to be free to marry in their chapels. But their ministers were of insecure tenure, their chapels impermanent, their registers chaotic. The lawyers demanded legal safeguards for the correct registration of marriage and provision against clandestine marriage. The parish register reposed in the parish church and under the care of the parson. The rector or vicar was the nearest official to a modern registrar. The evidence of his baptismal register was legal evidence of birth, of his marriage register legal evidence of marriage, of his burial register legal evidence of death. Earlier plans for dissenters' marriage insisted that the marriage be registered with the parson. Lord John Russell's abortive bill of 1834 proposed a marriage in chapel after banns in church, and this inequality caused the dissenting deputies to repudiate the bill. Peel's abortive bill of 1835 proposed marriage as a civil contract but registered with the clergyman.

Quakers and Jews had secured special acts of Parliament legalising their forms of marriage. No other marriage was legal except marriage in a parish church, in no other marriage was wife protected against misconduct of husband. The worst sufferers were Roman Catholics. In Liverpool there were 60,000 Irish Catholics, in Manchester 40,000. After they were married by an Irish priest, they nearly all refused to go to the parish church to be legally married. Apart from religious scruple, there were fees to pay. In London some Irish Catholics were married in the parish churches; and if the priest at Moorfields chapel married two of his flock, he always recommended them to have the marriage legalised at the parish church afterwards, and declared gloomily that almost every day the wife of an Irish labourer was deserted by her husband and could get no redress.[1]

---

[1] PP, 1833, xiv, 574; cf. Hansard, xxii, 6. The Irish nevertheless discovered advantage in the law. Under the old system of poor relief they could not receive settlement for their children except in the parish where the father received settlement; and Irish labourers soon found it useful to prove their marriage invalid and the child illegitimate in order that the child might be a charge upon the parish where he was born. By this use of the marriage law an Irishman named Brennan achieved the notoriety of drawing children's relief from four different parishes, St. Martin-in-the-Fields, Marylebone, St. Paul's, Covent Garden, and Lewisham, PP, 1834, xxvii, 99; xxviii, 107. The usual

Apart from Unitarians and Roman Catholics, not many dissenters objected on grounds of conscience to being married in the parish church. Most Methodists were perfectly accustomed to attending the parish church and almost always brought their children there to be baptised. Some Congregationalists and Baptists were more scrupulous. But the system was bad on grounds other than those of conscience.

Clergymen were not always efficient registrars. Under an act of 1812 they were compelled to keep the register in an iron chest at parish expense and the churchwardens were ordered to send copies each year to the registrar of their diocese. In 1833 a quarter of the parishes in England and Wales made no return, the returns were not indexed, the post office resented the provision that returns might be sent post free and refused to deliver them if they were improperly addressed. In 1831 the London post office burnt a large number of registers as not deliverable. Legal attempts to prove death were hampered. They proved the death of Mr. Robert Gibbons at Ninfield in Sussex by searching the graveyard for his tombstone. In 1831 they proved a marriage of fifty-eight years before by taking an affidavit from one of the bridesmaids. At a parish in Northamptonshire the daughter of the parish clerk was found to have used the old registers as lace-parchments.[1] These irregularities were rarer since the act of 1812. They were still common enough to argue that civil registration should be separated from parish churches.

In August 1836 twin acts of marriage and registration received the royal assent. The poor law of 1834 created a suitable officer in each district and the registration act extended his functions. It was provided that from 1 March 1837 any proprietor or trustee of a dissenting chapel might apply to the registrar to register his chapel as a place for marriages. He must produce a certificate from twenty householders that the building had been regularly used in religious worship for one year. Marriages might be celebrated in the presence of the registrar, either in these licensed buildings or in the registry office. The parson continued to act as registrar for marriages in the parish church, but the

mode was marriage in the parish church first and then marriage in the Catholic chapel. The Catholic authorities preferred the inverse order, but it made the officiating priest liable to penalty. There were still a few Catholics who followed the opinion that as the parties were validly married in the Protestant church, the Catholic ceremony ought to be dropped, but nearly all Catholics insisted on the need for a Catholic marriage. Cf. Ward, *Sequel*, i, 193 note.

[1] PP, 1833, xiv, 513, 528–9, 560–2.

sending of copies of the registers was rendered effective under penalty. Opposition to the act was slender. In the Commons Peel and Gladstone, wishing to discourage civil marriages, voted for an unsuccessful amendment that persons who marry in registry offices or in dissenting chapels should solemnly declare themselves to have conscientious scruples against marriage according to the rites of the Church of England. The House of Lords gallantly struck out a clause which required a lady to state her age.[1]

The government was right to pooh-pooh the amendment in the Commons, right to prophesy that 99 out of every 100 marriages would continue to be religious ceremonies. The habits of the English people were slow to change. In 1838 there were 5,654 marriages in Roman Catholic or Protestant chapels—1,629 in Roman Catholic, 1,360 in Independent, 728 in Baptist and 175 in Methodist chapels. By 1842 marriages outside the parish church rose to 8,034. Some Protestant dissenters, and most Methodists, continued to be married in the parish church.[2] Anglican marriages continued to rise steadily in number after 1836. Between 1838 and 1845 the increase of such marriages was much more numerous than the total number of marriages outside the establishment. But marriages outside the establishment increased rapidly. Year ending 30 June 1839, 6,451; year ending 31 December 1845, 14,228. In 1845 Anglican marriages were 129,515.[3]

The registration act appeared to the clergy more vexatious than the marriage act. Though they might regret the institution of civil marriage in a registry office, few of them regretted the new freedom not to marry persons who objected to their ministrations. They were more concerned over divorce between civil registration and baptism. Some clergymen put placards in their parishes that baptism was a sufficient registration for members of the established church; and a stonemason at Turvey in Bedfordshire was summoned and a Norwich housewife given four days' imprisonment because they obeyed their parsons and refused to give the registrar information.[4] The clergy were irritated that they must pay a £10 penalty if they buried a corpse without a registrar's certificate;[5] and a few early officers of the

---

[1] Hansard, xxxiv, 1021; xxxv, 692.   [2] PP, 1839, xli, 369.
[3] PP, 1847–8, xxv, 28.   [4] Br. Mag., 14, 1838, 326, 362.
[5] Against this claim as printed in the documents of the British Magazine in the copy of the Cambridge University Library a contemporary has written Stuff. Howley protested against it to Melbourne.

registrar were foolish enough, in search of information about new babies, to enter labourers' cottages or pester nursemaids with perambulators. The people, not understanding the act, hastened to be married or to christen their children under the old law. The collegiate church at Manchester, which was accustomed to baptise some sixty children a Sunday, baptised 360 children on the last Sunday before the act came into force.[1]

The head of all dissenting grievance was rate. It was impossible for a Whig government not to attempt the end of church rate. Melbourne exempted the rate from those bills which would be agreed with the bishops. A new bill to end the rate almost brought down the government and almost destroyed the Ecclesiastical Commission.

Archbishop Howley understood that the government intended to copy Lord Althorp in providing for church rate out of national taxes. When the agreement of May 1835 was reached, that was the intention of the government. A year later it was still the intention. But by summer 1836 the Whig leaders were no longer content with the old plan. Dissenters still clamoured their rejection of any bill to repair parish churches out of the taxpayers' pocket. The activities of the Ecclesiastical Commission invited suggestions that the resources of the church might be improved by better management and that the increased wealth be used to abolish church rate. Lord John Russell's answers to questions in the House of Commons showed the mind of the cabinet moving away from the old plan towards a plan certain to be disliked by bishops.

By the spring of 1837 a plan to use taxes was impossible. The Whigs, though just in power, were more dependent for their majority upon the support of radicals. They selected a more radical plan for dealing with church rate. Their whole procedure was penetrated with that carelessness typical in some moods of Lord Melbourne. They selected a plan which had no chance whatever of passing Parliament. They entrusted it to the minister who of all the cabinet was least likely to make the best of a bad case; Spring Rice, chancellor of the exchequer. He proposed (3 March 1837) that the government take over church leases, and from more efficient management create a surplus of £250,000 per annum to replace church rate. The proposal temporarily wrecked the Ecclesiastical Commission. For if the surplus

[1]Br. Mag., 11, 1837, 475, from *Manchester Courier:* cf. 10, 1836, 620.

money of the church was going to pay repairs of roofs, it would not go to pay poor curates or new parishes in slums. Howley and the four bishops promptly refused to continue the Ecclesiastical Commission and were violently attacked in the Commons as a vile cabal to upset the Whig ministry.[1] The motion passed the Commons by only twenty-three votes, in committee on 22–23 May a debate of two nights produced a majority of only five. The cabinet perforce abandoned the scheme. Church rate remained wherever it could still be enforced; abandoned in more and more of the cities, maintained without pain in squire-ruled country parishes, and destroying peace and charity in every town where the sides were almost equal in vestry votes.

Tory defenders of this mode of taxing the public were fond of saying how few were the parishes where the rate was resisted successfully. And it was true that tumults in the great cities, Birmingham, Manchester, Leeds, Sheffield, ensured limelight in the press and passion among the politicians which their number, reckoned as a fraction of the parishes in the country, did not warrant. A large number of parishes witnessed no strife because no rates were collected, either because they were otherwise provided by endowment, or because they were so richly sustained by pew rents that they needed no rates. In some other parishes, especially in London (for example in Whitechapel), resistance to the rate was more hazardous because of local acts of Parliament under which the rate was enforced by common law and therefore enforced more effectively than by the incompetent machinery of ecclesiastical courts. In many country parishes no resistance whatever was attempted to the system, which continued to work as smoothly as though it was nowhere challenged.

From this failure to abolish church rate parish life suffered more ill than it gained from all the reforms of the Whig government.

First, there were the men who refused to pay a legally valid church rate and suffered a penalty. Unlike the Quakers they saw no religious grounds against and much public advantage in favour of physical protest against distraint of goods. On 10 May 1838 the auctioneer at Truro tried to sell three japan waiters containing likenesses of John Wesley, linen drapery and other household furniture distrained for non-payment of the rate. A bugle summoned the inhabitants to procession, they hissed and hooted the auctioneer, smashed his shop window, broke his shelves and tore his coat. In the evening a brass

[1] Gisborne; Hansard, xxxvii, 1837, 469.

band paraded through the town and stones were thrown at the auctioneer's shop. Baron Gurney, himself a dissenter, imprisoned five rioting dissenters for a month; and on their release they were hailed by a triumphal march and a public banquet.[1]

Then there were men who wanted to be imprisoned for conscience.

In 1837 David Jones, a simple Unitarian weaver, was elected church-warden of the parish of Llanon in the county of Carmarthen. Under the toleration act of 1689 a dissenter (like peers, members of Parliament, barristers, non-commissioned officers in the army, customs officers and apothecaries while practising their profession) had the legal right to refuse the office of churchwarden. Jones consented and took the solemn oath to serve the church. He called a vestry to make a church rate. A handful of twenty-seven people attended the vestry and so carried the adjournment that no rate was passed. David Jones and one other voted for the rate.

The vicar of Llanon was the Reverend Ebenezer Morris, who was also the vicar of Llanelly, something of a pluralist in those parts, warm and strenuous worker for the Tory party, a preacher of such popularity that the gallery of Llanelly church is said to have cracked under the weight of his hearers. Morris sent David Jones a written notice requiring him to provide bread and wine for the sacrament. Jones replied that he had no funds and was himself too poor to pay for bread and wine. Morris provided the elements at his own expense and sent a letter to Jones asking that this might not recur. Jones took no notice. Evidence was given that he came on sacrament Sundays to a nearby alehouse and was heard using obscene and blasphemous language. The vicar cited him before the ecclesiastical court. Jones despised the law, was condemned for contumacy, lodged in Carmarthen gaol until released by a happy technicality, prosecuted a second time until he fled the police and died in flight. The vicar was left bearing the costs, and in appealing for funds declared that Jones died to all appearance under the most awful judgment of God. He then went bankrupt; perhaps, as posterity may think, a still more fitting judgment.[2]

[1] AR, 1839, Chron., 51–55.
[2] Ebenezer Morris contemporaneously secured the imprisonment of the church-warden at Llanelly for contempt of court in a suit against him for failing to discipline persons loitering in the churchyard during divine service and disturbing the congregation. He was in prison only a few days. For the two cases cf. NLW/SD/CCCM(G), 558; W. T. Morgan, 'Disciplinary cases against churchwardens in the consistory court of St. David's', JHSW X, no. 15, 17; Hansard, xlvii, 522ff. Morris won a libel action against the Welshman newspaper for impugning his motives.

The imprisonment of John Thorogood, though marked by less folly on the part of the prosecuting authority, gave bigger scandal. For they got John Thorogood into gaol and then found that no one could get him out again.

Thorogood was a Chelmsford cobbler who gained a reputation as heckler at vestry meetings. In September 1838 he was summoned before the magistrates to answer a charge of failing to pay church rate of 5s. 6d. Asked why he had not paid, he replied that he believed it inconsistent with his religious obligations to pay a compulsory rate for the support of religion—and, further, that he believed the rate to be improper because no sufficient estimates were laid before the meeting. This challenge to the validity of the rate removed from the magistrates all power of summary jurisdiction. In November 1838 Thorogood was cited to appear before the consistory court of the diocese of London. He failed to appear. The judge, Lushington, himself a keen opponent of church rate as a politician, was forced to commit Thorogood to prison for contempt of court. On 16 January 1839 he was seized by officers and lodged in Chelmsford gaol.

It required a special act of Parliament to get him out again.

A citizen, committed for contempt of court, could not be released without purging his contempt by submitting. A large number of citizens, friends or opponents, were ready and eager to pay the 5s. 6d. and subscribe to pay the mounting bill of costs—but the fullest payment could not purge Thorogood's contempt. Even if the prosecutors withdrew their prosecution (which many of the vestry were not inclined to do), Thorogood could not be released. Lushington would cheerfully have released him, but had no power unless Thorogood was willing to plead. When he had been in Chelmsford gaol for more than eighteen months and showed no signs whatever of coming out, the radical Duncombe produced an astonishing motion (24 July 1840) that the House of Commons should petition the crown to exercise its prerogative and release the prisoner, citing various Stuart precedents for such power in the crown. It required Lord John Russell and the attorney-general together to explain that this power was one of the claims of the crown which the revolution of 1688 fought to destroy.

Radical journals held Thorogood to be a martyr for conscience. Tory journals were cynical about the martyrdom. If Thorogood wished to make a conscientious protest, all that he needed to do was to appear before the judge, suffer condemnation, and allow his goods to be distrained like a Quaker. To effect a martyrdom he had no need to despise the legal system of the country. But the distinction was not clear to all the public, and certainly not clear to Thorogood.

He held court at Chelmsford gaol. He issued petition after petition for presentation to the House of Commons. Allowed a room near the road to see his wife on a Sunday, he went to the window, collected a crowd outside, and harangued them. He published a statement upon the severity with which he was treated, and forced a team of visiting magistrates to lay a refuting paper on the table of the House of Commons.[1] Advised by his friends to submit and come out, he replied, 'No power on earth shall cause me to yield to what I believe is not right.'

By July 1840 it was plain that Thorogood must be released and that only Parliament could procure his release. A special act allowed a judge to release a prisoner for contempt if he had been in prison for six months and if his debt and costs were paid by or for him.[2]

William Baines was a prosperous shopkeeper in the parish of St. Mark's, Leicester, the only parish in the town of Leicester where by the year 1838 the rate was still enforced. Like Thorogood, he challenged the validity of the rate before the magistrates, disregarded summons before the ecclesiastical court, and was held in contempt of court. He was arrested on 13 November 1840 and in gaol for more than seven months. Neither churchwardens nor vestry wanted to proceed against him. Leicester sympathised with Baines and not with the law. A society called the Leicester Voluntary Church society was formed to spread sympathy for Baines, and held a meeting at which there was voted into the chair no less a person than John Thorogood, recently released from Chelmsford gaol. His petitions were presented in the House of Commons, a petition signed by the mayor and most of the corporation, another petition signed by 7,000 females of Leicester. While incarcerated he was unanimously elected town councillor by one of the largest wards in the town. Vast numbers of people visited him in gaol. His lawyer attempted to persuade him to give way and come out for his family's sake. Baines refused, and the lawyer thought that his scruples of conscience were reinforced by the prosperity which martyrdom brought to his shop.[3] He was released under Thorogood's act at the latter end of June 1841.

---

[1] PP, 1839, xxxviii, 397.   [2] Hansard, xlvii, 685ff.; xlix, 1001ff.; lv, 939ff., 1161ff.
[3] Hansard, lvi, 257; lvii, 360ff.; PP, 1851, ix, 345.

The imprisonment of William Baines transformed one Congregationalist minister into a mortal enemy of the establishment. For six years Edward Miall ministered to the Bond Street chapel in Leicester where Baines was a member of the congregation. In November 1840 Miall took part in a meeting to express sympathy with Baines. He had long been a strong local fighter and journalist. He now resigned his charge and travelled England in search of capital to found a newspaper, *The Nonconformist*. The motto on the title page of each number was Burke's phrase 'the dissidence of dissent and the Protestantism of the Protestant religion'. The first number appeared on 14 April 1841. Many leading dissenters thought him and his party disreputable. But the circulation grew and he gradually acquired political influence. 'Depend upon it,' he wrote from Lancaster on 26 October 1840, 'I will ring a peal in the ears of drowsy dissenters, such as will startle the blood in their cheeks for very shame.'[1] He was determined to carry the war into the enemy's country, to organise dissent into a powerful body clamouring for disestablishment, to campaign for the total separation of church and state. He pounded away at every dissenter who was mealy-mouthed about fighting the state church. There was to be no more apology. Dissenters were no longer to be complacent in their parishes, seeking baptism or marriage or burial in their parish church. They were to be out-and-out fighters. Politically he was radical, advocating manhood suffrage, ballot, payment of M.P.s, annual parliaments, repeal of the corn laws, and a general destruction of the powers of church, squires, aristocracy. For those who read his leading articles or heard his oratory, it came as something of a shock to find that in private life he was quiet, meek and unassuming.

After herculean efforts against every kind of dissenting apathy, or contempt, he succeeded in organising a national conference to plan a campaign to separate church and state.

This conference met from 30 April till 2 May 1844, at the Crown and Anchor tavern in the Strand. It attracted some 700 delegates from dissenting bodies. Under Miall's inspiration, the meeting constituted a society to become celebrated in the English political history of the century. At first it was known as the British Anti-State-Church Association. In 1853 the name was changed to the Society for the Liberation of Religion from State Control, whence its short name 'the Liberation Society'. Miall immediately became one of the secretaries.

[1] *Life of Edward Miall*, 45.

He stood for Parliament, contested two constituencies unsuccessfully, and was elected for Rochdale in 1852. Since the revolution of 1688 the Church of England had not encountered so implacable a foe in public place.

These imprisonments, though not the only imprisonments, achieved national publicity. But they give little hint of the bitterness, scurrility, exasperation, entanglement of sacred things in hustings.

The parishes must live with the rate. Wherever there was a contest, the clergy and their supporters had only two courses. They could whip up support, turn the struggle into a triumph for the Tory party and the church, and face enmities in the town. They could refrain from laying a rate or, if they laid a rate, they could refrain from enforcing it. If they refrained from enforcing it, they had no idea how they could prevent the roof falling about their ears. They could try not to pollute the church, by avoiding riotous meetings in the nave; hissing, stamping, cat-calling, climbing on pulpit, sitting on communion table, wiping boots on pew-cushions, spitting on chancel carpet. Bills of 1838 and 1844 tried vainly to make it illegal to hold these public meetings in church. Even churchmen were not sure that they wanted such a rule. To discuss local business in the church kept the parish together, it was argued, and the meeting was not likely to be less tumultuous if held at a public house instead of in church.

Between 1833 and 1851 there were 632 contests: 484 successful in resistance, 148 unsuccessful.[1] Churchmen liked to point out the smallness of these numbers. The figures give no idea of the truth, that many others refused to levy a rate. The chief dissenter in South Hackney, the bookseller George Offor, after a battle with the much-respected vicar, Mr. Norris, offered a little treaty: 'Cannot we manage this thing pleasantly among ourselves? If you will promise me never to enforce the church rate, then you may make the church rate as you please?'[2] And so it was done. Miller, the new vicar of St. Martin's, Birmingham, refused to attempt a rate. Walter Hook soon reached the same decision in Leeds. At his first vestry meeting as vicar of Frome, in Somerset, W. J. E. Bennett advised the congregation to abolish the rate, and so pleased the dissenters that one of them sent him a cheque for £100 to restore the church.[3] The last Birmingham

---

[1] PP, 1851, ix, 465–6.
[2] PP, 1851, ix, 39–42.
[3] *The Story of W. J. E. Bennett*, 213; cf. W. J. E. Bennett, *Why Church Rates should be abolished*, 1861.

parish to abandon the rate was Edgbaston. The congregation could easily have continued to enforce it. They preferred the interests of the Christian religion to the interests of the treasury and Tory tea-cup politicians.

But others would not abandon the rate, for they saw their church falling into ruin. The churchwardens of populous Leeds or Birmingham might replace the rate with subscriptions. The churchwardens of little country towns could not see how the roof could be kept safe. When the rate was refused they were forced to stop the church clock because they could not pay the winder. They must dismiss bellringers and organists and sexton and pew-openers and singing men, must cut off the gas and cancel evening services. A clergyman complained in 1835 that it was no longer safe for churchwardens to incur the expense of transporting village children to towns for their confirmation; and that unless the bishops would begin to visit village churches the rite must be abandoned.[1] But the worst was roof, walls, churchyard. In 1844 the windows of St. Philip's at Birmingham were in fragments, rain fell through holes in the roof, the pavement was broken. In the same year a block of stone fell into the nave from the tower of St. Mary's at Nottingham and the church was shut for four years while the town fought over its repairs. Neither vicars nor churchwardens were accustomed to beg for money. And where they could have raised money without much difficulty, they felt it a sacrifice of principle to abandon the rate. At Boston in Lincolnshire and elsewhere the dissenters offered to pay voluntarily what they refused to pay under compulsion, but the churchwardens refused to concede the principle.[2]

[1] *Christian Remembrancer*, 17, 1835, 499.

[2] Cf. a conversation reported in *Nonconformist*, 1842, 634, between a visitor to Boston and a church cleaner:

'This splendid pile of building must cost a considerable sum in order to keep it clean and in good repair.'

'Yes, sir. But would you believe it, it is five years since there was any church rate!'

'Why, how is that?'

'Oh! the dissenters will not allow one.'

'Who, then, are these dissenters?'

'Methodists, Baptists, and Independents—but the Baptists are the worst.'

'Do you think they would not pay a voluntary subscription? They never, sure, would allow an ornament to the town like this to fall to ruin.'

'Aye—but don't you see, Sir, our folks won't let them pay it willingly!'

'Then you must be badly off between them?'

'Yes, bad enough. But our folks are the worst, for they will neither pay themselves, nor let anybody else! Would you believe, Sir, that I myself have to pay for the brushes and dusters!'

It was not certain whether the majority of the parishioners could legally refuse a rate. According to the law of England the parish was as responsible for the cost of keeping the nave and churchyard as for the cost of maintaining the highway or relieving the poor. But there seemed to be no penalty available. There was certainly a penalty in the court of queen's bench for refusal to pay a rate made by a majority of parishioners at a duly convoked vestry. But, so far as the lawyers could decide, though the refusal to repair the church was undoubtedly an offence, it was not an offence where the secular courts had standing.[1] The only remedy lay in the ecclesiastical court. What penalty could that court impose?

It could not excommunicate the churchwardens, for the churchwardens would with ease obtain a prohibition from the queen's bench, on ground of secular injustice, if it tried to do so. It could lay an interdict. No one was sanguine enough to suggest that laying an interdict upon the parish church would be effective. And that was all. In short there was no remedy. If the parishioners failed to repair the church, they were committing an undoubted offence against the law, but no one could penalise them for committing this offence.

Confronted by events at Sheffield or Leeds or Birmingham, the lawyers instinctively supposed that the proper solution was simple. Since resistance was 'illegal', it only needed proper penalty to be crushed. Since the ecclesiastical court could not penalise, Parliament must intervene to transfer the issue from the ecclesiastical court to the queen's bench. There was never any difficulty about compelling a parish to repair highway or pay poor rate, because they could be compelled to it by *mandamus* in the queen's bench. Make the church rate like the other rates, they supposed, and all would be well.[2]

In all those who later hankered after this remedy and nothing but this remedy, there was a failure in imagination, to which conservative

---

[1] In 1793 the churchwardens and parishioners of St. Peter's Church, Thetford, refused to repair their church. An application was made to the court of king's bench to compel the churchwardens by *mandamus*. The court declared that it could not interfere in such a case by *mandamus*, Campbell, *Letter*, etc., 5th ed., 1837, 11. From time to time the court of king's bench intervened by *mandamus* to compel parishioners to hold a vestry meeting, but they would not compel the vestry, when met, to make a rate. There was thus found to be an important distinction in law between the church rate and other rates. If a village failed to repair a highway, an indictment would lie against the inhabitants in the court of king's bench. If the village failed to repair a church, the king's bench was found to have no status.

[2] A commission of 1830–2 on church courts recommended this change in vain. PP, 1831–2, xxiv, 47–48.

lawyers are sometimes prone. They could not see the difference between attempting to enforce a poor rate which the parish refused to make and a church rate which the parish refused for different reasons. Nor could they see that successful resistance to the rate in Birmingham or Leeds made the proposed remedy into a torture sufficient to evoke riot and rebellion.

If it was the law that the parish must repair the church, perhaps the majority of the congregation could not refuse a rate? If the majority refused a rate perhaps it was void and the minority might proceed to levy a rate? Everyone agreed that if the parishioners failed to attend a duly convened vestry, the churchwardens alone might make a rate which would legally bind the parish. Was it possible that if the majority was recalcitrant their presence at the meeting should be treated as absence? Lawyers confessed the possibility, confessed that this had never been tested in court. Between 1833 and 1837 a few bold churchwardens at Wakefield or Portsea put on a brazen mask and declared a rate, though the parish refused it. They were not brazen nor instructed nor wealthy enough to prosecute defaulters.

In the spring of 1837 the advocates of doctors commons discovered a hitherto unknown precedent. The report of the case had never been printed. Even learned ecclesiastical lawyers had never heard of it.

The case of *Gauden v. Selby* (1799), thus discovered, supported the precise opinion of those who held that a minority could make a legal rate if the majority of parishioners refused.[1] Here was possibility for a bold litigant. If a churchwarden was willing to risk time and money in testing the law through the courts, it was just possible that all might yet be well. Such a churchwarden was found in Augustus Charles Veley, solicitor at Braintree in Essex. Not a man of imagination, but a quiet, sober, determined man, who disliked untidiness and was a fierce churchman, Veley was ready to spend time, energy and money in attempting to crash through the legal jungle in the interest of the Church of England.

The parish of Braintree was organised against the rate by a dissenter of rare distinction. Samuel Courtauld was engaged in building that

---

[1] The case had come before the court of the Peterborough diocese and thence on appeal to the court of arches. Not merely a minority, but one churchwarden alone, made a rate, though the parishioners dissented. Nor had the parishioners refused any rate, but offered a smaller rate than Selby the churchwarden deemed necessary. When Gauden refused to pay, Selby brought him before the two courts in succession. Sir William Wynne, the dean of arches, upheld the judgment of the consistory court that the rate was valid.

business which under his son and grandson became one of the leading industries of Britain. In the eighteen-forties he employed between 2,000 and 3,000 people in Braintree and the surrounding towns, the biggest employer of the district, an important manufacturer of silk and believed to be the largest manufacturer of crape in the country. Though he was a Unitarian, there was no Unitarian place of worship in Braintree, but strong chapels for Independents and Baptists, and an unusually numerous group of Quakers. Courtauld was not, like Thorogood, a refuser of legally made rates. All his life he paid church rate in the parish of Gosfield, because there he constructed a family vault and mausoleum and went to Gosfield church on the death of any member of the family. He once declared that he was moved, not by religious scruple, but by desire for civil justice.[1] From 1834 he campaigned against the rate in the three parishes where he exercised influence, Braintree, Bocking, and Halstead.

The dissenters of the three towns were not at first pleased with Courtauld's campaign. They were not used to taking hostile action against their parish church, and at first supported him with reluctance. But support him in the end they did; and so, unusually for country towns, the rate was refused simultaneously in Braintree, Bocking and Halstead. Since these were not populous half-slum parishes like Whitechapel or Hackney, but little towns (the largest, Halstead, had 6,987 people in 1851) division and bitterness were multiplied. Stiff churchmen changed their grocer or butcher if they found them joining Courtauld's campaign. It must be related in honour of Courtauld that he refused to carry the rate war into his social and business life. The manager of one of Courtauld's works at Bocking was an active propagandist for the rate and remained Courtauld's manager.

It appeared at first as though the campaign, thus successful in 1834, would be as permanently successful as in Birmingham or Sheffield. This view reckoned without the solicitor Veley. It must be related, to the honour of Veley, that he changed none of his tradesmen because they happened to be of Courtauld's party. The best butcher in the place is a dissenter, he once said, as though this were a sufficient explanation of just conduct.[2] At the Braintree vestry meeting of 2 June

---

[1] PP, 1851, ix, 71.

[2] PP, 1851, ix, 166. The incumbent of Braintree had been in office since 1796, and though he had begun with promise and enthusiasm he had gradually lost heart and energy, and in 1837 was already near to 70 years old. If the church was to be maintained in repair, it was plain that the laity of Braintree must organise it. In 1837 the

1837, Veley presented an estimate of repairs and incidental expenses of £532 10s. The repairs (£508 12s.) consisted mainly of the nave roof; the incidental expenses (£23 18s.) included clerk's salary, cost of cleaning the church, bread and wine, a new copy of the prayer book for the clerk, register book and copies, visitation fees, and 2s. worth of stationery. The motion for adjournment was carried by a large dissenting majority.

Veley was ready for this defeat. On 10 June 1837 the churchwardens declared a rate of 2s. in the £ upon their own authority. Professing himself anxious only to discover the state of the law, Veley proceeded against one parishioner for refusing the rate, a Mr. Burder, who had ousted the vicar from the chair at the vestry meeting. Burder, a respectable tenant-farmer, found himself the defendant in the consistory court of London, resisting a claim that he owed £41 16s. of church rate (acres 308, rateable value £418). A committee of dissenters was formed to support him, and a public subscription raised. So the Braintree case was hunted through court after court.[1] In the tangled conflicts of secular and ecclesiastical jurisdictions it took Veley fourteen years and hundreds of pounds to achieve a final answer. The question was heard by a total of twenty-six judges and eight courts. The lawyers of England were neatly divided. Four courts held for Veley and four

---

roof was already beginning to be unsafe, and the builders advised that a new roof was required. The chancel of the church was not in question; for the repair of the chancel was obligatory upon the owner of the great tithes, and that owner was the trustees of Felsted School. But to mend the roof of this miniature cathedral, which seated 1,600 people, Veley found that he possessed only a little charity of £6 or £7 per annum which was applied to mending windows.

[1] First Braintree case, Veley v. Burder (1837–41); London consistory court (Lushington) held for Veley (15 November 1837) on the basis of *Gauden v. Selby*, while the judge was rude about the precedent. Burder moved for prohibition in queen's bench: prohibition granted (Lord Denman) on 1 May 1840 holding that churchwarden had no power to make rate without consent of the parish. Veley appealed to exchequer court, which (8 February 1841) upheld the prohibition. But in giving this judgment Lord Chief Justice Tindal suggested that if the churchwardens made the rate *at* the recalcitrant vestry meeting, instead of *apart from* the meeting, it was possible that the rate would have been valid. Veley began again.

Second Braintree case, Veley v. Gosling (1841–53); Gosling was a wealthy local brewer who was one of the dissenting majority refusing the rate in July 1841. Consistory court (Lushington) held for Gosling. Veley appealed to court of arches, where the dean (Sir Herbert Jenner Fust) held for Veley, 25 March 1843. Gosling applied for prohibition, which (8 February 1847) Denman refused in queen's bench. Gosling appealed to exchequer, which (22 January 1850), upheld Denman by a majority of only four judges to three. Thus Veley secured three successive verdicts in his favour. Gosling applied to House of Lords, which held the rate to be invalid (12 August 1853).

courts against. On 12 August 1853, sixteen years after the fight began, plodding Lord Truro gave the judgment of the House of Lords. Veley's rate was invalid. But the people of Braintree were undoubtedly obliged by law to repair their parish church.

The verdict in the Braintree case left the right to make or refuse a rate in the power of a majority in the vestry. The judgment quickened the pace of campaigns against the rate. Parishes postponed their conflict by agreement until the Braintree rate should be settled. One competent observer calculated rhetorically that from 1853 onwards the rate of increase in opposition was multiplied by five.

It is one of the interesting and impermissible speculations of Victorian history to guess what would have happened if the Lords had wobbled and descended upon the other side of the fence. Every pair of churchwardens in the country would have been entitled to enforce a rate. In parishes like those of Birmingham no rate had been paid for twenty-two years. To enforce this suddenly revived rate in such cities would have required, not 2,000 summonses, but 100,000 and more. It appears a safe speculation that if the judgment had gone the other way, dragons would have breathed fire through the churches and political parties of north and midland cities. A judgment favourable (so-called) to the Braintree rate would probably have driven the government into immediate abolition.

The law still required that the parish must keep its church, like its highway, in repair. But it was found to be also the law that if the parish refused to keep its church in repair no one could compel it. Abolition became inevitable. It waited until 1868, that is for fifteen more years of irritation and war between dissent and establishment.

7. THE YOUNG QUEEN

King William IV died in July 1837, anxious for the stability of the establishment and muttering, 'The church! The church!' and the name of Archbishop Howley on his death-bed.

Victoria's mother, the Duchess of Kent, was a German, her governess Lehzen was the daughter of a German pastor. Her education was in the hands partly of Lehzen and partly of her tutor, the non-resident Dean of Chester, George Davys. For a span of formative years, while her strange and possessive mother kept her in purdah, he was almost the only clergyman whom she was allowed to see. He prepared her for confirmation, directed the subordinate tutors, read with her Hume, Blackstone, Virgil, Paley, Boswell and the New Testament, preached the weekly sermon at the said prayers of the household on Sundays. She was in the habit of noting, in her childhood journal—a journal which was open to the inspection of her mother and her governess and may therefore represent more aspiration than sincerity—such remarks as these: 'the dean preached a very excellent sermon'. She privately thought his delivery to be monotonous and soporific. He was plain, honourable, good-hearted, unintelligent, undistinguished, and was her tutor for fifteen years. His religious simplicity fitted the desires of the duchess and the governess Lehzen.

The prime minister surprised himself by affection and pity for the young queen, suddenly emancipated from her enclosure and ignorant of the world. For the sake of educating her he neglected the duties of his station. The critics said that the business of the country languished because Melbourne reclined on a sofa in Buckingham Palace when he ought to have sat at a desk in Whitehall. He taught her the Whig view of life, in politics, history, society, the constitution and at last religion. When she feared that Archbishop Howley would be so nervous at the coronation that her crown would fall off, it was Melbourne who undertook to tell Howley to put the crown on firmly. The archbishop took the instructions so literallyhat he rammed the ruby ring, designed inadvertently to fit her little finger, so hard upon the fourth finger that she could only get it off painfully after bathing it in iced water.[1] He tried to give her the orb when she already had it.

Belligerent newspapers gossiped that Melbourne was turning the queen against religion, making the court sceptical and atheistical. It was not true. For all his quaint, amused, critical, superficial air of a man-of-the-world, Melbourne respected religion and thought that the queen of a Christian country must be pious and churchgoing.

In one respect he had nothing to do with the change which came over her religious practice. Unlike most young people, she sprang in a moment from extreme of simplicity to extreme of formality. Accustomed to nothing but the said short worship of her household prayers, she found herself a sovereign expected to attend the solemn slow-moving grandeur of Anglican cathedral worship. If in Buckingham palace, she was expected to appear on Sundays at the Chapel Royal of St. James's; if in Windsor castle, at St. George's. This sudden

[1] Longford, 81.

change of worshipping habits dismayed her. At the Chapel Royal the music was deplorable and the service long, at St. George's there was bitter chill and the service longer. She often noted in her youthful journal the length of service, sometimes with an exclamation mark. A girl accustomed to a simple half-hour was now expected to bear two and three-quarter hours with patience; including endless sermons from the deans and canons of Windsor, none of whom was selected for his preaching ability. (The Dean of Windsor was that strange old gentleman, Hobart, who on the birth of the Prince of Wales, later King Edward VII, tried to congratulate her on thus 'saving us from the incredible curse of a female succession'.)[1] She found that Melbourne agreed with her in disliking long sermons and solemn music. She observed that during sermons he often went to sleep and sometimes snored, but then he even went to sleep after dinner in her drawing-room. 'There are not many good preachers to be found,' she said to him. He agreed, and said, 'But there are not many very good anything.'[2]

Melbourne would have no zeal and encouraged her to distrust zeal. But he recommended her to Dr. Arnold's sermons, and at least there was moral power. 'He's too vehement for me,' confessed Melbourne.[3] He told her that the Oxford school, Dr. Pusey and Mr. Newman, were very violent people of the high church character, that William Wilberforce and the evangelicals were enthusiasts, that all Quakers were sly, that Luther was a very questionable man and all hermits were rogues, that commonplace sermons were better than wild sermons. He wanted her to exchange that earlier fear of episcopal wigs and aprons, which she learnt from her mother and governess, for a faint air of aristocratic contempt. 'Bishops should be young,' he told her, 'else they go off directly, and don't learn anything.' 'Obstinate dogs, those bishops'; 'those clergymen,' he said, 'they are always poking themselves into everything.' 'You bishops,' he said to the Archbishop of York in her presence, 'are sad dogs.' He asked her if the chaplain to Windsor castle was a good liver—'which a clergyman ought to be; and a clergyman of the Church of England ought to be; it's the character of the Church of England; and I am all for keeping up the character of the hierarchy.' She told him that she disliked Archbishop

[1] Olwen Hedley, *Report of the Society of the Friends of St. George's*, 1961, 28.
[2] Queen Victoria's *Journal*, 29 October 1837.
[3] Queen Victoria's *Journal*, 14 January 1838, 19 January 1839.

Howley. 'He has an unfortunate manner,' said Lord Melbourne; 'a hypocritical, cringing manner, but I don't think he is so. He made a great fool of himself in that Hampden business, and I always tell him so.'[1] He taught her the difference between Arminianism and Antinomianism, between consubstantiation and transubstantiation.

Lady Holland sent the queen two thick volumes on the Gospels, and Melbourne thought that it must be an infidel book or Lady Holland would not have sent it. The queen heard with interest that Lady Holland thought it a crime if any visitor to Holland House went to church. But of the scepticism of Holland House he told her nothing. Though she knew he seldom went to church, he encouraged her to church; he said that it was a right thing to do. He told her not to puzzle herself with controversies in religion, but keep to the simple truths; that going to the Chapel Royal was her penance for her sins.

The worst of the religious education provided by Melbourne was the appointment of George Davys to the see of Peterborough. Melbourne did not normally trouble her young head about his appointments. But Davys had been her tutor and it was custom that the tutor to the reigning sovereign should become a bishop. It was agreed by all parties that Davys was unsuitable, and by Whigs that he was a Tory. But the mode of his appointment left something to be desired. Melbourne pointed out how convenient it would be because it would relieve the queen of paying him a pension. Melbourne needed Whig bishops badly and did not want Davys in the House of Lords. He was sure, he told her, that Davys was weak and would be led astray by strong Tory bishops. But when newspapers used the neglect of Davys as evidence of Melbourne's atheistical influence, it became even Melbourne's interest to prefer him. On these dubious grounds Davys became Bishop of Peterborough, where he was universally liked, where he steadily promoted his relatives to be canons of the cathedral, and where his record of votes was not what Whig ministers could wish. He lived a long time, peacefully and thriftily and without exertion, and when at last he died the *Times* remarked ambiguously: 'His ambition through life was rather to be good than great. Higher praise it is impossible to bestow.'[2]

Fascinated by his brilliance, his wit and experience, Victoria owed Lord Melbourne much during those first troubled years when she was

[1] Queen Victoria's *Journal*, 28 December 1839.
[2] T, 19 April 1864; cf. Baring-Gould, *The Church Revival*, 174.

free from her mother. He might have done worse for her by way of religious education. But he was a man of the eighteenth century, and the religious interests of that century were being replaced. Though she later reacted against Melbourne, he contributed something to her sense of estrangement from the main religious movements within the established church of which she was the supreme governor, a sense which had important consequences. The easy nonchalance about religion, as about all other subjects, which inspired his conversation, did not fit her stern and dutiful character. It was quickly shed when she married a husband who was never nonchalant, least of all about moral duty.

On 10 February 1840 Archbishop Howley married the queen to Prince Albert. The queen wanted the wedding to be private inside Buckingham Palace, and Archbishop Howley and Bishop Blomfield remonstrated that it should be in the Chapel Royal. She told Melbourne that these prelates always liked what was most disagreeable. At the wedding the archbishop became confused and tried to make the prince put the ring on her right hand.[1] 'The Archbishop of Canterbury', wrote an observer, 'did not spare us one word of the ceremony, which is very disagreeable, and when one looked at all the young things who were listening, most distressing, however he mumbles a good deal.' And now a different mind began to exert itself upon the queen. As Melbourne was soon to be ousted in politics and then from the palace, Albert slowly—less slowly after the birth of the first child Vicky—took upon himself the appropriate burden of being chief adviser to the sovereign.

The family of Prince Albert, though descended from that Saxon line which first protected Luther and the Reformation, divided into various branches, some of which were now Roman Catholic. A few Englishmen accused him of being a secret or open Roman Catholic. The rumour spread so far that pamphlets were issued to deny its truth; and it was given additional weight when Lord Melbourne's cabinet omitted the word *Protestant* from the declaration of the marriage to the privy council on 23 November 1839, and later in the declaration to the Houses of Parliament. Whether this was in origin a slip, or whether it was thought unnecessary because the queen could legally marry none but a Protestant, or whether it was omitted as a sop to the Irish Catholic supporters of the Whigs, it gave a useful stick

[1] Cf. *Journal of Mary Frampton*, 1885, 412.

to beat the government. Wellington carried an amendment in the House of Lords inserting the word *Protestant* into the congratulatory address to the queen.[1]

Nothing was less well grounded. Albert was not merely a confirmed member of the Lutheran Church. All his life he feared bigotry, clerical power, the pope, claims to ecclesiastical dominance; and he brought this fear with him into England, where it was not so easily fitted to the circumstances. The suspicion of his Catholicism, hinted in Parliament and rumoured in the country, was ludicrously wide of the mark.

But there was another rumour; that he was an infidel, or at least a dangerous radical in religion. Lord Palmerston wrote urgently to Albert's intimate, Baron Stockmar, to find out whether Albert belonged to any sect which would prevent him receiving the sacrament in the English church.[2] Stockmar reassured the English cabinet that there was no essential difference between the communion services of the German Protestant and the English churches.

This rumour, though still wide of the mark, was not so wild as the rumour that he was a Catholic. The religious atmosphere of the leading German universities was far different from the religious atmosphere of Oxford and Cambridge. There was more freedom of thought, harder study, more emphasis on enquiry and less on the duty of transmitting received truth. The philosophy of Kant shattered the old rationality of the eighteenth century, and in most German thinking the idea of development, of the continuous unfolding of an ordered world, loomed large. The more attention German professors paid to historical continuity and to vital onward forces, the more distrust they bestowed on static formulas, and the more loosely they sat to traditional religious dogmas.

When Albert of Saxe-Coburg studied at Bonn the leading professors of the university were fervent for the principle of historical development. The school of philosophy was headed by J. H. Fichte, son and intellectual heir of the great Fichte. Albert preserved a caricature of Fichte lecturing and soaked himself in philosophy of the Fichte tradition. Phrases redolent of Fichte reappeared in Albert's addresses and letters for the rest of his life. Moral freedom, activity and ceaseless endeavour, the wise man making himself perfect by steady effort,

---

[1] Martin, i, 58. Wellington privately thought the omission 'very childish and foolish', cf. *Wellington and his Friends*, 1965, 126.
[2] Martin, i, 58.

God as the principle and ground of the moral world, absolute obedience to the inward voice of conscience, kingdom of God attained by the advance of reason and science—those characteristic phrases of the Kantian tradition in its Fichte-clothing floated in and out of Albert's mind throughout his subsequent career. His adviser and confidant, Baron Stockmar, shared this metaphysical outlook, and was not ashamed of the vast moral platitudes which gave practical expression to this abstract standpoint. They sounded more convincing in their original German than when later translated into English by biographers of the prince consort.

But it must not be thought that because old dogmatic formulas were regarded as obsolescent, the German school of the prince's upbringing justified the English rumour that he was infidel. He was a devout communicant of the Lutheran church.[1] It was sufficient for the conservative English that he participated in a modern and metaphysical form of German religious philosophy. At that date the English were wont to regard most German teachers of religion as apostates. Albert regarded creeds as a barrier to mental development and wanted to adapt them to the needs of the day. He was inclined to look down on English religious conservatism compared with the liberal metaphysics of his German upbringing. He was neither biblical nor ecclesiastical in his language. His brother said of him, with some justice, 'he had no natural piety.' Though his phrases were not public, it will readily be understood that their author failed to capture the entire approbation of traditional English churchmen. The wife of the queen's private secretary, Lady Ponsonby, once said, 'Churchmen could not but distrust him.'[2]

Whether his religion was orthodox or not, it was certainly earnest. And although he had at first no power in the household, and grumbled that he was only a husband and not a master, he soon began to introduce changes into the habits of the palace. The Baroness Lehzen, who brought up the queen, resented the innovation when the prince started to read religious books to the queen on Sundays. His Sunday habits, however, were not so austere as those of some English churchmen whom he met. One Sunday evening he challenged Archdeacon Samuel Wilberforce to a game of chess, and caused a twinge of conscience in his opponent.[3]

This new earnestness in the royal household was not before time.

[1] Cf. Martin, i, 66.   [2] Fulford, *Prince Consort*, 183–4.   [3] Fulford, 63, 101.

The tone of morals in the queen's household was still Hanoverian. Together with the moral reformation which the prince conducted at court, he contributed something characteristic to the office of supreme governor in the established church. He started with the handicap that he was incapable of understanding or sympathising with the old Anglican outlook or the newer religious movements of the day. His liberalism feared the dogmatism of high churchmen or of evangelicals. He was disturbed and even shocked at the conservative practices of the Church of England and soon concluded that it had been insufficiently reformed during the sixteenth century. He began by being critical of the Church of England, and he continued to be critical. In his earlier days in England his secretary Anson needed to warn him not to be so outspoken in his reproaches. He never understood the rich dignity and scholarship of the English cathedral tradition.[1] When Lady Lyttelton, a most devout woman, was appointed governess to the Princess Royal, she insisted that the child kneel to say her prayers. The queen argued about it vehemently[2] and the prince disliked it. He decided that English religion was cold and that kneeling was part of this formalism. He told Lady Lyttelton that kneeling went out with the Reformation: 'I do not do it.' Lady Lyttelton replied that she thought sitting in prayer was irreverent. The prince gave way, telling Stockmar that as the princess was being educated in England her prejudices must be those of the English church. Albert kept telling the queen how much more impressive was the German communion service than the English, and confirmed her suspicion that the English service was cold and repetitious.[3]

He shared the queen's views about the services at St. George's, Windsor, and at the Chapel Royal, and was not so long-suffering as she. Accordingly, the prince created a new private chapel in Windsor castle, consecrated by Bishop Bagot of Oxford on 19 December 1843. Thereafter they seldom attended services except the simplest; at Windsor in the private chapel, in London at the private chapel of Buckingham palace. At Osborne they began in July 1845 to attend the little parish church of Whippingham, not without fear of being pestered by sightseers, and found it quiet and orderly.[4] The officiating

---

[1] Fulford, 183, 185, 193.   [2] Cf. *Letters of Queen Victoria*, i, 509.
[3] *Dearest Child*, ed. Fulford, 186.
[4] Anson to S. Oxon, 6 August 1845. Wilberforce Papers BL Dep. c. 193. Earlier sovereigns had private domestic chapels in the castle, but Wyatville demolished two such, of Charles II and George III, during his reconstruction of the twenties.

chaplains were few and select—Lord Wriothesley Russell, Gerald
Wellesley, the nephew of the Duke of Wellington, and later Arthur
Stanley, Charles Kingsley and some half-dozen others.

In 1846 Prince Albert marked for his queen a passage from the
advice to princes by Saint-Simon, that they should show their religion
by leading moral lives, not in slavishly attending services in church.[1]
But the royal pair were diligent in attendance at their simple short and
private worship. The childhood tradition of Dr. Davys was successfully established in adult life. All her life she wanted liberal and
scholarly clergymen. She had been taught to distrust extremists
whether high or low, demanded simplicity in ritual, thought of
religion as a way of life based upon a few simple truths, and had no
patience with the complexities of dogmatic theology. She was bored
by *Barchester Towers*; and the editor of her letter disclosing this view of
Trollope remarked justly that she was not in sympathy with persons
in holy orders.[2]

The supreme governor of the established church was not well
prepared to understand the strong religious forces of her day. An upbringing by Lehzen and her mother, and Davys, and Melbourne, and
finally Prince Albert, prevented her comprehending evangelicals or
Puseyites, who were beginning to dominate church life. But she was
moral, and dutiful, and a good example, and sincerely professed a
humane liberalism towards her various dissenters. Moreover, Albert
taught her that the crown must be above politics; and in all appointments, whether in army or justiciary or church, the royal pair moved
the choice away from party grounds. We shall see that she contributed
towards freeing the establishment from the old inheritance that the
crown could only choose bishops of the party in power.

[1] Longford, 340.   [2] *Dearest Child*, ed. Fulford, 164.

CHAPTER III

THE OXFORD MOVEMENT

In the autumn of 1835 the Church of Rome began to be abused more vehemently. O'Connell and his Irish radicals happened to hold the balance between the two parties and behaved unbearably in the House of Commons. Irish Protestant clergy were still in distress over tithe despite a million pounds which the Whigs of 1833 allotted to their relief. A wave of sympathy for Irish Protestants swept England. Meetings were held to collect money, the king gave £500 and Queen Adelaide £100, chapters voted money from their corporate funds, and twinkling eyes watched to see how Lord Melbourne and Archbishop Whately would subscribe. The undercurrent of *No Popery* bubbled again to the surface of English life. A Protestant Association was founded in London, others in the provinces. English Roman Catholics were readier to face abuse and so provoked it. Under the penal laws they retired behind high walls into owl-haunted mansions and preferred not to be observed. But now they saw no reason for secrecy and advantage in public notice. On 15 November 1835 the Roman Catholic chapel at Weobly in Herefordshire was consecrated with solemn and public rites, and the patrons believed it to be the first solemn and public consecration since the Reformation. Lord Althorp's brother, George Spencer, who became a Roman Catholic and turned into Father Spencer, was appointed priest at West Bromwich and alarmed the town by visiting all the dissenting ministers. The prior of Ampleforth came out of his rustic cell, preached in Helmsley market-place, distributed tracts and was drawn in a phaeton to the Black Swan.[1] The rector of the English College at Rome, Dr. Wiseman, whom few Englishmen yet knew, dared to appear in London during 1836 and give public lectures expounding transubstantiation and the Roman Catholic faith. If it appears odd that the lectures caused a stir and a scandal, it should be remembered that the last lectures of the kind were delivered in the reign of Bloody Mary.

[1] *Br. Mag.*, 8, 1835, 654; *Br. Mag.*, 8, 1835, 604.

English churchmen felt themselves under assault. Their obvious allies against the pope were Protestant dissenters, and after recent events they feared dissenters more than they feared the pope. The Church of Rome was the danger in Ireland, the dissenting churches in England; and the unnatural alliance of Irish radical Catholics with English radical dissenters kept Lord Melbourne in power and beleaguered the Church of England to right as well as left. The clergy saw themselves to be treading the middle way of truth, royal road between twin abysses—

> The floodgates on me open wide
> And headlong rushes in the turbulent tide
> Of lusts and heresies; a motley troop they come;
> And old imperial Rome
> Looks up, and lifts again half-dead
> Her seven-domed head,
> And Schism and Superstition, near and far,
> Blend in one pestilent star,
> And shake their horrid locks against the Saints to war.[1]

I. NEWMAN AT OXFORD

Since the affair of Hampden's professorship Newman, Keble and Pusey were notorious as leaders of a secret papist school of divinity in Oxford. Wits sometimes named this doctrine Newmania. But by the end of 1837 everyone knew the group as Puseyites. The sound was smooth and comic and disrespectful. Heads of colleges disdained to use so vulgar a word. A bishop solemnly forbade it to his clergy.[2]

The name suggested to the ignorant that Pusey led. Every Oxford man knew better. Newman commanded and Pusey followed. Newman had the life, the ideas, the pen, the poetry, the public influence, the guidance of a party; and the name Puseyite was quite misleading. By 1839 the *Tracts for the Times* generated ugly misshapen nicknames, Tractator or Tractarian or Tractite; and two years after that, just when the *Tracts* disappeared in smoke, Tractarian conquered and remained incongruously with posterity. But those without perfect manners continued to use Puseyite.

Newman divided Oxford. The old and the buttoned were not con-

---

[1] *The Angel of the Church*, in *Lyra Apostolica*, 139, Br. Mag., 8, 1835, 646.
[2] R, 19 May 1842. Keble became vicar of Hursley, Hants, in 1836.

verted. But the young fell under a thrall. The undergraduates first went to Newman because he was disreputable among their elders, because his name was exciting, because he banged the regius professor, because the chaplain of New College placarded Oxford against his popery. They stayed to discover an ethical power which led them to examine the unwonted doctrine and then to revere the teacher. From the pulpit of St. Mary's they learnt obedience, holiness, devotion, sacrament, fasting, mortification, in language of a beauty rarely heard in English oratory. Archbishop Whately believed that by October 1838 two-thirds of the steady reading undergraduates were Puseyites. Though this estimate is probably one of the pessimistic exaggerations to which Whately was prone, Newman commanded in 1837-8 a following rare even in English universities. The undergraduates paid him the compliment of crowding his sermons, of imitating his gliding gait, of holding their heads on one side and pausing long between sentences, of reading in hurried impersonal monotony, of kneeling down with a bump as he knelt, of arguing endlessly over his teaching. In later years nostalgic disciples remembered how every subject of discussion seemed to come round to Newman's doctrine, and how you could not talk of novels or philosophy, poetry or painting, Walter Scott or Jane Austen, Gothic architecture or German literature, without finding yourself in an argument over Newman. In November 1837 the senior common room of Queen's College told two Cambridge visitors after dinner that Pusey and Newman governed the university; that nothing could withstand their influence; that every man of talent who came up to Oxford during the last six years had joined Newman; that they went to hear him on Sunday afternoons even at the loss of their dinner; that his triumph over the mental empire of Oxford was complete.[1] Legends gathered outside Oxford, that at Littlemore chapel, which he built, candles were kept burning night and day, or that upon his surplice he wore a rich illuminated cross. Years later Newman hailed the time as the happiest of his life from the human point of view. 'I was truly at home . . . It was the time of plenty.'[2] He touched the summit of his influence in Oxford and the Church of England.

Young men will not become disciples unless they sense something

---

[1] J. F. Russell to a friend, 18 November 1837, Liddon, i, 406; R. W. Church, 159; Whately, *Life of Whately*, i, 418; Liddon, ii, 12.
[2] *Apologia*, 88.

revolutionary. Newman, high Tory defender of the established church, had a streak of revolution. The Church of England must appeal to the ancient fathers of undivided Christendom—that was common ground to all high churchmen. In Adam de Brome's chapel at St. Mary's, where vice-chancellor and heads of houses were in the habit of assembling before the university sermon, Newman devoted week-day lectures on theology to this old-fashioned Anglican groove. The main series was published in March 1837 as *Lectures on the Prophetical Office of the Church*. The book contained fierce condemnations of Rome and dissent, and propounded the appeal to undivided Christendom. It contained more. Newman confessed what made high churchmen nervous, and in the confession lay the revolutionary dynamic. 'The *via media* has never existed except on paper; it has never been reduced to practice.' By the providence of God the English church survived the discreditable episode of the Reformation with creed and ministry unimpaired. But it failed to value its treasure. Its Protestant practice did not agree with its Catholic theory. He allowed some truth in the Roman claim that you would hardly find ten or twenty neighbouring clergymen of the English church who agree together; that the laity wander like sheep without a shepherd, not knowing what to believe; that English churchmen have no internal bond, but are kept united by the wholesome tyranny of the state.[1] There is a great work to be done; to bring the practice of the Church of England to agree with its theory. We need a second Reformation.

Other high churchmen regretted these admissions. In London H. J. Rose, passionate and asthmatic, edited the *British Magazine* with sharp intelligence. Rose feared Rome in his heart, Newman condemned her in his head. Rose saw the Roman church through the eyes of an historian, admitted to his journal articles upon financial defalcations of Jesuits as though they might be relevant to divinity, allowed abuse of Roman censorship or of legendary absurdities. Since his visit to the city of Rome in 1832, Newman felt his heart drawn by Roman antiquities, breath of the primitive church among the catacombs, continuity of Catholic history, sanctity of Catholic ideals. Rose was more learned in history, Newman more sensitive to the grandeur of the past.

> O that thy creed were sound!
> For thou dost soothe the heart, thou Church of Rome

---

[1] *Proph. Office*, 20–21, 394–6.

was a couplet rising from his continental holiday, but first published in the *British Magazine*.[1] Newman was drawn by Roman history and judged her wrong by the intellectual standards of a divine. Rose felt his heart repelled by Rome and needed no systematic theology to reject her. Newman was more pessimistic about the condition of the Church of England. Rose was not uncritical of the existing church, but took a higher view of Anglican tradition. Newman conceived the task to be practising what had appeared only on paper. Rose conceived the task to be practising better what had been practised, not by everyone but in every generation.[2] The Oxford school slowly gravitated away from the *British Magazine* and began to use the *British Critic* as its organ. Newman dedicated to Rose the fourth volume of his sermons. Rose continued to support Newman with private misgivings and public applause until, losing the fight against asthma and dropsy, he died at Florence on 22 December 1838.

Before the end of 1837 the learned world perceived the difference between Newman's men and the high churchmen of tradition. They conceived Newman to be the head of an Oxford party, the apostle of a new kind of sect within the establishment. Newman denied that he was a man of party. He aspired only to be the leading writer of a school of divinity. He disliked the notion that he led a party.

But schools of divinity easily become parties. And as leader of a party Newman suffered from defects. His powerful mind was trained in dialectic by Whately. Enjoying clever argument, he was open to the logician's vice of being easily convinced by his own skill. In religious belief he heaped scorn upon dialectic, in religious controversy he relished subtle twists and turns. His subtleties puzzled his friends and fortified his enemies. And though secure in his cause, he suffered from sensitive shyness which made him hang back hesitant and self-questioning. He would have been a more formidable combatant, so disciples thought, if he had cared less for the opinions of his friends. He had the party virtue that he was willing to be fierce against antagonists in sharp provoking phrases, the party vice that answering

[1] 9, 1836, 147. Continental travel helped several Tractarians to see greatness in the Church of Rome: Faber, Hope-Scott, Bellasis, Allies. Bellasis in particular was moved when he saw the French helmsman take off his hat to the crucifix on Dieppe pier, and the workmen at 5 a.m. mass in thier overalls before going to the factory. *Memorials of Mr. Serjeant Bellasis*, 22–29.

[2] Cf. his review of *Lectures on the Prophetical Office* in Br. Mag., 11, 1837, 546–7, where the magazine uses the word 'Anglicanism' (I believe) for the first time, putting it into inverted commas.

pungencies found him prickly and left him sore. He was happy to stir the wasps, but could not brush aside the stings. Confident in the present, he suffered epidemic forebodings about the future. He knew that he was at the top of his influence and expected only to decline. He worked steadily and rapidly, filled with energy and zeal; but something about his self-distrust and something about his ardour robbed him of the quality of endurance.

Hurrell Froude left an indelible mark on Newman. No one took Froude's place in Newman's heart until Ambrose St. John joined him at Littlemore in 1843. He loved Froude as a man and believed that to him he owed his Catholic soul, his understanding of all that was noble in the Church of Rome, his devotion to the eucharist and the Virgin Mary. On Froude's death in 1836 Newman chose Froude's breviary as keepsake from his library. Newman studied it, published one of the *Tracts* about it, and used it daily in his prayers.

A man is blind in judging the qualities of another who has touched his heart. Affection led Newman to exaggerate Froude's gifts and so into the first blow which hit his movement; the publishing of Froude's *Remains*.

Froude's 'Remains'

Within three months of Hurrell Froude's death his father, the Archdeacon of Totnes, sent to Newman all the papers which he could find.[1] He said that Newman and Keble might do with them what they pleased and that he would bear the cost of publication. Newman collected Froude's articles printed in the *British Magazine* and the manuscripts of some sermons. None of these was remarkable. The dramatic element was supplied by fragments of Froude's private journal, by a few of Froude's private letters, and by recollections of his sayings and epigrams. Newman hesitated a little and consulted. He saw that sayings of Froude would shock and argued himself into believing that it would help the movement. He wanted the book to show Froude as he was and to display the *enthusiasm* of a Puseyite. Froude's private journal astonished him. The revelation of Froude's austerities blinded him further to sane judgment and good taste. The nearer came the date of publication, the more anxious he became. He was sure that some would judge parts of the journal silly and trifling

---

[1] Archdeacon Froude to Keble, 3 May 1836, Keble Coll. MSS.

and injudicious. Judge Coleridge was sent the proofs and was shocked. He tried vainly to prevent publication.[1]

In March 1838 the world was given the first two volumes of Froude's *Remains*, with more to follow in 1839. The first volume alone mattered. It contained the private journal, private letters, and sayings.

It was the private journal of a penitent aged 24 and would have been better burnt. Froude, whom all his friends found charming and vivacious, appeared as nervous and overscrupulous, introspective and morbid, battling against the flesh, sleeping on the floor, troubled with dreams and anxious mortifications, ashamed that he had muddy trousers, confessing an impulse of pleasure when Wilberforce was not in Oriel chapel one morning, or a disposition to sneak away when he broke one of Wilberforce's windows, bothered at eating too much toast after refusing wine. The atmosphere was wrong. It was like the moral register of an earnest schoolboy trying to be good after confirmation.

So, at least, it appears to modern taste. Archdeacon Froude professed to welcome it, the *British Magazine* and *British Critic* hailed it, Pusey allowed that it might check the movement, but was glad of it. We find a solitary instance of a Tractarian layman using the book to foster private devotion.[2] Filled with a sense of ethical responsibility, they called for sanctity and expected antiquity to interpret that word. In antiquity they found heroic mortification and rejoiced to see a shadow within the Church of England. When the hostile world abused the Church of England for secularity and said that among its purposes the gospel was second to good incomes for the children of aristocrats, Oxford men must be pardoned unbalance of retort. They were hardly familiar enough with Catholic standards of devotional writing to be able to recognise the journal as callow. Newman saw some of the defects. Prejudice of affection made him think the juvenile quality to matter little in comparison with the unveiling of secret mortifications. Half a century later a more private shock was administered by the publication of certain papers of Dr. Pusey which should have been burnt. But Pusey's papers were so unique, the penitential meditations of a strange saint, that even level-headed executors could not bring themselves to burn. Newman, without any such excuse over Froude's papers, was led by intimacy into the same affront to taste.

---

[1] Cf. Archdeacon Froude to Keble, 26 February 1838, Keble Coll. MSS.
[2] Liddon, ii, 45; Ornsby, i, 192.

The ideals of the Church of England had been one with the stream of Protestant devotion. They looked for the virtues of home and vocation in the world. Froude whispered rather of Ambrose or Athanasius than of Nicholas Ferrar or George Herbert, and hinted at archaic modes of self-discipline from which the Reformation was supposed to have freed Christian men. Readers wondered whether this unevangelical self-tormenting way of life was intended to be the practical expression of Puseyite ideas.

For several years Newman and Keble disliked the word *Protestant*. The Reformation was dusty in repute. Nothing riled English high churchmen more than the phrase *Protestant church*. It seemed to lump them with Germans against miracle or Swiss against Trinity or ranters against decorum. They chanted litanies to be delivered from contemporary claimants to the Reformation heritage. Newman and Keble wished never to line the Church of England with Protestant churches of Europe and America. Their middle way, they said, was neither Protestant nor Roman.

An older nostalgic Newman thought that the characteristic attitudes of the Oxford divines were encouraged by the romantic in contemporary literature. He selected the poetry of Wordsworth and the novels of Walter Scott. Historians followed Newman in declaring the romantics to be part-cause of the Oxford Movement. Like the link of Renaissance with Reformation, this link is easier to feel than define. Theology like literature moved from reason to feeling. But theology did not move because literature moved. They marched in hand because the human spirit yearned for new depth. A world of common sense yielded to a world which saw common sense as shallow and reached after beauty and truth beyond the easy fetters of prose. Religious men wanted poetry of heart in their hymns, sacramental sensibility in their worship, recovery of symbolism in art and architecture. But Keble and Newman and Hurrell Froude were not divines of the Protestant right wing because they were romantics. They expressed their divinity with the aid of romantic images and attitudes common to their day.

The romantics altered popular attitudes to the Reformation by deepening popular sympathy for the middle ages. In the thirties this new sympathy was more popular than scholarly; no-man's-land of *Ivanhoe*, new affection for whispering stones of Tintern abbey, new love of pointed arches and sedilia and piscinas. A sentiment for monastic ruins generates no love for a Reformation which ruined monasteries.

Hurrell Froude hated the Reformation. This hatred rose more from political attitude than from romantic sentiment. While the established church was in danger, the Reformation was thrown to the front of controversy. Might the state seize money from the Irish or English church? When Tory churchmen said that it was robbery, radicals replied that Tory churchmen now lived on endowments transferred by state power at the Reformation. By what right could a non-Anglican Parliament interfere with the Church of England? By right of royal supremacy, taken by crown and Parliament at the Reformation. So far as the Reformation stood for state interference with religion, the Reformation was vile to Froude; and the vileness of an erastian state spilt over to infect all the English Protestants except the puritans. Therefore in Froude's *Remains* the repudiation of Protestants appeared before the public in a new and shocking light. Newman's *Tracts* disliked the word Protestant, Froude disliked Protestants. Newman wanted to reform the Reformation, Froude seemed to want to destroy the Reformation. Critics picked out sentences like these:

Odious Protestantism sticks in people's gizzards.

Really I hate the Reformation and the Reformers more and more.

The Reformation was a limb badly set—it must be broken again in order to be righted.

I never mean if I can help it, to use any phrases which can connect me with such a set (i.e. as Cranmer, Ridley, Bucer, Peter Martyr, Luther, Melanchthon).

Newman inserted a defensive paragraph into the preface, that this was not popery, for Froude used equal harshness towards modern Roman Catholics, calling them wretched Tridentines. But these laconic and scornful condemnations lent themselves to the scissors. The biting epigrams caused foe to exult and friend to shrink. Newman believed that the transparent character of his friend would stand out from the pages and that the extremisms of his conversation would be pardoned. He miscalculated; not realising that he read the book in the correcting light of friendship while the world judged Froude by the book.

It mattered little that ignoramuses accused the Oxford divines of being Jesuits in disguise or that Lord Morpeth dragged irrelevant quotations from Froude into a parliamentary speech. It was a gain that publicity began to sell the *Tracts for the Times* faster than the publisher could print them.[1] But Newman committed a further error in triumphing over his least wild accuser. The slow and portly Lady Margaret professor of divinity, Dr. Godfrey Faussett, preached a university sermon against Froude in Newman's own church, and said that though not papists Newman and Keble were not safe nor consistent members of the Church of England. When Newman rose in wrath he could write cleverer pamphlets than anyone in England. He sat up all night writing a reply which danced amusingly round the Lady Margaret professor and left him ridiculous.[2] He would have been wiser to eschew the triumph. The university of Oxford was sore.

Newman soon felt the loss of confidence. In a charge of August 1838 Bishop Bagot of Oxford denounced the Ecclesiastical Commission and praised the *Tracts for the Times*, but took exception to various passages. Newman wrote some of his prickliest letters in consequence of the bishop's exceptions. His colleagues were more critical of his leadership. He had a fortnight's tiff with one, a second came into his rooms and condemned him to his face, a third told him that he was unsettling the country clergy. They threw him into a mood of self-distrust. 'It is just like walking on treacherous ice: one cannot say a thing but one offends someone or other—I don't mean foe, for that one could bear, but friend. You cannot conceive what unpleasant tendencies to split are developing themselves on all sides . . .'[3]

When England resounded with assaults upon Roman Catholics the university of Oxford was pained to find itself a gratuitous target. The provost of Oriel saw a slump in applicants which forced him to accept all comers.[4] Other colleges found parents nervous. Posthumous Froude wounded Oxford where it hurt.

Golightly, known in rueful affection or contempt as Golly, with wealth and high cackling voice, began the first of the campaigns which made him the notorious skirmisher of the age. He held a meeting at his house in Oxford. To purge the university from the stain of Froude's *Remains*, the company planned a memorial to the martyrs of

[1] Hansard, xliv, 817; LC, ii, 279. Arnold, who thought *Remains* the most impudent book that he had ever read, believed nevertheless that Newman's policy was right, and that the 'strength of the dose' would bring more disciples. Arnold to Hawkins, 5 August 1838, in Rugby School Papers.

[2] Faussett's sermon, 20 May; Newman's reply, 22 June, 1838. Both the pamphlets reached a second edition. Newman told J. B. Mozley that he had sold 750 while Faussett sold only 500, LC, ii, 255.

[3] Newman to Bowden, 21 November 1838, LC, ii, 272.

[4] Ashwell-Wilberforce, *Life of Wilberforce*, i, 130.

the Reformation burnt in Oxford; Cranmer, Ridley and Latimer. They intended more to vindicate Oxford than to strike at Newman, and were backed by several former colleagues of Newman. But the plan was welcomed by others as a good cut at Newman. First they proposed a cross to be erected on the spot in Broad Street. The evangelicals were not pleased with a cross and preferred a memorial church. Archbishop Howley and Bishop Blomfield each sent £50. Bishop Bagot of Oxford subscribed and tried to persuade Pusey and Newman and Keble to subscribe. Howley and Bagot thought the church less quarrelsome than the cross and gave their subscriptions on condition that it was a church. By 14 January Golightly was in the predicament of having £1,642 7s. 3d. if it were a cross and £1,173 1s. more if it were a church.[1] In March 1840 they agreed to have a cross and to add an aisle to St. Mary Magdalen near by, to be called the Martyrs' aisle.

Newman and Keble refused to have anything to do with the plan. They thought that they would appear to repudiate Froude. They shared his hostility to Reformers. Pusey, who was willing to commemorate the blessings of Reformation in general terms, dithered for several weeks, but at last determined to stand by Newman.

During 1839 every number of the *Christian Observer* and many numbers of the *Record* carried an onslaught upon the Oxford divines, as a group or as individuals. Newman, Pusey, Keble, Isaac Williams, Manning, Hook were held up to society as traitors to the Church of England. In a moment of not unusual wildness the *Times* repeated the scandal that Oxford housed secret Jesuits. But there was support and defence on the other side; Newman was keenly alive to the uses of publicity which sold thousands of copies of the *Tracts*. He and his friends knew that they were not traitors and were sure that they represented the authentic mind of the English church. He cared little for the *Record* or *Christian Observer* and thought abuse praiseworthy when it came from heretics.

The mental effect of being bombarded is difficult to predict. Newman's letters of 1839 do not show a mind unsettled by reason of public persecution. What mattered more was the inability of Oxford to listen without suspicion to what he wanted to say. Many years later he wrote[2] that in the spring of 1839 his position in the Anglican church

[1] *Times*, 14 January 1839. Subscription lists in Wadham College MSS.
[2] *Apologia*, 102.

was at its height. If *position* meant notoriety and sale of books and tracts, the verdict may stand. If it meant influence upon the Church of England his memory played him false by several months. The alliance which Hampden provoked and which turned Newman into the mouthpiece and guide of high churchmen was broken by Froude. In the country at large there were still many clergy who saw no other way of proclaiming the independent authority of the church and continued to wait upon his word. In Oxford he retained the heart-given allegiance of a strong band of the faithful. But senior Oxford as a whole despised or disliked him. The university could no longer make allowance for the extremisms of his group, for the eccentricities thrown up on the fringe of this as of every powerful movement of religion. In September 1839 Newman went on holiday and left J. B. Morris of Exeter College in charge of St. Mary's, with anxiety and a warning that he should preach no extravagance. On Michaelmas day Morris, who had a monomania about fasting, seemed in rhetoric to recommend that animals should be made to abstain on fast days. The next Sunday he preached what Newman called the Roman doctrine of the mass and said that everyone who did not hold it was an unbeliever.[1] Newman blamed Morris ('may he have a fasting horse next time he goes steeplechasing'), but was blamed for him, not without cause. His situation at St. Mary's threatened to be so unpleasant that he wondered whether to stop preaching. He talked of resigning St. Mary's and retreating to be a brother of charity in London, or looked wistfully at the village of Littlemore and began to think of living there in a little religious community.

He looked to the future with foreboding. The odium of the fight told upon him. He wondered whether the Church of England was heading for schism, whether the two parties which lived awkwardly together since the Reformation were now gathering their forces for a collision. The church seemed to be held together by the bonds of state, and he fancied that if allowed freely to meet in a Convocation the parties must split.[2] And he was beginning to be afraid that one or two of his people might become Roman Catholics. He collected all the hot sayings against Rome from the *Tracts* and republished them as a brochure. But he and Pusey were aware that some of their flock were

[1] The vice-chancellor summoned Morris, examined the sermon, formally admonished the preacher, and took away his family for a time from St. Mary's church, LC, ii, 291.

[2] LC, ii, 293, 297.

anxious, and that nothing could do the movement more harm than public secession by persons known to be under their guidance. Newman was the more anxious about these anxieties because he knew them in his secret heart. For a moment he felt the tug of Rome; and though he eluded it for a moment, he was despondent for others. If he, expert in the Roman controversy, felt himself pressed, what of disciples who had not studied the question?

His difficulty was the court of appeal in Christian authority, the fathers. The Puseyites appealed from the Reformation to the early and undivided church, and Newman had done more than any other author to recover the study of ancient fathers into English divinity and history. In 1836 Pusey and Keble and Newman began editing a library of the fathers, English translations of the main texts. The consensus of the fathers was the measure of Christian truth and practice. The high view of sacraments, and of the authority of bishops and ministry, the new interest in celibacy and mortification, were consciously based upon this appeal to the undivided church. Newman was soon aware that the fathers were a great pool in which swam many varieties of fish, not all savoury to modern palates.

In the number of the Roman Catholic journal *Dublin Review* published in August 1839 Wiseman drove home the judgment of the fathers. The Puseyites have appealed to antiquity and to antiquity they shall go. The fathers professed one axiom beyond others, that the church is one visible body. If there are two organised 'churches', each claiming to be the true Catholic church, the claim of one of them cannot be true. If you appeal to antiquity, you cannot pick and choose. You must allow that there can only be one true visible church, and so must join the Church of Rome.

Newman at first saw little in the article. But he talked of it with Robert Williams, the disciple who gave him most anxiety by confident assumption that the Church of Rome was right. Williams seized upon a phrase in the article, a judgment of St. Augustine upon the Church of Rome, *Securus judicat orbis terrarum* (the whole Christian world is assured of truth when it makes a judgment) and kept repeating the words till they rang in Newman's ears. Wiseman's point was sharp, and Newman took it to his belly. 'I must confess,' he told Rogers, 'it has given me a stomach-ache . . . It does certainly come upon one that we are not at the bottom of things. At this moment we have sprung a leak . . . It is no laughing matter . . . there is an uncomfortable vista opened which was closed before.' He used the same word *vista* to Henry Wilberforce as they walked in the New Forest.[1] Wilberforce understood him perfectly and felt fear like a thunderstroke. He said that he hoped Newman would rather die than become a Roman Catholic. If he were ever in serious danger, Newman replied, he thought of asking his friends to pray that he might be taken away before he took the step, unless that step was the wish of God.

The qualm was of the moment. Newman soon found his old assurance. If the fathers were decisive against the Church of England for schism, they were equally decisive against the Church of Rome for error. He comforted himself and his friends with an article to this effect in the *British Critic*, entitled 'The Catholicity of the Anglican Church'. But he was not quite the same. He said later that he had seen the shadow of a hand on the wall, and 'he who has seen a ghost cannot be as if he had never seen it'. His intellectual ground shifted. He had lately believed the Church of England to fail practically in reaching upwards to its Catholic heritage. Now he believed it wrong in theory; and the claim for it rested only on this, that everyone else was more wrong. This ground was unstable when he needed to help anxious minds. He discovered in himself a growing dislike of speaking against the Church of Rome, and asked himself whether only the Church of Rome was strong enough to defend religion against the league of liberal evil.[2]

In November 1840 happened the first of those secessions which Newman and Pusey awaited with foreboding. A young Englishman named John Biden, who was studying for ordination, visited an aunt in Bruges and there abjured the Protestant faith before a crowded congregation. He was neither an Oxford undergraduate nor known to any of the Oxford leaders. But he claimed to have been influenced by Pusey and said that he abstained for days from meat in order to buy Pusey's books and the fathers.[3] The question was before the public, whether the Oxford Movement led men towards popery or kept them away. On the one hand Puseyites evoked a type of devotion not then easy to express within the Church of England. They recommended a high view of celibate life to members of a church which contained no monasteries nor nunneries where the life might be practised. Casting

[1] *Dublin Review*, April 1869, 327–8; LC, ii, 287; *Apologia*, 120.
[2] *Apologia*, 121, 126; LC, ii, 300.
[3] T, 26 November 1840.

reproaches upon the Reformation, elevating the authority of the church, professing the utility of Catholic tradition, they diminished the obstacles to receiving Roman dogma. To the contrary it was argued that in the English scene of 1840 a demand for church authority was inevitable; that a church which by Parliament's action was ceasing to be national must be more aware of the universal Christian (as opposed to the national) inheritance; that the romantic literature and religious sentiment of the age must find expression in Catholic modes of prayer and mortification—in short, that Rome needed no stimulus from Puseyites to attract, and that Puseyites guided souls into a safer port.

In the summer of 1840 Newman bought ten acres and began to build a few cells at Littlemore; partly because he wanted to be away from the frigid air of Oxford, and partly because he was feeling his way towards a monastic community under rule.

Tract XC

The Thirty-nine Articles of the Church of England were a discomfort to Puseyites. This discomfort was not confined to Puseyites. For two hundred years the articles made members of the Church of England uneasy. A formula of the sixteenth or any other century, framed in the midst of dead controversies, must vex posterity if understood literally and in the original sense of the drafters. Since 1660 common sense demanded and accepted a wider liberty of interpretation than the drafters intended. The clergy subscribed the articles on taking office. But over doctrines of justification by faith and the authority of the church they retained much liberty. Some liberal divines, predecessors of Whately and Hampden, pushed liberty to the limit. The clergy, they said, were only required not to preach in contradiction of the articles. Everyone recognised that the courts preserved the threat of excluding from the ministry anyone whose teaching failed to conform to the articles. But the meaning put upon them by the subscriber must be left to his conscience.

In 1840 Archbishop Whately precipitated an argument over the articles by presenting a petition in the House of Lords. The petition carried thirty signatures of clergymen, Dr. Arnold among them ('not', said Arnold, 'that I believe it will do any good'), and thirty signatures of laymen. It complained of parts of the liturgy and articles, and asked the Lords to make the articles agree with the practice of the clergy.

Whately said that he agreed, but dissented from the view that the House of Lords had any business to tamper with the articles of the church. Archbishop Howley said that instead of making the articles and liturgy agree with the practice of the clergy it would be better to make the practice of the clergy agree with the articles and liturgy. There the matter might have ended; but an unlucky aside brought Bishop Stanley of Norwich to his feet and an unprepared speech. Stanley said that the Church of England had 'a sort of elasticity'; that the articles were framed upon a wide basis; that none pretended the clergy to agree in every part and every iota of their subscription; that because different minds are differently constituted everyone must be allowed a certain latitude. He misquoted with approval the words of the elder Pitt that the Church of England has a Calvinist creed and an Arminian liturgy.[1]

The words hurt the clergy. Bishop Blomfield rose in his seat to denounce them as a libel against the church. The clergy were never pleased at hints that inwardly they did not believe what outwardly they professed to believe. And a dictate by a bishop to Parliament that the articles were Calvinistic touched the Tractarians on their tenderest sore. It was bad that a prelate who patently did not believe the Calvinist doctrines should declare the official creed of the church to be Calvinistic. But a lot of clergy and divines would have challenged the statement by whomsoever it was uttered. And divines of the Oxford Movement, who believed that Protestants were not Catholics and that the Church of England was Catholic, must answer or perish.

The Oxford Movement was not friendly to liberty in dogma. The church had spoken. But the articles were the offspring of the Reformation and the Reformation was suspect. Examining the articles upon sacraments, future life, cult of saints, authority of the church, they found a discrepancy between their tone and the doctrines of the ancient Catholic church. If the Church of England was Catholic (that is,

---

[1] Hansard, liv, 552ff., 26 May 1840; cf. Kaye of Lincoln to Melbourne, 27 May 1840, MP; Melbourne to Kaye, 27 May 1840, MP, in which Melbourne deprecated as much as Kaye the idea that Parliament should tamper with articles and liturgy. Arnold was delighted with Edward Stanley's speech, Stanley, *Life of Arnold*, ii, 132, 219. The precise words of Pitt (Chatham) are now lost. The words are not recorded in the parliamentary history. The only early evidence is Horace Walpole's *Journal*, i (1910), 92: 'Their Thirty-nine Articles were Calvinistical, their creeds papistical, and both the church and dissenters were every day approaching nearer to Arminianism'. When Edmund Burke on 2 March 1790 (*Speeches*, iii, 1816, 474) summarised Chatham's speech he reported it as 'We have a Calvinistic creed, a popish liturgy, and an Arminian clergy'; and in this pithy form it was canonised.

faithful to the early and undivided church) its prayer book and articles must be interpreted in the light of antiquity and must be capable of being so interpreted. No one doubted the prayer book. Robert Williams and several others doubted the articles. Newman courageously essayed to treat the catholicity of the articles in a *Tract for the Times*. *Tract XC* was published on 27 February 1841. Newman did not expect it to attract notice.[1]

In the preface he declared his aim. The articles were formulated in an uncatholic age. Nevertheless by God's providence they are not uncatholic and may be subscribed by those who aim at being Catholic in heart and doctrine.

The tract took fourteen articles out of the thirty-nine, and treated them legally. Newman was not trying to reconcile the Church of England to the Church of Rome. He believed Rome to be in error. The articles taught, this tract showed, a number of doctrines which anyone else but Newman and Keble would have called Protestant—

that the church derives its faith wholly from scripture
that it is unlawful to kneel before images, light candles to them, go on pilgrimage to them or hang up crutches
that we are greatly offended at the received Roman view of transubstantiation
that the bread and wine remain in their natural substances
that no adoration ought to be done to the bread and wine there bodily received
that the papacy began in the exertions and passions of man; and what man can make, man can destroy.

It is odd that so Protestant a document should be accused of making it possible for English clergy to believe all the doctrines of the Roman Catholic Church.

Not even the university was accustomed to the word Catholic as not meaning Roman Catholic. They knew that Newman disliked the word Protestant and read in the tract that no Catholic need hesitate to subscribe the articles. The obvious meaning suggested that the articles were no barrier to Roman Catholic dogmas. And Newman added fuel by thinking the articles imperfect. During the previous ten

---

[1] LC, ii, 326. Keble read the proofs and was enthusiastic, Liddon, ii, 171; Isaac Williams read the proofs and tried to dissuade Newman from publishing, *Autobiog.*, 108.

years liberals made several pleas that the articles should be improved and redrafted by act of Parliament. The prospect of an O'Connell-infested Commons altering the doctrines of the Church of England caused the clergy to tremble with ire and anxiety. Newman and the Tractarians (as with contemporaries we may henceforth call them) stood square against this liberal plea. In *Tract XC* he protested again that Parliament must not alter the articles. But he evidently expected the church to alter the articles when the church of the future came by grace to agree. Meanwhile, he said in his most offensive sentence, 'let the church sit still; let her be content to be in bondage; let her work in chains; let her submit to her imperfections as a punishment; let her go on teaching with the stammering lips of ambiguous formularies . . .'; and he called the articles a body of death and a penalty of sins.

The sections of the tract which beyond other sections offended the enemy and dismayed the friend treated article XXII on purgatory and article XXXI on the sacrifice of masses. Here analysis of the literal phrase looked like evasion of the plain meaning. The articles condemning the Romish doctrine of purgatory could not be directed against the Roman Catholic doctrine formulated in the Council of Trent, since Trent had defined nothing when the article was drafted. To condemn the sacrifice of masses was not to condemn the sacrifice of the mass.

Golightly read *Tract XC* with horror. He went round Oxford waving it about, went into Parker's, bought almost all the copies, posted them to all the bishops, inviting them to condemn. He tried to see the rector of Exeter and was refused admittance, saw the warden of Wadham and gained him to the cause. Several tutors refused him their aid, the four tutors of Wadham (Griffiths), Balliol (Tait), Brasenose (Churton) and St. John's (H. B. Wilson) agreed upon a letter to the press. Griffiths was a zealot and Wilson a crank. The names of weight were Churton and Tait. Tait drafted the letter;[1] and all his life, even when he was Archbishop of Canterbury, long memories reproached him for 'hounding' Newman out of Oxford.

The four tutors declared in ugly English that *Tract XC* was dangerous because it mitigated the serious differences which separated the Church of England from the Church of Rome. Admitting the necessity of liberty in interpretation, they saw no security, if this proposed

[1] Liddon, ii, 167. Tait's correspondence over *Tract XC* is in Tait MSS., 77, 1–56.

latitude were allowed, against the teaching of Roman Catholic doctrine in the Church of England. They demanded the name of the
author. On 12 March 1841 all the heads of houses except Routh of
Magdalen and Richards of Exeter, who invariably backed Newman,
and Hampden of St. Mary Hall and Macbride of Magdalen Hall,
who were ill, resolved to censure the tract.

It was not easy. Senior members of the university wished the
reputation of Oxford to be cleared by a formal act rejecting Newman.
Such a formal act ought to proceed from convocation, the assembly
of all senior members. But in convocation non-residents possessed
votes. From all they heard of country clergy the heads were not sure
that they would win if they proposed a vote condemning Newman.
On 16 March 1841 the vice-chancellor published in the press a declaration of the hebdomadal board that the *Tracts* were in no way sanctioned by the university and that the suggested modes of interpretation
evaded the sense of the articles and were inconsistent with due observance of the statutes of the university. The popular press was less
dignified and less analytical. 'According to the authors of the *Tracts*,'
wrote the *Morning Chronicle*, 'we are all good papists without knowing it.' The defences between Lambeth and the Vatican were imaginary. 'I fear', wrote Newman to his sister, 'I am clean dished.' On the
same day, 16 March, he wrote to the vice-chancellor declaring what
nearly everyone knew, that he was the sole author of the tract.[1]

He had backers. Any corporate act by heads of colleges in an
ancient English university was likely to excite antagonism on constitutional grounds. Oxford men who had no sympathy for Newman
blamed the heads for acting beyond their powers. If the tract was to
be censured, it should be censured by convocation, and the heads
could no more commit the university than the tract-writers themselves. A number of Tories began to rally when Whig and radical
newspapers turned the quarrel over divinity into politics. Oxford
university was a bastion of the Tory party as well as of the church.
When the *Morning Chronicle* of 27 March cried that the alliance of
church with Tory party was shattered by the Puseyites and that
shovel hats would no longer serve for the eagles of Tory warfare,
the Tory press was sent to damp down the fires of controversy. Keble

---

[1] MC, 11 March 1841; LC, ii, 326. Golightly had told the bishops, in sending them
the tract, that Newman was certainly the author; cf. Golightly to Bishop Blomfield,
March 1841, Golightly Papers, box 1.

agreed in almost everything with Newman and wrote to the vice-chancellor accordingly. Pusey, though disliking some of Newman's language, worked earnestly and unavailingly on his behalf in Oxford, but Pusey's earnest support always harmed a cause. William Palmer of Worcester College, who since Froude's *Remains* refused to co-operate with the Tractarian leaders, now wrote to say how much he valued *Tract XC*. Arthur Perceval declared his public aid. From Leeds Walter Hook, who began by privately regretting the tract and disapproving its tone, was so irritated by the proceedings against Newman that, as he said, 'I have nailed my colours to the mast, and intend to stand by Newman'.[1] Newman helped himself by publishing (16 March) a letter to Dr. Jelf in which he clarified misunderstanding, and by preparing a second edition of *Tract XC* which omitted the offensive phrase 'the stammering lips of ambiguous formularies'.

Liberal divines were long accustomed to exercise liberty in interpreting and subscribing the Thirty-nine Articles. They disliked Newman's *Tracts*, none more. But if the quarrel over the tract ended in attempts to prevent liberty of interpretation, they knew where they stood. 'Seriously,' wrote Arthur Stanley from Rome to Tait, a little shocked at hearing what Tait was doing, '. . . do not draw these articles too tight, or they will strangle more parties than one. I assure you, when I read the monition of the heads I felt the halter at my own throat.'[2] If to censure Newman narrowed the terms of subscription, liberals would defend, not Newman's interpretation, but Newman's right to interpret. The heads were wise not to risk a vote in convocation.

Conservatives wanted to stop these opinions being lawful within the established church. They could be declared unlawful by decision of the university, guardian of Anglican divinity; but the decision would be like the barking of a chained watchdog. They could be declared unlawful by a united act of the bishops. The act would lack legal force, but would weigh heavy upon sensitive consciences, especially consciences of men who preached apostolic succession. The illegality of *Tract XC* could be established only by prosecuting Newman in court. As incumbent of a benefice (St. Mary's, Oxford) he could be prosecuted if his bishop were complaisant. And thus Bishop Bagot of Oxford, no divine but courteous aristocratic Tory pluralist,

---

[1] Stephens, i, 366.
[2] Davidson-Benham, i, 93.

became important. He was bombarded with letters demanding that popish Newman be suppressed.

Bishop Bagot preferred peace and found the affair of *Tract XC* tiresome. Bishop from an older age of tranquillity, he never felt at home among democrats and Whig reformers. He thought Newman wrong to cause controversy, but preferred Newman to Ecclesiastical Commissioners. With an irritated mildness he began by asking Newman not to discuss the Thirty-nine Articles in *Tracts for the Times*. Newman was relieved at this mildness and cheerfully promised. Four days later Archbishop Howley intervened. He told Bishop Bagot that it was most desirable to discontinue the *Tracts*. Under this august pressure Bishop Bagot asked that *Tract XC* be suppressed; that the series of *Tracts* should cease; and that Newman should tell the world that he suppressed them at the request of his bishop.[1]

Newman's hackles rose in resentment against Archbishop Howley. He contemplated obeying, but threatened to resign.

Bishop Bagot yielded a little, and Howley agreed with his yielding. It was simply arranged that the *Tracts* should cease; and that Newman should write a public letter to the bishop making clear his continued antagonism to the Church of Rome, and declaring that he ended the series because the bishop required it. In return the bishop would refrain from any censure upon the *Tracts* in general or *Tract XC* in particular.

Newman's spirits rose again. The extended liberty of interpretation was achieved. Near-Romanisers would not leave the Church of England because its articles were impossible to reconcile with the Catholic faith. Even into his letter to Bishop Bagot he managed, as he wrote to Keble, to wedge in a good many bits of Catholicism.[2] Pusey said that people would abuse *Tract XC* and adopt its main principles.

Despite his resilience it was hardly a victory. If the bishop of his own diocese refrained from condemning *Tract XC*, there were other bishops in the Church of England. Some were silent, some discouraged their clergy from agitating. But not many. The Archbishop of Armagh told his clergy that the Bishop of Oxford joined the censure of the Oxford heads and condemned the tract as evasive; Bishop Sumner of Chester condemned nine specific interpretations suggested as permissible in the *Tracts*; Bishop Monk of Gloucester shared the popular

---

[1] Liddon, ii, 185–90.
[2] LC, ii, 341: the letter was published on 31 March; Ornsby, i, 261.

opinion that the author wanted to reconcile the Church of England to the Church of Rome; Bishop Wilson of Calcutta called the tract one of the most dishonourable efforts of sophistry ever witnessed in theological discussions;[1] Bishop Phillpotts of Exeter, who of all bishops might be expected to be friendly, but never in his life hesitated for an opinion, regarded the phrase 'stammering lips of ambiguous formularies' as a way of jeering at the Church of England. The first question asked of Keble's curate was 'What is your mode of interpreting the Thirty-nine Articles?' and Bishop Sumner of Winchester refused to ordain him priest. The provost of Oriel refused testimonials to ordinands if they would not repudiate *Tract XC*.

'We are ducks in a pond,' Newman told his sister Jemima, 'knocked over but not knocked out.'[2] He told Keble to remember that the clergy left off wigs before the bishops. If he thought that by persuading Bishop Bagot not to condemn he won liberty of interpretation, his followers were not agreed. Unaware of the subtleties of diplomacy between bishop and divine, they saw only that the *Tracts* were ended on account of *Tract XC*. The *Tracts* were a public symbol of the movement. Why, asked his supporters, all these concessions? Why this timidity, apology, humiliation? Why were opponents allowed to boast that the *Tracts* were censured? Why, when they had nothing to be ashamed of, was Newman letting church principles be disgraced? The suppression of the *Tracts* looked like confessing error on top of weakness. So far from losing the stains of its Protestantism, the Church of England looked more Protestant than before. The Roman Catholic priest in Oxford, Newsham, reported that forty undergraduates came to question him.[3]

The battle over *Tract XC* ended Newman's usefulness to the Church of England.

Later he claimed in the *Apologia* that this crisis did not unsettle him. He had weathered the storm and his tract had not been condemned. His silencing he rather attributed to the charges of the bishops that summer, to the Jerusalem bishopric of that autumn, and to the inward movement of his mind. His contemporary letters show that his soul

---

[1] Sumner's charge of 1841, no. 4; Monk's charge of 1841; Wilson's charge of 1842; Phillpotts's charge of 1842; Bricknell, 533, 537, 541, 547.

[2] Keble to Newman, 19 July 1841, LC, ii, 343, 350; M. Trevor, i, 254.

[3] W. Palmer (of Worcester College) to Pusey, 1 April 1841, Liddon, ii, 205; Trevor, i, 260.

continued to be unsettled. He received intellectual blows from academic pursuits, like the study of the ancient Arians, which would have disturbed no settled mind. He still regarded himself as an Anglican and a leader. But his assurance was gone, his sensitivity was rising to the surface, he was a leader eschewing the responsibility of leading. By the end of that year, he said later, he was on his death-bed as an Anglican, though he realised it but slowly.

The Jerusalem bishopric

In October 1841 the British government and the Prussian king together sanctioned a Protestant bishop in Jerusalem. At bottom this plan was part of British and German policy in the middle east. The powers were manoeuvring for the loot which lay about as Turkey collapsed. The protection of Christians in decaying Turkey had long been an instrument of Russian and French policy. Russia protected the Orthodox, France the Roman Catholics. Britain and Prussia, whose political interests in the middle east were considerable, determined to protect the Protestants.[1] In these high policies of state it mattered little that Turkey contained no Protestants to protect; except a little congregation of six inhabitants, and a few visitors, gathered illegally in Jerusalem by the evangelical London Society for promoting Christianity among the Jews.

The Archbishop of Canterbury was not so complaisant as he looked and would not have sanctioned a crude act of state policy. Higher considerations entered the mind of Howley. In England he was pressed by Lord Ashley and the evangelicals who studied the apocalyptic books and hoped for a Christian Palestine at last. Ashley's mind united the practical with the prophetic in a fascinating harmony. He wrote a memorandum for the foreign secretary, based upon religion and apocalypse but supported by prudent reasons of commerce and politics. Then the Prussian diplomat, Chevalier Bunsen, intervened with a plan which achieved the aims of the British government without cost. His sovereign, King Frederick William IV of Prussia, wanted the union of the Protestant churches. To this end he wished to introduce bishops into Germany. To harmonise these various interests—British power and prestige in the Levant, Prussian power and prestige in the Levant, Prussian desire for Protestant unity, evangelical plan to convert the Jews—Bunsen proposed that the suggested

[1] Tibawi, 33; Hansard, lvii, 142, 608; Hodder, i, 233–5, 310–15.

bishopric be Anglo-German, and that Britain and Prussia join in compelling Turkey to recognise Protestantism as a legal religion.

In July 1841 the British government, Archbishop Howley and Bishop Blomfield accepted Bunsen's proposal.[1] The British ambassador in Constantinople was ordered to demand recognition of Protestants. Ashley selected the bishop:[2] Michael Solomon Alexander, born a Prussian Jew, professor of Hebrew at King's College, London. Since the bishop was not in British territory, Parliament passed a short act empowering the archbishops to consecrate bishops in any foreign country to exercise spiritual jurisdiction over Anglican clergy and congregations, or over other Protestant communities which might wish to place themselves under their authority. Under the agreement the bishop was to be consecrated by English bishops, and nominated alternately by the crown of Britain and the crown of Prussia. The Archbishop of Canterbury possessed a veto upon the Prussian nominee. German congregations were allowed their own form of service, but the clergy must be ordained by the Anglican rite. The King of Prussia gave £15,000 in capital to pay half the bishop's stipend, and the English subscribed to give the other half.[3]

Alexander was consecrated in Lambeth palace chapel on 7 November 1841, in the presence of Bunsen, Gladstone, Ashley and Sir Stratford Canning, the new ambassador to Constantinople. Under pressure from Ashley, who wanted a demonstration of British might, the admiralty was authorised to carry him to Palestine. They offered the frigate *Infernal*. Alexander refused to travel in a warship of this name, but did not object when they substituted the frigate *Devastation*.[4]

So unique a venture in ecclesiastical order did not go forward without enemies in Turkey, Germany and England.

The Turks had refused leave for a Protestant church and took less kindly to a Protestant bishop. They withheld their recognition. They had difficulty in keeping the peace of Jerusalem amid the rivalries of Orthodox and Latin, and were not eager to add another community of Christians. They reasonably suspected the bishop to be an agent of British power and an excuse for interference. They were prodded in their antagonism by Roman Catholic fears of incoming Protestant

---

[1] Negotiations described by R. W. Greaves in EHR, July 1949, 328.
[2] *Memoir of Bunsen*, i, 609.
[3] List of trustees and subscribers, *Times*, 17 November 1841.
[4] Tibawi, 51.

missionaries. French agents in Constantinople or Jerusalem did what they could to discourage the Turks. The Turkish envoy in London made several protests to the foreign office. Orthodox bishops of the east were resentful at the appearance of a new bishop in a much-bishopped land. The British authorities needed to provide many assurances. The foreign secretary (now Lord Aberdeen) told the Turkish envoy that the British were asking no special privileges for the bishop, but only the rights of every British citizen in Turkey; that he was strictly enjoined not to attempt to convert to the Church of England either Mohammedans or other Christian subjects of the Turks.[1] Archbishop Howley gave a similar assurance to the Orthodox prelates. These assurances narrowed the scope of Alexander's work. He was limited to the Jews, ten thousand in number and not readily convertible, and to the handful of Protestants. It was agreed that he should be entitled, not Bishop of Jerusalem, but Bishop of the united Church of England and Ireland in Jerusalem.[2] The foreign office was nervous that he might try to convert the Jews. The trumpeted bishopric became ridiculous.

Reformed Germans protested that alliance with so corrupt a church as the English stained the purity of German faith, and justly suspected Frederick William of a secret desire to introduce bishops into the Prussian church. Most English churchmen were friendly, and the plan divided the Tractarians. Hook supported it fervently, William Palmer of Worcester College defended it, Pusey knew Bunsen and hoped that it might indeed lead to bishops in the Prussian church.[3] But some high churchmen were uneasy that the Church of England was being committed to a revolutionary act of ecclesiastical communion on the sole authority of the foreign secretary, the archbishop and the Bishop of London. Few other bishops knew what was happening; and it is a tribute to the veneration so many of them felt for Howley that no bishop publicly expressed scruples on the score of authority. To meet private scruples it was written into the articles of agreement that the bishopric was provisional until a meeting of the English bishops. But since the English bishops could not meet until after the bishop was consecrated and money collected, this article was waste paper. Blomfield maintained that the article did not demand the later agreement

[1] Tibawi, 55.

[2] *Memoir of Bunsen*, i, 627; Howley to Frederick William IV, 18 June 1842, H. Smith, *The Protestant Bishopric in Jerusalem*, 1847, 90–91.

[3] LC, ii, 378; Liddon, ii, 250–1.

of the English bishops, but only a later announcement to the English bishops by Archbishop Howley.[1]

Newman had a horror of continental Protestants. Gladstone afterwards thought that the Jerusalem bishopric lost Newman to the Church of England.[2] Newman's recollections do not quite confirm this simple view. But it helped to destroy his faith in English bishops. Nine years before he had seen Archbishop Howley treading meek and brave amid the catcalls and howls of the mob. Unlike most churchmen, Newman and the group round him now ceased to revere Howley. In October 1841 he said: 'Now the bishops are at their worst.' Four weeks later he wrote to his sister accusing Howley of doing all he could to unchurch the Church of England.[3] Bunsen's large language about a church which would supersede existing churches made him aghast. The Germans were not popular among English churchmen. 'I utterly distrust you Germans,' said Hope courteously to one of them.[4] Newman called the bishopric miserable, fearful, atrocious. A friend who returned from Jerusalem told him that there were no Englishmen and less than six converted Anglican Jews. After much foreboding, and realising that he had nothing to lose, he sent the Bishop of Oxford a public protest, that 'Lutheranism and Calvinism are heresies, repugnant to Scripture . . . and anathematised by east as well as west'. Pusey was converted to Newman's side, but still refused to think it right to call Lutheranism heretical. Keble thought the protest disrespectful and better not published.[5] Bishop Blomfield talked about infatuation and said that Newman and his friends laboured under a nervous excitement which vitiated their judgment on every question. He remarked to Howley: 'We have been worse treated by the Oxford writers than we have ever been by the evangelical party in the whole course of our government in the church.' The archbishop assented.[6]

At this point the Prussian king became a royal godfather. In November 1841 the queen was safely delivered of the future King

[1] Ornsby, i, 296. Phillpotts objected to friends, ibid., ii, 4, 14.
[2] Ornsby, ii, 282.
[3] Newman to Hope (Scott), 17 October 1841, Oriel: Ornsby, i, 301; LC, ii, 352, wrongly dated.
[4] Ornsby, i, 292.
[5] LC, ii, 362-5.
[6] Liddon, ii, 253, 275. Bishop Alexander died in 1845. His successor Gobat was appointed amid similar protests, including a public protest from Bishop Phillpotts; and his conduct in Palestine continued to cause epidemic trouble.

Edward VII. Amid public rejoicing sounded notes of ecclesiastical anxiety. When it was stated that the prince would follow the old aristocratic custom of England and be baptised privately, Peel and Howley remonstrated with Prince Albert that the interests of religion and propriety required baptism in church.[1] Then there was question whether the Dean of Windsor would resist the archbishop's right to christen in his church. Then the privy council ordered the prince's name to be inserted in the liturgy after the name of Prince Albert, causing stiff clergymen to question whether such an insertion could be fitting before the baby was a Christian. Then it was announced that the King of Prussia was to be sponsor, causing Keble and some Tractarians to rise in public protest. As the little queen of England and the portly king of Prussia walked together after breakfast at Windsor, Bishop Blomfield remarked: 'The Reformed Church was seen on the terrace.' Finally the child was christened in St. George's, Windsor, and behaved with princely decorum through the sacrament and the Hallelujah chorus. Archbishop Howley infected the bystanders with such trepidation that the Duchess of Buccleuch feared lest the baby pull off his wig, and reached deep into his bosom to secure her charge.[2]

The retirement of Newman

In the month of the royal christening Newman fought the painters out of Littlemore and retired there to make his home.

He professed to want the chance of a more severe and prayerful life. He moved his library into the row of stables.

Rumours about Littlemore were already rife. It was said to be planned as a college for teaching Newman's version of popery. With a pun upon the Irish seminary at Maynooth, someone nicknamed it unwittily Newmanooth.[3] When he moved into the buildings the press printed rumours of an Anglo-Catholic monastery with cells, dormitories, chapel, refectory, cloisters. It was a grandiloquent description of Newman's row of converted stables. Oxford walked or rode out to see what was happening. Coming back one day, he found a flight of undergraduates inside. If Newman was building an Anglican monastery, everyone wanted to know what an Anglican monastery was like. Even the master of Balliol and warden of Wadham, hostile doctors, could not check their inquisitiveness and poked about the

---

[1] e.g. Add. MSS. 40495, 289–91.   [2] *Letters of Sarah Lady Lyttelton*, 324–6.
[3] S, 4 December 1841: 9 April 1842.

building uninvited.[1] Bishop Bagot demanded an assurance that he was not attempting to revive the monastic orders 'in anything approaching to the Romanist interpretation of the term'. Newman cheerfully gave the assurance. He told Bishop Bagot that his 'cloisters' were a shed connecting the cottages.[2]

On 23 May 1842 Bishop Bagot delivered a fateful charge in St. Mary's Church. He dreaded the day when he must speak about the *Tracts*, but could avoid it no longer. He called the Tractarians the most remarkable movement of the last three centuries, though exposed to calumnies of the most wanton and cruel description and to attacks from the dissenting, democratic and infidel press clothed in language which he would not trust himself to characterise; praised their stern call to discipline and self-denial and prayer, their love of external reverence and deference to authority; appealed for forbearance, and upheld their moderation in refraining from railing in answer to railing; said that despite faults and errors the *Tracts* had been beneficial.

He turned to the inescapable reproaches. He thought them to be obscure, and too indifferent to the discord and crisis which they caused. When he came to *Tract XC* he suddenly spoke out. It was objectionable and regrettable. He confessed that Calvinists had done worse in interpreting the articles, but believed the plain and obvious meaning to be the sense which members of the church were bound to receive. 'I cannot reconcile myself to a system of interpretation which is so subtle, that by it the articles may be made to mean anything or nothing.' Nevertheless, if the articles might be construed not to force Calvinists to leave the Church of England, they might surely be construed not to force out those whose opinions agreed with the anti-puritan divines.

Bagot passed to rebuke special acts of indiscretion. It was worse than folly to cause dissension by vestments. The anathema upon Protestantism (hurled by William Palmer of Magdalen) showed a lamentable want of humility, charity and judgment. The Reformers were frail and fallible men, but the church owed them much and the tone of hostility towards them was deplorable. The use of Roman Catholic devotions encouraged the young to be dissatisfied with their

---

[1] Dessain, xiv, 52; cf. *Apologia*, 166.

[2] *Apologia*, 167; LC, ii, 396. Kindly Bishop Bagot replied that his letter proved the charges to be calumny, and that he much approved his residing at Littlemore, which needed a pastor.

liturgy. To prevent this discontent they must see that the liturgy is reverently and prayerfully celebrated, churches no longer left to damp and dilapidation, rubrics of fast and festival observed, almsgiving increased, priesthood holy; and then Catholic aspirations and longings will find safe and sufficient vent in the Church of England.

Newman sat listening in St. Mary's and was pleased. The bishop not only condemned Golightly but spoke fairly, even generously, of the influence and ideals of the movement. But he was nervous of what the bishop said about *Tract XC*. His friends afterwards said that they understood the bishop to condemn the tract as making the articles mean anything or nothing.[1] Newman would not believe the bishop to have said it. He argued that the bishop condemned all interpretations which made the articles mean anything or nothing, not this particular interpretation. But he waited anxiously for the printed edition. Nearly a month later he still professed himself pleased with the charge. But something about the words rankled. A year before he had agreed to end the *Tracts* on the understanding that *Tract XC* was not condemned. Were not these words of the charge a breach of the understanding? But he was charitable to the bishop. 'The tide', he told Manning, 'was too strong for him.'[2]

By going to Littlemore Newman left the Oxford Movement headless. He was still a figurehead and symbol, but he ceased to guide events or divinity, as one who retired to the desert and fell on his knees. He still wanted to present the fathers to the Church of England, studied St. Athanasius, wrote for the *Lives of the Saints*, translated Fleury's church history, published an *Essay on ecclesiastical miracles* which showed his mind at its most tortuous and uncritical. Young men came to join him. The first was the immature enthusiast John Dobrée Dalgairns, the second William Lockhart, whom his family sent in hope that Newman would prevent him becoming a Roman Catholic. Newman received him on the sole condition that he stayed for three years. A third arrived in December 1842, the fourth in the summer of 1843. The fourth was older than the others: Ambrose St. John, aged 28, who at last filled in Newman's life the gap of affection left by Hurrell Froude. Many others came to stay for a day or few days, among them Mark Pattison and James Anthony Froude,

---

[1] Bagot's chaplain, F. E. Paget, told Bagot casually that *Tract XC* made the articles mean anything or nothing. Bagot adopted the words formally into the charge, to Paget's lasting regret. Paget to Eden, 24 January 1879, Liddon, ii, 286.

[2] Newman to Manning, 14 October 1843, *Apologia*, 202; cf. LC, ii, 398.

Hurrell's younger brother. Willy-nilly Newman became a kind of father superior. They lived simply, kept the monastic offices and a rule which in Lent was severe. Austerities increased till they acquired, not without embarrassment, hairshirts and a scourge from Belgium.

The world outside waited for Newman to announce that he was a Roman Catholic. The head of an Oxford college told Pusey in the summer of 1842 that it was soon to happen.[1] Wiseman and other Roman Catholics confidently awaited it. They waited long. Golightly and the more excitable newspapers inferred that Newman delayed because he wished to teach Roman Catholic faith surreptitiously in the Church of England, a spider gathering Protestant flies into his web.

A clergyman in Lincolnshire, Bernard Smith, suddenly became a Roman Catholic in January 1843, and it was untruly reported that Newman advised him to continue in his parish to pervert his people. In February 1843 Newman publicly withdrew his hard sayings against the Church of Rome. Few could understand why he did not go unless the reason were underhand. In March 1843 the vicar of Cheltenham, Francis Close, said at a public dinner that he would not trust the author of *Tract XC* with his purse. Travelling in a train from London, Newman heard a passenger quoting a Durham divine as saying: 'Depend on it, Newman, Newman is a Jesuit, a Jesuit.'[2]

Still the world waited. Newman was fastened to his place by an anchor of the intellect. If his argument contrasted the Church of England with antiquity to the discredit of the Church of England, it made a similar contrast to the discredit of the Church of Rome. Dr. Russell of Maynooth college sent him a pile of little devotional works which showed him that he judged harshly of Roman popular devotions. He knew that he was a Roman in his heart. But somehow he needed to see the Roman church as the single and authentic representative of the primitive church. Before the end of 1842 Ward began to talk and write about the idea of development. That winter Newman started to think seriously about its application to the history of the church.

The difficulty was not only intellectual. He loathed O'Connell and could hardly bear the prospect of joining a church which allied with Irish agitators. His security and comfort depended on being an Anglican. He could not resign St. Mary's in Oxford without also resigning the chapel at Littlemore which he had built and the people

[1] Liddon, ii, 292.   [2] Trevor, i, 286, 333.

to whom he was attached. It was not likely that a successor would allow him to go on at Littlemore. He tried to persuade the provost of Oriel to separate St. Mary's from Littlemore, but in vain. So he hung on, not clear that he should go, not clear that he should stay, until in August 1843 Lockhart broke his promise to stay three years and became a Roman Catholic. Then Newman knew that he could no longer hold St. Mary's. On 18 September he resigned. He preached his last sermon at St. Mary's on Sunday, 24 September, and his last at Littlemore, the famous sermon on *The Parting of Friends*, on Monday, 25 September. It is the crown of pathos, a lovely and poetic lamentation; but with the children, whom he had catechised and who could answer in chorus on the nine orders of angels, in new frocks and bonnets given by himself as a parting gift, with the offertory for new seats, and with a church full of villagers for whose souls he had long been responsible, it rings dramatic.[1]

The retirement of Newman spelled disaster to the Oxford Movement.

The Tractarians lost the single bold and original mind which they then possessed. The national influence of the movement was symbolised in Newman. The parochial sermons of St. Mary's, bound in successive volumes, were taken into many vicarages and some pulpits. The name of Newman rang with the ideals of self-sacrifice which his sermons propagated. He seemed to call the church to a higher life. With the confidence of one under authority he proclaimed the faith of the universal church and pointed to a treasure of sacrament and obedience after which men must reach. His dogma was too dogmatic for the followers of Arnold, too unprotestant for the evangelicals; and the tortuousness of *Tract XC* lost him some of his natural followers. But the retirement, amid sinister rumours, looked like a profession of failure. The morale of the Tractarians sank. And as always when morale collapses, the ranks of the party quarrelled and fell into confusion. Recrimination took the place of assurance.

The Tractarian mind looked for leadership from the two others, Keble and Pusey. And these two men had the merit of being almost unmoved by ill-repute. They were anxious, but their anxiety was tempered by a religious doctrine that truth will be unpopular. A church will only be loved by the world if it conforms to the world.

---

[1] The best description is by Bellasis in *Memorials of Mr. Serjeant Bellasis*, 52; cf. *Letters of J. B. Mozley*, 103; Robert Gregory, *Autobiography* (1912), 28.

They turned away from the social esteem of an older clergy. In identifying democrats with mobs they were not fond of public applause. Keble courted no popularity and in his quiet retirement faced little unpopularity. Pusey intended to court no unpopularity, but was so poor a judge of public prudence that he faced obloquy. Keble and Pusey at least had a stability. But as leaders of a party neither could compare with Newman. Keble's name was beautiful among high churchmen, but beautiful with the sound of poetry, of simple ministration in a country parish, of a character quaint and pure and naïve. He had neither the force of mind nor the breadth of vision to guide the troubled high churchmen of that day. Pusey could do more. By his public stature and by the nickname bestowed upon the Oxford writers, he inherited the mantle of leadership which Newman threw aside. If Newman had faults as head of a party, they were trivial to Pusey's. Ten years earlier Pusey might have managed better. In 1839 his wife died and left him a changed man. Many years passed before he entered the drawing-room of his own house. He wore crape upon his hat till he died, could not cross Tom Quad without a mental vision of the pall of her coffin fluttering in the breeze, would not dine out or in hall. He tried to see her death as punishment for his past sin, and his strictness and austerity were melancholy. He kept his eyes down when walking, used a hard seat by day and a hard bed by night, repressed all humour, resolved never to look at a beauty of nature without an expression of unworthiness, refused to wear gloves though his hands were liable to chilblains, made an act of internal humiliation when college servants or undergraduates saluted him, and prayed daily for gravity. He made Keble his confessor and asked to be allowed not to smile except with young children or in a matter of love. At one corner of the most splendid college in Oxford he practised the life of a hermit, with its remoteness and strictness, prayerful contemplation, command over select hearts, affection and simplicity, failure to understand the world or to influence the generality of men. It should rightly have been said of Pusey, what was later said of Christopher Wordsworth, that he had one foot in heaven and the other foot in the third century A.D. The Tractarians justly venerated his sanctity and disregarded his judgment.[1]

---

[1] 'Who be that . . .?' asked a village girl after service when Pusey preached at Horfield: 'a monstrous nice man but dreadful long.'

'Don't you know?' replied her friend: 'it is that Mr. Pewdsey, who is such a friend to the pope. But come along, or we'll be late for tea.' *Rural Rides*, by a Churchgoer (1847), 230.

Into the vacuum of leadership sprang lesser men. The Tractarian name was further damned in the public eye when Newman gave place to successors of paradox or fanaticism. If Newman refused to speak, some of his friends and followers supplied the need with zest. If the world accused Oxford divinity of damning Protestantism, Oxford men were willing to accept the challenge and invoke anathemas upon Protestants. Men who were publicly told that they had no place in the Church of England stood more hesitantly to their allegiance. During the summer of 1841 the Tractarian ranks publicly divided in their opinion of the Reformation. Pusey believed the Reformation to be an act of providence which helped the Church of England to remain Catholic, and was shocked to discover that Newman was as hostile as Froude. The younger disciples followed Newman in regarding the Church of England as rather harmed than improved by the Reformation, and went beyond him in saying that England had as much to learn from Rome as Rome from England. Out on a peninsula stood the odder William Palmer, of Magdalen College, who identified Protestantism with dissent and hurled excommunications at name and thing.

The Romanising group was led by two fellows of Balliol College, Frederick Oakeley and William George Ward. Their organ was the *British Critic*, now out of Newman's direct control and edited by his brother-in-law, Tom Mozley. In a series of pamphlets ostensibly defending *Tract XC*, and in the July number of the *British Critic*, Oakeley and Ward began a crusade against the Reformers. The Reformation, whatever its overruled benefits, was the origin of deplorable schism. Rome has imperishable claims upon our gratitude, and were it so ordered, upon our deference; is our mother in the faith; for her sins and for our own we are estranged from her in presence, not in heart; may we never be provoked to forget her, or cease to love her even though she frown upon us. The Thirty-nine Articles were constructed with an eye to comprehending all Roman Catholics except those who maintained the Pope to be lawful primate of Christendom. The Protestant doctrine of justification is heretical and unchristian. The Church of Rome has held up higher patterns of evangelical sanctity than any other church of modern times. . . . Pusey, distressed and vexed at the language, told Newman that Ward and Oakeley undermined the pillars of the Church of England by speaking as though the Church of England threw out a rope to drowning men and simultaneously doubting whether the rope would hold.[1]

Oakeley was quiet and gentle, Ward was neither. Ward had the ablest mind which Newman succeeded in converting. With a clumsy cumbersome frame, awkward hands incapable of tying knots or sealing envelopes, dress awry, and lumbering ungainly walk, he disliked his body and was full aware that it housed a clever intelligence. His mental background was liberal and utilitarian, and unlike so many of the Tractarian leaders contained none of the evangelical inheritance. So far as he owed anything to Anglican divines before he met Newman, they were liberals who attracted him, logic of Whately and ethical power of Arnold. He hammered away in dialectical conversation, giving his opponent the feeling of being a bit of paper blown up a chimney, revelling in paradox and shock, the liveliest conversationalist in Oxford, a logician who loved music and natural beauty but had no vein of poetic language; a believer in advancing truth by argument and therefore unique among Tractarian leaders in maintaining lively friendships with colleagues who hated his principles. His pupil Clough the poet never recovered firm ground after being plunged into the vortex of Ward's company.

Ward began by despising Newman's irrational or anti-rational streak, and the antiquarian dry-as-dust side of the Tractarian appeal to the fathers, until he heard a sermon which enchained him with its moral power. Disliking the Reformation on the older liberal grounds, he read Froude's *Remains*, admired the frankness and extremism, and was drawn into the Tractarian movement because it protested against the Reformation. On a Sunday in the summer of 1839 he walked out to Littlemore church with his pupil Benjamin Jowett, preached a printed sermon by Arnold with additions and alterations which, as he said, it would have driven Arnold mad to hear, and walked back in the twilight singing airs from *Don Giovanni*.[2]

Bored with Anglican sermons and patient of Anglican prayers, Ward pursued the doctrine that the Church of England needed to learn from the Church of Rome. When he was ordained deacon he subscribed the Thirty-nine Articles (not without question from his

---

[1] Oakeley in BC, July 1841, 1–3, 27; *The Subject of Tract XC Examined*, 14–16; Ward, *A Few More Words in Support of No. 90*, 71–80; Pusey to Newman, 20 July 1841, Liddon, ii, 219.

[2] Jowett's reminiscences in Ward, *W. G. Ward and the Oxford Movement*, 113.

tutor, Oakeley) in the liberal sense of Arnold; when he was ordained priest two and a half years later he subscribed them in the Catholic sense of Newman.[1] He therefore welcomed *Tract XC* as the best publication yet to appear from Newman's pen. After the censure of the heads he resigned his share in the tutors' work at Balliol because his own master was one of the heads. After his second pamphlet in defence of *Tract XC* he was required to resign his logical and mathematical lectureships at Balliol. 'What *heresy* may he not insinuate', the master is said to have exclaimed, 'under the form of a syllogism?'[2] Newman never intended *Tract XC* to enable Roman Catholics to subscribe the Thirty-nine Articles. Newman's enemies clamoured that this was its effect. Ward rapidly moved to the view that this was not only its effect but its great merit.

The crusade against Reformers, and the charges of Romanising flung hither and thither, weakened the force of Oxford in the movement. Its collapse was manifest when the *British Critic*, in the hands of the extreme party, was forced (1843) to cease publication because steady high churchmen refused to subscribe.

Other eyes than those of clergymen watched Tractarian chaos with dismay. By tradition high churchmen supported the Tory party unshakeably. Oxford was a bastion not only of the established church but of the Tory party. But if the public mind identified high churchmen with Puseyites, and the repute of Puseyites continued to sink into an abyss, the link with high churchmanship might weaken the hand of Tory politicians. No one doubted that most Tory voters were good conservative Protestants. The Tractarians were endangering the ancient idea that the Church of England was the Tory party at prayer.

The last public attempt to protect the Tractarian reputation was undertaken by the *Times* newspaper, which had lately turned into the national oracle which it has remained. Its proprietor, John Walter, was far from a Puseyite. But he was sensitive to the political and ecclesiastical needs of the moment. And his link with the Puseyites was fostered by an accident. His son studied at Merton College while Newman dominated Oxford, and persuaded the father to friendliness. Walter therefore allowed his editors much liberty in befriending the Puseyites. From June 1840 until 1844 the *Times* employed a struggling barrister,

[1] *Letters of Dean Stanley*, 40–41; Ward to Scott of Balliol, 27 April 1841, Ward, *W. G. Ward*, 168.
[2] Ward, *W. G. Ward and the Oxford Movement*, 175.

Roundell Palmer, the brother of the Tractarian fanatic William Palmer of Magdalen College, to contribute a long series of favourable leaders.[1] For three years the outspoken support of the *Times* was invaluable to the Puseyites.

But as Tractarian disaster developed these political shields were taken away. Tory writers reached a point where it was vital to their interest to jettison the Puseyites; and a coincidence turned the proprietor of the *Times* from a friend to a mortal enemy. It happened, first, because Oxford university kept its inward turmoil perpetually before the public eye; and secondly, for ritual reasons almost unconnected with the Puseyites.

The troubles at Oxford

By prestige and history Oxford university weighed heavily in the establishment. It nurtured English statesmen, guarded orthodoxy, educated future clergymen. Civil war in Oxford must weaken the established church; and during the four years after *Tract XC* civil war became insufferable. Fought under conditions of an ancient creaking constitution, amid the strife of parties which degenerated into faction, and under the glare of national newspapers, the fight in Oxford occupied a place in the public eye which its importance hardly warranted. The vice-chancellor, little silver-haired nervous Dr. Wynter of St. John's College, happened to be the least effective of vice-chancellors. Seated on a throne of briers during the stormiest years of unreformed Oxford, he mingled weakness with rigidity. It is fair to Wynter to remember that in a university divided by fierce suspicions few vice-chancellors could have sustained their reputation.

The hebdomadal council, governing body of the university, was composed of the heads of the colleges. If a measure required the approval of the university, it required a vote of convocation, composed of all senior members whether resident or non-resident. One party wished to preserve Oxford for the Church of England, and free it from the taint of Romanising in public repute, by condemning the Tractarians in formal vote of convocation. The other party regarded this as mere persecution by dry dons who cared nothing for the interests of true religion. Thus every question was a religious question; every question needed an appeal to non-residents and therefore the attention of London newspapers; every question needed an emotional

[1] Selborne, *Memorials*, i, 303-4.

and dramatic settlement in the Sheldonian theatre. No constitution could do more to harm the quiet and secret interests of faith.

In the end of 1841, the university must elect a professor of poetry to succeed Keble. The fellows of Trinity College had a poet in Isaac Williams and put him forward as a candidate. Williams was attractive among lesser Tractarians, a gentle peaceable clergyman whose model was Keble. If the mantle of Keble fell upon anyone, Williams was a natural Elisha. Though he wrote nothing so celebrated as *The Christian Year*, he published a poem called *The Cathedral* which, if not powerful, conveyed a sense of brooding mystery and contained some beautiful lines. He took no part in the controversies of the age. But he had written three of the *Tracts for the Times*; one on the duty of obeying the authority of the prayer book, and two on reserve in communicating religious knowledge. Accepting the principle of Newman that faith is deepened and confirmed by moral growth, he desired that the holiest mysteries of Christianity should not be thrown into the market-place of the profane, but should be communicated as men by moral development were able to receive them. It was a pious and hardly exceptionable opinion. But it was assailed by Bishop Sumner of Chester and by a few less discriminating critics who leapt to the idea that reserve was a weapon of the stealthiness popularly attributed to Puseyites.

Brasenose had a rival candidate named Garbett. He had written no poetry. But his translations of classical verse were esteemed and he was said to possess a rare knowledge of foreign literature. Williams was not so eminent a candidate as to command wide and immediate support. Then Pusey suddenly issued a circular which accused the principal and fellows of Brasenose of putting Garbett forward with the sole motive of preventing the election of Williams. If anything could prevent the election of Williams, it was support from Pusey and a public accusation that the other candidate was merely theological. Newman's friends thought Pusey's support outrageously injudicious.[1]

Neither Williams nor Garbett was so eminent that anyone now minded the poetic merits of the question. Neutral observers wanted Williams elected because he was the better candidate and believed that the theological opinions of candidates should not be considered. Such impartiality was rare. The election, declared a senior member of the

[1] *Letters of Lord Blachford*, 106–8. For the troubles at Oxford, W. R. Ward, *Victorian Oxford* (1965).

university, is a national question—whether Puseyism is to prevail or not?[1] Pusey, who quite lost his head, said that the election was more important than the election of a prime minister. A committee was formed in London to organise Garbett's backers, another committee to organise Williams's backers, a third committee to present a testimonial of esteem to Golightly. One side said that Williams was the only poet in the competition and that all opposition was religious warfare. The other side said that to be a professor of poetry it was unnecessary, if not disadvantageous, to be a poet, and that anyone who published middling verses must be incapable of appreciating poetical merit; that the university had condemned the *Tracts*, and this election was an attempt to get convocation to upset the censure and vindicate the *Tracts* by electing a Tractarian to public office; that the claim to separate poetry from theology was too subtle when Keble's last lecture as professor of poetry maintained their intimate bond. The *Standard* newspaper was the worst offender in converting the tea-cup election into a national no-popery wrangle, with cynics laughing a plague on both houses.

In December and January Gladstone and other eminent men tried to get both candidates to withdraw for the sake of church and university. Bishop Bagot of Oxford, Bishop Phillpotts of Exeter and 257 other members of convocation signed an address to the rival committees. Garbett's committee refused. Williams's committee was readier to compromise by testing pledged votes. On 20 January 1842 it was found that 921 votes were promised to Garbett and 623 to Williams. Though Newman believed that many of the 921, and the *Standard* that many of the 623, would not come to vote, Williams withdrew his name a week before the day of election. A day later the newspapers announced that Dr. Gilbert of Brasenose, chief supporter of Garbett, was to be the new Bishop of Chichester. The prime minister (now Peel) made it known that he selected Gilbert for his merits and not because of his conduct over the professorship of poetry. Few could believe that the timing was accidental. Gloomier critics consoled themselves with the bitter thought that it might have been worse, for the prime minister could have nominated Golightly.[2] Partly by Pusey's fault the contest had been turned into a trial of strength. A main reason why victory was so eagerly sought was fear or hope that the result would show a majority willing to condemn the *Tracts*. The

[1] S, 23 November 1841. [2] JB, 1842, 55.

rival strengths were now known. A Tractarian party which commanded 600 votes was potent, but not so potent as its enemies.

The next three years were marked or marred by a series of attacks
upon individuals of both sides. An attempt to remove the censure upon
Hampden (7 June 1842) failed at a public vote. A vice-chancellor's
court (27 May 1843) tried a charge of heterodoxy against a sermon by
Pusey in Christ Church, containing high sacramental language about
the Real Presence, and suspended Pusey for two years from preaching.
Pusey rummaged among courts and lawyers for remedy until his
advisers dissuaded him. To devout Puseyites and even others who
respected his clouds of glory, this attack upon Pusey felt not only
unjust but irreverent. Then Dr. Hampden tried to exclude a Tractarian
candidate for a B.D. degree, R. G. Macmullen. With the aid of the
vice-chancellor Hampden sought for two and a half years, and at last
failed, to keep Macmullen from his degree by a statutory and legal
obstructiveness which just bears examination on moral grounds. For
two and a half years the trivial case stirred Oxford mud before the
world, while the *Times* accused the heads of bullying and abused the
university for the absurdity of censuring Hampden for heterodoxy
and then making Hampden the test of orthodoxy.

The Tractarians gained sympathy and credit from these cases. But
on their side they still generated bad blood in Oxford. Newman and
Pusey in their retreats ceased to be Oxford politicians, Keble was
distant and hesitant, but their young men enjoyed being provocative.
At commemoration in June 1843 the university proposed to give a
degree to the American ambassador, Edward Everett. They discovered
that he was a Unitarian, and even for a short time pastor of the most
fashionable Unitarian church in Boston. Sewell, Macmullen, Morris,
Church, James Mozley and other zealots decided to *non placet* the
degree. But at the theatre the undergraduates greeted an unpopular
junior proctor, Jelf's younger brother, with such thunders of abuse
and catcalls that not a word could be heard and the oration of Garbett
the professor of poetry looked like dumb show. Above the din
reporters heard the *non placet* of Everett's degree. The vice-chancellor
disregarded the *non placet* and conferred the degree, claiming afterwards that he heard no *non placet* until too late. Four undergraduates
were rusticated; the United States was insulted; the objectors visited
the ambassador to express their sorrow at being impelled by conscience
to oppose him and assured him that they intended no discourtesy; they

also secured a legal opinion that the degree was null because the vice-chancellor gave no chance of a vote.

By his behaviour in the cases of Pusey and Macmullen, and by his courteous oversight at Everett's degree, Dr. Wynter caused a vexation against vice-chancellors. In the autumn of 1844 he came to the end of his term of four years. The next in rotation was Dr. B. P. Symons, the warden of Wadham, and the next in rotation had not been seriously opposed within the memory of man.

No one knows who started the most factious act which the press was ever able to fasten upon the Tractarian party. The eccentric John Morris may first have propounded the idea. An obscure fellow of Balliol named Wall formed the opinion that to oppose the election of the new vice-chancellor was a useful though symbolic protest. He went to James Mozley, who disliked the plan, but was won over. Keble disliked the plan, but was won over. Newman disliked it, but followed meekly. Gladstone thought it mistaken, Manning thought it madness.[1] Wadham was the leading evangelical college and its warden the leading evangelical. Known as Big Ben, with a hearty, florid countenance, the warden was something of an autocrat in his college, headed the attack upon *Tract XC*, was one of the court which tried Pusey's sermon, and had transferred his Sunday chapel to the precise time which prevented the undergraduates from attending Newman's sermons.[2] On inadequate hearsay he was rumoured variously to have said that the Tractarians should have been *exterminated* long ago, or that they should be *crushed*, or that 'I will put down Puseyism'. Dr. Symons was not a man to use so opprobrious and vulgar a term as Puseyism.[3] On none of these grounds could anyone object publicly to the vice-chancellor designate. He was confessed to be a man of business and personality. James Mozley gave the game away when he admitted the attack on Symons to be weak, but said that Wynter's policy had been steadily unconstitutional and Symons was sure to continue it.[4] To assail Symons because Wynter behaved badly did not commend itself to many honourable men. The Tractarians could not expect to

[1] Liddon, *Pusey*, ii, 413; Purcell, *Manning*, i, 296.

[2] J. Wells, *Wadham College*, 173. In view of this controversy Hawkins of Oriel was now regretting that he and the warden of Merton had both refused the office of vice-chancellor when their turn came, cf. Oriel College MSS. I, 43.

[3] *Letters with a few remarks concerning rumours*, ed. J. Griffiths, 1844, 8.

[4] *Letters of J. B. Mozley*, 154; J. S. G. Simmons, in *Bodleian Library Record*, V (1956) 37ff.

win. Their tally of 183 votes was higher than they hoped. The defence of Dr. Symons mustered 882 votes and so gave the Tractarian party the sorest thrashing which they had yet received. James Mozley, who could not understand why so many people troubled to travel so far to vote against them, used the word *swamped*. The numbers were a record. But there was a simple and physical explanation in the opening three months before of the railway link between Oxford and London. The railway suddenly increased the power of non-residents within the constitution of the university.

In June 1844 Ward published his first book, *The Ideal of a Christian Church*. Tractarian voters refrained from the Symons controversy because they feared that a vote against Symons would be taken as an approval of Ward; and as they finished reading his 600 pages during the long vacation they disapproved Ward quite as much as they disapproved Symons.[1]

The systematic mind of Ward combined the vague sense of liberal reformers that the Church of England was not doing its pastoral duty, with the vague sense of the Tractarians that the Church of Rome preserved devotional treasures which the Church of England had lost. He combined these two notions into a critical assault upon the practice of the Church of England when tested against the ideal of a Christian church; and that ideal, as portrayed in his book, bore a singular likeness to the contemporary Church of Rome. Nothing mattered to Ward except (what he called) 'the standard of saintliness' in a church, or 'the average of Christian attainment'. This standard, which he regarded as miserably low in the Church of England, was formed upon the ideals of medieval ascetic or of Counter-Reformation. But this contrast was not only a moral contrast. For Ward pushed to the limit Newman's doctrine that conscience was the guide to religious truth, until he preached (what Newman could not follow) conscience as the only guide to religious truth. Therefore a church which elicits more saintliness has an obvious claim to be teaching truer doctrine than a church which elicits less. The presence of a strong school of moral and ascetical and mystical theology was a clearer sign of an ideal church than any quantity of intelligent or critical history. He had been blamed for declaring that the Church of England would be wise to take the Church of Rome as a model. So far from accepting this as a matter of blame, he rejoiced in it, declared war upon the principles of the

[1] e.g. Hook; cf. T, 7 October 1844.

Reformation, and called upon England to expel the Lutheran and evangelical spirit from the national church. The best part of the book was a trenchant demand that the Church of England should cease to be dominated by rank or station and become the church of the labouring poor. It was a defence of his aims and attitudes while writing for the *British Critic*; and as the book of a man whose heart had left this Church before his reason knew whither he was moving, it gave readers a feeling of incongruity. Pusey defended him privately, so far as he could. Keble thought the book excellent in parts. Secular philosophers like John Stuart Mill were pleased at Ward's destruction of religious metaphysic and his assault upon the Church of England. Gladstone reviewed him intelligently in the *Quarterly Review*, saying that it ill became a priest of the English church so to speak of his own communion. Hook was enraged. Newman whole-heartedly disagreed with the theory that a man might subscribe the Thirty-nine Articles and at the same time hold all the doctrines of the Church of Rome.[1] He thought it shocking to common sense. He rejected Ward's idealising of the Church of Rome. But he thought it wanton and meaningless if the university degraded Ward.

Among the kites flown by Ward were ejaculations like this: 'We find—oh, most joyful, most wonderful, most unexpected sight!—we find the whole cycle of Roman doctrine gradually possessing numbers of English churchmen'. . . . 'Three years have passed since I said plainly that in subscribing the articles I renounce no one Roman doctrine'.[2]

Ward thus gave the assailants of the Tractarians the chance at last to condemn. The logical and religious standpoint was so paradoxical that the heads had only to put forward a resolution condemning it to be certain of victory. But severity or policy recommended two other resolutions: that this standpoint was so incompatible with good faith that the university should deprive Ward of his degrees; and that the Thirty-nine Articles must be interpreted in a Protestant sense. The form of the third resolution, as announced by the vice-chancellor on 13 December 1844, declared that the articles must henceforth be accepted in the sense intended by their original framers and now imposed by the university.

This third resolution was either absurdly narrow or meaningless. Few could determine precisely what sense the original framers

[1] Newman, *Cor. with K*, 361–2.
[2] Ward, *Ideal*, 565, 567.

intended, and no one knew in what sense the university now imposed its subscription. The words gave many, and not only Tractarians, a feeling that the heads were drawing a noose round their throats. Gladstone wondered what would happen to the favourite propositions of Archbishop Whately.[1] Three weeks before the vote was to be taken this third resolution was withdrawn.

The numerous Oxford men whom Ward enraged were not content. Sure that some regulation was necessary to prevent the teaching of Roman Catholic doctrine by men who subscribed the Thirty-nine Articles, they gathered a list of signatures asking the vice-chancellor to propose the censure of *Tract XC*, that is, to allow convocation now to accept the verdict of the heads four years before. The heads agreed. Five days before the vote the two proctors Guillemard of Trinity and Church of Oriel, both from Tractarian colleges and Church being an intimate of Newman, gave notice that they would veto the condemnation of *Tract XC*. Their notice was denounced in the press as monstrous and insulting,[2] but abuse would not overthrow it. *Tract XC* could not be condemned before new proctors took office.

Church himself, the junior proctor, thought that the sternness of the proposals was a gross mistake. A single resolution to condemn the *Ideal*, and even to censure its author, would have commanded an overwhelming majority. But the heads linked the resolution with a degrading of Ward, though they made no effort to take degrees from persons who had become Roman Catholics; and with an assault upon *Tract XC* and therefore upon Newman's person. The link made sympathy for Ward and transferred an astonishing number of votes to his defence.[3] From Littlemore fastness Newman still exercised a silent unseen power. He cared little for the controversy, felt himself remote and detached, rather hoped that *Tract XC* would be condemned to show that he was right in slipping quietly from the Church of England. But still men revered him, expected nervously that he would soon become a Roman Catholic, but longed to keep him in his place, and sometimes voted for Ward because they wanted to keep Newman.

Despite snow and sleet, nearly 1,200 voters gathered in the theatre

---

[1] Ashwell-Wilberforce, i, 251.
[2] S, 11 February 1845.
[3] Church, *Oxford Movement*, 327.

on 13 February 1845. Ward asked leave to speak in English instead of Latin, and so occupied the English rostrum normally reserved for the recitation of prize compositions. With him, as in a dock, stood Frederick Oakeley, who declared that he shared Ward's every opinion. Ward made a long uncompromising speech (of which Newman had approved the draft), denying the legality of the proposals, and asserting that every single person present signed the articles in a non-natural sense and that they *ought* to do violence to the language unless the church formally interfered. The proctors took the votes at the door, and found that the book was condemned by 777 to 386. The news was received in perfect silence, for the great size of the minority astounded even its members. Ward was then degraded from his degrees by 569 to 511; and Manning turned to Gladstone at his side and said: 'So begins disaster.'[1] When the resolution was put to condemn *Tract XC*, the senior proctor stepped forth with *Nobis procuratoribus non placet* and was loudly cheered or hissed. The undergraduates had been successfully excluded. As Ward came hurrying out of the theatre his clumsy frame slipped in the snow and fell headlong, scattering papers and pamphlets in all directions. Sixty or seventy undergraduates cheered and escorted him to Balliol. They hissed the vice-chancellor.

Nearly 200 voters signed an address of thanks to the proctors. Oakeley issued a letter to the vice-chancellor challenging him to action against himself. Other voters signed a request to the vice-chancellor to renew the third proposal next term with the new proctors, who were observed to be hostile to the Tractarians. But the heads were wise. Everyone was sick of religious strife in Oxford. *Tract XC* was allowed to rest uncensured. Oakeley challenged Bishop Blomfield by publicly claiming the right to believe (not to teach) all Roman Catholic doctrines while retaining his license to minister at Margaret Chapel in London. When Bishop Blomfield instituted a suit against him he resigned and became a Roman Catholic.

Ward had just become privately engaged to be married, and newspapers hinted at the incompatibility between matrimony and Ward's Roman opinions about priesthood. Ward was oddly nervous about it, and concealed the news until after the day of the vote. On 1 March 1845 he wrote to the *Times* and the *Morning Post* an egotistical letter so eccentric that his biographer-son would not print it. He said that he

---

[1] Purcell, *Manning*, i, 299.

regarded celibacy as a higher life than marriage; that priests ought to be celibate; that in a church with an effective system a person so wholly devoid of vocation as himself would never have been admitted to holy orders. 'How anyone can imagine that I have ever professed any vocation to a high and ascetic life I am utterly at a loss to conceive.' The tone of the letter was not complimentary to his fiancée. Not so much the marriage as the mode of announcing the marriage shattered the Tractarians. Arthur Stanley and Benjamin Jowett believed that the joke marked the collapse of the Oxford Movement. Certainly the Oxford Movement could never be the same after the Ward crisis. 'To ordinary lookers-on', wrote Church,[1] 'it naturally seemed that a shattering and decisive blow had been struck at the Tractarian party and their cause; struck, indeed, formally and officially, only at its extravagances, but struck, none the less, virtually, at the premisses which led to these extravagances . . . It was more than a defeat, it was a rout, in which they were driven and chased headlong from the field.'

Two hundred years before, weariness with religious strife nourished latitudinarian divinity. Now the same weariness favoured the liberals. Whatever else the Tractarian wrangle had or had not done, it proved the archaisms of the university and strengthened liberal demand for reform. The Tractarians had been the only party in the university with a coherent programme. Richard Church, in a retrospect wherein he charged Hawkins of Oriel with dealing the heaviest blows against Puseyites, wrote that the defeat left Oxford at the mercy of the liberals.[2] Henceforth liberal divinity, and the liberal programme of academic reform, grew slowly to eminence in Oxford. Once-devout Tractarians who would not follow Ward and Newman—a Mark Pattison, a James Anthony Froude—turned with reluctant hesitation towards the liberals. Ward and his wife became Roman Catholics in September 1845; Newman, who satisfied his mind by writing that summer the *Essay on the development of Christian Doctrine*, was received by Father Dominic the Passionist at Littlemore on 9 October; Oakeley a few weeks later; and several eminent Tractarian clergymen preceded or followed them. Pusey was still a name among the country clergy. In Oxford his school subsided and slithered towards ruin.

[1] *Oxford Movement*, 335.
[2] G, 4 November 1874.

2. THE DEVELOPMENT OF RITUAL

Everyone wanted to reform the worldliness of the Church of England and held the axiom that a more otherworldly reverence ought to inspire the services and fill the churches. Not only the Tractarians wanted the churches to be less like halls of preaching and more like temples where the mystic incense of the heart rises before a throne.

The Tractarians taught that the treasures of antiquity should be appropriated and that the contemporary Church of Rome preserved some of these treasures more lovingly than the Church of England. Their disciples saw old and harmless customs still in use, like the sign of the cross upon the breast, or the use of a cross on the altar. In the prayer book they were delighted to find provision for daily service, private confession, weekly celebration of the sacrament, and splendid ornaments if the ornaments rubric of the prayer book were correctly understood. As Newman claimed his new reformation to be only the practice of what the church ordered but neglected, so young men claimed only to be practising exact rubrics under the authority of the church. A few Tractarians, especially Bloxam of Magdalen College, enjoyed ritual revival, but as antiquarians, not as pastors. Newman and Pusey were not sympathetic to changes of trivial detail which might offend, to coloured stoles or rich hangings or unaccustomed postures. Pusey thought that the reassertion of Catholic truth must not be hindered by unnecessary provocation in ceremony, and that the simplicity of English practice was appropriate to the penitential state of divided Christendom. Oakeley on the contrary held that care about the smallest details was the mark of intense and reverent affection. His chapel at Margaret Street in London was loved or feared as a pattern of high Anglican worship.

In 1837 a few Cambridge undergraduates formed a group to study church architecture. Their leader was John Mason Neale, son of an evangelical clergyman. During his undergraduate years he neglected his studies to pursue the antiquarian hobby, taking brass rubbings, examining fonts, drawing pointed arches. His quest for the knowledge of ecclesiastical architecture and decoration was always a religious quest. His mind was imbued with the feelings of mystery in worship and of the power of symbolism. One evening in the Easter term of 1839 he and two others waited upon the senior tutor of Trinity College, Thomas Thorp, prominent among the residents as a high churchman. Thorp became patron and president of their society, and in May 1839 the Cambridge Camden Society was founded. Few undergraduate societies have achieved a comparable success. After four years its patrons or members included two archbishops, sixteen bishops, thirty-one peers or M.P.s, twenty-one archdeacons and rural deans, sixteen architects, and more than 700 ordinary members.[1]

A society with this membership was not Tractarian. Most of its members regarded it as antiquarian and architectural. In the age of church restoration, amid the flowering of Victorian Gothic, a society was needed to guide taste, afford a centre for information, disseminate comparative ideas. The Camden Society admirably met the need. As its organ they founded a periodical, the *Ecclesiologist* (November 1841). Its young leaders began at a different end from the *Tracts*. Newman and Pusey began with the doctrine of authority and asked how best to execute its ordinances. Neale asked a different question, How shall men be led to worship? The Tractarians were concerned first for truth and then for the issue in worship. The Camdenians were concerned for decoration, ritual, the structure and seating of churches, because these affect the way in which men worship. Neale criticised the tract-writers as 'unworthy' in blinding themselves to the principle of aesthetics.[2] The Camdenians believed with Pugin that Gothic was the only Christian style of architecture, and loved screens, priest's doors, sedilia, piscinas, gargoyles, concealed frescoes, fragments of brasses, poppy-heads, hammer-beams. They uncovered a mass of interesting and important facts about medieval churches, and propounded erroneous theories to account for the facts. They advised modern architects to make exact copies of medieval churches.

As the Oxford Tractarians dwelt upon the Catholic doctrines of the Church of England in the seventeenth century, so the Camdenians nursed the ritual solemnities which survived the Reformation. The churches most conservative of a solemn ceremonial were cathedrals and college chapels. Therefore the new fight for reverence meant that parish churches should be made like cathedrals. Their chancels, hitherto used as storehouses or even as schools except on the rare occasion of the sacrament, must be cleansed and filled with a choir in surplices. Hook, whose new church at Leeds was as grand as any

[1] Towle, *Neale*, 43; White, *The Cambridge Movement*, 37: E. J. Boyce, *A Memorial of the Cambridge Camden Society*, 1888, 10. Boyce and Benjamin Webb were the two others who accompanied Neale on the visit to Thorp.
[2] Towle, 51 (1844).

cathedral, first put his choir into a chancel; and the example was sporadically imitated in other parishes, though rarely with the choir instantly in surplices lest the congregation be vexed at the unfamiliarity. The said prayers of the old parish church began to imitate the sung responses of the cathedral. The Camdenians and Hook had discovered a use for the chancels.

The new cleaned chancel needed ornament. Thus the quest for reverence, and the restoration of churches and the opportunity of building so many new churches, threw up the ritual question; colour of altar frontals, lighting of candlesticks, wearing of surplices or stoles, use of pews or benches, posture of ministers. The ceremonial of the Church of England had been governed by custom slowly decaying. As with the Oxford doctrines, the innovators appealed from present custom to past authority. When past authority was investigated, it was found to be patient like the Thirty-nine Articles of more than one interpretation. The ambiguity of authority, and the ineffectiveness of means for enforcing or propounding it, propelled the Church of England into the age of ritual controversies. The church could only have avoided these disputes, either if Parliament disestablished, or if Parliament intervened with the same direct exercise of supreme headship as once it had imposed the prayer book. After 1835 the occasion of disestablishment vanished; and after 1832 the reformed Parliament had neither confidence nor power to exercise supreme headship in direct revision of forms of worship. The church had no self-government to settle its own disputes, and Parliament, which when Anglican used to settle such disputes, could and would no longer interfere.[1]

Though Bishop Blomfield could never command the arts of pleasing mankind, and could never by any possibility be revered, he had won sober respect since the days of reform. He proved himself diligent and earnest, and showed an efficiency reflected in the pastoral care of his diocese. Still impulsive and imperious, he was not suspected of sympathy with the Tractarians. He was the first bishop to resign from the Cambridge Camden Society because he disapproved its literature. In the autumn of 1842 his charge to the diocese of London, delivered by his beautiful clear voice in St. Paul's cathedral on

[1] Cf. Melbourne's refusal to countenance such an idea, Melbourne to Bishop Kaye of Lincoln, 27 May 1840, MP.

10 October, condemned *Tract XC*, Ward's inference from it, and the doctrine of reserve. He knew that he could not prevent high churchmen from tampering with the prayer book in one direction unless he forbade low churchmen to tamper with it in another. Practical and precise in thought and habits, and with no large quality of mind, he used the same charge to rush in where angels feared. He decreed that all clergymen must obey all the rubrics in every particular. If we are not to go beyond the ritual, at least we ought not to fall short of it. He thought the line of obedience easy to define and was not timid in defining it. By his sudden and rash definition of rubrics, and without the smallest intention to provoke, he precipitated the first of the ritual controversies.

He condemned the placing of flowers upon the holy table; the mixing of water with wine in the chalice; the beginning of service with a psalm or hymn; private confession.

He saw no objection to candlesticks upon the holy table provided that they were lit only at the evening service; thought that the Church of England insisted that all its members bow the head whenever the name of Jesus occurred in the liturgy; wished the preacher at morning service to wear a surplice (usual in cathedrals) and at evening service a black gown (usual in churches), but gave no final ruling; required the rubrics about feast and fasts to be kept, the daily service and more frequent sacraments.

The clergy, who normally ended the morning service (mattins/litany/ante-communion) with a sermon and hymn, were to obey the rubric and read the offertory sentence and prayer for the church militant before the blessing.

London was a vast diocese sprinkled with every variety of clergyman and congregation. Some clergy refused to obey, others took no notice of the bishop's decrees. Others obeyed in bounden duty and found that their congregation was indifferent. Others, especially round Chelmsford, obeyed with enthusiasm and infected their people with enthusiasm for offertory or daily service or more frequent communion. And others obeyed with reluctance or enthusiasm and discovered that their parishioners thought them popish or ridiculous. The editor of the *Record* was not pleased with the bishop's attitude to doctrine, and the more Protestant parishes were alarmed to hear that the bishop was a Tractarian. The *Times* newspaper, befriending as usual the Oxford divines, seized upon Blomfield's charge and, in the face of all his words against *Tract XC*, told the world that the charge held for Oxford theology in all fundamental points.

By the summer of 1843 Blomfield was obeyed only in parishes where the congregation liked the changes or did not care. In nearly all other parishes the clergy stopped obeying the rubric when they found that their flock disliked it. But in three or four parishes, headed by Ware and Tottenham, Blomfield unwittingly achieved parochial war. The clergyman felt in conscience bound to obey the bishop, and to preach in a surplice, or hold a weekly collection, or bow at each mention of the holy name, or use the daily service. His people resented these practices as innovations and sublimated their dislike of novelty into accusations of popery. Clergyman or congregation appealed to the bishop; and Blomfield by his charge had prevented himself from following the course of a sane pastor. Publicly he must back the clergyman and tell the congregation that their pastor was doing his duty. He began by rebuking congregations with the brusqueness which flowed from his pen. Soon he was privately advising his clergy not to provoke unnecessary prejudice, not to obey the rubric after all. But if one of his clergy insisted on the rubric, Blomfield could hardly avoid backing him against the people.[1] He found himself in the unusual predicament of writing private letters to some clergymen urging them to yield and public letters to other clergymen pronouncing them right in not yielding. His reputation hurried back down the hill.

The troubles in the London diocese moved across England. In every diocese a few conscientious clergymen wondered anxiously whether they obeyed lawful authority as they ought. In the dioceses of Lincoln and Chichester some parish priests felt obliged to introduce the surplice in the pulpit and a weekly offertory, and there was argument whether it was legal to ask for a collection except for the poor of the parish. In many parishes the people were indifferent enough, or respected the clergyman enough, to accept what he declared to be his duty. In a few of the parishes there was trouble among the congregation, without quite attaining to the clamour at Ware and Tottenham in the diocese of London.

[1] Cf. *Life of Blomfield*, 254; 'Rubrics and Ritual of the Church of England' in QR, spring 1843; 'Present and prospective results of the Bishop of London's charge', CR, 1843, ii, 113, and pamphlets there cited; T, 12 October and 19 October 1842.

The most important of the troubled parishes was Hurst in Berkshire, because it happened to be the church of John Walter, proprietor of the *Times*. The curate of Hurst tried to obey the rubric by holding a weekly collection for outside objects. Walter was roused at the innovation and took legal advice whether it was lawful to hold such collections without the authority of a queen's letter. On 20 October 1844 the churchwardens of Hurst refused to carry the plate, and clerk and schoolmaster perforce took their places. The curate at last gave way. But meanwhile the *Times* thundered against innovation, pursued the innovators into the remotest parishes of the country, printed news of parish troubles everywhere, and denounced in leader after leader the high-flying pretensions of the clergy. Roundell Palmer, who had written so many leaders in defence of Puseyites, parted from Walter over his attitude to rubric and ritual. The little parish of Hurst brought calamity to the Puseyites, stripping them of their weightiest advocate at the bar of public opinion. Newman regarded the loss of the *Times* to the Tractarian cause as one of the signs that the Oxford Movement was running into ruin.

In Exeter was a bishop more warlike than Blomfield. Henry Phillpotts would have felt at home in the casque and cuirass of a military prelate. By education and marriage a Tory of the extreme right, a genuinely religious man with his religion concealed behind porcupine quills, he constantly quarrelled in the House of Lords, exposing opponents' follies with consummate ability, a tongue and eyes of flame, an ugly tough face and vehement speech. His promotion to the bench was the last political act of the Duke of Wellington in 1830. He had won greenish laurels as a Tory pamphleteer, teaching the establishment that aggression is the best defence. He was too intelligent to be rigid. On some important occasions he was pliable enough to bow to the inevitable, but removed all the good effect of concession by the menace, the entrenched posture, the coat of mail, which he adopted until the last moment. It was a weakness that he relished fighting, and lacked human sympathy for that majority of the human race with which he disagreed. Anthony Trollope said of him in *The Warden* that the ring was the only element in which he seemed to enjoy himself. The House of Lords expected a humane and courtly manner in bishops, and was horrified at the fury of his tone, at the incongruity between his violence and his lawn sleeves. King William IV, even when he backed Tories to the limit, disliked the acrimony of the

Bishop of Exeter, and other bishops realised the danger in which he placed them and his cause. Earl Grey, Lord Goderich, Lord Durham, Lord Melbourne, Lord Brougham abused him publicly and were abused in return. Durham, himself violent and arrogant, loathed Phillpotts and assailed him with a rare command of coarse invective; and Greville[1] believed that he would have unfrocked him if he could. Phillpotts flowered under this treatment. He was never happier than when battered by the eminent in the land. It is not possible to study his career or to read his charges without gaining a rueful affection for this elephant trampling so conscientiously amid the porcelain. High churchmen often admired his stands for principle, and were grateful for this champion as an army will applaud a gladiator eager for single combat between the hostile ranks. Even an ordinand not likely to sympathise with his outlook, and resenting him before the occasion, could be moved to deep regard by the solemnity of his ordination charge.[2] It was inevitable that the first biographer of Phillpotts was only able to complete volume one because the bishop went to law to prevent him publishing selections of his letters. But if his ability and integrity and force of character are confessed, it is impossible to credit him with prudence or delicacy, impossible not to feel that his nomination to the bench was unwittingly the hardest knock to the English churches ever struck by a Tory minister of the crown.

Among the clergy who introduced innovations was the amusing and energetic curate of Helston in Cornwall, Walter Blunt. He found the surplice used in the pulpit and continued it without protest from the people. But he had that passion for exact obedience to authority which was the mark of the age, and was encouraged to be precise by private letters of advice from Phillpotts. He refused to bury persons who had not been baptised by a clergyman of the Church of England; refused to give the sacrament to, or even to say the Lord's Prayer with, a sick Irishman who had been baptised by a Roman Catholic priest but who brought up his children as Anglicans; refused to marry parishioners without receiving satisfactory evidence of their baptism; dismissed the church singers from the organ loft because they ate apples through the service, and substituted a little choir of schoolboys in the chancel, which was far from the organist and outside his control; and made a violent speech at the end of a sermon, declaring that he would refuse

[1] ii, 332.
[2] *Life of Henry Alford*, 91; Davies, 152-3.

communion to anyone who left church before the exhortation on sacrament Sundays, and by his vehemence brought tears to the eyes of ladies in the pews.[1]

The churchwardens complained to the bishop. Phillpotts supported the curate on all the trivial charges. On 19 November 1844 he issued a pastoral letter to the clergy of his diocese, requiring them to have a weekly collection and to preach in the surplice.

The ensuing quarrel was complicated, first by an argument in public between the bishop and his antagonists in the chapter, including the dean; and secondly by the political distrust and dislike which all Whig and radical citizens of Devonshire felt towards their bishop. But the principal conflict was neither political nor constitutional. The in-articulate laity learned from the press to identify the surplice, when used in a pulpit, with the badge of a party which declared war on the Protestant Reformation. They were not going to tolerate changes in their immemorial practice, least of all when a change made weekly inroads upon their pockets. Through Devon and Cornwall the people held parochial meetings, and passed resolutions to memorialise the bishop, the archbishop, and the queen. Placards appeared on the walls of Exeter, savage letters by anonymous hands were delivered in the post, the city could talk of nothing else. Despite bombardment from the diocese and abuse in the national newspapers, Phillpotts held out grimly for more than a month. He committed an error when he defended the need for a ruling by the plea that in November one cleric of the diocese preached neither in gown nor in surplice but in his great-coat—a story which he then believed, but which had been invented.

On 23 December he withdrew the order that the clergy should wear the surplice in the pulpit, and left the offertory to their discretion. On 8 January 1845 he received from Archbishop Howley of Canterbury a provincial letter, recommending that the services be left quietly as they were until further consideration could be given, and seized the opportunity to recommend the clergy to follow this advice and make no further attempts to get the rubrics observed. The *Times* crowed with triumph and self-congratulation. John Walter ascribed victory to his campaign.

At St. Sidwell's parish in Exeter the perpetual curate Mr. Courtenay

[1] For Helston, the report of the commission of enquiry in T, 15 November 1844, 6, cf. 16 November, 19–20 November 1844.

had not introduced the surplice, but found it when he arrived. Though the parishioners protested against its use, Courtenay said that he was now under authority to archbishop and bishop that services be left as they were, and would therefore continue to use the surplice. When Courtenay entered the pulpit on 12 January two-thirds of the congregation walked out. On going home from church in the evening he was escorted by a hooting and hissing mob of 200 or more people. On Sunday morning 19 January the mob rose to 700 or more, and Courtenay needed a strong corps of police to bring him home in safety. The afternoon mob rose to 2,000, though it was pouring with rain. A young barber, arrested by the police for hissing, was discharged without penalty, and the mayor wrote to Phillpotts that it might be impossible to keep the peace if Courtenay persisted. On 22 January Phillpotts requested Courtenay to desist at the request of the civil authority, and on Sunday, 26 January, though all the sermons at St. Sidwell's were preached in black gowns, the police and an uneasy crowd of 5,000 conducted Courtenay home.[1]

The surplice riots at Exeter were the symptom of distrust growing between ordinary layman and high churchman. If a bishop was abused by the national press for his politics, this harmed the parishes little. If he was repudiated in his ecclesiastical authority, suspicious laymen looked anxiously at their clergy, and saw the normal frictions of a parish in a new light. It could not help the parish of Newton Abbot that most of its population met at the Globe hotel to record its determination to resist the mode of conducting services which the bishop ordered. At St. Columb the rector lived for a time with the windows of his rectory barred, alarm bells fixed to the shutters, and dared not go forth to visit the people.[2]

But the informed were already aware that they would find little remedy without changes in the laws of ecclesiastical discipline, even changes in the Book of Common Prayer. The machinery of church

---

[1] *Times*, 14 January 1845, and *passim*: G. C. B. Davies, *Henry Phillpotts*, pp. 180ff. A visiting preacher reappeared in the pulpit of St. Sidwell's in a surplice at the evening service on three (widely separated) Sundays of 1848. On the last occasion, 29 October, there was a continuous uproar which prevented a sentence being audible, and the mayor of Exeter was fetched to get the preacher out of the pulpit and safe home: Davies 189-90.

The surplice was introduced to St. Sidwell's first by Courtenay's predecessor E. H. Browne, later Bishop of Ely and Winchester; cf. G. W. Kitchin, *E. H. Browne*, 1895, 73. The introduction offended parishioners and the offence caused Browne quickly to leave. Thus Courtenay arrived into an already embittered parish.

[2] *Times*, 3 March 1845, 7.

courts and law was too ill oiled to settle the disputes now likely to arise. Either the rubric and the church courts must be altered or the Tractarians could sooner or later establish their modes of worship within the Church of England.

This first ritual controversy destroyed the Cambridge Camden Society. One of the few precious relics of medieval Cambridge, St. Sepulchre's, commonly known as the Round church, fell into ruins when its tower collapsed into the nave. The Camden Society under-took the restoration. The round nave and tower in imitation of the crusading church of the holy sepulchre was cleaned and restored, the high baise-covered pews were removed and a chancel furnished to suit the abstract models of Gothic architecture. Even Queen Victoria gave money to this famous and fashionable restoration.

The incumbent resided in another benefice in Essex and took no interest in the reconstruction. He discovered at last that the Camden Society inserted a stone altar and a credence table, which objects he called most pernicious and soul-destroying heresies. He sued the churchwardens, behind whom stood Thorp, the senior tutor of Trinity College. Losing in the consistory court, he appealed to the court of arches. On 31 January 1845 the dean of arches (Sir Herbert Jenner Fust) held that a stone altar was not a communion table within the meaning of the rubric. The stone altar and credence table were removed and lay about indecorously in the churchyard.[1]

The legal battle rendered the Camden Society suspect. Between 1843 and 1845 several writers exposed the connexion between Puseyism and the zeal for church architecture. On the ominous date 5 November 1844 Francis Close, evangelical vicar of Cheltenham, preached a sermon entitled *The Restoration of Churches is the Restoration of Popery*. On 13 February 1845, the very day when Ward was condemned at Oxford, the committee of the Camden Society recom-mended that the society be dissolved, chiefly on the ground that Phillpotts of Exeter and Kaye of Lincoln and the vice-chancellor of the university had resigned. Another and turbulent meeting in the Cambridge town hall on 8 May issued in a crop of eminent re-signations. The society soon dropped its prefix of Cambridge, and reformed itself as the Ecclesiological Society administered from London.

[1] Romilly's *Diary*, 25 April 1845.

3. TORY AND TRACTARIAN

The troubles of Oxford and the surplice riots finally separated the Tractarians from the leadership of the Tory party. Not so long before Tory and high churchman were synonyms. They were now being sundered. The *Standard* newspaper, traditional organ of ultra-Tory politicians, led the assault upon Puseyites. The separation between Tory and Tractarian had far-reaching consequences in the political and religious history of England.

In May 1841 the weak government of Lord Melbourne collapsed at last, and a general election put the Tories back in power, only nine years after the reform act. Peel, prime minister for the second time, possessed for the first time a majority in the House of Commons and therefore executive power. The power, though real, was not so extensive as it looked. Since Catholic emancipation Peel was disliked and feared by many natural Tory supporters. The ultras suspected him of being more than half Whig.

Among his ministers he had a Tractarian in Gladstone. But Gladstone was junior and exerted no influence upon Peel's ecclesiastical policy. Among the backbenchers was another Tractarian, Lord John Manners, who was the most romantic of the little group in Parliament called Young England. Manners propagated a Toryism which valued the feudal link of lord and tenant and distrusted the middle class. He expected the church to save society from the materialism of modern industry, to rouse the gentlemen of the land to their responsibility towards the masses. Cynical critics mocked him and his few allies for wanting to save England by dancing round the maypole. The ideals were shadowy, and came out of the mist only because Disraeli presented them with imaginative power in the novel *Coningsby*. But Disraeli was Peel's bitterest critic, the most cruel assailant which any prime minister has endured in a backbencher of his own party. Peel and Manners seemed natural enemies; and the enmity symbolised the natural antipathy between the new Toryism and the new high churchmanship.

For not only were the high churchmen different, thanks to Newman. The Tories were different, thanks to Peel. He was a realist politician of the representative age. By tradition a Tory prime minister was expected to befriend the established church. Peel knew well that the reformed constitution made it almost impossible even for a Tory government to favour a single church.

Peel therefore gave old-fashioned Tory critics matter for grumbling. He started away from the protection of agriculture on which Tory landowners depended for prosperity. They wanted the corn laws and he moved step by step towards repeal. Tory churchmen wanted public money to build churches. Politically it was still not quite unthinkable and even Peel dallied with the programme. He said that the grant could not be carried without outraging the dissenters and at last refused absolutely to provide. He consented (1843) to introduce an act which permitted separate districts to be formed out of old parishes even where no church existed, and empowered the Ecclesiastical Commission to borrow £600,000 from Queen Anne's Bounty to pay the stipends of the ministers of new districts. He gave £4,000 from his pocket to build churches. The private generosity did not reconcile his Tory critics to the public refusal. Despite a mild prod from Archbishop Howley,[1] he refrained from attempting the measure by which a government could most have benefited the church, a revision of the law of church rate. He came nearest to helping the established church in a scheme of national education which was appended to Graham's factory bill of 1843. The collapse of the education clauses in that bill (see pp. 340–2) confirmed Peel in his view that such favour to the established church had become political suicide.

Extraordinary though it then appeared, and extraordinary though it still appears, Peel passed an act of Parliament to give money to the Roman Catholic church in Ireland. Scottish churchmen asked the government for money and were refused. English bishops asked the government for money and were refused. Catholic bishops from Ireland asked for money and extracted it from a Tory government. They said with perfect truth that their college for training priests at Maynooth was dilapidated. Early in 1845 Peel passed an act to raise the annual grant to Maynooth from £9,000 to £27,000 and to give £30,000 for capital expenditure.

Nothing displayed so shatteringly the gulf which divided Peel from the axioms which ruled so many minds in his party. The fact was, that the Catholics had to be given money because Ireland was almost ungovernable. Whitehall believed that Irish priests encouraged their flocks to sedition, used the threat of excommunication to influence votes, allowed placards on the walls of their churches, used churchyards for political meetings, threatened to refuse burial to political

---

[1] Add. MSS. 40521, 169.

opponents, or even put themselves at the head of mobs with bludgeons. The evidence was not all strong. When it was solemnly reported[1] that a priest at Clonmel threatened to turn into a serpent anyone who voted for Mr. Bagwell, we may suspect the English of less humour than the Irish. But in Ireland politics and religion were one. Peel believed that he must convince the Irish of his good will. Tory axioms or no Tory axioms, efficient government required that he show benevolence to the Catholic church. In public he tried to content the Irish by the grant to Maynooth. In secret he tried to content the pope by offering to check Italian revolutionaries in Malta.[2]

The no-popery campaign rocked the government, but did not destroy it. Dissenters, Wesleyans, the Scots, were loudest in their cries. Peel carried the bill into law by a union of Whigs and half the Tories. He continued steadily on the same tack by founding in Ireland three colleges from which religion must be excluded—Cork, Galway and Belfast.

The Tory party was falling apart.

Scottish disruption

During Peel's ministry the old plan of favouring a single established church was slowly seen to be untenable. In 1843 the total numbers of free churchmen, and therefore the religious neutrality of the British government, were strengthened by the tragedy in Scotland.

The constitutional changes of 1829–32 made all churches more self-conscious. In both the established churches a party stood decisively for the independent life of the church apart from the state. In England that party was Tractarian. In Scotland it was evangelical. The Scottish evangelical cry against the state was more formidable than the cry of the English Tractarian. The English owed their Reformation to the crown. The Scots forced through their Reformation against the crown. When Scottish evangelicals talked of the sovereign rights of the church, they meant rights reaching further than any Tractarians wished to claim for the Church of England. And they possessed an organ to declare their independence. The Convocations of the Church of England had been suppressed since 1717. The Scots possessed a General Assembly which met and governed.

An evangelical General Assembly of 1834 ruled that no pastor shall be intruded upon a congregation against their will. Since the law of

[1] QR, 1840–1, 568.   [2] Broderick, 179.

the state safeguarded the rights of patrons in Scotland as in England, this act (the so-called veto act) challenged the law. In the inevitable lawsuits at Auchterarder and Marnoch the state courts upheld the rights of the patron. The General Assembly adopted declarations of spiritual independence couched in high-flown language. A smashing of the union between church and state was now inescapable, unless church or state recanted. Scottish churchmen used such Bannockburn utterances that they could not weaken without ruin of character. Westminster politicians were not prepared to legislate under threats. Most Englishmen could hardly understand the fuss. Sydney Smith jested that it was surely something to do with oatmeal.[1] Peel regarded the Scottish evangelicals as a northern version of the Puseyites whom he detested. He exercised the patronage of the crown almost as decisively against Scottish evangelicals as against Puseyites.[2]

At the General Assembly of 18 May 1843, 203 representatives withdrew amid the cheers and shouts of the people and hisses for those who stayed. Scotland was divided into an established church, weak except among the upper classes and their tenants and in the north-east, and a free church, strong in the great cities and formidable in the Highlands and Hebrides. Out of 1,203 ministers, 474 joined the free church, among them many of the best.

Politicians were quick to sense the change. The established church, a minority in Wales and a small minority in Ireland, was now the barest majority in Scotland. The established church in England was a majority, perhaps a big majority. But its relation to the state was perceptibly altered by the new strength of the voluntary principle among the Scots. If money for church extension had been just possible before 1843, it became a hopeless dream after the Scottish disruption.

We are entering the years when the fear of erastian government began to dominate Anglican minds. The Church of England had no organ of expression, no government but the state. Once it cheerfully accepted the submission partly because the state was Anglican and partly because the state passed laws to benefit the established church. Now the state was no longer Anglican, and even a Tory minister could not pass laws to benefit the church. Yet the state continued to

[1] Letter of 31 January 1841, in Nowell Smith, 719.
[2] Cf. Wilson, *Memorials of Candlish*, 182; but Peel, unlike some of his supporters, took the threat of schism very seriously; cf. Peel to the queen, 30 December 1842, Add. MSS. 40435. 232.

exert its ancient control. A crisis not unlike the crisis in the Church of Scotland was looming in the Church of England.

Peel and patronage

Peel would never and could never use his patronage to promote a Puseyite.

But his conduct of patronage marked a reform in the behaviour of the crown. He resolved to reward learning, hard work, and 'professional usefulness'. He refused to please eminent friends by giving places to their clients. Political applicants were discouraged and told that the prime minister was determined to look for zealous discharge of duty. Among the Peel papers in the British Museum are numbers of such letters to applicants, whereas in Melbourne's papers it would be difficult to find one; and conversely, those demands for political pledges before promotion, which so amusingly sprinkle Melbourne's correspondence, are not to be found among Peel's. Dr. Merewether, the Dean of Hereford, who was promised a bishopric by the dying King William IV, and was politically suitable, since he organised the Tory party at Hereford elections, reminded Peel of the royal promise and said that a bishopric would be most congenial to his feelings. Peel replied that he considered the king's intention to lay no obligation upon him and that his principles precluded him from attaching weight to any considerations but those of professional character.[1] Thus he sacrificed grease which might have been used to oil the cogs of the party machine. His example in the use of crown patronage was his outstanding service, after the Ecclesiastical Commission, to the Church of England.

A Tory minister could afford to be high-minded. Melbourne desperately needed votes in the House of Lords, Peel commanded more than he needed. Since clergymen were usually Tories, his field of choice was larger. For all his professions of principle Peel never preferred a staunch Whig and would have thought such altruism as unnecessary as Melbourne would have thought it foolish. The five bishops whom he nominated were all solid members of the Tory party. As befitted a Tory prime minister he kept in close touch with the Archbishop of Canterbury and the Bishop of London. Melbourne consulted Archbishop Howley as a kind of formality and sought advice from a variety of unofficial Whig sources, Whately, Copleston,

---

[1] Add. MSS. 40499, 283–93; cf. 40302, 228.

Maltby, Lord John Russell. Peel treated the archbishop as a chief adviser.

It was not all altruism. Peel realised an important truth of the new political world. The national movement towards duty and responsibility demanded an end to aristocratic patronage and called for ecclesiastics chosen for merit and capacity. Peel saw that there came a point where a government would suffer more damage from a blatantly political appointment than by the loss of a secure vote or a single influence however eminent. He saw that to elevate the patronage of the church beyond politics would in the long run promote the interests of his party. It was characteristic of him to refuse an exchange of livings in favour of a radical parson, not because the parson was radical but because exchanges were liable to abuse and because (subordinately) the parson was an active politician.[1]

To the doctrine that personal influence should be excluded, Peel allowed important exceptions. He sent his nephew to the crown living of Munden in Hertfordshire and offered his brother John the choice between the deaneries of Canterbury and Worcester. In extenuation of the offer to his brother, it must be recorded that the queen pressed Worcester and Archbishop Howley suggested Canterbury, and no one questioned that the appointment was proper. Another piece of personal patronage was the gift of a canonry at Westminster to Christopher Wordsworth, headmaster of Harrow school. Peel told Queen Victoria that Wordsworth's chief claim consisted in the merits of his father, the old master of Trinity.[2] In fact, Peel was a loyal Old Harrovian and wished to rescue the school from an unsatisfactory headmaster. But for the most part his choice fell upon men accustomed to work. Lonsdale, who was sent to Lichfield, was one of the best bishops of the century, if the standard lies in kindness, sanity, fairness and hard endeavour. Samuel Wilberforce, who was sent to Oxford, had a reputation for boundless energy. The single exception was sedentary old Bishop Bagot of Oxford, whom Peel translated to the see of Bath and Wells. But Bagot held other benefices including the deanery of Canterbury, and Peel wanted to be rid of one of the scandalous cases of plurality. He promoted Dale of St. Bride's to a canonry of St. Paul's, partly because he had eleven children

---

[1] Parker, *Peel*, III, 414; Add. MSS. 40499, 29.

[2] Add. MSS. 40439, 70. Cf. Blomfield's view of Wordsworth, Add. MSS. 40549, 190.

and partly because of his indefatigable exertions in the parish.[1] Such a promotion was typical of Peel.

Plenty of advisers from the queen downwards told him that it would never do to prefer Puseyites. The evangelical Lord Ashley stood frequently at his elbow warning him that they were Jesuits in disguise and that he must beware their perilous pranks. Ashley even sent him a copy of that public letter from William Palmer of Magdalen which heaped anathemas upon Protestantism.[2] Peel needed none of this advice. As Gladstone once remarked, he had an anticlerical and anti-dogmatic streak, and though not an evangelical shared Ashley's opinion of the Puseyites. Before Ashley sent him Palmer's pamphlet he read it and discussed it. He feared Pusey and eyed Newman at Littlemore as an enemy concealed in the defending ranks, saying that it would be better if he were an open Roman Catholic.[3] He gave a conventionally liberal address about the benefits of education at the opening of the Tamworth reading room and found himself ridiculed by letters in the *Times* under the pseudonym *Catholicus*, who was none other than Newman. He was riled by the *British Critic* which used the same occasion to pour contemptuous invective upon his person and his principles.[4] His promotions were never Tractarian and occasionally anti-Tractarian. Dr. Gilbert, who led the campaign over the Oxford professorship of poetry, was announced as the new Bishop of Chichester on the day after Isaac Williams retired beaten; and although it was put about that Peel selected him on merit and not on the victory, he was not insensible of Gilbert's services in Oxford. 'His theological views', he told Queen Victoria, 'are entirely sound.'[5]

But he was too capable to make Melbourne's mistake over Hampden. He refused either to follow Melbourne in avoiding Oxford men or to select men who would harry Tractarians. He told Bishop Kaye of Lincoln, when they were trying to fill the newly created Oxford chairs of pastoral theology and ecclesiastical history, that decided opponents of the Puseyites might add to the dissensions of the university. In consequence his nominations were usually safe, solid, dull. To the chair of ecclesiastical history he sent Hussey, who contributed

---

[1] Peel to the queen, 11 October 1843, Add. MSS. 40437, 225; cf. 40534, 168.

[2] See p. 199; cf. Add. MSS. 40483, 14, 38, 55, 114.

[3] Peel to Henderson, 13 November 1844, Add. MSS. 40553, 307.

[4] BC, July 1841, 46–99; for Peel's anger cf. Peel to Ashley, 1 August 1841, Hodder, I, 347.

[5] Peel to the queen, 19 January 1842, Add. MSS. 40433, 196. At Gilbert's consecration the provost of Oriel preached against the Puseyites, R, 11 April 1842.

modestly to history, when he could have sent Brewer, who transformed Tudor studies. But they told him that Brewer was a Puseyite.

To this general rule of safety there were two remarkable exceptions who in succession filled the deanery of Westminster. In 1843 Samuel Wilberforce was suspect for his sympathy with the Tractarians. Bishop Blomfield warned Peel against him, declaring prophetically that he favoured high churchmen too much to control the Tractarians.[1] Between 1843 and 1845 Wilberforce made it almost too plain, both to Tractarians and their enemies, that he disapproved them. Charming and delightful in company, he was a favourite with the queen and the prince; and so he went to Westminster and quickly to the see of Oxford. Whatever else might be predicated of Wilberforce, he was not safe, not solid, and not in the least dull.

The successor at Westminster was odder. Peel liked to collect scientists and engineers round his table. Professor Buckland of Oxford was an eminent geologist and the most colourful scientist in the universities. A delightful mimic and buffoon, well known for lax views about the first verses of Genesis, carrying into decorous occasions a blue bag from which peeped bones and fossils, caricatured in drawings with an alligator in the pocket of his tail-coat, littering his staircase with ammonites and his dining-room with tanks of snakes and his hall with a stuffed hyena, Dr. Buckland came to Westminster and repaired its pavements and laid on gas and provided the school with better food and water-closets. When he showed visitors round the abbey he carried a light featherduster to brush the statues. He was the best company in the world, and devoted his energies to the sanitation of London and the diseases of the potato until three years later he went mad.[2]

Peel's fear of Puseyites affected his judgment adversely on certain ecclesiastical affairs. Since the act of 1836 united the sees of St. Asaph and Bangor when a vacancy should occur, English and Welsh churchmen, low as well as high, united in pressing the government that Wales must be allowed to keep its bishops. The matter assumed an importance out of all proportion, so that when Gladstone took office

[1] Add. MSS. 40534, 108.

[2] *Life and Corr.*, by Mrs. Gordon, 189–219. Peel put him above Wilberforce for Westminster and the queen and prince reversed the order, cf. Peel to the queen, 22 March 1845; the queen to Peel, 24 March 1845, Add. MSS. 40439, 352, 361. But on the second occasion Buckland was again put second, to Lord John Thynne, and was only appointed when Thynne refused; cf. Peel to the queen, 28 October 1845, RA, A17/186.

in Peel's cabinet he expressly reserved the right to differ from his chief on the Welsh bishoprics. By 1843 the very designers of the union, Howley and Blomfield, were convinced that they should bow to public opinion and advised Peel in this sense. Peel dug in. The decision of Parliament must be upheld, the government must not betray weakness, repeal would be a bad precedent—and all this obstinacy because, as he confessed, he feared that Puseyites led the campaign.[1]

The Puseyites weakened the Church of England in politics and popular esteem. They strengthened the Church of England in its soul.

They weakened the church in politics by dividing; and in dividing, by loosening its grip upon the Tory party and the crown. Some Tory newspapers belaboured them with bludgeons like radical or dissenting bludgeons. When in 1843 the Tory government tried an education measure (see pp. 340–2) which gave power to the Anglican incumbent, dissenters could cause the government to pause by the cry that they might give power to a Puseyite.

The Puseyites weakened the church in popular esteem by making laymen suspicious of clergymen. In face of the constitutional changes which so drastically modified (some said shattered) the old alliance of church and state, Puseyites stood for free and independent life in the church. They wanted to lift the Church of England from the national rut, to persuade Englishmen to see their religion as part of a world-wide apostolic inheritance. They could not succeed without attempting to discuss what was good within the traditions of Roman Catholics. Fear of Rome ran deep in English consciousness. Puseyite appeal to church authority generated changes in rubric and ritual. It has yet to be proved that tiffs over rubrics benefit religious life.

But beneath popular disesteem and public weakness they strengthened the soul of the Church of England. The devotion and character of Anglican clergy changed between 1825 and 1850. Let us not exaggerate. In 1825 there were many devoted clergymen, in 1850 there were a few who would have disgraced any church in any age. But the evidence of startling change for the better is widespread. 'We believe the Anglican clergy', wrote a dissenter of 1851,[2] 'to be the

---

[1] Add. MSS. 40527, 356. For the most important papers of the whole affair, see in the National Library of Wales the calendar of letters and documents in possession of the Earl of Powis, 1941.

[2] Drummond-Upton, *Life of James Martineau*, i, 216; *Westminster Review*, January 1851, 463.

most pernicious men of all within the compass of the church; but also the most sincere, the most learned, the most self-denying.' That same dissenter attributed the change to the sacramental and priestly ideals of Tractarians. Of course, the Tractarians were not sole authors of improvement. Evangelical earnestness; new dissenting rivalry; new power in press and public opinion; new laws to repress old abuses—in one aspect the Tractarians were as much symptom as cause of rise in standards. But if any single movement beyond others is selected, a great body of evidence selects the ideals of worship and ministry taught by Tractarian pastors. No one did more to drive Anglican worshippers out of formalism, to give them a sense that Christianity has a history and a treasure not insular, and to enable sympathetic hearts to perceive the beauty and poetry of religion.

The weakness and strength are seen in the three leaders. As public men, guiding controversy, facing the practicable, commanding a party, conciliating opinion, Newman, Pusey and Keble were sad incompetents. As moral guides, representing in their persons the ideals of sacramental and ascetic life which they commended, they sent out to the English religious conscience a call which sounded through the century.

CHAPTER IV

LORD JOHN RUSSELL

THE corn laws defended the interests of English agriculture and were supported by Tory squires and country parsons. They offended the interests of townsmen for cheap bread. The anti-corn law league was supported by middle-class politicians and dissenting pastors in the cities. Peel modified the corn laws when he came to power and was determined to modify them further. Irish potato famine compelled him to act; and after a resignation and a return to office he carried the repeal of the corn laws (25 June 1846). Since the Tory right wing now regarded him as a traitor, the repeal destroyed the already precarious unity of the Conservative party. Four days afterwards Peel resigned and Lord John Russell took office as head of a government weak because its legislative power hung on Tory disarray.

Lord John Russell was an obsolescent Whig. Obstinate, impulsive, and angular, he was nevertheless a likeable man, full of anecdotes and information, and at important debates commanded the house by simplicity and sincerity and courage. Something about his diminutive stature or his manner made everyone think of him as plucky. Neither subtle nor discriminating, he found difficulty in understanding even intimate colleagues. Without vanity or ambition himself, he could not appeal to other men's vanity or ambition, and even in a cabinet gave an appearance of solitariness. His principles were formed early and applied consistently through his long life—religious liberty, extension of the franchise, free trade, national education; but the principles were Whig and not radical. Believing that religion must be of the state and that Christianity is the source of enlightened legislation, he argued the necessity of an established church, and was abused as bitterly by radical nonconformist as by Tory churchman. Like some other Whigs, he was convinced that a clergy paid by the state was more amenable and less troublesome than a clergy paid by voluntary subscription. On such grounds, to the dismay of radical supporters, he steadily refused to countenance the abolition of the most irritating of all taxes, church rate, without providing alternative means of paying for the repair of churches.

He found more difficulty than any other prime minister in handling the delicate machinery of church and state. More forthright than diplomatic, he happened to be responsible at a time when clumsiness was fatal; and he found the machinery gritty because after Gladstone he was the most fervent and religious prime minister of the Victorian age.

Lord Melbourne sat loosely to religious doctrine, but understood it, studied it, respected it; and after he learnt his early lesson over the appointment of Professor Hampden, he used his ecclesiastical power skilfully and even wisely, with that common sense which was the leading habit of his cynical mind. Sir Robert Peel was a churchman of the middle class, generous and sensible, and so used the patronage of the crown as to gratify the moderate churchmen of England. Lord John Russell did not lack common sense, but an emotional streak in his religion rendered him less capable of balance and consideration. Direct and sincere, he could not sympathise with doctrine. He suffered from dogmatic anti-dogmatism, feared priests, hated Roman Catholicism like a conventional uneducated Protestant. Melbourne was amusedly anticlerical, Peel administratively anticlerical, Russell anticlerical in the heart. Though he worshipped regularly in parish churches, he disliked parts of the prayer book, finding its liturgical repetition to be tedious and its formality to be formalism. He was unceremonious and discovered nothing intelligible in a sacramental cast of mind. He not only loathed narrowness and bigotry but expected to find these vices in clergymen. Fearing Roman Catholicism, and finding no virtue in the more Catholic elements of the English Protestant tradition, he resented the contemporary attempt to revive Catholic forms or teaching in England. He wanted the Church of England to be a barrier against Rome, not an ally in reviving papal power. He considered baptism to be mere symbol of dedication and the eucharist to be bare commemoration of a death. Never confirmed, he thought this no barrier to receiving communion, and regarded the notion that confirmation was a necessary gateway to communion as a petty superstition. He disliked the catechism as unsuitable for children. 'He looked forward', wrote his wife, 'to a day when there would be no priests, or rather when every man would be a priest, and all superstitious notions—such as is implied in the notion that only a clergyman ought to perform certain offices of religion—should be cast aside by Christian men for ever.' While he normally attended a parish church in London, he sometimes sat at the feet of eminent dissenting preachers, and one Sunday, sitting quietly at home, he said to his wife, 'It conduces much to piety not to go to church sometimes.'[1]

Such was the man now able to exercise potent influence in the Church of England. His leading principles of action were three. First, the narrow-minded clergy must be kept in control by the broad-minded laity, to which end the royal supremacy was designed. Secondly, the Tractarians and Catholicisers of the Church of England must be beaten to the ground. And thirdly, he would use the patronage of the crown to encourage liberal theology. Peel had already adopted a conscious policy of refusing to promote Puseyites. Russell pursued the policy, which Peel thought dangerous, of promoting decided anti-Puseyites. And the worst of it was that unlike Peel he was liable to act impulsively. For the first time since the reign of Queen Anne bishops were to be chosen not only for their politics but for their theology. Melbourne made Hampden a professor not because he wrote the Bampton lectures on Christian doctrine but because he wanted dissenters admitted to the university. Russell wanted dissenters admitted to the university, but would have chosen Hampden because he delivered the Bampton lectures.

In nominating men to bishoprics he had no close advisers. The archbishop was consulted, but formally and not invariably. Blomfield, whose advice Peel often asked, was still asked occasionally, but soon lost all influence. Lord Ashley, who wrote freely to Peel, and who at Russell's first approach to office lamented in his diary that the reign of jobbery and improper appointments thus began, continued to advise, but in different language: '2 November 1849. Dear Russell, It is quite manifest that you hold my opinions, ecclesiastical and religious, in supreme contempt . . . Nevertheless you have always been so kind and good-humoured in allowing me to state what I think . . .' '7 November 1849. Dear Russell, . . . Pray allow me to qualify the words "supreme contempt"; I see that it is not quite so

[1] So wrote his second wife; Walpole, *Life of Lord John Russell* (1891), ii, 486. His wife was even stronger on these matters than Russell, and may therefore have described his attitudes as even more decisive than the reality. She was vehemently Protestant. Her influence on Russell was well known. Cf. Bertrand and Patricia Russell (edd.), *The Amberley Papers*, i, 30. The summit of Russell's public expression of anti-dogmatism was reached in November 1871, in a published letter to the Chairman of the Education League.

bad.'[1] Leading members of his cabinet, and his brother the Duke of Bedford, had their occasional say. That ancient Whig Bishop Maltby of Durham spoke frankly, but lived remote from affairs and from men. No one who represented the ordinary opinion of ordinary clergymen could get near Russell. The aristocratic drawl and shy manners kept him fenced among intimates. No prime minister knew less of the mind of the established clergy. The single strong influence from outside was willy-nilly the crown—which meant Prince Albert.

In the quest for liberal minds to rule the church, Russell was conscious of support from the crown. Prince Albert shared many of his views with a touch of the same fervour. He thought that the Reformation failed to reform the Church of England and must be carried farther. Like Russell, he found himself uneasy in the clerical age of English life. With his German education he was more eager than Russell to promote learned clergymen, supposing that learned clergymen were likely to be liberal. He asked that 'scientists' should be appointed to high office in the church. Russell became eminent among prime ministers for the habit of appointing learned men to bishoprics, deaneries and canonries. William Cureton, who shed light on the Syriac manuscripts of St. Ignatius, was promoted to be canon of Westminster. Milman, the liberal historian of the Jews and of the Latin Church, became Dean of St. Paul's. There had always been a tradition of scholarship upon the English bench of bishops. Russell extended it consistently, providing always that the scholars were sufficiently liberal in divinity and Whig in politics.

Russell was expected to be the foe of the established church. In the first year of his cabinet the new Whigs surprised churchmen by their friendliness. Against bitter radical onslaught he agreed to found the see of Manchester without insisting on uniting the sees of St. Asaph and Bangor; the additional bishop, that is the most junior bishop for the time being, not to have a seat in the House of Lords. The concession was greatly valued by the clergy, for Peel steadily met their requests for new bishops and divines by the argument that it was dangerous to have some bishops not in the House of Lords and impossible to increase the number in the House of Lords. For a moment it looked as though the Church of England could secure more bishops without delay. Russell gratified the clergy by proposing not merely the statutory see of Manchester but three more sees, St. Albans to

[1] Ashley to Russell, PRO 30/22/8B. Shaftesbury's *Diary*, 19 December 1845.

relieve the diocese of London, Southwell to relieve York and Lincoln, and Bodmin for the county of Cornwall. Under radical attack the plan was withdrawn, but seemed to show Russell an earnest well-wisher to the established church. Sir James Graham diversified the debate with an extraordinary speech, which afterwards reverberated in mockery down the Victorian years. Graham could not understand why more bishops were needed when the duties of the present bishops were so light. He thought them better bishops when they saw little of their clergy; better bishops when they communicated with their clergy through the post. 'I can conceive', he said in a much-quoted phrase, 'overactivity and overzeal on the part of bishops.'[1]

The credit which Russell gained by creating the see of Manchester was little shaken by his choice of a bishop for Manchester: James Prince Lee, headmaster of King Edward's School, Birmingham, a great teacher of schoolboys and liberal in educating dissenters. He formed his ideals of education as assistant master under Dr. Arnold, not without friction, and at Birmingham educated an exceptional series of scholars, including J. B. Lightfoot, E. W. Benson, and B. F. Westcott. The prime minister was unlucky in that a Mr. Gutteridge came forward and published pamphlets that Prince Lee was several times intoxicated, drinking two or three bottles at a sitting, and made himself quickly sober by wrapping wet towels round his head. There was no truth whatever in these accusations.[2] Russell was also unfortunate that this great headmaster turned out not to be a great bishop.

In the summer of 1847 Russell dissolved Parliament and appealed to the country, hoping for that working majority which in the end he failed to secure. Many candidates appeared as Protestants, men who would rescind the Maynooth grant or stamp on new ritual or purge the stables of Oxford university. In the election for Oxford Gladstone was vainly opposed as Puseyite. The general election was

---

[1] Hansard xciv, 355. Sir James Graham was perhaps unique only in saying this publicly. Goulburn told Manning in a private conversation that it was the social and not the spiritual character of the bishop which impresses the people and serves the church; that the chief social importance of the bishop is money and a peerage. Manning, reporting this to Sidney Herbert, was sufficiently ignorant of the world to say that he imagined such ideas to be extinct and thought the 'last specimen of this race had been some time in the British Museum'. Purcell, Manning, i, 424.

[2] Russell sought reassurance from Bishop Pepys of Worcester and showed the clearance to Howley, Pepys to Russell, 23 October 1847, PRO 32/22/6F. For Prince Lee cf. David Newsome, Godliness and Good Learning, 92ff. Prince Albert strongly pressed his claims.

one of the two most Protestant elections of the reign. Russell stood for the city of London. Tory churchmen were perturbed that the list of candidates with whom he consented to stand included the banker Lord Rothschild, who was a Jew not only by race but by religion. No Jew could take his seat in Parliament, for he must swear the oath 'on the true faith of a Christian', and all the bills to release Jews from this disability had failed. The example was infectious, and Jewish candidates stood at Hythe and Maidstone. Still worse, Rothschild was elected and became a member unable to take his seat. Tory clergymen found it bad that their church should be ruled by a non-Anglican Parliament, but worse that a non-Christian Parliament was looming. At the same time government seemed to be trying to loosen the hold of the clergy upon the church schools of their parishes. Everyone was beginning to be strained about the alliance of church and state; and in the midst of this strain Russell chose to mishandle the patronage of the crown.

1. BISHOP HAMPDEN

Early in October 1847 ancient Archbishop Vernon Harcourt of York, in his ninety-second year, was walking with his chaplain across a wooden bridge over an ornamental pool at Bishopthorpe, when the bridge collapsed, and they fell in the water up to their necks. 'Well, Dixon,' said the archbishop, 'I think we've frightened the frogs', and insisted on presiding that evening at a dinner party. On 12 October he presided at a meeting in York, though somewhat paralysed in his legs and in one hand, and on 5 November, amiable and blameless, he faded away. The *Times* obituary noticed his family connexion with powerful politicians, and observed that 'the progress of his professional advancement . . . though perhaps not much beyond his deserts, was at least fully equal to them'.

A week later Russell announced his intentions. Dr. Musgrave, Bishop of Hereford, whom Melbourne promoted for the sake of encouraging the Whigs in Cambridge University, was to become Archbishop of York.[1] To succeed Musgrave at Hereford, Russell

---

[1] Musgrave was son of a respectable Whig woollen draper of Cambridge, JB, 1847, 740. Howley recommended Kaye of Lincoln for York, Howley to Russell, 6 November 1847, PRO 30/22/6F. Whately seems to have had a wistful hope of the see. Cf. Whately to Senior, 16 November 1847, *ibid*. Maltby of Durham was, in fact, sounded about going to York, but refused, cf Russell to the queen, 6 November and 8 November 1847, RA, A19/130-1. It was as well for Russell that Maltby refused.

chose the regius professor of divinity in the university of Oxford,
Dr. Hampden. Melbourne was asked to make Hampden a bishop in
1840[1] and refused, declaring that he was in his right place as professor.
Russell was less wise. It was true that Hampden's lectures at Oxford
gave no offence, being heavy, dull and much occupied with dictating
long lists of books.[2] But the record stood against him, and an attempt
of 1842 to get the university to lift the censure of 1836 failed abjectly.
The appointment was declared to be a gratuitous insult to the
church, an aggression, that Russell should select for a bishopric the
only clergyman whose orthodoxy was stamped by the stigma of
authoritative censure. What was the object? Why was it necessary to
elevate the single person who would offend the vast majority of
churchmen?

In 1836 the nomination of Hampden to his professorship raised the
demand that the royal supremacy be controlled and checked. The
news of November 1847 instantly revived the demand. All the old
fear of Whigs rose to the surface. They were called the hereditary
enemies of the church, and within two days of the announcement
voices clamoured that the chapter of Hereford refuse to elect or that
Convocation, meeting next week, should break through the bonds of
silence and speak.

It was 1836 over again; meetings of clergy, meetings of laity, documents for signature, petitions to bishops, petitions to the archbishop,
petitions to the queen. Lord John Manners wrote a poem praying the
spirit of truth to upraise some man of God

> Who, strong in conscious rectitude, shall dare
> Resist the flagrant outrage, which repays
> The church's long obedience with the rod
> Of state oppression.

The *Guardian*, a weekly newspaper lately founded by young Tractarians like Church and Rogers, and edited with exceptional intelligence,
seized the occasion to become the organ of high churchmen. Thirteen
bishops, headed by Blomfield of London, ranging from the highest
churchmen like Phillpotts of Exeter to the lowest churchmen like
Sumner of Winchester, took the unprecedented step of remonstrating
publicly with the prime minister. Three other bishops were said to

[1] Cf. Maltby to Melbourne, 28 August 1840, MP.
[2] ER, 1883, i, 537.

agree, and Longley of Ripon, who did not sign the remonstrance, allowed a private letter of protest to be published in the press.[1] To make a nomination against which, for the first time in English history, fourteen bishops could agree to protest was ample sign of clumsiness in the nominator.

Archbishop Howley refrained from joining this protest. His temperament and office prevented him. And apart from his temperament and office, he was in the predicament that Russell consulted him about Hampden. In the previous August Russell suggested Hampden as first bishop of Manchester and enquired whether as professor at Oxford he taught any doctrine at variance with the Thirty-nine Articles. Howley replied that he had no reason to believe that Hampden taught from his chair any doctrine at variance with the articles; 'and in justice to him I must say that I have discovered nothing objectionable in the few publications of his which I have seen, and which are ably written.'[2] He said that he knew nothing of his discretion or talents for business, qualities so necessary to a Bishop of Manchester. Howley raised no objection on grounds of orthodoxy, and gave no hint that feeling among the clergy might make the appointment imprudent. Russell was able to reply publicly to the thirteen bishops (8 December) that he consulted the Archbishop of Canterbury and received no discouragement. He declared untruly that many of the most prominent among the Oxford assailants of Hampden had later joined the Church of Rome. 'It appears to me that, should I withdraw my recommendation . . . I should virtually assent to the doctrine that a decree of the

---

[1] G, 47, 724, 758. The thirteen bishops, among whom Phillpotts took the initiative, were Blomfield of London, Sumner of Winchester, Kaye of Lincoln, Bethell of Bangor, Percy of Carlisle, Bagot of Bath and Wells, Monk of Gloucester and Bristol, Phillpotts of Exeter, Denison of Salisbury, Gilbert of Chichester, Turton of Ely, Samuel Wilberforce of Oxford, Murray of Rochester. Of these only Salisbury had been nominated by a Whig prime minister (Melbourne). The three bishops (besides Longley of Ripon) supposed to agree boiled down to Davys of Peterborough, who was one of Melbourne's bishops, but a reluctant nomination, only permitted for the sake of Queen Victoria. All the outspoken Whig bishops—Thirlwall of St. David's, Maltby of Durham, Stanley of Norwich, Copleston of Llandaff, Musgrave of Hereford and York, Pepys of Worcester—would not sign; and with them was joined the moderate Sumner of Chester, an abstention momentous for his future. Blomfield's extremely illegible material on the Hampden case is in FP, 397. Copleston took the monstrous simple view that the attack on Hampden was due to his personal unpopularity, unattractive manner and conduct towards Macmullen, cf. Copleston to Hawkins, 13 February 1847, Oriel College MSS. Sumner of Chester took trouble to re-read the Bampton lectures and, deciding that Hampden's errors were only errors of expression, refused to sign the protest: J. B. Sumner to Longley of Ripon, Longley Papers, 2, 47–49.

[2] Howley to Lord John Russell, 9 August 1847, copy in RA, C55/1.

university of Oxford is a perpetual ban of exclusion against a clergy-man of eminent learning and irreproachable life, and that, in fact, the supremacy which is now by law vested in the crown, is to be trans-ferred to a majority of the members of one of our universities . . . I cannot sacrifice the reputation of Dr. Hampden, the rights of the crown, and what I believe to be the true interests of the church, to a feeling which I believe to be founded on misapprehension and fomented by prejudice.' He failed to tell the public that in a later con-versation Howley warned him verbally of a probable *explosion* if Hampden were promoted.[1]

It was politically impossible for the prime minister to withdraw the nomination. He must go forward. Russell's emotional character gave this going forward an appearance of trampling upon whatever puny opposition might arise. The Duke of Bedford urged him to read for the occasion Arnold's famous article on *The Oxford Malignants*.[2] The Marquis of Londonderry formally raised the impolitic nature of the nomination in the House of Lords on 17 December. Russell told Archbishop Howley that the opposition consisted of clergy who shared Newman's opinions, but had not the honesty to follow New-man to the Church of Rome. Rosaries, confessions, non-natural senses, monkish legends of saints floated mistily in Russell's mind. He suspected the bishops who failed to repress these errors. Howley tried vainly to correct the simple view that the remonstrants were New-manites.[3] Dr. Hampden himself had no doubt that Russell was right. He hinted to Russell that Howley's opinions might be neglected be-cause one of his chaplains was an intimate friend of Dr. Pusey;[4] and published a *Letter to Lord John Russell*, in which he maintained his entire sincerity, attributed the imputations to the Romanising party and professed orthodox propositions about all the central doctrines of the Christian faith. Some 250 members of Oxford University, in-cluding Tait, signed a counter-petition in Hampden's favour. The

[1] Howley to Russell, 26 November 1847, PRO 30/22/6G; Russell to Howley, 27 November 1847.

[2] Bedford to Russell, 21 November 1847, PRO 30/22/6G.

[3] Russell to Howley, 27 November 1847, PRO 30/22/6G; Howley to Russell, 29 November 1847, *ibid*; cf. Murray of Rochester in the House of Lords, 17 December 1847, Hansard xcv, 1339.

[4] i.e. Archdeacon Harrison, who had dissociated himself from the Puseyites. Cf. Hampden to Russell, 1 December 1847, PRO 30/22/6H. Not all the allies of the Tractarians joined against Hampden. Hook lamented the appointment, but refused to take part in the agitation because he could not bear the thought of 'baiting a man all his life because he has committed one error': Longley Papers, 2, 50–51.

Roman Catholic member Sheil talked in the Commons of the machinations of mitred mutiny.[1]

In 1836 the assailants of the prime minister had reason to hope that King William IV might repudiate Melbourne. In 1847 no one believed that Queen Victoria might repudiate Russell. Behind Russell stood Prince Albert, whose mind was also engaged to promote liberal divinity. Greville heard a rumour that at the height of the battle Prince Albert wrote Russell a daily letter to fortify him.

But unlike the professor of 1836, the bishop of 1847 needed to be elected by the dean and chapter of his cathedral. If the chapter failed to elect, the crown had power to appoint by letters patent. But the crown had not done this since the reign of Edward VI and was nervous at the effect upon the status of the future bishop. King Henry VIII attached the penalties of *praemunire* to refusal. The members of a recalcitrant chapter were liable in law to imprisonment for life and confiscation of their goods. Optimists talked of *praemunire* as an obsolete and bombastic noise, Phillpotts called it *the magna carta of tyranny*. The assailants of Russell and Hampden hoped that the dean and chapter of Hereford would risk the consequences and refuse to elect.

By an unfortunate circumstance the Dean of Hereford was that garrulous old Dr. John Merewether who laboured under a sense of grievance since King William IV promised him a bishopric. He wrote a letter about his grievance so absurd that Prince Albert wanted it published as part of the campaign for Hampden's election. He wrote the queen a verbose but restrained letter asking either that another name be recommended or that the election be postponed till the charges against Hampden had been investigated. He fixed the last legal day, 28 December 1847, for the election. Russell had again made history by driving a dean to mutiny.

The home secretary advised the dean (20 December) that her Majesty had not been pleased to issue any commands on his letter. On 22 December Merewether addressed another vast letter, this time to Lord John Russell. He said that he had now re-examined Hampden's writings for himself and discovered many assertions which were heretical, dangerous and objectionable.[2] He could not in conscience

[1] G, 47, 760. Hansard, xcvi, 274, 7 February 1848.
[2] G, 47, 774. By a curious coincidence both Hampden and Merewether applied vainly for the see of St. David's when it was vacant in 1840; MP, box 44. The application of the other was, of course, not known to either.

cast his vote to elect such a person to the bishop's throne. 'Having fully counted the cost . . . I have come to the deliberate resolve, that on Tuesday next no earthly consideration shall induce me to give my vote in the chapter of Hereford cathedral for Dr. Hampden's elevation to the see.'

On Christmas Day Russell replied to Merewether with one of his two famous letters:

'Sir, I have had the honour to receive your letter of the 22nd inst., in which you intimate to me your intention of violating the law.

'I have the honour to be your obedient servant,

'J. Russell.'

Even Russell's friends thought this letter a mistake.

In Hereford cathedral, on 28 December after divine service, the prebendaries first cast their votes, beginning with the most junior. Canon Huntingford made a little speech to explain why he was voting against. In breathless silence the dean read a prepared statement recording his dissent and protest. While the only dissenters were the dean and Canon Huntingford, three residentiary canons and eleven prebendaries voted for Hampden; but twelve prebendaries recorded their disagreement by not appearing.[1]

'Lord John Russell', wrote the *Guardian*,[2] 'has within the last six weeks destroyed, with an unparalleled rapidity, all notions that may ever have been entertained of his fitness for the position of premier. . . . His last letter to Dr. Merewether can only be characterised as worthy of himself.' The letter staked much on the chapter giving way, for if the chapter refused to elect, it committed Russell either to appoint Hampden by letters patent, with unforeseeable consequences for the relation of Hampden to his clergy, or to institute a process of

---

[1] The dean's solemn and religious protest contained an awkward little point. The non-residentiary prebendaries voted, and it was not certain that they had the right to vote. He found a statute of Hereford cathedral which ruled that the dean and three residentiary canons must vote in the majority, and therefore argued that the majority was not a legal majority. From the announcement of election he carefully erased the age-long words 'The dean and chapter' have elected, and carefully substituted 'a majority of the chapter'. When it came to the certificates to the crown, the archbishop and the bishop-elect, he tried to use the same phrases, but Canon Musgrave and Canon Lord Saye and Sele argued that 'dean and chapter' was the legal entity and ought to be used even when the dean voted against; and the dean let it pass, but added to all three certificates his personal protest against the legality of the election. He refused his traditional right to affix the chapter seal.

[2] G, 47, 777.

praemunire which was more likely to discredit the prime minister than the culprit. Keeping Christmas at Woburn, Russell felt a load off his mind when he heard the news of the election.

Meanwhile Bishop Wilberforce of Oxford got himself into trouble. By a personal letter he tried to persuade Russell to delay the proceeding while the charges were investigated and compared the government's pause in testing the charges of immorality against Prince Lee. Russell replied that while the charges of immorality were facts which could quickly be disproved or proved, the charges of unorthodoxy depended on varying clerical opinion, and so Hampden might be 'suspended between the cap and the mitre for years, to the infinite amusement of the idle crowd, but to the detriment of the church and of the royal supremacy'.[1]

The clergy of England in majority demanded that Hampden's orthodoxy be investigated before he was consecrated bishop. The university of Oxford could hardly investigate further, since Hampden refused to recant those opinions for which Oxford condemned him in 1836. But attached to the regius professorship of divinity was the parish of Ewelme in the diocese of Oxford, and an incumbent was liable to question in the courts under the church discipline act of 1840. For days Wilberforce closeted himself at Cuddesdon Palace, conning the Bampton lectures of 1832 and the objections lodged against them. On 16 December he sanctioned a suit of three incumbents of the Oxford diocese in the court of arches, so that these alleged propositions could be tested for heresy.

Wilberforce was the most brilliant and eloquent speaker of the day, the favourite of the queen and the prince, enthusiastic with the enthusiasm of his father. But he was young and inexperienced, and to tell the truth enthusiasm was not a useful quality in this realm of law courts and expediency and Whig politics which now he entered. Thinking again and again about the suit against Hampden, he wrote next day to Hampden, asking for an explicit avowal of sound doctrine and withdrawal of suspect doctrine, and declaring that he believed Hampden to hold the true faith and to have used language unconsciously at variance with it; that is, asking him to withdraw the language, not because he (Hampden) thought it unsound, but because it appeared unsound to his bishop and to most of the church. He demanded also that Hampden withdraw the Bampton lectures and

[1] Ashwell-Wilberforce, i, 447.

the *Observations on Religious Dissent*. And, well-meaning but imprudent, he told Hampden that the suit would be withdrawn if he consented to this withdrawal, thus turning a friendly letter into a menace.

On 18 December Hampden replied from Christ Church that though he regarded these elementary doctrinal enquiries as almost insulting, he affirmed all Wilberforce's propositions. He was silent on any withdrawal of his writings. The tone of the reply was uncompromising, even truculent. The suit, Wilberforce held, must go forward.

On 21 December Wilberforce held an ordination in Oxford and stayed the night with Hawkins, the provost of Oriel, who, like most of the Oxford heads of houses, was on Hampden's side. A letter arrived from Hampden to Hawkins, stating that *Observations on Religious Dissent* were being sold without his leave, and Hawkins passed the news to Wilberforce. Hawkins also said that Hampden had earlier expressed himself ready to remove incautious or obscure language from a reprint of the Bampton lectures. Wilberforce, who had received a letter from Archbishop Howley to the effect that the suit was an error and should not be permitted,[1] already wanted any excuse to quash the suit, was delighted to find evidence of a silent withdrawal, urged the promoters not to press the suit, and said that in his last reading of the Bampton lectures he was sure that Hampden was objectionable only in language, not in intention.

On 28 December Wilberforce published to the world that he was now satisfied with the 'virtual' withdrawal and with his renewed inspection of the Bampton lectures. The news was even utilised by an assenting canon of Hereford at the election that day. It was not consoling to Wilberforce or his friends that the unofficial grounds on which he based his acquittal of Hampden were later contradicted as insinuations in a letter by Hampden.[2]

Wilberforce never regained the royal favour which he lost in this turnabout. The court, where he had acted like an intimate chaplain, would have less to do with him, for Prince Albert condemned the 'persecution' of Hampden, and personally composed a long list of clerical councils pursuing the innocent down the centuries. The high church party, headed by Phillpotts, resented a betrayal; and between one side and the other Wilberforce's name was spattered with mud:

[1] Ashwell-Wilberforce, i, 468.

[2] G, 48, 36: the letter was to Faulkner, incumbent of the Round church at Cambridge. Hampden did not intend Faulkner to publish it, Hampden to S. Wilberforce, 26 January 1848, RA, C55/81.

So! you've watched the flying crow, Sam of Oxon—
Sniff'd the way the court winds blow, Sam of Oxon—
Trimmed your sails, and turned your coat . . .[1]

Before he became a bishop an affable and smooth manner already attached to him the nickname Slippery Sam. It became widely used after 1848, turning itself into the more cruel Soapy Sam about 1853, and preserving for this man of integrity a dubious reputation.

The next step to frustrate Lord John Russell was taken at the confirmation of the elected bishop in Bow church.

Inside Bow church gathered a multitude, crowding the sanctuary and pressing four or five into the pulpit. Dr. Merewether was there, and the provost of Oriel; many clergy and many women. The people had not expected the litany and showed signs of impatience while it was recited. The apparitor-general came forward to ask for objectors 'in due form of law and they shall be heard'. While Mr. Townsend the lawyer rummaged in his bag for a paper of objections, the vicar-general, Dr. Burnaby, said that by authority of the crown he conceived himself bound to confirm without suffering opposition. Dr. Addams, eminent among ecclesiastical lawyers, rose to speak. He secured leave to speak, not upon objections, but upon whether he possessed the legal right to speak. Under this cover he was able to insert a long cold history of episcopal election, and at the end became warmer. Look at the absurdity and mockery of the thing they were called upon to do. They were converting a solemn proceeding in a court into little more than a mockery. This was greeted with a few cheers, which were silenced by the court. The court held itself bound by law to proceed to confirmation, and amid laughter and cries of 'Shame', 'Order', 'Mockery', 'Farce', Hampden was confirmed. When he left the church he was cheered in the streets by most of the crowd, while others hooted and called out 'Mockery'. He could not get through the crowd to his own carriage and was trotted away by one of the lawyers.[2]

Dr. Addams and Dr. Phillimore were not exhausted. They

---

[1] MC, 1 January 1848. But Russell was just, and told the queen that the Bishop of Oxford had done much to end the persecution of Hampden, Russell to Prince Albert, 2 January 1848, RA, C55/61. For the history of the nickname cf. David Newsome in *History Today*, September 1963, 624ff. The *Record* was respectable enough to prefer the name Proteus.

[2] Description, e.g., in Arthur Wilson to Longley, 11 January 1848, Longley Papers, 2, 52–53; cf. *Memorials of Bishop Hampden*, 154–7.

promptly applied to the court of queen's bench for a mandamus to compel the Archbishop of Canterbury or his vicar-general to hear the objections against Dr. Hampden. On 14 January 1848, to the alarm of Russell's advisers, they secured from the judges a ruling that there was a case to answer. The Hampden affair had long passed quite beyond the question of the fitness or unfitness of Hampden to be a bishop. It had become a constitutional question, to test what safeguards the established church possessed if the royal supremacy were abused.

The case of Queen Victoria versus the Archbishop of Canterbury began to be heard on Monday, 24 January 1848, before the Lord Chief Justice Denman and Judges Patteson, Coleridge and Erle, in a court filled with spectators including Keble and Bishop Copleston of Llandaff, and with a crowd in the street; the case to determine whether the legal officers of the archbishop could be compelled to hear objections against a candidate. Dr. Hampden's consecration, fixed for 30 January, was postponed, and judgment was given on Tuesday, 1 February. The court was equally divided. Coleridge and Patteson (though Patteson was too deaf to hear the argument)[1] would grant the mandamus, Denman and Erle would refuse it; and by that equality of votes the mandamus was refused. The attorney-general carried the prerogative of the crown to the limit. Even if a man had been convicted of atrocious crime, the primate has no choice but obey the act of Parliament and must consecrate him. Denman and Erle would not proceed so far. But the crown lawyers had a potent case when they argued that to revive the reality of an old ceremony like confirmation would be inconvenient, because allowing any cross-grained crank to issue public pleas against a new bishop. The other side admitted that this was not a desirable way of resisting a bishop's appointment, but claimed than an undesirable way was better than no way at all. The advocates of reasonable independence for the church were not likely to look upon the confirmation at Bow with less interest when they found that the Whigs in Parliament whispered that the ceremony must be abolished, lest the future appointments of the crown be hampered.

A last safeguard remained, if indeed it were a safeguard. They knew that Howley remonstrated privately against the appointment and hoped that he might refuse to consecrate. The barrier was flimsy, because if the archbishop declined the crown could issue a commission to other bishops, and with Whig bishops scattered round England by

[1] Grey to Lord John Russell, 26 January 1848, PRO 30/22/7A.

Melbourne and Russell it was unthinkable that all would refuse to consecrate. It was hoped as a supreme measure of distrust.

It was never tested. For three years Howley had been slowly failing in health. Day by day he sustained his soul by repeating 'Leave off from wrath and let go displeasure: fret not thyself, else shalt thou be moved to do evil'. Amid the clamour of partisans he walked quiet and serene, beloved even by Queen Victoria, who at first had so disliked his timid manner[1] and came at last to deep sorrow at his passing. Amid the splendours of Lambeth palace, last of the prince-archbishops with gilt-edged paper and solemn torchlight processions and banquets in the great hall, yet bearing on his person no whiff of grandeur, as one walking through the fire unscathed, the gentlest and wisest archbishop of the century died as he had lived, fading peaceably and unobtrusively to his grave. It was 11 February 1848, the day before his eighty-third birthday.

The usual game of prophecy produced the hair-raising proposal that Russell would nominate Archbishop Whately of Dublin. By far the ablest academic mind on the bench was the historian Connop Thirlwall, Bishop of St. David's, and his name was rumoured. But Thirlwall, brilliant and coherent on paper, was hesitant and remote as a pastor, and would hardly do. Indeed, when they omitted the fourteen bishops who remonstrated, and Prince Lee because he was only just a bishop, and Davys of Peterborough because he was a Tory, and Maltby of Durham because his age was 77, and Stanley of Norwich because his person was quaint and his orthodoxy suspect, there were only three or four from whom to choose. In the House of Lords Bishop Phillpotts talked openly of Russell going about like Diogenes with his lantern to find a dishonest man who would consent to become Archbishop of Canterbury for the express purpose of consecrating an unworthy man to a bishopric.[2] Russell considered the names of Sumner of Chester, Lonsdale of Lichfield and Pepys of Worcester.[3]

---

[1] Churton, *Joshua Watson*, 287, 344; Queen Victoria's *Journal*, 11 February 1848; Longford, 218.

[2] Hansard, xcvi, 637, 15 February 1848.

[3] Letter of 12 February 1848, PRO 30/22/7A. Sumner had refused the offer of St. Asaph in October 1846, cf. Russell to the queen, 3 October 1846, RA, D15/58. Russell consulted Sir George Grey whether Sumner was too old and received a favourable reply: Russell to the queen, 31 January 1848, RA, F32/48. The queen laid it down that the new archbishop must be a liberal man. She seems to have mentioned Sumner's name to Russell before anyone else suggested it, for she put the idea fourteen days before Howley died. Prince Albert strongly supported Sumner as best.

On 22 February the *congé d'élire* to Canterbury was announced, and the name was Bishop Sumner of Chester.

Sumner's name gave Russell the credit of selecting a good honest religious man, and for not selecting another 'insult' to the church like Whately. Several bishops were greatly relieved.[1] Yet Sumner had the reputation of being inadequate to such eminence, of being a kind, earnest and weak man, with little judgment, and an adherent of the evangelical party. In truth almost anyone tolerable to Russell, and to Prince Albert behind him, would have been intolerable to large numbers of clergy in the prevailing weather.

Hampden was therefore consecrated in Lambeth palace chapel on 26 March, the archbishop being assisted by three bishops all of the Whig party, Copleston of Llandaff, Pepys of Worcester and Stanley of Norwich. He did not have to wait for the House of Lords, since the new Bishop of Chester was his junior. The carpers called him 'the Russell bishop' and a few sticklers said that, since his election was invalid but his consecration undoubted, he should be addressed as Bishop Hampden, not as Bishop of Hereford.[2] As Bishop of Hereford he retreated shyly into the episcopal library and ministered innocuously for twenty years. On the rare occasions when he emerged from his heaped folios he surprised everyone by a strong orthodoxy. Not a

[1] Cf. Denison of Salisbury to Longley of Ripon, 23 February 1848, Longley Papers, 2, 60–61.

[2] Only a year and a half later Dr. Hampden had the odd experience of being singled out for public praise by the most intransigent of his former press enemies. He was the first bishop to set aside a day for public thanksgiving at the cessation of the cholera. At the end of October 1849 he appeared to preach at Abergavenny, and dissenters flocked to hear him, but Hampden preached on the sin of schism, G, 49, 671,696. He was strong for condemning *Essays & Reviews*.

After various rumours of the succession to Chester—Hampden (!); Whewell; Peacock, Dean of Ely; Waddington, Dean of Durham—it was given to Graham, the master of Christ's College. He had wanted to admit dissenters to Cambridge in 1834 and was reported to have proposed transferring the services from chapel to hall, but was otherwise of good name, even among Tories. He had taken a prominent and delicate part in the campaign of 1847 to get Prince Albert elected chancellor of Cambridge University, cf. Romilly's *Diary*.

Russell also played safe in the succession to Hampden as regius professor. Whately advised Hinds, and if not Hinds, Baden Powell. Nassau Senior advised Milman, though he had been told in Oxford that Milman was suspect of infidelity for his *History of the Jews*, Senior to Russell, 19 November 1847; Whately to Senior, 14 and 16 November 1847; Hampden wanted Archdeacon Ormerod, Hampden to Senior, 14 November 1847. Russell selected the sober and competent Jacobson whom Hampden had not wanted, Hampden to Russell, 28 November 1847. Archbishop Howley put in a good word for Jacobson, Howley to Russell, 29 November 1847; all these letters in PRO 30/22/6G. Oxford talked of Arthur Stanley as possible, but he was thought too young.

single liberal divine of the Victorian age derived even one idea from Dr. Hampden.

To understand the troubles of the next few years it is necessary to remember that Russell had given a large body of churchmen cause to think that he was a tyrant, and that the royal supremacy in its present form was intolerable. The attorney-general publicly maintained that even if the crown appointed a vile man the chapter had no choice but to elect and the bishops no choice but to consecrate. The lay resentment at clerical assaults upon Hampden produced further comments calculated to arouse hatred of the state's interference in religion. A radical member of Parliament talked of removing from cathedral chapters all power to check the government in appointing 'learned theologians' to bishoprics.[1]

Russell, realising that he could never stamp out ritual innovation without quicker and more effective courts, and stimulated by Prince Albert with his knowledge of German consistory courts, contemplated setting up an ecclesiastical court which bore a strange similarity to that old high commission which smelt so high in English history. He privately proposed a committee of the privy council for ecclesiastical affairs, of which all the members must be Anglican, some laymen and some bishops. But he found that even Archbishop Sumner hotly disapproved the plan, and desisted.[2] Amid these schemes and rumours high churchmen leapt to their armour. A church, they said, committed suicide if it lost the power to determine its faith and entrusted that power to an external body.[3] Many churchmen regarded the state as now an external body. And meanwhile the reputation of the Reformation sank a little lower, and the magnetic power of Rome tugged a little harder; for in the Reformation English governments seemed sometimes to have been guilty of that act which was now so feared, altering the faith of the church without leave of the church. The clergy were alert, sensitive, prickly, their consciences not at ease. Some wise men, who thought that Russell made a calamitous error of judgment, nevertheless deplored the campaign against Hampden. For prolonged agitation could only result either in partial victory or in seething discontent.

England was not yet finished with orthodoxy and patronage.

---

[1] Heywood, in Hansard xcviii, 1105, 16 May 1848.
[2] Sumner to Russell, 18 September 1848: PRO 30/22/7D. [3] G, 48, 257.

In the same week that the Hampden affair was at last ended an ominous little notice appeared in the paper. Dr. Phillpotts pronounced Mr. Gorham to be unsound in doctrine, and therefore refused to institute him to the living of Brampford Speke in the diocese of Exeter.

2. MR. GORHAM

Upon certain subjects—of which the sacraments were the most important—the language of the prayer book was more traditional, more 'Catholic', than the language of the Thirty-nine Articles. Long before the Oxford Movement began, the argument between high churchmen and evangelicals focused upon the sacrament of baptism. The evangelical was anxious to lay before men the need for conversion, for moral regeneration; and was afraid of any doctrine that man had been unconditionally regenerated in infant baptism and needed no subsequent regeneration. He knew that the baptismal service of the English prayer book described the baptised infant as regenerate, and wrote books to prove that he might use the service with a good conscience, interpreting the liturgy in a charitable sense.

The doctrinal argument, keen enough early in the century, was sharpened by conscientious men during the eighteen-forties. The extended awareness of 'Catholicity', and of the claim to teach orthodox truth, meant that everyone was more insistent upon the necessity of subscribing to what he believed to be the truth. If the liturgy declared the infant to be regenerate, and evangelicals interpreted the act to mean a conditional sign of future regeneration, high churchmen were readier to insist and less ready to make allowances. They were encouraged in their mood of insistence because they felt Lord John Russell to be weakening the strength of traditional doctrine. If a 'heretical' state started breaking the safeguards against heresy, some people who had not hitherto troubled themselves much on orthodoxy would become exceeding orthodox. It seemed to them as though the Parliament of England was suddenly trying to pass a law to change the doctrines of the Roman Catholic Church in England, or the Presbyterians, or even the Plymouth Brethren. An ominous story was circulated during the summer of 1848 that Lord John Russell was in communication with the new Archbishop of Canterbury about permitting various doctrinal passages to be omitted from the prayer book,[1] and few high churchmen felt confidence in the orthodoxy of Archbishop Sumner.

The battle over doctrine was joined by that combative champion, Bishop Phillpotts of Exeter.

George Cornelius Gorham was a fellow of Queens' College in Cambridge. Educated by a Quaker schoolmaster, he became an evangelical at Cambridge, was threatened with a refusal of ordination by the Bishop of Ely because he held the evangelical doctrine of baptism, and served as curate of Clapham when it was still the Zion of evangelical leaders. Not so much a theologian as a learned antiquarian, he was presented by the Tory lord chancellor, Lyndhurst, in January 1846, to the parish of St. Just with Penwith in Cornwall, then containing a population of 8,000 miners. Bishop Phillpotts welcomed the appointment and installed Gorham without a qualm. Six months later Gorham appealed for funds to build a district church connected with the evangelical Church Extension Society, and applied in his circular to the bishop. Phillpotts disliked the circular because it called the Church of England 'the national establishment'; and though willing to subscribe £50, he was only willing if the district church was withdrawn from communion with the Church Extension Society. In September 1846 they were arguing over a curate; and Phillpotts, shocked to see in the *Ecclesiastical Gazette* that Gorham advertised for a curate who should be 'free from Tractarian error', demanded to interview the prospective curate and test his doctrines, especially upon baptism. He said that to advertise in such a manner was to encourage party spirit and invite applications from unsound and dangerous men. The irritated Gorham protested against the bishop's desire to add a test of doctrine behind the Thirty-nine Articles, and reaffirmed that he was determined to fight Tractarian error. The two gladiators loosened the swords in their scabbards.[2]

Meanwhile Gorham found that at the western tip of Cornwall he could scarcely educate his children, and asked the lord chancellor—

---

[1] G, 48, 518; including Athanasian Creed, portions of marriage, baptism and burial services. In 1848 the word *doctrinal* was normally pronounced as a dactyl with a short i. It achieved its modern pronunciation by 1870, cf. G, 70, 495.

[2] Phillpotts regularly interviewed curates and incumbents and examined them before licensing or instituting them. In the winter of 1833–4 he was in trouble with radical newspapers for the practice, and already claimed that it was his habit; cf. *Standard*, 28 December 1833; JB 1834, 13; *Standard*, 8 January 1834. For his conduct during 1846 in examining at least two other Devonshire clergymen, see the letters of Savile and Bowden in the Gorham Papers.

now the Whig, Lord Cottenham—for a living nearer a town. In August 1847 the lord chancellor offered him the parish of Brampford Speke, a little farming parish of 400 souls, not far from Exeter; and though the income was less by £300 a year than that of St. Just, Gorham determined to accept it. Upon the required documents, Phillpotts wrote that in view of the letters of the year before he could not conscientiously countersign the testimonials. There was then a long delay while the lord chancellor enquired the cause of this episcopal refusal, and the Church of England would have profited if he had seen reefs ahead and steered Gorham towards some other diocese. But Lord Cottenham, like all Whig lawyers, was neither friend nor admirer of Phillpotts. Informed by Gorham of the nature of the controversy, he at last issued the legal presentation to the living of Brampford Speke. Gorham had already removed much of the furniture from St. Just when he received a letter from Phillpotts refusing to institute him until he should have examined him, to be satisfied whether he was sound in doctrine. On 17 December, at Bishopstow outside Torquay, the examination began.

The examination was unusual. It was solely concerned with the doctrine of baptismal regeneration. It lasted for thirty-eight hours, on five days divided by a Sunday; and even at 5.30 p.m. on 22 December Gorham removed some more questions to answer by letter. On legal advice he said he was willing to be further examined, and they hammered at it again for fourteen more hours on 8–10 March 1848. On 11 March Phillpotts finally declared that he found Gorham's doctrine to be unsound and declined to institute him to the living of Brampford Speke. He had required answers to 149 questions. Meanwhile the three eldest Gorham children were staying with various friends, Mrs. Gorham and the youngest children were living dismally in the quarter-furnished vicarage of St. Just, the newly built national school at St. Just was closed all the winter, and the parishioners both of St. Just and Brampford Speke were stirred to suspicion and contempt of their present or future incumbent.

On 3 April 1848 there were amused comments in Parliament at the length of the examination, and the attorney-general disclosed that the lord chancellor had asked his advice on what should be done. On 12 April Gorham sent a circular letter to the public. He described the circumstances as a 'cruel exercise of episcopal power, stretched beyond the boundaries of reason and decency'. He said that if the precedent were established a Tractarian bishop would be able to exclude from his diocese everyone whose views did not conform to his own. Bishop Phillpotts was serene. He had excluded from his diocese a teacher who would teach error and he knew that to be his bounden duty. He carried the war further by appointing a commission to examine charges that Gorham had on several occasions omitted the Lord's prayer at its proper place in the liturgy.

In June 1848 Gorham asked the court of arches to compel the bishop to institute. The case was delayed for six months because Phillpotts did nothing until threatened with another action in the queen's bench.

The question at bottom was the same question as that over the nomination of Dr. Hampden, and the same question as that which six years before destroyed the unity of the Church of Scotland; had the patron, crown or other, the right to present whomsoever he liked, without regarding objections lodged by the relevant authority of the church? In Scotland the lawyers contended that the ecclesiastics were interfering with the rights of property, and the party of Dr. Chalmers contended that the church could never surrender the right, necessary to its existence, of testing the candidate presented by the patron. In England the controversy was in one respect less acute and less calamitous in its consequences, since far fewer English churchmen resented the proper exercise of state authority, or presumed to claim that the church alone could determine the boundary between church authority and state authority. In another respect the controversy ran deeper in England inasmuch as it touched doctrine. No one contended that Mr. Gorham was unsuitable because his future parishioners would not accept his ministrations, for no one contended that his parishioners had any right or standing in the matter. Nor was it denied that the bishop had the duty of satisfying himself about a candidate, and that if he found the patron presenting an atheistical or immoral or unordained person, he must act. But it was contended that the crown was presenting a heretic, and that the church must possess the right to exclude a heretical teacher from its pulpits. Thus the questions in England came to be, first, whether Gorham was in truth a heretic; and secondly, more momentous, what authority possessed the right to determine whether he was a heretic or not.

In the arches court the doctrine of baptism was hunted through the liturgy and articles, through Luther and the Augsburg Confession, through the fathers of the ancient church and the fathers of the

Reformation, through the English divines of the Protestant centuries. The chasm which divided the parties was the effect of infant baptism. Gorham refused to assert that regeneration was always given in baptism, though he allowed that it might so be given, and that baptism and regeneration were so connected that baptism was made truly efficacious when regenerating grace was given. He sometimes represented the bishop as teaching that baptism was always and unconditionally efficacious to regenerate; but this was not just to Phillpotts, and his advocate publicly accused Gorham of being dishonest in this representation. For the parties were agreed that scripture and the church linked baptism with regeneration. They were agreed that by hypocrisy or atheism an adult might bar the working of sacramental grace at the moment of baptism. But the schoolmen of the middle ages argued that infants, having committed no actual sin, were incapable of putting a bar to the entry of grace, and therefore that with the baptism of infants 'regeneration' was linked indissolubly. The language of the Book of Common Prayer supported the opinion that this was the teaching of the Church of England; for immediately the baby was baptised the priest was made to say unconditionally 'Seeing now that this child is regenerate . . .', and in the catechism the child was taught to affirm that in his baptism he was made a child of God and an inheritor of the kingdom of heaven. Phillpotts derived his most cogent pleas from the language of the liturgy, and from the historical circumstance that several ministers could be shown to have resigned their parishes because they believed Gorham's doctrine. Gorham derived his most cogent pleas from the circumstance that the language of adult baptism, which the bishop admitted to be conditional, was hardly distinguishable from that of infant baptism; and that English ministers could be found who had not resigned their livings nor been ejected, though they held the doctrine of Gorham.

The dean of arches, Sir Herbert Jenner Fust, was never guilty of haste in his judgments and his health was delicate. While the churches breathed expectantly and the parish of Brampford Speke degenerated, he took four and a half months before he was ready to deliver judgment. He was well aware that whichever way he decided someone might leave the Church of England, and that though the case was nominally of a single pastor he was in danger of contributing unwillingly to doctrinal definition. He found himself ill at ease among the ramifications of historical theology.

On 2 August 1849, two years after the lord chancellor's presentation, the dean of arches was carried into court by two footmen and
delivered his judgment. He entertained no doubt that (though the
meaning of regeneration was imprecise) the infant was regenerated in
baptism. Mr. Gorham had maintained a doctrine opposed to that of
the Church of England, the bishop had shown sufficient reason for his
refusal, and the case must be dismissed with costs to the bishop.

To many members of the evangelical party the decision if upheld
was fatal. They had learnt to press for conversion, for repentance and
faith, and to associate the word regeneration with the heart-renewal
of the already baptised man. If they were orthodox Calvinists, they
were able to attribute saving grace to sacraments administered to the
elect, but to none others. In 1849 most of the English evangelicals were
not orthodox Calvinists. But they preferred to think of the sacrament
less as a vehicle of regenerating grace than as a sign or pledge or
promise of a future regeneration, itself under conditions of growth in
penitence and faith. The language of the liturgy, they believed, was
always conditional language. Few of them were perplexed at the need
to use the prayer book. Certain allies of Gorham denounced the oppos-
ing doctrine as a popish fiction and declared that it destroyed souls.
But not many of that party wanted to exclude from the Church of
England those many churchmen who understood the prayer book in
the medieval and traditional sense. They wished to maintain their
liberty. The decision of the court of arches seemed to menace that
liberty and foreshadow a disruption in England, the exodus of the
evangelicals. The threat was not immediate; partly because the decision
applied only to one parish and one pastor, and declared that this one
pastor had rightly been refused institution; and partly because the
judgment was under appeal. But no evangelical could doubt that if
the judgment were upheld the consequences for the Church of
England would be grave and damaging.

Conscientious men had once interpreted their subscription to
articles and prayer book with breadth and freedom. But since *Tract
XC* and the contest over Ward and Oakeley and the 'non-natural
sense', conscientious men were more anxious in wishing to make a
literal subscription. *Tract XC* and its aftermath seemed paradoxically
to have diminished for the time the comprehensiveness of the Church
of England.

If the term is understood narrowly, the evangelicals of 1849 were

not a numerous body. They were never numerous, and the events of
the thirties and forties drew many of them into the high church movement. But under this pressure they rallied their forces. They were
joined by everyone who feared Tractarians, everyone of the liberal
school in theology, everyone for whom the name of Phillpotts was
anathema; and by a mass of English laity, who were hazy in dogmatic
theology and could hardly distinguish the argument. Archbishop
Musgrave of York issued a charge holding the effects of infant baptism
to be an open question, and declaring that Gorham's doctrine was
legitimate within the Church of England; and in the same month the
Archbishop of Canterbury preferred to the rectory of All Hallows the
Great in London William Goode who was the leading evangelical
theologian. The two archbishops could hardly have declared more
openly what they thought of the theological question and of
Phillpotts.

But some of the Tractarians were as perplexed and anxious as the
evangelicals. They were content with the judgment and declared that
no other judgment had been possible. But they were now confronted
with the court of appeal in ecclesiastical cases, the judicial committee of
the privy council. Their anxiety arose not only because they awaited
its verdict with concern, but because they were forced to examine the
nature of the final court of appeal. The court might decide 'wrongly';
but even if it decided 'rightly', was it a suitable court to be determining
doctrine? We are reminded of Lords Brougham and Cottenham
giving the final verdict for the patron in the Auchterarder case of
1839 and thereby throwing the Church of Scotland and the state into
their postures of antagonism. In the months before the court sat, some
Tractarian writers set out to prove in pamphlets that the verdict of
the court would not touch the church at all, even if it condemned
Phillpotts and upheld Gorham.

The constitution of the court of appeal became momentous.

The judicial committee of the privy council judged appeals only
after 1833. When King Henry VIII abolished the Roman jurisdiction
the final appeal was given to a court of royal commission, appointed
for each case of appeal, and known as the high court of delegates.
Until 1640 this court appears not to have exercised jurisdiction in
suits over doctrine or ritual, for such suits were brought before the
court of high commission. Anyone might be appointed as a delegate,
and in its earlier years the court often contained bishops as well as

civil and common lawyers. There were always ecclesiastical lawyers from doctors commons, but no bishop sat in the court after 1751. The court declined with the decline of doctors commons and of the profession of civilian lawyer compared with common lawyer, and there were many grumbles against the court of delegates during the eighteenth century. It was complained that the court was slow, inefficient and expensive; that the law was uncertain because the judges never gave public reasons for their judgments; that the court was unable to grant costs and therefore injured appellants; that appeals were heard by junior and inexperienced lawyers; and that the mode of payment— a guinea a day paid to each judge at the end of the case by the winning party—was undignified.

In 1830 the working of the court of delegates was examined by a royal commission, which reported in 1832. The commissioners suggested that the court be abolished and its jurisdiction transferred to the privy council. They argued that the judges of the privy council were more experienced, that the tribunal was permanent and need not be constituted for each appeal, and that in this tribunal the reasons for the judgment must be publicly stated. The government accepted this recommendation, and in 1832 carried it into effect for almost all purposes.[1] In the next year they created out of legally qualified privy councillors a judicial committee to hear all appeals to the king in council. An act of 1840 added to this committee bishops who were privy councillors if the case were ecclesiastical.

In this constitutional change no one distinguished appeals on points of doctrine from appeals on other ecclesiastical matters. The sole criterion was the efficient working of legal machinery. Even in 1832 no lawyer or ecclesiastic[2] questioned that there must be appeal to a crown court. And the high court of delegates became hazily romantic to a generation which learnt to regard the judicial committee as a juggernaut to be resisted. It must be remembered that the court of

[1] Recourse was still allowed to the delegates by a provision in the patents of colonial bishops: cf. *Ecclesiastical Courts Commission* (1883), vol. i, pp. xliii–iv. Though the commission reported in 1832, it made a special report in January 1831 recommending the transfer to the privy council. The act of 1832 is 2 & 3 William IV, cap. 92; of 1833, 3 & 4 William IV, cap. 41.

[2] The theoretical question was used as a stick to beat the establishment by Childs of Bungay as early as 1842–3, after the judicial committee decided in the case of Mastin *v.* Escott that baptism by a dissenter was valid: cf. the rector of Topcroft to W. E. Gladstone, Add. MSS. 44360/93. For doubts whether the privy council would be ecclesiastical enough, see the evidence of H. B. Swabey to ecclesiastical courts commission on 13 December 1830, PP, 1843, xix, 524.

delegates, equally with the judicial committee, derived its jurisdiction from the crown, and was no more a specially church court than the judicial committee. But the change had this serious consequence: it removed the final appeal from a court where the judges, even when junior and inexperienced, were trained in the canon and civil law; and transferred it to a court where some of the judges, though vastly more eminent, were less accustomed to the system of ecclesiastical courts.

There is no doubt whatever that the change, regarded as a change in machinery, made for more effective administration of justice.

As soon as Gorham appealed from the court of arches, both the entrenched parties in the church perceived what might lie ahead. If the judicial committee upheld Phillpotts, many evangelicals might be compelled to secede from the Church of England; and if the judicial committee upheld Gorham, the powerful body of high churchmen might secede from the Church of England or try to insist upon its disestablishment. Both sides attempted a faltering wistful approach to Parliament for a remedy even before the case was settled in the court of arches.

A bill was introduced into the Commons to make the Thirty-nine Articles alone (instead of the Thirty-nine Articles and the prayer book) the test of doctrine in the Church of England. This bill looked to the clergy like an effort by the non-Anglican state to alter the doctrine of the church without consulting the church. On the other side Bishop Blomfield, seeing the rocks ahead, introduced a bill to Parliament with the object of reforming the final court of appeal. He proposed that in cases of heresy, false doctrine, blasphemy or schism, the court of final appeal should consist of the two archbishops, the lord chancellor, three other bishops, eight other lawyers including the dean of arches, and the regius and Lady Margaret professors of divinity at Oxford and Cambridge. It was provided that no one might sit in this court unless he were a member of the Church of England. The bishop could hardly have expected to change the court of appeal before Jenner Fust's decision came for review.

The arrangements for hearing the appeal were in the hands of Lord Lansdowne and of the clerk to the privy council, Greville the diarist. It was soon agreed that the two archbishops and Bishop Blomfield should attend. Blomfield never answered the invitation, and was unreliably said by Greville to have wished that the prelates should not be present,[1] but attended the court when the time came. There was difficulty in securing a common-law judge to attend.

The court met on 11 December 1849 in the crowded committee-room of the privy council office, with a fine arched ceiling, and in the centre of the room an oblong table. On one side of the table sat the three prelates, Lord Campbell, and Mr. Pemberton Leigh, a retired Tory lawyer; on the other side sat Lord Langdale, the master of the rolls, a lawyer with a clear dry intellect and a reputation for fussing in court, Baron Parke (the common-law judge who at last consented), Vice-Chancellor Knight-Bruce, and Dr. Lushington, while Greville sat at a side table and Lord Lansdowne moved restlessly about the room, sometimes at the fire, sometimes whispering with Campbell or with Greville or occasionally with the spectators beyond the rails, and after a time going away. It was not quite certain that the judicial committee was in the formal sense a court, and therefore, though the advocates wore wigs and gowns, the judges were in undress coats and black cravats, so that spectators found the atmosphere not like that of a court. High churchmen were nervous about Lord Campbell. He was known to be the son of a Scottish Presbyterian minister, was fondly supposed to have imbibed Calvinism with his mother's milk, and was alleged, a few days before, to have declared privately that the decision in the court of arches was sure to be reversed.[2] But then high churchmen were equally nervous about the Archbishops of Canterbury and York. Lord Campbell himself seems to have sensed a certain oddness in finding himself a member of a tribunal to decide a question of dogmatic divinity.[3] But for all his Scots blood, he was now a communicant of the Church of England, and even a patron of the Sisters of Mercy, whom under Pusey's guidance Miss Sellon gathered in the slums of Devonport. Strong Protestants, who feared Miss Sellon's ladies as nuns, talked with painful humour about Campbell's 'Miss-Sellon-ies', and were not quite confident. A few people found it unfortunate that Lord Langdale was a Bickersteth, the son of one eminent evangelical clergyman and the brother of another who had published a pamphlet for Mr. Gorham. Mr. Pemberton Leigh was a Tory, the chancellor of the Duchy of Cornwall and a friend of Prince Albert, a lawyer who was wealthy enough to need no practice and therefore devoted himself to organising the procedure of the judicial committee of the privy council. He was a pious member of the Church

---

[1] Greville, vi, 190.   [2] G, 49, 847–8.   [3] Cf. *Life of Campbell*, ii, 266.

of England. Stephen Lushington was the only trained ecclesiastical lawyer in the court; a Whig with radical affection in politics, and a steady churchman. Sir James Knight-Bruce, the vice-chancellor, was a deep-hued Tory who had been employed to defend cathedrals against the depredations of the Ecclesiastical Commission, and was in high repute for the speed and accuracy of his legal mind.

The arguments of counsel before the judicial committee repeated in substance the arguments alleged in the court of arches. On the one side it was pleaded that there was sufficient vagueness in the idea of spiritual regeneration, and in its connexion with the baptismal rite, to warrant liberty of opinion in Mr. Gorham; that the doctrinal language of the articles was more important to the decision than the devotional language of the liturgy; that the mind of the Church of England was friendly to comprehension. On the other side it was argued that the belief of a church was expressed as well by its forms of worship as by its formal articles, that English law had always admitted this, and that the words of the liturgy were inescapable.

The arguments were tranquil and courteous; but at the end, on the fifth day (18 December 1849), there was a touch of drama. Phillpotts's lawyer, Edward Badeley, at the close of a long and learned development of the English theology of baptism, turned upon the two silent archbishops and declared that he laboured under some disadvantage because at least one of them, if not both, had committed themselves to the opposite side; Archbishop Sumner by preferring William Goode, known to be a partisan for Gorham. One of the spectators said that the effect in court was like an electric shock. All three prelates looked uncomfortable. The watching clerk to the privy council thought this assault injudicious and indecent,[1] but Sumner replied mildly, though not without a touch of emotion, that he had no thought of Goode's book on baptism, not yet published, when he preferred him. Badeley apologised to the archbishop, and Lord Campbell said severely that the remark was most indecorous; but Badeley secured what he wanted, a public statement by Archbishop Sumner that the patronage of Goode was not a befriending of his doctrine on baptism.

When the pleadings were ended on the afternoon of 18 December, Lord Langdale said that they would consider their judgment, and the

---

[1] G, 49, 848; Greville, vi, 191–2. It was as well that Badeley knew nothing of a letter of sympathy from Bishop Sumner of Chester to Gorham dated 31 January 1848, and now to be found in the Gorham Papers.

court was cleared. The judges, the three prelates and Greville the clerk remained in the chamber to partake of an elegant dinner at the public expense, and there they briefly discussed the case in private. It was at once evident that all the laymen except Knight-Bruce thought the judgment of the court of arches to be wrong, and that it should be reversed. Lord Campbell was afterwards alleged to have hesitated inwardly what the answer on legal grounds alone ought to be, and to think that public policy demanded a decision against Phillpotts, later justifying the intervention of policy into a purely legal argument by the plea that the judicial committee was not a normal court, but a body advising the crown. The bishops said that they would like time to consider, and would deliver their opinions in writing. It was accordingly agreed to adjourn.

On 15 January 1850 Blomfield, hesitant and undecided, gave an opinion for Phillpotts, Knight-Bruce was strongly for Phillpotts; all the others, including the two archbishops, were strongly for Gorham, and Lord Langdale agreed to draft the judgment. Blomfield said that he hoped nothing would be said to condemn the doctrine of Phillpotts, and they all exclaimed that they would take care nothing of the kind was done; they would 'steer as clear as possible' of any declaration of opinion about doctrine, and affirm only that Gorham had not taught so clearly and undoubtedly against the articles and formularies as to warrant the bishop's refusal.[1] Lushington said that he had the greatest difficulty in understanding what Gorham taught.

On 9 March 1850 they met at the council office to deliver judgment. Knight-Bruce refused to come. They first considered Lord Langdale's draft and omitted various expressions. Langdale, Campbell and Lushington wanted to give Gorham costs, but Pemberton Leigh objected, and so it was agreed to say nothing of costs.[2] The argument kept the public out for nearly half an hour after the main doors had opened and there had been a rush of clergy up the staircase. Lansdowne and Brougham were there, Chevalier Bunsen and Dr. Wiseman, and a good number of ladies. Lord Langdale delivered quite a simple judgment, for just over an hour, and at the end there was applause and cries of *Bravo*. Langdale insisted again that they were not attempting to define the truth of a doctrine. They were not satisfied that this single clergyman contradicted the formularies of the Church of England.

Thus some evangelicals and broad churchmen were saved for the

[1] Greville, vi, 193.   [2] Greville, vi, 210.

Church of England. The Tractarians Robert Wilberforce and James Hope (Scott) walked silently down the steps of the privy council office, heads drooping. But William Goode's face shone with bliss.[1]

Now began the tragedy of the other side. Was the Church of England Catholic if exponents of non-Catholic doctrine were allowed to teach in its parishes? Was the judgment a definition of Anglican doctrine or not? If it was a definition of Anglican doctrine, had it any authority over the Church of England? Was the pronouncement of the judicial committee no more relevant to the church than a pronouncement by the Great Mogul, with the important exception that it possessed the tyrannical power of enforcing its orders against the church? If the pronouncement was not a church declaration, what could the church do to repudiate that pronouncement as untrue? Was anything possible short of disestablishment and a free Church of England? Since Convocation was suppressed, there was no organ nor mouthpiece to make repudiation. To press for the revival of Convocation would be nothing, for the high church party had pressed the revival for at least three years. Would a corporate declaration by the bishops suffice—allowing that the two archbishops, and perhaps others, must be omitted? If not by the bishops, by whom?

Manning went to Gladstone's house, and found him in bed with influenza. Gladstone threw up his arms and said, 'The Church of England is gone unless it releases itself by some authoritative act.'[2] Two days later, on Sunday, 10 March, George Denison gathered the churchwardens and other witnesses into the vestry of East Brent church in Somerset, and read them two solemn protests; first, that no judgment of the privy council in a matter of doctrine could be accepted by the church, and secondly, that the church must without delay make a public declaration upon the truth of baptism.[3] The protest was imitated in several parishes. Manning convened the clergy of the Chichester archdeaconry in the cathedral library and by 92 to 8 they voted a formal address to their bishop.[4] Keble denounced the crown as heretical; Pusey declared the court to be improperly constituted;

---

[1] *Memoir of Bunsen*, ii, 246.

[2] Purcell, *Manning*, i, 528, late reminiscence. Cf. Wilberforce Papers, BL. Dep.c.93, where Blomfield is seen trying and failing to collect signatures of bishops to a declaration, during April-May 1850.

[3] *Notes of my Life*, 193–5. On 18 March Hume asked Lord John Russell whether the government would prosecute Denison. Russell replied in the negative.

[4] Purcell, *Manning*, i, 533.

sixty-three eminent laymen, including eleven English peers and eighteen members of Parliament (among them Gladstone and Lord John Manners), published a letter to the Bishop of London[1] that the Church of England was in danger and that the judicial committee was unfit, and asked him to take counsel with other bishops. Bishop Bagot of Bath and Wells issued a circular to his diocese declaring the unconditional regeneration of infants in baptism to be the doctrine of the Church of England. Miss Sellon compelled Lord Campbell to withdraw his name from the list of patrons of her nuns because he had assisted at a judgment 'fatal to the Church of England unless absolutely rejected'.[2] The most spectacular of these protests was the publication, towards the end of March, of a powerful and sarcastic letter from the Bishop of Exeter to the Archbishop of Canterbury, repudiating the judgment, declaring that he would not obey it, and threatening (though without mentioning Sumner's name) to withhold communion from Sumner if he obeyed it; and the idea of the Bishop of Exeter excommunicating the Archbishop of Canterbury caused amusement, indignation and alarm.

But the most ominous of the protests was a series of resolutions of 19 March, by only thirteen names, headed by Archdeacons Manning and Robert Wilberforce, and including Thorp, Mill, Pusey, Keble, Dodsworth, Henry Wilberforce, W. J. E. Bennett, J. C. Talbot, R. Cavendish, Badeley and J. R. Hope. The Church of England will be bound by the sentence unless it openly rejects the erroneous doctrine. The abandonment of one essential doctrine destroys the divine foundation of the church and so separates it from the Catholic body that it can no longer assure its members of the grace of sacraments and the remission of sins. The resolutions allowed only three possibilities of remedy: the restoration of Convocation; an act of Parliament giving legal force to the decisions of the collective episcopate; or (as a *pis aller*) a declaration by the bishops.[3]

The talk of secession and disruption was no longer vague. Like Chalmers and his followers in Scotland seven years before, Manning and his followers were driving forward towards a situation where they must secede or be untrue to themselves. Manning wrote to Robert Wilberforce as early as 26 February, 'How can a priest, twice judged

1 *Times*, 28 March 1850.
2 *Times*, 19 March, 30 March, 15 April, 18 April 1850.
3 Resolutions in *Times*, 20 March 1850.

unfit for cure of souls by the church, be put in charge of souls at the sentence of the civil power without overthrowing the divine office of the church?'

As in Scotland, those driving towards secession were not united. In Scotland the more moderate among them were few in number. In England Manning and his friends at first expected to carry all the leading Tractarians. At a very early point in private argument they discovered that the two most eminent of the surviving Tractarian leaders were not prepared for these lengths. Even in the discussion which drafted the declaration of 19 March, they found that Pusey and Keble wanted to weaken its menace. Hope said, 'I suppose we are all agreed that if the Church of England does not undo this we must join the Church of Rome.' There was an outcry of protest, and Keble said, 'If the Church of England were to fail, it should be found in my parish.'[1] Though the thirteen met at Gladstone's house to sign the resolution, Gladstone himself, not without hesitation, refused to sign. Hope thought that the judgment committed the Church of England and must be reversed if the church was to remain a true church; that it was the final act in a long history of erastian government quietly accepted since the Reformation. Keble thought that the judgment was that of a secular court and touched the true church not at all. By 7 April 1850 Dodsworth was convinced that if they meant to be faithful to the truth they must break with Pusey and Keble. He even published a letter reproaching Pusey for jettisoning his friends, shrinking from the fight, and hiding behind ambiguous statements.[2]

Phillpotts was not quite finished with his happiest home, the law courts. He found an old unrepealed statute of Henry VIII making an appeal to Convocation in matters touching the king, and argued that since Brampford Speke was a crown living this was a matter touching the queen. His lawyers, who cannot have expected success, applied to the queen's bench vainly, then to the common pleas, and finally to the court of exchequer. It was hardly a serious plea, and more a means of spending money, of keeping his repudiation before the public, and of not knowing when he was beaten.

On 3 June 1850 Bishop Blomfield tried the parliamentary remedy by introducing a revised form of his former bill, this time turning the bishops into a court of appeal in matters of doctrine. The royal

[1] Purcell, i, 529, later reminiscence by Manning.
[2] Purcell, *Manning*, i, 540; Liddon, *Pusey*, iii, 262.

supremacy was still to be supreme, the source of all legal jurisdiction. It was to be exercised by lay judges in temporal matters, by episcopal judges in spiritual. It was first considered by the bench, and was believed by the *Times*[1] to be approved by all the bishops except three. Even Archbishop Sumner agreed with Blomfield that the judicial committee was unsatisfactory as a judge of unsound doctrine.[2] In the House of Lords it was strongly backed by Bishop Wilberforce of Oxford, who declared that if the bill failed a disruption like the Scottish disruption was possible, and a free episcopal Church of England might appear; and by Lord Redesdale, who attacked Lord John Russell for his erastian desire to keep the church under the heel of the state, and professed the unlikely belief that the prime minister would soon make Mr. Gorham into a bishop.[3] The Whig peers shared the view of Russell, of Prince Albert, and of the *Times*, that such a court of legally unqualified clergymen would establish clerical domination in the church and narrow the terms of comprehension by a series of dogmatic definitions; and after Bishop Thirlwall of St. David's supported them in a telling speech, the bill was lost in the Lords by eighty-four votes to fifty-one. If it was lost in the Lords, it would never have passed the Commons. And its recognition that even in spiritual cases the jurisdiction would derive from the royal supremacy made it impossible for the extreme antagonists of that supremacy. Before the bill was even debated Archdeacon Manning told Robert Wilberforce that he thought it a total failure.[4]

For although (or because) this was the clerical age of England, it was also the age of an anticlericalism not seen since the reign of Queen Anne, perhaps not since the Reformation. To read radical pamphleteers is to realise that the laymen of England were painfully conscious of being lay, and understood the ecclesiastical history of England as a righteous and on the whole triumphant struggle of the laity to free themselves from the yokes of rival factions of clergy. Part of the reason for this crude stance was the political power of Irish Roman Catholics since the reform act; part, the ill repute of Irish priests; part, the English fight over church rates and the claim that the state's money

---

[1] *Times*, 17 April 1850, 8.
[2] So he told Lord John Russell, 17 February 1850, PRO 30/22/8C. Blomfield's second bill included only three laymen in the courtroom, lord chancellor, chancellor of London and dean of arches.
[3] Hansard, cxi, 602–3, 640–2, 663–8.
[4] Purcell, *Manning*, i, 538.

could go to build the churches or schools of the establishment and none others; part, the rising political power of evangelical dissent; and part, the flying truculence of priestly theorists. The Reformation vindicated the rights of the laity by asserting the rights of the godly prince over the clergy. And now the godly prince had yielded his power to a parliament which need not be godly. While high churchmen refused to allow parliament to exercise the power which once they yielded to its sovereign, low churchmen wanted parliament to continue the plenary exercise of the old royal supremacy, as the only way of achieving what the Reformation sought to achieve. They conceived themselves to be fighting for the tolerance, breadth, and Protestantism of the Church of England; and Blomfield's proposed court of bishops had not the least hope of achieving a place in the constitution against these tormented memories of English history.

The Church of England knew itself called to the vocation of a national church. To be national a church cannot be narrow in creed and practice. If not so broad as Arnold wanted, it must be sufficiently broad to meet the worshipping needs of a majority in the nation. In the past this breadth was achieved. But it was possible only if most of the English people were sufficiently agreed in their doctrine and religious practice. A national church could not simply reflect the religious kaleidoscope of the nation. A church must be something. It needs a message or a practice to propose. The Anglican tradition of religious thought and practice, however tolerant or controversial on its fringes, was hitherto decisive and coherent. Its decisiveness had been compatible with its national claim because nearly all the governing class shared its doctrine and discipline. But in the fifty years after 1800 Irish immigration and urban proletariat and leaping dissent and better education and philosophical criticism made the religious or irreligious opinions of the English people ever more varied. Low churchmen wanted the Church of England to be so broad that it was still national. High churchmen feared that if it was broad enough to be national it would be nothing. Sooner or later the question must be fought even if Phillpotts had never spent weary hours in examining Gorham.

The comparative weakness of the extreme party was shown in July when Manning, Robert Wilberforce and W. H. Mill circulated for signature a declaration that they understood the royal supremacy to mean only supremacy over the temporal accidents of spiritual things, and that they could not acknowledge the power recently exercised, which was 'committed to the church alone by the law of Christ'.[1] Perhaps because the declaration was not dramatic enough; perhaps because it was circulated above their three names alone, and Pusey and Keble were excluded from the plan; perhaps because the average high churchman was not so definite, and partly because some clergy disliked the latent threat to secede to the Church of Rome, the declaration attracted only 1,800 signatures. Manning later in life regarded this as signal failure. The contemporary evidence shows that though some pooh-poohed it, the high church party as a whole regarded it with respect. If this interpretation of the oaths to the supremacy were accepted and not challenged by the crown, it would ease everyone's conscience. The *Guardian*[2] thought it the sharpest blow yet struck against the Gorham decision.

After the bill of Blomfield failed, there were anxious negotiations to persuade the bishops to a public declaration. It was soon evident that the bishops were not willing to take corporate action. When at last a great meeting was collected, on 23 July 1850 in the concert hall of St. Martin's in Long Acre, only one bishop consented to attend— aged Bagot of Bath and Wells. Not even Blomfield, not even Samuel Wilberforce, not even Henry Phillpotts were there.[3] The bishops were becoming more anxious to save the unity of the Church of England than to fight the royal supremacy. People were beginning to leave it— William Maskell, chaplain to Phillpotts, and Mrs. Robert Wilberforce were among the trickle received in June into the Roman Catholic church.

The day, or The Day as high churchmen called 23 July, resounded success in everything but the absence of the eminent. Fifteen hundred persons crammed St. Martin's hall under the chairmanship of J. G. Hubbard, and another thousand or more moved to the Freemasons tavern and held an overflow meeting under the chairmanship of Viscount Feilding. By special request the audience refrained from applause and gave the halls an air of religious solemnity. Bishop Bagot presented to the meeting a protest asserting baptismal regeneration,

---

[1] The declaration was drafted by Manning during the night after The Day of 23 July. Pusey signed it. Cf. Purcell, *Manning*, i, 540–1; Liddon, *Pusey*, iii, 273.

[2] 50, 765. It reached the pope, who took the occasion to speak contemptuously about the royal supremacy to the English agent in Rome: Petre to Conyngham 21 December 1850, RA, C51/91.

[3] Phillpotts warmly approved the meeting, but felt it better to abstain as too personally concerned; cf. his letter to Bishop Bagot from Durham, 22 July 1850, G, 50, 540.

solemnly repudiating the judgment of the judicial committee, and petitioning the crown and the bishops for a spiritual court and the right to synodical government. Here was the public repudiation by which the church should clear itself of uncatholic heresy. 'I thankfully believe,' declared Pusey in his speech at the overflow, 'that the judgment passed is not, as yet, the judgment of the church; that the church is not yet responsible for it.'[1]

But was repudiation by high churchmen equivalent to repudiation by the Church of England? The *Times* and the *Daily News* were bitter against the meeting, the *Standard* regarded it as monstrous, the *Morning Herald* was violent, the *Record* pooh-poohed it as the Baal of Tractarianism. Bishop Turton of Ely thought it all a fuss about nothing, and said so in a visitation sermon at Holy Trinity church in Cambridge. Bishop Sumner of Winchester disapproved of platforms and agitated meetings. A day or two after the meeting the secretaries of the Metropolitan church union appealed to Archbishop Sumner not to institute Gorham, and secured 2,700 signatures to their appeal. Sumner refused to receive the appeal on the ground that he was being asked to reverse the sentence of a law court. When they replied that there were times when it was right to obey God rather than man, Sumner agreed, but said that before anyone took the responsibility of disobeying the law of men he ought to be very certain that in doing so he would be obeying the law of God. The archbishop was showing himself a less weak person than had been confidently predicted on his appointment.[2]

On 20 July 1850 Henry Phillpotts solemnly and with his episcopal seal excommunicated anyone who should institute and induct Mr. Gorham.[3] On 10 August, after finding (as was alleged) the lock of the church door blocked with mortar and breaking in, Gorham was inducted to the parish of Brampford Speke by commission, and on 15 September preached his first sermon to a vast devout congregation on justification by faith. Phillpotts drew in his horns. Pressed by the intransigent to appoint a curate to the parish and attempt to defy the incumbent—that is, the solution adopted a few years before by the General Assembly of the Church of Scotland in the Marnoch case,

[1] Liddon iii, 247ff.; G, 50, 53–58. Keble, Manning, Sewell, Marriott, Palmer, Robert Wilberforce were among the speakers. A protest, signed by the participants, was bricked up by Hubbard in the walls of St. Alban's, Holborn, until 1868, when a deputation removed it and presented it formally to the Lambeth library, not without a hint that the archbishop in 1868 was a different person from the archbishop of 1850.
[2] Letters, in G, 50, 588.   [3] G, 50, 527; JB, 50, 552.

the solution which smashed the Church of Scotland—Phillpotts refused. He refused for the sake of obeying the law and for the sake of the parishioners. Pressed to order the parishioners not to attend their parish church but to attend others, he refused, declaring the plan to be schismatical. He issued a solemn warning to the churchwardens to watch carefully over the doctrines of their vicar and charge him if necessary, and directed their attention to Article XXVI, that the unworthiness of the minister hindereth not the effect of the sacrament. He sent to every house in the parish of Brampford Speke a copy of a sermon by Archdeacon Bartholomew, containing the true doctrine of baptism. He gave encaustic tiles to the new church in Brampford Speke. He steadily continued to refuse licences to curates or institutions to clergymen whose baptismal doctrine he found erroneous. No one else dared the expense of challenging him in a law court.[1]

The pace of secession quickened. Viscount Feilding once stood as an anti-papal candidate for Cambridge University, and moving a little higher presided at the overflow meeting in the Freemasons tavern on 23 July. On 30 August he became a Roman Catholic convinced, as he wrote to the *Times*, that there was no living authority of faith in the 'so-called Church of England'.[2] The change of allegiance by Lord Feilding, itself grave enough in one who had consented to take the chair on The Day, gave rise to an incident which exacerbated feelings beyond measure. He was building a new parish church at Pantasaph, near his seat in North Wales. He now withdrew the merely verbal undertaking, and designed it for Roman Catholic worship; and North

---

[1] G, 50, 606; 53, 181. Gorham's friendship with Brampford Speke was never secure. He refused to invite the churchwardens to the annual tithe dinner and only one tithepayer came (1853). There was a brawl between Gorham and a farmer over a funeral (1854), a wrangle in church in 1856 over an inscription on the new organ, causing Phillpotts to appoint a commission of enquiry which decided that the case against Gorham for brawling was doubtful. In October 1856 Gorham personally cleared the inn after 11 p.m. and had a piece of turf thrown at him. He charged the landlord with keeping the bar open at an unseasonable hour, but the magistrates dismissed the case. He died on 19 June 1857 after an agony of several months, and left £20,000. On his death-bed he sent a message of reconciliation to Phillpotts and friendly letters were exchanged. Gorham's son, G. M. Gorham (then vicar of Walkeringham), was offered the living but declined. G 53, 96, 181; 54, 224; 56, 275, 402, 57, 489, 535, 599, 618. G. M. Gorham's opinions did not altogether agree with those of his father. A skilled photographer, he made money for Walkeringham church by selling photographs of Keble, Hursley church, and Hursley vicarage, G, 66, 602. He had been a close friend of Fenton Hort at Cambridge. Cf. also friendly letter of G. M. Gorham to Liddon, 14 January 1859, Keble College MSS.

[2] *Times* of 2 September 1850; G, 50, 641, 650, 858. It was rumoured that the viscountess, who was received on the same day as himself, pulled his mind that way.

Wales reverberated with cries of broken faith, amidst which Lord Feilding preserved a silence of dignity.[1]

Lord Feilding's departure, after his recent eminence, caused a near-panic. High churchmen started talking of oaths, and tests, and binding assurances that their members would not join the Church of Rome. Gladstone proposed that the discontented should pledge themselves not to leave the Church of England without giving notice of two months and opportunity for discussion.[2] Manning thought that he was trying to tamper with personal convictions and conscience. Christopher Wordsworth laid it down in a sermon at Westminster abbey that there is no just cause for separation from a church even if mistaken ministers are suffered to preach in it.[3] William Palmer tried to get signatures for an anti-Roman declaration, and the nervousness in the movement won the scheme a surprising measure of support. Some of Palmer's friends tried to turn the proposed declaration into a kind of test for membership of the church unions which were formed as local fortresses in the Hampden crisis and now extended their support. Pusey and many others disapproved such tests; and others disapproved the unions as likely to become ecclesiastical cliques and to foster narrow minds.[4]

In mid-September went T. W. Allies of Launton, and Henry Wilberforce. Wilberforce had written a famous essay upon church extension, and his name was respected by thousands who had never met him. The secession was far weaker than that of the Church of Scotland, partly because it was secession by stragglers instead of a great army, and partly because the obvious home of the seceders, the Roman obedience, was a palace which many English high churchmen, however discontented with an erastian state, were for other reasons never going to enter. Keble talked largely of the non-jurors and of a Free Episcopal Church, as Bishop Wilberforce threatened in the Lords; but such a plan had no chance in the climate of English high churchmanship. Robert Wilberforce asked Manning about setting up a Free Church of England, and Manning replied,[5] 'No. Three hundred years

---

[1] Cf. the correspondence, G, 50, 838: and cf. the church at Erdington, G, 50, 850; contrast West Lavington, built by Manning's curate, Laprimaudaye, who became Roman Catholic in the building, but completed the gift to the Church of England, Purcell, i, 445.

[2] Purcell, *Manning*, i, 538.   [3] *Times*, 16 April 1850, 5; Liddon, iii, 274-5.

[4] So Joshua Watson and H. H. Norris; cf. Churton, *Watson*, 358.

[5] Purcell, i, 592.

ago we left a good ship for a boat; I am not going to leave the boat for a tub.' If the Free Church was impracticable and perhaps (as Phillpotts thought) schismatical, and Rome was impossible except to those already inclined towards it by theology or devotion, the seceders could not by Scottish standards be numerous. But if not numerous, the Anglicans were beginning to be agonised about the quality of those leaving. Henry Wilberforce had been respected as among the salt of the church.

New ordinands looked nervously at their subscription, and wondered if they could subscribe with a good conscience that the queen's majesty was the supreme governor of the realm as well in things spiritual and ecclesiastical as in things temporal. The high church movement in England, so lately raised up by Lord John Russell and Dr. Hampden to a confident fighting united army, was beginning to be demoralised.

A week after the press reported the secession of Henry Wilberforce, the entire crisis was metamorphosed into a different crisis. On 30 September 1850 the pope himself entered the arena.

3. PAPAL AGGRESSION

Roman Catholics 1829–50

The Roman Catholics after 1832 blinked like owls at the daylight. They came into the sun and found its rays benevolent and exciting. For three decades their eyes suffered difficulty in focusing. Confronted with unforeseen opportunity and unexpected converts, they struggled to rise to the moment, feeling like a kindly pauper who has wages just enough to support a little family and finds his home besieged by a hundred orphans. They ran into crisis; and like all societies which run into crisis, they passed through strain in deciding how to act.

The crisis was twofold, of money and of men. The religious mood of the age, mood of reaction and romance and feeling and poetry, drew educated men and women towards Catholicism and no penal laws made them hesitate on the brink. The needs of England for cheap labour brought Irishmen in an ever-swelling stream, first to Liverpool and Manchester, then to London and Birmingham, then as navvies to build embankments or dig tunnels for the railways. Freedom and religious mood drew Catholics to splendour, even to ostentation, to display the majesty and mystery of Catholic faith, to build cathedrals prominent in the city square. Irish labourers tied them to back streets and slums, to tin sheds and converted halls. Whether they aimed at splendour or whether they aimed at sacraments for uprooted Irishmen, no one had money for either purpose.

The full tide of Irishmen was reached during the years of the Irish famine after 1845. But the flow was steady before the famine. The poverty of Ireland was worse than the poverty of the English or Welsh countryside. They heard of employment and wages to be had in England. Sometimes they came for a few months or few years, sometimes they settled and became part of English life. They were ready to take the lowest-paid work. By 1851 no less than 3 per cent of the population of England and Wales was born in Ireland, and this statistic took no account of babies born in England of two Irish parents. Probably 400,000 Irish entered England in the ten years 1841 to 1851.[1] In 1851 108,548 persons born in Ireland were living in London. The mountain of travail is pictured by the contrast between these figures and the numbers who attended mass. On 30 March 1851 about 252,500 Catholics attended mass in England and Wales. Yet at that moment 519,959 persons born in Ireland were living in England and Wales. The Catholics were witnessing a calamitous wastage of the Irish poor who lived in slums without churches.

Wherever they went they congregated in an Irish quarter. By language, by religion and by social habits they were distinct from the English and not easily assimilated. Nearly half the total of worshipping Catholics in 1851 lived in London or Liverpool. In London they had a quarter round Smithfield, in the parishes of St. Sepulchre, St. Bartholomew the Great and St. Bartholomew the Less. They worked in the docks at Limehouse and occupied a sewerless region near Drury Lane. They were thought to drink more than the English and to be more improvident. Earning lower wages, they repelled by their readiness to eat uneatable food like bad bacon, old pigs' heads, salty fish.[2]

Roman Catholic chapels were as ill equipped to receive these Irishmen as the parish churches to receive the English labourer. While the Anglican made temporary use of corrugated iron chapels at £500 or £700 a time, Roman Catholic priests often began like other dissenters in small and dingy rooms. In Charles Street off Drury Lane, where the thieves of London congregated, they hired a coach factory believed to hold about 1,000 persons. Six weeks after the opening the factory was crammed with Irish on a Sunday night when an alarm of *fire* was raised outside, and in the stampede the wooden staircase crashed in pieces amid screams of agony, and 500 people were got out of an upper window down the ladder of a fire-engine. The scum of London assembled outside to watch the fun and was not displeased at such a calamity to papists.[1] Two drunken women molested the priest when he came out last.

The crying need for so many temporary and cheap chapels was used as a battle-cry against the wing of Catholics who called for Gothic magnificence. Pugin found that ornate plans for Catholic chapels were constantly set aside or pared. With the indignation of which he alone was capable, he said that the welfare of the poor was made the pretext for stripping the altar of God and rendering his temple as bare as a Quaker's conventicle.[2] He stood for chancels, embroidery, vestments, frontals, screens, and believed that by a rich solemnity no one would benefit more than the poor. 'They actually propose deal and plaster', he wrote incredulously. '. . . Ere long they will advocate a *new service*, suited to these conventicles—a sort of *Catholicised Methodism*.' The labourer from his factory must not be given a room with deal walls and iron-girded roof and skylight dripping with steam, serving only to remind him of his workshop, but a palace where he may dwell with the king and inhale fragrant odours and hear solemn chants, and stand at last equal to the most dignified of the land. His friend the Earl of Shrewsbury wanted to inspire the English people to Catholic reverence. Gothic, castellations, battlements, ruined abbeys, romantic medievalism took hold of Roman Catholics as well as Anglicans. The Goth of the Catholics happened to be the wealthiest or at least the most generous of Catholic peers. Shrewsbury built a Gothic fantasy at his home of Alton Towers. He discovered (1832) Pugin, made him his personal architect, encouraged his employment in building churches, and lived out of England for several months of every year to save money with which to build churches. He only built three churches and all in or near his estates; a little church at Uttoxeter, a grand church at Cheadle, a church on his estate of Alton. But he gave munificent donations else-where,[3] and his fostering influence generated a legend among Catholics that he built noble and expensive churches all over the country.

[1] *Weekly Register*, 4 August 1849, 9–10; 25 August, 59.
[2] *Weekly Register*, 6 October 1849, 145.   [3] Gwynn, *Shrewsbury*, xiii–xiv.

Irish immigrants needed churches quickly and cheaply; and that meant tin roofs, deal altars, tawdry ornaments, paper pots with artificial flowers, dingy discarded vestments. Pugin and the idealists wanted no buildings that were not expensive. Meanwhile the chapel at Merthyr Tydfil was a low dark loft above a slaughter-house, reached by a ladder flung across a brook; the floor of the chapel at Swansea was collapsing into a hole; at Pontypool they used a room in the village inn; and those Welsh priests were paid only from collections, one receiving 9s. a week and another 2s. 6d.[1]

Between the different tugs Catholic bishops found it vexatious to decide how to spend the money which they had not got; whether in the cheapness of many little chapels or the ornament of a few great churches. They pursued both policies at once. Consequently Bishop Baines sank all the money of the western district into the bottomless pit of Prior Park at Bath, bought in 1830 on borrowed money to be a school and a seminary and perhaps even a university, almost burnt to the ground in 1836, and sold again in 1856 at a loss. Bishop Walsh left the Midland district groaning under a load of debt and would probably have gone bankrupt but for timely help from Lord Shrewsbury.[2] He even issued a writ to extract money from his colleague Bishop Griffiths of the London district. Walsh explained affairs to his successor Ullathorne, but seems to have been hardly aware how cavernous looked the exhausted treasury. The old haphazard modes of administering money, appropriate to little societies round a few lordly families, could not compete with slum tabernacles, still less with Gothic fanes. Bishop Walsh kept no accounts. If Bishop Baines kept accounts, no one could ever find them. Dr. Wiseman, who often complained of the deficiencies of his predecessors, graphically pictured the entire chancery of episcopal papers wandering round with the bishop in gig or stage-coach.[3] It is only just to remark that the debts of Oscott were far from diminished while Wiseman was its president, and that he spent many years of his life in a suit at Rome over money with the Catholic Bishop of Southwark. Some vicars-apostolic were like financiers living on overdrafts without ever knowing the deficit except when the bank issued sharp reminders. In the effort to save his district from ruin, Bishop Ullathorne had recourse to

[1] PA Congregazioni Particolari, 157, 500; cf. Beck, 276–7.
[2] Gwynn, *Shrewsbury*, 27.
[3] Ward, *Sequel*, ii, 6, from Southwark archives; Wiseman to Lingard, 11 November 1840.

the agony of reducing the exiguous stipends of his priests. Through an investment in the Monmouthshire and Glamorganshire Banking Company, rashly accepted by Walsh, Ullathorne went bankrupt and spent ten days in Warwick gaol.[1] The joint policies of impressing the English upper classes with temple-glory and of finding quick tabernacles of God for Irish labourers were painful to their administrators.

If they despaired of money to build, they were almost as troubled to find men. English priests were by ethos like chaplains to noblemen, by instinct men of the private chapel and the library. In blue top-coats and high lay collars and white ties, they were not easily discovered to be priests. Quiet, well read, unostentatious and gentlemanly, they were even less fit to cope with Irish navvies than Anglican parsons with new town labourers. But they were the tradition of Catholic ministry in England. Whatever modes of ministry were new devised must be married to this tranquil priesthood. It was too much to hope that the marriage could be celebrated with natural affection.

England and Wales were divided into four districts under four vicars-apostolic in episcopal orders. With the rising numbers of Catholics the four districts and vicars-apostolic were made eight (1840). In England and Wales there were 357 chapels in 1824; 423 in 1835; 453 in 1839. For Irish immigrants they could and must import Irish priests, though Irish priests never came in sufficient quantity. But Irish priests, whether numerous or few, were not likely to lead educated Englishmen to the splendour of Catholic faith. In the eyes of some English worshippers their culture was low and their habits deplorable. Pugin, who was fanatical for splendour, talked off his irritated head to a few Protestants. 'What's the use of decent vestments with such priests as we have got? a lot of blessed fellows! Why, Sir, when they wear my chasubles, they don't look like priests, and what's worse, the chasubles don't look like chasubles.'[2] Nor on their side were all Irish priests confident that they would receive fair dealing from English ecclesiastics. Occasionally they complained of their alleged ill-treatment to Rome,[3] occasionally even to English Protestants.

Another source of priests besides Ireland was the continent of

[1] Butler, i, 171–4; Dessain, xv, 94. It was not a limited liability company.
[2] Ferrey, 112.
[3] e.g. PA Scritture Riferite nei Congressi, Anglia, xii, 663, Father Thomas Geoghegan of Clapham to Cardinal Fransoni, 18 November 1850.

Europe. In penal days foreign chaplains served the Catholics of London, and the Sardinian and Portuguese and German and Spanish and Belgian chapels were still important among the Catholic churches of the city. Several French or Italian priests already ministered in English chapels. In 1835 Bishop Baines invited the Rosminians to take charge of Prior Park. Father Gentili came with two other Italians and two years later three more Italian priests and three Italian lay brothers joined them. The experiment was melancholy. The fervent and attractive Gentili took a low view of English priests. He screwed discipline to a rigour which bred mutiny and was requested to depart. Ambrose Phillipps invited him to be chaplain at his country seat of Grace Dieu near Leicester. As a missionary to the poor he was striking and effective. His habit, the mud thrown at him, even his comic English, attracted crowds of non-Catholics to his mission-sermons in Leicestershire villages.[1]

The vicars-apostolic did not at first share the opinion that foreign missionaries could be useful in England. Ambrose Phillipps invited Father Dominic Barberi of the Passionists, and Father Dominic felt a vocation to the English mission. The vicars-apostolic were not pleased to discover that without their knowledge Dr. Wiseman in Rome applied to the pope for such a body of missionaries. 'We are like parents', wrote Bishop Griffiths of the London district, 'struggling to provide necessary food for our rapidly multiplying children, and compelled to neglect superfluities.'[2] Father Dominic knew so little of England that he landed at Folkestone on 5 November and was perplexed at what he saw. He went to Oscott to teach, and after becoming the laughing-stock of the students retreated sadly to Belgium. Wiseman brought him back in 1841 to Aston hall. The Passionist habit was spectacular, with sandals and a great red cross in the breast, and his missions attracted crowds of sightseers. Father Gentili received into the church William Lockhart, the young truant from Littlemore, and Father Dominic received Newman himself. But Italian religious resembled the splendour of a Gothic cathedral more than the modesty of an Irish chapel. Though tonsures and habits served to remind the English people of the grandeur of Catholic monastic life, they were less useful as pastors than the Irish priests. Newman said of himself that he was not converted to Roman

[1] Pagani, *Life of Gentili*, 153, 181, 194.
[2] Griffiths to Wiseman, 28 February 1840; Ward, *Sequel*, i, 165.

Catholicism by the Roman Catholics but by the university of Oxford. The born Catholics of England distrusted the foreigners. On his dismissal from Prior Park, Father Gentili offended the taste of some English Catholics by summoning the students, kneeling down before them, and begging public pardon for all the faults which he might have committed.[1] The most eminent of English priests, Dr. Lingard, proposed caustically that Dr. Wiseman's debating society should discuss 'how to send away those swarms of Italian congregationists who introduce their own customs here, and by making religion *ridiculous* in the eyes of Protestants, *prevent it from spreading here*'.[2]

Distrust mounted between English Catholics and Rome. For the Italians reported to Rome. Knowing little of English language or society, they disliked what they found. Rome was told how unecclesiastical were English priests, how cautious, how little devout, how devoid of ardour. Dr. Gentili was not the only one to share these impressions. Dr. Wiseman, though half English, lived for so long in Rome that he took an Italian point of view. It was reported to Rome that when a statue was introduced into Prior Park it had been removed with the sentence, 'Let us have no Romanising here'. English priests on their side were conservative enough to dislike the slow growth of Roman custom and devotion. When veterans could remember penal days and the trial of Bishop Talbot for saying illegal mass, they felt it hard that they who had borne the burden should now be accused by enthusiasts of torpidity towards the Catholic faith. They distrusted public processions and loud devotions and holy water and the Roman fashion of neckwear. The clerical collar with black coat was prescribed by Dr. Griffiths for the London clergy, and in consequence some abandoned knee-breeches for trousers. Others thought that trousers were affected and many priests refused at first to wear the collar. Dr. Lingard continued to wear a white cravat and hoped that they would 'let the old man alone as to his throat, and not suffocate him with a Roman collar'.[3] Sensing that the English were more likely to be converted by quietness and prudence than by noise and colour, they were little pleased at strange music, at opening churches with Italian tenor solos, at Pugin's rood screens or Pugin's rich vestments. They hardly perceived that the

[1] Ward, *Sequel*, i, 138. But amend Ward's view of Gentili by Leetham, DR 1963–4, 395.

[2] Haile-Bonney, *Life of Lingard*, 353.

[3] Ward, *Sequel*, i, 170. Haile-Bonney, *Life of Lingard*, 309.

Roman Catholic church in England faced the crisis of Irish labour. Since their knowledge of ecclesiastical Latin was sometimes rusty, they found difficulty in making their meaning plain to the Roman curia, and thereby bred misunderstanding.[1]

Thus the conservative Catholics of England disliked uncomprehending interference by the Congregation of Propaganda in Rome. The vicars-apostolic were shocked by two Roman decrees in 1838 which removed the religious orders from their jurisdiction.[2] Since the relation between secular priests and religious orders had long caused strife between bishops and monks and led to breach between Bishop Baines and the Benedictines of Downside, the vicars-apostolic were convinced that Rome understood little of their predicament.

To gain more independence of Propaganda there was only one way; remove England from its status as a mission and secure a constituted hierarchy of bishops. While the vicars-apostolic wanted a hierarchy because they wanted more freedom from Rome, their clergy wanted a hierarchy to secure more freedom from vicars-apostolic. The missionary status of England meant that no priest had security of tenure. He could be moved hither and thither at the beck of the vicar-apostolic. Nor had the priests a voice in choosing their vicar-apostolic. The usual practice was a curious form of personal succession whereby the vicar-apostolic chose a coadjutor who then succeeded him. In the then state of soreness between secular priests and religious orders the very rumour that the northern district would have a bishop from the regular clergy threw the secular priests of Manchester into ferment.[3] Therefore the priests of England wanted missionary status ended, canon law introduced, chapters to advise at the selection of a bishop, and no removal from office without due process. They formed a London club called the Adelphi to forward their aims. For different but parallel reasons both vicars-apostolic and priests wanted a hierarchy. Always in turmoil because they lacked a constitution, they naturally wanted its settlement.

Rome refused their requests. Pope Gregory XVI is declared by one important witness to have wanted an English hierarchy and to have

---

[1] Cf. the extraordinary case cited in Ullathorne, *Hierarchy*, 56–57.

[2] Ward, *Sequel*, i, 143, and appendix F: the first decree allowed the religious to grant indulgence, the second to set up chapels wherever they liked, without in either case referring to their vicar-apostolic. The worst effects of the decrees were withdrawn in the following year, through the mediation of Mgr. Acton at Rome.

[3] Ward, *Sequel*, i, 140.

felt frustrated that he could not grant it.[1] The implied culprit who thus bore the guilt of refusal was the English Cardinal Acton. Acton disapproved the plan. Thinking, like the vicars-apostolic, that a hierarchy meant freedom from Propaganda, he believed, unlike the vicars-apostolic, that a hierarchy was therefore undesirable. English priests could not be trusted and must be kept on a leash. Acton told the pope that the English clergy had always been factious and opposed to authority, and must not be granted more independent power. So long as Acton exerted influence at Rome the plan for a hierarchy was shelved. When he died in 1847 the pace quickened astonishingly.

The desire for bishops owed something to the Oxford Movement. Instructed controversialists sometimes resented Tractarian argument from vicars-apostolic to prove Anglican bishops to be the sole authentic bishops of England. They confessed that they secretly smarted at the open Protestant claim.[2] But the Tractarians and at last Mr. Gorham affected the manner in which bishops were restored. The predicament of the establishment turned that manner from courtesy to rudeness, from modesty to flamboyance, from gentleness to provocation. The hierarchy was needed for the internal constitution of the Roman Catholic church in England. Calamitous timing, and unlucky choice of persons to introduce it, made it look like assault upon the Archbishop of Canterbury or even upon Queen Victoria, and generated disaster to English religion whether Catholic or Protestant.

Ambrose Phillipps of Grace Dieu in Leicestershire was a wealthy Roman Catholic squire. At the age of 15 he insisted on becoming Catholic and while an undergraduate at Cambridge needed to ride twenty-five miles to hear mass on Sundays. He and his friend Father George Spencer (who became Father Ignatius Spencer when he joined the Passionists in 1846) bubbled with unquenchable optimism about the goal of the Oxford Movement. They were sanguine that it would issue not only in conversions but in reconciling the bulk of the English church to the see of Rome. Phillipps was a romantic visionary who saw the faults in his own communion and hoped that reunion with the Church of England would infuse new blood. In his chapel an epileptic girl was alleged to be healed by a miraculous medal brought from France. In Charnwood Forest he gave 230 acres of land to build a monastery and revive the Cistercian order in England. He sighed

---

[1] Wiseman, *Recollections* (1858), 521.
[2] Cf. William Palmer, *On the Church* (1839), i, 459; Ullathorne, *Hierarchy*, 5 and 19.

pleasurably over each number of the *British Critic*. At a meeting to refuse church rate in Whitwick, where he was accused of supplying voters with refreshments, he caused offence by declaring the Church of England to be the best Protestant sect in the kingdom and prophesying that at no distant time it must reunite with the Church of Rome.[1] The two friends travelled on the continent, exhorting a crusade of prayer for this object. Phillipps even stopped the circulation in his neighbourhood of Wiseman's pamphlets against Tractarians because he thought them ungrateful after what the *British Critic* had done to vindicate the pope from being antichrist. He told Lord Shrewsbury improbably that Archbishop Howley and Bishop Blomfield approved the design for reunion, but were restrained by the other bishops.[2] Phillipps communicated to the enthusiastic Wiseman a measure of his own optimism, and urged Lord Shrewsbury in Rome to persuade the Vatican to conciliate and encourage, 'not to call upon these men to quit their own communion in order to join ours, but to proceed on courageously with their holy and glorious intention of *reconciling* their CHURCH to OURS'. He was conciliatory in his interpretation of Roman Catholic doctrine and told his Anglican friend Bloxam that almost all Roman Catholics repudiated the infallibility of the Roman see.[3] He drew glowing pictures to Cardinal Acton of the new Anglican devotion to our Lady, the severity of Anglican fasting, their whole nights in prayer, their floods of tears over their fallen mother the Church of England, and claimed that this piety was practised by hundreds. 'Oh yes, England is ripe for the harvest, England will again be an island of saints, she will be one of the brightest jewels in the church's diadem, but the hour is not yet quite arrived . . .'[4] He tried to dissuade the conversions of leading Tractarians like Newman and Pusey on the plea that their departure would leave the Church of England in the hands of ultra-Protestants. He urged Lord Shrewsbury to propagate this doctrine among cardinals and Jesuits at Rome.

This deluded optimism was not so naïve as it looked to posterity. Accustomed to steady Protestants, Roman Catholics found Tractarian sympathy wonderful, almost miraculous. They were dazzled and excited by the sight of Protestants translating the breviary or commending monks or approving Father Gentili when he visited Oxford

[1] Purcell, *Life*, i, 79, 107, 208; *Br. Mag.*, 10, 1836, 245–6, 634.
[2] Purcell, *Life of Phillipps*, i, 217.
[3] Purcell, *Life*, i, 221.
[4] Phillipps to Acton, 1842, *Life*, i, 237; cf. 257–9, 275.

in his habit, or defending the mass and the sacrifice and the Catholic miracles of the later centuries. On All Saints' day of 1845 Wiseman saw ten former Anglican clergymen gathered in Oscott chapel and wondered whether such a gathering had happened since the Reformation.[1]

Other Catholics did not share the optimism. *The Tablet*, founded in 1840 and edited by Lucas, was fierce against Puseyites as hypocrites. Even Lord Shrewsbury, who loathed the *Tablet*, thought Newman and Pusey fanatical illuminés in their defence of the Church of England. Conservative priests and vicars apostolic, struggling to keep heads afloat amid a sea of Irish, thought that these country squires and Roman ecclesiastics and recent English converts were wild and foolish. Bishop Griffiths of the London district, already so unpopular with Rome that rumours of his deposition kept circulating, eyed Wiseman as a thruster who knew nothing about England. Bishop Baines of the western district printed a Lenten pastoral of 1840 which denounced Spencer's prayers for the conversion of England as encouraging Catholics to deluded hopes of moral impossibility, as impossible, he wrote in a phrase which angered the Roman censors, as the return of the negro's skin to its antediluvian whiteness.[2] Summoned to Rome by Propaganda to answer for his language, he told Cardinal Fransoni that a few neophyte converts were bringing disrepute upon the Catholic religion, that they were a bustling, noisy, conceited untractable little party, which affected extraordinary piety without knowing what piety meant.[3]

The old traditions of Roman Catholics in England were slowly being superseded. They were austere and restrained and more devout than Rome or Gentili or Wiseman imagined. But they were being swamped; partly by Irish labourers who knew nothing of these traditions, and partly by converts who joined the Church of Rome because it was *not* like the Church of England, and therefore put high value upon whatever in Roman tradition was neither austere nor restrained. Converts came into the Roman Church because it was not insular like the Anglican and therefore regretted whatever among English Roman

---

[1] Ward, *Sequel*, ii, 119.

[2] PA Congregazioni Particolari, 156/39ff.

[3] *Catholic Magazine and Register*, xii, 93ff. Baines was compelled to make a declaration (15 March 1841) that his language had been misunderstood; and on his return to England printed a history of the pastoral, which Rome found even more objectionable than the pastoral.

Catholics was found to be almost as insular as among Anglicans. They loved the dramatic. When they travelled on the continent they were conspicuous by demonstrative conduct in Catholic churches, by bowing lower to priests than native Catholics, by prostrations and ecstasies, by genuflecting in public places to anyone who looked the least like a bishop. In Oscott, Gladstone's convert sister Lucy appeared at mass with a large dark cloak which she threw off dramatically at *Gloria in excelsis*, displaying a bright coloured dress as token of resurrection.[1] Conservative English Catholics, though loyal to the pope, were more than familiar with the irritations of being governed from Rome and had no desire to bring Roman rule any closer. Converts who had been unable to bear the stammering lips of the Church of England, saw the immediate power of Rome as the decisive voice of religious authority which they sought.

Two kinds of Catholic devotion, English and Roman, rubbed against each other. The centre of trouble was the convert Frederick Faber, who after 1849 stood at the head of the London Oratory. Faber's attitude was uncompromising. The born Catholics, he believed, were incapable of seizing the moment. They wanted to seem English. They were not aware that the time for conservatism was passed, and suffered from what he called a chronic and unreasoning timidity.[2] He denounced them as jealous of Roman usage, taking a light view of Protestant heresy, biased towards materialism, afraid of promulgating controverted doctrines like indulgences or pope or images or miracles or Virgin, comfortable, failing to practise the ascetic life, moving in society without being known as Catholics, corrupted by the engulfing atmosphere of heresy. To convert England they must cry up Rome and Roman ways—'God has put a spell into them'.

What was happening was a kind of restoration to Europe of English Catholics. Under penal laws Catholics had not been isolated inasmuch as many priests were educated perforce upon the continent. But in penal conditions the stream of European devotional practice left them behind; and Dr. Griffiths and Dr. Baines were not unlike Celts who discovered when St. Augustine landed in England that Romans now wore a different shape of tonsure. They had their own discipline. But practices familiar to Italians were bizarre and repellent to old-

[1] Ward, *Sequel*, i, 114.
[2] *Notes on Doctrinal and Spiritual Subjects*, ii, 99; the address is of 1850.

fashioned English Catholics. And meanwhile the new railways made Belgian and French and Italian Catholicism known to more and more Englishmen.

English Catholicism was restored to Europe at a time when European Catholicism was peculiarly Roman. The French Revolution and its aftermath rallied political Europe to authority and Catholic Europe to the pope. A half-liberal and half-anticlerical France no longer professed a Gallican mind in the councils of Catholicism. Rome was elevated as the source of religious authority. The ensuing movement called Ultramontane was a rippling wave of Italian influence upon Catholic devotion throughout Europe. The Italian pronunciation of Latin with *ch* instead of *c*, benedichere for benedicere, became fashionable and was mocked by conservative Catholics as chees and chaws. While the northern world went Gothic in its medievalisms, Ultramontanes preferred baroque because it was Italian. Devotions before the crucifix, public processions, wearing of habits by monks in the street, affection for the Sacred Heart, kneeling before statues, votive candles, gentleness of the Lady Virgin and the saints, fostering of miracle and dislike of rational thinking, sermons of harrowing enthusiasm, familiarity instead of fear, cradle of Bethlehem instead of thunders of Sinai, soft penance instead of rigour, frequent communion and frequent confession, mass daily; Ultramontanism was the Catholic version of an onslaught to convert the escaping city crowds, of an emotional missionary stance found also in the revivalism of the Protestant left. As steady conservative Wesleyans were just then regretting the loud techniques of itinerant American evangelists, steady conservative Catholics regretted the fervent excess of itinerant Italian missioners. Methods usual among Neapolitan peasants were found fertile among French villagers and Irish navvies and Belgian miners and London intellectuals.

Dr. Nicholas Wiseman, formerly rector of the English college in Rome and since 1840 Bishop of Melipotamus *in partibus* and coadjutor to Bishop Walsh of the Midland district, became quickly identified with the movement to Romanise the English Catholics. His mind was intelligent and his person exuberant. On paper and on platforms he was capable of recommending the Catholic religion with compelling brilliance. His attitude to Tractarians was friendly and understanding; and by his articles in the *Dublin Review*, which he founded in 1836, and by his welcoming enthusiasm he made the awkward transition

easy for converts. He shared the Roman view that the prudence of
the older vicars-apostolic was tepid, that the English clergy needed
stimulus to fervour, that Roman habits should be encouraged.
Eminent as a public figure, he was capable of superb appearances and
telling gestures. In the conflict of interest between splendid fane and
Irish chapel, he was wholly for magnificence. Details of diocesan or
collegiate administration bored him; the college at Oscott sank under
his rule; his diocese was never a happy family. If Pugin imagined
Catholicism resurgent in the hallowed associations of Gothic ornamental ritual, Wiseman conceived it resurgent in a great prelate. The
vicars-apostolic of old days, digging their vegetables in braces or
riding on buses or carrying carpet-bags, were dying. Pugin asked a
priest, 'How can you expect to convert England if you use a cope like
that?' and Wiseman in his different situation asked himself a similar
question.[1] The Catholic bishop, he supposed, would not make his
mark in English society until he was awarded that place which Roman
society gave him naturally and which by long history English society
gave to bishops of the Church of England. For most of the converts,
for Italian missionaries, and for the needs of Rome, he looked almost
ideal. Newman and Oakeley, Gentili and Shrewsbury told Rome that
he was ideal. For the Irish labourer he was less ideal, since he saw them
only in the corner of his eye. For clergy, who must suffer his administrative incompetence, he was far short of ideal. And his affection for
magnificent gesture, his inability to distinguish ceremony from
flamboyance, led at last to national calamity.

Among the statutes of England remained a number of obsolete or
semi-obsolete enactments against Roman Catholics. In the summer of
1842 a commission of legal reformers drew attention to these statutes
in forcible language. An act of 1844 repealed various obsolete penalties
(7 & 8 Vict., cap. 102), but only about half those originally proposed
and after another commission a government act of 1846 repealed
more (9 & 10 Vict., cap. 59). These benevolent measures encouraged
Roman Catholic members in the Commons to press for the repeal of
the securities enacted by the emancipation act of 1829, especially the
securities against Jesuits and the ban upon public funerals. The
Trappists of Mount St. Bernard in Leicestershire, the community
founded under the protection of Ambrose Phillipps, sent a petition to

---

[1] Ward, *Sequel*, i, 116.

Parliament, supplying voluntary evidence that they had all violated the law and were all liable to be banished or transported. Parliament was not prepared to repeal those securities of 1829 which were already obsolete. And there were more ancient disabilities. It was still illegal under penalty of *praemunire* to bring a papal bull into this country; and it was still illegal for the British government to conduct any negotiation or business with the pope.

The desire to establish control in Ireland made even Tory statesmen anxious to influence the Irish clergy by establishing a concordat or at least a diplomatic exchange with the pope. Peel used surreptitious agents in Rome, Lord John Russell found the same necessity. This necessity was not concerned only with Ireland. His foreign secretary, Palmerston, was engaged in a policy of supporting liberal Italians against illiberal Austrians, and Pope Pius IX, on his accession in 1846, showed signs of putting himself at the head of the popular cause in Italy. English politics needed a representative in Rome to sustain the liberal cause. If the Austrians crossed the Po, the British government could hardly pretend that the papal states did not exist, for Palmerston was threatening to send the British fleet to Trieste; yet the British were prevented from recognising the existence of the pope by an act of Parliament. In September 1847 Wiseman appealed to Lord Palmerston. Within a week the newspapers announced that Lord Minto, lord privy seal and father-in-law to the prime minister, had been appointed ambassador to Rome, and the *Times* (15 September 1847) needed to explain that no one could be appointed such an ambassador. Early in 1848 the government introduced a bill to legalise this diplomatic representation. Irish Roman Catholics were hostile to it lest it give the British government power over their independence in Ireland, Lucas denounced it bitterly in the *Tablet*, W. G. Ward declared that it was an unexampled piece of political impudence, Archbishop M'Hale of Tuam went to Rome to agitate against it, Bishop Phillpotts opposed it on principle, but Wiseman and Lord Shrewsbury and the leading English Catholics wanted it, most Tories approved of it, and it received the royal assent on 4 September 1848. A Lords' amendment carried the clause that if the pope accredited a minister to London that minister must not be an ecclesiastic. Another amendment by the Duke of Wellington called the pope not 'sovereign pontiff' but 'sovereign of the Roman states'. The amendments made the law futile, for on these terms the pope declined to send an envoy.

Amidst these negotiations it was rumoured that the pope intended to create new Catholic dioceses in England. As early as September 1847 the *Salisbury Herald* announced that Wiseman was coming back from Rome with authority to establish a hierarchy of archbishops and bishops, who should take their titles from towns not the seat of Anglican bishops—Westminster, Birmingham, Derby, Nottingham, Liverpool. There was rumour that Newman was to be made one of the new bishops, and that Wiseman or Walsh would be the Archbishop of Westminster, and later still that Walsh refused on grounds of illness and old age.[1] The plan was even printed in the *Tablet*. So confident was the rumour that there was surprise when nothing happened. Stout Anglicans suspected that Lord Minto told the pope that Russell's government would make no objection to a hierarchy. Stout Roman Catholics believed that nothing happened because the pope was persuaded by Lord Minto not to go forward, and expressed resentment that the needs of Catholic discipline were sacrificed to pressure from a Protestant government.[2]

The letters from Minto to Lord John Russell are now accessible at the Public Record Office and prove that neither of the contradictory rumours about him was true. But the general rumour was well founded. The vicars-apostolic, who for two previous years applied vainly for a hierarchy, were astonished in 1847 to find that the attitude of Rome had changed from resistance to encouragement and that they were no longer pushing a boulder up a cliff. Whether the change of air should be ascribed to the death of Cardinal Acton, or to the new pope, or to the new secretary of Propaganda, Monsignor Barnabo, the vicars-apostolic rejoiced when on 4 October 1847 the cardinals of Propaganda, and on 5 October Pope Pius IX himself, approved the plan for an English hierarchy with an Archbishop of Westminster and seven other bishoprics. On 1 November 1847 the brief was printed ready to issue.

At the last moment it was not published. Dr. Wiseman, who conducted the negotiations in Rome, returned to England and found reason for delay. A legal difficulty appeared—whether new bishop would be entitled in law to the property of old vicar-apostolic.[3] He

---

[1] G, 47, 569, 581, 732.

[2] Sir Robert Inglis asked about Minto in the House of Commons on 17 August 1848, Hansard, ci, 211–16; Catholic suspicions of Minto reported by Wiseman to Grant, 8 March 1848, PA Congreg. Partic., 157/261.

[3] PA Congreg. Partic., 157/231ff.

also suffered a little fit of nerves that publication of the brief might cause a new flaring of religious fanaticism in England. While Rome delayed, critics of Wiseman started complaining. The plan expected Wiseman to succeed eventually to the see of Westminster and the archbishopric. Among many English Catholics Wiseman was not popular. They told Rome that he was incompetent as an administrator, ran into debt, was harsh to his clergy, encouraged converts at the expense of born Catholics, was too subservient to the English government. An anonymous pen told Propaganda that he was greedy for worldly honour and double-tongued.[1] Rome took these grumbles sceptically, for it received other and far more friendly portraits of Wiseman from Englishmen who believed his preferment necessary to the advance of English Catholicism. The Irish bishops were also afraid that the plan might lead to a concordat with the English government and were not backward in expressing doubts. Bishop Ullathorne went to Rome in May 1848 to find the cause of the delay, and was told by Barnabo that they doubted who should be the archbishop.[2] Propaganda nevertheless reaffirmed (26 June 1848) that the plan should go forward. On 17 July they decided after consulting Ullathorne that there should be twelve sees instead of eight.

But while Rome paused the Romans revolted, the pope fled to Gaeta, Barnabo fled to an Armenian monastery under Turkish diplomatic protection,[3] and ecclesiastical business stopped. For nearly two years nothing could be done. Pius IX re-entered Rome in March 1850, a pope who had lost his liberalism. The cardinals slowly took up the threads of business. They saw no reason to hurry.

That summer of 1850 the plight of the Church of England afforded sudden reason to hurry.

Catholic optimism grew rapidly after Newman's conversion. Wiseman almost astonished himself by finding at work in London, or founding, sixteen convents of nuns and four male communities—Passionists established in 1848, the Redemptorists in the same year, who occupied the old headquarters of the Bible Society in Lord Teignmouth's house at Clapham, the Oratorians under Frederick Faber, and the Jesuits at Farm Street from 1849. On 4 July 1848 Pugin's cathedral of St. George's in Southwark, which had been

[1] PA Scritture Riferite, Anglia, xii, 379.
[2] Ullathorne, *Hierarchy*, 35.
[3] Ullathorne, *Hierarchy*, 77.

eight years in building,[1] was solemnly opened. When the site was acquired in 1840 the sellers stipulated that no image nor religious emblem should appear on the outside of the building. When its foundation-stone was laid the same year the little service was held in the early morning and without publicity, to avoid trouble. In July 1848 the opening was celebrated by thirteen bishops and 240 priests, a choir with eminent soloists from the Italian opera, and full airing from the press. Such a contrast in eight years could not but fire the naturally excitable spirit of Wiseman. He had eyed the Tractarian Movement since its birth, argued with it, declared its logical end to be Rome, fostered its converts, welcomed and provided for those who came. He expected the Oxford Movement to end in the Roman Catholic church, and now he observed more leaders of the party threatening publicly to leave the Church of England. The day after the Gorham judgment he preached a sermon of one hour and three-quarters in St. George's, Southwark, directed at the waverers. Two Sundays later on Easter Day he preached for two hours and ten minutes on the same theme.[2]

Other Roman Catholics besides Wiseman stretched out their invitation to the Tractarians. The voice of Father Newman had not been heard so clearly for five years. Trained to the priesthood at Rome, he was engaged in founding the Oratory at Maryvale in Birmingham, and since 1845 had spoken nothing outside his communion. The leader of the original Movement had taken his course to Rome; and it seemed to him that the Gorham case stripped the blinkers from the eyes of other Tractarians and showed them that they ought to follow where he had led. He considered how best he could turn the Anglican crisis to account.[3]

Wiseman persuaded him to lecture in London. Newman was reluctant. Whatever he said, if it were to the point, it must offend many Anglican friends. Though he wanted to take advantage of the Anglican disarray, he saw that interference in the Gorham imbroglio might do his cause more harm than good. Never blessed with a thick skin, he was already more than sensitive to the imputations, some silly and most untrue, which scandalous journalists rumoured about him.

---

[1] Characteristically, Pugin's original plans were so elaborate, that the committee refused to meet their cost and time, and with great difficulty persuaded him to withdraw his resignation and produce something more manageable.

[2] Bogan, 50, 167.

[3] Dessain, xiii, 460.

But eschewing the reluctance in May 1850 and writing long hours and too late at night, he delivered to his discredit and published the *Lectures on certain difficulties felt by Anglicans in submitting to the Catholic Church*. It was the only book by Newman which many Anglicans found it impossible to forgive.

It was an appeal to members of the Oxford Movement. He considered that Movement historically, to show that its logical end was Rome, that it was always an excrescence upon the Church of England and never at home there. He compared its aims and its ideals with 'the facts'—with surplice riots, Sumner's opinion of baptism, Phillpotts refusing to obey the law, the elevations of Prince Lee and of Hampden. The most offensive utterances of the book, to the persons at whom it was directed, were the violent onslaughts upon the Church of England—in the eyes of faith a mere wreck—a mere collection of officials depending on and living in the supreme civil power—but one aspect of the state—its life an act of Parliament—we thought it so unearthly and we find it so commonplace or worthless—it does not know what it holds and what it holds not—it has no love for its members—it is an imposture—a body of yesterday—you must leave it, you must secede. A long passage was directed against the only rival to Rome as a home for the seceders, the non-jurors or a free episcopal church.

Ten years later Newman would not have written in this language. He was suffering a little from the disease of being a new convert, of burning what once he had adored; but the occasion, while the high church party tottered upon the precipice of disruption, persuaded him to shout louder than his inward judgment truly approved. He confessed to Faber that he was writing them against the grain of his intellect.[1] And even in these most hostile of lectures he never lost that characteristic sense of continuity evident in the *Essay on Development* five years earlier and the *Apologia* fourteen years later. He was not contending that the Oxford Movement had been uncatholic, but that, though Catholic and because Catholic, the Movement was always strange in the Church of England. He received from Rome an honorary doctorate of divinity, and though he still wanted to be called Father, he became Dr. Newman. But the lectures were too extreme to persuade minds not already more than half persuaded.[2]

[1] Dessain, xiii, 470.
[2] They appear to have influenced T. W. Allies, M. Trevor, i, 521. For their influence upon Bellasis and Hope (Scott) cf. *Memorials of Mr. Serjeant Bellasis* (1893), 71–72. Thackeray and Charlotte Brontë are said to have attended, Bowden, *Faber*, 372.

Though the creation of Roman Catholic dioceses in England was a plan which owed almost nothing to the Tractarians and nothing at all to the Gorham case, the timing of it could not help being influenced by the ecclesiastical crisis of the Church of England during the spring and summer of 1850.

The conversion of Lord Feilding after presiding at *The Day* caused sensation in Rome. Propaganda received descriptions of the utter disorder and confusion of the Anglicans and imperative requests to act.[1] By 1 September 1850 Wiseman knew that the hierarchy was going forward. On 13 September the Pope interviewed him and gave final approval.

Aware that a brief to establish bishops might cause trouble in England, Rome steadily insisted on three conditions for its promulgation.[2] It must be done while a Whig government ruled England; must be published at a time of year when Parliament was not sitting; and must establish sees of which the titles did not transgress the emancipation act of 1829, and therefore avoided all titles used by bishops of the Church of England. The titles of sees were long discussed. Practical minds wanted bishops to have titles in cities where many Catholics lived, that is the great cities, several of which grew through industrial revolution and were therefore not the sees of Anglican prelates: Birmingham and Liverpool were obvious candidates. Doctrinaire or romantic minds suspected that Anglicans would rejoice if the titles of sees were not ancient, and therefore wanted ancient Anglo-Saxon sees no longer occupied by English bishops: such sees as Hexham, Beverley, Selsey, Thetford, Dunwich; and above all Westminster, once a see in the age of Reformation but untenanted by Anglican prelates and therefore legal for a Catholic bishop. The proposal of Westminster raised qualms among conservative English Catholics. Though not the title of an Anglican bishop the name rang loud with the history of England. Dr. Lingard thought that if they chose Westminster they risked cries of *No popery*.[3] The vicars-apostolic were permitted within reason to choose whether they would be practical or

[1] PA Scritture Riferite, Anglia, xiii/15.
[2] Cf. PA Congregazioni Particolari 157/224ff. Wiseman was summoned to Rome in August with the intention not of sending him back but of keeping him there as cardinal. Monsignor George Talbot, the English convert who had the ear of Pius IX, claimed to have influenced the pope to send Wiseman back to England as cardinal and Archbishop of Westminster, Dessain, xiv, 110 n. 1. But Talbot was never wont to underestimate his influence upon the pope.
[3] Haile-Bonney, *Life of Lingard*, 361.

romantic. Two ancient names were selected, Hexham and Beverley; eight cities of modern industry—Birmingham, Liverpool, Nottingham, Northampton, Plymouth, Bristol (called Clifton to keep the law), Manchester (called Salford to keep the law), Southwark (for south London and the southern home counties, legal because no Anglican see of Southwark existed until 1905); one see at Shrewsbury, convenient for North Wales and respectful to a noble lord and benefactor; one see which combined ancient with modern, Newport and Menevia; and the archbishopric of Westminster. On 29 September 1850 the pope issued the brief establishing these thirteen sees and next day made Wiseman a cardinal.[1]

The conditions exacted by Rome to avoid English anger were thus fulfilled. The government was Whig and partly dependent on the Catholic votes of the Irish. As Parliament was not sitting, no questions could be asked in the House of Commons. The titles of sees kept the law of England. The pope and his advisers at Propaganda believed that they had done all that was necessary to secure favourable circumstances. They overlooked considerations of moment. They wanted speed while the Anglican soul was in turmoil, and therefore failed to realise that the brief would look like a spoon to stir the boiling pot. Propaganda was not sufficiently aware how hallowed to England was the name of Westminster. And above all they reckoned without the exuberance of Wiseman. He found himself a cardinal and an archbishop, the first in England since the reign of Bloody Mary, and his heart was moved to exult.

Wiseman's pastoral

On 7 October 1850 Cardinal Wiseman issued a pastoral letter 'from out of the Flaminian Gate', or in less florid language Porta del Popolo, the northern gate of the city of Rome; for it was a breach of etiquette to issue a pastoral from within the papal walls. He announced the hierarchy and his elevation to be Cardinal and Archbishop of Westminster. He declared that the greatest of blessings had just been bestowed upon England. 'Your beloved country has received a place among the fair churches, which, normally constituted, form the splendid aggregate of Catholic communion; Catholic England has been restored to its orbit in the ecclesiastical firmament, from which its light had long vanished.' The martyrs of later ages had mourned

[1] Text in Maziere Brady, *Annals of the Catholic Hierarchy*, 358.

over the departure of England's religious glory and now bless God that they see the lamp of the temple kindled again. The language was emotional and rhetorical. If it were a message to the faithful of the new diocese of Westminster, it was little more than normality. It came to be regarded, and there was something about its tone which gave ground for the suspicion, that it was less a message to faithful Roman Catholics than a manifesto or challenge to the English people. Intending to exult over the new beauty of English Catholic order, Wiseman was believed to be exulting at the downfall of English Protestants. A modest song of gratitude was orchestrated like a conquering hymn of pride.

Wiseman expected little trouble. He supposed that no-popery riots were obsolete. He visited Lord John Russell before he set out for Italy, and a conversation was exchanged of sufficient vagueness to allow Wiseman afterwards to claim that he informed the prime minister of the plan, and to allow Russell to deny that he knew anything whatever about it. Pope Pius IX thought that he spoke of the plan to Lord Minto, but Minto afterwards denied all knowledge. Wiseman ordered the pastoral to be read from the pulpits of all the churches in his new diocese, on the next possible Sunday. Seldom had a cardinal of the Roman church been guilty of less foresight and more imprudence.

The papal brief broke upon an astonished England at the end of the second week of October. On 21 October several newspapers were attacking, and on 22 October the *Times* produced a leader of rare severity, fastening upon the use of a Westminster title. 'If this appointment be not intended as a clumsy joke, we confess we can only regard it as one of the grossest acts of folly and impertinence which the court of Rome has ventured to commit since the crown and people of England threw off its yoke . . .' The London newspapers regarded it, or claimed to regard it, as an attempt by the pope to restore his dominion in this island, as a way of expressing contempt for the English church, as a mode of denouncing the Archbishop of Canterbury as an intruder, and as a deplorable and preposterous effort to revive sectarian feelings. Many priests doubted the wisdom of reading the pastoral in the London churches, but obeyed. Lawyers started searching the statutes to prove illegality, clerical and lay meetings issued the inevitable protests.

Ullathorne, the new Catholic Bishop of Birmingham, wrote a

letter to the *Times* on 22 October attempting to undo the damage. This was no pretension to rule the English people, but an internal affair of church government, entirely concerned with spiritual matters. So far from the pope bringing Englishmen more under the direct control of Rome, the act liberated Englishmen by allowing them more independence. There was no intention to be aggressive and no political object. Other apologists reminded the public that there were Anglican bishops in Orthodox Jerusalem, and Catholic Gibraltar, and Presbyterian Scotland, and asked what was the difference? When Ullathorne was enthroned in the see of Birmingham on 26 October, Newman preached a partly inaudible but nevertheless unfortunate sermon.[1] Like many English Catholics who suspected that the hierarchy proceeded from Gothic pageant-minded romantics, Newman doubted the wisdom of the plan, but with battle joined he stepped out to fight. The sermon undid the cooling effect of Ullathorne's letter by seeming to adopt an extreme interpretation of the brief common among some of the ex-Tractarian converts; that the brief was indeed directed to the whole country. The people of England (he was reported to have said), who for so many years have been separated from the see of Rome, are about, of their own free will, to be added to the holy church. The people of England were restored to the bosom of the church. The hierarchy was restored—the grave was opened, and Christ was coming out.

Thus Newman made his own the rhetoric of Wiseman, and drew upon himself a shower of missiles, from the crude vulgarities of *Punch* to the urbane severity of Dean Tait of Carlisle. He thought that the only way of dealing with the prejudices of the English people was to trample upon them, and justified himself to Ullathorne by the plea that he wanted to draw the fire from his bishop to himself.[2] Roman Catholics of a forward mind contributed to the popular uproar. Looking hopefully towards the Tractarians, they believed that the pope demolished the Tractarian argument about schism. Their extremists talked joyfully of the Anglican sees as ghosts of realities long passed away, and gloried that they were ignored.

A few sensible Anglicans could not see what difference was made by the new titles, and thought thus early that popular indignation diverted ecclesiastical energies from more important tasks. But these critics were rare. For the first time for centuries the Bishop of London

---

[1] Published as *Christ upon the Waters*, 1850.   [2] Dessain, xiv, 121.

requested his clergy to preach controversial sermons.[1] The Fulham
papers at Lambeth show Blomfield stoking the flames, anxious to
keep public wrath at high temperature. The usual meetings of protesting clergy in diocese or archdeaconry or rural deanery were accompanied or supplemented by meetings of dissenters to the same end.
Some meetings were sober and dignified, others were marked by the
worst kind, now vile and now absurd, of anti-popish vituperation.
The latent and historic prejudices of the English people rose to the
surface.

Guy Fawkes day occurred awkwardly on Tuesday of the following
week. The Catholics were afraid of mob assault upon St. George's
cathedral in Southwark and on the Oratory in King William Street,
and barricaded the cathedral against an onslaught. Detachments of
police were sent to protect these and other possible posts of danger.
The Oratorians kept to their house while crowds hooted outside and
paraded with guys and threw fireworks up to the roof of the chapel.
The procession of guys often included Cardinal Wiseman as well as
the pope, and sometimes twelve more bishops. At Salisbury they were
all burnt after a torchlight parade with a brass band and fireworks, in
the presence of a mighty crowd which sang the national anthem.
At Ware the crowd paraded to Musley Hill, where an effigy of
Wiseman was hung on a gallows over a pyre of faggots and tar-
barrels and burnt amid roars and curses. A few Catholic churches had
their windows broken, and more were disturbed by trampling hatted
intruders at service time. A few priests were pelted and hooted.[2] The
Catholic clergy were afraid that Wiseman would be lynched when he
landed in England and advised him to delay crossing the Channel. In
Fleet Street there were fourteen guys, with a colossal guy sixteen feet
high upon a van drawn by two horses, and a man dressed in a red
robe and wearing a red broad-brimmed hat, on his right a comedian
dressed as a nun and on his left a jolly fat monk who leered im-
pudently at the passers-by from under a mask. One of the guys
carried a pail of whitewash, labelled *Holy Water for the penitent*. A
squad of police marched with it into the city, lending it an air of
pageantry and solemnity, and despite the great crowds, there was no
rioting.

The Oratorians were among the worst hit, chiefly because Faber's
rash nature insisted that they walk abroad in their habits, and they

[1] G, 50, 762.   [2] Ward, *Wiseman*, i, 552-3.

were followed by jests, hoots and hisses. An Anglican clergyman went out in a long cloak and was pursued by a rabble, until he turned round and showed them that he was wearing trousers, which so satisfied them[1] that they gave him a cheer and departed. It would be wrong to exaggerate the tumults; they were not to be compared with the riots against popery of old days. Though the Oratory at Birmingham was almost besieged, Oratorian fathers in the streets were sometimes greeted with cheers. Few windows of Catholic chapels were broken. Dr. Pusey himself arrived at Bristol on Guy Fawkes day and preached unhindered next day to an attentive congregation of 2,000. One of the worst acts of violence was committed at Cheltenham as late as 22 November, when a mob seized an effigy of the pope exhibited in a draper's window, carried the guy to the front of the Catholic chapel where they burnt it and then smashed the chapel windows. At Birkenhead 250 policemen needed the aid not only of 700 special constables but two companies of the 52nd Regiment. Father Ignatius Spencer insisted against advice on wearing his habit and was assaulted in the streets.

Wiseman delayed a few days at Liège. But he had the courage to proceed. He arrived in London on 11 November, in what was supposed to be secrecy but was reported widely in the press. On 12 November he boldly went to St. George's, Southwark, and was observed by a crowd of the reporters to be enveloped in a large blue cloak, and in his hand what was perhaps his breviary, but which the reporters called a superbly bound missal. The mayor of Boston suggested to the prime minister that he be exiled as a Spaniard under the aliens act and Lord Winchilsea urged the government to declare war against the papal states.[2]

At the anti-popery meetings the drum was beaten not only against the Pope or Dr. Wiseman but against their supposed friends within the Church of England. The placards of *No popery* carried on 5 November were accompanied by other placards, *No Puseyites* or *No Tractarians*. At Exeter influence was needed to prevent Bishop Phillpotts being burned in the same bonfire which consumed the pope and the cardinal.[3] In a charge at the end of October Bishop Blomfield not only denounced the aggression of the papists, but the insidious imitations of Rome lately introduced into Anglican worship, and English

[1] Dessain, xiv, 118.   [2] G. 50, 814–15, 918.
[3] PRO 30/22/8F: Fortescue to Russell, 11 November 1850.

clergy who led their flocks 'step by step to the very verge of the precipice'. In the emotions of that day many of the English people dimly believed that somehow the pope had been encouraged to his assault by the weakness of English Protestantism, and that the Protestant fortress was weak because there were traitors within the bastion. From the Bishop of London and the editor of the *Times* and Lord Chancellor Truro to the ranting orator of Limehouse and the ignorant hooligan of Pimlico, many were sure that the Tractarians emboldened the pope, by deceiving the world about the deep Protestantism of the English people. Every meeting to repudiate the pope was vociferous for the Protestantism of the Protestant religion and insisted upon the glory of the Reformation. Wiseman had not only put Catholic chapels in peril but unwittingly caused an upsurge of English feeling against the disciples of the Oxford Movement.

At this moment the prime minister lent a willing hand to stoke the flames.

In judging the most foolish act of Russell's political career, it is important to remember that he could not avoid saying something. Public opinion, and the members of both Houses of Parliament, required him to explain the attitude of government to pope and cardinal. It was important to speak because Wiseman publicly claimed that Russell knew and consented, because the politicians suspected that his father-in-law Minto was told at Rome and agreed. Downing Street issued an official denial that either Minto or the cabinet knew the plan beforehand.

Neither Russell nor his sovereign professed alarm at the papal bogey. Though Queen Victoria was loudly told by the press that the pope intruded upon her prerogative, she felt no undue anxiety. She had long ago learnt to treat Roman Catholics with tolerant justice and to fear Puseyites. She told Russell that the real danger was not the pope but the enemy inside the established church. Russell agreed with her that the new dioceses need cause no alarm and that the Tractarians were the dangerous enemy. He quoted Dr. Arnold to her—'I look upon a Roman Catholic as an enemy in his uniform; I look upon a Tractarian as an enemy disguised as a spy.'[1] He thought privately that anger against the pope would do good, not because he was afraid of

---

[1] *Letters of Q. Victoria*, i, ii, 273. The quotation is not exact. Arnold used even stronger language; Stanley, *Life of Arnold* (1844), ii, 280. Original in Rugby School Papers.

the pope, but because he saw that it would be bound to strengthen the Protestant feeling of the country, and so encourage popular hostility to the high churchmen who were his political and religious enemies.

His old friend Bishop Maltby of Durham wrote him a lament that the pope's aggression was insolent and insidious. On 4 November Russell replied from Downing street, and with his leave Maltby published the letter on 7 November.[1] He said truly that he agreed with the bishop, but that his alarm was not equal to his indignation. He promised that the law would be examined, the possibility of further legislation would be considered. 'There is a danger, however, which alarms me much more than any aggression of a foreign sovereign. Clergymen of our own church . . . have been most forward in leading their flocks' (and he quoted the recent charge of Bishop Blomfield) 'step by step, to the very verge of the precipice.' He seized upon some of the usages which Blomfield attacked in his charge—honour paid to saints, infallibility claimed for the church, superstitious use of the sign of the cross, muttering of the liturgy, auricular confession. 'What then, is the danger to be apprehended from a foreign prince of no great power, compared to the danger within the gates from the unworthy sons of the Church of England herself? . . .'

The informed and unprejudiced[2] thought the letter was imprudent, undignified, and unbecoming to a prime minister. The queen disapproved of it, Russell's closest colleague Lansdowne regretted it, Lord Clarendon reported its effect in Ireland to be disastrous, relations with the papacy were shattered, and the animosities of Guy Fawkes day were perpetuated for several weeks. A majority of the English liked it.

What Russell intended to do is not known, and probably he acted without much thought of consequences. Against a politician with fewer scruples might lurk the suspicion that he was diverting the onslaught of prejudice from Roman Catholics, some of whom voted for the Whigs, towards Tractarians nearly all of whom voted for the Tories. In the autumn of 1850 his enemies denounced him as unscrupulous. But Russell was neither subtle nor unscrupulous. He

---

[1] In the campaign which followed Russell was abused for causing the riots; and most modern books, misled by the date 4 November, when the letter was written, make Russell responsible for the Guy Fawkes riots. He was innocent of anything that happened on Guy Fawkes day.

[2] Greville, vi, 258.

clumsily expressed the popular mind, and received many messages of thanks, especially from the common council of the city of London.

First, he made it impossible for himself not to legislate against the Roman Catholics. The Whig leader, devoted all his life to the principle of toleration, and politically relying on votes from Irish Roman Catholics, committed himself inadvertently to some kind of penal law. Secondly, he partially diverted the force of anti-papal feeling against alleged traitors within the gates. Pusey and Manning were to suffer because of Wiseman. Some of Russell's friends doubted whether he cared.[1]

To the dismay of his timorous priests Wiseman continued to think that lying low was not the right policy. On 20 November the *Times* and four other newspapers published a pamphlet of thirty-one pages called an *Appeal*. He now explained that the new hierarchy was exclusively directed to the better organisation of his own church; but admitted another reason, namely that Anglicans treated them with contumely because they possessed no ordinary bishops and were therefore schismatic, and taunted them because the pope dare not institute such bishops. He belaboured Lord John Russell and Lord Chancellor Truro for their incitement, mocked the royal supremacy in its power of nominating bishops, and the Anglican bishops for countenancing agitation, claiming that the Roman Catholic was no more touching the prerogative of the queen than any dissenter who equally would have nothing to do with the bishops of the Church of England. Anglican bishoprics were founded in Jerusalem and Gibraltar without complaint. And finally, the pope showed the plan to Lord Minto three years before.

This clear and powerful appeal was still aggressive and continued to embitter members of that church which its author so openly affected to despise. Greville thought that the pamphlet was uncommonly well done, and that though incapable of quieting passion, it betrayed a consciousness of being impregnable amidst the storm. It claimed toleration as a right. The English consented to tolerate Roman Catholicism, bishops were essential to Roman Catholicism, therefore the English must tolerate those bishops.

Wiseman's controversial ability was the least of the reasons for the quietening of the agitation. Sensible Englishmen were ashamed of the hooligan prejudice which they saw around them; Whigs wanted

[1] Greville, vi, 259.

the Irish not to be too offended; high churchmen resented the papal aggression bitterly, but resented the Protestant outburst even more bitterly; radicals demanded toleration on principle.

Russell's onslaught rallied English and Irish Catholics. Many priests and eminent laity thought that Wiseman had been foolish, but were prepared to close ranks in self-defence. The Irish bishops, always afraid of concordats and attempts to rule Ireland through Rome, had suspected Wiseman of being intimate with Russell and were now gratified to find him at fisticuffs. But not quite all the Catholic laity were willing to rally. A few conservative Catholic peers resented the pope's act and wondered whether they would be loyal to their queen and country if they supported it. Lord Beaumont declared that English Roman Catholics could not accept the new hierarchy without violating their duties as citizens. The Duke of Norfolk announced that he agreed with Lord Beaumont and publicly became an Anglican by receiving holy communion in his parish church. Some English priests were not satisfied that the coldness or worse which they now met in the streets was either necessary or useful, and laid the blame upon the cardinal. Despite a front of steel, the Catholic body showed signs of internal stress.

But if the Duke of Norfolk left, there were compensations. Whatever the lightning damaged, it shed a blaze of light upon Catholicism. Priests and chapels found a sudden increase in enquirers or postulants, more interest among the people and sometimes more sympathy by reaction.

Among the convenors of special meetings of Anglican clergy to protest against papal aggression, Bishop Gilbert of Chichester summoned his archdeacon to gather the clergy. Manning was confronted with a crisis of conscience. Required to summon the clergy to protest, he found that he believed there to be no grounds for protest, and that the pope's bishops were more legitimate than the English bishops. On Gilbert's advice, he agreed to call the meeting if he might state his dissent. He asked to resign his archdeaconry at the end of the month, thinking of travelling to Gladstone at Naples, and so to Jerusalem. But he went to London and regularly attended Anglican worship. His friends—Dodsworth, his curate Laprimaudaye, Lord Campden and his wife—were received first into the Church of Rome. It took Manning three months longer, part study and part hesitation. He attended Anglican worship for the last time on 23 March 1851; two days later he legally resigned his archdeaconry and benefice at a notary's office in the city, and then crossed Blackfriars Bridge to St. George's in Southwark and knelt before the reserved sacrament and said his first *Hail Mary*. With Hope (Scott) he was received into the Roman church on 6 April 1851.

Manning and Newman were contrasting types and leaders of Anglicans attracted towards Rome. Newman was a divine, Manning a churchman. Newman looked for theological truth and found it in that church which, he came to believe, represented with least unfaithfulness the doctrine and ethos of the first Christian centuries. Manning knew that the church possessed the truth, but the English establishment allowed the state to adulterate the possession. Newman left the Church of England because it spoke to his conscience with stammering lips. Manning left the Church of England because it let a non-Christian state within its borders and surrendered its guardianship of truth to state officers. Newman left the Anglicans because they were Protestants, Manning because they were established.

The true Manning had few intimates and was therefore mysterious to discern; and the historian's difficulty is multiplied by Purcell's famous and discreditable biography. A man of action with a coherent mind, Manning was revered by high churchmen for clarity and courage and judgment. Thirty years later the old cardinal was dry and brittle, emotions impoverished, life drained away before death. Seeing a death-mask, the biographer pushed it over a young face and refused to see that the mask would not fit. The Manning of 1850 concealed his heart like a widower of thirteen years, but was still rich in feeling and sympathy. He was always an extremist. Whether as Anglican against the Ecclesiastical Commission in the thirties and state education in the forties or as Roman Catholic against mixed education and in favour of papal infallibility, he always defended positions so clear and unsubtle that they could be crude. Newman's mind was more hesitant and delicate. Manning would therefore exert more influence. In a short run the world follows him who proclaims that difficulties do not exist, in a long run him who faces them with candour and humility. Catholic posterity has rated Newman's mind so high that it cannot think Manning even comparable.

The establishment laboured under the handicap that despite the poverty of curates and loneliness of pastoral care it stank of fleshpots. Clergymen striving to deepen devout lives in the Church of

England became abnormally sensitive about the temptations of high office in the establishment. In their different ways Manning and Samuel Wilberforce were conscious of ability and aware that by practising silence and conformity they could hardly avoid preferment. It therefore became a duty neither to conform nor to keep silence. During these years when the Church of Rome drew Anglican clergy with such unusual magnetism, one of the tugs was freedom from the smell of secular advantage. Rome preserved the grand image of Catholic might and nevertheless invited Englishmen to yield their interest and their comfort. How sensitive Manning became to this tug is demonstrated by the form of an aspiration which he entered in his diary during the mental struggle:[1] 'Certainly I would rather choose to be stayed on God than to be in the thrones of the world and the church.'

Wiseman confirmed Manning a week after his reception, gave him the tonsure, ordained him subdeacon and deacon, and on the day before Trinity Sunday 1851 made him a priest. After the ceremony Wiseman embraced him and said: 'I look upon you as one of the first-fruits of the restoration of the hierarchy. . . .'[2] It was not quite true. The Gorham judgment and not papal aggression converted Manning. The speed of ordination caused severe criticism of Wiseman among Roman Catholics. Wiseman had to defend himself to Rome.[3] He claimed that Manning was unique, the most distinguished of converts, upon whom depended many conversions.

W. J. E. Bennett, vicar of St. Barnabas, Pimlico, was one of the signatories, with Manning and Pusey and Keble and others, of the declaration against the Gorham judgment and the royal supremacy. He was confidently expected to be among the seceders. He had been curate-in-charge of St. Paul's, Knightsbridge, a new church which was consecrated in 1843 and became in a few years one of the wealthiest parishes in London, with Lord John Russell and his wife among its regular worshippers. In 1846–7, with the aid of wealthy subscribers including the prime minister, Bennett built the new church of St. Barnabas for the poor districts of the parish and formed a little college for choristers and four priests. By a misfortune of timing this church was consecrated on 11 June 1850. Bennett was a devoted and able pastor, whom the poor revered.

[1] Purcell, i, 283.   [2] Purcell, i, 633.   [3] PA Scritture Riferite, Anglia, xii/1009.

For three or four years the subject of ritual usages[1] by Bennett had
been matter for complaint or correspondence between Bennett,
Bishop Blomfield and a minority of aggressive parishioners, until at
last Bennett offered his resignation, threatening (15 July 1850) to
become a Roman Catholic. When in October 1850 Bishop Blomfield
made charges against the Romanisers in the Church of England many
supposed him to be referring to Bennett at S. Barnabas. The press
pointed its accusing finger. On the morning of 10 November 1850
the church was filled with a curious crowd. As the congregation was
leaving a handful of people called out 'That is popery', or 'No
popery', and hissed, and in reply there were a few muttered cries of
'Shame'. This little scene, reported in the press, produced an outrage
a week later. When the church was full the doors were shut, but the
discontented crowd of several hundred left outside yelled away that
they would have neither popery nor Puseyism, and would pull the
church down. A party headed by the butler of Mr. Henry Drummond,
M.P., tried to break in, but were foiled by a strong body of police.
The butler was charged, but the magistrate, in dismissing the charge,
made hostile criticism of the Romish worship at S. Barnabas. Bennett
received letters threatening his life and parcels filled with dung, was
hooted when he walked in the streets, and suffered a siege of his
house. On 24 November he was coughed down when he mentioned
the two lighted altar-candles in his sermon, and a final organ voluntary was hissed, but the police slowly calmed the public.[2] In December,
by a *Letter to Lord John Russell* (seven editions), Bennett damaged
Russell further, first by revealing Russell's long connexion with his
church at a time when the practices were hardly different from those
now attacked by him as mummeries, and secondly by making the
Durham letter responsible for the outrages at S. Barnabas. On 16
November Bishop Blomfield called upon Bennett to fulfil his offer
of resignation. In mid-December Bennett's resignation was one of
the main topics of public conversation, for it was to be the first open

---

[1] Especially the eastward position of the celebrant at the eucharist; retaining hold
of the chalice at the administration; allowing six of the communicants (two of them
ex-Roman Catholics) to receive directly into their mouths; beginning sermons with
'In the name of the Father, and of the Son and of the Holy Ghost'; the use of the sign
of the cross (Blomfield to Bennett, 1 July 1850). The bishop charged him on hearsay
with ministering extreme unction to a dying lady, but Bennett denied it (Bennett to
Blomfield, 15 July 1850). Cf. G, 50, 913.

[2] The still Anglican Manning was said to have offered to harangue the mob outside
the church on 15 December, but was persuaded to desist. G, 50, 901.

step, as the *Times* declared, towards making secure the Protestantism of the Church of England. On 5 December Lord Ashley declared at the Freemasons tavern, 'I had rather worship with Lydia on the banks of the river than with a hundred surpliced priests in the temple of S. Barnabas.'[1] Bennett resigned, and was found an Anglican living at Frome.

Papal aggression made England more conscious of its Protestantism. During the next few years the Anglo-Catholics attained the zenith of their unpopularity, the government of the Church of England moved towards the evangelicals, the alliance between low churchmen and dissenters was restored and cemented. Parochial life was subject to strain. Laymen pestered bishops or archdeacons with complaints about their parsons and demanded discipline. Vicars who wanted to introduce a new and reverent custom into their church looked nervously at their flocks. The vicar of East Dereham erected over his daughter's grave a tombstone surmounted with a cross and was afraid that parishioners would desecrate it in the night. Observers, called spies by the unfriendly, were sent to parishes of notorious Tractarians to report on ritual. Suspicion divided parishes[2] and estranged pastors from their people.

Meanwhile the cabinet sadly and regretfully addressed itself to plan the now inevitable penal legislation. At a meeting of 13 December, with several members disliking the plan but seeing no way of avoiding it, they agreed to introduce a bill to make all territorial titles illegal for Roman Catholic bishops. 'I disapprove of such legislation very much,' wrote Earl Grey in his diary, 'and most reluctantly assent to its being attempted, but the country has got into such a state that I believe still greater mischief would result from doing nothing. . . .'[3] The bill, when introduced to the Commons on 14 February, was found to provide a penalty of £100 for any assumption of a territorial title by archbishop, bishop or dean, and a far fiercer penalty that any endowment of such sees or persons or their subordinates should be forfeit to the crown.

In February 1851 the government, now at sixes and sevens, almost fell and was propped with difficulty. From February to July of 1851

---

[1] F. Bennett, *The Story of W. J. E. Bennett*, 1909, 107. Cf. *Punch* at the time. Protestant wits called it S. Barrabas.

[2] *Armstrong's Norfolk Diary*, 23. Cf. Brasted and Dr. Mill, G, 51, 759.

[3] *Diary* of 3rd Earl Grey, 13 December 1850, HP.

Parliament devoted a proportion of its time to making the sees of
Roman Catholic prelates illegal. Every sectarian orator had his chance.
In the Commons the climax was reached by that Henry Drummond
whose butler distinguished himself in Pimlico. The bill was attacked
by Gladstone and the Peelites, by Roebuck and the English radicals,
by the Irish Catholics, by Archbishop Whately,[1] who compared it
to firing at a mob with a blank cartridge, and by some Anglican newspapers who thought it puerile and frivolous.[2] In its course it was much
modified. First it was pointed out that the Scottish (Anglican) bishops
would be rendered illegal by the bill, and a clause was needed to
exempt them. Then the government dropped the plan to confiscate
endowments and so extracted the real penalty. The resulting rump of
a bill caused cynical merriment to its critics and shamed the majority
who could not avoid carrying it. In its final form it included in the
illegality any publication of a bill or rescript for creating territorial
titles, and received the royal assent on 30 July 1851.

Thus Dr. Wiseman, and Irish immigration, and the Tractarians,
and Lord John Russell, and the people of England, forced Parliament
into a constitutional anachronism: a penal law, a law discriminating
against a religious denomination otherwise tolerated and containing
many subjects of the queen. For a moment it seemed as though the
old union of church and state as it existed before 1829, was rising
out of the mists of past history. It was its dying flicker. The ecclesiastical titles act was the last act carried by a British government with the
intention of discriminating between religious denominations.[3]

Though most of the Catholic bishops in England obeyed the law
on principle, their flocks took no notice whatever. The only vexatious

---

[1] *Life*, ii, 232–3.

[2] e.g. G, 51, 93, 109. Prince Albert regretted the clause exempting the Scottish
bishops, for they also were rivals to the establishment: the prince to Russell, 16 January
1851, RA, C19/1.

[3] Dr. M'Hale had called himself Archbishop of Tuam since the thirties, and he continued to do so. The new Bishop of Hexham used his title from the first; a reference in
Dublin to Dr. Cullen as Archbishop of Armagh was received with cheering, G, 51,
589, 605. Newman gave his *Lectures on the Present Position of Catholics in England* and
dedicated them to 'the Lord Archbishop of Armagh', with an ironical expression of
regret that in so dedicating them he appeared to show disrespect for an act of Parliament. At a Catholic meeting in Birmingham on 5 September 1851, for the purpose of
thanking Newman for his lectures, the tickets announced that the Lord Bishop of
Birmingham would preside. For the effects of the act, cf. the evidence and reports of
two parliamentary committees contemplating repeal; PP, 1867, viii, 15 (in which the
evidence of Hope-Scott and Manning is particularly important), and PP, 1867–8, viii,
185; and in education, PP, 1852, xxxix, 376–89.

consequence of the act was discovered by accident. The trust deeds of some Roman Catholic schools, phrased to attribute a large power to the bishop, were found now to be illegal and therefore to exclude those schools from receiving grants from the committee of privy council. It was a temporary alarm and soon cleared by administrative action. As every sensible man had foreseen, the law was a noise. No one was ever prosecuted under it. Gladstone, who forcibly argued against it, carried the repeal twenty years later.

The gains and losses to Roman Catholicism in England are difficult to balance.

They achieved a public face towards England: bishops, an Archbishop of Westminster, a resident cardinal. If the pope was worth this abuse and this law, he must be more powerful than most informed Englishmen supposed. They achieved this public face against the cries of mobs and the debates of the House of Commons. Parish priests reported interested enquirers, increase of conversions. Majesty appeared in the pageantry of the Cardinal of Westminster, driving unrabbled through London in a carriage bedecked with finery, writing his letters on splendid paper, insisting at first on being received by torch-bearers when he dined out, serving four courses of fish at his table in Lent.[1] The splendour of Gothic fane was now reflected in the dignity of its hierarch. Wiseman was prone to exaggerate. But the feeling which he overdid was widespread among Roman Catholics. They passed through the darkness and came unscathed into the day. Newman expressed this feeling in heartfelt poetry when he preached the sermon *The Second Spring* at the synod of Oscott in July 1852. The synod was the summit of Wiseman's career, president of thirteen bishops, with the greatest of converts Newman and Manning preaching sermons. Newman touched beauty in contrasting the old state of Catholicism and the new; the church renewing its youth, hopes budding amid blasts of spring winds, memories of sacrilege and martyrdom and profanation and contempt, a people who once shunned the light coming into the sun, from lowly chapel of the alley to storied edifice with cloisters and corridors and fronts and courts; the winter is past, the rain is over and gone, the fig-tree has put forth her green leaves, the vines in flower yield their sweet smell. Canterbury has gone its way, and York and Durham and Winchester. But the church lives again; and Westminster and Nottingham,

[1] Ward, *Life of Wiseman*, ii, 188–9.

Beverley and Hexham, shall be names as musical to the ear and as stirring to the heart as the glories that are lost.

Persecution may help a church, always helps it if the persecution is trivial and ineffectual. But it has the invariable disadvantage of encouraging minds to feel besieged. It was no advantage to Catholicism that gentle housewives started refusing to employ Catholic cooks, that Catholic priests were cut by old friends in the street, that fanatical parliamentarians accused Catholic converts of kidnapping nuns, that *Maria Monk* went through a huge edition, that *Punch* drew vile pictures of Wiseman and Newman, that in June 1852 the English labourers of Stockport rioted in the Irish quarter and sacked two Catholic chapels. In that same month the government at last gave notice that it would suppress public processions, and the Oratorians and other religious orders yielded and henceforth refrained from wearing their habits in the streets. By the emancipation act of 1829 Peel hoped to bring Roman Catholics out of the mood, retiring or aggressive, of being a minority in a hostile state. Papal aggression ended these hopes. English Catholics felt as besieged as ever and closed ranks against the foe.

The worst blow struck by papal aggression to the Roman Catholic cause was the trial of Achilli versus Newman.

In his *Lectures on the present position of Catholics*, given in the Birmingham corn exchange during the summer of 1851, Newman intended to expose the more ludicrous and revolting forms of anti-popish prejudice. He mocked the number of the Beast, and John Bullism, and tried to expose *Maria Monk* and the ex-priest Achilli.

Achilli was an Italian who had been a Dominican and then held various posts as a secular priest. Fleeing from the papacy, he came in 1847 to join the staff of the Protestant college at Malta. An obscurely discreditable incident compelled him to leave. He came to England, where the Evangelical Protestant Alliance welcomed him, gave him a chapel near Wiseman's house in Golden Square, used him as an itinerant preacher, and helped him to print a popular book entitled *Dealings with the Inquisition*. His addresses up and down the country were tuned to the popular mood.

In July 1850 Wiseman published an article to expose Achilli in the *Dublin Review*. Achilli, the article alleged, was tried before the inquisition for misconduct, expelled from the Dominican order, and imprisoned in an Italian monastery for sexual offences. Newman included in his lectures a detailed catalogue of Achilli's offences with dates, and sold a printed copy at the door. In bitter and ironical language, with a tone of seeming relish in its nervous power, he pilloried Achilli as a profligate under a cowl. Newman consulted Hope before he printed or reprinted his charges, asking whether he could be accused of libel. Hope thought an action possible but not probable and was inclined to pooh-pooh the risk. Newman supposed that Wiseman had all the Italian documents necessary to prove what the *Dublin Review* asserted.[1]

Thus Newman imprudently compelled his own prosecution. He put Achilli into a cage from which the only door of escape was a suit against him for libel. He wrongly supposed that Achilli would not dare to prosecute because he would render himself liable to transportation if the charges were proved.

The news of a libel suit put Newman into a torment of apprehension. He applied several times to Wiseman for documents which justified the charges. Wiseman behaved cavalierly. He poked vaguely among his papers, but failed to find the relevant documents and helped Newman with a less useful gift of £100. The lawyers warned the culprit that he was likely to lose the case, and told him that the penalty might be a year in prison. He collected affidavits that prison would have a serious effect on his health. Emissaries scoured Italy for witnesses, but failed to open the prison records sufficiently to produce documents useful in English courts. At last Wiseman found the missing papers, documents were sent from the Roman inquisition, and two Italian women were brought from Italy to say of Achilli what was necessary. The accounts of the trial made nauseating reading; witnesses coming forward to testify to rape in Italian sacristies, *Maria Monk* stories brought to reality in the cold decorum of an English law court. If this were represented as a contest of gladiators, between a Protestant convert from the Church of Rome and a Catholic convert from the Church of England, the Church of Rome had infinite advantage. Few sane men believed in the innocence of Achilli. But in truth, though Newman might save himself, the Roman Catholic church could only lose whatever the verdict. If the charges were untrue, Newman was liar and knave who hired Italian harlots to commit perjury. If the charges were true, they disclosed a sordid pit of priestly depravity.

---

[1] For the Achilli trial, lives of Newman by both Ward and Trevor; W. F. Finlason *Report of the trial and preliminary proceedings*, 1852; Giacinto Achilli, *Dealings with the Inquisition: or Papal Rome*, 1851, 2nd enlarged edition 1851; Dessain, vols. xiv–xv *passim*. For a young man's unfavourable view of the tone of these lectures of Newman, see *Life of Westcott*, i, 163–4, where the letter is wrongly dated.

Fanatics of the English Protestant underworld preferred to destroy Newman, but were content if Newman should win. Achilli as a Protestant was expendable. What mattered to them was his conduct while a priest in Italy.

On 25 June 1852, after a slanted summing-up from Lord Campbell, the jury found that of twenty-three charges the defence had proved only one, the charge that Achilli was deprived of his professorship and forbidden to preach. In the atmosphere of those years it would have been hardly possible to find a London jury willing to give any other verdict. An application for a new trial was refused; and on 31 January 1853 Mr. Justice Coleridge, whose son Henry was newly a Roman Catholic, read a misjudged lecture to Newman that he had deteriorated in character since he became a Roman Catholic and to the joy of Newman's friends fined him only £100. He needed to pay £12,000 in costs, which were paid by the affection of a relieved Catholic community, and for which Wiseman asked for collections in all churches. His true penalty was the agony of two years' expectation.

The Achilli trial stimulated the salacious excitement of the British public and must not be forgotten in estimating the results of papal aggression. Some said that another such trial would destroy the morals of the English people.

Thus the gains and losses were mixed if we contemplate public face. If we turn to pastoral utility, they were still mixed, but weighed more evidently towards the side of temporary loss.

The Catholics now had bishops. But they had bishops before, and found difficulty in filling the new sees worthily. They now had cathedral chapters by a papal brief of 19 November 1850, and the possibility of independent parishes. But the clergy who had wanted the hierarchy because they wanted security of tenure and a settled constitution felt defrauded. They were not released from the control of Propaganda. They were even afraid that the brief removed their existing rights by giving the bishops power over charitable trusts. Expecting more liberty, they feared that they now had less.[1] The rights awarded to the chapters were exiguous. Few priests qualified for the parochial status which now carried a measure of independence. Priests started appealing to Rome. If the troubles of the Catholic body had

---

[1] Cf. the evidence in the report of the select committee on Mortmain, PP, 1851, xvi, 152, 298–300, 390ff., 531–2.

been due to lack of constitution, those troubles now went from bad to worse. Rights of bishop versus rights of bishop, bishop versus religious orders, rights over old seminaries, cathedral chapter versus bishop, priests versus bishop—so far as the hierarchy was expected to create government and therefore peace, it failed. The priests of England had to wait more than half a century before Propaganda released its hold and their status ceased to be missionary.

If the choice of Wiseman to introduce the hierarchy proved bad, his choice as archbishop ended worse. With some of the converts—Faber, Ward, Newman, Manning—he was wholly in sympathy. But the archdiocese of Westminster needed organising, and Wiseman as administrator was somewhat inattentive. Over the next ten years every party among the clergy came to loggerheads with every other party, often for reasons which tactful government might have averted.[1]

4. CONVOCATION

From the time of the reform act of 1832 churchmen of every religious school put forward suggestions for an organ to express the mind of the church, on the avowed ground that neither Parliament nor the bishops of the House of Lords expressed that mind. This desire assisted the birth of Peel's Ecclesiastical Commission. Archbishop Whately and others made divers proposals for some kind of church assembly or committee under the authority of Parliament.

But Convocation quickly attracted the strongest backing. Few knew much about Convocation. They knew that it was once an assembly for church discussion, that its history in the British constitution ascended as far as the history of the House of Commons, that since 1717 it had

---

[1] Realising the necessity for administration, Wiseman secured the appointment (1855) of a coadjutor in a former colleague and friend George Errington, whose administrative power had long been known to him. The precise Errington, who wanted an account of every penny, could never work with Wiseman, who spent money without knowing which pocket banked it; and after five years and a troubled suit at Rome was dismissed from office. Since Errington represented to the clergy their rights and a steadiness against convert enthusiasm, the dismissal was intensely unpopular and left Wiseman isolated and almost friendless among his clergy. Cf. Morris, in Ward, *Life of Wiseman*, ii, 255. His own vicar-general, Maguire, refused to resign and was dismissed, the rector of his seminary at St. Edmund's, Ware, was in rebellion.

The chief disputes concerned property, the rights of the chapter, the rights over the seminary at Ware.

But for a favourable view of Wiseman as diocesan, though not as administrator, see David Norris in DR, 1963-4, 158.

not been allowed to meet except formally. This ceremony at the beginning of each Parliament preserved the name and memory. Tractarians when buffeted by bishops were consoled because bishops must give way to higher authority in the church, a resolution of Convocation—if Convocation were ever allowed to resolve. Convocation contained an upper house of bishops, all of whom were appointed by the crown. It also contained a lower house of clergy, about forty of whom were elected by the clergy. They were provincial synods. The Convocation of York was independent of the Convocation of Canterbury. At a new Parliament the Canterbury Convocation met for a service and Latin sermon in St Paul's cathedral; was prorogued for a few days till a meeting at Westminster, where the upper house of bishops drafted an address to the crown and the lower house of clergy amended a word or two to prove their independence. Between general elections there was only a formal proroguing from time to time by the archbishop's representative. To a few parochial clergy the revival of Convocation seemed the natural way to secure their proper and neglected status in the government of the church. When they presented the address to Queen Victoria on her accession, they added new solemnity to show the dignity and historic right of their assembly.

The ignorance of the clergy was slowly diminished. In the *British Magazine* Newman wrote a series of coherent articles upon the history of the assembly. In 1842 a strenuous advocate for the cause, Thomas Lathbury, published a *History of Convocation* which became a textbook for the reformers. In November 1847 the nomination of Hampden to the see of Hereford coincided with a new-elected Parliament and therefore the meeting of Convocation. The coincidence, at a time when the fury of the clergy was going about like a roaring lion, began the effective campaign to restore Convocation, to allow it to debate and legislate for the Church of England. On 24 November 1847 ten bishops and more than 100 clergy attended Archbishop Howley. They debated the address for the whole day, which was the sole time permitted, and a bold spirit carried an amendment praying the crown to revive the active powers of Convocation. The foolhardy proposed a petition to the queen to delay the *congé d'élire* of Hampden, but the majority doubted whether this came within the sphere of Convocation. That autumn there were at least two contested elections of proctors to sit in Convocation and at St. Sepulchre's, Snow Hill, the sitting proctors were ejected because they never went to a meeting. Neither an attendance of these numbers nor rival candidates had been known for more than a century. Since the duties were meaningless, no one wanted to be a proctor. Few knew how to elect a proctor or whether they could vote. Shortly before his death Archbishop Howley told Blomfield that sooner or later the time must come; but (he would not have been Howley if he had not added) the time should come slowly and they must act moderately. Howley's opinion was important. He had ruled so long, so imperturbably, so consistently, so courageously in substance while timidly in manner, that when he died his words were hallowed. The many who distrusted his successor were disposed to appeal from Sumner living to Howley dead.

For Archbishop Sumner and his colleague Archbishop Musgrave of York had no desire to revive Convocation. Nearly all the laity and half the clergy agreed with them. The *Times* pictured a flood of denunciation, and recommended cynically that to avoid theological rhetoric or wrath all speakers should be compelled to talk Latin.[1] Sumner looked back upon the disruption of the Church of Scotland and saw the General Assembly as a forum of schism and bitterness. He thought that the revival of Convocation would establish an assembly rent asunder by the cries of partisans. Evangelicals and liberals feared that a new authority would narrow liberty of opinion. The opponents of Convocation noticed how some advocates of Convocation hoped to exclude Gorham and his opinions. When the advocates of Convocation proclaimed that the church must speak with the voice of authority they seemed to proclaim that they would excommunicate evangelicals by the doctrinal decrees of a new synod. The laity were afraid of heresy-hunts and saw Parliament as the pledge of liberty.

It was a paradox which first appeared in 1849-51, but which plagued the Church of England for another fifty years and more, that the laity clamoured simultaneously for discipline in ritual and liberty in dogma. These contradictory aims destroyed the chance of effective discipline. In the long run freedom triumphed because no one would tolerate restriction in thought; and freedom in thought carried freedom of ritual, for in the English constitution the same organs of discipline regulated both.

The Tractarians talked about the independence of the church and inalienable rights which the state could not touch, and so instilled

[1] T, 25 April 1844.

more fear of Convocation into the breasts of the laity. Archbishop Sumner could not imagine what this proposed assembly would do. If it did much—if it altered the prayer book, defined doctrine, redrafted the articles, reconstituted the organs of discipline—it would be an axe to split the church down the middle. If it did little—altered a few rubrics, made a new table of lessons, removed a few obsolete words in the prayer book—is this little worth so drastic a constitutional innovation? If it did much, it would breed dissension; if little, frustration.

An assembly of the Church of England, it was argued, ought not to be revived. But granted that an assembly was needed, Convocation was the wrong assembly. It was not representative because only about forty clergy in the lower house were elected and the remainder sat by virtue of their office. The majority of the lower house consisted of deans, archdeacons, proctors from cathedral chapters; and deans were nominated by the crown, while the others were nominated by bishops who were nominated by the crown. It was not representative because the laity were not allowed to sit. It was divided into a Convocation of York and a Convocation of Canterbury, a partition justifiable when men rode horses, but absurd when a railway whisked them from York to London in five hours. Its past was a history of taxing the clergy and not of giving laws to the church. If an assembly were unfortunately necessary, it should be a national synod, an assembly new-constructed by act of Parliament.

So argued the opponents of Convocation like Archbishop Sumner of Canterbury, his still more hostile brother of Winchester, or Hampden of Hereford.

The defenders of Convocation cheerfully confessed its imperfections. They did not deny that the ingenuity of man could devise a paper constitution more adapted to the present needs of England. But like most Englishmen they preferred history to logic. This assembly was rooted deep in the history and constitution of Britain. Convocation was the only synod with a right to exist. Its friends distrusted new and paper constitutions. They disliked the unlikely prospect of machinery fabricated for the church by the act of a non-Anglican Parliament. They wanted Convocation to be allowed to meet and then to reform its constitution.

In the House of Commons Gladstone led the movement. Outside Parliament the banker Henry Hoare raised funds and chaired meetings and organised opinion.[1] But the leaders were not all Tractarians. In the House of Lords Bishop Wilberforce of Oxford and Lord Redesdale were their trumpets. Wilberforce slowly became an indispensable captain. By his energy and force and mastery of the subject he raised himself in the favour of high churchmen until at last they owned him as their spokesman.

The friends of Convocation quickly found that they were divided, not on the need for Convocation, but on the kind of Convocation. Politicians like Gladstone saw that the laity feared a narrow and exclusive clerisy. They believed that the revival would meet less resistance if Convocation included lay members. Their schemes to this end collided with Pusey and Keble. In Pusey's eyes Convocation was the living authority of the Church of England, the judge of orthodoxy and heresy. Pusey yielded buildings and money to the laity. In doctrine it was impossible, unscriptural, to allow them a voice. The bishops taught the faith, the presbyters by delegation from the bishops. The laity had no vocation to teach, only to receive. Pusey believed that if laymen were admitted to Convocation the Church of England would be finished. Bishop Phillpotts of Exeter agreed with him that very few of the laity could be deemed orthodox.[2] Archdeacon Robert Wilberforce said that the church would cease to be Catholic if it accepted lay votes. On this question the London church union came near splitting into two.

Thus the notion of securing leave to meet by inviting laymen to join the meeting was perforce abandoned. If Convocation met, it must be an old unreformed Convocation.

No one doubted that on the first day of a new Parliament Convocation could meet to discuss an address. If Parliament lasted six years, one day in six years was not sufficient to display the powers or responsibility of the assembly before the British public. The meetings of 1837, 1841 and 1847 saw nothing but hurried hugger-mugger speeches in expectation of the message which prorogued the assembly. But by custom the assembly was prorogued for a few months, to a date when the sole business was further proroguing for a few more months. At these purely formal meetings no business had been done since 1717. In 1850 it suddenly became a question whether these mournful ceremonies could be turned into real meetings. In February 1850 a

[1] J. B. Sweet, *Memoir of Henry Hoare*, 1869. Archdeacon Julius Hare of Lewes and Bishop Monk of Gloucester were leaders among the anti-Tractarians who supported the revival of Convocation.

[2] Liddon, iii, 343–52.

proctor tried to attend the session. But all the session which he could find consisted in Archbishop Sumner walking through the rain beneath a cotton umbrella.[1]

The mountain of papal aggression piled upon the mountain of Gorham incited everyone to action. They were further incited by seeing a 'synod' of Anglican bishops meet freely at Sydney in Australia, and a 'synod' of Catholic bishops meet freely at Thurles in Ireland. On 14 January 1851 Henry Hoare held at the Freemasons tavern a meeting imposing enough to elicit two hostile leaders from the *Times*. It sent a petition not to Parliament but to Convocation. The Convocation of February 1851 received this petition and by that tiny act made the first independent motion outside the established ritual. In June 1851 Bishop Phillpotts held a diocesan synod at Exeter, despite hostile placards and a bedraggled riot in the cathedral close and a protest from eighty clergymen headed by Gorham. Lord John Russell asked the law officers of the crown whether it was legal to hold a synod without leave from the crown. The law officers replied that the act of Henry VIII applied only to provincial synods, and did not think a diocesan synod to be unlawful.[2] On 11 July 1851 Lord Redesdale introduced into the House of Lords the first formal debate of Convocation by Parliament. He made an unusual and barbed speech. To the plea that Convocation would increase discord between church and dissent he replied that the discord was such that to increase it was impossible. To the plea that the movement was started by high churchmen to befriend the movement towards Rome, he replied that the surest way of repressing that movement was by giving freedom.

The Convocation of 4 February 1852 took another step forward, almost imperceptible. The 1851 session proved that they could receive a petition. The 1852 session received twenty-four petitions in the upper house, twenty-seven in the lower. In the upper house Samuel Wilberforce asked for an address to the queen praying for the revival of synodical powers. Archbishop Sumner tried to stop him, and appealed to the queen's advocate, Sir John Dodson, whether it was illegal. Dodson said that there was no precedent for 135 years and that the act of Henry VIII prohibited Convocation from doing business without the express sanction of the crown. Phillpotts of Exeter said that *business* meant making canons, not petitioning the crown.[3]

---

[1] G, 51, 68. [2] G, 51, 395, 400.
[3] Ashwell-Wilberforce, *Life of Wilberforce*, ii, 138; G, 52, 96.

At York, Archbishop Musgrave locked the door of the meeting-place and by this simple device prevented anyone from doing anything. Russell's government fell at last and Lord Derby came to power at the head of a weak Tory cabinet. In the late summer of 1852, to strengthen his government, Lord Derby attempted a general election. New elections of proctors were needed for the new session, and this election, for the first time, approached a real instead of a nominal election—though still to an assembly which might have no functions except to receive petitions. There were contested elections in several ecclesiastical constituencies, but the voters were not numerous. No one knew whether curates were allowed to vote; and the boundaries of dioceses changed by the Ecclesiastical Commission, or dioceses amalgamated and new dioceses created, caused confusion to the organisers and their lawyers. But they were not handfuls of clergy. In the archdeaconry of Lewes 81 out of a possible 160 clergy turned up to vote at St. Michael's church. In most areas the number who bothered to come was more like 40. 112 clergy out of 800 voted in the diocese of Lincoln, 56 out of 330 in the diocese of Hereford, 54 out of 500 in the diocese of Ely.[1] It was natural that those who attended should be those who wanted Convocation, and natural that they should elect proctors who wanted Convocation. The voting numbers suggest that about a fifth of the clergy of the Church of England felt strongly enough to travel, sometimes long distances, to record their votes.

In the diocese of Winchester, Bishop C. R. Sumner strenuously discouraged these proceedings. Evangelicals were much opposed to the revival. Clergy in London and the north signed petitions against it. Meanwhile Samuel Wilberforce took legal opinion whether Convocation could legally debate so long as it did not prepare canons. The attorney-general (Sir F. Thesiger) and Dr. Phillimore and Sir William Page Wood were sure that these debates were legal. When Bishop Phillpotts was sitting in his place in the House of Lords an eminent lawyer[2] said to him: 'So long as you keep from either framing canons, or consulting to frame canons, there is nothing which can restrain you from debating in law; it was mere folly to think differently; no lawyer would dare to give you such an opinion.'

But if they could debate legally, they could only debate while they

---

[1] *Times*, 25 October 1852.
[2] ? the lord chancellor; Phillpotts did not say, G, 52, 759.

were meeting, and at any moment they might be prorogued. The
crown could prorogue by direct intervention; but for nearly a century
and a half it had left this duty to the archbishop, and it was not easy to
imagine an easier way to precipitate ecclesiastical fury and disruption
than by proroguing Convocation through an act of the prime minister.
Already it was evident that if an archbishop were friendly enough to
refuse to prorogue, Convocation could not be stopped from debating,
or could only be stopped by crisis in church and state.

Archbishop Sumner was not friendly to Convocation. His brother
the Bishop of Winchester was its most determined opponent upon the
bench. But the archbishop was wiser or weaker than his brother—
Wilberforce thought him weaker. Archbishop Musgrave might for
years lock out the Convocation of York with impunity. But the
Convocation of York was smaller and more lockable. Sumner of
Canterbury was confessed by everyone to be an amiable mild man,
not a man to lock the clergy out of their rights if they were rights. He
possessed nothing like the force of personality, the argumentative
power and the theological coherence of his suffragans like Phillpotts of
Exeter and Wilberforce of Oxford. Modest, and unconvinced of his
infallibility, he found himself in a situation which would have tested
an entrenched Napoleon. He must prorogue Convocation on the day
of its meeting, by an exercise of his single authority, and encounter
obloquy from a high-minded section of his clergy and two or three
giants among his suffragans. In this predicament no man of Sumner's
temperament and character could have persisted unless the friends of
Convocation were shown to be a contemptible minority. By 1852
they were far from contemptible. Therefore he slowly reached an
important resolution. He would prorogue Convocation. But he would
perform this controversial act only in a ministerial capacity. He would
prorogue the assembly because otherwise the crown would intervene
to prorogue and thereby provoke acts against an erastian state.

During the summer of 1852 Samuel Wilberforce took the advice of
the lawyers to determine whether the archbishop could only prorogue
Convocation *cum consensu fratrum*, with the assent of a majority of the
bishops present in the upper house. To nearly everyone's astonish-
ment, the attorney-general gave an opinion that the archbishop could
only prorogue with the consent of his suffragan bishops. If it were
established, remarked the *Times*,[1] that Convocation might legally

[1] 15 November 1852.

hold debates, and that a majority of the bishops could prevent it from being prorogued, the powers of the assembly would suddenly become important. Nearly all the lawyers seemed to be agreed upon the first; and one eminent lawyer had produced an opinion for the second.

Towards the end of October 1852, with Convocation due to meet in early November, it was rumoured that Lord Derby had given the long-sought leave to transact business. Newspapers were filled with articles of alarm and anger because it might be the prelude to expelling the evangelicals, defining new dogmas, or seceding to form a Free Church. The *Times* could hardly conceive an act of the state 'more perilous to the Church of England or more inimical to the order and tranquillity of society'.[1] Derby was indifferent or unsympathetic to Convocation. But he could only preserve his government if he tried to unite conservative voters and could therefore afford to alienate no voters among the clergy who helped him at elections and who lately helped to elect him chancellor of Oxford University in succession to the Duke of Wellington. Whether he sanctioned or repressed Convocation he would alienate powerful churchmen. In this predicament he adopted the classical policy of doing nothing.

The rumours multiplied and for some time were not contradicted. Even Archbishop Sumner believed that the crown might shortly sanction the business of Convocation. At last a letter from Derby's secretary to some clergymen at Bath denied that he had any intention of the kind. Convocation held its opening service in a St. Paul's cathedral being prepared by workmen for the funeral of the Duke of Wellington, and nearly a hundred clergy clambered in procession over scaffolding and watched but failed to hear a sermon by Professor Jeremie of Cambridge. At Westminster on 12 November the lower house retired to the Jerusalem Chamber while the bishops met in the dean's library. The lower house crammed as much as possible into its hurried speeches until the usual messenger should arrive to prorogue them; but after six hours of unaccustomed debate, they were astounded to find themselves allowed to meet again on 16 November. Sumner showed signs of wanting to prorogue the house. But he was overborne by a threat from Wilberforce that if he insisted on proroguing without the consent of his suffragans, it would be their painful duty to sit in his absence. On the second day of debate both houses broke new ground by appointing committees, the upper a

[1] T, 18 October 1852.

committee on clerical discipline, the lower a committee on grievances
to consider all manner of questions; and then they adjourned to a
third day.

It was not without protest.

On 10 November 1852 Lord Shaftesbury presided over a meeting
at Freemasons hall on Confession and Convocation; two things said
Shaftesbury, 'so much akin, and so necessarily inseparable, that I
should just as soon think of separating in Guildhall Gog and Magog'.[1]
On 19 November the home secretary (Walpole) was asked about the
debate of three days and the committees. He said that he had no
power to interfere, but nothing would induce him to advise the crown
to grant a licence to make canons. Three days later Lord Derby
repeated the assurance in the House of Lords. He said that he was not
prepared to sanction an active Convocation and thought the powers of
the appointed committees to be null and void.[2]

A month later Lord Derby resigned and nearly as weak a government, the Peelite-Whig coalition under Lord Aberdeen, took office.
From the point of view of the church this uncomfortable cabinet contained the ecclesiastical opposites Lord John Russell and Gladstone.
But Aberdeen was fair-minded. High churchmen later looked back
upon his ministry as the first time since the reform act that they were
treated with understanding. And for handling the battle over Convocation, Aberdeen had the rare qualification that earlier he had engaged
in a similar dispute. In the strife between government and the Church
of Scotland during 1838-43, Aberdeen had struggled to avert the
disruption and to minimise its ill consequences. As a good Scot he
never saw the church as a mere department of state. Therefore in
theory he recognized that even an established church should possess its
independent organs of government.

Lord Aberdeen once professed a sympathy for the movement to
revive Convocation.[3] But he remembered with distress the disruption
of the Church of Scotland and in the back of his mind feared a
Convocation which might turn into a Scottish General Assembly.
The public quarrel of last November confirmed his fear and distrust.
Sitting with Russell on his left and Gladstone on his right, he preferred

---

[1] T, 11 November 1852.

[2] H, cxxiii, 1852-3, 247-9, 277-9; cf. J. A. Smith's question to Walpole on 15
November.

[3] Gordon's letter, in Ashwell-Wilberforce, ii, 161.

like Lord Derby to do as little as possible. But to do nothing was beginning to be beyond the power of a prime minister.

For Convocation must have a future if permitted to meet in February 1853. The question was a test. Such a meeting would not have the excuse of a recent general election. If Convocation met it would meet no longer as a ritual act but because it had agenda to consider. And Archbishop Sumner refused to act except as instrument of the government. The *Times* thought it unreasonable to place so heavy a burden upon such drooping shoulders and called upon the government to save Archbishop Sumner by proroguing Convocation with a royal writ.[1]

Samuel Wilberforce was a friend of Aberdeen's son and secretary. Through this intermediary he tried to work upon the prime minister and found the result dispiriting. Aberdeen had no desire that Convocation should meet. 'It can't go on,' Aberdeen told his son, 'it must be stopped. . . . Do you think I am going to tolerate them by a side-wind because the archbishop is a poor, vain, weak, silly creature whom they can bully with impunity?'[2] He wanted to prevent evangelicals appealing to the crown and saw the whole country and half the clergy as dead against the restorers. His gloomy memories of the Scottish disruption returned. 'They would only hasten the inevitable smash. Your friend is right who says the Church of England is *two* churches only held together by external forces. This unnatural apparent-union cannot last long, but we may as well defer the separation as long as possible.' Yet if he prorogued by royal writ he might himself precipitate this crisis which he wished to avoid.[3]

Samuel Wilberforce went down to Windsor and tried to reconcile Prince Albert, who always disapproved assemblies of clergymen. The cabinet discussed whether they ought to appoint a commission of enquiry into the whole constitutional question. Aberdeen agreed at last that Convocation should go forward provided that its speed was imperceptible to the public. He proposed the bargain that if the crown refrained from proroguing, Convocation should confine its debates to a single day. Despite Bishop Phillpotts, who prepared for war, the bargain was struck. The Houses of Convocation met at the Bounty office on 16 February 1853; received the report of a committee on

[1] *Times*, 8 February 1853.
[2] Ashwell-Wilberforce, ii, 161.
[3] Ashwell-Wilberforce, ii, 163; cf. P. J. Welch, 'The Revival of an Active Convocation of Canterbury 1852–5', JEH, 1959, 188 ff.

clerical discipline appointed last November; argued whether colonial
bishops might sit; proceeded to Buckingham Palace to present their
address to the queen, surrounded by Prince Albert, Lord Aberdeen and
all the leading members of the cabinet except Lord John Russell;
heard the queen read a gracious reply to their address, in her clear
silvery voice pronouncing the words *my supremacy* emphatically and
incisively;[1] briefly considered the marriage law; appointed another
committee to consider the claims of curates to vote; extended the
proceedings for about six hours and were suddenly prorogued by the
archbishop until 18 August. In the upper house Wilberforce, though
consenting to the prorogation, tried to persuade Archbishop Sumner
to admit that he was proroguing with the consent of his suffragans.
When Sumner refused, four bishops—Phillpotts of Exeter, Gilbert of
Chichester, Denison of Salisbury, and Wilberforce of Oxford—
entered a formal protest that in assenting they were not assenting to
any claim by the archbishop that he could prorogue without their
agreement.

This further appointment of a committee, to act in the intervening
space, was not expected by Aberdeen and the cabinet. Again they
consulted the law officers of the crown on its legality, and again
questions were asked in the House of Commons, and again the
cabinet, this time by the mouth of Lord John Russell, was forced to
declare that no illegality had been committed.[2]

In 1851 they received a petition. In 1852 they met and debated for
three days. In February 1853 they debated for a single day without the
usual excuse for the meeting. The next rung in this constitutional
ladder was whether they could meet more than once a year. Archbishop Sumner had prorogued them until 18 August 1853, and upon
this meeting hung the aspirations of advanced advocates. But Archbishop Sumner and Bishop Wilberforce struck another bargain.
Sumner agreed to allow discussion at future meetings and Wilberforce
agreed not to press for a session on 18 August. While Convocation was
supposed to be meeting, Wilberforce cantered across the downs in the
Isle of Wight and Sumner conducted a fashionable wedding at St.
James, Piccadilly.

The inferior clergy were more resolute. Twenty-one of them met in
the Jerusalem Chamber at ten o'clock, to find no archbishop and there-

---

[1] G. W. Kitchin, *E. H. Browne*, 144–5, wrongly dated.
[2] Hansard, 3 March and 4 March 1853; cxxiv, 977–8, 1070.

fore no session. A rumour spread that he would appear at three o'clock, and there were mutters that he was treating them with great want of courtesy. At 3.15 p.m. they were arguing in groups when Sumner appeared unaccompanied. The prolocutor stiffly said that they had been waiting since ten o'clock and amid supporting cheers requested that there be no recurrence. Sumner apologised and said that he supposed the meeting to be generally known as only formal. The archbishop had been irritated for a moment into adopting the tactics of Archbishop Musgrave of York. The story of Sumner's 'discourtesy' reached distant country parishes in a corrupt form, how he kept the lower house waiting for hours in doubt while he coolly performed a fashionable wedding.[1] That autumn Archbishop Sumner issued a charge explaining his reasons against the revival. He still held[2] that the revival would rather hinder than help the progress of religion, and asked the clergy whether they ever felt hampered in their pastoral duties because Convocation did not meet.

If meeting more than once a year was impossible, even the annual meeting was not quite secure. In February 1853 they had at least the pretext of an address to the queen. In February 1854 they had no pretext. But Aberdeen was beginning to be friendly. He conceded a debate of one day or even two if the business warranted. While Wilberforce was securing this concession a note arrived from Archbishop Sumner hoping that the government would intervene— 'fishing for a government interruption', Wilberforce called it. He helped Aberdeen to draft the answer. It was now certain that Archbishop Sumner had determined to abandon the policy of Musgrave of York.[3] In spite of protests and menaces from Shaftesbury and Lord John Russell, the opponents of Convocation were now powerless. It was too late. The power of meeting regularly though briefly, debating a little, and appointing committees to report and advise, had been conceded. When Convocation met on 1 February 1854 even Thirlwall of St. David's and Sumner of Winchester, respectively the most intelligent and most intransigent opponents hitherto, seconded resolutions to appoint committees. Thirlwall had been convinced by observing the last two sessions and seeing that good was done and fears

---

[1] Ashwell-Wilberforce, ii, 196–207; *Armstrong's Norfolk Diary*, 19 August 1853.
[2] *Charge*, 1853, 11–12.
[3] The actual note which Wilberforce described as fishing is in Add. MSS. 43195/119, Sumner to Aberdeen, 3 January 1854.

absurd.[1] Bishop Wilberforce wrote in his diary: '. . . *Deo gratias* most marvellously succeeded. The bishops who heretofore had been our chief opposers moving and seconding our motions . . .' On the next day Aberdeen strongly expressed to Wilberforce his contentment at the proceedings in Convocation.[2]

Among the advocates of Convocation two parties began to appear. One, strongly represented in the lower house, still wanted a free assembly to legislate for the church and would be satisfied with nothing less. But nearly all the influential members saw that this was impossible and doubted its wisdom even if it were possible. They were attacked with the axiom that if Convocation could not legislate it could do nothing. They replied that Parliament must still legislate; that church and state had not grown so far apart in England as to make it wrong for Parliament to be the final authority. But under the new conditions of church and state, Parliament needed a consultative body, an assembly to focus the mind of the church and proffer advice upon those ecclesiastical questions which Parliament now confessed itself incompetent to determine.

On 20 July 1854, still limited by Aberdeen to a meeting of one day, Convocation received the reports of its committees, and even accepted an offer of an endowment for a bishopric of Cornwall. Lord Harrowby, once an opponent, confessed that he was now converted. The *Times* began to treat the assembly with a little more respect, Lord Shaftesbury sat silent in the House of Lords, and, as Wilberforce noted, though Archbishop Sumner was so gentle that you could not easily tell his inner feelings, his opposition appeared to be greatly modified.[3] Sumner was impressed with the utility of the report of the committee on church services. The hostile bishops steadily came round to the view that this organ was doing useful work, and that the prophesied dangers had been fanciful. Bishops and proctors who once refused to serve on committees were now willing to be nominated. In the upper house of Canterbury only Bishop Sumner of Winchester held out uncompromisingly.[4] 'Something', noted the *Spectator* with surprise, 'may yet be got out of this church Parliament, if it do not itself exhibit a spirit of reactionary usurpation.'[5]

The next rung of this weary ladder was to achieve a meeting longer than one day.

[1] *Remains*, I.198–200, 221; *Charge* of 1854.
[2] Ashwell-Wilberforce, ii, 133.   [3] Ashwell-Wilberforce, ii, 248.
[4] Ashwell-Wilberforce, ii, 248; G, 54, 586.   [5] *Spectator* 1854, 765.

On 18 January 1855 Aberdeen went to see Archbishop Sumner, not about Convocation, which he had resolved not to mention. Sumner surprised the prime minister, and astounded Bishop Wilberforce when he heard the news, by expressing the hope that Aberdeen would see no objection to a prolonged session of Convocation—'as it was very essential that business should be transacted by Convocation which could not properly be considered by any other body'.[1] Aberdeen, feeling no personal objection, but remembering his cabinet, asked whether Convocation could do anything which the bishops could not do as well. Sumner said that there were many things and instanced the division of services. The archbishop, in short, was a convert to the revival. He thought that clergy who disobeyed bishops might obey a recommendation from Convocation. Aberdeen promised nothing. But he said he 'should be very unwilling to incur the responsibility of refusing a permission which the Archbishop of Canterbury, whose moderation everyone knew, and who was not generally supposed to be overfond of Convocation, had declared to be required by the interests of the Church of England'. Aberdeen wanted the request in writing, because he knew that he would be challenged in the Commons by Lord John Russell and in the Lords by Shaftesbury. For his own sake he must be able to declare that the archbishop wished it.

Wilberforce was instantly anxious lest the archbishop change his mind. That letter must be secured, before Sumner of Winchester got at his brother. Blomfield set to work; and four days later, on 22 January 1855, the archbishop wrote to Aberdeen confirming that he considered a meeting of two or three days desirable, but 'it may be well to limit the consent to two or at the most three days'. It was only just in time. Aberdeen's government was beaten in the Commons on the sufferings of the army in the Crimea and on 1 February resigned— 'for church matters', wrote Wilberforce in his diary, 'how dark a prospect! the only government which could be or was minded to be fair to the church overthrown, because six miles of road not made from Balaclava to Sebastopol'. 'The best minister possible for the church' was Gladstone's obituary on Aberdeen as prime minister.[2]

The Earl of Derby tried to form a government and failed. Lord John Russell tried and failed ('thank God', wrote Bishop Wilberforce

---

[1] Gordon to Wilberforce, 18 January 1855, Ashwell-Wilberforce, ii, 268.

[2] Ashwell-Wilberforce, ii, 269-72. The letter secured by Blomfield from Sumner on 22 January is in Add. MSS. 43195/154.

in his diary). Shaftesbury and other opponents of Convocation argued that Convocation could not properly meet while there was no cabinet. Blomfield told Archbishop Sumner that Aberdeen was 'in' till another prime minister took office,[1] and Sumner accepted the opinion.

So Convocation sat for three days in February 1855 and even Bishop Sumner of Winchester was observed to be taking part in the business without protest. The proceedings were neither inspiring nor decisive, the debates rambled aimlessly, the body felt no corporate spirit. But it existed.[2]

Thus the clergy of the Church of England gained the right to utter a voice; through an instrument clumsy, unreformed, inexperienced, unpopular, but at least independent. Its debates were wearisome, trivial, verbose, but not more wearisome than those of a more powerful assembly, and it was a relief to consciences and a safety valve to discontent. A writer remarked in 1869[3] that the clergy of the Church of England no longer suffered from that morbid sensitiveness and burning sense of injustice which marked so many of them during the Hampden and Gorham cases. If not the constitutional revolution which its extreme advocates wanted, it was nevertheless observed to be neither useless nor likely to split the Church of England. It was the most important change in the relation of established church and state since the passing of the reform bill.

The editor of the *Times* believed that none of it would have come about if Lord John Russell had not mismanaged the patronage of the crown.

[1] Ashwell-Wilberforce, ii, 276.

[2] For the first time in 1855 Convocation asked the crown for leave to make a canon; namely to reform its own constitution. In August 1855 the crown refused to sanction any canon to reform Convocation. Petition in PP, 1854–5, xii, 79. But as prejudice declined unpopularity was diminished and Palmerston became less unfriendly. The government first sanctioned new canons when four canons were revised after the new statute on clerical subscription in 1865. Hansard, clviii, 1860, 1714; clxii, 1861, 1374: clxiv, 1861, 1865. Cf. PP, 1865, xli, 519, 643; 1872, xlvi, 39.

In 1860 died Archbishop Musgrave of York, impenitent despite more than one attack upon him from high churchmen in Parliament. In 1858 they even tried to force him by threatening a mandamus from the court of queen's bench. Musgrave was a match for them all, refusing even to attend the most menacing assault in the House of Lords on a plea of important business in the diocese. He continued to the end consistent in proclaiming that the Convocation of York would serve no useful purpose and that most of the working clergy had no confidence in it. The utmost point which he reached was to confess that he watched with interest the proceedings of the Convocation of Canterbury.

His death ended the ban. His successor Longley instantly allowed the Convocation of York to behave like that of Canterbury. From 1861 it met regularly.

[3] J. B. Sweet, *Memoir of Henry Hoare*, 408.

CHAPTER V

RELIGION AND THE LABOURER

I. RELIGION IN THE SLUM

THE middle classes of early Victorian England went to church or chapel. An older generation of Hanoverian aristocrats, a Melbourne, a Waterford, a Hertford, a Sussex, continued to absent themselves. But by the end of the thirties Melbourne remarked how religious everyone was becoming.

Everyone did not include most of the city labourers.

Between 1780 and 1860 a large number of Englishmen, whose families worked upon the land since families existed, moved into towns and cities. Whether or not the father attended the country church, the son was not likely to attend the city church. So far as the churches or chapels possessed the allegiance of the working class of England and Wales, they lost that allegiance when the country labourer became a town labourer.

In the countryside the tradition of the community, and the social might of squire or parson, usually held the parishioners to a minimum of religious duty. The first obvious breaches in the social-religious unities of the countryside did not appear till the third quarter of the nineteenth century. In the industrial city was no squire, no parson, no tradition, no community. Instead there was a proletariat. Ten millions were added to the population between 1801 and 1851. Most of the increase lived in large cities. In 1851 more than half the population of London aged 20 and over had not been born in London.[1]

The parish churches, the dissenting chapels, the Roman Catholic chapels, were not equipped to cope with this tide of immigrants. The churches and chapels were not unique. Nothing in the cities was equipped to cope. Municipal government, building, sanitation, health, cemeteries, hospitals, roads, paving, lighting, police, dentists, schools—all the organs of city life were strained till they were bursting.

[1] PP, 1852–3, lxxxviii, pt. 1, cvi.

So came the slums of east London, of Manchester, Liverpool and Leeds. Habits natural in the open air of the country bred filth and disease in the gutters and alleys of Whitechapel and Stepney. In 1840 more than 39,000 people lived in cellars at Liverpool, nearly 15,000 lived in cellars at Manchester.[1] In districts of east London they lived, family to a room, in wooden sheds or closed courts or tenements, without privies and sometimes with an open sewer running down the centre of the street and likely to overflow in wet weather; the houses dirty beyond description, potato peel or gristle or bones thrown into corners. At Bethnal Green a row of pigsties emptied their refuse into a neighbouring pool of stagnant water, and in some streets lay pools polluted with dead cats and dogs and rubbish. These barbarised areas were the worst symptom of the entire English predicament: to make the new cities habitable and their citizens civilised. To maintain the traditional pattern of English life they must have drains, lavatories, paved roads, houses, policemen, nurses, schools, parks, cemeteries and churches.

The cemetery illustrates how the life of the country needed converting into the life of the city. As pig-keepers of the country must be prevented from keeping pigs among the tenements of Bethnal Green, the sentiments about interment needed adapting. The church was the home of the dead as well as the living. The countryman passed the graves of his father and grandfather on his way to worship God, his churchyard was the resting-place of his rude ancestors. Round the London churches lay the churchyards, some small some big, suitable to old London, not well equipped to be the home of more and more of the dead. But the dead poured in. A few prudent parishes, like St. Pancras, bought extra land. A few far-sighted speculators observed the coming need and opened private cemeteries. In 1838 the Kensal Green cemetery opened and relieved the pressure. And still the old churchyards continued in use. Hideous stories were told: how the floor of the Enon Street Baptist chapel off the Strand was bare planks dividing the congregation from mounds of skeletons beneath and how the Baptist verger found hundreds of winged bugs in the chapel and took them home in his hat;[2] how some of the bones from Enon Street helped to make the streets by Waterloo Bridge; how gravediggers were suspected of loathsome methods of clearing space within the crammed graveyards, especially by digging up coffins and selling their

[1] PP, 1840, xi, 284.   [2] PP, 1842, x, 368, 373.

lead and wood; how a gravedigger of St. Anne's, Soho, gave evidence that they used to play skittles with the skulls. During epidemics of cholera or influenza there were indescribable scenes at the churchyards, with the ground looking like a ploughed field, queues of mourners miserably waiting their turn, and navvies hired as extra gravediggers cursing or jumping on the coffins. A commission was appointed in 1842 to survey the need, and assembled a mass of macabre and erroneous evidence.[1] The commission recommended that within towns of over 50,000 people at the last census all interments should cease, except in family vaults already existing, or in cemeteries recently constructed, or in Westminster abbey and St. Paul's cathedral, and that the rates should provide new cemeteries outside the boundaries of the city. For ten years the churchyards continued to deteriorate. In September 1847 part of the rubbish for making the road at Ampthill Square in London consisted of broken bones and coffins, and children were seen raking for teeth among the remains. At last the government by the public health act of 1848 and cemetery acts of 1852 and 1853 carried out the main recommendations of the commission, empowering the closure of cemeteries by order. Bishop Blomfield predicted that the public would have a strong feeling against sending funerals by train.[2] He was wrong. The public was found to have no such feeling.

The closing of London churchyards touched the pockets and affected the labours of the clergy. They were earning substantial incomes in fees. During the year 1838 the vicar of St. Giles-in-the-Fields earned £764 16s. 6d. in funeral fees, the rector of St. George's, Hanover Square, £597 17s.,[3] and in addition was presented with numerous black hatbands and scarves. The opening of the Kensal Green cemetery cost the vicar of Paddington £200 a year. The act of 1852 cost Bishop Blomfield about £300 a year which he had paid into a fund to repair the new churches built in Bethnal Green[4] and forced him to raise subscriptions for the purpose. The act contained a vague clause about compensation, but compensation was never obtainable. Several other London clergymen lost £200 a year or more in burial fees. Not only Anglican clergymen suffered. The opening of public cemeteries hit private speculator and dissenting chapel. An undertaker remarked casually of a Wesleyan Methodist chapel in the New Kent Road that 'they gain more money by the dead than the living'.[5]

[1] PP, 1842, x, 349. It included Lord Ashley and Sir Robert Inglis.
[2] PP, 1842, x, 549.   [3] ibid., 546.   [4] PP, 1857–8, ix, 48.   [5] PP, 1842, x, 381.

The cemeteries illustrate the universal predicament of churches and chapels in a city. No item of the city's old equipment could manage the new numbers efficiently. New equipment was necessary. This new equipment, from hospitals to schools, must be on a scale to be provided only by the money of the state. In supplying the need the state diminished the direct influence of the churches. Some curates regretted the end of the religious association between church and graveyard, the distance of several miles between a field where the dead lay and a church where the living worshipped. They mourned the breaking of a hallowed nexus.[1] But no sensible curate wished to retain the nexus when it meant irreverent and insanitary graveyards.

So it was in every organ of community life. The churches struggled heroically to educate—and at last the state must step into the yawning breach, educate the people and unwittingly diminish the direct influence of Christianity in education.

If there was not room for the dead in cemeteries, there was not room for the living in churches. In Shoreditch or Stepney or Whitechapel or Newington most of the population could not have got into the churches (of all denominations added together) even if by some miracle they decided to go. The churches and chapels were respectably filled with people. But this was more due to the packed numbers of the surrounding inhabitants than to any steady habit of churchgoing. The parish of Shoreditch was one of the worst shepherded in England. But in its nine Anglican churches there was an average morning congregation of more than 400 persons. Whitechapel under its great evangelical vicar Champneys was one of the best shepherded among slum parishes. In its eleven churches there was an average morning congregation of more than 500 persons. The churches were far from empty. But if every seat in all churches and chapels in Shoreditch had been occupied on a Sunday, more than eighty in every hundred inhabitants would have absented themselves from worship.[2] And the seats in the chapels and churches of Shoreditch were not all occupied at the same moment.

Everyone agreed that more churches and chapels were needed. Everyone knew that for fifty years before 1840 the parish churches were not sufficient for the growing population. In respectable suburbs and artisan cities the dissenters built chapels and flourished upon the voluntary contributions which they collected. They were rarely chapels

---

[1] Cf. PP, 1842, x, 427.   [2] PP, 1852–3, lxxxix, cclxxviii.

for the slums. Few dissenting congregations could survive as independent communities in a slum, for the money of the working poor could pay neither the rent of the chapel nor the stipend of the minister. Sometimes, as in Poplar, a wealthy dissenter devoted his personal resources to maintaining a chapel or a school or a minister. English Roman Catholics were munificent and self-sacrificing in building temporary chapels and in finding priests for the Irish, who were the poorest of the poor. Ancient endowments assisted the old parish churches of the slums. Their ministers were more numerous, their alms collected with less persistence, their churches easier to repair. But these old parish churches were few. The Church of England needed new churches in the slums. As soon as they built a new church in a slum they found it as hard as the dissenters to maintain the minister or the structure—or harder, for they were accustomed to a minister of high education, a church of dignity, and parishioners not accustomed to frequent and obtrusive collections.

The financing of new churches was not easy. It was easier to build the church than to keep it going. The established church started with the long advantage of the million and a half pounds of public money from the old unreformed government, and the Church Building Commission used this money intelligently to elicit voluntary subscriptions. All churches found their parishioners readier to pay for a building than to pay the consequent minister. 'I find no difficulty', said Bishop Robert Bickersteth of Ripon, 'in getting funds to build a church. But when you remind persons that the clergyman must live, and ask for an endowment, there is the greatest possible difficulty in obtaining it.'[1] Several east London churches tried the experiment of a weekly collection or offertory, but the troubles of 1842–4 caused it to be suspect as popish. It raised little money, and was usually abandoned after a short trial.

The familiar arrangements of old parish churches were not well suited to the new slums. In country churches the gentry possessed private pews and the poor sat on benches at the side or back of the church. In many of the new town churches there were few or no gentry in the parish. But where poor and rich were mixed it was difficult to arrange the seating.

An illuminating example is the Roman Catholic Oratory in London, which was at first founded in King William Street and moved to

[1] PP, 1857-8, ix, 57.

Brompton in 1854. The Roman Catholics were proud that the seats of their chapels were free, and were in the habit of contrasting their excellence with the ill arrangements of the Church of England. A visitor to the Oratory chapel wrote to the press a glowing account of this Christian freedom, declaring that the spirit of pews and reserved seats lived not there.[1] But behind the scenes the superiors of the Oratory corresponded anxiously about their predicament. Father Faber wrote to Father Newman[2] that the upper classes of Catholics, and the merchants and even the tradespeople, were leaving the Oratory chapel, driven out by stink and dirt; Father Dalgairns wrote to Newman[3] that the dirt and stink of the Irish were intolerable and that the English were swamped. 'Is the Oratory sent exclusively to the Irish?' Apart from higher considerations, like the loss of their religious influence with the educated classes, they were in the predicament of any dissenting chapel, that if the poor drove away the rich the chapel would not continue. Newman advised that the poor might be guided by tickets to a separate mass in the lower chapel. Other educated Catholics resented the constant rattle of collecting boxes in churches and preferred to pay a fixed contribution as a rent for their seat.[4]

Roman Catholics were committed by sentiment to free seats and by the Irish labourer to ministry to the very poor. If they found themselves in such a plight, others were likely to find the same trouble. Many Methodist chapels adopted pew rents; and even where seats were not formally allotted various devices (like Newman's tickets) ensured the same result. A chapel in Leeds carried a notice that the trustees, 'wishing to accommodate the respectable friends who may attend on this occasion', would reserve the gallery for their use and take a silver collection at the foot of the stairs.[5]

When many of the new parish churches were built it was made a condition that all the seats be free.[6] But the older parish churches inherited pews from the seventeenth century or before. The law about pews was as complex as all ancient ecclesiastical law. Even where the seats were all free, parishioners liked to occupy the same seat by

[1] *Cath. Mag. and Register*, xi, 48.

[2] Faber to Newman, 9 July 1849; Newman to Faber, 10 July 1849; Dessain, xiii, 211.

[3] Dalgairns to Newman, 14 August 1849, Dessain, xiii, 253.

[4] *Weekly Register*, 11 August 1849, 30.

[5] Hammond, 244.

[6] In churches built from the million grant of 1818 20% of seats must be, and 60% were, free. But the free sittings were made 2 ft. 4 in. from back to back and were uncomfortable, whereas pew sittings were 3 ft. from back to back. PP, 1857–8, ix, 51.

custom, and enlightened incumbents encouraged their sense of property in their church and a pride in their cushion or hassock.[1]

It was an axiom that the building of new churches brought light and civilisation to the slum. In 1858 people contrasted the present condition of Bethnal Green or Stepney with their condition twenty years before, and attributed the favourable change to new churches. This comparison was inclined to overlook other changes which happened to the slums during those years: better lighting, paving of roads, better drainage. But there was truth in the doctrine that more churches meant a more civilised people. The churches brought into the district educated men and women, leadership, relief, social amenities and schools. Not all the slum pastors were of high excellence. When Bishop Blomfield built ten churches in Bethnal Green he had an arduous task in finding men to staff them and some of the selected men proved a grave disappointment.[2] It took time to persuade the clergy of the Church of England, or of other churches, that this was a heroic challenge. By the eighteen-fifties the devotional appeal of the east end of London and of the less salubrious areas of Nottingham or Manchester or Leeds was recognised. In 1858 the rector of Bethnal Green resided in Cheshire, where he had another living. The vicar of Shoreditch was incompetent or idle or both. The rector of St. Dunstan's, Stepney, was not resident, and the parish was sequestrated. Even the vicar of St. Matthias's, Bethnal Green, Mr. Colbourne, who had a name as an effective and zealous pastor, refused to accept the living if he were required by the bishop to reside in the parish, because there was not a house to be had, and the parish was unhealthy for a clergyman to reside in.[3] He refused to subject his children to the trial of growing up in a sewerless, fever-ridden alley among a gin-drinking, fornicating rabble. But the ideals of clerical life were rising. There was no doubt about the zeal and devotion of the younger priests and pastors attracted during the fifties into the east end of London.

The people exchanged hostility for friendliness. When, in 1839, the first of Blomfield's churches was built in Bethnal Green a canvasser for sixpences was told that they would give him a shilling to hang the bishop but not a sixpence to build a church. They said that they wanted food, not churches. And when the lord mayor came to lay the foundation-stone in the bishop's presence an infuriated cow was

[1] Cf. PP, 1857–8, ix, 62, 74.
[2] So William Cotton said, PP, 1857–8, ix, 41–42.   [3] PP, 1857–8, ix, 71–75.

driven among several hundred children assembled to sing a hymn. Eleven years later the foundation-stone of the tenth church was laid. Strong bodies of police were present to keep order, but were not needed. The Eastern Counties railway company lent a building for a mammoth tea. A procession which included 7,000 children and pupil-teachers walked across the parish and was received with the utmost friendliness. It was quoted with satisfaction that a rough-looking man was heard to say with an oath, 'I will not believe anything they say against bishops again. Look at those children.' The wives and mothers of the clergy could not at first pass through the streets without meeting insults, but after ten years were greeted with kindness. A police inspector told the incumbent of St. Luke's, Berwick Street, that before the church was built no single policeman would dare to arrest a man in the wretched streets behind the church; and by 1858 ladies visited the street habitually.[1] Champneys in Whitechapel saw a great change for the better over twenty-one years, despite more inhabitants in the same number of acres; in a lower rate of drunkenness, and in education.

The new churches were often nearly empty, or at least empty by the standards of that day. But something like one in ten people of the great slum parishes attended a church or chapel. And good curates were astonished at the quality of life which under adverse conditions the east Londoner could display. The curate of St. Dunstan's, Stepney, said in 1858 that the 'steady poor' (that is the permanent residents, not part of the shifting population) who occupied the free seats in his church practised the highest standard of Christianity that he had ever known.[2] The perpetual curate of St. Peter's, Stepney, T. J. Rowsell, had 112 confirmation candidates in the year 1858, and every Sunday night 600–700 parents or friends remained behind after service to hear the children's instruction. His population was 13,000 and his normal attendance at service 1,400 persons. The evening congregation in the old parish church of Whitechapel under Champneys was 1,500, in a church which could hold 1,700. These big figures were rare. A number of new east London churches have never in their history been more than half full.[3]

[1] PP, 1857–8, ix, 42–7, 132.

[2] PP, 1857–8, ix, 97.

[3] The smallest congregations were in the city churches. Among the smallest of all in 1858 was St. Mary's, Somerset Street, which had thirty-five persons at the morning service, PP, 1857–8, ix, 108, 117, 169, 179.

Pastors and politicians were grieved at the failure of the people to attend church or chapel. We should be wrong to receive their grief sceptically. Dr. Ryder, the evangelical Bishop of Lichfield and Coventry, issued a charge of 1832 lamenting that the churches of the diocese had seating capacity for less than a third of the population, that less than a quarter of these seats were free, that only a quarter of those who attended church were communicants. Analysing the figures, we find that about $2\frac{1}{2}$ per cent of the population of that diocese were communicants.[1] Fifty years later Easter communicants in England and Wales numbered about eight per cent of the population aged more than 15 years.[2] In 1840 Tom Mozley calculated[3] that three-quarters or nine-tenths of the poorer classes practised no religion, and never or rarely saw in church a working man with wife and children. If the calculation is applied to the poorest in slums, it was wildly optimistic. Henry Mayhew met a costermonger and asked him what was St. Paul's. 'A church, sir, so I've heard. I never was in a church.'[4]

Why did they not come to church? Clothes were much discussed. It was said that they could not come because they had nothing to wear. The women came covering their shabbiness with shawls,[5] the men could not wear shawls. Some Anglicans, especially in the north, talked about the iniquity of private pews. No one thought to examine the effect of large movements of population upon a society. By the forties there began to be questions about *infidelity*.

Most slum pastors agreed that they were free or almost free of infidelity. They found apathy and indifference and hostility, not unbelief. The labourer disregarded the church not because he disbelieved beforehand the doctrine which might be taught there. The literature of the working man was violently anticlerical, antichurch, antimethodist, antichapel. It rollicked in abuse of the establishment. But it was not usually heathen. Pamphlets and newspapers used simple texts of scripture to beat church of merchant and chapel of shopkeeper. Most working men would have been horrified to be told that they were not Christians. The Chartist leader Lovett, asked for his religion when he was admitted to prison, said that he was 'of that religion which Christ taught, and which very few in authority practise', if he might judge by their conduct.[6] There were many 'infidel' publications, but one clergyman of the east end thought his people too poor to buy

[1] CO, 1832, 735–7.   [2] *Facts and Figures*, 29.   [3] BC, xxviii, 1840, 337, 346.
[4] Mayhew, i, 22.   [5] PP, 1857–8, ix, 152.   [6] Lovett, *Life and Struggles*, 229.

them. Another said that the trouble was obscene publications, not infidel. Others talked of a floating, doubtful scepticism among the poor, but nothing so definable as infidelity. Some took a gloomier view. The rector of St. Clement Dane's in the Strand, a parish containing many of the London brothels, said that there was 'a frightful amount of infidelity', a mass of people with no idea of the existence of God. Occasional meeting-houses for infidels could be found. At the Obelisk in Southwark they were in the habit of holding open-air meetings to disprove the existence of God or the immortality of the soul, in Stepney there was a kind of atheist chapel, infidelity was alleged to be rampant among the Clerkenwell watchmakers and there was a lecture-room used by a body called *The Free-thinking Christians*. But nearly all witnesses agreed that where infidelity was positive it was apathetic and mournful.[1]

It could also be curiously religious. About 1841 Goodwyn Barmby founded a communist church at Bow Lane in Bromley, with a meeting-house of whitewashed walls and white deal furniture, and a liturgy of lessons-business-epistles-discourses-conversation.[2] Thence he edited the *Communist Chronicle* and offended more stalwart rationalists by insisting that he was a prophet sent from God and even had a direct command from God to change his lodging. His communism was modelled upon the primitive church of Jerusalem. At this level there was a strong link between atheism and extreme opinions on society and the constitution. A man who thought that the clergy sometimes did good was expected to be both superstitious and reactionary. Conversely the vast majority of society believed that all atheists were immoral and disloyal.

The conduct of the Chartists illustrates the odd air of religion which accompanied so much antichurch and antichapel feeling. The Chartists were the political and intellectual heirs of Tom Paine and the English friends of the French Revolution. Satisfied for a moment by the reform act of 1832 they quickly discovered that the act did little or nothing for the labourer. Their Charter of 1838 demanded votes for every man, the ballot, annual parliaments. For a short time Chartism focused the seething discontent of labourers throughout the country. Some of their leaders were professed atheists or deists, one was an expelled Methodist minister, two were Quakers. In Scotland and the Midlands sprouted for a moment little Chartist churches. Their congregations were hostile

[1] PP, 1857-8, ix, 81, 117, 128, 151, 167, 195.   [2] *The Reasoner*, i, 13, 109.

to other churches, but professed Christian faith, attracted a few dissenters, and held their meetings in schools or halls or houses.[1] Some of them never knew whether they were attacking Christianity or were defending Christianity by attacking the churches which betrayed Christianity. Most of them thought the second.

This ambiguity was strangely displayed in the Chartist visits to churches during the late summer and early autumn of 1839. A half-ironic resolution at a monster meeting on Mousehold Heath recommended the Chartists to display their strength by appearing in church. They formed a procession somewhere in the town, marched to church before the doors were open, tried to cram every seat before the regular congregation could appear, and sent the vicar a request that he should preach on certain texts, usually 'Go to now, ye rich men, weep and howl for your miseries that are coming upon you' or 'Hear this, O ye that would swallow up the needy, and cause the poor of the land to fail', or 'If any will not work, neither shall he eat'. Thus they demonstrated their numbers at Stockport, Newcastle-upon-Tyne, Blackburn, Bolton, Manchester, Norwich, Cheltenham, Dowlais, and even St. Paul's cathedral in London. Their success varied. At Manchester a band of only 150 listened meekly to a sermon on obedience to constituted authorities. At St. Paul's cathedral a band of 500, with red ribands in their button-holes, was persuaded by a single verger to remove their hats. There was only occasional irreverence. Once they left in a body when the clergyman gave out his text as 'My house shall be called the house of prayer but ye have made it a den of thieves'. At Bolton a few of the congregation smoked pipes during the service. At St. Stephen's in Norwich, where 5,000–6,000 crowded the church and churchyard, the clergyman preached pointedly on contentment with the state of life in which we find ourselves, and evoked a menace of sticks and cries of 'You get £200 a year, come and weave bombazine', or 'Put out the gas'; and the congregation dispersed amid feminine shrieks and without injury. But most of the visits were orderly displays of good temper. At St. James, in Bradford, Parson Bull belaboured the sins of rich and poor impartially for nearly two hours, exhorting them to attend church regularly and not to take Sunday newspapers. The packed congregation was still and devotional, made their responses with fervour and sang the final hymn with delightful harmony. After attending Anglican services in Norwich on two successive Sundays

[1] Faulkner, 42–43.

and menacing Bishop Stanley, who found himself among a hostile crowd,[1] the Chartists went by invitation to the Roman Catholic chapel, where the priest was alleged to have preached an inflammatory sermon on the text, 'He that hath two coats let him impart to him that hath none', and to have told them that their sufferings were caused by the robbery of Catholic endowments at the Reformation. At Blackburn, Dr. Whittaker told them in his sermon that it was the height of injustice to apply the text 'Go to now, ye rich men' to an England of equal laws.[2]

Chartists nevertheless continued to believe that they could make their voices heard through churches. In 1842 and 1843 they took the trouble to control the election of churchwardens at Leeds parish church. Dr. Hook handled them bravely and humorously. He told the meeting of 1843 that he had never had such honourable, straightforward and gentlemanly churchwardens, and that he could not wish for better unless they were to give him members of the Church of England.[3]

2. EDUCATION

The answer to Chartism, nearly everyone agreed, lay in more churches and more schools. But nearly everyone agreed that the need far outran the resources of the religious denominations who provided churches and schools. It was therefore a question how or whether the state should provide. Most members of the Church of England believed that the state should pay money to build more churches. Sir Robert Inglis astonished himself and everyone else by coming within seventeen votes of passing a motion friendly to state aid in the House of Commons. When Peel came into power in 1841 staunch churchmen hoped that at least a Tory government would pay to extend the number of established churches. At the time the mirage looked glittering. But Peel refused all help; except that he passed his exiguous church building act to enable parishes to be created more easily.

If they hoped for the aid of the state, they meanwhile collected money and planned churches and ministers. Glasgow and Manchester

[1] A. P. Stanley, *Memoir of Edward Stanley*, 52–53.

[2] Faulkner, 35–37; CO, 1839, 574; T, 2–6 August, 13–14 August, 21–23 August, 2 and 9 September 1839; Whittaker's sermon at Blackburn and Close's sermon at Cheltenham were printed and are in the British Museum.

[3] AR, 1843, *Chron.* 53.

set the example in collecting funds to build churches. Bishop Blomfield adopted the plan in April 1836 and founded a society to build churches in the metropolis.[1]

Just as the heathen poor must be brought under religious instruction by a programme of building churches, so their children must be taught to be loyal citizens and to refrain from crime by being given the chance to go to school. The axiom *education is good for everyone* was not accepted universally. Lord Melbourne is reported to have said that he did not believe in education, 'because the Pagets got on so damned well without it'.[2] Some moralists observed that the people could only be given a little learning and knew a little learning to be notorious. Not everyone thought it a blessing for the uncritical poor to read the worst newspapers of the day. According to the Reverend Stephen Cassan, the church should educate the poor, because otherwise the dissenters would. 'The people at large', wrote this fierce clergyman, '. . . have no business with minds.'[3] Even Cobbett asked why you should teach a ploughboy to read and write when these accomplishments would be useless for mounting a cart-horse.[4]

In the thirties this old-fashioned opinion became eccentric and faded away. The axiom that education was first religious education remained. The Central Society of Education was formed (1836) upon a secular basis, to persuade the state to pay for a system of national education which excluded religion from schools. This society attracted a few able supporters, but its plans had no prospect of being adopted by any government. Educated opinion wanted voluntary schools, teaching religion as well as the three Rs, and assisted by state money but

---

[1] The head benefactor was a London banker named William Cotton. The first church to be completed was Christ Church in St. Pancras, consecrated in the summer of 1837. The appeal was disappointing. Blomfield asked for £250,000 and got scarcely more than half by 1839. Inglis in Hansard, lv, 1840, 297. The king gave £1,000, Blomfield £2,000, Howley £1,000, Pusey £1,000, Golightly £1,000, Hoares the bankers £1,000, an anonymous 'Clergyman seeking treasure in heaven' £5,000 (afterwards said to be Keble, but Liddon, i, 330, had evidence that he was Pusey). Mrs. Pusey sold her jewels and contributed the proceeds, Liddon, ii, 82. In 1839 Blomfield launched an appeal for ten new churches in Bethnal Green, which then had two churches and a chapel for 70,000 people. He got his ten churches during the next eleven years. All over the country public attention was drawn to villages and suburbs without enough churches.

[2] Sanders, 384.

[3] *Bath and Wells*, ii, 221–2.

[4] Cf. Best, 'The religious difficulties of national education in England, 1800–70', in *Cambridge Historical Journal*, xii, 155–73.

uncontrolled by the state. From 1833 the Treasury paid £20,000 a year to assist the building of schools.

The main division of opinion, therefore, was not between religious education and secular education, but between two different notions of religious education. One opinion wanted a general and simple education in religion without any instruction characteristic of a particular church. Its instrument was the society known since 1814 as the *British and Foreign Schools Society*. This society attracted nearly all the dissenters, who were afraid that any alternative meant religion under the control of the established church; but it also contained many liberal Anglicans. The other opinion held that religious instruction was useless unless it included training in membership of a church. Therefore all schools ought to be controlled by Christian denominations. The schools of the Church of England ought to be controlled by the *National Society for promoting the education of the poor in the principles of the established church* (founded 1811), and in those schools all the children should be taught the liturgy and catechism of the Church of England. The parson was expected to hold his traditional place in the education of the people. The village school was 'his' school, the schoolmistress under his direction.

The new grants of state aid raised in a new form the difficulty whether the taxpayer rightly paid money to particular churches, especially to the established church. The Treasury paid the annual grant of £20,000 to the two great societies in proportion to the amount which they raised. Since members of the Church of England were richer, the resources of the National Society outstripped those of the British and Foreign Schools Society and so qualified for a larger part of the state grant. Of £100,000 paid in five years, the National Society secured £70,000.[1] Dissenters perceived that an apparently neutral distribution of money steadily favoured the established church. During 1838 and 1839 the movement for church extension formed twenty-four diocesan or subdiocesan boards of education. In 1839 the Whig government was a little frightened at the progress of the National Society by means of its fostering grants. At the same time experts knew that the self-sacrificing efforts of voluntary education were not keeping pace with the expanding needs of the population. The state must pay more money. Who was to get it?

In 1839 Lord John Russell proposed a modest increase from £20,000

[1] PP, 1837–8, xxxviii, 325.

to £30,000 a year. This money might be paid to reputable schools even outside the two main societies—thus a dissenting or Roman Catholic school might now receive a direct grant from the state. No grant should be paid unless the right of inspection was conceded; and the inspectors should be under the control of a committee of the privy council which is the ancestor of the modern Ministry of Education. The members of this committee were not chosen on religious grounds. Not a single bishop was selected to sit upon the board. Russell also proposed to establish a 'normal' or model school to train teachers. In this normal school there would be 'general' instruction in religion to everyone; and also 'special' or denominational instruction by visiting clergymen or dissenting ministers to the members of their churches. This proposal for a normal school was the first wistful attempt at a system of education which should be religious but not denominational.[1]

Churchmen agitated against the plan. Their highest members, who for this purpose included not only a warrior like Bishop Phillpotts but a diplomat like Bishop Blomfield, believed with the old and vanished world that the government of England could not and should not pay money to the schools of any churches but those of the established church. Moderate churchmen denounced the normal school. On the 4 June 1839 Russell gave way to pressure and abandoned the normal school. But he stuck to the proposals for a committee of education, the right of inspection, and the possibility of grants to dissenting schools. Archbishop Howley deplored that so momentous a change should be made without act of Parliament and in this sense carried through the House of Lords an address to the queen.

The most important person of the new committee, the most important person in the earlier history of English education, was its secretary, Dr. Kay, who three years later changed his name to Kay-Shuttleworth.

Son of a Lancashire nonconformist, and himself once a teacher in a Congregational Sunday school, he qualified as doctor at Edinburgh university. By ministering in the slums and fever hospitals of Edinburgh and amidst the cholera of Lancashire, he acquired a social passion for the poor, their health and welfare. He interested himself in district schools, and so became known to Russell and Lansdowne. His appointment as secretary did nothing to encourage the Tories.

[1] Cf. Hansard, 12 February 1839, xlv, 274–80.

Though now a practising Anglican, he was known as a liberal and a friend of dissent, as well as a supporter of compulsory rates to provide local schools. He suggested the normal school which caused the fiercest controversy of 1839. The Whig leaders told him privately that their object was to frustrate the claim of the church to the national system of education, and to assert the claim of the civil power to control the education of the country—'to prevent the growth of inordinate ecclesiastical pretensions . . . to vindicate the rights of conscience, and to lay the foundation of a system of combined education in which the young might be brought up in charity with each other, rather than in hostile camps . . .'[1] It was Kay-Shuttleworth who advised that the constitution of the committee should be purely civil and should not contain a single clergyman.

Archbishop Howley was roused. Under his quiet and inflexible leadership the clergy refused to apply for state grants, and after a year's struggle compelled the government to compromise. A concordat of 15 July 1840 agreed that the archbishop of the province should possess a veto upon the appointment of all inspectors of schools connected with the National Society and the power of ending their appointment. The church conceded the right of inspection and preserved a control over the inspectors. Under the concordat the National Society renewed its applications for state money. Its intransigent members were not content.[2]

Chartist disturbances of 1839–40 and riots of 1842 revived the demand for church extension. It was alleged, even by the *Times*[3], that children educated in church schools refrained from participating in the disturbances. Though Peel refused money to build churches, he was prepared to pay churches money to educate the poor.

Sir James Graham's factory bill of 1843 included a plan for educating children in state schools, a plan which was the nearest Peel's cabinet ever approached to helping the established church in an old-fashioned Tory manner. Children aged between 8 and 13 and working in factories must not work more than six and a half hours and must attend school for three hours, the school to be supported from the rates and from small deductions of the children's pay. The schoolmaster must

---

[1] Smith, *Life of Kay-Shuttleworth*, 148.

[2] Joshua Watson, the layman who rendered unique service in building up the National Society, resigned from being treasurer rather than ask for government grant for a new training college of St. Mark's, Chelsea.

[3] T, 17 June 1843; Hammond, *The Age of the Chartists*, 192–3.

be a member of the Church of England and approved by the bishop of the diocese. The schoolmaster should teach from the authorised version of the Bible and from no other book of religion. But the school was to be managed by seven trustees of whom the clergyman and two churchwardens were three; and the schoolmaster might also teach the catechism and the prayer book for not more than an hour daily. From this latter instruction parents might withdraw their children on grounds of conscience. The clerical trustee could determine the syllabus and books. The child was compelled to attend church on Sunday unless his parents objected. On Sundays the child was to be instructed in the catechism and prayer book for not more than three hours. Roman Catholics were exempted from religious instruction. If parents wished, licensed ministers might attend one day a week to instruct the children of their denomination.

The extraordinary thing about this extraordinary proposal was the failure of the government to expect opposition from dissent. Even Kay-Shuttleworth supported it. Peel and Graham rather feared the antagonism of churchmen who would observe the mild aid to dissenting children and claim it contrary to the principles of the English constitution. High churchmen disliked the conscience clause. They said that the state's duty was to educate its children in the truth. But upon the other side dissenters raised a campaign of a fury which had not been seen since the war between church and dissent during 1833 and 1834. Many dissenters had wavered between fear and hope in their attitude to government money. If the state paid no money, they saw no hope of educating the people. If the state paid money, they were afraid that the Church of England would get it. Graham's factory bill convinced them that their fears were justified and that any state aid to education must end in danger to the dissenting cause. They now declared national education to be an engine of oppression and an assault upon the liberty of the individual. The most foolish clause was the provision that the schoolmaster must be an Anglican. For Lord John Russell and others could easily show the numbers of good teachers who would be excluded by the clause; and Russell claimed that by this means the Tory government was subtly going back to the test act, creating a public office, paid by public money, from which many persons were excluded on grounds of religion.

In the dissenting campaign the Puseyites were a useful weapon. The local parson was to be given great power in the schools. If the parson were a Puseyite, the state was said to be subsidising the teaching of popish doctrines. Even the Wesleyan body, which steadily refrained from joining dissenting attacks upon the established church, joined battle upon these clauses, because of the spirit hostile to the Reformation which filled so many of the clergy.[1] Bowing to the storm, Graham drastically modified the educational clauses. But the new bill was declared almost as bad as the old, and there was every prospect that dissenters would refuse to pay rates. On 15 June 1843, with the utmost pain and reluctance, the government dropped all the educational clauses of the bill.

The Tory plan for national education was thus frustrated by the religious division of the country. Peel knew that the electors of Britain would never allow him to pay money to build Anglican churches and that it was useless for churchmen to tell him the state's duty. He now knew that dissent was strong enough to thwart a more moderate plan which recognised the influence of the established church in national schools. The campaign of 1843 was a victory for dissent, a final blow to the notion that the new Tory government could resuscitate the old alliance of church and state. The education committee had earlier refused to allow to the British and Foreign Schools society that control over inspectors which Archbishop Howley had already secured for the National Society. In November 1843 it reversed its decision and gave way. A Tory government confessed that even in that work which was traditionally allotted to the established church the religious denominations of England must now be treated as equal.

The arrangements under the concordat of 1840 befriended the established church. The National Society garnered more and more of the state grant which in the year before Graham's failure began to rise: 1842, £40,000; 1845, £75,000; 1846, £100,000; 1848, £125,000. As a result of Graham's bill the dissenters were convinced of the danger of state tyranny in education, and organised their denominational societies to found schools. If Peel's ministry was believed to have done little to help the established church, Tory administration at least made churchmen content with its policy over schools.

Content, except that children were still increasing faster than schools. A stalwart Anglican like Hook was convinced by experience in Leeds that the government must do far more to make schools and

---

[1] Minutes of the Wesleyan Conference, Sheffield, 26 July 1843, 557.

teachers, and that this far more could only be done without strings to denominations.[1] With the Whig return to power under Lord John Russell, Kay-Shuttleworth continued to move slowly forward towards more money from the state *and therefore* more control by the state of denominational schools. Kay-Shuttleworth pushed his way with the utmost civility, unruffled by political ambushes, retiring for a moment under bombardment, but soon appearing to renew the slow advance with an air of reasonableness and courtesy, devoid of abuse or emotion.

In 1846 he agreed with Archbishop Howley and the committee of the National Society to a series of 'management clauses' for schools receiving state money. Every school must be placed under a committee of management. Kay-Shuttleworth wanted a more permanent body than the incumbent, whose policy might change at every vacancy; and he further supposed that a single clergyman would be more likely to exclude dissenters from the school than a committee of laymen with the clergyman possessing a single vote. Many founders, needing state money and seeing no objection and perhaps advantage, accepted the new condition without a qualm. But it shocked incumbents of parishes accustomed to control the school of their village. Bishop Bagot of Bath and Wells protested on behalf of one of his clergy that a committee of management might even extinguish the authority of the clergyman.[2] Kay-Shuttleworth was clumsy in first imposing the clauses, with curt letters from a Whitehall desk which every right-minded Englishman wished instinctively to fight.

The incumbent was given sole charge of moral and religious instruction. The members of the committee of management must be members of the Church of England. But some lawyers held that dissenters were legally members of the Church of England until they were excommunicated. Country clergymen were afraid that a school, founded to educate children of the established church, would slowly be prised away from all connexion with the Church of England. Just at the time when Hampden and Gorham persuaded so many clergymen to fear government, Kay-Shuttleworth looked like an underhand manipulator through whom the state interfered in the private affairs of the church. The campaign became very confused, because in the

[1] W. F. Hook, *Letter to the Bishop of St. David's on the means of rendering more efficient the education of the people*, 1846. Hook had consulted Kay-Shuttleworth, cf. Smith, *Life of Kay-Shuttleworth*, 175–6.

[2] G, 47, 587. The clauses were agreed with the National Society in 1846, but not published till 28 June 1847.

absence or silence of Convocation the annual meetings of the National Society turned into a forum where country clergymen could make speeches about more ills than the management clauses. The National Society blushed to find itself at the centre of the quarrel between church and state. As with all conflicts of this epoch, the word *Tractarian* was thrown to and fro. The supporters of Kay-Shuttleworth said that his opponents were Tractarians. The word Tractarian fast degenerated into meaningless billingsgate.

George Anthony Denison, vicar of East Brent in Somerset and brother of the Bishop of Salisbury, led the battle to refuse all money from the state. 'We reject their thirty pieces of silver,' declared a prebendary of Bath and Wells amid emotional cheering.[1] Denison told Kay-Shuttleworth that he would refuse to admit the inspector to his schools. Kay-Shuttleworth replied his inspectors were busy elsewhere for the time, but if necessary would go to law to enforce inspection. Denison wrote to the clerical inspector of schools: 'My dear Bellairs, I love you very much; but if you ever come here again to inspect, I lock the door of the school and tell the boys to put you in the pond.'[2] At the annual meeting of the National Society in 1849, which hammered the subject for eight continuous hours, he declared open war on Kay-Shuttleworth and the committee of council. The climax of his campaign was reached at a meeting of 7 February 1850 (a date very near to the Gorham judgment), which condemned all co-operation between church and state because the clergyman of the parish and the bishop were not allowed sole control of the school.

Kay-Shuttleworth conceded a little. The members of the management committee might be required to declare themselves communicants. The schoolmaster or schoolmistress might be required to be a member (but not necessarily a communicant) of the Church of England. An appeal to the bishop on religious matters had always been conceded; now an appeal on non-religious matters was conceded, not to the bishop but to a tribunal of three, of whom one was a clergyman selected by the bishop, another an inspector who must be approved by the authority, and a third agreed by the previous two.[3] These concessions were generous. Archbishop Sumner and many members of the National Society were content. That they failed to content many

---

[1] G, 49, 712.

[2] Smith, *Life of Kay-Shuttleworth*, 188.

[3] Success of negotiations between committee of council and committee of National Society tabulated G, 49, 355.

of the parochial clergy, and high churchmen generally, may be ascribed to the murky atmosphere of Russell's erastian age. The clergy feared state action; and the person of Archbishop Sumner was not likely to reconcile them to a plan for a tribunal which the archbishop helped to constitute.

Meanwhile Kay-Shuttleworth made matters worse by doing in 1849 what he was forbidden to do in 1839. He founded a 'normal' or model school for teachers at Kneller hall. Though he conceded that the principal should profess the doctrine of the Trinity, the college would train schoolmasters of every religion and its examinations in divinity were purely biblical. He was then careful to conciliate opinion by appointing as first principal a fellow of an Oxford college and a clergyman, even though a liberal clergyman—Frederick Temple, later to be Archbishop of Canterbury and father of an Archbishop of Canterbury.

The National Society worried its way towards schism. Liberals and evangelicals disliked its quarrel with the government, and finding that high churchmen were too strong for them turned to found other institutions to train teachers. In 1850 papal aggression strengthened their hands and weakened the high churchmen. Everyone was suddenly suspicious of clerical claims to control anything, school included. Many were convinced that the National Society must not repudiate state aid, for the people could not be educated without state money. The annual meeting of the National Society in 1851 was conducted in a continuous uproar, but negatived Denison's motion and ended in deadlock. In 1851 the moderates formed a separate society on Protestant principles, the Church Education society.

Through the system invented with so much friction by Kay-Shuttleworth the labouring poor were educated in greater numbers, though not in sufficient numbers. England's ideal continued to be schools in the hands of the leading Christian denominations, each assisted in some just proportion by the purse of the taxpayer. But by numbers and wealth the Church of England secured the bulk of the money. As late as 1859 the establishment received two-thirds of the state grant. And therefore dissenting consciences in the many districts where there was only a church school became more troubled. For by its foundation the National Society must teach the catechism to the children in its schools.

By the middle of the century half the Anglican clergy were allowing dissenting children to absent themselves on grounds of conscience from religious instruction and worship. The sticklers over management clauses were equally firm over the duty of church schools to refuse a conscience clause. It was said that a clergyman was bound by the rubric in the office of baptism to instruct children in the catechism. Denison wrote numerous pamphlets to this end, of which the most characteristic was entitled *Seventeen Reasons why the Church of England may have nothing to do with any manner of Conscience clause*. Kay-Shuttleworth and the committee of council did all they could to persuade schools receiving state aid to allow a conscience clause; and took power to compel such a clause, but did not dare to insist upon it until 1860, when they began to insist in Wales. A revised code of 1862 required a conscience clause in all schools aided by the state, and a renewed controversy ensued till 1870, when the state insisted by act of Parliament.[1]

Everyone with responsibility was agreed that the education of the poor must be Christian. But two ideas of religious education contended for the nation's money. Religion, said one side, cannot be taught like arithmetic. It is a life, a community, a tradition. The child must be educated in worship and the community of the church, and without that education will understand little of the meaning of biblical information. Religion, said the other side, cannot be given to the labouring nation unless we give them that which is common to religions, for today each denomination has its equitable place in the sun. And that which is common to the Christian denominations is the Bible. Whether the Bible could sensibly be taught without interpretation remained to be seen.

3. CHRISTIAN SOCIALISM

'You think', the Duke of Somerset asked an experienced clergyman from the east end of London, 'that the first thing towards the spiritual and moral improvement of the people would be to improve their physical and social condition?'

'Yes,' replied Mr. Stooks, 'unquestionably. That lies at the very root of the whole.'[2]

The priests and pastors of the slums knew well that the lives of their flocks must be made more tolerable in this world if they were to look

---

[1] Adamson, 129–30; Burgess, 105 ff.   [2] PP, 1857–8, ix, 134, q. 1298.

with friendliness upon the next world. Few of the priests and pastors of the slums were inclined to be radicals. Many of them were Tories; and if they voted Whig they were likely to vote Whig more for political than for social reasons. They received from the tradition of the countryside a doctrine of vocation which assumed a hierarchy of classes and bade men to be content with the state of life to which they were called. In 1848 Miss Humphreys[1] published her *Hymns for Little Children*, with a preface by John Keble, and the stanza

> The rich man in his castle,
> The poor man at his gate,
> God made them, high or lowly,
> And ordered their estate.

Miss Humphreys was living in a remote feudal world on the borders of Donegal and Tyrone. The words betray the romantic medievalism of early Victorian poetry. Even when they were written they were not appropriate to the contemporary society which came to love Mrs Alexander's verse. But the traditional doctrine of the old countryside was taken into the growing towns and found itself an uneasy stranger, like other rural traditions from pigsties to sanitary habits.

To declare that a man must try to be content in that station of life to which he was called was not to declare that society must be content with sweated labour, chimney-boys, open sewers, fever-ridden tenements. Priests and pastors of the slums cried for better houses, better drainage, better education, better laws about drink, or hours of work. They did not cry for better wages, because no one believed the level of wages to be controllable.

The plan which attracted a few clergymen was a Christian version of Robert Owen's social experiments at New Lanark and later (from 1825) at Harmony, an estate on the Wabash river in Illinois and Indiana. Owen's condemnations of religion and his idea of socialist co-operation continued to influence Chartist and radical. From 1835 to 1846 there were fourteen 'socialist congresses', of which Owen was frequently chairman. After 1847 he became feeble in mind. An American medium converted him to spiritualism. He produced spiritual communications from Jefferson and some posthumous plays of Shakespeare. But all through the forties and fifties of the century his ideas, or rather his one idea, stirred those who had to do with working men.

[1] Two years later she became Mrs. C. F. Alexander.

For example: on 28 May 1846 a meeting was held at Exeter hall where Bishop Edward Stanley of Norwich proposed to adopt a Christian version of Owen's village communities. Villages of 300 or 400 families were to be formed, the land to be common, the labour to be for the community, half of the surplus (estimated at £500 a year) to go towards paying off the capital of £45,800, until the land and houses became the property of the labourers. The village was to include a church at £3,000 and houses for the clergyman and the director. The capital was to be provided by a society now to be formed and called the Church of England Self-Supporting Village Society.[1] Since on these figures the community needed 183 years of stable prices to pay off the capital and it would be the year 2030 before it finally acquired the land, the proposal had a utopian side. The authentic disciples of Robert Owen were shocked at the waste which proposed to spend £4,500 of the capital upon a church and a parsonage.

Evidently there was nothing unchristian about the idea of co-operative labour with profits distributed among the labourers. The communist prophet Goodwyn Barmby was not alone in justifying it by the primitive church of Jerusalem. The first to apply a Christian sanction to industrial socialism was a young and educated barrister far from the world of communist churches or rationalist radicals: by name John Malcolm Ludlow.

Ludlow was brought up by a radical widow in Paris and always looked at socialism with half-French eyes. Among French Protestants he found a sympathetic understanding of the political left. At the age of twenty he wrote in French an apology which taught Christianity to be the fulfilment of whatever was good in socialism.[2] In 1846 he met in Paris the Lutheran pastor Louis Meyer, who created philanthropic organisations among his labourers and wished to establish a celibate brotherhood to educate, relieve and evangelise the poor. Meyer suggested that Ludlow should do the same work in London.

Ludlow came back to England and determined to persuade the barristers of Lincoln's Inn to undertake social and missionary work in the slums which surrounded them. He asked for help from the preacher of Lincoln's Inn. The preacher referred him to the chaplain.

---

[1] *The Reasoner*, i, 27–29. The author of the plan was J. M. Morgan, who published a pamphlet on these lines about five years before. The motion was seconded by Lord John Manners, another though more Tractarian idealist.

[2] Masterman, 27–28.

The chaplain, Frederick Denison Maurice, said that he had no right to interfere in the surrounding parish and recommended him to go to its vicar. Ludlow was shy, Maurice very shy. To external observers Maurice had an air of quaint and sincere enthusiast. Ludlow found him a good man, but very impractical. With the complaisance of the vicar he began to visit the slums.

On 24 February 1848 revolution broke out in Paris. Ludlow hurried across the channel to see that his sisters were safe. He had a sudden vision of socialism spreading out of France and conquering the world. Socialism must be made Christian if the world were to be saved. He returned to England filled with the decision to christianise English socialism. The first practical step which he took was to write a letter to the impractical Maurice of Lincoln's Inn. This time he discovered, or thought that he discovered, a revolutionary Christian mind.

Son of a Unitarian minister, Maurice began as a Tory clergyman in revolt against Whigs after the reform act, and at various times was believed to be an unusual and valuable member of the moderate party of high churchmen. In 1838 he published a substantial work of historical and philosophical theology, *The Kingdom of Christ*. To this combined reputation he owed two professorships, in history and theology, at King's College, London.

His face was noble and his expression reverent. He exalted his hearers, but could not make them understand what he said. In lecturing or preaching he visibly reached upwards towards God, pouring forth words, contorting himself and his language, passionate for truth yet believing truth to be found only in hints and shadows. His better students loved him. His worse students abandoned the exhausting effort and ragged his lectures. Whether his students were better or worse, they could make nothing of the notes which they took from his lips. But a lofty purpose and a reverent mien did better for some of them than information or coherence. They could see and feel the grandeur and mystery of truth.

His selflessness was doubted by none. Its manifestations were sometimes so intense that they made others jumpy. Hostesses suffered paroxysms of nerves because he insisted on helping with the kettle and would absently pour the water into the sugar-basin.[1] He continually shrank from thrusting himself forward and never acted without pain and self-distrust. Often he would decide not to act and end by acting.

---

[1] *Letters of Jane Welsh Carlyle*, i, 68.

This travail gave birth to vehemence and even violence in attack or denunciation. On paper he easily made enemies.

Behind the strained and verbal paradoxes, behind the vast opaque generalities, lay the mind of a Platonic mystic. His youth was lived in a world of tidy systems of theology or philosophy, the world of Paley and Jeremy Bentham. Like so many of the romantics, he turned against the barren neatness of this shallow common sense and found a kindred spirit in Samuel Taylor Coleridge. Those systems packed religion into a box too small to hold it. Formulas of the dead throttled the breath of truth. The direct knowledge and experience of God was beyond language and could allow no substitute in the religious catchwords of the sects. This was part of the obscurity in Maurice's style. He reached towards the indefinable while he struggled to avoid defining it. He wanted to paint a picture which would hint at the living being with impressionistic brush, not a portrait of hard lines and dead likeness.[1] Maurice believed that every man could apprehend God, that every man possessed a spiritual vision. He therefore expected to find a measure of truth in every form of religious or moral experience, Christian or not.

This confusing and struggling prophet opened his mind to Ludlow's socialism.

Stirred by the victory of the French Revolution and by the news of revolt from Germany, Austria and Italy, the Chartists uttered threats of violence. They summoned for 10 April 1848 a monster meeting which should march from Kennington Common to the House of Commons and present a petition said to contain five million signatures. Their incendiary language sent the government and middle class into panic. The queen left London, the Duke of Wellington was given command of the troops, the home office enrolled special constables, noblemen sent to the country for gamekeepers with double-barrelled guns, 1,500 Chelsea pensioners were told to defend Battersea, the clerks at the general post office received rifles, the foreign office barricaded its windows with bound copies of the *Times*. The meeting on Kennington Common ended in quiet fiasco and pouring rain. The petition reached the House of Commons through back streets in a hansom cab.

---

[1] Whately said that Maurice's word-painting reminded him of a Chinese portrait where each single object is drawn with accuracy, but no one could make head or tail of the landscape: *Life of Whately*, ii, 302.

Maurice tried to enlist as a special constable, but found that they refused clergymen. On the day he had a cough and could not go out. During the morning his disciple Charles Kingsley called on him to talk about what was to be done. Maurice sent him with a letter of introduction to Ludlow.

Kingsley was the vicar of Eversley in Hampshire. Of all the romantic idealists of this age he was the most romantic. His breast was animated with chivalry. To describe Kingsley as a warm-hearted enthusiast is to understate. He poured forth a torrent of noble aspirations and felt them all in his heart. In his childhood nursery he arranged the chairs to form a congregation, made himself a pulpit, and imagined his pinafore to be a surplice.[1] He was a preacher by natural constitution. His mind thought in the imperative mood. He rather ejaculated than spoke. His punctuation was littered with notes of exclamation.

The ejaculations were not platitudes. His mind was as energetic and ardent as his emotion and his body. He read wisely and assimilated what he read. Kingsley wrote nothing of the first rank, nothing that was fully coherent or precise. But he was nearly always interesting and sometimes fascinating. So generous and joyous an idealism could not fail to attract. It attracted the more because it was mingled with a miscellany of unusual information. The information was not always correct. The leading defect of Kingsley's mind was vagueness. Large-minded and high-souled, he was neither thinker nor scholar. Contemporaries could not be neutral about Kingsley. They loved him or despised him. According to their cast of mind they found him elevating or absurd.

The Chartist fiasco of 10 April 1848 brought together the three men who together gave Christian socialism its name and being: Maurice the Platonic philosopher and Anglican divine, Kingsley the preacher, and Ludlow the socialist. Ludlow proffered the social ideas, Kingsley the prophetic fire, Maurice the anchorage in Christian doctrine. In this unusual crew Ludlow stood at the helm, Kingsley flew the flags and sounded the horns, Maurice poked round the engine-room to see that the engines were of authentic Christian manufacture.

It took time before they found their course. Maurice suggested that

---

[1] *Life*, i, 8. This game of the Victorian nursery was not confined to the childhood of future clergymen. It is recorded of the childhood of such future hammers of orthodoxy as Thomas Hardy the novelist and T. H. Huxley the scientist.

they should copy the Oxford Movement by issuing tracts to remind the upper and middle classes of their duty to the poor; Kingsley was possessed with the idea of doing something by means of handbills. Kingsley drafted a placard. Two days after the Chartist meeting, when London was quiet, a few copies appeared of a poster headed WORK-MEN OF ENGLAND!

On the same evening they agreed to publish a penny journal. The first number of *Politics for the People* appeared on 6 May 1848. The editors were Maurice and Ludlow. Maurice announced on the first page that they intended to consider questions of the day, like the extension of the franchise, the relation of capitalist to labourer, and what a government can or cannot do to find work or pay for the poor. The standpoint of the journal was to be sympathetic to the poor and based upon the acknowledgment that God rules in human society. The journal regarded God's government as the pledge that Liberty, Fraternity, *Unity* (italics not original)[1] are intended for every people under heaven. They addressed themselves to workmen. They confessed that they were not workmen, but asked for workmen's help in bridging the gulf that divided them.

Politics for the People achieved few readers, but contains strong and intelligent writing. Almost all the best came from the pen of Ludlow, who wrote more than a third of the whole. He contended for a vast extension of the vote, treated old Tory squire with sympathy, had little use for Whig, was not ashamed of the proposition that to be a Christian was to be in some form a radical. The paper was prepared even to treat the union with Ireland as an open question and suggested an increase of income tax and estate duty to allow a reduction of indirect taxes. It was reasonably against universal suffrage and the ballot, vehemently against monster meetings and the party of violence. Most of its contributors believed in a class society as an inescapable (and therefore God-given) fact of life. Their finest writing sought to convince the working man that the machinery of government was but a means. To end oppression and secure justice needed moral change as well as reform of law.

The most outspoken writing came from Charles Kingsley under the pen-name of Parson Lot. 'My only quarrel with the Charter is, that it

---

[1] The change from *Equality* did not go unobserved or uncriticised by the friends of the Chartists. Cf. the correspondent in *Politics for the People*, no. 3, 45. Fenton Hort also disapproved the change, *Life of Hort*, i, 143.

does not go far enough'. 'Instead of being a book to keep the poor in order, it [the Bible] is a book, from beginning to end, written to keep the rich in order.' 'It is our fault. We have used the Bible as if it was a mere special constable's handbook—an opium-dose for keeping beasts of burden patient while they were being over-loaded.'[1] Kingsley paraded the biblical texts which, nine years before, the Chartists sent up to the pulpits of harassed clergymen; 'He that will not work, neither shall he eat'; 'Go to now, ye rich men, weep and howl'. 'You cry, and I cry, "A fair day's wages for a fair day's work". And is not this the doctrine of the whole Bible. . . ?' This was plain and courageous utterance. The extremism vanished on close analysis, but Kingsley never wrote for analysts. If more of the contributors had resembled Kingsley, more of the workers might have read the paper.

By the end of June 1848 they expected to close. It limped along till the end of July and the seventeenth number. The writing was irretrievably educated, the editing amateur. It was not a total failure, since it was attacked by the Chartist *Commonwealth* for its clerical tendency and by the *Oxford Herald* for its democratical tendency.[2] Kingsley was for drawing the sword and throwing away the scabbard. Maurice pushed the sword back to safety. There was not enough in the paper to attack. 'Why—' Maurice asked Ludlow plaintively—'why spend your time in trampling upon people's corns and gouty feet?'[3] The newspaper was too gentle, too rational, too donnish. It committed the worst fault of the journalist by preferring meekness to ferocity. In the expiring number Maurice printed an apologia penitent of blunders and melancholy with failure. A born editor does not stand in sackcloth as he bows himself modestly from the desk.

The workers suspected the paper of designing to keep the poor in order and their station. Its failure lessened their distrust. They became readier to converse across the gulf which divided them from the middle class. The brotherhood round Maurice was uneasy with the knowledge

[1] *Politics for the People*, 28, 58–59.
[2] Christensen, 89; *Politics for the People*, 144; *Life of Kingsley*, i, 183. Archdeacon Julius Hare protested to Kingsley against his language about the Bible as the poor man's book, Christensen, 83. He said that the Chartists already believed the clergy to be impostors and that Kingsley encouraged them in the belief. Hare told Maurice that Kingsley and Ludlow were very conceited young men. *Life of Maurice*, i, 477. He succeeded in frightening Maurice to suppress a story by Kingsley called *The Nun's Pool*. This was already in type and so the paging of *Politics for the People* jumps suddenly from p. 64 to p. 81. The novel was afterwards published in the *Christian Socialist*. Christensen 84: Raven 110, n. 2.
[3] *Life of Maurice*, i, 479.

that they still knew little of what passed through the labourer's mind. Ludlow arranged a meeting with one of the antichristian Chartist leaders, the tailor Walter Cooper. He persuaded Cooper to come to two services when Maurice preached in Lincoln's Inn. Cooper was sufficiently moved to suggest that Maurice ought to meet the working men.

The first meeting was held at a coffee-house on 23 April 1849.[1] Here Maurice was at his best. He freely allowed criticism, encouraged the men to talk frankly, guided the discussion without dominating, and tried to give a fair summary at the end. Whereas most clergymen of the day wished to promulgate truth to the workmen, Maurice wished to learn from them. They had never met a parson like him. Over a hundred workmen were expected at the meeting of 4 June. Kingsley was present at the meeting a week later and found it unforgettable. Maurice, he wrote to his wife, 'was inspired—gigantic . . . He stunned us!'[2] The meetings drew some of the ablest and most hostile of antichristian leaders—even on one occasion Holyoake, editor of the *Reasoner* and king of atheistic socialism. If Kingsley enthused, Holyoake sneered. Not all the meetings were harmonious. Tom Hughes, the gentleman-boxer who was later to write *Tom Brown's Schooldays*, once jumped on a chair and offered to fight if they hissed the queen again. On another occasion the speeches waxed bitter against church and clergy until Kingsley struck a stance and stammered 'I am a Church of England parson'—long pause—'and a Chartist'.[3] But universal harmony is not an invariable sign of success, and all witnesses are agreed that Maurice uniquely threw down barriers against sympathy and understanding.

The brotherhood round Maurice discovered that the labourer was more interested in social than political reform. Ludlow returned from a holiday in Paris with a programme of founding co-operative societies, or associations where the workers would own the business and receive the profits. The plan was not new to England. The stores opened by the Rochdale Pioneers in 1844 are celebrated in the history

---

[1] It has been suggested that it was at this meeting that Kingsley broke the ice by stuttering that he was a Church of England clergyman and a Chartist. But the *Life of Maurice*, i, 536, 538, proves that Kingsley was not present on 23 April. The *Life of Kingsley*, i, 195ff., shows that Kingsley was in Devonshire from January to May 1849 and first attended the meetings in London on 4 June and 11 June.

[2] *Life of Kingsley*, i, 206.

[3] *Life of Kingsley*, i, 166; *Life of Maurice*, ii, 10.

of the co-operative movement and the north saw several examples of co-operative societies. A variant of the plan was called home colonisation. The village communities of which Bishop Stanley of Norwich dreamed were a fulfilment. The workmen at Maurice's meetings demanded help to found home colonies. Maurice characteristically welcomed the plan and even talked of founding a community himself, perhaps in the west of Ireland. Ludlow at once promised to join the colony if Maurice would lead it. In August 1849 Maurice was talking to the men about Christian communism and referring them to the primitive church of Jerusalem and to the monasteries.[1] Maurice was certain that the state never could be nor should be communist, for the state must conserve the rights and property of the individual. But the church was 'communist in principle'. In December 1849 they determined to establish a working tailors association under the management of Walter Cooper. In January 1850 Maurice publicly accepted the name of Christian Socialist. He allowed Ludlow to plan a series of *Tracts on Christian Socialism*, declaring it the only title which would define the object and would commit him at once 'to the conflict we must engage in sooner or later with the unsocial Christians and the unchristian socialists'.[2]

The associations worked for a time. Middle-class capital launched twelve workshops scattered over London from Tottenham Court Road to Pimlico: tailors, builders, shoemakers, pianomakers, printers, bakers, smiths. The Christian Socialists (as they may at last be called without anachronism) were enabled to extend their practical endeavours when they were joined by a wealthy philanthropist, Vansittart Neale, who put sums of money calculated at £60,000 into the various ventures. Dr. Wiseman and Bishop Wilberforce ordered suits from the tailors, doubtless for their footmen rather than for themselves. Kingsley wrote a passionate pamphlet, *Cheap Clothes and Nasty*, which had at least the effect of persuading a few officers in the Guards to order coats from the association. Lord Shaftesbury, greatest of English philanthropists, came into the movement to help found an association of needlewomen in Red Lion Square. Applications for capital began to multiply.

On 2 November 1850 appeared the first number of a new penny journal, under the title *Christian Socialist*. Ludlow founded it and was the sole editor. The unpractical Maurice deplored the use of the

---

[1] Christensen, 105: cf. *Life of Maurice*, ii, 7–9.   [2] *Life of Maurice*, ii, 35.

press to propagate Christian socialism, saying that the newspaper was the great idol-temple of the day. Ludlow was therefore free. He decided the policy and wrote nearly all the leading articles. The *Christian Socialist* thus contained the first coherent attempt to state the Christian view of a socialist society.

The church must be taken out of the sanctuary and into the world. Christianity becomes chilly when cramped within the walls of its churches and chapels. It must go out to assert the rule of God over every act of common life and embody its gospel in forms of social organisation.[1] Socialism was the livery of Christianity for the nineteenth century. Christian socialism was a message and a programme of action. Its message told the worker that the eternal king would have them sound in all their being and by his power their sicknesses might be healed; and that these sicknesses included sweated labour and commercial fraud as much as the diseases of the body and the soul. Its programme was a practical attempt to embody this message in reconstructed forms of society. No godless system of socialism can stand. For socialism rests upon moral grounds of righteousness and self-sacrifice and common brotherhood, which at last are inseparable from religious faith. Christian socialism intended 'to vindicate for Christianity its true authority over the regions of industry and trade, for socialism its true character as the great Christian revolution of the nineteenth century'.

Ludlow set before his readers the ideal of a state where every citizen was well employed and well educated. To this end the economy of the state must be controlled. He attributed the ills of 'godless' society in the slums to the theories of political economists who proposed that economic life must be allowed to follow its laws without interference. Christianity is not compatible with a system of trade and economy based wholly on profit. Free economy ended in unemployment and the wages of starvation.[2] In a free economy the interests of the employer and of the employed are opposite and can agree in nothing better than an armed truce.

Therefore associations or co-operative societies must be formed to end the antagonism of capitalist and labourer by making the labourer his own capitalist. The movement must spread over England and

---

[1] Masterman, 102; *Christian Socialist*, i, 1; Christensen, 153.
[2] *Christian Socialist*, i, 1. Cf. Ludlow's lecture of 12 February 1851, *The Christian Socialism and its Opponents*.

beyond, until it embraced the nation and was able to fix wages and prices for the well-being of all the citizens of the nation. In the associations the worker would be schooled in the duties of a citizen and prepared for the parliamentary vote. Ludlow had no desire that all men should have the same wage and an equal position in society. He said that this was the counterfeit of communism. But so long as the citizen was able to labour for the society instead of himself, 'Communism, pure communism, will, I feel sure, exhibit the very type of a flourishing society'. Unlike nearly all his Christian colleagues, he wanted the state to control the economy. He neither expected nor desired the direct control of a modern communist state. He expected a control of prices primarily by the associations of workers. But he wanted the state to intervene decisively by using the money of the taxpayer for such purposes of the whole society.[1]

Since the base of a socialist society was moral its foundation was the Christian church. Ludlow did not suppose that the existing churches could serve that high end. He looked at squires and dignitaries, lethargic congregations, sectarian dissenters, corruptions which he partly attributed to establishment. True to his background he wanted a more democratic church, 'Americanised', as he called it, with popular self-government. 'It seems quite clear to me', he wrote in a private letter, 'that, with what I have called an Americanised church, we could fairly conquer the working-classes of this country, that is to say, the very heart of English society, for Christ, and that if we do not, nobody else will, and that we never shall without sweeping church-reform.'[2]

Posterity accused the Christian Socialists of being milk-pudding socialists. That is because they have been judged by Maurice. Maurice was elevated as leader and interpreted the Christian philosophy to which many of the brotherhood subscribed. But he was not a man for programmes. Christian socialism as a platform should be judged by the *Christian Socialist* and its editor Ludlow.

In the late summer of 1850[3] Kingsley published the novel *Alton*

---

[1] *Christian Socialist*, i, 225, 234, 262; Christensen, 157–9.

[2] Christensen, 161, quoting a MS. letter of 23 September 1850. Maurice would have been alarmed at such a drastic attitude to the existing churches.

[3] Kingsley himself said afterwards it was published in 1849, (Preface, 1861). Hughes (Preface to 1881 edition) says it was 'the winter' of 1850 (i.e., 1850–1). It was reviewed in the *Guardian*, 16 October 1850; welcomed by the *Northern Star*, 7 September 1850; and in Hughes's Preface to the 1881 edition, i, 27, is a letter of August 1850 to Ludlow which shows that it was already out.

Locke. Though a work of fiction in autobiography, it was founded upon the life of the Chartist tailor-poet Thomas Cooper.[1] It proved that Kingsley could write and established his literary reputation. Despite inconsistent characters, muddled plot, tailing end, and lack of literary depth, Kingsley justly won his fame. He couched his moral vehemence in language of graphic power and range. Though not the best of all his novels, it interests historians the most. Every chapter is a denunciation. Kingsley released his pulpit reproof against Calvinists and Tractarians, cathedral dignitaries, bishops who leave fortunes out of their preferment, Tory parsons, aristocrats, undergraduates, ill-behaved choirboys, the fellows of Dulwich College and the fellows of all Cambridge colleges, Chartists of violence, purveyors of obscene and blasphemous literature; and behind everything the contemporary society which allowed the brutality and squalor and poverty of the slum. Kingsley followed the success by collecting and revising earlier articles into the novel *Yeast*, a miscellany of reflections about the rural poor.

In June 1851 Kingsley attained the national press by getting himself publicly denounced in church.

The Great Exhibition in Hyde Park that summer drew crowds from all over England and the London clergy planned courses of sermons to instruct the visitors. The incumbent of St. John's in Charlotte Street was an intelligent man, G. S. Drew. His church was too near for comfort to the celebrated John Street Literary Institution, palace of London socialistic atheism. With the aid of Maurice he arranged a course of six evening sermons[2] on The Message of the Church and allotted to Kingsley (22 June) the sermon on The Message of the Church to the Labouring Man. The sermons were advertised in the press and on placards. A crowd of working men came. Drew's plan succeeded in drawing audiences beyond those of ordinary piety. Even a pair of John Street critics came to hear Kingsley.

Kingsley delivered sermons like a man wrestling with demons.[3] In the Charlotte Street pulpit he seemed to identify his enemy with the English clergy. He sounded as though he was telling the people that the gospel was liberty, equality and fraternity and that any priest who

---

[1] *Life of Cooper*, by R. J. Conklin, 1935, 132.
[2] The preachers were to be (1) Maurice, (2) F. W. Robertson, (3) Kingsley, (4) Septimus Hansard, (5) Maurice, (6) Drew. R. B. Martin, *Kingsley*, 127: cf. *Reasoner*, xi, 102.
[3] *Letters of J. B. Mozley*, 239.

did not preach liberty, equality and fraternity betrayed his God and his church. In trumpet-tones he said that the message of Christ was Freedom, that all systems of society which favour the accumulation of capital in a few hands or which oust the masses from the soil are contrary to the kingdom of God. He besought the poor not to judge the church by its diseases. Let the clergy be as tyrannical, luxurious, bigoted, ignorant, careless as they may, the Bible proclaims freedom to the poor, baptism proclaims the equality of all men, the Lord's Supper proclaims their brotherhood, not as a dim and distant possibility but as an absolute and eternal right. It is God's will that the degraded masses shall share in the soil and wealth and civilisation and government of England.

In the midst of the sermon came definitions which weakened the theoretical force of this equation between the gospel and the principles of the French Revolution. Freedom is to do not what I like, but what is right. Equality is not giving equal power to wise as well as foolish or to bad as well as good, but equality of opportunity in developing unequal talents. The cry was qualified. But neither the manner nor the matter caused his hearers to mark what was reserved.

Drew the vicar thought that Kingsley equated Christianity with socialism. He waited until Kingsley gave the blessing from the pulpit. Then he stood in his surplice at the reading-desk and told the congregation that he must perform the most painful duty. 'Some things which the preacher has said may be very useful; much that he has said I think very imprudent; and much I consider to be very untrue. I must also say that I think the subject which he was to have brought before you has been utterly forgotten."[1] There were cries of No no from a section of the congregation. Kingsley stood in the pulpit with folded arms and then came down without a word. His friends thought that he had only to speak a word of retort for the poor in the church to break into riot. Two friends, F. W. Robertson and Septimus Hansard, quietened groups of men who began to hiss. Outside the church knots of people stood and argued. The national press seized the drama and heightened it.

The sermon at St. John's church was important to the Christian

[1] Best account in *Record* and *English Churchman*, 26 June 1851. Kingsley understood the last sentence to mean that he was accused of violating some pledge and resented it more than anything else: cf. his preface to the printed sermon. But it seems clear that this was not Drew's intention. The account by Tom Hughes in the preface to the later edition of *Alton Locke* is inaccurate. Mrs. Kingsley founded her account (*Life and Letters of Kingsley*, i, 288–91) partly on Hughes. Drew was a man of parts who attained DNB, though DNB drew a veil over this incident.

Socialists. They could no longer be dismissed by the workers as parsonical amateurs and by the Tories as silly and harmless sentimentalists. To be denounced by a parson for equating Christianity with socialism was the quickest route to the confidence of the Chartist labourer. Antichristians took a stance of respect towards the Christian socialists, antichristian institutes offered their platforms, the redoubtable Holyoake abandoned his sneers. The Christian Socialists achieved among working men an influence astonishing in so small a group. They were driving their coach through the multi-barred gate which sundered upper and middle classes from labourer. The leading Chartist newspaper confessed them to be the leaders of the co-operative movement.[1] In the spring of 1852 labouring leaders in the strike of wireworkers, the first national conflict between employer and labourer in English history, looked for advice and sympathy to the Christian Socialists. In the same summer Ludlow and Neale and Thomas Hughes helped to secure an act of Parliament (Slaney's act) securing adequate legal protection for co-operative societies and their business.

Ludlow was troubled on three sides: by the associations, by their chief promoter Vansittart Neale, and by the nominal head and real theologian of the group, Maurice. The associations were composed of men or women whose human nature was not higher than ordinary and tottered on their way with financial unease and personal friction. Not even the working men would bring custom to the associations. Their wives refused to abandon their habitual shops.

As serious were the internal strains of the brotherhood directing the movement. It was a miscellany of awkwards. Maurice perpetually shrank from practical measures lest they corrupt the kingdom of God and his disciples perpetually pushed their way over barricades of tangled trepidation. Kingsley pictured himself as a robust athletic carnivorous Englishman and could not bear the beards and vegetarians which the brotherhood collected. He was depressed for days after finding himself on a deputation with a bearded colleague wearing a straw hat and blue plush gloves.[2] The austere Ludlow could be truculent and clothed his silken vest in a coat of mail. He toiled under the Victorian burden that in duty bound a man must reprove his best friends for their faults. He lectured away at Maurice, Kingsley, Neale, Hughes. Maurice reverently took the arrows to his breast and tried to

---

[1] *Northern Star*, 19 July 1851; Christensen, 226.
[2] T. Hughes, Preface to *Alton Locke* (1881), i, 24.

learn. The others found this discipline insufferable. Neale was not such a disciple of Maurice as most of the brotherhood. If a Christian at all, he was misty and lax. He never came to the Bible classes which Maurice gave and which Ludlow and others regarded as the Christian power-house of the brotherhood. The philanthropy meant more to him than the theology. He disliked the name Christian Socialist. To provide capital for associations he gave his money liberally or recklessly. He went into the new London co-operative stores, enlisted the aid of trade unions, made the Christian Socialist group into a small though important agency within a vast national movement. Neale was an enthusiast for expansion. Ludlow believed that the mission would prosper if the Christianity were as plain as the socialism and this could only be achieved by slow development of compact responsible groups not dependent on lavish gifts. He grieved when he found that Maurice agreed with Neale. Maurice thought that Ludlow's viewpoint narrowed their work until it was sectarian.

At the end of October 1851 Ludlow tried to force Neale out of the council for promoting the associations. He failed hopelessly. Accordingly he resigned from the council and (as soon as a new editor could be found) from the *Christian Socialist*. The process of finding a new editor brought him to an agony. First Maurice refused to take the editor's chair. When Tom Hughes agreed to do it Ludlow was horrified that Maurice decided to drop the name *Christian Socialist* from the title of the journal. He thought it surrender, desertion, a hauling down of the flag in face of the foe. The disagreement between them mounted. Ludlow was a Christian Socialist, Maurice an evangelist who wanted to christianise socialists as well as Tories. To Maurice the name stood for no principle and could be jettisoned without qualm. Ludlow felt the bitterness of frustration. He accused Maurice of abandoning the name because he wished to keep his professorship at King's College. Maurice did not quite feel able to deny it. Ludlow told him acidly that he had better keep to the college, as he was doing no good among the working men.[1]

For Kingsley's sermon at St. John's church had the unforeseen result of putting Maurice into jeopardy. The pair Kingsley and Maurice were linked as target for ultra-conservative journalists and pamphleteers. Critics accused Kingsley of confusing the body with the spirit,

---

[1] Masterman, 130. Maurice's son, though using the letter, omitted this passage from the biography, *Life*, ii, 105.

of mixing social with sacramental equality. Christ said that his kingdom was not of this world and the Christian Socialists virtually assert
that it is of this world.[1] That autumn John Wilson Croker, leading
journalist of the Tory party and once the friend of Wellington and
Peel, stoked the fires against Maurice and Kingsley in the *Quarterly
Review*.[2] This allegedly responsible Tory writer in an unquestionably
responsible Tory journal accused them of teaching revolutionary
doctrines which led at last to shooting landlords or practising communism in wives. Croker taxed Kingsley's sermon with being the
worst of their productions, with wresting scripture to downright
communism, with expecting a world of no capital, no merchandise,
no wages, and no rich. Even the Whig *Edinburgh Review* joined more
moderately in the hunt.[3] The *Edinburgh* confessed its sympathy for the
poor and acclaimed Kingsley's power of writing. It only taxed
Kingsley with disreputable ranting and the Christian Socialists with
ignorance in assailing the political economists. If for the sake of
journeymen tailors Kingsley raved against cheap clothes, should he
not be consistent and rave against cheap bread?

Were these well-meaning clergymen liable to penalty for teaching
error? Could they be stopped? On the news of Kingsley's sermon
Bishop Blomfield of London inhibited Kingsley from preaching, but
cancelled the inhibition after Kingsley explained the printed text of
the sermon at an interview.[4] Maurice might be damaged more easily.
The council of King's College could dismiss him from his professorship of divinity. Maurice had not preached the offensive sermon. He
had been rash or courageous enough to allow an approving letter to
be printed with its preface. Croker seized the chance. He wrote that it
was surprising to find this teacher of socialist and theological error
occupying the chair of divinity at King's College.

The triumphant ejection of Maurice from his professorship (see
p. 548) did not shake the Christian Socialists. It rallied them for a short
time. The brotherhood continued to work uneasily until the end of
1854 and uttered its last whimper in March 1855. Hughes lost faith in
the group because he believed that they worked better as individuals.[5]

[1] So the *Record*, 7 July 1851: illustrating that dualism which Maurice and Kingsley
denounced as unchristian.
[2] 89, 1851, 491: 'Revolutionary literature'; esp. 522, 524.
[3] January 1851, 1ff., 'English Socialism and Communistic Associations'.
[4] Letters of Blomfield to Kingsley, 27 June and 3 July 1851, in Blomfield Papers,
FP, 385/242, 385/249.
[5] Christensen, 362.

Maurice turned his interests from co-operatives to the education of working men. Ludlow brooded gloomily over Maurice's betrayal of the cause. The failure of several associations and the rising prosperity of England ended the Christian Socialists.

Almost all retained their social sentiments. Neale and Hughes continued their endeavours for the same causes. Only Kingsley came near to recant. Two new prefaces in succession were given to later editions of *Alton Locke*. Each preface spoke louder against his disreputable past. By 1855 he ceased to believe in tinkering with the economy and even respected economists.[1] To the manager of an association who wanted government to store cheap bread for the poor of Manchester he said mockingly, 'Yes, and why ain't you and I flying about with wings and dewdrops hanging to our tails?' He told Hughes that he was becoming an optimist and that the world would go right in its own way. 'We've all tried our Holloway's pills, Tom, to cure all the ills of all the world—and we've all found out, I hope, by this time that the tough old world has more in its inside than any Holloway's pills will clear out.'[2]

4. THE RELIGIOUS CENSUS

The government of Lord John Russell determined to organise a religious census in connexion with the normal census which fell in the year 1851. No mention of this plan appeared in the census act. But the act empowered the secretary of state to issue questions about any further particulars that might seem advisable. Sir George Lewis, then under-secretary at the home office, suggested that under this vague clause it would be desirable to seek religious statistics.

The government therefore appended questions about religion to the questions which must be answered under penalty. When members of Parliament doubted the legality of the questions and the efficacy of the penal claims so far as they applied to religious statistics, the law officers of the crown advised that the penalties were probably not legal in these clauses. The public was informed that they could not be compelled to answer; and on this voluntary basis the registrar-general recommended that the census proceed.

---

[1] T. Hughes, Preface to *Alton Locke* (1881), i, 54–55.

[2] T. Hughes, Preface to *Alton Locke* (1881), i, 70: the date was 1856. Hughes regarded it as the end of the Parson Lot age of Kingsley's life.

The registrar-general employed an agent, Horace Mann. He appears to have been responsible for the plan. The enumerator in each district provided the names and addresses of ministers. Mann's office sent a form to the minister of each place of worship. This form asked for the number of buildings used for public worship; the number of sittings provided in them; and the number of persons present at each of the services held on 30 March 1851, the day before the general census.

Three days before census Sunday Bishop Wilberforce, in presenting a petition to the House of Lords, said that the only result of the present arrangement would be wrong information, and that he was inclined to advise the clergy not to answer the questions. Absence of episcopal enthusiasm meant that many clergymen of the established church returned the forms blank. To those ministers who gave no answer Horace Mann made a second application, and this produced a significant diminution in the number of blanks. For the remainder Mann tried to secure information from the churchwardens, and this further diminished the blanks. Out of 14,077 places of Anglican parochial worship, there remained 989 which continued to refuse any return of attendance. In view of the circumstances, this was an achievement.

Mr. Horace Mann then disappeared into the dust of enumerators' reports, and emerged nearly two years later with his report, ready towards the end of December 1853, published on 3 January 1854.

No government report can be compared with that of Horace Mann. Not merely did he give a catalogue of thirty-five different religious sects in Britain. He described their history and analysed their tenets. His style was marked by a certain indefinable air of the historical amateur. He began with the Druids, and pursued a devious and doubtful course through St. Alban and Hengist, hurrying from the character of Saxon paganism to the Revolution of 1688. The long introduction afforded easy openings to the knives of critics who wished to question the value of his statistics. Mann gave the impression of a well-meaning warm-hearted latitudinarian who wished not simply to provide the country with facts, but to stir the country to act, to preach the country a sermon.

The statistics themselves were not without vagueness. After the returns were analysed, Mann made estimates for the blanks; and adding these allowances to the returned numbers, he produced the following totals for the population of England and Wales which attended churches on 30 March 1851 (total attendances):

The Church of England	5,292,551
The Roman Catholics	383,630
The main Protestant dissenting Churches (Presbyterian, Methodist, Congregationalist, Baptist)	4,536,264

Total population of England and Wales disclosed by the census, 17,927,609.[1]

The first question which Mann asked himself, and wished the country to consider, was whether the population was going to church. Mann's estimates for the persons who could not go to church were precise in appearance though vague in calculation. Of the nearly eighteen million persons who could have attended church, he refused to make a deduction for Sunday traders or criminals. He postulated three million children under ten and deducted them as not church-going. Then he deducted 7 per cent of all the remaining adults, or about a million, on the ground that they were invalid and infirm, and then one person in each house to look after the old or the infant, and then a certain number necessarily engaged on public transport, estimating, for example, that 6,000 men were employed on London omnibuses every Sunday; and so arrived, not without leaps in the dark, at the figure of 58 per cent of the population, or just over, as that which ought to be worshipping God somewhere in England on Sunday; reckoned at 10,398,013 persons. But these are those able to be present at one and the same time; and if we allow for services at different times of day, we should desire an attendance as high as 70 per cent of the population; or 12,549,326 persons.

Adding the figures of attendants on 30 March at the morning, afternoon and evening services, we find a total of 10,896,066, comfortably more than 58 per cent of the population. But some persons attended twice, and others may have attended thrice; but if we suppose (and Mann pleasantly added a note that the calculations here 'are mainly conjectural') that half the afternoon attendants had not been present in

[1] From Mann's figures were inferred the following imprecise estimates for separate attendants (*Congregational Year Book*, 1855, 39):

	Estimated Total	Per 1,000 of Population	Per 1,000 of attendants
Church of England	3,773,474	210	520
Methodists all sections	1,385,382	77	190
Independents	793,142	44	109
Baptists all sections	589,978	33	81

the morning, and that a third of the evening attendants had not been present in the morning or the afternoon, we should obtain a total of 7,261,032 persons who attended service once or more on census Sunday. Comparing this figure with the 70 per cent who ought to have attended church, Mann reached at last the gloomy result that over five and a quarter million persons, who ought to have gone to church or chapel and were physically capable, failed to do so. He added in a footnote a grain of comfort: 'It must not, however, be supposed that this . . . represents the number of *habitual* neglecters of religious services. This number is absent every Sunday; but it is not always composed of the *same persons.* . . . The number of *habitual* non-attendants cannot be precisely stated from these tables.'

In the eyes of Mann, this was the significant statistic. About five and a quarter million people failed to do their duty—here was a great mission field in England, which the churches must co-operate in attacking.

In his introduction he continued, unique among census officials, by trying to diagnose the cause and to plead for a remedy.

He assumed that the upper and middle classes, especially of late years, regarded their attendance as among the recognised proprieties of life. This five and a quarter million was of the labouring myriads—educated perhaps in a Sunday school, but soon 'as utter strangers to religious ordinances as the people of a heathen country'. Mann reported the supposed reasons. They dislike social distinctions in churches, the division into respectable pews and free seats, and regard religion as a middle-class propriety or luxury; suspect the churches of being indifferent to their poverty, and think that the message of the clergy is vitiated because they are paid to deliver it. They live in such physical squalor that they cannot rise to the things of the spirit. The number of ministers of religion is at present too few to reach them. From his statistics Mann tried to answer the question how far they failed to go to church because there was no room for them. Behind the enquiry into church 'sittings', and a main part of the report, can be seen the assumptions of the church extension movement—people do not go to church because there is no church where they can go.

The census form asked for sittings; and this part of the form was returned blank more often, even, than the question of attendants. But by a similar mixture of enumeration and guesswork, he concluded that in large towns, and in large towns only, it was physically impossible for over a million and a half people to attend church or chapel even if they wished, and that about 2,000 new churches and chapels were needed. But Mann's emphasis did not lie upon this statistic. For in the slums the churches were even now half empty; and Mann therefore exhorted Britain rather to provide living agents, without whom the new churches would remain as empty as the old. It was less difficult to build new churches than to fill them when built.

From this point of view the most interesting statistics of the census are the local variations on which Mann made no comment in his preface. London was grossly under-churched—sittings for 30.2 per cent of the population; while North Wales and the North Riding could house over 90 per cent—and in some of the London boroughs the ratio of sittings to population was even lower, as in Shoreditch, which provided 18 per cent or no seats for over 43,000 people. It startled critics to find that Durham, where the ecclesiastical endowments were splendid, had one of the lowest percentages of sittings to population.

These statistics were formidable. It was natural that attention should be focused upon other statistics—those of dissent and the establishment. The newspapers fastened upon them, each after its kind. The *Times* was chiefly astounded at the size of the Roman Catholic population; after all this fuss, after the agitation over papal aggression, it was found, said the *Times* with an exclamation mark, that they were less than the known population of Irish immigrants—the agitation had been an absurdity, and so had the pope's imposing hierarchy. But, except for the *Times*, the newspapers pushed their noses into the relations now disclosed between establishment and Protestant dissenters.

According to Mann's figures and estimates, over five and a quarter persons attended the worship of the Church of England, and over five and a half the worship of other religious bodies. Admit that more dissenters may have attended their chapels twice or thrice, deduct Jews and Mormons and even Roman Catholics, and the statistics still pointed to the uncomfortable fact that in gross the dissenting churches commanded the allegiance of nearly half the population of England and Wales.

This was a state paper where the dissenters were treated on perfect equality with the church, where no hint appeared that their religion was less beneficial. Edward Miall confessed to a curious sensation. He said that as a dissenter he felt like the son of a peer, treated from birth as a menial, and suddenly finding himself in his ancestral home, recognised and receiving the attention due to his rank.[1]

The census figures became at once the missiles of a new controversy called the 'arithmetical war'. The war was taken up into party politics. The Tory Lord Derby pointed out the fallaciousness of the statistics. Lord Palmerston had no doubt at all of their reliability.[2]

To discredit Mann's statistics was not at first sight difficult. Easily exhibiting the absurdities of the introduction, the critics seized upon the numerous gaps, the estimates, the cloudiness whereby the statistics were reached. Some parishes or chapels estimated the Sunday schools within their lists and others not. Mann largely omitted cathedrals and entirely omitted college chapels, workhouses, schools, almshouses, prisons, asylums. He took no notice of early services. At Leeds two lines of figures were so transposed that the numbers of Mormons were those of Roman Catholics and vice versa.[3] The Baptist Union found Mann's Baptist numbers impossible to reconcile with their private records, and appointed an officer to investigate the discrepancy.[4] There were improbable cases where the hearers were more numerous than the sittings. Modern students of this census, who dig into Mann's heap at the Public Record Office, do not breathe trust in Mann's enumerators. The critics at last drove Mann to write a letter to the *Times* (11 July 1860) confessing that the census made no attempt to estimate the numbers of the different denominations. He continued to be confident that the *general* picture of the country's religious practice was authentic.

For whatever its vagueness and unreliability, however absurd some moments in the preface, there was something about Mann's report which was inescapable, and which made it a landmark in the history of England. The statistics, once given so largely, were seen to contain something probable enough. They showed the strength of the Church of England to be in the home counties and the east. In the big towns dissent was shown to be the stronger. In Leeds (assuming each attendance as one person) 15 per cent of the population went to church, 31 per cent to chapels; in Bradford 12 per cent went to church, 27 per cent to chapels. In the big towns of the West Riding like Halifax and Huddersfield, in Manchester and Bolton, in Newcastle-upon-Tyne and

[1] *Nonconformist*, 1854, 1.
[2] Palmerston was asked by Apsley Pellatt in 1854: cf. H, 1860, clix, 1717.
[3] Hansard, clix, 1860, 1699–1700.
[4] *Nonconformist*, 27 April 1854, 349.

Hull, in Birmingham and Stroud, and in the Cornish towns like Penzance and Redruth, dissent was in the majority, often a comfortable majority, of actual attendants at worship. The worst for the establishment was Wales, where in the entire principality the number of persons who went to chapel was more than four times the number who went to church.

No sensible man had believed that the dissenters were as strong as they were now shown to be. The census therefore acted in England somewhat as the disruption acted in Scotland.[1] It finally established the impossibility of treating the establishment as privileged on the ground that it was the church of the immense majority of the country.

It was the last, as well as the first, religious census in English history.

In 1860 the cabinet considered the forthcoming census, and planned that the religious enquiry be repeated, this time under penalty for refusal to answer. The dissenters objected to answering religious questions under penalty, and the government again consented to make the questions voluntary. But dissenters objected even more to the proviso that profession of faith be filled in. The government had learnt that a study of attendance was not reliable and therefore asked heads of households to state their denomination on the form. The dissenters would not countenance such a proposal. They feared the effect of a mere 'C. of E.' on the return of a person with vestigial relation to his church. Most churchmen, and the government, would not countenance Mann's method, and so the home secretary dropped the proposal for a religious census. Despite suggestions at more than one later census, the idea was never revived successfully, and Mann's report remains, in more ways than one, unique.

---

[1] The Scottish census report was published separately in March 1854. It showed the attendants of the Church of Scotland at 19.9 per cent of the population, of the Free Church at 19.2 per cent, of the United Presbyterians at 11.7 per cent, and of others at 10.1 per cent—or just over 60 per cent in all. The statistics rested on a far larger amount of mere estimate even than in England. Scottish enumerators were less willing to deliver forms, Scottish ministers even less willing than ministers of England to fill them up. Cf. PP, 1854, lix, 309. Mann himself became registrar and secretary to the Civil Service Commission from 1855.

CHAPTER VI

THE DISSENTERS

THE phrase *free church* to mean Protestant dissenting church is not found in early Victorian England and is a tribute to the changing idea of establishment. In the earlier part of the century many dissenters regarded themselves as eschewing privileges for conscience. In the later part many dissenters regarded themselves as escaping state shackles, and the name *free churchman* slowly began to oust the name *dissenter*. It was first formed by analogy from the Free Kirk of Scotland and began to appear in an English context about 1869.

1. METHODISTS

The Methodists were not sure whether they were dissenters. Wesley bequeathed the puzzle of his attitude, that he wanted not to separate from the Church of England while his acts led towards separation. A Methodist of 1834[1] said that he was like an oarsman who faced the Church of England while he rowed steadily away. After his death Methodist societies fell easily and inevitably into two attitudes: Methodists who believed that their societies would lose influence if they identified themselves with dissent; Methodists who found a gospel ministry in Methodism and suffered the establishment like dissenters.

Since 1795 each local society had been permitted to have the sacrament celebrated by authorised persons and to hold services at times when the established church was holding services. The decision of 1795 recognised that Methodists were a denomination separate from the established church. But long afterwards most of their members continued to be married or buried by the incumbent, many members worshipped at the parish church in the morning and the Methodist chapel in the evening. As late as 1870 a few chapels refrained from celebrating the sacrament or from holding worship during the

[1] Joseph Beaumont; Smith, iii, 219.

hours of Anglican services.[1] Many chapels used the Book of Common Prayer with slight alteration; a prayer book somewhat as the puritans of the seventeenth century wanted, baptism without sign of the cross, ordination without charge to bind and loose sins, place for extempore prayer, no surplice nor solemn ceremonial.[2] In London this use of varied forms of liturgy was almost universal, in the provinces there was more diversity; in London many collects and some extempore prayer, in the provinces much extempore prayer and a few collects.[3]

Conservative Methodists valued the reverence and decorum of evangelical Anglicans, a decorum which others feared as a formalism that shackled worship. Conservative Methodists, if not Tory in politics, were friends to the established church and refused to agitate for its overthrow. Radical Methodists looked with understanding upon old dissent and its hatred of a state church. As the movement spread it made converts among dissenters and the children of dissenters, whose stance towards the Church of England did not resemble the benign posture of John Wesley or high Methodist ministers.

The ruptures which plagued early Victorian Methodism derived in part from this tension within John Wesley's soul. But calamitous stress would still have troubled Methodists even if there were no state church to respect or repudiate. The constitution of the Connexion was ill suited to the facts of Methodist life.

They were strong in the midland cities except Birmingham, in the West Riding of Yorkshire, in the south-west, among the miners of Durham and the farm labourers of Lincolnshire. They were weak in the home counties round London except Kent. Their social structure was chiefly of the lower middle class and artisan. At Kettering, where the numbers were insignificant compared with those of the Church of England and old dissent, the flock of 1843 consisted of: a retired and rich gentleman from Bradford, a Yorkshire brother of the preacher, a cultivated and intelligent widow, one well-to-do farmer, the leading druggist of the town, a brush manufacturer, the town crier (who cried with a solemn clerical voice), a bank manager, a prosperous tailor; and the others were farm labourers or hands in the Northampton boot trade.[4] This social composition was typical of much Methodism in the

---

[1] Workman, i, 386.

[2] Cf. *The Order of administration of the Lord's Supper and Baptism . . . as used by Wesleyan Methodists, 1848.* For account of editions of this and of *The Sunday Service of the Methodists,* see Wesley Swift in PWHS, xxix, 1953, 12; xxxi, 1958, 112.

[3] Jackson, *Life of Robert Newton,* 75–76.   [4] Gregory, *Autobiog. Recoll.,* 356–7.

towns of the provinces; a composition not naturally firebrand. The preachers were usually of simple origins. The fathers of nine ministers eminent about the year 1850 were five Methodist preachers, one tailor, one draper, one small farmer and one naval surgeon. The preachers expected and were expected to maintain a social status comparable with customs officers, surgeons, or shopkeepers of respectability.[1]

The golden age of Methodist preaching faded. Giants of the second generation with the mantle of Wesley upon them, an Adam Clarke or a Richard Watson, died and left few successors of equal stature. The days of hooligan persecution passed away and ceased to embattle Methodist faith. When Queen Victoria ascended her throne the Methodist preacher still rode out, saddlebags stuffed with tracts, and returned after many days, saddlebags stuffed with cream cheese and pork pie from many a farm;[2] austere God-fearing men blessing each home where they passed a night, riding into remote valleys and hurrying across country to catch the coach. The coming of the railways stripped outward romance and heroism from the travelling preachers. When stage-coach yielded to express train their journeys became faster but more prosaic. The circuits, always a system of pastoral care to be judged on merit, lost their nimbus of Franciscan beauty. Yet moments still recalled the prodigies of John Wesley; hundreds of people crying *Glory* enraptured in Halifax chapel, folk roaring amid a congregation of eight thousand at Gwennap Pit in Cornwall.[3] They were still expanding fast; in Great Britain from 245,194 in 1828 to 338,861 in 1848, overseas from 36,917 in 1828 to 97,451 in 1848. These figures are of members. According to Horace Mann 654,349 persons worshipped in Wesleyan Methodist chapels at the evening services of 30 March 1851.

Liturgy mattered less because the Methodists gave hymnody to England. Their hymns bore the impress of two or three poetic minds. The new 1831 edition of Wesley's hymnbook contained 769 hymns of which 668 were written by one of the four Wesleys (father and three sons), 66 by Isaac Watts, and only 35 by nineteen other authors.[4] The collection possessed a rare doctrinal coherence important to the

---

[1] Coley, *Life of T. Collins*,[2] 221.

[2] Gregory, *Autobiog. Recoll.*, 5.

[3] *The Reverend John Rattenbury*, 1880, 36.

[4] Julian,[2] s.v. *Methodist hymnody*.

continuity of Methodist teaching. It was marked by catholic sympathy and by heart-assailing directness characteristic of Wesley, simple words of agony or exultation.

The government of the Connexion rested with Conference, a hundred itinerant preachers chosen by a deed of Wesley to succeed him in managing his societies and their property. These preachers elected their president and secretary annually and members of the Legal Hundred chose district committees to act during the year. All preachers beside the Legal Hundred could attend Conference. The Legal Hundred originally filled up its own vacancies by seniority. But since 1814 every fourth election was by and from ministers who had travelled fourteen years.[1]

That is, government by senior clergy. But Methodist chapels resembled dissenting chapels in being unendowed and dependent on voluntary endeavours. The constitution provided for central and clerical government over societies where local laymen carried the burden and responsibility. Conference aimed at strong government as the only way of directing Methodist expansion. To overrule a decision by determined local officers who controlled the money invited collision between Conference and its congregations; between central government and local authorities; between high clerics and low laymen. The centralised polity groaned and creaked along.

Within these constitutional conflicts rumbled the attitudes of high and low Methodism (these names are modern). Central government was clerical, local government was lay. Therefore the authority of itinerant ministers was pressed by Conference and diminished by congregations. The high party in Conference wished itinerant preachers to be seen as commissioned by the authority of God. By 1820 they jettisoned the pretence of a distinction between a Wesleyan preacher and an ordained minister, a pretence maintained at first that they might not appear to dissent from the established church. In 1818 preachers were authorised to entitle themselves the Reverend. For some years Conference ordained foreign missionaries by laying on of hands, but eschewed the rite for home preachers out of tenderness to their right and left; the right objecting because it would be a schismatic act not authorised by the Church of England, the left objecting because its use might doubt the validity of existing ordinations. Conference of 1836 approved laying on of hands in all ordinations, not as

[1] Workman, i, 405.

required for validity but as most proper and advantageous.[1] Very high Methodists preferred clerical costume (gown and bands) in the pulpit. But in Hull and Manchester ministers who wore gowns and bands[2] caused uproar among their congregations. Conference of 1841 ruled that no one might wear gown in the pulpit without leave of Conference. This pacific half-measure failed to content anti-ritualists in the northern congregations. Conference of 1842 forbade gowns, cassocks, bands, surplices.

The central government of the Methodist societies was directed towards the right wing; and it was their advantage and misfortune that the occasion threw up a leader so able as to guide Conference towards its goal and so overbearing as to bring Wesleyan Methodism within distance of destruction.

Jabez Bunting was the manager thrown up by the need for management. The Connexion needed organising; its ministry, missions, property, trust deeds, theological training, finance, discipline, polity. No one could exert influence in Conference without the name of a great preacher and Bunting was a great preacher. He was pulled out of the itinerant ministry in northern industrial cities and made the indispensable assistant secretary of Conference. He became secretary in 1814 and president for the first time in 1820; editor of the *Wesleyan Methodist Magazine*, secretary of the Wesleyan Missionary Society, member of every important committee, weighty speaker at every Conference, and three more times president of Conference. He managed Conference because the majority supported his policy; because he formed his mind with rare speed; because he mastered every subject; because he was more moderate in proposals than in manner; because he was a realist; because no one could rival his knowledge and experience; because he bludgeoned opponents with pomposity and rudeness. No one could imagine him young, radical or incompetent. He seemed like a Hercules from his cradle. Across the colonies and Pacific islands, from Jamaica to Tonga and Fiji, spread the Methodist preachers and missions, and Bunting as a secretary of the Wesleyan Missionary Society financed adventure and directed policy. In 1831 he was revered, an Atlas with the care of all the churches. A station among the Bantu was given the name Buntingville. A cultured minister composed lyrics on Methodist patriarchs, and began in lively

---

[1] Workman, i, 405; Smith, iii, 324–6.
[2] 1841: B. Gregory, *Side Lights*, 303–5.

anapaests *Great Jabez the Wesleyan head*.[1] An irritated Mancunian declared with hyperbole that 'the whole Methodist Conference is buttoned up in a single pair of breeches'.

Conference was an assembly of ministers meeting for a few days once a year. Constitutions obey the notorious rule that a temporary assembly cannot control a permanent executive. The ministers were selected for their preaching ability and godliness, and most lacked experience of business. A few able preachers needed to make policy and commend it to an ignorant assembly. The only effective thing which Conference could do was negative; to reject proposals or to change officers and committees. Since the existing officers and committees ran the business efficiently, and since few others wanted this unMethodistical variety of work, Conference was dominated by indispensable officers. When Bunting was absent from sessions of Conference they found that they could not conduct sensible discussion, and adjourned or talked about nothing till he came back.[2] They were pious and charitable men without relish for controversy. An artless preacher came with Sinai-shining face from lowly pulpit into Conference, tried to follow what was afoot, admired the wisdom of the platform, rejoiced in the common worship, and returned with relief to his cottagers.[3] In the complexity of affairs they preferred being governed to governing. An acid critic once told them during a storm, 'It is the misfortune of Methodism that you are always moving special votes of thanks to Dr. Bunting.'[4]

To the itinerant ministry and the circuits a coherent order was indispensable. Yet the strength and expansive power of these societies rested upon a charismatic spirit. Save souls by the power of God and let church order take care of itself—something of this mind was deep in Wesley and kept overflowing among Methodists. The societies practised meetings of personal witness and fervour, love-feasts and watch-nights, unknown to the dull solemnity of contemporary Church of Englandism; and in these assemblies the pentecost of evangelical revival leapt with flame upon simple heads. Bunting and his executive needed to govern Christians suspicious that government

[1] B. Gregory, *Autobiog. Recoll.*, 64. Chew, *Everett*, 379 note. Friendliest study of Bunting in LQR, 69, 1887–8, 115, 'the greatest man, take him for all in all, that Methodism has produced since its founder died'; more balanced in J. H. S. Kent, *Jabez Bunting*, 1955.

[2] Gregory, *Side Lights*, 250, 259, 335.   [3] Cf. Coley, *Life of Thomas Collins*,[2] 218.

[4] Joseph Beaumont in 1848; Gregory, *Side Lights*, 429.

obstructed divine spirit; to prove that office stool and pulpit are not necessary enemies; to show that extraordinary charismata can be reconciled with decency and order; to uphold the apostolic authority of ministers among people who saw the dove alighting upon women and ignorant; to persuade that saving souls and church order need not be incompatibles. Probably no one could have succeeded completely. And the measure of Bunting's success is a measure of his stature and moderation.

The young Connexion was inflaming a sore which afflicts every church; natural antipathy between front-line infantry and general staff, between otherworldly vision and worldly business, between pastors and managers, between missionary priests and Roman Curia, between Anglican vicars and Ecclesiastical Commission. But in Methodism the antipathy was sharper; since the *raison d'être* of the Connexion was conviction that law and discipline which hampered the free course of gospel were bad law and worse discipline.

The spirit of Methodist preachers sometimes resembled a Catholic religious order more than a denomination. The ideal of itinerant ministry was not so remote from the ideals of friars; and like friars the ministers needed to obey their superiors and go unquestioning whither they were sent. Conference stationed ministers in their circuits. But the right to move families from house to house and from Northumberland to Cornwall gave Conference power over ministers, much greater power than any Anglican bishop could expect over his incumbents or their curates. Humble ministers at Conference had a feeling that they should stand well with the managers. And this feeling gave Conference the air of voting for what the platform wanted, and left opposition to a few independent or truculent minds.

Ministers and high Methodists claimed that the preachers were given apostolic authority. The people wanted to receive sacraments from their preachers, but regarded them as incurably lay. The preachers' doctrine of the ministry was higher than the people's doctrine of the ministry. The people had this feeling because so little but a black coat set ministers apart. Many of the preachers had little education, less than their leading laymen. They were not separated from their flocks by vows of celibacy, nor by bishop's hands, nor by knowledge of divinity, nor by literary education, nor by social convention, nor by exclusive right to the pulpit. They were respected only in their religious character. Therefore the rub of the constitution was not only between Vatican and local church. It was the ancient Christian feud between layman and clerk.

Charismata descend from heaven and need no preparation. Cornish Methodists were apt to offend by boasting the ignorance of their preachers.[1] Yet sensible ministers agreed that some preachers were incompetent or eccentric and needed training. Old dissenters who possessed established colleges and trained their ministers rebuked the comparative illiteracy of Methodist preachers. A committee recommended to Conference of 1834 a plan for a theological institution at Hoxton which they shrank from calling a college. The institution roused stern debate. Critical of university-trained Anglicans, simple Methodists feared culture in a pulpit. The college was declared to be antiMethodistical, to reflect upon present preachers, to threaten the moulding of ministers in a uniform pattern, to encourage knowledge of speculative divinity instead of experimental knowledge of saving truth, to 'manufacture' ministers.[2] The opponents uttered long against a recommendation that Bunting be head and theological tutor. Conference bowed to the critics and turned Bunting into visitor. When it saw the word visitor in print it disliked it and turned him into president. Since he was left to define the exercise of his powers as president, he ended as effective head of the institution.

Dr. Samuel Warren used the chance to assail Bunting and autocracy. There came a shower of pamphlets[3], and disgraceful scenes in chapels of the Manchester circuits where Warren was superintendent. Warren's party demanded that Conference vote by ballot and allow laymen at least as spectators. They wanted local societies to be given more independence, Methodist money to be controlled by laymen, no legislation without consent of a majority of the local societies, and the theological institution to be abandoned. No programme could better illustrate the inward tugs of Methodism between local lay responsibility and a central government of preachers. When Warren went to court to secure his reinstatement Lord Chancellor Lyndhurst (25 March 1835) refused to interfere. The decision confirmed that the government of Conference was legally valid. A verdict to the contrary would have made Wesleyan Methodism unrecognisable.

The ardour of Cornish miners or Lancashire cotton-spinners flamed

---

[1] W. H. Rule, *Recollections*, 5.   [2] B. Gregory, *Side Lights*, 171.
[3] Begun by Warren's *Remarks on the Wesleyan Theological Institution*, 1834.

into absolute demands, not patient of ecclesiastical statesmanship or moderation. During the middle thirties a growing movement for temperance turned towards teetotalism. The word *teetotal* was invented by a Lancashire working man in 1834. For it was quickly discovered that a demand for temperance was morally weak compared with a demand for total abstention. And so began the bands of hope, pledges, processions which reached national influence and even the Irish people in the campaigns of Father Mathew. In England they were usually led by Methodists or old dissenters. In 1837–8 the Methodists of Penzance and St. Ives adopted teetotalism as a gospel. They began to desert worship led by ministers who would not sign the pledge and to demand sacraments with unfermented wine. Conference of 1841 prohibited unfermented wine, and closed the chapels to teetotal meetings. They were not in sympathy with local zeal. A prudent Cornish superintendent prevented worse schism by allowing the chapels to Penzance teetotallers and by turning a blind eye to some use of unfermented wine. But by 1842 there was a group of about 600 separated from Conference and organised as the Teetotal Wesleyan Methodists.[1] No one will underestimate the difficulty which faced Conference in preserving the unity of the Connexion. They faced what the Anglican bishops had faced when confronted with Wesley's more enthusiastic assistants.

Ways of worship were as diverse as in the established church. At one end was a respectable London congregation like the Queen Street chapel, where Lord John Russell might occasionally be found, where the atmosphere was solemn and liturgical, where the Book of Common Prayer was largely used. At the other end was the worship of revival. Methodists confessed that every preacher ought to be at heart a revivalist. But they were sometimes perplexed when they met revival. A young minister came in 1840 to visit a class meeting at Guiseley and was mystified to hear strange outcry proceeding from the neighbouring schoolroom, where a crowd of people knelt by the ranged benches and beat upon them in furious anguished wailing penitence. As he gazed upon the scene, the preacher felt out of tune; for he remarked with singular bathos, 'Dear me! in what an agony of earnestness they all seem!'[2] Yet he respected revival while he was surprised at its manifestation.

---

[1] M. S. Edwards, 'The Teetotal Wesleyan Methodists', PWHS, xxxiii, 1961–2, 63.
[2] Gregory, *Autobiog. Recoll.*, 233.

No woman became a Wesleyan Methodist minister. Primitive Methodism, little conscious of difference between lay preachers and ordained preachers, used women as ministers. In Wesleyan Methodism a few women became eminent among local preachers, though some stood within the communion rail and not in the pulpit when they preached.[1] Several of the most celebrated were wives of preachers. Mary Barritt was an itinerant revivalist before she married the preacher Taft; and after marriage the people of Sandiacre somehow felt of the Reverend Zechariah and Mary Taft that the Reverend applied to them both. Conservative Methodist ministers objected to women preaching, some because St. Paul ordered women to keep silence in church, and others on what were described as 'aesthetic' grounds.[2]

Modes of revival were another rub between central and local. Bunting, who stood for decency and order, steadily maintained the rightfulness of revivals. 'As in nature there are thunderstorms,' he said, 'so in grace God sometimes goes out of his ordinary way.'[3] But controlling revival by wisdom is as futile as ruling gusts of wind by opening or shutting windows. Let loose the fire of emotional preaching and it burns unpredictably. The high ministers of Conference disapproved ranting and sought to repress it. They were careful to dissociate themselves from the passionate shouts of Primitive Methodists. From 1843 onwards there were long arguments over an itinerant evangelist from the American Methodists, James Caughey. American methods were organised like a machine, and Caughey had enemies. English preachers of Leeds and Sheffield and Birmingham testified that he wrought wonders in their parishes and had rare gifts of bringing the indecisive to decision. They protested that interference with Caughey would obstruct the work of God. Others could not bear his devices and dodges. They accused him of using decoy penitents to lead others forward to the communion rail,[4] and of pretending to miraculous knowledge about individuals in his congregations. He divided Methodists wherever he went. Conference of 1846 at last resolved to ask the Americans to recall him. It was not easy to persuade Methodists in York or Huddersfield to respect the ban.[5]

Bunting was devoted to the interests of Methodism and commanded the respect of nearly all the best ministers in Conference.

[1] e.g. Mrs. Pattison of Belper; cf. Gregory *Autobiog. Recoll.*, 318.
[2] ibid., 274–5.   [3] Gregory, *Side Lights*, 246.   [4] Gregory, *Side Lights*, 345.
[5] Friendly portrait of Caughey in R. Chew, *Everett*, 347–8; Gregory, *Side Lights*, 401, 412.

But he was a portentous clergyman; and he had the misfortune to arouse obsessive hatred in the breast of one Methodist minister, James Everett.

Everett was a tangled nervous bookseller who accepted a post on circuit out of duty to Conference of 1834, but never forgave Conference for demanding this duty. He peeped quizzically at majestic preachers and mentally stripped them of vesture. He fell into a habit of anonymous pamphlets and justified himself by the plea that Conference could ruin an open critic. His fancy was tickled at finding friends guessing the author. The pamphlets began by housing reasonable arguments. But during the next thirteen years habit or immunity or hatred turned these anonymous sheets into phials of venom without parallel in English religious history since the Marprelate tracts of Shakespeare's day.

The first to be noticed by Conference was a volume called *Wesleyan Centenary Takings*. As early as 1834 Everett wrote a portrait of Bunting not unsympathetic but picturing a lion in the forest among a menagerie of satellite beasts; 'he is great in mind, and great in influence —too great to be forgiven; if he were less so, it might be borne'.[1] After the centenary he extended it into a hundred portraits or caricatures of Wesleyan preachers, the dead under names, the living under asterisks equal in number to the letters of their name. Much of it was delicate and skilful, some of it even charitable, the whole was distasteful; a wit who prided himself on his wit. 'The book,' said Bunting scornfully, 'would not kill a flea.' 'No man should do as a Christian minister,' said Bunting's son, 'that for which he would be horsewhipped if he were not a minister.'[2] Conference of 1841 passed a mild resolution of regret that the book was published.

It is orthodox doctrine that anonymous pamphlets are below notice. If orthodoxy could have triumphed, Methodism would have suffered less agony. But circumstances prevented Conference adopting a posture of silent dignity. Beneath English Methodism bubbled a cauldron of discontent with government by Bunting and his majority. Anonymous pamphlets, if plausible enough, could focus the discomforts of the ungainly Connexion. When Everett started his next row of poison bottles in 1845[3] he gathered all those suspicions of the

[1] *Wesleyan Takings*, 6. For the growth of *Wesleyan Takings* cf. Chew, *Everett*, 322.
[2] Gregory, *Side Lights*, 308.
[3] *Minutes of Conference*, 1849, 276: no. 1 was 1844 or 1845; no. 3 and an enlarged edition of no. 1 in 1847.

London centre which afflicted local preachers, lay financiers, revivalists, radical politicians, friends of dissent, and everyone who feared Methodism becoming respectable. Everett had sufficient grace not (at first) to publish the *Fly Sheets*. They were privately printed, sent to the address of every Methodist minister, and posted in different towns to avert discovery. Everett never acknowledged the authorship. Contemporary Methodists, who knew the man and his books, had no doubt. Apart from the style, they had evidence that he bore all or part of the cost of printing.

About the year 1847 Methodism began to suffer a touch of melancholy, shadow of that partial loss of assurance which afflicted contemporary Anglicans. The people of England resisted conversion. The discovery that membership declined by 5,000 during a year inflicted self-scrutiny and penitence on Methodists. They observed that more than 1,000 emigrated from Cornwall and nearly 3,000 fled from Irish plague.[1] But though decline was explicable and temporary, advance was no longer a plunging rush. Their leaders began to diagnose a familiarity among Englishmen, as though old methods lost their freshness; to regret that the English people were pursuing wealth on a scale unthinkable to their fathers; to condemn newspapers because they inserted political passion into the home; and to attribute something to popular education, because the more men could read, the more men could read infidel books. But whether this diagnosis was true or not, the Methodist air was heavy with criticism and sadness.

The *Fly Sheets* belaboured Robert Newton and a few other ministers in passing, but were aimed to knock Bunting down. Wesleyans had a noble passion for missions, for itinerant preaching, for independence. Bunting rules the missionary society, but has never been a missionary. He has taken station for years on end in London, never itinerates and seldom preaches. He intrigues, bullies, packs committees, breaks rules which he enforces against others. Conference moves at the nod of the dictator . . .

And again the friar-bent of Methodism entered to prevent contempt. They were a godly society of religious men, intent on maintaining standards above the world. Conference was the government of a pastoral superior. Every year it enquired publicly into the qualities of candidates, every year it conducted formal examination of ministers

---

[1] *Minutes of Conference*, 1847, 564.

in office, inflicted rebukes and exhortation. It bore the duty of maintaining high moral standards among Methodist ministers. It now felt as responsible as a superior would feel who knew that one of his monks was defaming the monastery.

On the motion of George Osborn, Conference of 1847[1] allowed Osborn to collect signatures to a declaration that the signatories had nothing to do with the *Fly-Sheets*. Osborn intended the declaration as a test. But 256 ministers refused to sign, partly because they were discontented with the régime, and partly because they objected on principle to this kind of test. In the next eighteen months the dominant and offended party in Conference made trouble infinitely more troublesome by replying in kind; anonymous pamphlets (*Papers on Wesleyan Matters*) against anonymous pamphlets, scandal about ministers, columns of the *Watchman* printing matter of a taste almost as low as that of the *Fly Sheets*. These guerrilla tactics were disastrously blessed by the officials, who treated the *Watchman* as an official organ and sold *Papers on Wesleyan Matters* from the Book Room. These publications gave Everett an excuse for publishing the *Fly Sheets* to the world.

The Hull Conference of 1848 was the first Wesleyan Conference to wear the image of a bear garden, with ill-feeling hanging like a fog over the sessions.[2] Across Europe that year ran the fever of revolution. English Chartists and democrats added their fuel to the inward turmoil of Methodism. Conference proclaimed its allegiance to the throne and constitution, reproved the disloyal and disaffected, urged Methodists to avoid all attacks upon the establishment, asked them not to travel by train on Sundays nor take Sunday newspapers nor share in the Sunday promenade. But its members departed feeling that they did not know whom to trust.[3]

At the Manchester Conference of 1849 the majority, seeing all Methodism in ferment, determined upon expulsion. The *Watchman* recommended Conference to ask the suspects whether they were guilty. George Osborn proposed that the question be put to suspected brethren and amid noisy shouts flung charges that they aimed to subvert Methodism. Everett was called to the front. He was asked, 'Are you the writer or author of the *Fly Sheets*?' He refused to answer.

---

[1] With a large minority voting against, Gregory, *Side Lights*, 410.
[2] Jackson, *Life of Robert Newton*, 279–81.
[3] *Vindicator*, ii, 139; *Minutes of Conference*, 1848, 121–3.

With only two dissentients Conference expelled Everett;[1] then expelled an ox-like radical firebrand, William Griffith, for refusing not to report for the *Wesleyan Times*; and then expelled Samuel Dunn for refusing to stop publishing another reforming newspaper *Wesley Banner*. Samuel Dunn had nothing to do with the *Fly Sheets*. There is evidence that William Griffith read the proof sheets. But this was not the ostensible reason why these two ministers were expelled.

To expel Everett alone might have averted calamity. Whatever virtues he did not display, no one ascribed to him popularity. But the expulsion of the two others bore an appearance of partisan rigour. The day after expulsion Dunn and Griffith preached at the Manchester corn exchange. The expelled ministers appealed to the country—to reforming Methodist critics of Conference, to old dissenters long hostile to conservative Methodists for refusing to ally Methodism with dissent, to everyone who loved the underdog, to the public sense of fair play and the tradition that a man is not required to incriminate himself, to anyone else who would listen. They stumped the country preaching in mechanics' halls or corn exchanges. Their purpose was not to divide Methodism but to compel Conference to become representative and allow elected laymen. In their appeal to the public they were triumphant, in their assault upon Conference they had hardly a chance of victory. The British public could not see that justice had been done and was quick to think of Conference as a hundred popes of England's Jesuitry. The liberal journals joined in national abuse. Even the *Times* thought that members of Conference must be tender hothouse plants to be so shocked at vile pamphlets. 'We are accustomed to see everybody treated in this manner, from the premier to a station clerk, from a bishop to a curate, from an archdeacon to a sexton . . . The *Fly Sheets*, therefore, have not that unusual and pro-digious character in our eyes which they evidently have in the eyes of Conference.'[2] The broad flippant semi-religious public made no allowance whatever for the atmosphere of a religious order, for the polity of entire sanctification. Conference looked worse than Bishop Phillpotts then trying to divest himself of Gorham. 'Talk of the Star Chamber!'

At meetings round the country collections were raised to buy the three expelled men an annuity. But the rebels could not break the iron front of Conference. Aware that they were legally impregnable,

[1] Gregory, *Side Lights*, 456.   [2] T, 3 September 1849.

Conference drew tight and began a long series of local expulsions; members expelled for 'stopping the supplies', not paying their quarterly subscription to the support of ministers.[1] When a few hecklers tried to interrupt the annual meeting of the Wesleyan Missionary Society Bunting was given an ovation of cheers.[2] They clung to the connexional polity and stoutly resisted plans for lay representation. They contended that Wesley's deed made laymen at Conference illegal.[3] Though in London and Bristol and northern cities groups of malcontents broke away, though suspicion seethed through the Connexion, though ministers were hissed as scoundrels, though a few chapels were raided and a few brawls fought in the street and a few sermons shouted down, though the tutor of Richmond theological institution was rumoured to persuade students to do homage to a marble statue of John Wesley, though a count showed that membership of the Connexion fell by 57,000 in 1850–1, though Dunn walked unheralded into Conference and was ejected by force, scattering six sovereigns as he went, Conference of 1850 expelled a fourth minister,[4] and Conference of 1851 mustered only five votes in favour of negotiating with the enemy; five bold men, instantly and publicly advertised by the president for their treachery. After the first error Bunting was no participant. He withdrew thin-skinned into the shadows and was big enough not to be vindictive. The period 1851–2 showed a further fall of 20,946. The worst disaster hit the African missions, which were suddenly starved of funds. After 1852 the loss slowed, and in the five years to 1855 reached 100,469, or a third of the Wesleyan Methodist Connexion. But these are numbers of ticket-holders. The number of those who attended worship as hearers may have been as many again. It was a calamity like the disruption of the Church of Scotland.

'The world,' said simple-hearted Thomas Collins to Dunn, who

---

[1] For account of expulsions, cf. *Life of Joseph Beaumont*, 314ff.; R. C. Swift, 'The Wesleyan Reform Movement in Nottingham', PWHS, xxviii, 1951, 74.

[2] WMM, 1850, 783.

[3] C. Welch, *The Claims of Lay Delegation fully examined*, 1850.

[4] T. Jackson, *Recollections of my own Life and Times*, 339–40. *Wesley Banner*, 1850, 352. Gregory, *Side Lights*, 480. The fourth minister was James Bromley, who voted in 1849 against the expulsion of Dunn and Griffith and joined the agitation. When Dunn came to campaign at Bath, Bromley received him into his house, advertised his meeting with a placard at the front of the house, and attended in sympathy. When the President of Conference visited Bath Bromley published letters against Conference. Cf. *Vindicator*, i, 43ff. Gregory, *Side Lights*, 493. For Samuel Dunn's apologia, see his *Recollections of Thomas Jackson and his acts*, Plymouth 1874.

came to destroy his circuit at Camborne, 'is no proper court of appeal against decisions of the church.'[1]

By July 1852 Dunn was convinced that they had no hope of forcing Conference to yield and became an Independent minister.[2]

Some seceders formed Wesleyan Congregationalist churches; others gravitated towards the Primitive Methodists; others faded out of organised worship; and others succeeded (1857) in joining their various associations in the United Free Methodist Churches; which yet retained a polity more akin to that of Congregationalism than that of Wesleyan Methodism. For ten years more morale sank. 'I used to think', wrote the blind and retired preacher James Dixon in 1870, '. . . that Methodism was the most glorious development of the grace and truth of God ever known in the world; but the horrors of that dreadful time shook my confidence . . .'[3] Fear and suspicion were slow to fade. A member of the 1852 Conference looked back upon it with nausea as an assembly where a clique oppressed into silence a discontent which must be dissembled and obsequious for fear of expulsion. Ten years later, enjoying again liberty of debate, he remembered a saying of Guizot, that a man 'must have breathed under a pneumatic machine to feel the complete enjoyment of free respiration'.[4]

The Wesleyan split left the seceders more radical and the survivors more conservative. The expelled William Griffith held violent republican doctrine, wanting to deport Queen Victoria and destroy the establishment. The survivors returned a little towards their neutrality or friendliness towards the Church of England. The growth of Puseyism shook old allegiances; the Tractarian refusal to allow Anglicans to attend the evening services of Methodism; the rigidity over baptising or burying Methodists. Bunting told Conference of 1841 that 'unless the Church of England will protest against Puseyism in some intelligible form, it will be the duty of the Methodists to protest against the Church of England'. In the year of the Scottish disruption he even wanted an English disruption, that the Puseyites begone.[5] Many students believe that the growing strength of high Anglican doctrine helped Methodists to be finally conscious that they were a

[1] Coley, Life of T. Collins,[2] 307.

[2] Wesley Banner, 1852, iv.

[3] J. H. S. Kent in PWHS, xxxi, 1958, 150. Dixon was writing to Tyerman, on the appearance of his Life and Times of Wesley, a book which he felt to have very much revived his confidence. Dixon had been degraded from superintendency by Conference of 1850 for his sympathy with the agitators, cf. Wesley Banner, 1850, 442.

[4] B. Gregory, Autobiog. Recoll., 418.   [5] Gregory, Side Lights, 317, 348.

separate denomination. But the separation happened by its own momentum. And the secession or expulsions of the early fifties made Wesleyan Methodists more suspicious of old dissent than before. The evangelical phase of Anglican government helped them to recover their friendliness to the established church. Lord Palmerston and Lord Shaftesbury protested against Puseyism in an intelligible form. Methodists praised good Archbishop Sumner as the property and pride of all the churches.[1] Many of the younger ministers after 1860 held an outlook much nearer to that of the old dissenters. Yet the secession of the radical wing allowed Bunting's policy to triumph and kept Wesleyan Methodism to its *via media* between dissent and the Church of England. No more in 1860 than in 1834 were they eager for disestablishment.

2. PRIMITIVE METHODISTS

The evangelical revival was a mighty movement of religious spirit; running from a far right wing in those who carried their ardour of soul into Puseyism or the Ultramontanism of Roman Catholics, to a far left wing in Primitive Methodism. The splinter-groups of Methodism were various; Kilhamites (New Connexion) from the end of the eighteenth century, Wesleyan Association who were an amalgam of the Leeds organ seceders with the Warren seceders, Bible Christians whose congregations were almost all in Cornwall and the west, and a few smaller groups. Far the largest and most important were the Primitive Methodists, formed in 1811 after Hugh Bourne and William Clowes were expelled for holding camp meetings. By 1851 they were five times as large as any other seceded Methodist group, and were nearly a third as numerous as the Wesleyan Methodists. On the evening of 30 March 1851, 229,646 persons worshipped in Primitive Methodist chapels.

All these groups were broadly Methodist in respect for Wesley, doctrine, hymnody, worship, constitution by Conference. But the Primitives were less like the Wesleyans than any other group except a small tribe of heretics in Derbyshire. Their methods included everything that was most abhorrent to Dr. Bunting. They were simple street revivalists of the open air. In Belper they were given the old name of Ranters when they marched singing through the streets. The

---

[1] *Life of Bunting*, i, 51.

name was resented, but stuck. When Victorians talked of Ranters they meant Primitive Methodists.

The social level was lower than in Wesleyan Methodism. Far more Chartists came from Primitive pews. At Bavington Hall in Northumberland sat Squire Shafto, a devout Primitive Methodist who entertained no one but Primitive Methodists and the local parson, believed that the Church of England was collapsing and that Primitive Methodism would take its place. But he was unique; the only house in England, it was later remarked, where Primitive Methodism obtained a vital connexion with the gentry.[1] Squire Shafto died on 5 April 1848 and his successor knew not the Primitives and transferred the chapel to other hands.

By 1850 they were strong in the Potteries, among Durham and Northumberland miners, in the West Riding and Hull and southward into Lincolnshire, where they were unusually strong in remote villages. In Norfolk they were numerous, and Norfolk parsons regarded them as the most ardent of East Anglian Nonconformists. Many of their chapels were called by the address of the street, like the chapels of Wesleyan Methodists; but there were also Bethel, Ebenezer, Providence, Zion, Rehoboth, Moriah, Canaan. Usually the chapels started as cart-shed, joiner's shop, forge, hayloft, converted house or shed. When they were built as chapels they retained the classical façade rather longer than the Wesleyan Methodists, who turned to Gothic about 1848, mainly on a plea of cheapness.

Well into the reign of Queen Victoria the Primitives suffered for their ranting. The Salvation Army is the nearest parallel in the twentieth century and is a direct descendant of revivalist Methodism. The British long ago accepted the brass bands of the Salvation Army as part of a delightful and varied scenery and told their children not to stare. In the first years of Queen Victoria a procession of Ranters singing hymns through the streets, a preacher standing on a box at a fair to denounce its vanity, a camp meeting held on a race-course, might rouse the people to that violence and mob law which fifteen years later attacked the London ritualists. Bulls were released into their street congregations, carts were trotted through them, boys banged kettles and drums and saucepans, vergers rang bells to drown their short sermons and long prayers. Several preachers were beaten or had

[1] H. B. Kendall, *The Origin and History of the Primitive Methodist Church*, 1906, ii, 159–60.

clothes torn in shreds, others were spattered with dung and rotten eggs, buckets were emptied over their heads. A few were convicted of riot or of obstructing the highway and were imprisoned. A few cottagers who gave them shelter had their windows smashed.

These popular games diminished through the thirties and became exceptional in the forties. The Winchester magistrates of 1834 behaved justly and thereafter it was less difficult for the assailed to get redress.[1] The population became accustomed, and found old antics to be new and godly respectability among the poor. But while the heroic age of ranting and persecution lasted it befriended the Primitives by advertising their wares and their courage. They kept a martyrology, and told how a Sandbach bull was headed for the congregation, but kept kneeling down in the field as if to do obeisance;[2] how a chapel was wrongly converted into a stable, but the horses died so frequently that the owners reconverted to a chapel; how at Dalton-in-Furness three horns and a rattle were sounded in the preacher's ears as he prayed by the village cross, and how he rose from his knees with the cry 'I can praise thee amidst all the din of hell'; how at Newark market the parson caused the fire-engine to be wheeled out and the preacher hosed, and half an indignant crowd turned and broke the engine into fragments. When a ranting preacher arrived at a Hampshire village of the thirties the parson went round telling the people to keep indoors and shut all the doors and windows—and was obeyed. We can imagine that a Denison would thus have protected the parishioners of East Brent, or a Hawker the parishioners of Morwenstow. But even in the thirties not so many villages of England would thus have obeyed an order not to see the fun. In the north rare crowds assembled. About 10,000 people assembled at a camp meeting during the Sunderland Conference of 1833. They grew fast. In 1830, 35,733 members were ticketed; 1839, doubled; 1850, 104,762; 1860, 132,114. They grew quickest in their youth of rant and missile. The last arrest of a preacher was 1843, the first temporary decline in numbers 1842.[3]

Hugh Bourne was no preacher (except in Sunday schools) but a tough argumentative organiser, William Clowes the preacher. The life of Clowes is a fascinating study in the flowing of spirit among

---

[1] Petty, *History*, 1864, 346.

[2] H. B. Kendall, *History*,[2] 1919, 60.

[3] Cf. Petty, *History*, 404–5, 485–6, 542–3, for statistics; Davison, *Life of Clowes*. 90, 202–5; H. B. Kendall, ii, 62.

little chapels or camps. Demons tried to throw him from the pulpit, while glorious unction streamed from heaven and confusion smote the hosts of hell.[1] Like the Quakers and seekers of the Commonwealth, these preachers were assured of their inspiration. Wesley himself taught the doctrine of entire sanctification, and Wesleyan Methodist preachers interpreted the doctrine in language consistent with evangelical orthodoxy. Some Primitive Methodist preachers pressed not only instantaneous conversion but instantaneous holiness upon their simple people. The meetings on occasion became uncontrollable. While worshippers banged at the tops of the pews or struck the collection plates with their fists or ejaculated wildly from the singers' pew, and while wicked men crowded at the door jeering and cursing, the divine power would descend like a rushing wind and overpower the elect with its glory.[2] Their evangelism was passionate pleading. In February 1830 two young Primitives met in a wood near the county boundary and hidden by the undergrowth of a coppice they knelt in snow and pleaded hour after hour the prayer 'Lord, give us Berkshire!' At last the younger rose from his knees with assurance and a sense of possessing the earth, 'Yonder country's ours! Yonder country's ours, and we will have it.'[3] Two years later this younger preacher, Thomas Russell, evangelised Wantage and was bruised with stones, his clothes torn in rags, his body coated in slime and mud and stinking eggs. He washed the clothes in a canal and went to Farringdon, washed his clothes in a pond and went to Shrivenham, washed his clothes in a brook and preached a fourth sermon, this time encountering nothing but a stone which cut his lip. That day he walked thirty-five miles, preached four sermons, was three times stinking with eggs and filth. Next Sunday he went back to Wantage and Farringdon. A wealthy Quaker of Farringdon gave him a stand on private ground for three Sundays. On the fourth Sunday he returned to Wantage market and was pelted till his spirits broke. Thereafter he rose early and preached in Wantage at 5 a.m. on weekday mornings. But there was no congregation in Wantage until twenty years later.

The more property the less corybantic. The more they met in chapels the less they shouted in streets. Through the thirties Conference slowly established control of building and stipends, not without a few secessions. Their preachers now looked like pre-Tractarian

---

[1] Davison, *Life of Clowes*, 198–9.   [2] Davison, *Life of Clowes*, 199.
[3] Petty, 268; H. B. Kendall, *History*, 1919, 55–56.

clergymen. William Clowes began his ministry by dressing like a commercial traveller or tradesman and ended in a white tie and black coat like Bunting or Gorham.[1] Conference of 1842 suddenly retired their founders Hugh Bourne and William Clowes, to the vexation of Bourne. In 1844 there was even talk of a theological institution for training preachers, but the plan was squashed like a fly. Sooner or later a sufficient number of immoral or otherwise calamitous preachers would infallibly strengthen the arguments of those who demanded training. As late as 1860 the people were said to fear the idea of a college. Five years later the college was open.[2]

Conference moved towards conservatism. It was distinguished from Wesleyan Methodism in that districts sent laymen as well as preachers to represent them. In 1845 Conference ruled that these representatives must be senior; no preacher eligible until he had travelled eighteen years, no lay official until he had been a member for ten years. Conference became an assembly of Nestors. The youthful wildfire spent itself in district meetings. Thus Primitive Methodism underwent a constitutional tension similar to that endured by Wesleyan Methodism, centre versus circumference. Conference was secretive and surrounded its sessions with high prickly hedges. The published minutes of early Conferences look designed to give the minimum of information. In 1845 an association was formed to reform Conference. But there were two momentous differences from Wesleyan Methodism, which prevented fission; first, tension was not agonised by the antipathy of clerk versus layman, for in Primitive Methodism the laymen felt superior; and second, the district felt sufficiently strong and sufficiently independent to go its own way. The Hull circuit kept its preachers on a tight rein. Each quarter day they enquired into their preachers so far as their cut of hair and coat. In 1832 they suspended a preacher for being late at chapel, not getting up early, speaking crossly to some children at breakfast, and eating the inside of a pie while leaving the crust.[3]

Temperance, as meaning total abstention, was still rejected by Wesleyan Methodists, but gained wide support from Primitives in the twenty years to 1850. Conference of 1842 passed a resolution backing temperance societies. Hugh Bourne became a preacher for

[1] Davison, *Life of Clowes*, 237.
[2] September 1865: H. B. Kendall, *History*[2], 1919, 97. Sunderland was opened 1868 and closed 1882; Manchester College (which later developed into Hartley College), 1881.
[3] H. B. Kendall, ii, 84.

teetotalism. But the practice varied with the district. Occasionally a decision of Conference led to a small district schism. In 1853 Conference approved a new hymnbook, revised from Bourne's hymnbook and edited by John Flesher, who four years before consolidated the rules of the Connexion in a single volume. The Andover district could not tolerate the new book and broke away. From the standpoint of literature, poetry, and scholarship Flesher's hymnbook was the most botched and mangled production in the history of Christian hymnody. But the Old Hymnbookers of Andover did not make schism on grammar, poetry or scholarship.

Most Victorians still despised them as Ranters. But as they came out of the ranting epoch they won a repute from gentry for elevating the moral standards of the poor. John Walter of the *Times* enclosed a plot of waste ground at Wokingham and gave it for their chapel. It was suspected that poachers were fewer when the Primitive Methodist chapel was strong. A sad Wesleyan Methodist of 1853 said that now the only denominations to possess the confidence and affection of the poor were the Church of England and the Primitive Methodists.[1] George Borrow published a description of a Primitive meeting on Mousehold Heath, with half-dozen men in sober coats preaching from a wagon; the crowd entirely of labourers and their wives and children —'dusty people, unwashed people, people of no account whatever, and yet they did not look a mob'. And Borrow thanked God in 1851 that there were plenty of such preachers to persist through poverty and contempt 'amidst the dark parishes of what, but for their instrumentality, would scarcely be a Christian England'. But Borrow was very odd.[2]

3. PRESBYTERIANS

A. *Unitarians*

The old Presbyterian congregations, descendants of the seceders at the restoration of Charles II, had slowly departed from the doctrine of the Trinity. By 1830 the majority were Unitarian in creed.

[1] T. Ensor, *The Crisis*, 1853, 9.

[2] Lavengro, 1851, chapter 25; the meeting is supposedly of 1820. Borrow till late in life professed himself an Anglican, and was indignant when the *Times* inferred from *The Bible in Spain* that he was not. He said in *Romany Rye* (1900 ed., 346) that he was a sincere member of the old-fashioned Church of England, in which is more religion and less cant than in any other church. His evangelical friends protested because he subscribed to nonconformist as well as Anglican schools. But his attitude to Anglican clergy was detached. His leading religious conviction was hatred of the pope. Cf. H. Jenkins, *The Life of George Borrow*, 1912, 141–2, 348, 355–6, 373, 445.

As lately as 1828 this departure from traditional doctrine mattered little. Most of them were not philosophical in their doctrine. They accepted the miracles of the New Testament and professed old-fashioned orthodoxy; though their orthodoxy denied the Trinity and questioned the received teaching about atonement and hellfire. Their sermons were more addressed to the head than those of dissenting pastors. Their congregations were educated. They were more varied in their beliefs, and readier to confess in the pulpit that they did not know. Lant Carpenter at Bristol used the language of *Examine for yourselves* instead of the language *Believe as I do*,[1] and was wont to avow publicly his difficulties about atonement or infant baptism. Despite these differences, they had worked harmoniously with other dissenters. But in the age after 1832 doctrinal difference mattered.

Leading Unitarians proclaimed their tenet openly. Independents were uneasy that under the umbrella-name of dissent they were allied with religious groups to whom some denied the name of Christian. Oxford men said that dissent led to heresy. Orthodox dissenters were determined to prove the criterion untrue. They could not prove it without loosening their connexion with Unitarians. Like the Anglican right wing, the dissenting right became more orthodox in its orthodoxy, more precise in its dogmatic system. Outspoken Presbyterians and outspoken Independents headed for breach.

The breach was caused by two lawsuits.

Unitarian congregations occupied the property and used the endowments of their Presbyterian forebears. Sooner or later the continuity between old Trinitarian and new Unitarian was likely to be tested. Were they the same body or a new body masquerading under the old name and teaching doctrines contrary to the doctrines of the old? If they were a new body, had they any right to the property and endowments of the old?

In 1816 the minister of the Unitarian chapel at Wolverhampton was discovered to be a Trinitarian. The congregation dismissed him. Encouraged by one of the trustees, the minister refused to be ejected. The congregation took legal action to eject him and failed. It left the chapel and retired to a large room. The vice-chancellor held that the chapel was built when it was penal to be a Unitarian, that the law could therefore have upheld no endowment to support Unitarian worship; and that money later collected, even in a confessedly Uni-

[1] *Memoirs*, 159, 222.

tarian trust, was married to the old endowment and must be allotted to Trinitarians.[1]

The Wolverhampton case put into jeopardy the chapel and the endowment of every Unitarian congregation founded before 1813, when Unitarian opinion nominally ceased to be penal.

In 1704 Lady Hewley left a fund to maintain poor and godly preachers of Christ's holy gospel, or their widows, in the six northern counties of England. In 1830 the income was about £2,900 and in the hands of Unitarian trustees. Independents at Manchester began a lawsuit to prove that the endowments were in the wrong hands. In 1833 the vice-chancellor's court held that only Trinitarian dissenters were eligible to benefit by the endowment; and on appeal the judgment was confirmed by the lord chancellor in 1836 and by the House of Lords in 1842. It was evident, though not fully evident till 1842, that anyone could challenge a Unitarian congregation and strip its endowments provided that the congregation existed before 1813.

The Wolverhampton chapel case and the Lady Hewley case divided English dissenters. The schism was not consummated until March 1836, when a majority of Unitarian congregations of London separated themselves from the Protestant dissenting deputies and so marked the break in the alliance of old dissent.

Irish Presbyterians who were Trinitarians observed that they could acquire the chapels and endowments of Irish Presbyterians who were Unitarian. The wealthy Eustace Street chapel in Dublin possessed an endowment of £2,600 a year. The suit over this chapel was passing through the courts in the spring of 1844; and the verdict, as everyone knew, must follow the precedent of Lady Hewley's case. And this was not the only consequence. Every Unitarian chapel in England might be the subject of litigation. Unitarian congregations dared not use their money to repair the chapels. Lawyers predicted that there might be 200 or 300 cases in the courts if nothing were done. A heart-rending example of a widow named Mary Armstrong was put forward; her husband had been a Unitarian minister, and she was just able to support herself and four daughters on an allowance from a trust which was now in doubt. Lady Hewley's case put £12,600[2] of Lady Hewley's money into the hands of the lawyers; and not even the lawyers could contemplate with equanimity the time and trouble and ruin of trusts which might ensue.

[1] *Unitarian Mag.*, 1835, 124.   [2] Cf. J. E. Carpenter, *Martineau*, 233.

With Peel's help the law lords of both parties—Lyndhurst, Cottenham, Brougham, and Campbell—introduced into the House of Lords
on 3 May 1844 a bill to remedy injustice. This bill was not to reverse
the Hewley decision, but intended to prevent the 200 or 300 suits
prophesied. The first form of the bill, known soon as the dissenters
chapels bill, simply declared that where there is no trust deed determining doctrine, usage or polity, usage of a certain number of years
(twenty-five years was soon agreed) should be taken as conclusive
evidence of the right of any congregation to possess a chapel, or
schools, burial-grounds or endowments. But in the committee of the
House of Lords a third clause, invented by Lord Cottenham, was
added; namely that in pending suits the defendants should have the
benefit of the act. The clause was designed to protect the Eustace
Street chapel, and interfere in another suit already started in Ireland,
that over the Strand Street chapel in Dublin.

The dissenters chapels bill encountered opposition on a scale which
Peel and his cabinet seem not to have expected. The Roman Catholics,
moderate Anglicans, the small body of General Baptists, the Unitarians, and various sensible or uncommitted persons were friendly to
the bill. But religious England, especially evangelical England, was
opposed to it. Petitions rained upon both Houses. There were those
like Henry Phillpotts, Bishop of Exeter, who believed that though all
the penalties against Unitarians had been abolished in 1813, it was still
illegal to be a Unitarian (Lord Cottenham asked the bishop in the
lords where he would try to prosecute them)[1] and certainly wrong
that the government should encourage 'a heresy of the gravest and
most malignant character'. Wesleyans and orthodox dissenters were
vehement against the bill, and the evangelical clergy of the Church
of England joined with them at Exeter hall and on public platforms.
Bishop Blomfield of London believed that the provision of twenty-
five years' usage invited the peril that trusts would be put to many
uses; that a chapel designed for Christian ends might later be found
to be preaching, as he said, socialism or atheism. There were others
who thought the third clause, giving the defendants the benefit of the
act in suits now pending, was equivalent to retrospective legislation,
and were quick to point out how the Eustace Street case had been so
postponed and further postponed that it was still pending, though
everyone knew what the verdict must be. There was some popular

[1] Hansard, lxxiv, 601.

feeling in the country. Passers-by pointed at Unitarian chapels as filched from sleeping Presbyterians, or eyed their ministers as persons living on embezzled money.[1]

The Church of England as a whole was not deeply moved. The Bishops of Exeter and London spoke against the bill, the Whig Bishops of Norwich and Durham voted for it; but most of the English bishops attended a charity festival instead of the main lords debate.

The act was important as a further extension of the toleration act to others besides 'orthodox dissenters'. And it was carried by a Tory government.

Unitarians like many dissenters were Whig or radical. They expected religious equality from Whig cabinets. Dr. Lant Carpenter of Bristol, doyen among Unitarian pastors, published an *Apostolical Harmony* in the autumn of 1838. Bold beyond all precedent, he wished to dedicate the book to Queen Victoria. He applied to Lord Holland, whom he knew in friendship, as a member of the Whig cabinet. Holland asked Lord John Russell as home secretary; and on receiving an assurance from Holland that the work was uncontroversial, Russell advised the queen to permit the dedication. Dr. Carpenter received Lord Holland's sanction for his choice of words. In October Lord Ashley, who deplored the moral descent down which hours of Melbourne's company was leading the queen, assailed Melbourne fiercely. Melbourne shrugged his shoulders. He picked up the book from Queen Victoria's table and said, 'I don't know that it was the most prudent thing to recommend, but it is difficult to say to a man, I can't allow it because you are a Unitarian.'[2]

This neutrality was long in descending from crown to people. In 1842 the lord chamberlain felt bound to refuse to present to the queen a sermon by a most orthodox dissenter on the birth of the Prince of Wales.[3] For many years the *Times* continued to refuse Unitarian advertisements. As late as 1866 a good candidate was excluded from a professorship at University College in London because he was Unitarian.[4]

[1] Cf. *Times*, 7 June 1844, 4.
[2] *Memoirs of Lant Carpenter*, 419–21; Queen Victoria's *Journal*, 18 October 1838, RA; Shaftesbury's *Diary*, 13 October 1838.
[3] Hansard, cxiv, 252; *Life of Joseph Fletcher*, 480–2.
[4] Drummond-Upton, *Life of James Martineau*, i, 408.

The Unitarians were not an expanding body. In 1851 they had 229 places of worship in England and Wales, and the number varied little through the century. Their educated constituency is shown by the single fact that on 30 March 1851 the morning worshippers in chapel were more than twice the evening worshippers; 27,612 in the morning and 12,406 in the evening. They attracted sympathy from non-Christian philosophers who suspected deism of being more rational than Christianity. But the needs for which they contended were in part met by the slow liberating of orthodox divinity.

To minds troubled by Victorian doubt they often appeared a resting-place which was at best temporary, a wobble between confident faith and confident scepticism. They grumbled sometimes that they only grew by other men's doubts.

Whether Unitarians were Christians was hotly argued in the heyday of early Victorian dogmatism. Yet they begot one of the leading Christian divines of all the Victorian churches: James Martineau. In the course of a life of ninety years Martineau changed the face of the Unitarian denomination and influenced the advance of English liberal divinity.

Martineau's first charge was the Eustace Street chapel in Dublin, which he promptly resigned because half the congregation refused to back him in declining the government grant called *Regium Donum*. For twenty-five years after 1832 he ministered in Liverpool; became professor (1837) and later principal (1869) of the training college for preachers, Manchester New College, which moved from Manchester to London in 1853.[1]

Unitarianism was compounded of two incompatible traditions: evangelical biblicism and the rational deism of the Enlightenment. Some Unitarians were Bible-Protestants, orthodox and rigid, accepting miracles and plenary inspiration, fervent in religious life, distinguished from evangelical dissenters only by the conviction that the Trinity was not a doctrine of scripture. Others were the heirs of old deism; preaching rational religion, unpoetic common sense, anti-evangelical, suspicious of fervour and enthusiasm, calm in religious life and arid in religious thought, believing that more good was done

---

[1] He retired in 1885 and died at the age of 90 in 1900. The theological works of chief importance were published at or after retirement: *Types of Ethical Theory*, 1885; *A Study of Religion*, 1888; *The Seat of Authority in Religion*, 1890. He was another of Huguenot descent.

by books than by emotional sermons. Observers found them wanting
in earnestness. They seemed readier to assail orthodoxy than sin.
James Martineau gave Jane Welsh Carlyle the impression of being
'singularly *in earnest* for a Unitarian'.[1]

Even attitudes to the Trinity divided the denomination. One group
denied the Trinity because it was unscriptural and thought its reasonableness nothing to do with the question. The other group denied the
Trinity because it was unreasonable and thought the evidence of
scripture nothing to do with the question. Among biblical Unitarians
revelation controlled reason, among deist Unitarians reason controlled revelation. The name Unitarian gave discomfort to both sides.
The evangelical came to question it because the label tied them to such
unevangelical philosophers as Blanco White or Frank Newman or
James Martineau. The philosophers disliked it because the label proclaimed them to share in a sect which wasted strength in banging
texts.

The philosophers slowly established dominance. The Lady Hewley
case encouraged progressive minds, for the plea in law rested upon the
claim that within living societies doctrine cannot be static. Converts
strengthened the philosophers; for though the denomination made
few converts, its eminent converts came there to find a more rational
faith: Blanco White and Frank Newman and John Sterling and Arthur
Clough. As ex-Tractarians brought new ability and stimulus to the
Church of Rome, ex-Anglicans brought ability and stimulus and
social prestige to Unitarianism. But James Martineau was no convert.
And in Martineau devotional fire derived from evangelicals married
philosophical power stemming from deists.

Martineau was naturally impassioned and was brought up on the
writings of Anglican evangelicals. From early years he wished to
destroy the dry old-fashioned rationalism which led a Unitarian
hymnbook of 1819 to exclude the word *soul* because the doctrine
of a soul had no rational foundation.[2] He preached in high philosophical language with an excess of flowering eloquence, and congregations found him impossible to follow.

To feed devotion upon the lyrics of the Christian centuries he

[1] *New Letters & Memorials of Jane Welsh Carlyle*, 1903, i, 150.

[2] Hymn-book issued at Warrington. The term *soul* 'cannot fail to excite unpleasant
feelings in many serious minds while engaged in the solemnities of public worship':
Carpenter, *Martineau*, 75.

published a hymnbook of 1840 which dared to use hymns from the Roman Breviary and Keble besides the evangelical hymnody of Watts and Doddridge and the Wesleys. Like so many religious teachers of the Victorian age, he appealed to affection and imagination. In harmony with this poetic soul lived a philosophical mind of courage and power. At first he retained his inherited belief in all the miracles of the New Testament and denied the name of Christian to anyone who rejected this belief. Blanco White, with whom he was never intimate, wrote to criticise the view; and by 1840 Martineau shared White's opinion, and made his change of mind public five years later. Henceforth his philosophy developed; a Platonic idealism fighting against a religion of doctrinal words, demanding a religion of feeling and consciousness; sympathetic to every movement of the religious heart; sitting lightly to the history of the New Testament, but confident in the character of Jesus as revelation of God; contending that true revelation is of a person and not of statements. Until 1860 non-Unitarians took little notice and half the Unitarians were afraid. But there came a time after Darwin when even orthodox Anglicans were grateful for this champion who linked devotion of soul to freedom of mind and wove from them a harmonious system of religious thought.

B. *Presbyterian Church of England*

The few surviving congregations of Trinitarian doctrine looked for aid to Scotland. Year after year deputations were heard in the General Assembly at Edinburgh. But the established Church of Scotland was reluctant. To a great majority of laity in both countries common establishment meant more than difference of polity. Most Englishmen worshipped with the Church of Scotland when they crossed the border; Scotsmen as naturally worshipped with the Church of England. Army officers thought it their loyal duty as servants of the queen to worship with the established church in either country.[1] Keble and other Tractarians were reminded too vividly of Oliver Cromwell when they went to Scotland; and took far more interest in communion with the little episcopal church in Scotland. But the established Church of Scotland was not eager to justify episcopal dissent in Scotland by cherishing Presbyterian dissent in England. To moderate Scottish divines the dissent of English Presbyterians was

[1] Cf. Hope-Scott's father, in Ornsby, i, 60.

more momentous than their nominal Presbyterianism. Even under Scottish evangelical dominance the General Assembly acted cautiously. In response to the English requests the General Assembly of 1839 acknowledged the independence of the Presbyterian Church of England and offered friendly intercourse by deputations.

Meanwhile the English congregations attempted to organise themselves into a polity more agreeable to their name. Scotsmen steadily immigrated into England and swelled the demand for Scottish polity and Scottish modes of worship. Many Scotsmen settled in the great Lancashire cities or in Northumberland and Durham. The Presbyterian Church of England was built when Scottish immigrants in the north were brought into constitutional union with the scattered remnants of an older English Presbyterianism. At a convention of May 1836—the year of the London schism with the Unitarian congregations— congregations of Lancashire and the north-west agreed to form a synod of two presbyteries and to adopt the Scottish (Westminster) confession of faith. In 1839 the presbyteries of London and Newcastle upon Tyne were brought into the synod; Berwick in 1840, Northumberland in 1842, and Birmingham (hitherto part of the London presbytery) in 1848. The changing attitude of the synod was illustrated by the change of name. More than half of them began by thinking themselves a church for Scotsmen in England. It took them forty years to think of themselves as indigenous and to revalue the older English tradition. The synod of Manchester in 1839 called it 'the Presbyterian Church of England in connexion with the Church of Scotland'. The synod of London in 1849 changed it to 'the Presbyterian Church in England'. Finally the synod of Liverpool in 1876 changed it to 'the Presbyterian Church of England'.[1] They steadily protested the harm which they suffered because Unitarians preserved the name of Presbyterian.

Towards the end of the Victorian age they became a channel by which the best of Scottish divinity influenced Christian thinking in England. But the Scottish disruption of 1843 weakened Scottish divinity for nearly half a century. The Presbyterians in England strongly sympathised with the seceders. The synod of 1844 passed a resolution asserting a church independent of the state. But true to their desire to be a home to visiting Scotsmen, they continued friendship with both sides of the Scottish schism.

[1] Leone Levi, *Digest*, 1877, 8.

4. INDEPENDENTS

Between 1830 and 1860 the chapels of Congregational dissenters turned from a loose federation into something like a modern denomination. This feat was not accomplished without disquiet. To organise a denomination meant a version of central authority. Central authority must mean that the chapel was not supreme. Independents held the axiom that each chapel was sovereign. In aggregate they represented something over half a million souls, perhaps as many as three quarters of a million, in 1851. Mann reckoned that their chapels housed 515,071 persons at the best attended service—significantly the morning service—of 30 March 1851. But Independency made for a larger element of guesswork even than usual in Mann's calculation.

The chapels had different histories. Some of them could trace a continuous existence to Cromwell and Commonwealth. Some were once Wesleyan or Presbyterian chapels, others were once Anglican proprietary chapels where in 1830 the liturgy of the prayer book was still used. Several were offspring of the evangelical revival, founded to belong to no named denomination. The old description Independent still flourished.

The first centripetal force was disability in civil justice. The rights of dissenters over marriage or burial or church rate were more easily protected by county associations than by little powerless groups. The establishment roused common interest among its enemies. The crisis of the reform bill stimulated the sense of political necessity. County associations had long existed and slowly began to act in still wider associations. The ministry was a national link. For Congregational dissenters rarely shared a Methodist suspicion of learned ministers. They were proud of their old colleges (though slow to call them colleges) and of their education. Confessing that the ministers could not rival the classical and mathematical attainments of Anglican clergy, they reminded the public that they selected their ministers only from pious persons. If the refusal of Cambridge and Oxford and Durham to give degrees to dissenters was a grievance, it hardly affected the educational standards of their pastors. They confessed that their pastors were poorly paid; and yet reminded the public that the best stipends were as high as £500 or £700 a year, that 4,000 clergymen of the established church were paid less, and that ministers did not need family influence or patronage to receive such stipends.[1] Most of them were better cared for than the Primitive Methodist preacher with his basic £1 or 22s. a week. One minister in Stepney is believed to have earned £1,500 a year. But some ministers were at the Primitive Methodist level. In 1853 ninety-seven Independent ministers received less than £50 a year.[2]

The chapels drew ministers from several colleges; and the need to support colleges and then to make stipends adequate could be met only by national endeavour. The existence of old trust funds and bequests for Congregational dissenters meant that trustees dispensed money from a centre in London. The earliest existed since 1695 as the Congregational Fund Board, which raised money by annual collections to assist poor ministers in the country and students for the ministry. But many Congregationalists of 1830 had never heard of this Board. The need for central funds became always more clamorous. A new chapel in a poor village could not be built without outside help. Independents found a useful parallel to this central need in the acts of the London Missionary Society, a strongly organised authority without which foreign missions could neither expand nor survive. In theory the London Missionary Society was non-denominational. In fact its members and missionaries were nearly all Congregationalist. The leaders of the London Missionary Society, who experienced the benefits of union abroad, were prominent in pressing for union at home. The advance of their nearest evangelical neighbours the Methodists also fostered the opinion that central government offered benefits.

Some Congregational dissenters thought that the union ought to be of all Independent congregations, whether Congregational or Baptist. But the Baptist chapels successfully formed their own union[3] and the early thirties were years when doctrinal disagreement loomed large. Doctrinal disagreement gave the final impetus to the movement for union. For it was observed that everyone else had now a central office and library, and that Dr. Williams's library, which Independents were accustomed to regard as their home, was in the hands of Unitarian trustees. A building at Finsbury Circus was secured in 1831 as library and office. They awaited officers to put inside the office.

Twenty years before an attempted union failed because Independents wanted to guard their independence. The union of 1831 almost

---

[1] CM, 1836, 12, 15.   [2] Tudur Jones, 229-30.   [3] See below, pp. 414-15.

failed because various ministers wanted too much union. They wanted a representative assembly with debates, though they allowed that decisions could only be sent to separate chapels as recommendations. They spoke rashly of protecting trusts and meeting-houses, of improving architecture, of remedying defects of baptismal registers, of providing pensions for ministers. This rashness almost wrecked the union. Opponents argued that hierarchies spring from inconsiderable beginnings. They had no desire for a new organisation which cumbered the ground, and feared that Independents would become a new sect or denomination. 'It is our glory', wrote one, 'that hitherto we have been no sect. We subscribe no creed. We submit to no synod or conference. We are not properly a body . . . Incorporation would go far to constitute us a sectarian church, whether we accept the designation or reject it.'[1] The opposition manifested some of the same suspicion as the anti-Bunting party in Methodism. They were upper room versus grandiloquent Goth, village versus London, prophet versus official, personal versus impersonal, pulpit versus desk.

On 13 May 1831 the union was proposed at a meeting of eighty-two ministers and nineteen laymen in the Congregational Library. The basis of union was perforce self-contradictory, an agreement among men who agreed not to unite; a union, said the resolution, 'founded on a full recognition of their own distinctive principle, namely, the scriptural right of every separate church to maintain perfect independence in the government and administration of its own particular affairs; and therefore that the union shall not in any case assume legislative authority or become a court of appeal'. The Congregational Union was founded as a consultative body, to collect statistics, make representations to government, send an annual letter to the constituent churches, and hold an annual meeting where every minister or official of a congregation might attend and vote. They sent the plan to the English county associations. Of the thirty-four English county associations, four made no reply, four refused to join 'for the present' and the remaining twenty-six were most favourably disposed. The 1832 meeting allowed individual churches as well as associations to be represented. They asked all the churches for subscriptions.[2]

At the end of a year the expenditure was £27, the receipts £9. Evidently union was not a Vatican nor even a standing committee of

---

[1] Peel, *These Hundred Years*, 54: Peel's is the fullest account of these negotiations.
[2] At least twelve county associations, in fact, stood out; cf. Peel, 65, 82, 116, 193.

the Methodist Conference. The meeting of May 1833 adopted a declaration of the faith, church order and discipline of the Congregational or Independent dissenters. This was extraordinary; for many Independent churches were decided that they subscribed to no human creed nor formulary. The declaration stated that it was not intended that it should be put forth with authority, nor as a standard to which assent should be required; that the Union disallowed the utility of creeds and articles of religion as a bond of union; that they were only informing the public what was commonly believed among them. They nevertheless claimed with pride that they were far more agreed in doctrine than any church which enforced a human standard of orthodoxy. The declaration (with the exception of memorialist language about the Lord's Supper) is a fair and large statement of moderate Calvinist doctrine. Article 9 asserted despite Oliver Cromwell that the union of church and state was wrong. Time came when Calvinism and Congregationalism parted company. Even in 1833 there were a few who resented this 'creed' and could not see why if creeds were useless it was useful to publish this. But at first they were rare. Twenty-one thousand copies were sold in a year, the walls of vestries were hung with it, and as lately as 1858 it was taken into the Congregational Year Book. Once there, it was difficult to dislodge and remained until 1918,[1] long after it was obsolete.

During the thirties the officers of the Union uneasily expected it to die. In 1837 the committee urged that it would be wrong for the churches to let it die. Slowly county associations joined; among the latest Oxford and West Berkshire in 1841, Cornwall 1846, Hampshire 1848. But they did not send money. The Union could do nothing to help home missions or pensions. Even in 1839 the income was £117 and the expenditure £574.[2] So far from helping the debts on poor chapels, the committee expended energy in wondering how to pay its own debts.

The Union was saved by the patience and skill of Algernon Wells, a delightful emotional pastor who was secretary of the Union from 1837 until his death in 1850; and still more by the Congregational Hymn Book. The usual hymnbook was *Psalms and Hymns* of Isaac Watts. To edit the necessary supplement the Union selected as editor the layman Josiah Conder. The excellent book was published in 1836 and by 1839 sold 40,000 copies. Since the profits went to the Union,

[1] Peel, 77. [2] Peel, 83, 92.

the worst financial troubles were past. If the separate churches would not support their Union efficiently, the Union would support itself by publications.

Independent churches were fortunate in the men at their disposal. After selecting a notable editor for their hymnbook, the Union was lucky or intelligent enough to discover a brilliant journalist to run their newspapers. John Campbell was from 1829 the minister of the London Tabernacle, second in succession to George Whitefield himself.

By 1845 the Union was more organised than its money or its function yet warranted. There was a general committee, a literature committee, an education committee, a superannuation committee, a publication department; and under the Union were affiliated Colonial and Home Missionary Societies. This structure bore little relation to the still anarchic facts of Independent life. The historian of the Union[1] compared it to a kneeling camel with an unwieldy ill-balanced load.

For a dozen years from 1845 the Union ran into such storms that it might easily have been destroyed. The trials of the Methodist Conference brought central church governments into further disrepute. By instinct and tradition Independents befriended the underdog and were quick to join the assault upon Bunting. Campbell knew that good journalism needed targets for battery and pounded away at Methodist autocracy. The relation between Methodist and Independent was never comfortable. Methodist held consciously aloof from dissenter and dissenter resented the implied repudiation. Meanwhile the death of Algernon Wells in 1850 removed a secretary who understood how to manage miscellaneous assemblies.

Campbell irritated members of his denomination. Not only did he edit the two official newspapers under the Union. He added to his giant labours a third newspaper, the *British Banner*; and although he muted his thunder in the official press, he used the *Banner* for grand noises. About the assault on the Church of England he held moderate views, and assailed those Congregationalists who planned for a political programme of disestablishment. He greatly disliked the Evangelical Alliance, which most Congregationalists loved. He lashed about him with a flail. Members of the Union found it hard to prevent doctrines of Campbell being mistaken for doctrines of the Union. He was official editor of the Union's newspaper, and what he said or

[1] Peel, 163.

shouted outside official newspapers was not easy to separate from his beetling personality. He seemed to commit the Union to programmes which many members rejected. In the *Nonconformist* Miall, whom Campbell attacked for the programme of the Anti-State-Church association, called him *Bombastes Furioso, Brag and Co* and demanded that the Union dismiss its editor. At the annual meeting of 1850 a curious twisted minister T. T. Lynch, whose unmuscular personality was as distant as possible from Campbell, declared that the publications must be amended or extinguished. 'Is he, or is he not, a voice from the heart of the Independents of England? We must disown him as we distrust him.'[1] A knot of young men in the public gallery hissed Campbell. The culprit cheerfully consented to remove from his title-pages the statement that they were 'The Official Organ of the Congregational Union'. He said caustically that he never pretended to represent the opinions of a body of whom no two were agreed. Rubbing salt into the wound, he hinted that if the magazines went out of the Union, the Union would have no money. Though the declaration of the title-page disappeared, Campbell continued to be official editor and, like Dr. Bunting from the Methodist Conference, continued to receive an annual vote of thanks from the annual meeting of the Union. The Union depended on funds. Most of these funds were supplied by newspapers which caused division in the Union. If the Union ended the newspapers it might end its usefulness in poverty. If the Union kept the newspapers it might destroy its precarious life in disruption. In 1850 it kept the newspapers and hoped.

In the fifties the loose bond was tested by a bigger tug, which pulled the entrails of every Christian church; doubt, German theology, biblical criticism. This tension appeared a little early among the Congregational dissenters. A church with strong government was protected against doubt by power of expulsion. Methodists of the fifties were almost untroubled. Roman Catholics of the fifties were troubled only because they defended every inch of every outwork. To be protected against doubt was not always useful. Strong government could postpone, but could not shelve indefinitely. In England it could not be shelved, because other churches had weak governments. That ancient series of corporations, the Church of England, possessed government so antique as to creak mournfully whenever doubt poked up its head. Independents had strong local government, but no central

[1] Peel, 217.

government whatever. Eschewing creeds and subscription, they were fertile soil for the seeds of German divinity and history.

Campbell's critic of 1850, T. T. Lynch, was the minister of a tiny congregation in Highgate. Lynch was a tender effeminate aesthete who with hardly a vein of true poetry imagined himself a poet; strange pastor, with a refined congregation of eighteen adults. He described himself with pathetic accuracy as a bird's heart without a bird's wings.[1] In November 1855 he published a little book of hymns called *The Rivulet*, with a preface that they were suitable for chamber or church. A few of these hymns are worth singing, a few have touches of genuine feeling, and a few embarrass.[2] The verses are innocuous. The ensuing rumpus is only explicable because journalism even when religious needs targets, and because orthodox divines trembled. The restful sparkling rills of Lynch were found to be nature-worship and pantheism. The *Morning Advertiser* said that the book contained no particle of vital religion or evangelical piety. The friends of Lynch foolishly came to his aid by issuing a protest; and when Campbell joined the fray against the friends of Lynch the conflict was almost forgotten in the general tension of Congregational Union. Campbell behaved outrageously; no more outrageously than others on both sides, but he happened to be the official representative of the Union.[3] The meeting of the Congregational Union planned for autumn 1856 had to be postponed. There was talk of the eclipse of the Union. Lynch declared the Union to be an obstruction to the advance of spiritual religion. Good men who believed that Lynch was harshly treated said that they would never enter the Union again. The magazines were separated from the Union and vested in trustees who should use the profits as before. In 1859 the income of the Union was only £193.[4] Impoverished, suspect, impotent, but standing for Catholic brotherhood and denominational strength, the Union survived.

An instructed ministry could not avoid the intellectual doubts of the fifties. Its students read widely, and could not be kept from Emerson or Carlyle. Congregationalists were far quicker than Methodists to sense the troubles ahead. The relative freedom of their polity enabled

---

[1] White, *Memoir of T. T. Lynch*, 312.

[2] Our heart is like a little pool/left by the ebbing sea/. . . And see what verdure exquisite/within it hidden grows!

[3] Even Spurgeon and the *Record* and Anglican evangelicals joined the quarrel, R, 13 June 56; White, *Memoir of Lynch*, 165–6.

[4] Peel, 244.

them to adjust their Calvinism to a non-Calvinist world with surprising ease.

In 1856 Samuel Davidson was accused of teaching error to students at Lancashire College. He had just published a volume called *The Text of the Old Testament Considered*, which abandoned the Mosaic authorship of the Pentateuch and limited biblical inspiration to religion and morals. In June 1857 a motion demanding his resignation was carried at the college committee by eighteen votes to sixteen, and Davidson resigned.[1] The breadth of Independent doctrine is demonstrated not by the dismissal but by the sixteen votes recorded against it. Once the process began, the Calvinist doctrines of Congregationalism disappeared with unusual speed and equally unusual absence of discomfort.

The Union diminished the variety of use in chapels. The gown and bands of minister slowly died away. Clerical dress was less common at the end of our period than the beginning. The Congregational Board (1834) voted that Independent ministers who used the Book of Common Prayer should not be admitted to the Board.[2] The vote was afterwards rescinded. Union chapel at Islington continued to use the prayer book until 1844. But pressure was always towards free worship. And as old Anglican evangelicals who once worshipped in Independent chapels found their needs satisfied by Anglican evangelical preachers, they ceased to be important in London chapels and the demand for their liturgy disappeared.

Under the impact of evangelical revival evening services became common. In the older tradition of Anglicans and Congregationals, Sunday evening was used for quiet meditation and prayers in the home. But in church and dissent the Methodist evening services evoked imitation, more slowly among the established than among the Independents, for they were usual in Independent chapels by the end of the thirties.

Congregational dissenters lamented that their chapels were not the homes of the poor. They observed the poor huddled on benches behind the pews of parish churches, but thought no good done because the gospel was seldom preached from those state-infested pulpits. In Ranters' chapels or camps the poor might be found, but Congregational leaders disliked ranting as cordially as Bunting or Pusey. They

---

[1] Cf. J. Thompson, *Lancashire Independent College*, 127 ff; Tudur Jones, 254.
[2] Bennett, *Hist. Dissenters*, 341.

criticised Unitarians not only because they were Unitarians but because they were almost all members of the upper middle class. In their own chapels were the shopkeeper and the tradesman, rising on occasion to aldermen and mayors and masters of city companies.

But evangelical revival wrought inevitably among the Congregational and Baptist churches. Though faithful to Calvinism, they could not watch Methodist advance without absorbing that missionary enthusiasm and adopting some of its devices. They gained from the Sunday schools and the village preaching, while epidemic Methodist disorders bowed a number of souls into Independent chapels. A few of their ministers tried to rouse them to revivals.[1] And in the years between 1820 and 1840 Independent ranks were thinner in the upper and educated ranks of society. The political quarrels of church and dissent which tortured the thirties and forties, the fear that Independents were natural allies of Irish and radicals, meant that the Congregational churches of 1850 were more unvaryingly of lower middle class than the same churches in 1800; though they housed many more worshippers.

But if it was sometimes complained that the poor could not be expected to come to chapel when the sermons were addressed to a level of education above their heads, the congregations were instructed in theology as nowhere else in English religion of the nineteenth century, a few Anglican churches excepted. Their best sermons were less warm and direct, but more profound, than those of Methodists. When young R. W. Dale (1855) attacked the theology of original depravity in the chapel of Carr's Lane, Birmingham, he used language which in no way brought the difficulty down to easy understanding; and if the same sermons had been preached in an Anglican or Roman Catholic or Methodist place of worship, we can imagine a contemplative doze afflicting pew or bench. Yet at Carr's Lane, we are told, excitement deepened into alarm, and alarm rose to the height of a panic. The congregation was like one great Bible class; there was a Bible open in almost every hand. Wave upon wave of emotion rolled through the congregation as the preacher developed his theme.[2] This is a sign both of education and of that lay responsibility which is the *raison d'être* of a Congregational polity.

Much of the preaching was without notes. In 1830–40 read-

[1] e.g. Dale, *Life of James*, 257.
[2] A. W. W. Dale, *Dale*, 111.

ing sermons from manuscripts was obnoxious to most dissenters.[1] John Angell James, famous minister in Birmingham, delivered a sermon of two hours from memory, but took the precaution of having his brother sit in the pulpit with the manuscript to prompt.[2] At the end of the first hour, when he asked leave to pause, members of the congregation lobbed oranges into the pulpit to refresh him. William Jay claimed the virtue of brevity, by which he meant forty-five minutes.[3] We know of one preacher who normally preached for two hours, and of a funeral sermon of three hours. Services of ordination could last three to five hours. The sermon hour of the Reformation was still normal. Once a boy sitting by the gallery clock slowed the pendulum to make James's sermon longer, and James apologised when by looking at his own watch he saw that he had spoken for ten minutes over the hour. Prayer was always extemporary and usually lasted half an hour.[4] Independent pastors distrusted formal prayer, but their flocks bought little books of prayers in great numbers. The hymnody was sometimes 'lined' (reading a line before singing it, to help the illiterate) but more commonly not, and Independent church music improved markedly in the early Victorian period. Organs and choirs grew steadily, and without controversy. Gothic architecture was adopted from 1847 or 1848. The barn-chapel of the side-streets was becoming the church of the market-square.

As the assault upon a state church became more vociferous, the inconsistencies of Congregational practice received painful denunciation. Since 1723 the crown paid £500 a year, later increased to £1,000 a year, finally to £1,695, to relieve the necessitous widows of nonconformist ministers; later, necessitous ministers themselves. But in early Victorian England they could not press the attack upon state endowment of religion, or even upon church rates, without being uneasily aware that they received state money in some form. For though in origin the king gave a personal gift, the revenues of the crown were later transferred to the state under arrangements for the civil list. The ministers' money became a charge upon the consolidated fund and was voted annually by the House of Commons among miscellaneous estimates, together with pensions to former spies in France or to American loyalists from the War of Independence,

[1] Cf. J. Bennett, *Hist. Dissenters*, 417.
[2] Dale, *James*, 1861, 143. The date is 1819, in Surrey chapel.
[3] *Autobiog.*, 143; Tudur Jones, 221–7.
[4] Birrell, *Life of William Brock*, 34–35; Tudur Jones, 223.

allowances to the chaplain and porter at the Lutheran chapel in St. James's, relief to refugees from Napoleon, and the maintenance of the bridge at Berwick-upon-Tweed.

The prime minister chose as receiver a minister from one of the three denominations of old dissent. During the last years of this charity the receiver was the Unitarian Dr. Rees, whom Lord Melbourne appointed. Rees then chose two ministers from his own denomination, three Congregational ministers and three Baptist ministers. The treasury paid the grant to Rees in half-yearly instalments. He divided it into ninths and gave one-ninth to each of the nine ministers, who spent it as he thought fit, not necessarily on ministers of his denomination. The nine met annually to compare accounts, but the names of the recipients were secret even from the treasury. Most of the money went to Wales, where dissenting ministers lived in grinding poverty. The average income of a Welsh pastor was £50; and within that average there were many lower stipends.

The normal grant was £5. To the exchequer the total sum was paltry. To pastors who could not afford shoes for children or butter for bread or sugar for tea, the gift was true blessing. If there was a dissenting principle not to receive money from the state, the principle was not shared by recipients of the bounty. Desperate applications loaded the tables of Dr. Rees, far more applications than he could satisfy.[1]

But harassed pastors and more harassed wives found themselves unwilling arrows in the war between church and dissent. Foolish Anglicans endangered their alms by defending establishment with this shield. Even Sir Robert Inglis, who despite large heart and beaming humanity was hardly conscious of near-starving Welsh pastors, habitually taunted dissenters with inconsistency. At the Pontefract election of winter 1847 campaigning Tories issued a circular called *The Puritan's Purse*.[2] Ministers' money was a bastion of the established church. No one knows whether dissenters hated it on principle or because it hampered their tactics in the political fight.

No one knows whether their principles would have been so strong if the grant had been larger. They felt its size to be an insult, government treating them as tramps and beggars. Statistics of 1847 proved that if the money was divided equally it would have given each recipient 22s. These were not the days of George I. When wealthy

[1] PP, 1847-8, xviii, i, 635-6.　　　[2] C Witness, 1849, 22-23.

dissenting communities embarked on expensive schemes for building chapels out of their resources they were not pleased to be offered sixpence from the plate. It was annual insult, badge of servitude, monument of oppression. Dissenters with comfortable incomes denounced it. They forgot the bread with no butter and the child with no shoes; or, if they remembered, declared that it would be easy for dissenting congregations to make up the trivial sum. And while the argument raged, postbags of heart-rending appeals reached Dr. Rees.

The nine distributors repelled insinuations that they were state employees or paid to truckle before government. They professed that religion should be supported by voluntary offerings and not by public money, and maintained that royal bounty was voluntary offering; that this onslaught cost high-minded attackers nothing if it were successful. They blamed the ill grace which wished further to impoverish persons poorer than the high-minded.[1]

The case was a little worse because Dr. Rees was a Unitarian. It galled orthodox dissenters that their distributors should act in so unholy an alliance. Complaint rose noisier in the forties. One of the Baptist distributors, Dr. F. A. Cox, was given a post as secretary of the Anti-State Church Association and resigned because the distribution of alms looked incompatible with his new duties. Then the Maynooth grant was the last straw. Government money to Roman Catholic dissenters was better assailed if Protestant dissenters refused government money. Petitions from dissenters against ministers' money began to pour into Parliament. In 1848[2] Charles Lushington began an annual assault upon the miscellaneous estimates. In 1848 numerous dissenting ministers sent petitions. In 1849 the only petition came from a remote village in Derbyshire.[3] But protests came again and again; until at last Dr. John Campbell of the London Tabernacle denounced the three Congregational distributors, harmless benevolents, as adversaries of the gospel and enemies of the cross.[4]

The chancellor of the exchequer was not accustomed to cries not to take his money. He did not mind paying so small a sum and resented the noise. The obligation descended from the crown. He

---

[1] Public statement of 1837 by distributors in J. Bennett, *History of Dissenters*, 281–90.

[2] In 1845 Charles Hindley moved in a hostile spirit for a return of the names of the recipients, and collected only two other votes; Hansard, lxxxi, 528.

[3] Hansard, cv, 1849, IIII.

[4] *C Witness*, 1849, 22–24: For fierce attack on Campbell in reply cf. Junius Secundus, *Individual Despotism dangerous to public liberty*, 1849.

remembered, what some so easily forgot, the rags of children and the tea without sugar. For four succeeding years Lord John Russell and his cabinet insisted on paying the exiguous charity. In the early hours of a parliamentary morning of 1851 the chancellor gave notice that in 1852 they would not propose the grant.[1] So everyone with a voice was satisfied. Sir Robert Inglis lost an osier from his wickerwork shield, and three hundred meagre ministers tightened their belts.

5. BAPTISTS

The Baptists were Independent congregations which condemned infant baptism and practised the baptism of believers. In happy circumstances there was little to distinguish them from Congregational dissenters. They were allied in all political grounds and the common interest of underprivilege. We find Baptists hearing Congregational sermons, Congregationalists hearing Baptist sermons, Baptist preachers in Congregational pulpits and vice versa, Baptist deacons of Congregational chapels. In 1833 Baptist and Congregational chapels at Bristol joined in a common celebration of the Lord's Supper.[2] Some Baptist chapels, as at Bedford and Luton, were used in common with the Congregationalists.

At their educated end in London or provincial cities some Baptist congregations were distinguishable from Independents only by their doctrine of baptism. There the preachers could stand comparison with any occupant of a Congregational or Methodist pulpit. Their educated laity demanded as solid a content of instruction. A few of the Baptist flock at Norwich would test their pastor by quoting largely at him from the original Greek or Hebrew of the Bible.[3] The leaders of the Baptist denomination worked easily and harmoniously with Congregationalists.

But this harmony concealed the extent of divergence. Congregational chapels contained few labourers. Many Baptist chapels of 1835 were of a low level in society. They bore to Congregationalists somewhat as Primitives bore to Wesleyans. Their pastors were less educated, people more illiterate, Calvinism more rigid, doctrine more conservative, liturgy more bald, polity still more independent.

Except Calvinistic Methodists who were strong in Wales, almost

---

[1] Hansard, cxviii, 970.   [2] J. Bennett, *Hist. Dissenters*, 359.
[3] Birrell, *Life of William Brock*, 92.

all Methodists were Arminian (Christ died to save all men), almost all Congregationalists were moderate Calvinists (Christ died to save those whom God has chosen to be saved). Baptists divided into three groups: General Baptists who were Arminian, Particular Baptists who were moderate Calvinists, Strict and Particular Baptists who were Calvinists but not moderate. Most of the old General Baptist congregations, which went back to the Commonwealth and before, faded during the eighteenth century into Unitarian belief. But since 1770 a small group, General Baptists of the New Connexion, preserved the orthodox Arminian faith and were recognised by some Particular Baptists as brothers.

Particular Baptists led the denomination in numbers and learning. But at Queen Victoria's accession they were themselves divided over Congregationalists and other evangelicals. Was the Lord's Supper to be ministered only to the baptised, i.e. to those baptised as adult believers? Or might a church admit to the holy table persons who shared evangelical faith but were not baptised as adult believers? Robert Hall, who died in 1831 the greatest Baptist preacher of the day, contended for open communion. During his life the opinion favouring open communion was held by a small minority of ministers and meetings. But between 1830 and 1860 it became ever more common, until it dominated London and the south. Its spread accompanied a steady decline of Calvinism within the denomination. Not only did this cleavage hamper united action. It was a case where different doctrines issued in different decisions of conscience and caused schism in congregation after congregation.

As the number of chapels with open communion grew, so grew the number of little groups who withdrew towards associations of Strict Baptists. On these grounds the Particular Baptists of Suffolk and Norfolk remained outside the general Baptist Union.[1] The doctrine of election and predestination was still potent and alive, the doctrinal controversies of the Protestant Reformation still meaningful and agonising. In Accrington, Liverpool, Leeds, Norwich, Manchester, Baptist people divided, the men of open communion turning towards liberal divinity and away from rigid Calvinism, the men of closed communion becoming ever stricter and less willing to fraternise.

[1] The oldest church in Liverpool split over the question in 1838, Underwood, 205. n Congregational churches we occasionally find laity banging pew doors and leaving the chapel when the preacher failed to preach high Calvinism; cf. Newman Hall, *Autobiography*, 61.

In Norwich the controversy came to law. William Brock believed in open communion, but was appointed (1833) to St. Mary's chapel (of course not dedicated to St. Mary, but so called because in the parish of St. Mary) on condition that he did not preach against closed communion. The pledge led to manifest inconvenience and suspicion. Five years later he resigned and was re-accepted on condition that he would not admit to communion without leave from the congregation. He could now preach what he thought, but could not practise. He began private services for the unbaptised at his house; but about 1844 the numbers became so large that he moved to the chapel by leave of the congregation, open communion being always on a day different from the regular monthly closed communion. On the first Sunday in the month communion was closed, on the third Sunday communion was open. Trustees objected that this practice was contrary to the trust deeds of the chapel, but counsel's opinion was secured that the objection was ill-founded.

Brock's successor George Gould reversed the order. He opened the regular communion and gave special services for the closed. Strict Baptists withdrew to maintain purity in a separate meeting. This time a trustee sued for the property, and at last the master of the rolls (1860) held that the congregation was free to alter the practice.[1]

To create a 'union' was therefore more difficult than among Congregationalists. The same needs for union existed—a missionary society in want of money and direction, training of ministers, stipends of pastors, chapels with debts. An embryo General Union was founded in 1813, and reorganised in 1832, as a meeting for mutual acquaintance and support of mission. The objects stated in 1832 were less practical than those of the contemporary Congregational Union. The Baptist Union got less support.

At first it was confined to Particular Baptists, but the stricter disciples of Calvinism and closed communion usually suspected or disregarded it. It started as an innocuous gathering of friendly ministers, able and willing to do nothing but censure. It grew in importance and influence only as more chapels turned from closed to open communion, usually losing a few members in the change. The Union became ever more fraternal towards the General Baptists, and in 1842 invited Gregory Pike of Derby, leader of the General Baptists, to preside at the annual gathering of the Union.[2] It had critics because

---

[1] Underwood, 206–7; Birrell, *Life of William Brock*, 72, 120.   [2] Payne, 65.

it was too fraternal and other critics because it was aimless; a committee travelling at the cost of their chapel to talk trivialities and audit accounts and return. Why should anyone bother to travel, or his chapel bother to pay his fare, to a meeting so destitute of meaning?[1] As late as 1863 the income of the Union was £90 and its deficit £49. It still had no building. The profits of the *Baptist Magazine* and of hymnbooks were used to help widows of Baptist ministers and missionaries, but unlike Congregational Union the Baptist failed to achieve influence through publishing. The president of the Union in 1863, Howard Hinton, said gloomily that there was no union among Baptists, there never had been and never would be.[2]

The census of 1851 showed about 366,000 Baptists at the best-attended service of the day. Particular Baptists had 1,491 chapels in England and 456 in Wales. New Connexion of General Baptists had 179 chapels in England and three in Wales. Old General Baptists (Unitarian) had ninety-three chapels.

The Strict and Particular Baptists[3] threw up grand angular characters. The most rugged were the Gadsbyites, called after William Gadsby, who ministered to the Angel Meadow chapel in Manchester until his death in 1844. Gadsby was a rough and clownish-looking ribbon weaver married to a terrible jealous wife. He preached in coarse brown coat and drab trousers, eschewed the title Reverend and instrumental music in chapel, and dodged away when ministers tried to lay their hands upon his head at ordination. He was a humorous and direct labourer who preached to labourers in their broad language. His ally Thomas Godwin taught himself how to write four years after his ordination.[4] Gadsby and his fellows preached a grace so sovereign that they offended by seeming to condemn the moral law. A minority of Gadsby's chapel in Manchester left to found a rival chapel. Though the humour was quaint, the language was stern. The Strict knew themselves a remnant or little flock, and the favourite name of their chapels was Zoar. Hearers of these exclusive elect preachers testified that sermons cut them up root and branch. Like all extreme Calvinists,

---

[1] *Baptist Record*, 1846, 772; Payne, 67.

[2] Underwood, 212; Payne, 91–93.

[3] The Scottish Baptists were different from English Strict Baptists. Though in northern England and Wales, they were so-called because they came into England from Scotland. They differed from every other body with the Baptist name by having no proper ministry, and were in many ways nearer to the Plymouth Brethren than to the Baptists. They refused communion with other Baptists.

[4] Godwin's *Autobiography* 41.

they delighted in particular providence, and gave glory to God when a minister's wife was struck dumb four days after condemning a Strict and Particular pastor, or when a spy committed suicide after taking notes of sermons. A few of them entered the heritage of religious ecstasy. The uneducated Gadsbyite John Warburton fell upon his knees under a hedge as ecstasy struck him, and when he rose to his feet danced along the road, bantering the devil and calling him names.[1]

In the excitable years 1830–5 these Strict Baptists gathered a surprising number of converts from the Anglican clergy. If priests of the Church of England were going to leave their mother, they did not usually join Methodist or Congregationalist churches. They ended with views distant from the Church of England. Joseph Philpot, fellow of Worcester College, Oxford, joined the Gadsbyites and ministered at Stamford. William Tiptaft, vicar of Sutton Courtney, founded a Strict chapel in Abingdon. J. H. Newman's brother Frank was baptised on the fringe of the same group. Henry Battiscombe of King's College in Cambridge resigned his fellowship and set up as a Baptist pastor at Zion chapel in the town.[2] The most famous of the converts was the evangelical preacher Baptist Noel, who in 1847 left the Church of England and ministered quietly as a moderate Baptist pastor.

The days of open popular persecution were long over. At the extreme end of the denomination a few windows of pastors might occasionally be broken, a front door smashed, a poison letter pushed over the sill.[3] But the Strict Baptist pastor did not draw opprobrium like the Ranter. A change of friends or customers was still to be expected. Dr. Keal was the most fashionable doctor in Oakham. When he left the parish church and founded a Calvinist chapel in a derelict silk factory many profitable patients forsook him.[4] But no more do we hear of baptismal pits polluted with filth by hooligans.

In 1836 the Strict Baptist pastor at Pewsey was paid £25 a year out of which he must pay £15 in rent and taxes. He could only live by

[1] J. H. Philpot, *The Seceders*, i, 102, 110, 218; Godwin's *Autobiography*, 33.

[2] For others, cf. Brenton in Philpot, *The Seceders*, i, 94, 181, cf. T. Mozley, *Reminiscences*, i, 228, Bulteel; Husband in Philpot, i, 133; Hitchcock of Devizes, Philpot, i, 182, 341. F. Tryon, vicar of Deeping St. James, built a chapel in his village, cf. *Baptist Quarterly* vi, 367; Underwood, 242; and the various clergymen who seceded to found the Plymouth Brethren. Battiscombe afterwards returned to curacies in the Church of England.

[3] Godwin's *Autobiography*, 33–34.

[4] J. H. Philpot, *The Seceders*, i, 76.

earning fees as a supply preacher elsewhere. When a pastor was absent
or unobtainable a deacon conducted prayers and read a printed
sermon. In many smaller places all the members of the congregation
were very poor. Debts on the chapel were a melancholy burden and
repairs were often oppressive. At Godmanchester Thomas Godwin
preached for three years not knowing at each sermon whether the
pulpit floor would collapse. But these Calvinists were not weaklings.
Walking two miles beyond Swindon to undertake new work,
Godwin's soul felt the Lord breaking in with the words *Thy shoes shall
be iron and brass, and as thy days, so shall thy strength be.* 'My soul began
to sing and rejoice in the Lord, and I took my little Bible out of my
pocket and soon found the words, and they so enlarged within my
heart and soul that I walked on to Marlborough as strong as a giant
refreshed with the new wine of the everlasting kingdom of our Lord
and Saviour, Jesus Christ, and as happy as I could live.'[1] They wrestled
with demons through agonised sleepless soul-searing nights, locked in
dungeons, trembling in valley of shadows, at moments on the brink of
insanity, but at last confident in cleansing blood and tingling with
sensible gratitude.

In 1835 Baptist and Congregational chapels were still obscure and
in back streets. Like the old Catholics who resented Dr. Wiseman's
flamboyance, some good dissenters preferred obscurity and disliked
the growth of meeting-house into chapel and then into church. By
instinct they were men of the upper room. But between 1830 and 1850
the mood changed. New chapels were necessary to house new town
congregations. Building a new chapel, they inevitably sought for good
sites and suitable architecture. By 1850 Gothic architecture became
synonym for reverent building. And therefore even Baptist chapels
began to be built on prominent sites in a Gothic style. The air of upper
room hung a little longer round the buildings. When the Baptist railway contractor Morton Peto built Bloomsbury chapel in 1848 the
planning authorities stipulated that if a public site were conceded the
edifice must have an ecclesiastical character. Peto beaconed his chapel
with elegant twin spires. It was necessary to defend these spires as
useful both for staircases and ventilation.[2]

The cathedral of this new dissenting architecture was not Gothic.
The Metropolitan Tabernacle near the Elephant and Castle owed its
building to the young genius, Charles Haddon Spurgeon, who

[1] Godwin's *Autobiography*, 28, 63–64.   [2] Birrell, *Life of William Brock*, 172.

strengthened the impact of dissent and of the Baptists upon the nation. The Tabernacle was completed in 1861 and cost over £31,000. 'Every Baptist place of worship,' said Spurgeon at the laying of the foundation-stone, 'should be Grecian, never Gothic.' It was to be called Tabernacle because God's people are still in the wilderness. It had seats for 3,600 and flap-seats for 1,000 more. The critics accused its builders of folly and ostentation. They predicted that it could not be kept half-full. The prophecy reckoned without Spurgeon.[1]

Of a family of Essex Independent ministers, Spurgeon supplied the pulpit of the Baptist chapel in Waterbeach at the age of seventeen, with results astounding enough to reach the ears of a deacon in London. The new Park Street chapel in Southwark was famous in old Baptist history, but now dingy and down-at-heel and unable to find a satisfactory minister. In 1853, when Spurgeon was nineteen, he was invited to preach at Southwark. A congregation of eighty smiled at his bumpkin voice and giant cravat and blue handkerchief with white spots, but four months later invited him there to be settled. So began a preaching career without parallel in modern history.

Spurgeon was no miracle. If he preached good sermons, England knew men who could preach great sermons. Sunday evening was still an evening for home or for church. The cities were increasing in size, their transport improving, their people a little less uneducated, a little more thirsty for instruction and entertainment. The revivalist method met their need for tough, popular, intelligible gospel. In one light Spurgeon was the man who tamed revivalist mission into a chapel and congregation. In another light he was part of the shock of Horace Mann's religious census, the sudden evangelical consciousness of the gulf yawning between labourer and Christianity. Well read and intelligent, he preserved the direct and colloquial address which spoke to the artisan, though he collected not many labourers among his crowds. In another light he was a sign of new power in publicity.

A man who can fill the pews of a church and see men standing in the aisles finds his congregation growing by curiosity. Spurgeon was assisted by two accidents of publicity. After he had preached in Southwark for a few months, and people were sitting on the window-sills or waiting outside in hundreds, the deacons enlarged the chapel

---

[1] Fullerton, 137. The Metropolitan Tabernacle was burnt to the ground but for walls and façade on 20 April 1898. It was rebuilt with smaller seating capacity at cost of £45,000. The reconstruction had its critics.

at a cost of £2,000. During the builders' mess Spurgeon took Exeter hall for his services. He was a brash and impudent youth of five foot seven, still of only twenty years. Wise heads shook over the conceit of taking so vast and so secular an auditorium. The alleged impropriety of holding services in a hall caused controversy, and the controversy blocked the Strand with carriages, and London began to talk about Spurgeon. Journalists attended Exeter hall to anatomise or caricature what they saw in the pulpit. When he returned to the enlarged chapel in Southwark on 31 May 1855 the money was found to be wasted, for the disappointed crowds were larger than before. He began to preach in the fields, to 10,000 people at Hackney. He returned to Exeter hall, and Exeter hall, which held between 4,000 and 5,000, was now found to be too small.

In the Royal Surrey Gardens on the south bank stood the Surrey music hall. Exeter hall might be quarter-hallowed by the May meetings of evangelical societies. The Surrey music hall was unhallowed and was known as a place of worldly entertainment with a zoo. But it held 10,000 people. Even Spurgeon feared that it would be half empty. On Sunday evening, 19 October 1856, 10,000 people filled the hall and another 10,000 filled the streets outside.

Hymn, reading, hymn, prayer; and in the middle of the prayer someone screamed, 'Fire! The galleries are giving way, the place is falling.' Spurgeon's flock always believed that the cry was criminal. In panic rush the balustrade of the stairs collapsed and several people fell into the pit, others were trampled in a rush to the doors. Seven were killed and twenty-eight badly injured. Spurgeon stayed in the pulpit, seeing only a tumult and ignorant of the slaughter. Some in the congregation cried loudly to him to preach, and he tried to preach, but vainly, for the rest of the congregation was moving out. So he urged them to retire, and fainted.

He afterwards believed that he was near to being sent out of his mind. Tough and resilient, he was back in Southwark chapel a fortnight later, still determined to use Surrey Gardens. The disaster gave more power to his critics and finally established his national fame. For three years his congregations used Surrey Gardens, but in the morning for safety; for a London morning congregation was likely to be middle class. It was said that Society first rallied to Spurgeon after the false panic.[1] There was an incredible rumour that

[1] Fullerton, 95.

Queen Victoria once appeared at Surrey Gardens in disguise. Spurgeon ended the connexion in December 1859 because the proprietors determined to break Sabbath by opening the hall for concerts on Sunday evenings. It was observed with satisfaction that shortly afterwards the company went bankrupt.

When every allowance is made for the circumstances of Victorian Sunday and crowded city and new education and new publicity, Spurgeon was a very extraordinary man. It is less astounding that he gathered a congregation of 4,000 to 5,000 than that he kept it so long. He had little personal magic and commanded devotion only from intimates. Outside the pulpit he was fat, podgy, unimpressive. He reminded Lord Houghton of a barber's assistant. His fellow ministers found it difficult to tolerate his youthful bounce, and at a prayer meeting in his presence prayed for 'our young friend who has so much to learn, and so much to unlearn'. Spurgeon could be vulgar. Visiting a country chapel, he gazed at the shiny suit of the reigning minister, commented to the people, and ordered the collection to a new suit.[1] People found him vulgar in a London pulpit. But what some found vulgar, others loved. It was partly the humour. He dismissed the old belief of the Reformation that to make people laugh in church is irreverent. He knew the sentimentality of the English people and understood that they loved serious truths best if they met them in a comic frame. As an orator he possessed not only a lovely voice but a rare range of moving his audience in a moment from laughter to tears, joy to pathos, heaven to hell. He was not profound. He approached the burning bush with cheerful aplomb, gave forth little awe or veneration. He shook his audience by the hand, patted it, made friends with it, and led it into the temple parlour.

But mere ease in a pulpit holds minds not more than a week or two. Something about Spurgeon was bigger than his methods. Swallowing the bounce of the natural man was a vaster confidence. He was a Calvinist preaching a Calvinist gospel. The assurance of the saved transformed him in a pulpit and filled his being with power. The jokes welled out of a spring of deeper gaiety. His neighbour the Strict Baptist at the Surrey Tabernacle doubted his conversion and would have nothing to do with him and mocked him as the boy round the corner;[2] and the moderation of Spurgeon's Calvinism broadened his appeal to

---

[1] Carlile, 127; Fullerton, 66–67, 84.   [2] Carlile, 202.

many not Calvinist. He believed in open communion and wrote the practice into the deeds of the Metropolitan Tabernacle. He founded a college to train pastors (now called Spurgeon's College) and placed a Congregationalist as its first tutor and later principal. About himself he was less moderate. He held ordination otiose and refused to be ordained at the Southwark chapel. He abandoned the white tie and frock coat of ministers and disliked the title Reverend. No instrumental music was permitted in his chapel, choirs and anthems he loathed. The Baptist denomination found him uneasy company. When he went to preach at Tring none of the three Baptist chapels wanted him. One chapel refused because he was a Calvinist, another because he was not a sound Calvinist, and the third let him into its pulpit fearfully.[1] But he knew his Bible, was widely read outside his Bible, never preached without preaching a cross, and perfectly understood how to array his gospel.

Keble and Spurgeon, Arminian and Calvinist, were opposite types of Victorian religious leader. Keble was all godly fear, Spurgeon all assurance. Keble believed in reserve and shrank from showing pearls of beauty to men who would not see. Spurgeon disbelieved reserve and wanted to speak highest truth to the crowd, that out of the crowd a few might be converted. Keble thought jest in the pulpit worse than unfitting and of set purpose preached dull sermons. Keble was quiet, slow, restrained, buttoned, high-collared, prayerful; Spurgeon quick and abounding with gusto or panache, overflowing with illustration wise or gay or piercing. Keble wanted to make holy, Spurgeon to make Christian. Keble was English religion of the past, shepherd in ordered peaceable squire-ruled village of farm labourers; Spurgeon was English religion of the future, preacher to a waste of London, more brash, aggressive, public, biting, and worldly, because haunted by multitudes of souls athirst.

Dissent stepped out of the back streets and spoke to the nation.

6. THE SOCIETY OF FRIENDS

The Friends were more removed by religion from Victorian society than any other group outside Catholic monasteries. At Queen Victoria's accession many Quakers kept their ancient testimonies against the world. Passive suffering of distraint for tithe and church

[1] Carlile, 127.

rate held them with sufficient sense of persecution to remain apart. They continued to testify against war, oaths, paid ministers, and all fixed ceremonies; refused to sue at law or accept relief; denied that the sacraments of baptism and the Lord's Supper were instituted by Christ; would not call the days of the week or months of the year by their names, as given in honour of false gods, and talked or wrote of First Day instead of Sunday and Seventh Month instead of July; eschewed all forms of conventional salutation, bows, curtseys, titles of Sir or Mrs or my Lord, doffing the hat, and were famous for entering houses hatted; allowed no gravestones nor black in mourning. They accepted the public ministry of women; and being first of Englishmen to expect equal education in women begot a prodigious series of conversable and public-spirited ladies, of whom the great prison-reformer Elizabeth Fry was chief. Strict male Quakers wore drab breeches, coats without lapels and broad-brimmed beaver hats. Strict female Quakers wore dresses cut plain and straight without plaits or ribbons (in some families with hooks and eyes to avoid buttons, which were regarded as ornamental), bonnet and muslin shawl. They addressed each other naturally as *thee* and *thou*, often ungrammatically, as *thou sees* or *thee were*. They disapproved of learning music or reading novels. If they were especially strict they let no newspapers into the house, used no silver forks at table, kept out the plays of Shakespeare and avoided laughter as unfitting. These customs or peculiarities assumed importance as badge of remnant or hedge against mankind. A few simpletons believed *thee* and *thou* to be the language of Eden and even of heaven. But for most they had the meaning which a Franciscan found in his habit. To adopt Quaker garb for the first time felt like ordination, experience of affection, committal of soul. To deviate from the customs was suspect as a first step down the broad way that leads to the world and the end of religious profession.

The Quakers aimed to conduct all affairs under immediate guidance of the divine Spirit. Their worship was silent waiting upon God until a member be moved to speak. Though rejecting all forms of ordination they recognised that some were especially entrusted with the ministry of the word, and such Friends the Monthly Meeting 'acknowledged' or 'recorded'. The ministers were paid their travelling expenses but no stipend, and the presence of a minister was not necessary to worship. At least half the meetings assembled without a minister. In 1700 male ministers outnumbered female by nearly two to one. But during the eighteenth century women steadily overhauled and passed men, and by about 1835 there were twice as many female ministers as male.[1] The ministers stayed where they were called unless 'liberated' to travel. One meeting might have six ministers, most had none. At meetings for worship men and women sat apart, both hatted, male hats being removed for prayer but not for sermon. The meeting-house contained no pulpit, but a long raised gallery in front of the congregation, where male ministers sat opposite the men and female ministers opposite the women. In this gallery sat the elders, two or more persons of either sex appointed by the Monthly Meeting to watch over the ministers; and often two or more overseers, whose duties included a watch for unbecoming behaviour at the meeting. Sermons were delivered by custom in a curious singsong intonation. Neutral observers found the sermons commonplace and rambling.[2] For speech arose from waiting upon the Spirit and therefore eschewed preparation and rhetoric. The text came haphazard. They distrusted words vehement or enchanting.

Their reputation was odd, but not displeasing. Educated Britons were interested in eccentricity, and Carlyle, Coleridge, Charles Lamb, Sydney Smith painted sympathetic portraits. Stern churchmen would not give the name of Christian to a sect which refused the two gospel sacraments. Even into the forties an old saw persisted that Quaker shopkeepers were sly. During one evening rush-hour of 1846 Friends filled a train from Croydon to London and at a station passengers baffled on the platform raised a storm against Quakers.[3] But they were respected for quaintness, honesty in trade, passive suffering, the appearance of their women like goddesses of innocence or purity, and their marvellous repute for philanthropy; not to be imitated, but distantly and sometimes mockingly admired. In 1835 Friends were still a little separated community behind a pale; marked off like friars or Mennonites by special usages, marrying within the Society, educating in their own schools, mocked but not despised, keeping themselves unspotted from the world. Like every other denomination of the troubled Victorian age, they suffered deep internal controversy. But the tradition of quietness and silence, though it made wills as firm as anywhere, prevented arguments from turning raucous. It was their habit to utter fierce judgments in undertones.

[1] Numbers of deaths of ministers with dates in *Memoir of J. S. Rowntree*, 252.
[2] *Ency. Brit.*[7] (1842, by William Howitt), 772.
[3] *London Yearly Meeting during 250 years*, 1919, 70.

Not all Quakers were strict about the customs. In the eighteenth century we hear of ribbons and lace and scarlet boots. In the early Victorian age a rich Quaker family of Bolton rented grouse moors in Scotland, though every variety of hunting was supposed to contradict their religious profession. But in this religious age of England strict Friends grew stricter. 'Gay Friends', like some of the Gurneys, might avoid the plain dress and call Sunday Sunday. But when the two noblest Gurneys turned to an earnest life they each adopted many of the peculiar customs—Elizabeth Fry in a flutter of heart at needing to say *thee* for the first time at dinner, her brother Joseph John Gurney in three weeks' agony of apprehension that he must enter a county drawing-room wearing his hat. An Anglican convert to the Friends found it a cross to stop wearing her wedding-ring.[1] The force of conservatism was strong within the Society.

Quakerism was not a religion of the poor. A few dependent paupers attended. But in high proportion to the numbers it contained men wealthy in the way of business, banker, coal-owner, wholesale grocer, railway director, cotton-spinning magnate, corn factor, farmer, Norfolk Gurney and Barclay and Buxton, Rowntree of York, Pease of Durham, Richardson of Cleveland, Ashworth of Bolton and Bright of Rochdale. In 1852 a working man of Bacup resigned from the Friends' meeting because he wanted to marry and the Society contained not a girl of his level of society. 'The daughters of Friends,' he said in resigning, 'are mostly brought up with notions of affluence and ease and a style of living not consonant with that of a working trades-man.'[2] Friends recognised the loss and regretted. But this mode of worship required unusual aptitude or training. Among mill-hands silence could not compete with lusty Methodist hymnody.

Comfort destroyed neither simplicity nor public service. In proportion to numbers, their social endeavour became legendary. Elizabeth Fry in prisons; Joseph John Gurney in abolishing slavery; Joseph Sturge among Chartists and in the Irish famine; John Bright in repealing the corn laws; Samuel Tuke in care of lunatics—a century and a half of passive resistance bred unique compassion for suffering. Vigour and security and sensitive conscience joined in Quaker character. If they had few poor of their meeting to tend, they circled the ocean to tend the poor whom others oppressed.

The record of social endeavour was more astounding in that it

---

[1] *Diaries of Edward Pease*, 171–2.   [2] J. Travis Mills, i, 439.

appeared contrary to Quaker custom. The old Anabaptist tradition from which they descended wished not to save the world but to save men out of the world. The Society was retired behind a wall of peculiarities. To be a magistrate was thought to be incompatible with religious profession. When the municipal corporations act was passed and Quakers were likely to become aldermen, the Meeting for Sufferings recommended that no Quaker should become a magistrate as inconsistent with his religious profession; and after prolonged discussion the Yearly Meeting of 1838 came within a knife-edge of deciding that no Friend might be a magistrate or member of a corporation. Joseph Rowntree offered no opinion, but felt that the meeting was not far from believing that you can escape the spirit of this world by avoiding public duties. In 1853 Rowntree allowed himself to become an alderman of York, but five years later felt obliged to refuse the office of lord mayor.[1] Many Friends believed that Joseph Sturge acted shockingly against his religion by agitating for Chartism. And if a man used words like *radical* in conversation he might be asked coldly whether he thought that a word for a Friend to use.[2]

The test came in 1833 over the righteousness of becoming a member of Parliament. Joseph John Gurney was offered a seat. He discussed it with advisers from the Society and was left free to make his own decision, but they were glad when he refused. Samuel Tuke was offered the Whig seat for York and refused. Joseph Pease was invited to stand in Durham and wished to accept. His father was astonished that he should contemplate the idea. Pease was strenuously opposed by father, mother-in-law and a weary session of the Monthly Meeting which lasted so long that it had to adjourn to the inn.[3] When Pease insisted, he refused to canvass and publicly announced that if elected he would maintain his practice and profession as a Friend. His father resigned himself, but was never comfortable at seeing a son in the House of Commons. Every election distressed him by din and intemperance. In the House his son refrained from addressing the Speaker as *Sir* or his colleagues as *honourable members*. John Bright was elected to Parliament in 1843, and the Yearly Meeting inserted into its annual epistle the pointed words *We desire ever to be found of those who*

---

[1] *Life of William Allen*, iii, 219; R. M. Jones, 945.

[2] Mary Howitt, *Autobiog.*, 139.

[3] *Memoirs of Joseph John Gurney*, i, 469; *Samuel Tuke*, 112; *Diaries of Edward Pease*, 64–66.

are quiet in the land. Bright leapt to his feet and said that he hoped the sentence was not intended to condemn those striving to repeal unjust laws (meaning the corn laws). The clerk rose to call for order, and Bright said, 'Now the clerk need not fear that I will introduce politics into this assembly' and made a speech defending himself without using the word *corn.* He got a little tapping as a grave and reverent form of applause, but the Yearly Meeting never reconciled itself to Bright. The yearly epistle of 1846 used language which seemed faintly to frown on using the vote where it was possessed; if used, then without entering the spirit of party politics.[1]

Social service, so far as it required public office, thus arose not out of the Society of Friends as a society, but out of character generated by the Society and sometimes in revolt from the special ethos of the Society. The typical Quaker service was not political programme but private charity like the *Retreat* near York which started to treat madmen humanely. As the Victorian age matured the Society lost its suspicions and stepped out into the world. In the last third of the century Friends accepted public office freely. Birmingham had seven Quaker mayors before 1892.[2]

This step from walled garden to market-square was not taken without pains and blushes.

As England grew smaller with roads and railways, and education more common, and public life more intense, young Friends resented the barriers by which their parents kept them enclosed. Instead of valuing the uses of their forefathers, they felt like egrets ready to fly and beating wings against a cage. The *thees* and *thous* and clothes were disliked by many youths and girls of Quaker family. Boys and girls found urchin mockery a strain. As they walked to school rude lads shouted *quack quack* at the duck-like bonnets. John Bright as a boy was too pugnacious for Quaker silence and shook his fist at them and mocked back. Little Mary Botham and her sister found the garb a crucifixion, and understood the text *take up thy cross* to mean adopting the peculiarities.[3] Girls were educated beyond the wont of girls and refused leave to read novels or plays or newspapers; and so in Quaker bedrooms there was secret or winked-at reading of romances, of disreputable authors like Carlyle and Dickens. By 1830 Mary Howitt

---

[1] Trevelyan, *John Bright*, 105; J. Travis Mills, ii, 6; *London Yearly Meeting*, 89.
[2] *Memoir of J. S. Rowntree*, 226.
[3] Travis Mills, *Bright*, i, 182; Mary Howitt's *Autobiog.*, 26.

determined not to bring up her own children in the dress, and six years later was so dropping *thee* that she used a strange mixture of *thees* and *yous*.[1] The men's costume went out more rapidly than the ladies', but then the ladies' costume was becoming. The Yearly Meeting of 1846 made general complaint at departure from plain language, attendance at amusements, and music in Friends' houses.[2] In the following year William Forster went into the women's Yearly Meeting and denounced loss of time through ornamented needlework. For some the dropping of the peculiarities felt like a monk throwing aside his habit and was first step to leaving the Society. For others it was freedom and stimulus to devout membership.

In the thirties and forties reforming Quakers felt their way towards strength. The constitution of the Society became important. Each meeting had a sitting for business, called a preparative meeting. The preparative meeting chose representatives to the Monthly Meeting, which governed a group of congregations, judged candidates for membership and administered discipline. The Monthly Meeting chose representatives to the Quarterly Meeting, which was a court of appeal over one or two counties. This received the answers to the Annual Queries sent to investigate the morals and state of the Society, reduced the answers to a simple report and sent them onward to the Yearly Meeting. It chose representatives to the Yearly Meeting, the supreme government of the Society. From 1794 the Yearly Meeting met towards the end of May at Devonshire House in Bishopsgate. Though the Yearly Meeting was technically open only to representatives, such ministers as might be in London, and members of the Meeting for Sufferings, the doors in fact were open to all Friends. To the distress of conservatives those who were not representatives began to take an increasing part in the deliberations. In 1861 the doors were formally thrown open to all male Friends.

The Yearly Meeting was an important social occasion. Coaches were full of the unusual costumes, the favourite inns were *The White Hart* and *The Four Swans*. Friends went on expeditions to the British Museum or the Zoo, in the City the slow unhurried pace was observed on the pavements. A traveller in a coach full of Quakers was interested to see the plenty of the picnic hampers of hard-boiled eggs, Stilton cheese, radishes, a pint of sherry.[3]

---

[1] Mary Howitt, *Autobiog.*, 119, 132–3.
[2] *Diaries of Edward Pease*, 228. [3] *Tait's Magazine*, 1838, 287ff.

At nearly all meetings for church affairs women met separately from men. The supreme government was the male Yearly Meeting. A man might be inspired with a concern to visit and address the women's meeting and a woman with a concern to address the men's meeting. This happened every year, but was often an awkward interlude. When Sarah Grubb visited the men's meeting the men were not comfortable[1]; and during the Beaconite controversy Luke Howard roundly charged her with trying to affect the decisions of the men by visiting them under the guise of a 'concern for preaching'. A doorkeeper kept out strangers[2] and proceedings were secret to Friends; no reporter was allowed, no journal of debates was printed or published. In the acid controversies of 1836-7 indiscreet Friends gave reports to dissenting journals and were regarded as breakers of honour and faith. The Yearly Meeting chose a clerk who was both chairman and secretary, summed the debate and drafted resolutions. It received the reports of Quarterly Meetings in answer to the queries, appointed committees on public causes like slavery or schools or distraint, and drafted an annual epistle which was sent to Quarterly Meetings, Monthly Meetings, and preparative meetings, and was finally given at the door of each meeting-house to heads of families. Only the (male) Yearly Meetings could change the rules of the Society.

The meeting waited upon the spirit impassively. No one might applaud, or dissent, utter *hear-hear*, exclaim with surprise, laugh at wit. A speaker knew only that he would be uninterrupted and saw nothing of what was passing in the minds of his audience. An eloquent or vehement orator might alarm or even shock. This constitution was radical because it waited upon inspired speech and demanded minds open to the winds of Horeb, conservative because it refused to countenance voting. The answer must be reached by divine inspiration bestowing a common mind. No one asked for votes or recorded majorities. The clerk gathered opinions and formulated the mind of the meeting.

This polity was suited to a family. A constitution which hopes for unanimity is conservative among constitutions. The tradition of the

[1] Cf. Edward Pease's comments in *Diaries*, 75. The first joint session of men and women was held in 1880.

[2] In the thirties it was seriously believed by some Friends that one of the children of George III (either the future George IV or the Duke of York) once penetrated the Yearly Meeting disguised as a female Quaker, but was discovered, cf. *Tait's Magazine*, 1838, 291.

Society had no belief in equality of opinions. Like St. Benedict in his monastery, they expected the judgment of the wise and senior to prevail. Young malcontents could not collect voters to reform, because they could not vote. Their discontent was swallowed into the bottomless pit of prayerful silence. The system had the strength of making every decision of business into a religious act, the weakness that when a group faced radical and conscientious cleavage the remedy was doubtful. In a moment of frustration John Bright wrote of the grievous errors in Quaker polity and organisation.[1] Angry Friends charged the government with being a dangerous oligarchy. When anyone might come and speak the charge of oligarchy is at first sight wild. It arose because opinions of *weighty Friends* demolished a mass of argument. A proposal at Yearly Meeting could be stopped without reason given because weighty Friends, persons of acknowledged experience and character and seniority, rose and said that they *felt* against it. Reformers wanted Friends to be allowed freely to pay tithe where it was owed to laymen, and at last (1855) achieved victory, but only after years of feeling being pleaded. Reformers wanted elders appointed for limited tenure and not for life, and the motion was repeatedly destroyed without counter-argument. 'To solve questions', wrote Bright, 'merely by what Friends "feel" is to subjugate the reason, and the domain of fact and experience, to a delusion; and, it may be, to subjugate the course of the Society to the guidance not unfrequently of the feeblest heads in it . . . I should like to see a little more plain common sense in the Yearly Meeting, and less of senti-ment.' The critics were also suspicious of the Morning Meeting, a conclave of ministers and elders which ineffectually censored books on the doctrine or polity of Friends.

Conservative Friends thought that their Society declined because its younger members were disloyal to tradition. They warned the Society that if members continued for another generation to abandon the peculiarities, no Society would exist.[2] Liberal Friends thought that the Society declined because its conservative government adhered to tradition. But whichever had the truth, neither side doubted the fact. If fewer means worse, the Society was declining. In an age of English history when every other denomination was increasing in size, the number of Friends was falling fast. In autumn 1843 Joseph Rowntree

[1] Bright to John Pease, 26 December 1851, JFHS, 43, 1951, 24.
[2] *Diaries of Edward Pease*, 292.

tried to trace the history of the 1,869 boys who left the Quaker school at Ackworth between 1800 and 1839. For obvious reasons he published no report. But he found frightening loss to the Society and disturbing loss to Christianity. Cassandra-like Rowntrees, father and son, kept uttering cries of doom upon the Society if nothing were done. John Bright in a savage moment warned Quakers of extinction.[1]

	Members	Attenders	Total
1799	19,800	8,000	27,800
1861	13,844	3,190	17,034

At the best-attended meetings on 30 March 1851 were 14,364 Friends. In 1775 the Wiltshire Monthly Meeting comprised 13 meetings; 1785, 11; 1800, 7; 1827, 3; 1828, 2.

Nothing puts more power into the speech of reformers than fear of extinction.

When loss was analysed three causes could be distinguished: evangelical revival; poverty of Quaker religious education; marriage discipline.

The doctrine of inward light was open to various forms of rational interpretation. In America, Elias Hicks interpreted it in a deist sense; and the resulting shock and orthodox reaction divided and almost ruined American Quakerdom. English Friends were more evangelical. Though conservative Friends constantly used the Bible in devotion, they opposed its study, believing it too sacred to be openly dissected and discussed. It was not read publicly in meetings until after 1860. But many English members were touched by evangelical faith. They preached atonement and faith alone and at times even election. They were like Independents who eschewed outward baptism and communion, whose liturgy was silent waiting upon God. Joseph John Gurney was the leading minister of the twenties and thirties to interpret Quaker doctrine in evangelical sense.

The authority of the Bible was the root of controversy. Was scripture the sole and unique revelation of God, or was it secondary to the immediate leading of the heart and mind by the spirit of God?

Shocked by Elias Hicks and American disruption, and defensive against English critics who accused Friends of gross heresy in despising

[1] *Memoir of J. S. Rowntree*, 315, 346; J. Travis Mills, ii, 13; JFHS, 44, 1952, 5ff. The religious census of 1851 caused as much concern among Friends as among members of the Church of England. Cf. Hodgkin's speech in *Diary* of J. S. Rowntree, 1854: cf. *Friend*, 1854, 108.

the Bible, the Yearly Meeting of 1829 made formal profession of faith in the inspiration of scripture. Joseph John Gurney, who was intimate with Charles Simeon and William Wilberforce, tried to persuade families and schools to read and even study the Bible. But something about *scripture alone* was uncomfortable with the customs of Quaker worship and family life. The Society risked dividing like the Americans into evangelical Friends and inward-light Friends.

In 1835 Isaac Crewdson, minister in Manchester, published *A Beacon to the Society of Friends*. Analysing the deism of Elias Hicks, he launched into an onslaught upon inward light, if understood to mean that the soul is enlightened by immediate revelation apart from revelation through the Bible. Inward light is delusion, and silence is not of the essence of true worship. The ensuing conflict lasted from 1835 to 1837. Gurney believed that Crewdson was right, but tactless. In an effort to preserve unity the Yearly Meeting of 1836, in an epistle whose leading phrases were suggested by Gurney,[1] defined scripture as the 'only divinely authorised record of the doctrines which we are bound as Christians to believe . . . whatsoever any man says or does which is contrary to the scriptures, though under profession of the immediate guidance of the Spirit, must be reckoned and accounted on mere delusion'. But when ministers in Lancashire preached against atonement and so seemed to deny Christian truth, it became impossible for many Lancashire Friends to remain within the Society.[2] When Crewdson and his followers organised separate worship with public reading of scripture and kneeling in prayer and even sacraments, the schism was complete. About 300 Friends of Lancashire and Kendal and London left the Society. For a time they maintained a separate denomination, called Evangelical Friends, which renounced the notion of a universal inward light.[3] But soon they found little to divide them

---

[1] *Memoirs*, ii, 55.

[2] Cf. the harrowed letter of resignation in J. Travis Mills, i, 382.

[3] R. M. Jones, 505–7; J. Bennett, *Hist. Dissenters*, 364–70; *Diaries of Edward Pease*, 167. The Kendal division was still separate in 1862, cf. *Memoir of J. B. Braithwaite*, 145. Braithwaite was a strenuous advocate and writer on the *Beacon* side of the controversy. Most of his family, including his twin sister, left the Friends because of the controversy. He much admired Crewdson, wrote anonymous articles on his behalf to the *Patriot* in 1835–6, was secretary to Elihu Bates (the visiting American minister who was strong for Crewdson and became a Methodist), and in 1840 had almost decided to leave the Society and seek instruction from Baptist Noel, under whose guidance his brother and sister had left. He attended the Yearly Meeting of 1840 meaning to leave, but was convinced by listening to the meeting that he must remain a Friend and in 1843 adopted the stricter garb which he wore into the twentieth century.

from other denominations. Some joined the Church of England and some joined the Plymouth Brethren.

The departure of the Beaconites delayed reform of religious education. Strict Quakers (like extreme Calvinists among Strict Baptists) taught little religion to their children. The young were expected to conform to the customs and attend worship, but in many homes the Bible was not read, and in some the children did not acquire the words of the Lord's Prayer. Education was a secondary means which might obstruct simple waiting upon the word. Evangelical influence and the statistics slowly altered these practices.[1] Quaker Sunday schools (First-Day schools) were started in the forties. Once the binding nature of customs was questioned, the young might also question the mode of worship. Samuel Bright as a boy used to float bits of cotton wool down from the gallery upon the broad-brimmed hats below.[2] All boys find it difficult to acquire hallowed associations of worship, but Quaker silence was said to be more difficult to take into the heart. Freedom of speaking had disadvantages as well as advantages. Persons whom one most wished to hear sat mute in contemplation, persons whom one had small desire to hear were voluble in discourse. But the hazard of sitting under Anglican or dissenting pulpits was equal.

The marriage of a Friend must be approved by his meeting. He or she must not marry in church or chapel. Nor must he marry in a registry office. Nor must he marry a spouse not a Friend. If he committed any of these acts, his meeting was bound to expel ('disown') him. No rule was so grievous. As English communities became less isolated young Friends fell in love and were disowned. Devout Quakers were lost to the Society in this way. The future cabinet minister W. E. Forster was son of a godly minister and was disowned for marriage. John Bright's brother Thomas and two sisters were disowned for marriages. Their father Jacob Bright was Spartan in decision that his meeting must disown, and John Bright was the solitary voice which spoke for them. One of the sisters, Priscilla Bright, was a devout Friend and was marrying a devout Scottish Presbyterian. Yorkshire Quarterly Meeting disowned 151 Friends between 1837 and 1854.[3] Marsden (Lancashire) Monthly Meeting dis-

[1] Cf. Mary Howitt's account of her religious education or non-education, *Autobiog.*, 24–25.
[2] Travis Mills, i, 437.
[3] Rowntree, *Yorkshire Quarterly Meeting*, 29; R. M. Jones, 190.

owned 177 Friends between 1800 and 1850: two were disowned for fraud, one for enlisting, fourteen for immorality, seventeen for non-attendance, twenty-five for insolvency, and 118 for marrying out of the Society. Of 851 boys of Ackworth school whose marriages Rowntree traced, 304 were found to be disowned for marrying outside the Society.[1]

Godly and old-fashioned veterans[2] saw the hardships of marriage discipline, but no alternative. To remove the discipline made unsuitable marriages easy and probable, introduced doubt and laxity into households and made it hard if not impossible to bring up children faithful to Quaker customs. Reformers loathed the rule as obsolete and uncharitable. Joseph Rowntree worked against it for thirty years, John Bright was scathing. Bright assailed the Society for visiting the marriage of two religious persons with the same penalty as flagrant immorality. 'The Society may well not extend. It is withering almost to nothing. Its glorious principles are made unsightly to the world. Its aspect is made repulsive. It keeps out multitudes by the imposition of tests and observances which can never be of real importance . . . Can the Society reform itself, or will it slowly sink?'[3] But Bright's advocacy was little use to the cause. The most eminent of English Friends was at first distrusted if not resented at the Yearly Meeting. He engaged in political acts doubtfully consistent with his religion; was strenuous against the peculiarities; refused to wear the costume though he used *thee*; was brusque and vehement, and amid the meek quietnesses of Quaker debate sounded like a bass lost among trebles. At one Yearly Meeting he kept standing up and perforce sitting down because the clerk would not let his eye be caught.[4] They heard his blistering denunciation peacefully and adjourned. He harmed the cause as much as he helped. His eloquence plopped into the listening coolness like a stone into a bog.[5] It was only after years that he became a weighty Friend.

[1] J. Travis Mills, i, 424–5; Rowntree, *Quakerism past and present*, 154.

[2] Cf. *Diaries of Edward Pease*, 294.

[3] Bright's *Journal*, 5 April 1849, the day when Priscilla Bright was disowned; J. Travis Mills, i, 277.

[4] A. Vernon, *A Quaker Business Man* (1958), 51–52. Cf. *Diary* of Joseph Rowntree the younger (24 May 1858). 'I should think that since the time of Samuel Tuke no such speech has been heard in Devonshire House. In a few sentences he struck at the heart of the question; swept away the cobwebs so diligently and so painfully spun in the great difficulty of suitable marriages—it was no use to attempt to put persons into straitjackets.'

[5] Cf. J. Travis Mills, ii, 38. J. Bevan Braithwaite enjoyed Bright's oratory, cf. *Samuel Tuke*, 115, but it commanded few judgments.

Joseph Rowntree, the York grocer, assailed the barriers with more outward tranquillity. He wore the garb and Friends were readier to hear pleas for change of custom from those who kept custom unchanged. Collecting horrifying statistics, he knocked gently away at the Society. During the fifties the pace of change quickened. In 1853 two Friends who did not wear the garb were nevertheless appointed to office in the London and Middlesex Quarterly Meeting. In the *Friend*, which was the more liberal and evangelical of the two Quaker journals, letters were allowed to appear on either side of the question, one side recommending the end of the garb as a needless separation from other Christians and acting as a burlesque on religion,[1] the other reminding the Society of their value as a hedge to the young, a protection to the female, and a badge which on stagecoach or steamer caused other passengers to refrain from swearing. The Yearly Meeting of 1856 discussed plainness of speech and Joseph Sturge raised the question whether the whole discipline of the Society was too strict, arousing a debate so stern that John Pease even urged men and women who did not hold with the principles of the Society to leave it. At the Yearly Meeting of 1857 Sturge again assailed the peculiarities of garb as a stumbling-block to the young, and the question could only be postponed by getting it referred to committee.[2] The Yearly Meeting of 1858 at last agreed, on request from Rowntree's Yorkshire meeting, to consider the difficulty of mixed marriages; and again Sturge hammered away at plainness of speech, that Mr. no longer means Master, that the plural pronoun has ceased to do homage, that the names of the days are harmless despite their heathen ring. By the end of the 1858 meeting everyone saw that change must come.

Rowntree's son, John Stephenson Rowntree, precipitated a new controversy. A prize was offered for an essay explaining the decline of Quakerism, with Frederick Denison Maurice as one of the umpires. At the age of 24 Rowntree entered the competition and won the prize with a book entitled *Quakerism past and present*, 1859. This essay was the boldest utterance yet by a Quaker reformer. Silence has become a form and could never meet the needs of more than a few. Scriptures should be introduced into public worship. In many parts of England two-thirds of the meetings have no acknowledged minister because Friends insist (wrongly) that ministry must be a direct miraculous call

---

[1] *Friend*, 1853, 91, 104, 129.
[2] *Friend*, 1857, 99.

like the inspiration of a Hebrew prophet, and therefore the call to ministry is rare. He charged the Quakers with disparaging all secondary means and pretending that everything must be done under direct fiat of God; with isolating themselves in education and literature and so becoming a body fossilised in the past. Rowntree wanted the peculiarities of dress and speech to disappear as hindrances which magnified trivial into important. But he attributed the main cause of decline in numbers to the discipline that Friends must marry Friends. A third of Friends who married between 1809 and 1859 (he reckoned) had been disowned for marrying outside the Society. He urged Friends to come out and live for the world instead of for themselves; to avoid rules on trivialities which should rightly be left to the individual conscience; to end disowning for marriage; and to educate members and their children in religion.

The essay was confident and not quite accurate. It excited alarm and indignation. But the aspirations of younger Friends were triumphing without this aid. From 1859 the marriage discipline became steadily less draconian. Many conservatives so disliked the omission of the query on plainness of speech that the clerk of 1859 preferred not to record a minute. The query however was quietly omitted in 1860 as part of a general revision. The Yearly Meeting of 1861 adopted a mellower attitude towards change and revised the disciplinary code while it still condemned music and plays and novels and gravestones.[1] Thereafter change was rapid. In 1865 they even founded the provisional committee of a society to evangelise the heathen. Few Friends wore the garb after 1900. Smiling to the world brought converts:

	Members	Attenders	Total
1861	13,844	3,190	17,034
(Bottom was touched in 1864 with a total of 13,755 members)			
1899	17,031	7,904	24,935

[1] From 1850 it permitted a plain stone of which the inscription stated only name, age, and date of death. The stones must be uniform to guard against difference between rich and poor, and horizontal: *British Friend*, 8, 170, 175; *Extracts from the Minutes*, 1862, 138. The Norwich and Norfolk Meeting came back next year with the plea that horizontal stones were difficult to achieve in practice; cf. *Friend*, 1850, 206; *British Friend*, 1851, 135. The change of attitude to marriage required two successive changes in the law of the land. The law allowed Quaker marriages to be legal only if both parties were members of the Society. In 1860 they secured an act legalising Quaker marriages between a Quaker and one who 'shall profess with' the Society. This caused further disciplinary problems. In 1872 another act of Parliament dropped the condition of Quaker profession, and from 1 January 1873 liberty was complete.

But quaint survivals long remained. 'Thee dresses thy children in a very *bright* drab,' was a reproach to a parent whose child remembered it in 1945.[1] And at Fritchley in Derbyshire a little group of Friends became a separate group to preserve clothes and customs and truth.

7. LATTER-DAY SAINTS

In 1841 or 1842 Englishmen became aware of a new religious sect, Mormons. At first they sneered or smiled. Six years later everyone opened eyes of alarm. England was discovered to have more Mormons than Quakers. And still they spread fast.

America, land of frontier-religion and revival, exported its methods and fervour into English dissent. An American revivalist, Lorenzo Dow, preached at the birth of Primitive Methodism. An American revivalist, Finney, published lectures on revival which influenced respectable Congregational or Wesleyan ministers. An American revivalist, Caughey, ran wildfire amid the tidy corn of Bunting-Methodism. And at last the frontier exported under modes of revival a doctrine so strange that no one knew whether it was contemptible or pathetic.

The first Mormon missionaries landed in England during 1837 and claimed to have converted 2,000 persons. The next mission of 1840 included seven of the prophet's apostles, headed by Parley Pratt and Brigham Young. Based on Liverpool, they sent missions round the country; preaching in streets or parks, invited like other extreme itinerants to preach in little independent chapels, early thought akin to Primitive Methodists or Baptists, drawing many converts from splinter-Methodists or splinter-Baptists. At Liverpool, Pratt, who seventeen years later was to be murdered by an outraged husband in Arkansas, printed a monthly (later fortnightly, still later weekly) newspaper the *Millennial Star*. Wales was the most fertile field, especially round Merthyr Tydfil and Dowlais. Mormon preachers delivered an apocalyptic gospel of atonement and immersion with a hymnbook taken from Methodist hymnody. To this they added adornments. They declared that the word of God was not only in the Bible but in the *Book of Mormon*, a history of American Indians since biblical times and written on gold plates which the prophet Joseph Smith dug out of a hill. They preached that the kingdom of Christ

---

[1] Anne Vernon, *A Quaker Business Man*, 53. For the whole subject, see E. Isichei, *Victorian Quakers* (Oxford 1970).

would shortly appear at Nauvoo in the state of Illinois, and that it was the duty of true Christians to fly thither and to fulfil the ordained number of Zion. Israel shall live with the Lord upon the banks of Mississipi. They interpreted signs literally. They taught that God possessed a body in the form of a man. They practised prophetic tongues and miracles of healing, instituted an elaborate hierarchy of elders, bishops, priests, deacons. They cast 319 devils out of a woman in Leamington Spa, spent seven and a half hours driving a devil out of a meeting at Merthyr Tydfil, healed cholera in Huddersfield, opened the eyes of the blind in North Wales, made a crippled woman walk in Lambeth and cured a girl of St. Vitus's dance in Soham. Earthquakes, murders, eruptions, floods, tornadoes, fires, shipwrecks, thunder, blood-red flag in sky over Hull, luminous electric ball over Winder-mere, were observed as signs of the end.[1] It was raw religion. Joseph Smith hoped to convert Queen Victoria and Prince Albert, and sent a copy of the *Book of Mormon* to each. He warned the queen to avoid pride, luxury and extravagance.

To English poor, hungry with the poverty and squalor of the hungry forties, Nauvoo towered dreamlike amid meadows flowing with milk and honey. Mormon missionaries described a city of high wages and low prices, best cattle-feeding country in the world, pasture smiling with fat hogs and turkey and hens, fruit trees loaded with grape and apple and peach, soil rich as Eden, millions of acres of park-land unoccupied and ready to plough; a kingdom fit for saints to possess. Pratt and Brigham Young organised emigration out of Liverpool. In that age the Mormon shipping office held high place for efficient transport amid the insanitary reek of most emigrant shipping. They chartered ships and established agencies in Liverpool and New Orleans and St. Louis to protect the travellers. Some 1,190 English Mormons sailed from Liverpool in the winter of 1841-2; 1,199 in the winter of 1842-3. Mormons were almost all of the poor. Of the recorded trades of emigrants during the years after 1840, the highest were 457 labourers, 226 miners, 120 farmers, 96 cobblers, 74 tailors. Trades which pro-vided a solitary emigrant included tobacconist, brewer, bookseller, sweep, corkscrew-maker, footman, dancing-master, bus conductor, jeweller, physician, dentist and pawnbroker. Two butlers sailed, two innkeepers, and two mysterious graduates.[2]

[1] MS, i, 215; ii, 136; xi, 39-40, 139; xv, 853.
[2] J. Linforth, *Route from Liverpool*, 13-17.

Brigham Young left for America in April 1841. In Missouri and Illinois the Mormons for several years defended themselves against the imputation of horrible crimes. As emigrants came steaming up the Mississipi they must close their ears to stories from loungers at the wharves. The rumours were discredited in England. The citizen of the Potteries or Birmingham or Lancashire or Wales found authentic gospel in the Mormon preachers and longed for a blessed kingdom overseas.

On 27 June 1844 Joseph Smith was shot dead by the lynching mob as he climbed, spent six-shooter in hand, out of the window of Carthage gaol. Martyrdom of the prophet set the seal upon his doctrine. Fewer emigrants from England sailed during the next two winters, for one winter no emigrants at all, and barely 200 in the winter of 1847–8. But the reason was less scepticism of faith than doubt of the loveliness of Zion. Bitter schisms of succession tore the church asunder. Missionaries rival to Brigham Young arrived in England on 1 August 1845 to denounce the new government of the church. The call to emigrate sounded as loud as ever, but the people doubted while their leaders struggled.

And still the church grew. In Illinois and Missouri mob-settlers hounded and pillaged the almost defenceless people. In February 1846 Brigham Young began the great exodus from Nauvoo across the plains and all emigration was suspended. That November the English Mormons petitioned Parliament, setting forth the poverty of the queen's subjects, and asking money and a small military force to help them emigrate to Oregon or Vancouver Island.[1] Lord John Russell acknowledged the petition, but gave neither money nor military force. On 23 December 1847 the twelve apostles issued an epistle to all the saints, urging them again to emigrate to Zion, now in Salt Lake City. Brigham Young established (1849) a perpetual emigrating fund to assist the poor. Between late 1848 and early 1854 Mormon agents helped nearly 11,000 converts across the ocean.

Mormon statistics of January 1850 showed 30,747 members in the united kingdom and nearly 17,000 who had emigrated. Several hundred had been excommunicated. According to these figures 50,000 Englishmen were converted to Mormon faith in twelve years. The religious census of 1851 was less encouraging in its count of 16,628

---

[1] The border on the 49th Parallel had been agreed in 1846. Petition in Linforth, 2–4; cf. MS, viii, 142.

Mormons at the best-attended (evening) service of Sunday. On the one side gold plates, crude dogma, rumours of vice; on the other the desperate forties, social revolution by faith and travel, bodily God and earthy heaven.

The year 1853 marked the end of their first flowering in England. The fifties paid better wages to the poor. And during 1852 Brigham Young announced that eleven months before his death the prophet received a revelation that polygamy was God's will. The revelation was published in the Utah *Deseret News* of 14 September 1852 and in the *Millennial Star* at Liverpool, not without hesitation, on 1 January 1853. Plunging into the pool, the English editors struck out boldly. They defied the world to prove polygamy unscriptural. When English newspapers and pulpits accused them of immorality they asked whether monogamy caused chastity in London streets. But the slur was fatal to evangelism in England. Brigham Young and his twenty-five wives, Heber Kimball and his forty-five wives became as laughable in England as in America. Outside the Mormon mission-house in Soham 1,200 people watched village youths enact a Mormon wedding, to which seven brides rode on donkeys.[1] A yellow-back entitled *Female Life among the Mormons* sold 34,000 copies by 1855. The number of Mormons in England sank back slowly to 2,000.

[1] MS, xv, 269.

CHAPTER VII

THE CHURCH OF ENGLAND 1853–1860

I. THE EVANGELICALS

PAPAL aggression gave a fillip to the evangelical party. Five or six years after Dr. Wiseman was made a cardinal, in part because Dr. Wiseman was made a cardinal, the evangelicals attained the summit of their influence in the Church of England.

From time to time newspapers of high churchmen announced hopefully that the evangelical party was dead or moribund or exhausted or obsolete. From time to time newspapers of low church-men rejoiced with equal justice or hyperbole that the Tractarian party was extinct. Wish begot hope and hope begot assurance. The *Times* of 1879 compared the once powerful and triumphant evangelicals to a harbour whence the sea has ebbed, with mouldering buildings and forsaken quays to attest its vanished trade.[1] But between 1851 and 1862 high newspapers were more chary in claiming that evangelicals were extinct, low newspapers more confident in believing that Tractarians were finished. It was the evangelical day of national authority. The evangelicals were never triumphant. But there was an epoch when they were powerful; the epoch after 1855, while the memory of papal aggression still rankled, while Sumner was still Archbishop of Canterbury, while Lord Palmerston presided over the cabinet, and while Shaftesbury the noble head of evangelical laymen was stepson-in-law to the prime minister.[2]

Parties are never monolithic. Whenever they are powerful they are numerous, and whenever they are numerous they contain a wide range of opinion. Evangelicals were as various as Tractarians. They held certain broad principles. They were men of the Reformation, who

[1] T, 31 January, 1879; cf. Francis Close's protest, 6 February 1879.
[2] For assertions that evangelicals are obsolete, cf. G, 47, 364, reviewing Carus on Simeon. For assertions by *Record* that Tractarians are nearly extinct, e.g., R, 18 June 1855. See an interesting comparison in E. B. Denison, *Life of Lonsdale*, 196.

preached the cross, the depravity of man, and justification by faith alone. Some of them were Calvinists and more of them were not. Most of them had little use or time for doctrines of predestination and reprobation. But they loved the song of sovereign grace, and respected Calvinist dogmas where they did not share them, and sheathed their daggers when they met Calvinists. They pondered long and daily over the Bible, were decisive and orthodox Protestants, embraced a Pauline interpretation of the Gospel, and were friendly to orthodox and Protestant dissenters. Rome they feared with the fear ot antichrist. Romanisers within the Church of England rallied them to the defence of truth.

With Protestant dissent it was different. Evangelicals owed their origins or revival to men who generated Methodism; and beyond Methodism they could join in doctrine and charities with conservatives of the three denominations of old dissent. Shoulder to shoulder with dissenters they stood on platforms of the British and Foreign Bible Society and worked to distribute cheap editions of scripture. They were sometimes content to hear sermons from famous dissenters. When travelling in Scotland they liked to worship and to communicate with the established church. The evangelical clergyman of St. George's in Bloomsbury met the Baptist pastor of Bloomsbury chapel every Sunday morning, each on his way to his flock, and every Sunday morning they blessed each other with the ancient greeting of the catacombs, *The Lord be with you, And with thy spirit*.[1]

This friendliness to dissent had edges. Leading evangelicals were attached to the doctrine and discipline of the Church of England. They exalted the prayer book, valued the establishment, resented assaults upon a state church. Edward Bickersteth, most colourful and godly of the evangelical clergy, helped to found the Evangelical Alliance which from 1846 organised annual meetings for Reformed Protestants from England, Ireland, Scotland, America, France, Geneva, Germany. But Bickersteth was unusual. Amidst the halls and speeches of the Evangelical Alliance rose the stink of disestablishment. Most English evangelicals conquered their sympathy for its aims and refused to touch it. Even Bickersteth regarded the anti-church spirit as poison in the veins of dissent.[2] They believed dissent to be contaminated with

---

[1] Stoughton, ii, 297. The two men were H. M. Villiers (later Bishop of Durham) and William Brock.

[2] *Memoir of Edward Bickersteth*, ii, 307.

politics, to be losing its spirituality, to be selling itself to the mammon of power. Most of them were conservative in politics and wanted the established church to control education.

Extempore prayer was golden to them. Their religion was sometimes ecstatic. And yet they loved the prayer book and found its ordered forms to be marrow and fatness. Stories were told of men roused to penitence as by the majestic words of the litany *From everlasting damnation Good Lord, deliver us*. Charles Simeon declared that no book outside the Bible was so free from faults as the prayer book, and that he never found himself nearer to God than he often was in the reading-desk.[1] Others suspected Simeon of being too much of a churchman. They accused him of being more of a churchman than a gospel-man. When Archbishop Howley accepted the dedication of his book Simeon thought it the greatest of blessings.[2] He caught his death of cold when paying formal respects to Bishop Allen of Ely. But Simeon was not unique among evangelicals. They were prayer-book men, establishment men, Tories. By reform of the established church they did not mean new machinery. Reform was of the heart. They had little faith in devices, laws, canons, convocations. To the Ecclesiastical Commission they were indifferent. The church might thus be reformed and still be dead.[3] To tidy the administration might be nothing but decorous crossing of the hands of a corpse.

They wanted sermons to be gospel. There was no reserve. They knew that men needed blast of judgment and sweetness of promise. The pulpit was their joy and throne. They were contemptuous of meatless sermons like the sermons of Bishop Allen of Ely.[4] Their sermons were long. Edward Bickersteth preached for an hour and three-quarters on an important London occasion. Some preachers still expected the hour demanded by the Protestant Reformation. In a great London church with a fashionable and instructed congregation it could be exalting and transforming. In a distant country church with rambling parson and ignorant people it could be wearisome beyond measure. But whether powerful or tedious they preached to convert. They wanted to identify regeneration with true conversion and found it complex to explain what happened in baptism. Uncomfortable with

---

[1] Abner Brown, 62, 221.

[2] Carus, *Simeon*[3], 504; Moule, *Simeon*, 109. Simeon refused to have prayers at his religious meetings lest he disobey the conventicle act.

[3] *Memoir of Edward Bickersteth*, ii, 359.

[4] CO, 58, 663.

the rasping saw-edge of Mr. Gorham's personality they were sure that he championed a gospel cause.

Their enemies confessed that they laboured. Some of their parishes were shepherded as diligently as any parishes in the land. Their hostile critics said that they were redeemed by the working of their parishes.[1] In slums like Whitechapel or Bethnal Green, in fashionable watering-places like Brighton and Bath, in remote country parishes, they could be found foremost in every scheme of charity, supporting church extension at home, distributing tracts and coals and blankets, stirring the people to support foreign missions, summoning the elect to their Bibles and their prayers. 'It is better', said Edward Bickersteth, 'to wear out than to rust out',[2] and he obeyed his precept. They instituted more frequent communion, increased the number of services, pro-moted new standards of reverence.

The distribution of tracts took no account of seasons. They were handed out in pleasure-boats and omnibuses, left open on the tops of hedges, proffered on sticks to galloping horsemen, sent to criminals awaiting the rope, given to cabmen with their fare. Occasional recipients tore up the gift or greeted it with *Don't read nuffin*, or left the inside of the stage-coach to demand a safer seat on top. Newman Hall always travelled third class in trains because he found that the people in those compartments received his tracts with more gratitude. Tracts were often received with courtesy or interest.[3] Stevenson Blackwood travelled by train from Aberdeen to London. While waiting a quarter of an hour at Aberdeen he visited the quay, gave tracts to the dockers and fishermen, and preached aboard a collier. In the ticket queue he gave a woman a book. Between Aberdeen and Perth he persuaded a drunken man to kneel down in the carriage and pray with him. At Edinburgh he gave a lady a tract as she got out and in exchange she gave him a sermon by Spurgeon. Between Edinburgh and Newark he got a snoring man to read a tract in his waking moment. After Newark he distributed books to two new gentlemen. Finally he spent the last hour in composing an address.[4]

The pistol among tracts was *The Sinner's Friend*, first published by the Methodist layman J. V. Hall in 1821, revised and altered in

---

[1] *Macmillan's Magazine*, November 1860, 119.

[2] *Memoir of Edward Bickersteth*, ii, 63.

[3] Cf. the record of tract-distributors in the crowds of the Great Exhibition of 1851, Weylland, *A Thought for the World*, 26–27.

[4] *Life of Stevenson Blackwood*, 211ff.: the journey was of 1858.

numberless editions. By 1845 it sold more than 800,000 copies, reached its 140th edition, and was translated into all the main European languages, several Indian languages, and a good many other tongues. Twenty thousand copies were distributed in Tahiti. It was evangelical gospel in direct attacking format. There were sixty pages, but they included lines of great black-letter capitals like placards—SEE! *The dreadful gulf is beneath you. A few more steps in the way of sin and headlong down you go into eternal fire* . . . ESCAPE!—*for your life*!!! And then came the promises of love and mercy. We hear of many simple people converted by its reading; and not only simple people. An undergraduate of Trinity College in Cambridge left his profligacy after reading it, Colonel Holcombe was changed by it, and the professor of Greek at Cambridge University, James Scholefield, had it read to him on his death-bed.[1] In 1853 the aged Hall went to see Archbishop Sumner at Lambeth palace and mentioned his little book. 'Not a little book,' said Sumner. 'I call it a great book, for it has done great good in the world.'[2]

The children of evangelical pastors lived austere lives without novels or cards or dancing. Waltz and polka reeked of vice, but all dances were odious. They were kept from entering worldly society. But they were given the run of good libraries, were encouraged to varied interests of natural history or music or good literature, and were early used to help in Sunday school or visit poor parishioners or copy important letters. Shakespeare was bowdlerised and idle words excised from the songs of the music room.[3] At Christmas their festivities were rather devout than gluttonous, and they were not allowed Christmas trees.[4] They were expected to have straight hair and not curls nor ringlets, eschewed gauze bonnets ornamented with bows and wore straw bonnets without bows, preferred green and grey colours to red or lilac.[5] Sometimes their fathers used the text of 1 Timothy 2.9 to ban gold or pearls or elegant dresses. But they varied. Henry Venn Elliott, the moderate and eirenic minister of St. Mary's chapel at

[1] J. V. Hall, *Autobiography*, 191, 196, 275. Cf. *Memoir of Colonel Holcombe*, 18. By March 1867 it had sold 1,800,000 copies, G 67,307.

[2] Hall, *Autobiography*, 274: 18 April 1853. Hall's son Newman Hall sold four million copies of a tract *Come to Jesus*: Newman Hall, *Autobiography*, 200.

[3] *Memoir of Edward Bickersteth*, ii, 192–6. A midland evangelical required a visitor to keep his Shakespeare locked in the portmanteau lest the servants see it, Baring-Gould, 102–3.

[4] CO, 1857, 78ff. The Christmas tree was introduced to England by Prince Albert.

[5] *Vicar Wrexhill, of* ii, 16; iii, 28.

Brighton, wrote a defence of plaited hair and ornaments and fine attire; or if not a defence, at least a confession that scripture does not condemn such decorations in their proper place, and that the Epistle of St. James speaks of a Christian with gold ring and splendid apparel.[1] Evangelicals disapproved fox-hunting parsons, shooting parsons, cricketing parsons, ballroom parsons. They did not disapprove of wine.

Tractarians shared such severities. Newman disliked dancing. Hurrell Froude was a fox-hunting parson, but when he edited Froude's *Remains* Newman omitted the moments of fox-hunting. Bishop Lonsdale of Lichfield, who loved the theatre in imagination, regretted all his life that convention prevented him from attending theatres.[2] Wilberforce of Oxford expressed the opinion that a resolution to attend theatres or operas disqualified a man for the parochial ministry. Ex-Puseyite Roman Catholics were attacked on the charge that they used their abandonment of Anglican orders as excuse to go to theatres. Books of etiquette prescribed that if you offer cigars round the room you shall not offer them to clergymen present,[3] and did not distinguish among clergymen. A curate was thrown forcibly out of a ballroom at Bury in Lancashire (1854) because the assembly objected to his presence. Sunday divided Tractarian severity from evangelical severity. Tractarian pastors like Keble encouraged their villagers to cricket on Sunday afternoon. No evangelical pastor would so have occupied Sunday.

The Victorian parent was stern with his children. The evangelical parent, receiving biblical order not to spare the rod, was severe. Maurice's sister used to put delicious puddings on the table before her child and just as he was expecting to eat would order him to carry them away to the poor of the village.[4] Solitary confinement in a dark room was an accepted punishment for the very young. Some of the books on bringing up little children must surely have been written by milk-dry desert-bred nannies. By chance or by law of average evangelical parents or schoolmasters succeeded in breeding distinguished rebels. In *Jane Eyre* Charlotte Brontë portrayed an evangelical

[1] *Life of H. V. Elliott*, 254ff.

[2] *Life of Lonsdale*, 184–5; *Recollections of Sophia Lonsdale*, 19; *Diaries of Lewis Carroll*, i, 152.

[3] *The Habits of Good Society*, 1855, 256; Laver, *Victorian Vista*, 150; G, 54, 777. The *Habits of Good Society* enacts: 'One must never smoke, without consent, in the presence of a clergyman, and one must never offer a cigar to any ecclesiastic over the rank of curate.'

[4] A. J. C. Hare, *The Story of My Life*, i, 112, 180–6.

parson as grim, gaunt, canting, prim, and hard as black marble—and yet other sources revere him as a devoted pastor.[1]

The impression exists that evangelical parents bred more revolts, or worse revolts, than other parents. This impression is partly derived from the terrible and classical description of the battle in Edmund Gosse's *Father and Son*. But Philip Gosse was not an evangelical in Shaftesbury's sense of that word. He was a Plymouth Brother, and an unusual one. The impression is partly derived from Samuel Butler's *The Way of All Flesh*, which was not an evangelical conflict. Other forms of education could also breed revolt; among the Puseyites, it is sufficient to name James Anthony Froude. And we find many examples of pious evangelical children of pious evangelical homes, a father-son relation of perfect naturalness and friendship, in families like Bickersteth, Moule, Villiers, Sumner, Ryle, Wilson.

Evangelical parsons were reckoned by a critic of 1853 as about a third of the English clergy.[2] The estimate was too high. A few years earlier an evangelical clergyman reckoned his brethren at 3,000 maximum and condemned nearly 10,000 ministers of the establishment as neither earnest nor God-fearing. But the edges were not sharp. One useful guide is the list of clerical subscribers to the Church Pastoral-Aid Society, which was founded in 1836 to supply evangelical curates and lay-workers in neglected parishes. In 1841 nearly 1,700 clergymen were members of the society. The Gorham case or its atmosphere added another 200 clergymen, papal aggression another 200.[3] Other evangelical institutions like the Church Missionary Society and the Bible Society showed parallel rise in numbers. The evangelical leader in Manchester, Hugh Stowell, calculated that in these years the number of evangelical pastors in Manchester rose from twenty to sixty.

They did good work, sometimes great work, in the parishes. But they were unpopular. No more unpopular than the Puseyites and usually less unpopular, they collected nearly as bad a reputation. The British public feared Puseyites and despised evangelicals.

One after the other the novels of two Trollopes held up evangelical clergymen to reprobation. In Anthony Trollope you almost miss the distorting burlesque of the character because it is hidden in the

[1] William Carus Wilson is Mr. Brocklehurst in *Jane Eyre*. For a defence against the charges see H. Shepheard, *Vindication of the Clergy Daughters School*, 1859.

[2] Conybeare, 'Church Parties', ER, 1853, ii, 338.

[3] E. J. Speck, *The Church Pastoral-Aid Society*, 53, 75. CO, 1856, 145.

humorous sunlit nostalgia of a Barset landscape. In his mother the portrait is a distasteful extravagance.

In 1837 Frances Trollope published in three little volumes a novel entitled in draft *The Unco' Guid* and in the press *The Vicar of Wrexhill*. The new parson of Wrexhill in Hampshire, appointed by Lord Melbourne to favour the Whig interest, is a blackguard who by religious profession and pseudo-sympathy creeps his vileness to the breast of the squire's widow and marries her for fortune and property; meanwhile seducing another woman of the parish and trying to dis-inherit his new wife's children by the dead squire. The second volume carried a terrible frontispiece of the vicar exhorting the soul of a kneeling and penitent girl—or is it of the vicar making love to a worship-struck adolescent? The discrediting of this villain was used by Frances Trollope to blacken Calvinist doctrine, extempore prayer, emotional religion, foreign missions, the *Christian Observer*, and all puritanism as canting, snivelling, sanctimonious hypocrisy. She claimed to have heard of such a living incumbent; and one parson amused or vexed her by insisting that she intended the book to be a portrait of himself. But in truth the novel failed; for whether or not such a Tartuffe existed in an English village, Frances Trollope general-ized from the single crude character to all evangelical clergy. No man of judgment believed it. Tractarians rebuked the book as immoral.[1]

But some people liked to believe it or were amused to believe it. For otherwise Anthony Trollope would not have tried the same on-slaught, twenty years later, in Mr. Slope, chaplain to the new Bishop of Barchester. Slope is a blackguard with the same desire to use his religion to achieve a fortune. But villainy is more subtle, personality more complicated, situation so rich in humour that no reader can miss its caricature. Anthony Trollope did not suggest that Slope was a type.

Their unpopularity was the odium of the godly and the puritan. As late as 1837 they were still known as Church Methodists.[2] As late as the fifties Cambridge evangelical undergraduates (247 on the list in 1856)[3] were known to the university as Sims, after Simeon. When evangelical sisters visited a neighbouring church the congregation

[1] Cf. BC, 1838, January–April, 85ff.   [2] *Vicar of Wrexhill*, ii, 261.

[3] CO, 1856, 145ff. It is curious how another part of the undergraduate world over-looked their existence. Samuel Butler, who went up to St. John's College in 1854, said later that by that date the evangelicals at Cambridge had become a matter of ancient history: H. Festing Jones, *Life of Samuel Butler*, i, 59.

broke into titters because they joined in responses and knelt to say their prayers.[1] Some of the charges were identical with charges against Puseyites: they get influence over silly women, are earnest and humourless, are so self-denying as to be fanatical, their religion is gloomy . . . Puseyite and evangelical were each accused of disloyalty to the Church of England, not only by each other but by Englishmen who were neither. The one caused secession to Rome, the other secession to dissent. Some Englishmen thought extempore prayer to be an outrage on the feelings. Some Englishmen thought private confession to be an outrage. Some Englishmen thought both were outrageous.

Evangelicals repudiated the charge that they were a faction in the Church of England. But they were not ashamed of the word *party*. They had a defined programme for the church and were organised to further it. A man must choose his side. They confessed that a party-man might become small-minded, censorious, affected. But these vices might be avoided, and to be valiant for truth was badge of honour. Of their two journals the *Christian Observer* practised charity and had few subscribers, the *Record* acted vituperative partisan and had many subscribers. No faction-spirit touched their best men—Sir Robert Inglis of the beaming countenance in Parliament, Bishop Robert Bickersteth of Ripon intent upon being bishop of a diocese and not of a party within a diocese. But others had the spirit of minority and knew that their conscientious opinions barred preferment. Through the forties and fifties partisans multiplied as high and low churchmen drew asunder. It had long been easy to distinguish evangelical from old high churchman by entering the house and examining books, pictures and conversation. By the late fifties the dress of clergy was distinct; evangelicals still in high collars and white shirt-fronts and cutaway tailcoats, looking (their critics said) like waiters in a restaurant, Tractarians with long black frock-coat and cassock waistcoat and neckwear which jettisoned the high lay collar and turned the white tie into something like a modern clerical collar. At least one Tractarian, when appointed to a new office, asked whether his future colleagues would mind that he did not wear a collar.[2]

---

[1] Shelford, *Memoir of Cadman* (1899), 7.

[2] H. P. Liddon, on appointment to St. Edmund Hall in 1859, Liddon to Barrow, 24 March 1859, Keble Coll. MSS. Cf. *ER*, 1853, ii, 301ff.: clipped shirt-collar, stiff and tieless neckcloth, cassock, waistcoat, cropped hair, unwhiskered cheeks as typical of Tractarians. It was noticed that the old-fashioned Tractarian, like Keble, continued to look like a waiter, Baring-Gould, 149.

Their habits of worship were beginning to differ more widely. When Archbishop Sumner and Bishop Blomfield both attended St. Paul's Cathedral it was observed that London turned east for the creed and Canterbury did not.[1]

The behaviour of two trusts lent substance to the charge that evangelicals were partisan: Simeon Trust and Church Pastoral-Aid Society.

Charles Simeon observed that under the law of patronage an evangelical vicar might be succeeded by an idle or fox-hunting parson. He therefore constituted (1817) the Simeon Trust, contributing his wealth and raising large sums from donors to buy advowsons which enabled the trust to appoint incumbents and so ensured evangelical succession. Shortly before his death the municipal corporations act ordered advowsons of corporations to be sold and allowed him to extend his purchases. The trustees[2] were not sectarian. The trust deed spoke lofty ideals of choosing clergymen. But the trustees were committed to choosing evangelical clergymen. They eschewed idle clergy, fox-hunting clergy, dancing clergy, gospel-less clergy, Anglo-Catholic clergy and at last non-evangelical clergy. Their opponents said that in exercising patronage the liberty of the Church of England was sufficient; that while it was right to exclude idle and immoral it was wrong to exclude good men because they did not hold the narrow orthodoxy of evangelicals. The evangelicals denied that their orthodoxy was narrow and said that it was nothing but the reformed doctrine of the Church of England. But this exercise of patronage opened them to the charge of party.

The Church Pastoral-Aid Society suffered like onslaughts. Founded in 1836 to pay for more curates and lay-workers, they were first suspect because they paid lay-workers. Stiff churchmen broke away to found 1837 the Additional Curates Society, which never equalled its rival in income. Then supporters of the Church Pastoral-Aid Society fell away because the society insisted on paying only for evangelical curates. It was asked why an unofficial society should test the opinions of a curate whom a bishop agreed to license. Few were

[1] *Armstrong's Norfolk Diary*, 22 June 1854.
[2] The original trustees of 1817 were Lord Calthorpe, Simeon, J. Thornton, J. Sargent, Daniel Wilson, W. Carus Wilson, William Marsh. For their successors cf. A. J. Tait, *Charles Simeon and his Trust*, 1936. Twenty-one livings went to the trust when Simeon died, including Newcastle-under-Lyme; Bradford; St. Peter's and St. Margaret's, Ipswich; and from the corporations Bath, Derby, Macclesfield, Bridlington, Beverley Minster. In 1936 there were 150. Pollard and Hennell, 174; A. J. Tait, 61.

the bishops who consented to join. Henry Phillpotts of Exeter refused with éclat, Samuel Wilberforce of Oxford joined and seven years later resigned, Prince Lee of Manchester joined and three years later resigned. But they had two Sumners, ancient Bathurst of Norwich, and a few others. The veto upon curates was called partisan interference with the authority of the church.[1] The managers were charged with using for a party purpose money raised for a church purpose. They continued unwavering. By 1858 they spent nearly £46,000 a year on curates and lay agents. The friction continued all the century; its climax when they discovered (1879) that they were paying for a curate at a church in Swansea which invited the Anglo-Catholic Father R. M. Benson to preach.

If Puseyites were distrusted as much as, or more than, evangelicals, in two respects they were admitted to have the advantage; in learning and in social class. Bishop Lonsdale of Lichfield, perfect type of the dry devout inarticulate shyness of Anglican middlemen, Howley redivivus, distrusting both sides, preferring the gift of an umbrella to the gift of a pastoral staff, confessed that the Puseyites had far more learning and ability; and he would generally add 'And they are gentlemen.'[2]

Nothing is commoner than the charge that evangelicals were ignorant. You can find learned evangelicals; James Scholefield, the harsh-sounding professor of Greek at Cambridge; William Farish, sweet-natured professor of Chemistry at Cambridge; William Goode, famous in the Gorham fights, whose learning bore comparison with that of any English divine. Nor did they all wear blinkers. George Wagner of Brighton (not to be confused with his uncle H. M. Wagner, the Puseyite vicar of Brighton) was a pupil of Julius Hare as well as of James Scholefield and sought to find the best in German divinity. In riposte to Tractarian editions of the fathers they constituted (1840) the Parker Society to republish the classics of the English Reformation; and the standard of editing was not inferior.[3]

But what has learning to do with religion? They were men with flocks, and spoke to simple hearts, and knew that little children shall

---

[1] J. E. N. Molesworth, the militant vicar of Rochdale, attacked the veto in a series of pamphlets of 1840-1; list of pamphlets and replies in Speck, 34ff.

[2] Denison, *Lonsdale*, 207-8; 121.

[3] Stoughton, ii, 207; *Memoir of Scholefield*, 289-90—Scholefield generally superintended what was printed by the university press, at first without pay, until in February 1845 he was appointed editorial secretary at a stipend.

inherit the kingdom of God. One of their favourite books after the Bible was *The Dairyman's Daughter*; not a novel but a true story of a girl in Legh Richmond's parish of Turvey who died of consumption; only ninety-two pages, but enchanting sentimental portrait of a godly quiet rustic arbour, with forelock-touching peasants in smocks, friendly gospel-preaching parson, simple consciousness of eternity in the fragrant sunlit countryside of England; and with a child who proves that the expert in religion is not the professor but the pure, and that humble insight penetrates deeper than learning.

Their daily meditations upon the Bible probed the apocalypse. They saw visions of a millennium, a recalling of the Jews to faith, a judgment of terror. They believed that biblical honesty ordered them to preach these visions. The minds of their more colourful leaders were dark with shadows and brilliant with sparks from the Second Coming. They pondered the predictions of Daniel or St. John and tried to detect the history of Europe. Students of prophecy eyed the Chartist rebellion, or the year of revolutions, or the Crimean war, and conned the signs of the times. The focus and arbiter of instructed evangelical opinion, the *Christian Observer*, announced in January 1860 that Garibaldi's imminent destruction of the papacy showed the Second Coming to be near. Dr. William Marsh of St. Thomas in Birmingham was known in the city as Millennial Marsh. Such doctrines did not lessen a congregation. Radicals and Chartists came from far and near to hear Marsh read from the Book of Revelation and discourse of a city paved with gold and built upon precious stones. In 1845 Marsh declared in a sermon his expectation that antichrist would be revealed within about twenty-five years and the Second Coming would be at hand.[1] The congregations did not depart. They knelt in soul before the throne of judgment. But it is easy to see why Christian sceptics mocked the learning and sense of evangelical preachers; why Dr. Arnold defined an evangelical as a good Christian, with a low understanding, a bad education, and ignorance of the world.[2]

It is difficult to see why they were said not to be gentlemen. The vicar of Wrexhill and Mr. Slope were vulgar beyond redemption. But remove them from the covers of novels and examine the lists of Oxford or Cambridge (especially Cambridge) graduates and they

[1] *Life of Marsh*, 86, 161; CO, 60, 53.
[2] Stanley, *Life of Arnold*, ii, (1881) 246. The hard saying was not included in the first edition of 1844. Its inclusion in later editions illustrates how it became fashionable to say hard things about evangelicals.

seem gentle. Noblemen sat as packed upon their platforms as at any other form of religion. Bankers and retired officers may be found in plenty. The filial biographer of the clergyman William Marsh studded his pages comically with titled relations or converts; so comic in bulk that a shadow of question rises whether the biographer dragged in his titles because he knew the accusation and thought that titles made weight in the balance. The suspicion should be dismissed. All Victorians attached importance to titles. The Duchess of Sutherland, the Duchess of Gordon, the Duchess of Manchester, the Duchess of Beaufort befriended evangelicals, but no dukes to overtop the Earl of Shaftesbury. As lately as 1860 Brighton was the fashionable watering-place for nobility, and among the churches of Brighton the most fashionable was St. Mary's proprietary chapel, where the beloved Henry Venn Elliott delivered thoughtful sermons to a remarkable congregation for thirty-eight years.

An old-fashioned English churchman, neither high nor low, look-ing back in 1868, dated the decline and fall of the evangelicals from the elevation of J. B. Sumner to the see of Canterbury in 1848.[1] This old-fashioned churchman happened to be son-in-law of the alternative choice for the see and therefore had an inward motive for severity towards Sumner. And yet it is certain that evangelicals were more unpopular in 1865 than in 1848. Place and authority damaged a decisive and unpopular minority. We must determine whether the evangelical Archbishop of Canterbury was guilty.

Sumner was not unpopular except with high churchmen. He was a temperate evangelical, and had none of that rigidity or aggression which cause unpopularity. He was moderate and gentle and amiable. Everyone who knew him enjoyed his affection. He was more active than he looked and more learned than he uttered. His early works on records of the creation and apostolic ministry were still sold. His voice was monotonous and jerky, but his sermons were sane, and after the bald inconsequences of Howley even eloquent. He dis-tinguished his former diocese of Chester by the number of new churches built. At most it could be said of him that he was decorous; and against archbishops this is not a just complaint. All men respected the man, high men despised the archbishop. A few evangelicals thought him great as well as good.[2] Men who yearned for the trap-

---

[1] Denison, *Lonsdale*, 193–6.

[2] e.g. Earl of Chichester, in *Memoir of Henry Venn*, 396. For Sumner's voice, J. P. Boileau's *Diary*, 22 May 1849.

pings of tradition and regretted the end of prince-archbishops were vexed at the indignity when Sumner walked out with an umbrella. Men who wanted the clergy to come down among the people were pleased with that umbrella. To them it seemed a symbol of the church casting aside imprisoning grandeur to turn towards the masses.

Lord John Russell aimed to check Tractarians by elevating Sumner. The choice had no such effect. He was believed to be partisan and known to be weak. Everyone liked him and disregarded him. He gave high churchmen a pleasant feeling that they resisted spineless government. The high-church wife of the Tractarian dean of Barchester was wont to assume a smile of gentle ridicule when Sumner was named in the conversation. While Howley's public speeches sounded imbecile, he was trusted as fair-minded; and had the singular advantage of being the archbishop who brought the church so imperturbably through the storms of the thirties. Sumner had no reserve of credit. After the Gorham judgment many high churchmen eyed him as a respectable and woolly-minded heretic. He gave offence by declaring in a private letter, which was secured by an unscrupulous Roman Catholic under false pretences and published in gross breach of confidence, that bishops were not necessary to Christian ministry. He confirmed the belief that he was partisan by dismissing the high and learned S. R. Maitland from the library at Lambeth.[1] Badly advised and lacking legal knowledge, he entangled his reputation in a series of legal blunders. Not incompetent, he presented the appearance of incompetence. The archives of government show that they barely consulted him on the choice of bishops at home and abroad. Though the first of modern archbishops to be enthroned at Canterbury, he was rarely prominent, had no desire to be prominent. At a public day of fasting it was remarked that the archbishop 'is, as usual, nowhere'.[2] He produced no watchwords, sounded no tocsin, marched along with the army and watched others command. Whenever he seemed to act with decision men believed that sharp goads prodded him behind. He could be dull. But it is doubtful whether sparkle was wanted for the post. The *Times,* contemplating Sumner's virtues, declared that the qualities of an English primate must be very sober and not at all brilliant.[3] It was vastly more momentous to be a good man than to be somewhere.

[1] *Life of Lonsdale,* 194.
[2] *Saturday Review,* 1857, iv, 321.
[3] Obituary of Sumner; cf. T, 8 September 1862.

Sumner therefore was not an important cause of growing evangelical authority. Nor was he a cause of growing disrepute.

From the senior evangelical clergyman it was a long stride to the senior evangelical layman. The Earl of Shaftesbury had qualities which Sumner lacked; courage, decision, prominence, toughness. If Shaftesbury had driven in Sumner's seat, the ancient coach of the Church of England might have ended its friendly lumbering journey in a smash.

Shaftesbury was the noblest philanthropist of the century. He promoted more good causes, and was therefore more cordially disliked, than any other politician of the Victorian age. He poked his long and charitable nose into sewers of London and hovels of Dorset, mills of Manchester and mines of Durham; enquired into children in factories or up chimneys, lunatics in asylums, milliners and needlewomen, burglars and pickpockets; attended tea-meetings in schools, read lessons from the Bible at services in theatres, encouraged the movement for ragged schools to educate the urchins of east London. When he succeeded his father as earl and inherited estates encumbered with a crushing tonnage of debt he signified his arrival at the little Dorsetshire village by closing the tap-room at 9 p.m., hiring a scripture-reader for the outlying hamlets, redecorating the village church, starting three schools and several new cottages, and arranging cricket matches in his park. He hardly read a book but the Bible. To read other books he had no time; writing hundreds of letters in his own hand, presiding at meetings of godly and philanthropic societies, devising bills for the Commons or the Lords, vainly urging policies upon ministers of state, never concealing his mind. He once talked proudly or wearily of meetings by day and by night on every imaginable subject.[1] His stature was national; partly because working men knew that for all his aristocratic conservatism he was their friend, partly because his unbending consistency gained the rueful respect of gentlemen who saw more clearly the need to compromise, and partly because he spoke for evangelical religion in an age when evangelical religion seemed suddenly to be the most potent religious and moral force in England. Cabinet ministers liked the idea of having him publicly on their side provided that he was given no post with power to act.

The death of the Reverend Edward Bickersteth in 1850 was a

[1] Hodder, ii, 356, 365.

disaster to Shaftesbury. Bickersteth was his private counsellor. A man of apocalyptic hope and puritan conduct, Bickersteth possessed an enchanting humane godliness and little interest in ecclesiastical politics. For a short time after his death Shaftesbury had no evangelical intimate beyond his wife. Five years later a lay Scotsman took Bickersteth's place in his cabinet counsels: Alexander Haldane, proprietor and leading writer of the *Record*. For thirty years Shaftesbury came into almost daily communication with Haldane. The exchange of Bickersteth for Haldane was not a blessing. Haldane encouraged the less agreeable side of Shaftesbury's evangelical faith—clamour for evangelical truth or puritan morals, concern for ecclesiastical politics and appointments, innate anticlericalism and antipopery, gaunt pessimism about church and Christian society. An air of harshness surrounded Shaftesbury as he walked and talked. A kindly preacher once directed a sermon against gloom to his personal pew.[1] Inside he was a simple person with a clear head, a troubled conscience, and a few fixed ideas of evangelical religion. But as the years passed the childlike quality became harder to discover behind the precise mouth and cold passionless eyes of a marble public face. Age did not ossify his mind, for it was ossified before he was old. Nor did it dry his emotions, for they remained as charged and hot as ever. But he poured torment of soul into his diary, spreading it out like Hezekiah in the Temple, and let no one see but posterity.

2. SUNDAY

Shaftesbury believed that the laws of England should conform to the laws of God; and the law of God ordered no man to work on the Sabbath day. With perfect consistency he stumped platforms and campaigned in Parliament for a godly Sunday as he campaigned for shorter hours or slum education. And evangelicals who pleaded the Sabbath encountered more obloquy than other evangelicals. For success—that is, compelling Englishmen to keep their Sabbath willy-nilly—meant inconvenience and discomfort and gloom for everyone; but especially for the poor. If no one was allowed to work on Sunday, no bus-drivers nor pilots of pleasure steamers nor park-keepers nor musicians nor stokers, the only occupation left to the poor of the London slums was drinking gin; an occupation which they pursued with zeal, and consequences far from sabbatarian.

[1] H. V. Elliott; Hodder, ii, 143.

At the beginning of Victoria's reign Sunday was quietly 'Victorian' in the homes and districts of the upper and middle classes. In some poor districts the streets were more like fairs, shops open, market stalls, fishmongers, cobblers, butchers, greengrocers, sheds, barrows; and on the Surrey side of the Thames pigeon-shooting and gambling. Thames steamers carried cheery loads of gaily-dressed Sabbath-breakers (as Bishop Blomfield called their passengers)[1] up to Richmond or down to Margate. The evangelical curate of Richmond gave evidence that the evil was very great. More barges with cargo sailed along the Thames on Sunday than on any other day. Droves of cattle were herded to Smithfield market. By law the people were turned out of public houses at service time, and so families on their way to church encountered drunkards ejected from bars. The congregation of St. John's church in the Waterloo Road could not hear the lesson because mackerel were cried in the street outside and the curate sent the beadle to stop the cries. Carriers were not allowed to ply on Sundays, and in 1828 a van travelling from London to York was stopped at Stamford and fined 20s. for travelling on Sunday. But stage-coaches and hackney-coaches had secured exemption from this law. Men with money to spend could travel easily. In the stirring times of 1832 a committee of the Commons[2] reported that the systematic violation of the Lord's Day was injurious to the best interests of the British people and calculated to bring down divine displeasure upon the country. They recommended that wages should be paid on Friday and not on Saturday, and that laws should regulate the hours when public houses might be opened. They reported with pleasure that the decorous observance of Sunday was increasing among the higher classes.

The evangelical who began the easy process of making sabbatarians disliked was Sir Andrew Agnew, who had been affected by *The Dairyman's Daughter*[3]. Early in 1831 he helped to found the Society for Promoting Due Observance of the Lord's Day. In 1833 he secured leave to bring in a bill. Its provisions astounded the public. It not only made any meeting illegal for the purpose of gaming, wagering, and betting, or for any wake, fair, hunt, baiting, cockfighting, and shooting, but added the ominous words 'any pastime of public indecorum, inconvenience or nuisance'. It forbade public lectures or speeches,

---

[1] *A Letter on the Present Neglect of the Lord's Day*, 1830. Cf. *Westminster Review*, July 1830, 135ff.

[2] PP, 1831-2, vii, 253, 331.   [3] *Memoirs*, 1850, 56, 60-61.

consumption of drink in hotels except by travellers, the hiring of carriages (except by clergymen and doctors), and the sailing of ships over 200 tons if for foreign ports and of any tonnage if for British ports. Turnpike-keepers were forbidden to open their gates, and lock-keepers their locks. But nothing in the act was to extend to works of piety, charity, or necessity. Mr. Beaumont said it should be entitled a bill to promote cant.[1] The bill was only lost in a late house by six votes, and both Sir Robert Inglis and the future Earl of Shaftesbury voted for Sir Andrew Agnew and the Sabbath. The press called Agnew a Scotch fanatic and caricatured him as a huge bird snatching off Sunday dinner in his bill.[2]

The odium of sabbatarians partly arose because their proposals seemed to hurt the poor and not the rich. The bus-driver must be forbidden to work and therefore the poor could not travel. But no one suggested that you could ban the rich from driving out in their carriages with coachmen and footmen. The poor who had no ovens were not to be allowed to roast their joint in bakehouses, while the rich enjoyed comfortable hot beef. In 1839 the lord mayor of London summoned various poor fishermen for using illegal nets in the Thames on Sundays. The fishermen retorted that gentlemen were allowed to fish with rod and line on Sunday. The argument that they were earning their living and the gentlemen were enjoying a holiday was not persuasive. The lord mayor accordingly summoned various gentlemen and let them off without penalty on receiving promises that they would not do it again. In the House of Commons the plea that Sabbath laws meant one law for the rich and another for the poor was deadly against every proposal. Lord Melbourne received two simultaneous Sabbath deputations with resigned endurance, lounging in his arm-chair and spitting into the fire.[3]

It might have been expected that the campaign to stop Sunday trains would have power. The Scots were fierce enough to force the cancellation of an express from Edinburgh to Glasgow on Sundays and Sir Andrew Agnew vainly pushed a clause forbidding Sunday trains into the bill establishing the Glasgow and Ayr railway. But English resistance was spiritless. Londoners must get out of London to breathe. Radicals in the House of Commons taunted Agnew that he dare not

[1] Hansard, 29 March 1833; xvi, 1232.
[2] *Memoirs of Agnew*, 164. For Agnew's bill cf. J. Grant, *Random Recollections of the House of Commons*, 1836, 339, and cf. Halévy, ET, iii, 163.
[3] AR, 1839, Chron., 159, 5 September; G, 48, 729.

try to abolish Sunday trains to Greenwich. Rare shareholders at company meetings protested against Sunday trains and were told by complacent directors that they must not deprive the public of health and exercise. A canal company petitioned wanly for laws against Sunday carrying of goods by canal or by railway,[1] but it is easy to suspect mixed motives. Joseph Sturge, who was one of the first directors of the London and Birmingham railway, kept proposing to the board that the company's engines and carriages be not used on Sundays. He got strong support, but could only secure that the railway be partially closed to prevent travel during hours of divine service; and, after two years, he confessed failure and resigned his directorship in protest against a course which involved such an incalculable extent of moral evil. The evangelical preacher at Brighton, Henry Venn Elliott, declared from the pulpit that the proprietors of the Brighton railway might be mere heathens if judged from their regulations, and that they sacrificed every religious obligation to mere money speculation. Occasional enthusiasts posted placards about swift and pleasant excursions to hell, and a Sunday crash afforded matter for sermons. Even high churchmen saw divine providence when a train carrying horses and racegoers to Newmarket fell off an embankment on Sunday. One Yorkshire jury after a crash added a rider deploring Sabbath desecration by the directors.[2] Queen Victoria travelled by train on Sunday for the first time in 1844, on her way to open the Royal Exchange; and not without comment. In 1850 the vice-chancellor, mayor and inhabitants of Oxford city sent a formal protest to the Great Western railway against Sunday excursion trains which brought visitors to disturb the town and offend the religious feelings of the respectable inhabitants. As late as 1861 a terrible collision in the Clayton tunnel between two trains running from Brighton to London, then the worst accident in the history of English railways, with 23 dead and 175 injured, was taken into many sermons.[3]

[1] Hansard, liv, 1840, 1100-1. C. F. Dendy Marshall, A History of the Sotthern Railway, 1936, 82. For taunts cf. Roebuck, Hansard, 1837, xxxviii, 900.

[2] Memoirs of Joseph Sturge, 251ff.; Romilly's Diary, 3 September 1843; placards of a visiting Scottish minister at Newcastle against the Newcastle to Carlisle excursion, 29 August 1841; W. W. Tomlinson, The North-Eastern Railway, 1914, 372-3; G, 1846, 218; Tomlinson, 427. Even Dr. Arnold, though refusing to support a resolution to ban all Sunday trains on the North Midland railway, was prepared for a resolution that a single train should run each way on Sunday, and offered to subscribe for extra help to relieve the employees: Stanley, Life of Arnold, 1844, ii, 198; 19 February 1840.

[3] CO, 1844, 704; Dendy Marshall, 309-10.

But for the most part the directors of railways rolled comfortably along on Sundays provided that they did not cross the border. All sensible men confessed that a few trains were necessary, though they were less confident about the 102 trains on the Greenwich line. An aggressive member of Parliament even attempted a bill to compel the Scottish railways to run trains on Sundays.[1]

It was agreed that shops should not open and that the drunken market hubbub of streets in south London was a scandal. It was agreed (except among extremists) that some work was necessary on Sunday—by milkmen, policemen, coastguards, men driving that minimum of public transport which alone allowed the city-dweller to breathe fresh air in parks or countryside. Sunday newspapers, under dropping shrapnel, continued unscathed on the plea that they were Saturday work and not Sunday and that Sunday was the day when men had leisure to read. Would the country's business come to a halt if Sunday postmen were forbidden to sort, deliver or collect letters? In the provinces the Sunday delivery was the heaviest of the week.[2]

The men or women who were required to work on Sundays wanted new laws. Shopkeepers of south London wanted to close provided all shopkeepers were forced to close. Postmen wanted their day of rest and were delighted with evangelical and dissenting agitation to close post offices. Penny post and extension of business caused the Post Office to make new regulations which caused a limited extension of work on Sundays at the London headquarters. On 8 October 1849 a mass meeting of protest was held at Exeter hall. The name of Rowland Hill, who was not the postmaster-general but whom everyone knew to be the brains in the Post Office, was hissed repeatedly.[3]

Lord Ashley, who did not succeed his father as Earl of Shaftesbury until 2 June 1851, headed this upsurge of feeling against Sunday work at post offices. On 30 May 1850 he disclosed in the House of Commons

---

[1] The perils of early railway travel were treated somewhat as the perils of early travel by air. The Catholic Bishop Thomas Grant said the psalm *de profundis* every time his train entered a tunnel, K. O'Meara, *Grant*, 166. For Dean Buckland's astonishing precautions when the railway line was wet cf. *Letters of Dean Stanley*, 97. Samuel Wilberforce once said that he never entered a railway carriage without reflecting that he might never leave it alive, Liddon, *Easter Sermons*, i, 121.

[2] So Rowland Hill, according to Ashley, Hansard, 30 May 1850, cxi, 469.

[3] H. G. Swift, *History of Postal Agitation*, 16ff. The October argument is reflected in the prime minister's papers: letters to Lord John Russell from Ashley on 6 October 1849, Inglis on 6 October, Archbishop Sumner on 10 October, and on the other side Lord Clanricarde, 6 October: PRO 30/22/8B. The clerks in the Post Office refused to work on Sundays unless compelled, Clanricarde to Russell, 24 October.

that he had petitions with more than 700,000 signatures and proposed that the Sunday collection and delivery of letters be forthwith ended. He rejoiced, he said, that here the voice of the people and the voice of God were in harmony. The government opposed the motion as inflicting hardship upon the majority of the people. To everyone's surprise it was carried by ninety-three votes to sixty-eight; and the surprise was more furious or delighted when the government of Lord John Russell decided to obey the motion. The postmaster-general announced that on and after 23 June 1850 delivery and collection of letters would cease on Sundays. It is doubtful whether Lord John Russell or Lord Ashley was the most unpopular man in the country. Men talked of organised fanaticism, of Russell's practical joke, of barbarous government. They compared the sudden attack upon English habits to an unheralded ukase banning tobacco or all plays but the sacred.[1] The government bowed willingly to the storm and appointed a committee of enquiry. In less than two months they rescinded part of the measure. They permitted one delivery and one collection on Sunday, and ordered Sunday work at post offices to be cut to the minimum.

While Shaftesbury was trying to sanctify Sunday, radicals in the House of Commons were trying to help the poor to enjoy Sunday. They wanted to open exhibitions and allow sports.

English Sunday was still controlled by the act of Charles II (1677). Under this act the depredators of Sunday quiet were prosecuted. The penalties were small, and the barrow-boy of south London cheerfully faced a fine of 5s. for Sunday trading and if caught opened a pitch in the next street. In August 1853 a Jewish outfitter at Shields was sentenced to a fine of 5s. and costs, and to sit in the stocks for four hours, for not observing the Christian as well as the Jewish Sabbath.[2] This act prohibited taking of money, and therefore no entertainment could be provided if a fee must be paid. But the poor of east London were not in a condition to pay fees. And therefore the argument, trivial but hot, developed upon certain public institutions or exhibitions which might be opened free to the people—British Museum, National Gallery, Crystal Palace—and upon the parks and whether free entertainment might lawfully be offered upon their swards. The radicals said that galleries and grass were better occupations than drinking gin. The conservatives said that you could not distinguish;

---

[1] e.g. *Times*, 31 May, 22 June 1850.   [2] G, 53, 583.

open the portals of the British Museum and you open the doors of other less solid institutions. They sometimes argued that if these institutions were open they would diminish attendance at church by the poor. The radicals said that this was impossible. You cannot diminish zero.

The Great Exhibition of 1851 was spun from the heads of Henry Cole and Prince Albert to be a symbol of peace through free trade among the nations. Prince Albert's doctrines were less than evangelical. The exhibition was to be a symbol of progress, of divine development through science and invention and industry. In the spring of 1850 Prince Albert raised qualms by a speech at the Mansion House, in which Man approached fulfilment of his great and sacred mission in the world. Devout critics thought offensive the display of religious jargon which so consecrated heaps of machinery and artefacts.[1] But most people shared the enthusiasm, even Lord Ashley, while he soliloquised that steam engines and china plates may consist with the vilest hearts. The British and Foreign Bible Society applied for space to exhibit the Bible in 130 languages. At first it received a blank refusal. For three months the argument was tossed. Lord Ashley intervened. He had a long interview, and a long correspondence, with Prince Albert. The prince said that the Bible was nothing to do with the products of modern industry and had no right to a place. Ashley said that the translation into 170 languages and 230 dialects was a wonderful proof of intellectual power. Prince Albert said, 'You have proved your right to appear.'[2] They won space, but in an obscure back room off a side passage upstairs. With grief they saw that the art of Pugin and other popish exhibitors was displayed to best advantage.

But here was a mighty assembly of wealth, and many Englishmen felt profound religious sentiments when they saw it. Observers looked at the crowd and saw, more than admiration, a quality of adoration.[3] Charles Kingsley found tears in his eyes.

The exhibition attracted unknown numbers of foreigners to London and something must be done for them. Bishop Blomfield of London appointed a Church Exhibition committee which considered the difficulty that services in a foreign language were illegal in churches. Courses of sermons were organised, the S.P.C.K. undertook

---

[1] Cf. *The Theology and Morality of the Great Exhibition of 1851*; by a Spiritual Watchman of the Church of England.
[2] Hodder, ii, 343. [3] Cf. J. P. Boileau's *Diary*, 19 August 1851; Hodder, ii, 343.

to distribute editions of the prayer book in French and German, tracts were distributed to the crowds. A prize of a hundred guineas was offered for an essay on the moral advantage to be derived from the union of all nations at the Great Exhibition. Prince Albert approved the plan. The essays made fascinating suggestions—that the queen should give an amnesty to prisoners; that the Houses of Parliament should eschew controversial business for the session; that ministers of religion refrain from their special tenets and enforce the grand principles of love of God and love of man; that estranged families resolve to meet; that Sabbaths be better kept; that bad characters be watched by police and so foreigners protected; that reading-rooms be opened in London; that evangelists take rooms in hotels next to foreign visitors; that Bibles be distributed free to visitors; and that over the area assigned to the Bible Society be framed an inscription, *The Charter of human liberty—the Book by which England has become great*.[1] After its first distrust of mammon and Prince Albert, England was warmed by the Great Exhibition. It stood grateful at the splendour of modern industry and saw a true symbol of peace among nations.

Men weakly and vainly suggested that the Crystal Palace in Hyde Park should be opened on Sundays. It was said with satisfaction or vexation that in no other European country would so splendid a promenade have been closed on Sunday. There was a proverb, *Ennui was born in London on a Sunday*.[2] In the next year the Palace was reconstructed at Sydenham Hill, and government must consider the charter of the company which acquired the right to use it. The directors pressed for Sunday opening. They asked only to open the parks and water-garden, not the industrial exhibition, and only after I p.m. They promised not to sell alcoholic drinks on Sunday. The *Times* startled everyone by announcing that the prime minister (Lord Derby) had agreed.[3] A deputation headed by Archbishop Sumner of Canterbury, Bishop Blomfield of London, Bishop Sumner of Winchester, the Earl of Shaftesbury and Sir Robert Inglis called weightily upon the prime minister to counter the plan. Dissenters and evangelicals said that the prime minister was advising Queen Victoria to abrogate the fourth of the ten commandments; that the principle once conceded must concede every shop and theatre after I p.m.; that it would

[1] Report on essays in J. A. Emerton, *A Moral and Religious Guide to the Great Exhibition*, 1851.
[2] Hodder, iii, 27.   [3] T, 2 August 1852.

be national crime. A dissenter[1] declared that the principle would be a deeper stab to public morality, and afford a greater triumph to popery and infidelity, than any act of the British government since the days of James II.

Men observed how those nations which neglected the Sabbath—and they pointed the finger at Spain, France and Italy—suffered revolution and bloodshed. Placards summoned the people to the rescue of England. The Crystal Palace (which in reality proved to be sober and even, when the novelty had worn, dreary) was described as a gorgeous temple of rampant pleasure.[2] Lord Shaftesbury delivered a fiery address to an enormous audience of Sunday-school teachers in Exeter hall.[3]

To the contrary it was argued that opening would be conducive to religion and morality; not only by promoting the health of London, but by leading minds upwards through architecture, sculpture, and the wonders of nature; by replacing the glass of gin with the glass of a palace; by fountains of pure water instead of intoxicating bowls; by rich flowers and rare shrubs in exchange for the bottle, the pipe and the gambling table; the song of birds for the rattle of dice; pure air and sweet perfumes for the stupefying fumes of the alehouse; the prattle of happy children for the revelry of brutal jests.[4] And between the contending parties stood moderate divines who knew that art unaided could not Christianise, but would have no part nor lot in agitation, lest Christian men set themselves aloft as prophets of doom and substitute pharisaic clamour for their own penitence and charity.[5]

The Crystal Palace stayed shut on Sundays.[6]

A month before it was due to open at Sydenham in June 1854 a campaign for fig-leaves began. The nude statuary caused adverse comment, and the adverse comment caused uproarious ribaldry in

[1] Dr. Josiah Conder, *The Law of the Sabbath*, 1852, 4.

[2] *The People's Palace and the Religious World*, 7; D. F. Jarman, *Proposed Opening of the Crystal Palace on Sundays*, 6.

[3] Hodder, iii, 29.

[4] Cf. Lord Chief Justice Campbell in House of Lords, 22 November 1852, Hansard, cxxiii, 277; *Much Ado about nothing: or the Religion of England staked on the opening or shutting of the Crystal Palace on Sundays*, 1853. The *Nonconformist*, alone among the leading dissenting or evangelical journals, discountenanced the agitation.

[5] See above all a fine sermon by F. W. Robertson of Brighton, *Sermons*, 1855, ii, 180, 'The Sydenham Palace and the religious non-observance of the Sabbath' preached 14 November 1852.

[6] Cf. T, 30 October, 3 and 18 December 1852. The directors in 1858 attempted to circumvent by giving life-tickets in exchange for surrendered shares and admitting the holders 'free'. A shareholder alleged that this would lead to revocation of the charter, and secured an injunction restraining them, G, 58, 259.

Punch, while the Crystal Palace was still in Hyde Park.[1] With nude statues in prospect at Sydenham, a formal remonstrance was sent to the directors requesting fig-leaves. Archbishop Sumner and his brother of Winchester, Bishop Blomfield of London, and various lords including Shaftesbury, thought it their religious and public duty to apply for fig-leaves.[2] The directors yielded to modesty. They were doubtful whether they would be able to secure a sufficient quantity of fig-leaves before the date of opening.

The triumph at the Crystal Palace stimulated demand for Sabbath laws. The leaders in the movement were evangelicals of the Church of England. But their power rested upon a constituency wider than the Church of England. Wesleyans, Baptists and Independents were decisively behind Lord Shaftesbury and Archbishop Sumner. The campaign for a godly Sunday was another wave in English politics of what later in the century was called the Nonconformist conscience. When the petitions for Sunday laws were analysed they were found to include a large number of petitions from Wesleyan congregations; still more from the united inhabitants of villages; fewer from Independents and Baptists; and an occasional oddity like gardeners from the Clifton nursery or a memorial from Bedford which cited the example of King Dosumo of Lagos who banned the beating of drums and other disturbances on Sundays near places of worship.[3]

The campaign was an attack by the country upon the city. Distant villagers with a silent Sunday heard what was planned in London and bombarded Parliament. Resolved to secure their peace, and fearing the immoral mammonish city, they could not imagine the conditions of east London. The city labourer toiled six full days a week, often with late hours on Saturday night, and could attend an exhibition only on Sunday. The evangelical and dissenting clergy of London knew that if they restricted Sunday pleasure in the name of God they must demand leisure for the labourer on a weekday; and the campaign therefore included a lukewarm cry for a half day—still sometimes spelt half 'holy-day'—on Saturdays. It was easier to prevent government relaxing Sunday than to persuade government into shortening hours of labour; and for that end much easier to blow bugles. To hallow Sunday was a divine command. To get rest on half Saturday was an expedient of statecraft.

---

[1] R, 5 May, 12 May and 29 May 1851.
[2] T, 8 May 1854; G, 54, 379.   [3] PP, 1856, lii, 123.

In June 1855 the London poor were stirred to protest against proposed Sunday legislation.

Lord Robert Grosvenor produced in the House of Commons a new Sunday bill. It was a moderate and sensible bill, confining its provisions to trading in London.[1] The timing was unlucky in that the previous year a public houses act established licensing hours (opening prohibited 2.30–6 p.m. and after 10 p.m.) which were resented as a Shaftesbury curfew and modified next year. Lord Robert Grosvenor was rightly believed by the public to be friend and colleague of Lord Shaftesbury, who by this time was feared as the general of a campaign to make England puritan. Placards summoned London to Hyde Park on Sunday, 24 June, to see how religiously the aristocracy kept Sunday. That afternoon several thousand people shouted and hooted and hissed and yelled at the carriages of the rich, crying 'Go to church!!' 'Why allow your servants to work on Sundays?' or 'Down with the Sabbatarians!' 'Away with the Sunday bill!'

The powerful began to be nervous. Lord Palmerston, now prime minister, was privately asked to persuade Grosvenor to withdraw. Palmerston refused. Grosvenor was asked in the House of Commons if he would withdraw. He refused.[2] Next Sunday 150,000 people assembled in Hyde Park, the police wielded truncheons, parts of the crowd tore up hurdles and used them as weapons, a few soldiers from the barracks helped the crowd, forty-nine policemen were assaulted and hurt, seventy-one people were arrested, ten for picking pockets and the rest for riot. Lord Robert Grosvenor, whose house was surrounded by a menacing crowd, withdrew the bill. A mob had dictated to the House of Commons. Riots in Hyde Park form habits, and next Sunday a crowd of boys went hooting carriages, pelting Palmerston and other occupants, and breaking windows, including those of the Archbishop of York.[3]

Three years later an ecclesiastical commission of enquiry reported that half the shops in London were still open on Sundays,[4] and that Sunday trade was increasing.

---

[1] It was given a second reading without a division on 3 May 1855, despite a radical's prophecy that it would mean riot, Hansard, cxxxviii, 1855, 55.

[2] Hansard, cxxxix, 158–60.

[3] Report of enquiry, PP, 1856, xxiii, 5. G, 55, 533 and 537.

[4] *Report presented to the Lord Bishops of London and Winchester*, 1858. Several of the most eminent evangelical London clergy were among its members, Dale, Pelham, Cadman, Champneys.

The fact was, Sabbath legislation was impossible. It was too entangled with religion. By the fifties wise men saw that they must design laws on grounds of social expediency and not of religious principle. The Victorians at last secured their Sunday by enactments in the title of which the word Sunday did not appear; by other acts, regulating licences or opening hours, by acts for shops and acts for transport and acts for public houses and not by acts for Sunday. These occasional laws grew into an interlacing thicket of briars which lawyers of the twentieth century needed to hack about.

Meanwhile officers of a Whig government could still try to provide leisure for the poor of east London. Sir Benjamin Hall was chief commissioner for works under Lord Palmerston; active in improving the government and amenities and parks of London. With the help of the colonels he installed the band of the Horse Guards to play martial airs in Kensington Gardens on Sundays.

In February 1856 a motion in the House of Commons to open the British Museum and National Gallery on Sundays was lost by a great majority (328-48), after Archbishop Sumner and Shaftesbury headed another enormous evangelical deputation to Palmerston, with representatives of the Religious Tract Society, the Pure Literature Society, the Evangelical Alliance, the Wesleyan Sabbath Committee, and numerous other bodies. The size of majority and the course of argument encouraged the campaigners to turn their attention to Sir Benjamin Hall's band—indeed bands, for this spring he installed the band of the Second Life Guards in Regent's Park and another military band in Victoria Park nearer the slums. He talked of installing Sunday bands in every garrison town when regiments returned from the Crimea. On Sunday, 4 May, 140,000 persons, a tenth of the entire population north of the Thames, assembled in the three parks to hear the bands, in good order and humour. On the following Sunday 250,000 persons listened to martial music.

What riled consciences was less the desecration of Sunday than government organising the desecration of Sunday. Colonels were compelling bandsmen under discipline to work outside their regimental duties. Shaftesbury went privately to Palmerston and warned him of the consequences. Palmerston approved nonchalantly of the bands. Shaftesbury went to Archbishop Sumner and wheeled his reluctance into a letter to the prime minister. Sumner wrote the letter, Shaftesbury hurried with it to Palmerston in the country. Palmerston yielded.

He told the House of Commons and the nation that he yielded to the request of the Archbishop of Canterbury. It was privately believed that the Scottish members were so militant that the government was in danger of falling unless it yielded to Sumner's letter.[1]

Placards whipped the crowds to fury for the following Sunday. Charles Dickens gave £10 to the cause, Holyoake and the *Reasoner* joined.[2] The police were alarmed. Shaftesbury shuttered windows and drew blinds and prepared for assaults. Lambeth palace expected siege and protected the stained glass of the library with a shield.[3] Luckily the weather on Sunday, 18 May, was bad. A small melancholy huddle in Hyde Park watched fifty teenagers antic on the empty bandstand and blow penny whistles. By 25 May enterprising persons hired private bands for the parks. Government stopped the band of the Brighton Pavilion from playing in Kensington Gardens. They professed to have no authority to stop the other two bands. Both sides were sufficiently satisfied. Londoners got their bands and the English government was halted from commanding desecration. Sir Benjamin Hall had the last word when he re-erected the dismantled bandstands at public expense.

To prepare Lambeth palace for siege had not been necessary since the lowering revolutionary days of the reform bill. Archbishop Sumner was groaned at at a public meeting. Evangelicals and dissenters, the Protestant conscience of Britain, admired their courage and praised their victory. Sumner was said to have won a crown of immortal honour. The Swiss Protestant scholar d'Aubigné went on pilgrimage to Kensington Gardens as an Englishman visits (he said) the field of Waterloo, and sat on a seat by the silent bandstand to offer his devotions.[4] But the repute of evangelicals was not advanced by this stand for principle; when responsible newspapers called them Exeter hall fakirs, fanatical gaolers, wet blankets, gloomy phalanx, ascetic party, parading their cheap and noisy goodness, wasting religious zeal away in yelling and howling.[5] Anthony Trollope

---

[1] Hodder, iii, 31–32. The letters in PP, 1856, lii, 137. Cf. the United States minister's report of Palmerston plumping on his knees before the archbishop in G. M. Dallas, *Letters from London*, i, 47. Palmerston's report to the queen in B. Connell, *Regina v. Palmerston*, 1962, 201–3. The queen replied that she could not 'sufficiently express her regret at the incomprehensible blindness and mistaken piety of the so-called "Evangelical Saints" '. Greville (Strachey-Fulford, vii, 228–9) thought that Palmerston deliberately sought for Sumner's intervention to save himself.

[2] McCabe, *Holyoake*, i, 285.

[3] G, 56, 400.

[4] R, 12 and 23 May 1856; T, 24 May 1856.

[5] e.g. T, 21 February, 14 and 17 May 1856.

embarked upon *Barchester Towers*, with evangelical Slope as the most odious clergyman in all the parson-blest county of Barset.

3. THE PALMERSTON BISHOPS

The fifteen years after 1847 put a new complexion upon the English episcopate. The bishops of Howley's day, high and dry, still partly bewigged, were not friendly to extremists, but understood the high churchmanship which prevailed among so many of their clergy. The revered personality of Archbishop Howley contributed to Tractarian affection for bishops; Bishop Bagot of Oxford and of Bath and Wells treated Newman and Denison and Bennett with sense and tenderness; Bishop Kaye of Lincoln was a learned and intelligent divine; Bishop Blomfield's vacillations were almost forgiven because they were seen to be more misjudgment than lack of comprehension; George Murray of Rochester was a blue-blood Tory; Bishop Denison of Salisbury always judged with sympathy. The bishops of a pre-Reform epoch, and the bishops of moderate Hampden-chastened Melbourne, and the bishops of Peel, composed a bench different in shape and angle and quality from the bench of Lord John Russell and Lord Palmerston.

In the days of Sumner high churchmen were less fond of bishops than in the days of Howley. If they looked wistfully round for leadership representative of their mind, they could find it only in a rare antique Ozymandias of a former age, or in an accident of the political whirligig. From far to the west came stories of giant unbowed Phillpotts, still hunting Gorhamite clergymen into law courts, still bristling with injunctions and mandamuses, but ancient and dusty and remote like a monumental ruin. And otherwise there was a space when Lord Aberdeen could nominate; and Walter Kerr Hamilton, once a famous evangelical preacher but now a Tractarian, was elevated to the see of Salisbury. Queen Victoria discovered afterwards and protested crossly that Aberdeen misled her, but too late.[1] Hamilton was the first disciple of Dr. Pusey to be an English bishop; the first English bishop

---

[1] Ashwell-Wilberforce, *Life of Wilberforce*, ii, 410. Denison of Salisbury on his death-bed in 1854 sent a message to Aberdeen asking him to nominate Hamilton, then a canon of Salisbury. Aberdeen passed a sleepless night and pressed the see repeatedly upon Professor J. J. Blunt of Cambridge. After Blunt's third refusal, he consented to nominate Hamilton. Aberdeen's correspondence with Queen Victoria in Add. MSS. 43048, 308ff.: Aberdeen told the queen in answer to her protests that Hamilton was moderate and that it would be unwise and unjust to exclude good men in consequence of a tendency either to high church or low church.

to carry a pastoral staff; the single Tractarian bishop until Gladstone became prime minister later in the century. But as a leader Hamilton was so self-distrustful as to be indecisive in public affairs.

The national reputation of English bishops was lower in 1857 than in 1847. Sumner was not Howley. Russell bishops were not Melbourne bishops. And bishops under the Ecclesiastical Commission were not the same as bishops before the Ecclesiastical Commission.

Lord Palmerston succeeded Aberdeen as prime minister in February 1855 when the government fell because the British army froze in the ice and stuck in the mud of the Crimea. He remained prime minister, with an interval of fifteen months in 1858–9, until his death in 1865. Ten years of a near-Whig prime minister must make a difference to the public predicament of the churches in England. Anthony Trollope symbolised the change in the story, how the downfall of the Conservative ministry meant the end to all hopes that the Tory archdeacon of Barchester would ever become a bishop. Those ten years of Palmerston continued to raise the authority and lower the prestige of the evangelical party.

Shaftesbury's wife was daughter of Palmerston's wife by her first marriage. Palmerston was like Melbourne in being a survival from an aristocratic age; bold, sensible, humorous and rakish, but without Melbourne's idleness and without his reading. By temperament and by moral code Palmerston found it gentlemanly to sit lightly to religious obligations, though he conformed to the services at Romsey abbey when he was in the country. It might have been predicted that he would flee from Shaftesbury's embrace. He was more ignorant about religion and the churches than any other prime minister of the nineteenth century; and enjoyed pretending to be more ignorant than he was. Shaftesbury began by desponding over his relative's ecclesiastical incompetence. 'He does not know, in theology, Moses from Sydney Smith.' He wrongly guessed that Palmerston had not spoken to a clergyman in his life except the vicar of Romsey. Palmerston smiled inwardly at Shaftesbury's fears and pulled his leg. He shocked him by pretending not to have heard of the Puseyites until a short time before he headed the government.[1]

Newspapers prophesied that Shaftesbury would now be able to influence the ecclesiastical policy of government. Shaftesbury himself thought the prophecy wild. 'He has never in his life, and never will, so

[1] Hodder, ii, 505.

long as he has breath, consult me on anything. It is not very likely that he will consult anybody; but, if he do, it will not be one connected with the evangelical party.' He expected Palmerston's appointments to be detestable.[1] It turned out that in this prognosis Shaftesbury was wrong and the newspapers were right.

For Palmerston admired Shaftesbury as a man of religion. It was no ordained minister but Shaftesbury who administered the consolations of Christian faith to Palmerston on his death-bed. Palmerston would never dream of making Shaftesbury responsible for policy. But being straightforward and direct, and without desire for influence through intrigue or clever management of his party, he professed to eschew the art by which Whig ministers made the church subservient to high policies of state or party.[2] 'If the man is a good man,' he used to say, 'I don't care what his political opinions are. Certainly I had rather not name a bishop who would make party speeches and attacks on the government in the House of Lords; but short of that, let him do as he likes.'[3]

His portrait of a good bishop was hazy and idealised. But he shared with Shaftesbury a belief of cardinal importance to the course of events. Shaftesbury thought that learning was no qualification for a bishop. Palmerston thought that learning was no qualification for anything, least of all for a bishop. The two men agreed on a fundamental principle of selection. What the church needed was neither scholars nor divines but simple, godly pastors of the people. Palmerston surveyed the theologians on the bench of bishops. He observed Bishop Phillpotts of Exeter. He observed the donnish Bishop Hinds of Norwich, driest of all the prelates whom Lord John Russell had nominated, and the learned Bishop Thirlwall of St. David's, more capable of managing the peacocks on his terrace than the clergy of his diocese. The queen once asked him for a learned man as bishop. Palmerston replied at forcible length. 'Viscount Palmerston would beg to submit that the bishops are in the church what generals of districts are in the army: their chief duties consist in watching over the clergy of their diocese, seeing that they perform properly their parochial duties, and preserving harmony between the clergy and the laity, and softening the asperities between the established church and the dissenters. For these purposes it is desirable that a bishop should have practical knowledge of parochial functions, and should not be of

[1] Hodder, ii, 490, 505. [2] Cf. Hodder, iii, 192. [3] Ashley, ii, 319.

an overbearing and intolerant temperament. His diocesan duties are enough to occupy all his time, and the less he engages in theological disputes the better. Much mischief has been done by theological bishops . . .'[1]

And so this strange pair of yokefellows agreed. Cavalier Palmerston wanted simple godly non-theological bishops. Roundhead Shaftesbury wanted evangelical bishops. Most evangelical clergymen were simple and godly.

The profession of evangelical opinion had until this moment erected a fence against preferment. In February 1855 the fence collapsed and reappeared as a ladder. Everyone was surprised; none more surprised than the evangelical clergy.

But Palmerston, if straight and unsubtle, was shrewd. The target of political advantage could not vanish from his mind. Though he never bargained, as Melbourne used to bargain, for the votes of future bishops, he had not attained the ethical plateau of appointing men best for the church. He thought that they were best for the church in the manner of unpalatable medicine, and did not care that they infuriated half the clergymen of the Church of England. The clergy could tolerate an evangelical bishop, even two evangelical bishops, even two or three evangelical deans. But to have no one placed above them except evangelicals whom they distrusted or despised caused them first to grieve and then to grumble and finally to vituperate. But Palmerston perceived that the hostility of clergymen harmed him little. Many of them were Puseyites or high churchmen whom England resented worse than papists and few of them would vote for his candidates. By identifying his ecclesiastical policy with Shaftesbury and the evangelical party, he gained a number of Anglican adherents and some anti-Puseyites; and he attracted many dissenters and Scottish votes. The closure of the Crystal Palace and the silencing of military bands proved how powerful, in these years after papal aggression, was the alliance of evangelicals and dissenters and Scotsmen. In the election of spring 1857 the use of crown patronage to promote evangelicals was an exciting cry at the hustings. When Prince Albert passed him a memorandum about the need for moderate men Palmerston replied that it was safer to err towards low churchmen because high churchmen were few and low churchmen were many.[2]

---

[1] *Letters of Queen Victoria*, I, iii, 416.
[2] Palmerston to Prince Albert, 3 August 1856, RA, D13A/2.

Palmerston's policy for the Church of England was not unpopular in the country. It was unpopular only in the Church of England. And Palmerston cared much for the country and not much for the Church of England.

Two of Palmerston's bishops (Philpott of Worcester and Wigram of Rochester) were not quite of his politics. In the mid-Victorian age that is still matter for notice and praise. But Palmerston was not so unmoved by political advantage as he professed to be. He was as eager as any prime minister not to have bishops who would speak against the government in the House of Lords. And he saw a merit in appointing Shaftesbury's shepherds, that they would not be interested in the House of Lords. Nor were all his nominations free of political taint. Wanting to keep Gladstone as member for Oxford University because he thought that Oxford tamed his wildness, he sent Jacobson to the see of Chester because he was Gladstone's Oxford agent in the election.[1] Gladstone wanted it on political grounds; Shaftesbury allowed that Jacobson was 'a proper man'; Palmerston nominated. The new evangelical bishops were pastoral and godly men. But some of them happened also to be members of great Whig families. Villiers, who became Bishop of Carlisle in 1856 and four years later Bishop of Durham, was younger brother of that Lord Clarendon whose diplomatic talent made Palmerston's ministry possible. Baring, who became Bishop of Gloucester and Bristol in 1856 and five years later Bishop of Durham, was younger brother of Lord Melbourne's chancellor of the exchequer. Pelham, who became Bishop of Norwich in 1857, was descended from an old and eminent Whig family. Palmerston took credit that he never asked future bishops about their political opinions. He was overheard to say that the worst way for a candidate to commend himself would be to mention his politics. But he seldom needed to ask.

Palmerston was ignorant of the clergy and professed to be more ignorant. In the now far-off days of William IV, and even of Peel, Archbishop Howley had exercised the quiet influence due to his office. Poor Archbishop Sumner was hardly expected to offer advice. Shaftesbury told Palmerston that he had better consult the bishops and received the answer, 'No no, you are quite enough; I had rather take your advice than that of all bishops put together.'[2] Whenever he

[1] Hodder, iii, 199.
[2] Shaftesbury's *Diary*, 1 November 1865. I owe much help on this question to an unpublished thesis by B. E. Hardman in the library of Cambridge University, *The Evangelicals 1855–1865*.

received a letter from a bishop he passed it to Shaftesbury for comment. In reality he listened to other voices besides Shaftesbury's; willingly to William Cowper and some of the Whigs, occasionally to leading clergy, and perforce but not always willingly to the queen. The rumour that he did whatever Shaftesbury wanted was untrue. But he trusted Shaftesbury more than anyone else; and when he died Shaftesbury lamented that a great and mighty door for good was now closed.[1]

In his ten years of office Palmerston nominated to nineteen English sees and six Irish sees and thirteen English deaneries, including the see of Canterbury once and the see of York twice. When he died more than half the bishops of England were Palmerstonian. He could influence the complexion of Anglican leadership.[2]

But between the earlier nominations and the later was a difference. When Palmerston first formed a cabinet no one expected the ministry to last. Shaftesbury felt an urgency about appointing leading evangelicals while there was time. Together they made a series of nominations which might justly be called extreme. But as criticism mounted, and as the evangelical alliance lost some of its political authority in the Commons, Palmerston saw, and Shaftesbury claimed afterwards to have seen, the need for more breadth. In the second ministry of 1859 Palmerston took Peelites into his cabinet, and to have Gladstone as chancellor of the exchequer was not compatible with an extreme evangelical policy in church affairs.

Therefore the ministry after 1859 preferred some persons whom the ministry of 1855–8 would never have dreamed of promoting; for example, Frederick Denison Maurice to a London parish or Arthur Stanley to the deanery of Westminster. After Gladstone joined the government Palmerston said to Shaftesbury, 'I should like to be a little cautious in the selection of bishops, so as not unnecessarily to vex my colleagues, some of whom are very high. It is a bore to see angry looks, and have to answer questions of affected ignorance. This must not stand in the way of fit men, but if we can now and then combine the two, so much the better.'[3] The principle remained of finding anti-Puseyites and men who would befriend dissenters. The single absolute impossibility in the plot of *Barchester Towers* occurs when Lord Palmerston appoints a Tractarian clergyman to the deanery of

---

[1] Hodder, iii, 191.
[2] List extracted from *Record* of 1 November 1865 in Hodder, iii, 194.
[3] Hodder, iii, 197.

Barchester. But these principles were interpreted more liberally from 1859, or rather from 1861, for despite Gladstone the first preferments of the second ministry resembled those of the earlier. The appointments from 1855 to 1858 and from 1859 to 1860 are mainly known to historians as the Palmerston evangelicals.

Governments had long expected rival policies to be represented on the bench. They had not expected rival theologies to be so represented. There were Tory bishops and Whig bishops because there were Tory and Whig prime ministers. About 1853 it dawned upon a few public men—among whom the Earl of Aberdeen is pre-eminent—that the theological groupings of the church also needed representatives among the bishops. In a world of newspapers and public opinion such representation had become necessary to the health of the church. But except Aberdeen no prime minister before Gladstone realised the new need in the administration of patronage. Melbourne, a moderate Whig, nominated none but moderate Whigs. Peel, a moderate Tory, nominated none but moderate Tories. Russell, an immoderate latitudinarian, nominated latitudinarians. In their first phase Palmerston and Shaftesbury nominated strong low churchmen.

Gerald Wellesley was the first to confront the prime minister with the harm which the policy caused. Wellesley, a man with the laconic sense of his uncle, the Duke of Wellington, refused Aberdeen's offer of the see of Bath and Wells in 1854 and accepted the deanery of Windsor in the same year. At Windsor he began to exert a healthy and independent influence upon the minds of the queen and prince. At the end of July 1856 Wellesley sent to Prince Albert a memorandum[1] declaring that all governments were conducting the nomination of bishops in a manner which undermined feelings of reverence towards the bench. The partisan selection required the choice of 'very inferior specimens'. Since the Church of England necessarily contained parties, the best representatives of each party should be selected in turn, provided that they are sincere and honest and moderate. Wellesley condemned the policy of choosing bishops who would not be capable of speaking in the House of Lords; for in consequence one or two leading and eloquent bishops dominated in that House, and the true opinions of the bench were not heard.

Palmerston thought, or told Prince Albert that he thought, this memorandum to be full of good sense. But he continued to transgress

[1] RA, D13A/1.

nearly all its principles. Neither he nor the crown would yet countenance high churchmen, still bearing the banners of the Puseyites
among their ranks. And therefore an important party in the Church of
England, the most important party among the clergy of the Church of
England, continued to be excluded from preferment by the crown.
Palmerston was creating a new difficulty for the church, or a new
extension of an old difficulty. The events of the thirties forced the
clergy to look with independence at the state. The events of the fifties
forced the clergy to look with independence at the bishops. Palmerston
generated new questions about the lawful authority of bishops.

The Palmerston evangelicals were denounced as ignorant and
factious enthusiasts; were watched with lynx-eyes that they might
stumble; were mocked and humiliated. When a man only wanted to
be a godly bishop in his diocese it was hard to be abused in national
newspapers as one of Palmerston's. Bishop Bickersteth of Ripon used
ruefully and deprecatingly to call himself a Palmerston bishop. Bishop
Wilberforce of Oxford thought the appointments wicked insults to
the church.[1] Lord Campbell congratulated Shaftesbury on the appointments. Shaftesbury received the praise with an air of complacency,
declaring that the dissenters would soon join the Church of England.
'Yes', said Campbell, 'and all the Church of England men leave it'.[2]
The question must therefore be asked whether the appointments were
bad; not only bad because partisan, but just bad.

Bickersteth, who went to Ripon in 1856, was a quiet and solemn
pastor. (It was rumoured that Palmerston thought himself to be
nominating his father, and was surprised to see so young a man.)
There was nothing to condemn as partisan, and much to admire as
diligent and devout, in the administration of the diocese of Ripon.
Pelham of Norwich shines out as pastor the more brilliantly because
he succeeded Hinds, and came among the Norfolk clergy like a stream
of living water after years of drought. His public utterances were not
splendid. In the House of Lords he hardly existed, in theological discussion he was nowhere. But he was a man of the Bible and of prayer,
and went about the vicarages reading his Bible and joining in prayer,
carrying everywhere good sense and cheerfulness. The worst that

[1] Ashwell-Wilberforce, iii, 84; *Life of Robert Bickersteth*, 131.

[2] Fitzmaurice, *Life of Granville*, i, 222.

For Gerald Wellesley see G. Battiscombe in *Report of the Friends of St. George's*,
1963, 126.

could be said was that he tactlessly befriended dissenters. Tait of London was a big man, intelligent and able and rock-like and not in the least narrow; not even an evangelical but just a low churchman. Villiers of Carlisle (and afterwards for a few months at Durham) was a kindly man of simple piety. The worst that could be said was that he presented his son-in-law to a wealthy living. The worst that could be said against Bishop Wigram of Rochester was that he fulminated too warmly against clergymen who played cricket or grew whiskers. Bishop Baring of Durham was afterwards confessed by nearly everyone to be a poor appointment.[1]

The Palmerston bishops were good bishops. Tories had charged Lord John Russell with nominating learned and dry persons like Hampden and Hinds and Prince Lee. They now attacked Palmerston for the opposite vice; that he nominated persons whose minds were unlearned and wet. The Palmerston bishops were not in truth ignoramuses. But the policy was called flinging mitres to third-rate professors of ignorance and obscurantism.[2]

The consequence, wrote a hostile writer in the *Times*,[3] is that never has the high church party been so numerous, wealthy, fashionable and enthusiastic. It was not true. The high church party was not fashionable at all, certainly not fashionable because Palmerston/ Shaftesbury appointed evangelicals. But this monochrome of patronage was no friend to evangelicals in the Church of England. It lifted them from the pulpit or school where they spoke words of life and buttoned them in a pillory of gaiters.

4. THE THEORY AND PRACTICE OF CHURCH AND STATE

The theory of church and state

In a perfectly Christian state the commands of Caesar conform to the commands of God. Few early Victorians did not think that the law of England must seek to conform to the law of God. Men dis-

---

[1] Waldegrave was at least due as much to Tait as Shaftesbury. Cf. Add. MSS. 48581, 156; Hardman, 64. Tait was pressed upon Prince Albert by Dean Wellesley of Windsor, and partly because he was not an evangelical and patronage must be bestowed upon other parties in the church. It was also expected that he would be no vulgar puritan and would take no narrow view of Sunday observance. Cf. Wellesley's memorandum of August 1856, RA, D13A/1.

[2] *Saturday Review* 1858, i, 366.

[3] T, 8 April 1857, on Pelham's elevation.

agreed not upon axiom but application. We have seen anxious clergy-men reminding Archbishop Sumner that we ought to obey God rather than Caesar, and Archbishop Sumner retorting that before we disobey Caesar upon grounds of conscience we must be very sure that we know the will of God. If Caesar intruded schismatic presbyter into Marnoch or heretic priest into Devonshire, men must disobey. But they might still argue whether presbyter was schismatic or priest heretical.

Nearly all members of the Church of England, and many Method-ists, believed that a state ought to establish a church. They were divided on the question which church a state ought to establish. Should the state choose the church to which the majority of its people belonged, or should it choose the church which, in the opinion of government, taught the truth?

By the fifties of the century this alternative became unreal. Despite the ecclesiastical titles act few instructed people believed after Gorham and the census that the state, meaning the House of Commons, was fit to determine which religious doctrines were true. The question had been framed in this form, partly because the old tradition of union between church and state was still strong in the constitution, and partly because the established Church of Ireland harassed those who saw that it was easier to maintain on truth than on majority. Through-out the fifties evangelical divines continued to maintain that the state had a duty to propagate true religion and could discern true religion by opening the scriptures. An eminent evangelical like T. R. Birks of Cambridge found it obvious that a government ought to encourage a religion which opened the Bible and to discourage a religion which closed it, to encourage a religion which befriended the domestic affections of its pastors and to discourage a religion which condemned its priests to lifelong celibacy. If the state failed to encourage Protestant truth, it was apostatising.[1] Evangelicals covered their eyes in order not to see the reality of Parliament. In condemning the religious neutrality of the state Birks was forced to condemn the entire development of the English constitution after the emancipation act.

We can follow year by year the mind of a high churchman as he changed from belief in a confessional state to belief in a neutral state; from the establishment of truth to the establishment of majority. Gladstone published in 1838 *The State in its relations with the Church*; a

---

[1] T. R. Birks, *The Christian State*, 1847; restated in response to new problems in *Church and State*, 1869.

book too heavy and convoluted in style to become the classic state-ment of high theory, but at least a strenuous attempt to claim ancient privilege for the united Church of England and Ireland on the sole ground of truth. Amid vast phrases which hinted at the philosophical idealism of Coleridge, he contended that the state possessed not only a conscience (which everyone confessed if it meant that government should encourage and practise good behaviour) but a conscience which could discern between religious truth and error. The governors of any state have a duty to profess the religious truth which they see, to pro-vide for the worship of God in public rites, and to encourage this truth and worship by its laws. In practical application to England he seemed to attribute to Parliamentarians a nice discrimination in theology, and claimed for the Church of England an exclusive right to the money of the state. Later in life he said that the book was obsolete when it appeared, that he found himself the last man on the sinking ship.[1] If he meant that no one approved, he was forgetful. Howley, Blomfield, the Duke of Newcastle, Keble, Newman were eminent among a multitude of strong churchmen who approved. But he soon found that practical politicians eyed it askance. He could not expect that Lord Melbourne and O'Connell would like his plea for the Church of Ireland, and bore Macaulay's savage bite. But he was dis-mayed to find that Tory politicians were as cold. Down in the country Peel said, 'That young man will ruin his fine political career if he per-sists in writing trash like this.' Gladstone discovered that no weighty group among the Tories was prepared to act upon his thesis. Lord Aberdeen told him a few years later, 'No one reads your book and those who do don't understand it.'[2]

Despite the disappointment, Gladstone changed these confessional principles very slowly. Looking back later in life, he thought that his naïveté was excusable. Everywhere around him he saw the Church of England reviving in pastoral care and beauty. Seeing the advance of piety and unworldliness, of purity and energy, he hoped that the Church of England might yet revive the love and allegiance of the estranged mass of dissenters. In retrospect he thought of those days as bright and happy for the Church of England, and pleaded that his dream was not wild.[3]

Six years later he resigned his cabinet post when Peel proposed the

---

[1] *Gleanings*, vii, 115.   [2] Longford, 182; Queen Victoria's *Journal*, 30 January 1845.
[3] *Gleanings*, vii, 140-3.

grant to Maynooth, not because he disapproved the grant (for which indeed he voted) but because he thought it inconsistent to be responsible when he had dogmatically attacked the grant to Maynooth in his treatise. As he looked back over his life he saw his education completed, and his crossing from Tory to Liberal party made easy, by a variety of decisions which proved the old Tory constitution to be obsolete; the increased power of the voluntary principle by the disruption of the Church of Scotland, the failure of a Tory state to educate the poor, above all the destruction of the early Tractarian party by the loss of Newman and his successors, and afterwards the suspicions within the establishment. To assert exclusive claims had become absurd. Even Samuel Wilberforce confessed that after the census the established church could not expect money from the state. In the year of the ecclesiastical titles act Gladstone published a letter to the Bishop of Aberdeen in which he proclaimed the need for a free church in a free state. You cannot secure your own freedom in religion unless you secure the freedom of everyone else. Several other Tractarians followed this road from the Tory towards the Liberal party. By extraordinary paradox Lord John Russell, whom extreme churchmen loathed, drew some of them out of Toryism by making them fear establishment and so removing their ecclesiastical motive for adhering to the Tory party.

In the fifties the union of church and state achieved an uneasy equilibrium. So long as the political parties remained even and so long as Lord Palmerston was prime minister the constitution would remain much the same. Whatever stirring plans Palmerston might forward overseas, he maintained quiet in politics at home. Though the Liberation Society agitated and church rate was still sour, the establishment was accepted as a practical and useful expression of Christian profession by the state and a public means to encourage Christian morality. Abandoning Gladstonian or evangelical theories of a confessional state, Englishmen took lower ground. And upon this lower ground various rules of the constitution began to look unnecessary and vexatious. During the fifties these changes in the law continued the drive towards state neutrality in religion and helped Gladstone a little farther from his Tory ancestry: the admission of dissenters to the universities of Oxford and Cambridge, a change in the law of divorce, and the admission of Jews to sit in Parliament.

The universities

In the Tractarian quarrels of the forties the university of Oxford failed to maintain its public esteem. The spectacle of quarrelling dons entertained the public and invited interference. In 1850 Lord John Russell surprised everyone by appointing a commission to enquire into the discipline and studies and revenues of Oxford. Russell did not blunder by selecting an impartial commission. Its president was Whately's little bear Samuel Hinds, then Bishop of Norwich; its secretary was Arthur Stanley, the biographer of Arnold; its members included Tait and Baden Powell. But the religious question was excluded from the commission's terms of reference. Although many colleges and individuals returned a blank refusal to help, the commissioners reported in August 1852. Influenced by the ideals of German universities, they put enthusiastic faith in lectures and professors. Remembering the Tractarian troubles, they substituted a new elected governing body for the old board of heads. They wished to free college fellowships from local restrictions. The argument did not divide by ecclesiastical allegiance. Pusey wanted the old board of heads, other Tractarians found themselves in the company of radical reformers, Gladstone was responsible for the bill in the Commons. In 1854 Lord Aberdeen carried partial reforms of the constitution into law, and in 1856 a second act extended similar reforms to the university of Cambridge. While the Oxford bill was passing through the Commons, Heywood (22 June 1854) proposed that religious tests be abolished at matriculation and (four days later) that religious tests be abolished at the first degree. The heads astounded everyone by refusing to resist the amendment. Gladstone reconciled himself that it was expedient. Bishop Wilberforce supported it, and the distance which the world had revolved since the university crisis twenty years before is proved by the failure of opponents to generate zeal. 'The new generation', mourned Pusey to Keble, 'seems wholly different from the old.'[1]

Thus dissenters slipped easily and at last into the right to be educated at Oxford and Cambridge. They were still excluded from fellowships and the government. If their college insisted, they must still attend the Anglican worship of the chapel. But they had arrived in surprising

[1] Liddon, iii, 399. The Oxford act allowed dissenters only to the bachelor's degrees. The Cambridge act allowed them any degree in arts, law, medicine or music but not membership of the senate or any office in the university hitherto always held by a member of the Church of England.

tranquillity, and one more of the five dissenting grievances found a partial remedy. Whether their arrival would tend to separate Oxford from the Church of England remained a question to which optimists gave a different answer from pessimists. And how many dissenters would wish to take advantage of so Anglican an education was also a matter of guessing. Newman was still trying to erect a Catholic university in Ireland, because it seemed unthinkable that the Roman Church would allow Catholics to go to Oxford. Lucas of the *Tablet* promised in the Commons that Catholics would never take advantage of the concession and so helped Protestant liberals to vote for the motion. The new government of the university had no revolutionary force. The first elected board included Hawkins of Oriel, Gaisford of Christ Church, Symons of Wadham, stout conservatives all. The residents elected Pusey second on the list of professors and went on electing him for a quarter of a century. Pusey found himself strange in harmony with Hawkins.

Divorce

In the year 1857 the partial jurisdiction over wills and marriages was removed from the ecclesiastical courts. The old system was an archaism. Its end did not touch the alliance of church and state. But in reforming it the law of divorce must be changed. And the interest of the church in safeguarding the indissolubility of marriage was found to differ from the interest of the modern state in evenhanded justice.

Many Protestant states allowed adultery as ground for divorce since the Reformation, and after the French Revolution the grounds were in some countries extended. Catholic countries maintained the absolute ban found in canon law, with the momentous exception that the pope's dispensing power could at times cut the knot. England was unique in maintaining the absolute ban and abolishing the dispensing power. By the lapse of time this rigour became intolerable to English aristocrats. From the late seventeenth century Parliament provided the required dispensations by passing acts of Parliament to divorce ill-yoked but eminent spouses. The law of England refused divorce to everyone, but allowed it to anyone influential enough to procure a special law. After 1800 an average of two, after 1840 an average of four such acts were passed annually.

Reason argued the absurdity of needing acts of Parliament and the wisdom of providing a divorce court. Reason looked across the border at the laxer law of Scotland and paraded the inconveniences of two different marriage laws in Britain. A royal commission of 1853 recommended a divorce court. It was no longer a commendation of any system that it could be worked only by the wealthy. But the public fact of Christianity in Victorian England was never more marked than in the framing of a suitable law. A few radicals might demand several grounds of divorce. The argument in Parliament and the country centred upon the meaning of the scriptural texts which allowed a wife to be put away for her adultery. Gladstone wrote a vast article in the *Quarterly Review* on the meaning of the text. And when Gladstone's biographer lifted his hands in mock amazement that at this age of the world men would suffer the solution of a far-reaching social problem to be affected by the disputed meaning of a few Greek words, he pretended to forget how the moral face of Britain still lived in the Christian past.[1]

The nation was far from desiring easier divorce. Simple labourers could not conceive the horrors of dissolute England. 'If this bill passes,' said a village gardener, 'there will be so much wickedness the country will not be fit to live in.' Rustics said that if the bill passed we should soon be Mormons or Socialists.[2]

Lord Cranworth's act was sufficiently backward-looking to provide that adultery in the man was more pardonable than adultery in the woman. The man might achieve divorce if his wife were an adulteress, the woman only if the man's adultery were incestuous, or bigamous, or accompanied by rape, sodomy, bestiality, cruelty or desertion for two years. Peers and prelates in the House of Lords argued at length the true interpretation of the Gospel texts. The Duke of Norfolk wanted a select committee to consider what scripture warranted. Not even the bishops were quite agreed. Archbishop Sumner was satisfied that the New Testament allowed divorce for adultery and forbade the remarriage of the guilty party. Hamilton of Salisbury was sure that the scripture, though allowing divorce for adultery, meant separation and no remarriage. To the plea that an innocent person would suffer hardship and indeed temptation to immoral conduct, he was persuaded that every Christian man could have the gift of continence. Wilberforce of Oxford believed that scripture permitted divorce of the guilty wife and forbade her remarriage but not her

---

[1] Morley, i, 424.   [2] G, 57, 576, 596.

husband's. Tait of London based himself upon the universal opinion of Protestant churches that warranted more grounds than adultery and voted steadily for the bill. Thirlwall of St. David's believed that the gospel intended no temporal legislation. Wilberforce tried and failed to make adultery liable to imprisonment. Sumner tried and almost succeeded in preventing the guilty party from remarrying.

The main question was whether the law of England could contradict the law of scripture. On this ground Parliament had refused bills to legalise marriage with a deceased wife's sister. The difficulty over divorce was settled, partly on the plea that a bill which commanded the votes of eleven bishops could not plainly contradict scripture, and partly on the more forcible argument that a Christian country should nevertheless legislate for its non-Christian citizens. This second argument was weaker than it looked. Hitherto the law of the state was the law of the established church. If the defenders of the bill argued that a Christian state might legislate for non-Christian citizens, they recognised that the laws of state and church might diverge; that the Christian citizen might lie under the duty not to take advantage of a liberty allowed to the non-Christian citizen.

This difficulty touched the clergy of the Church of England in conscience. A man might secure a divorce and remarry. Was the vicar, who believed remarriage forbidden by divine law, to be compelled to remarry the divorced man and liable to penalty if he refused? Lord Cranworth thought it scandalous if clergy were allowed thus to asperse a marriage which the state recognised as lawful. Pressed in the House of Lords to save the consciences of the clergy, Cranworth refused to budge. Six thousand priests petitioned Parliament, the old cries of schism and disruption were heard again. Gladstone and his disciples tried to make it compulsory that divorced persons when remarrying must be married in a registry office. The government refused, but consented to modify the bill in the Commons. A clergyman was exempted from all penalty if he refused to marry the guilty party in his church. But he must surrender his church if the couple could find a clergyman of the same diocese to celebrate the wedding. The concession was large. The clergy disliked the loopholes and continued to petition, without menace. When they applied to Bishop Phillpotts he dismissed the affair with the sanguine verbosity of his fourscore years. He prophesied that the youngest curate in his diocese would not live to see his church invaded by an alien celebrant.

Later in life Gladstone still regretted that the law passed. In the year after the act successful suits, which lately averaged four a year, rose to 179. They then declined, and did not recover that figure for ten years. They first topped 200 in 1872, 300 in 1875, 400 in 1890, 500 in 1897, 600 in 1901.[1] In proportion to the rising number of marriages these figures were far from proving a decline in marital faithfulness.

The bane of the act appeared in the invitation to squalid collusion by confining the grounds to adultery. Fifty years later government needed to consider the entire question afresh. And fifty years later the clash between church canon and state law sounded again. Phillpotts was too sanguine in his prophecy that the youngest curate of his diocese would never need to worry. In 1857 the clergy were barely satisfied by the freedom from penalty bestowed upon them in certain cases. Convocation passed several resolutions praying that the law be amended. As time passed high churchmen found mere protection grossly inadequate. They thought it insufferable that any clergyman should exercise his legal right to marry a divorced person in church. Gladstone's demand that all marriages of divorced persons should be civil was renewed by Bishop Gore.

The Jews

Since the emancipation of the Roman Catholics the Whigs could see no reason why Jews should not have the same privilege. In 1828 dissenters gained the right, in 1829 Roman Catholics, in 1833 the Quaker Joseph Pease was elected for South Durham and the lawyers held the House of Commons justified in allowing him to take his seat.[2] The Whigs argued that the oath excluded conscientious Jews but not unconscientious atheists and played with the argument that the historian Gibbon or the philosopher Bolingbroke took seats in Parliament. Tories held that the declension from Anglican Parliament to Protestant Parliament, and then from Protestant Parliament to Christian Parliament, afforded no reason for falling to non-Christian Parliament. Every member must take his oath on the faith of a Christian. Christianity was a pillar of the constitution. The Tory defence was pleased to find that so stern a Whig as Arnold agreed with them on the necessity for a Christian Parliament. Lord Ashley pro-

[1] PP, 1912–13, xx, 682.
[2] Report in PP, 1833, xii, 137.

nounced the solemn warning that if they failed to stand for a Christian Parliament they would soon have to stand for a white Parliament or even in the end for a male Parliament.[1] The defenders on high principle were hindered or helped by the vile insinuations of an anti-Semitic rabble. It is not easy to decide whether they were more hindered or helped, but melancholy evidence suggests that they were supported by silent prejudice.

Relief bills to allow the Jews to take a different oath passed the House of Commons in 1833 and 1834 and apathetically in 1836. By the time Russell came to power the question was more pressing, because the Jews were more prominent in the state. The merchants of London, Rothschild, Montefiore, Goldsmid, Salomons were powers in England whether they sat in Parliament or not. They were indispensable to the banking system of the country, gave munificent donations to charity without regard to religion, even building churches for the Church of England, and were respected in the City of London. David Salomons[2] led the campaign for Jewish rights. From 1835 he was permitted to be a sheriff in the City; and after he had been elected alderman twice, Peel's government passed a bill (1845) to enable Jews to hold office in municipal corporations. The bar against Parliament was the sole remaining disability.

Encouraged by the success of Salomons, Lionel Rothschild stood as a candidate for the City in the election of 1847, with Lord John Russell as his colleague, and was comfortably elected. Confronted with a member unable to take his seat, Russell began again the attempt to get a Jewish bill through Parliament. He had the advantage that Peel and Gladstone now favoured relief. The old fate continued to befall the new bills. Weary of waiting for the relief which government promised, but which was always postponed or defeated, the friends of Rothschild tried direct action. On 26 July 1850 Rothschild presented himself at the table to take the oaths in the usual manner and claimed to be sworn on the Old Testament. Sir Robert Inglis protested in a voice trembling with emotion.[3] When Rothschild was heard in his favour a few days later (29 July) he said that he wished to swear upon the Old Testament because this was the form of oath most binding upon his conscience. The House of Commons then agreed by 113 to

[1] Hansard, 16 December 1847, xcv, 1278.
[2] A. M. Hyamson, *David Salomons*, 1939; Cecil Roth, *A History of the Jews in England*, 2nd ed., 1949, 239; H. S. Q. Henriques, *The Jews and the English Law*, 1908.
[3] AR, 1850, 183.

59 that there was nothing to stop him swearing on the Old Testament.

On 30 July Rothschild reappeared amid the cheers of Whigs and radicals. The resolution of the House was read, ordering the clerk to swear him on the Old Testament. As Rothschild recited the oaths after the clerk he came in the oath of abjuration to the words 'on the true faith of a Christian'. He said, 'I omit these words as not binding on my conscience', and quickly 'So help me God'. He picked up a pen with the evident intention of signing his name on the parliamentary roll. Then the uproar began, and on the motion of the attorney-general the House passed a resolution that he could not legally take his seat.

A year later Salomons made an entry still more brazen. Elected member for Greenwich at a by-election, he entered the House (18 July 1851), took the oath on the Old Testament, refused to repeat *on the true faith of a Christian*, but unlike Rothschild refused to withdraw, and sat down on one of the benches at the right side of the chair. The Speaker again ordered him to withdraw; and he went as far as a bench within the bar usually reserved for peers and distinguished visitors. Three days later he again entered, amid vehement cheering and cries of *Order*, and sat decisively upon the government benches. He then proceeded amid a storm to vote in three different divisions upon his case. At last the sergeant-at-arms touched him lightly upon the shoulder. Salomons stood up and said that he yielded to sufficient force. He wanted to be prosecuted. The government refused to prosecute, but a common informer obliged, and Salomons was fined £500.

In such an atmosphere the victory was only a question of time. The old Tory argument that Parliament must be Christian fell more and more to zealots like Inglis and Shaftesbury. In 1855 Salomons became lord mayor of London. The House of Lords continued to reject bills for altering the oaths, but with little heart. It passed the Lords at last in 1858 (21 & 22 Victoria, cap. 48) and on 26 July Rothschild became the first Jewish member of Parliament. A second act provided that the Jew should suffer the same disability as the Roman Catholic in the exercise of high ecclesiastical patronage in the Church of England. He was excluded from administering patronage which fell to him by virtue of an office of state, and the patronage passed to the Archbishop of Canterbury. But he might still own an advowson as part of his property and unlike the Roman Catholic was not excluded from using the advowson to nominate the incumbent of a benefice in the Church of England.

Thus the Jews and Roman Catholics remained the sole citizens disqualified, if one of them became prime minister, from advising the sovereign on the appointment of bishops.

5. THE PROTECTION OF RELIGION

Blasphemy

By 1860 religion was still protected in respectable conversation. But its legal defences against critics were lower. The blasphemy laws still operated. But they no longer confined intelligent minds who wished to publish sane and reasoned criticism.

It was (and is) illegal in England to blaspheme God or question the truth of the Bible. Under this law of 1698 Robert Taylor was convicted of blasphemy in 1831, Gathercole in 1838, Abel Heywood and Hetherington in 1840. Under this law publishers of the late thirties refused to risk printing English translations of the *Life of Jesus* by Strauss. Charles Southwell began publishing an atheist journal called *Oracle of Reason* and after the fourth number was sentenced to prison for a year and a fine of £100.

Authority was not happy. Every case produced columns in the press and petitions in Parliament. When Archbishop Howley drew the attention of Sir Robert Peel to the spread of atheistic pamphlets Peel replied that government only sold more copies if it prosecuted.[1] In 1842 an assize judge delivered an opinion which successfully changed the law in the public interest.

In May 1842 Holyoake went to Cheltenham to preach socialist communities. A questioner asked him why he failed to mention chapels in his communities. The words of his reply were disputed at the time. Hostile witnesses alleged that he said, 'I do not believe there is such a thing as a God' and that he would place God upon half pay. According to his own account he said, 'I appeal to your heads and your pockets if we are not too poor to have a God. . . . Read the mental degradation and oppression of your race, and there you read the history of religion'; and that so long as Charles Southwell lay

---

[1] Add. MSS. 40499, 144, 146. In 1842 Strauss's *Life of Jesus* circulated in cheap numbers, and the law officers of the crown were consulted, but did not advise prosecution.

immured in Bristol gaol he shuddered at religion, fled the Bible as a viper and revolted at the touch of a Christian. Despite warning he repeated himself at Cheltenham in June and was arrested at the lecture. At Gloucester assizes he defended himself in an enormous and irrelevant harangue of nine hours. Judge Erskine behaved with exceptional courtesy and tried to persuade him that he only meant the incomes of the clergy to be reduced, as this was the sole practical effect of his words. Holyoake refused this charity, was judged to have spoken with improper levity, and was imprisoned for six months. On release he returned to Cheltenham and repeated his sentiments.[1]

At this trial, and at another trial (Shore *v.* Wilson) in the same year, Judge Erskine laid it down that though it was blasphemy to impugn Christ scoffingly, any man may soberly and reverently examine the truth of the doctrines. This judgment commended itself to succeeding judges. Christianity was still the law of the land. Trusts or bequests to propagate atheist doctrines were still invalid. In 1844, 1850 and 1861 bequests to propagate doctrines subversive of Christianity were held void by the courts.[2]

Thus the blasphemy law of 1698 was altered without legislation and solely by the judges, who regarded public opinion and public interest. Intelligent publishers benefited. Chapman ran little risk of prosecution when he published (1846) George Eliot's translation of Strauss. He would have welcomed attack.

In 1857 a demented Cornish well-sinker of Liskeard named Thomas Pooley was charged with blasphemy. He believed that the earth was a living animal, feared that in digging wells he might hurt the earth by breaking its skin, and thought that he could cure potato disease by scattering the ashes of burnt Bibles. For fifteen years he scrawled blasphemous and disgusting sentences on gates. A clergyman at last lodged information and Pooley was committed for trial. It was unfortunate that the judge was the high Tractarian, Keble's biographer, J. T. Coleridge; and still more unfortunate that the prosecuting counsel was John Duke Coleridge, son of the judge. Though the neighbours believed Pooley mad, neither of the Coleridges saw evidence of madness in court. Pooley was sentenced to twenty-one months of imprisonment for blasphemy and pardoned on the score of insanity in

[1] McCabe, i, 63, 92.
[2] Halsbury, iv, 123. Cf. G, 50, 439. This view was reversed by the House of Lords as lately as 1917.

December of the same year. Severity of sentence and circumstances of trial put guns into the hands of every liberal critic. The case became celebrated above the inevitable pamphlet by Holyoake because John Stuart Mill took it into his essay *On Liberty* and H. T. Buckle printed a severe letter against the judge.[1] England slowly moved out of an age when men were successfully prosecuted for blasphemy. If sane they were reasonable enquirers, if insane they needed treatment.

Moral discipline

The penances of ecclesiastical courts still existed in theory. In the old days church law enforced moral discipline. Almost all this discipline was obsolete and unenforceable, so that (for example) fornication was no more subject to legal penalty than failure to attend church. Fornication and absence from church on Sundays were still in theory acts against the state. But the state had ceased to touch them. Church law was not unique. The pillory was only abolished in 1837, and there were still rare sentences to sit in the stocks.

But in one respect penance survived: for defamation. It was possible to charge a man with defaming character before an ecclesiastical court which could inflict public penance. These penances were infrequent, unpopular, and absurd. The convicted person must stand in a white sheet at church and solemnly read to the congregation a confession of guilt. A woman forced to public penance at Walton church in December 1838 was not compelled to wear a white sheet. But a brewer at Bristol was made to wear the sheet in 1847.[2] At Fen Ditton near Cambridge on Sunday 6 May 1849, the village fiddler, convicted of calling the rector's wife a whore, did penance amid cat-calls and riot and hassock-throwing and pew-breaking, and was carried shoulder-high for drinks at the Plough after service. At Wakefield in 1850 a Congregational corn merchant did penance with a procession which would have been triumphant but for pouring rain.[3] Defamation was at last transferred to the civil courts in 1855, and brawling by laymen in 1860. Obsolete laws harmed public morals and Christianity.

---

[1] Cf. *Life of J. D. Coleridge*, i, 246ff.; Huth, *Life of Buckle*, i, 235ff.; *Fraser's Magazine*, May 1859, 533ff., June 1859, 635ff.; H. T. Buckle, *A Letter to a gentleman respecting Pooley's case*, 1859.

[2] AR *Chron.*, 1838, 165; G, 47, 545.

[3] JB, 12 May 1849; *Bury and Norwich Herald*, 11 September 1850.

National days of prayer

Government was in the habit of ordering national days of prayer either of thanksgiving as in victory or of fasting and humiliation as in plague. After 1830 governments became wary about ordering such days. Every day so ordered encountered criticism; from radicals who thought it superstition, from dissenters and Roman Catholics or extreme Puseyites who thought it unwarrantable interference by government in their religion. The queen, in whose name these proclamations must go forth, developed a sensitive reluctance to countenance superstition. The theology of God's providence perplexed her mind. She approved of Peel when he took offence at the drafting of a prayer of thanksgiving for victory in India, which almost made it appear that gunfire into a confused mass of Sikhs, struggling in the waters of the Sutlej, was directed by divine providence and an agreeable sign to a merciful God.[1] Even clergymen behaved strangely towards days of prayer. Dr. Buckland caused a sensation by preaching on the text *Wash and be Clean* on the cholera day of 1849, exhorting the people of London to improve their sanitation.

In October 1853, troubled by cholera again, the presbytery of Edinburgh requested Lord Palmerston as home secretary to appoint a day of national fast and supplication. Palmerston replied that overcrowding and insanitary habits among the poor caused the infection and that the country ought to take all steps to remedy these sources of contagion. 'When man has done his utmost for his own safety, then is the time to invoke the blessing of heaven to give effect to his exertions.'[2] The language caused indignation elsewhere than in Edinburgh. Next spring war in the Crimea demanded a day. The queen and prime minister exchanged critical letters before a form for the day could be agreed. Partly because of Palmerston's language, the day of prayer held on 26 April 1854 caused open expressions of doubt. Philosophical men were declared to have abandoned the belief that providence would specially intervene as a result of prayer. Yet churches and chapels were fuller on such a day than any other. Collections were given to the widows and children of fighting soldiers. Roman Catholics and some dissenters refused to observe the day itself, though not its object, as a protest against religion by royal command.

At the Indian mutiny the queen appointed 7 October 1857 as a

---

[1] Add. MSS. 40441, 170: cf. *Life of F. J. A. Hort*, i, 37.   [2] G, 53, 731.

public day of solemn fast, humiliation and prayer. Events in India caused men and women to flock to church, though the weather was stormy and the day Wednesday. It was one paradox of Victorian England. While philosophers theorised of superstition and bigots complained of official religion, men who never otherwise entered a church or chapel fought their way through mud and sleet to attend. Mr. Spurgeon went down to the Crystal Palace and preached for thirty-five minutes to a congregation of 23,654 persons.

State Services

Appended to the prayer book of the Church of England were four special services added by authority of the crown: the days of the queen's accession, of the execution of King Charles I, of the Restoration in 1660, and of the gunpowder plot. The highest churchmen objected to these services because they were authorised by state authority only, and after 1840 ceased in increasing numbers to use them. The worst of them was the service for the gunpowder plot, which was also the day to celebrate the arrival of King William III and the Revolution of 1688. Strong Tories had often doubted the Christian propriety of celebrating the Revolution of 1688. And the language of that service was as hostile to the pope and the Roman Catholic faith as could be predicted. Provost Hawkins once refused a testimonial to a man who would not attend gunpowder plot services in the chapel of Oriel College.[1] 'How is this, Mr. Wingfield,' asked Bishop Blomfield of a London curate, 'that you would not read the 5 November service?' 'My Lord,' said Wingfield, 'it is not a church service but a state service, and I could not conscientiously read it.'[2] The queen disliked liturgical attacks by royal authority on her Roman Catholic subjects. Lawyers argued long whether they could be abolished without act of Parliament, but at last it was agreed that what the crown had done the crown could undo. The accession service was preserved. The others were celebrated for the last time during the year 1858.

6. THE TROUBLES OF EUCHARISTIC WORSHIP

The Denison case

George Anthony Denison, vicar of East Brent in Somerset and Archdeacon of Taunton, resembled Bishop Phillpotts in loving the ring. Square and tough, he wished to continue the Gorham battle for

[1] Ornsby, *Life of J. R. Hope-Scott*, i, 315.   [2] *Memorials of Mr. Serjeant Bellasis*, 43.

truth in the Church of England. The Tractarians told him that the doctrine of the Church of England was the doctrine of Catholic antiquity, and that doctrine of high points was therefore defined. A rugged personality, he stumped among the rocks of reality and arranged them into rows. Examining the candidates for the Wells ordination of Christmas 1852, he told them that before they became priests he would expect them to confess that the inward reality of the sacrament was received by all, wicked as well as faithful.[1]

The divines of the Church of England had been guided by article XXIX of the Thirty-nine Articles, which declares that the wicked are in no wise partakers of Christ. One of the Wells ordinands was troubled by the archdeacon's uncompromising declaration, and sought advice. The diocese began to argue over the truth or falsehood of the proposition. The bishop was Richard Bagot, formerly Newman's Bishop of Oxford, a strong high churchman, but now dilapidated in health and living partly at Brighton. For episcopal duty in the diocese he employed a retired colonial bishop, Spencer, formerly Bishop of Madras. Spencer was a low churchman. After fruitless argument with Denison, who insisted that an auxiliary bishop had no rights whatever in examining the candidates, Spencer resigned his episcopal duties in the diocese of Bath and Wells (May 1853) and published the correspondence. Denison resigned his examining chaplaincy pending enquiries, and asked poor Bishop Bagot to prosecute him.

At this stage Denison had no one's sympathy. Bagot did not see why he should pay large sums of money to prosecute his own archdeacon in order to define the doctrine of the Church of England. Accordingly Denison preached three sermons in Wells cathedral between August 1853 and 1854, and printed them. He looked forward with joy to the fight.[2]

Early in 1854 the evangelical vicar of the next parish, Joseph Ditcher of South Brent, produced extracts from the earlier sermons and asked Bishop Bagot to prosecute. Behind Ditcher the evangelical Archdeacon Henry Law hurried round organising evidence. Behind Henry Law stood the Evangelical Alliance and Lord Shaftesbury, eager to contribute the funds which Bishop Bagot lacked.

---

[1] *Fifty Years*, 69: Denison to Archer Gurney, 20 December 1856. Denison is probably the prototype of Archdeacon Grantly in *Barchester Towers*. There is a good modern study of the whole theological question by A. Härdelin, *The Tractarian understanding of the Eucharist*, 1965.

[2] *Fifty Years*, 53: Denison to Wolff, 1 August 1853.

And now began a comedy of the English legal system; cross-fire of jurisdiction, gold-mine of barristers, ineffective church courts and effective state courts. Denison revelled like a Hercules in these serpentine coils.

Ditcher applied again to Bishop Bagot to prosecute. Bagot refused, because the mystery was too high for legal judgment. In a vain effort to stop the looming suit, his advisers guided his dying hand to write an admonition against Denison's indiscretion. Ditcher applied to Bagot's successor Lord Auckland. Auckland refused. Ditcher discovered that as Denison's living was in the patronage of the Bishop of Bath and Wells a clause protected the incumbent from a bishop-patron by allotting the duty of proceeding to the Archbishop of Canterbury. Ditcher applied to Sumner.

Archbishop Sumner behaved oddly. Two diocesan bishops in succession had refused to proceed. Yet now, under a clause intended for Denison's protection, he nominated a commission of enquiry. The commission consisted of five low churchmen. Denison applied to the court of queen's bench to stop the commission. The queen's bench refused. By November 1854 the question of Denison and his doctrine was becoming ominous. Few of the Tractarians believed that Denison was right, and many thought his behaviour silly. But Keble and Pusey worried whether if the opposite of Denison's doctrine were defined the Church of England could still be called Catholic. 'However much Denison may have provoked it,' wrote Pusey to Keble,[1] 'the Low Church, I fear, mean a war of extermination against us.'

Sumner's commission of enquiry sat at Crason's Royal Hotel in Clevedon from 3 January 1855. The commissioners overruled objections that they were biased against Denison and then refused to hear doctrinal evidence on either side. Evidence was given amid laughter in court that Denison was 'an evangelical in the best sense of the word'. The commission found unanimously that there was a *prima facie* case to answer before Archbishop Sumner's court.

Whether because he saw where this was leading, or because he freed himself momentarily from the handcuffs of Lord Shaftesbury, Sumner did nothing. After consenting to a prosecution at stage one, he now refrained from proceeding at stage two. Ditcher applied to him for a prosecution. In August 1855 Sumner refused to proceed. Ditcher

[1] 1 October 1854: Liddon, iii, 428–9.

applied to the court of queen's bench to compel the Archbishop to hear the case against the Archdeacon of Taunton. In April 1856, nearly three years after the first sermon in Wells cathedral, the mandamus was confirmed. By the law of England Archbishop Sumner must proceed whether he thought it right or not. Lord Chief Justice Campbell, in granting the mandamus, regretted that Sumner did not refuse to proceed in the first instance.

On 21 May 1856 Sumner summoned Denison to a court in London. Denison applied to the court of queen's bench that the archbishop was acting as the diocesan Bishop of Bath and Wells and must summon him to a place in the diocese. On 22 July 1856 Sumner appeared in the Guildhall at Bath with Lushington as the legal mind on the bench and two anti-Tractarian assessors from the clergy.[1] The court (12 August 1856) found Denison's doctrine repugnant to articles XXVIII and XXIX, and gave him until 1 October to recant. On 30 September Denison lodged in the registry of the diocese of Bath and Wells a paper declining to recant. On 22 October he was deprived. Keble, Pusey, W. J. E. Bennett, Isaac Williams, John Mason Neale and other Tractarians issued a public appeal from the Bath judgment to a synod of the Anglican communion. They feared secessions to the Church of Rome as numerous as those after the Gorham case. Again there was talk of non-jurors. Pusey had to issue a public statement that they had no such intention.[2]

Denison appealed from the archbishop's court to the court of arches. The court of arches is the provincial court of the Archbishop of Canterbury. The dean of arches, Sir John Dodson, held that it was legal nonsense to appeal from Archbishop of Canterbury to Archbishop of Canterbury, and refused to hear the appeal. Denison applied to the queen's bench for a mandamus to compel the dean of arches to hear the appeal, and won. On 23 April 1857 the reluctant Dodson found that since the prosecution must begin within two years of the offence the whole prosecution was invalid from the beginning; for the two relevant sermons were preached in 1853 and the prosecution began formally in June 1856. Ditcher appealed to the judicial committee of the privy council; and in February 1858, amid singular lack of interest, the judicial committee held that the prosecution was invalid and the case against Denison fell.

[1] Dr. Heurtley, the Lady Margaret Professor of Divinity at Oxford; Dean G. H. S. Johnson of Wells.
[2] Liddon, iii, 443.

A case, in which both the relevant courts refused to sit and were compelled by the queen's bench, did not recommend the prevailing system of ecclesiastical courts. The failure of the prosecution benefited high churchmen. It was ignominious that it failed on legal technicality and contributed nothing to determine the lawfulness of Denison's doctrine. But over the years Denison as stalwart martyr achieved a popularity which he was far from possessing at the start of the suit. In the Bath court even the tradesmen clapped him, and when he returned from the judicial committee every man, woman and child in the parish met him and drew his carriage a mile and a half to church and home.[1] The evangelicals suffered partly because the prosecution seemed so persistent, partly because dissenting money helped to finance the attack upon an Anglican archdeacon, and partly because Sumner appeared before the world as an archbishop in a muddle.

Higher language about the eucharistic presence became customary among the Tractarians. Their theologians began writing on the Real Presence. Pusey published a volume called *The Real Presence*. Keble published a beautiful little book called *On Eucharistical Adoration* (1857), which meditates poetically upon the reality of the sacramental gift and the response of the heart. Robert Wilberforce, a year before he became a Roman Catholic, published (1853) an austere scholastic treatment of *The Doctrine of the Holy Eucharist*. And meanwhile younger men in the parishes were busy translating this high sacramental language into external symbol and ritual. When the Denison case ended, ritual controversy had passed far beyond the old troubles over surplice and collection. Outward honour to God's presence within the sacrament was in question; vestments, genuflections, candles, ornaments of the altar.

St. George's-in-the-East

Men are moved by ritual symbols, hallowed associations of custom. Whether these symbols are simple or elaborate, they are valued as they are inhabited, vessels for aspiration of conscience and yearning of soul. The Reformation pushed the focus of worship from altar towards pulpit; and the rational divines of the eighteenth century pushed it still farther from the chancel, into a pulpit which sometimes resounded like a rostrum, as preacher lectured or lecturer preached on moral duty

---

[1] *Notes of my Life*, 263. This parochial triumph did not prevent parochial battles later in his life.

and historic evidence. But now they peered into temple clouds, and made obeisance before throne invisible.

The Book of Common Prayer avoided the word *altar*. But the law of England and therefore of the Church of England sanctioned the use of that word,[1] and popular parlance used *altar* and *communion table* without discriminating. As the chancel was cleansed and restored to beauty, so the holy table demanded ornament. It possessed already a fair linen cloth; in some churches two candlesticks stood upon it, though rarely lit except for light; in a few churches a cross stood upon it; and in the fifties the quest for altar reverence issued in a few chancel screens, in sanctuary rails, in lighting the candlesticks, and finally, though rarely, in Roman-like vestments for the celebrating priest and his assistant ministers. A violent argument and subsequent lawsuit at St. Paul's, Knightsbridge, and its notorious chapel of St. Barnabas, Pimlico, drew everyone's attention to the state of the law about ornaments; and the law was found to be unexpected.

Everything hung upon the ornaments rubric of the prayer book; ordering that 'Such ornaments of the church, and of the ministers thereof, at all times of their ministration, shall be retained and be in use as were in the Church of England, by the authority of Parliament, in the second year of the reign of King Edward VI.' Historical investigation proved that in this year of 1549 the ornaments of church and minister were more elaborate than in any subsequent year of Protestant England. Under this rubric a cross behind the altar (provided it be not 'attached' to the altar), a credence table in the sanctuary, candlesticks upon the altar (provided that they were used for light) and a cross on the chancel screen were formally held legal by 1857.[2] In that year the judicial committee of the privy council made a sensible but ominous declaration: that though in the performance of rites and ceremonies nothing might be added to the prayer book and nothing might be omitted from it, this rule could not apply to the articles used in the church; for otherwise there would be no authority for necessary or familiar objects like organs, pews, pulpit cloth and hassocks.[3]

But these were the years after papal aggression. The conscience of those with invincible repugnance was alive and pulsating; and the

---

[1] 59 George III, cap. 134, sect. 6; 2 & 3 William IV, cap. 61, sect. 1.

[2] Liddell *v*. Westerton and Liddell *v*. Beal: consistory court (Lushington), December 1855; court of arches (Dodson), December 1856; judicial committee of privy council, February 1857; judgment in Brodrick and Fremantle, 117.

[3] Brodrick and Fremantle, 153.

more they manifested that repugnance in irreverence, the more strongly attached to these objects grew the conscience of Tractarian priests and their flocks. Blaspheming rabbles did as much as thickets of law to establish Anglo-Catholic ceremonies within the normal practice of the Church of England.

Parishes of unhappiness were few. Most Tractarian priests were moderate men who knew that the highest reverence was charity. Most objectors preferred desertion to clamour. But in east London window-smashing hooligans were easily conjured from their alleys. In the parish of St. George-in-the-East hooligans and ritual innovation collided with a clang that sounded through the land. The established church could never be quite the same after the vileness of St. George-in-the-East.

St. George-in-the-East had a population of 30,000, a church to hold 2,000 or more, dunes of empty pews and fifty or sixty faithful worshippers. It was the land of docks and sailors, of dining-saloons and filthy bars, of public houses offering squads of harlots. The 733 houses within four streets of the church included 154 brothels. The handsome rector, Bryan King, suffered the misfortune to arrive at that moment of 1842 when Bishop Blomfield's charge about rubrics was damaging the London diocese. In the tedious conflict over surplices or collections or intoning, rector and parishioners were alienated for ever, and everyone who hated church rates joined the campaign to elect churchwardens hostile to the rector. For fourteen years King struggled along with a loyal band and tumultuous vestries. In 1856 he discovered an ally in one of the great slum priests of the century, Charles Lowder. Lowder was one of the college of curates at the troubled St. Barnabas, Pimlico, and long accustomed to choral services which roughs interrupted, rowdy elections of enemy churchwardens, and a church where reverence was secured by a bodyguard of gentlemen. Lowder valued elaborate ritual and ornament; partly because it was assailed sacrilegiously, and partly because he saw its impact upon the heathen poor. He temporarily lost his licence from Bishop Blomfield for giving boys sixpence each to throw rotten eggs at a sandwich-man parading on behalf of the wrong churchwarden.[1] He was very penitent.

Convinced of the necessity for colleges of slum clergy, he helped to found a group of priests under a rule, the Society of the Holy Cross, and looked round for a missionary area. In August 1856, with Pusey's

[1] Trench, *Life of Lowder*, 34, 57, 171.

blessing and alms, he became Bryan King's curate and the head of a little mission-house at Calvert Street in dockland. It was five minutes' walk from Ratcliff Highway, renowned among sailors as the market of prostitutes. He was a brave withdrawn man with a steely will. By May 1859, when calamity began, Lowder was in charge of the Danish church in Wellclose Square, which he rented for Anglican services, another little chapel built of iron, schools with 400 children, a convent formed by the sister of John Mason Neale, and a country home for redeeming harlots. His two first assistants left for the Church of Rome. In their place he was joined by another young Anglo-Catholic of formidable courage, Alexander Heriot Mackonochie. The congregations remained small. Lowder, no preacher, had not the immediate gift of speaking intelligently to this strange mixed population. He heard regular confessions. His ritual included two lighted altar candles and the use of vestments at the eucharist. In common with many Tractarians he believed that the privy council judgment of 1857 sanctioned, if it did not order, the use of vestments by its interpretation of the ornaments rubric. No one doubted that in the year 1549 the clergy of the Church of England wore chasubles; and the ornaments rubric ordered the ornaments of 1549. Since none of the population but a few Irish knew about churches, they were neither shocked nor surprised to find chasubles. Friends gave Bryan King a set of vestments, a white silk chasuble with golden edging.

Attached to the church of St. George's was an old lectureship, for which the parishioners elected the lecturer. Canvassed by placards and mounting cries of no popery, the hostile parish elected an evangelical clergyman named Hugh Allen. Bryan King tried vainly to veto the appointment. Bishop Tait of London believed that he could not refuse to license Allen; and if he is defended from responsibility on the pleas that refusal might be illegal and that he could not see the future, an elementary knowledge of Hooker and English church history should have taught him that vicar and lecturer preaching against each other end in strife to get rid of one of the antagonists. He wanted to rid the diocese of what he called childish mimicries of antiquated garments.

On the first Sunday after his licensing, 22 May 1859, twenty minutes before the usual afternoon service, Hugh Allen walked unbidden into the church with a crowd of supporters and cries of *Bravo, Allen!* Finding the vestry locked against him, he robed in the church. A curate foolishly blocked his way to the pulpit. A vast congregation, assembled to see the game, started hissing, and ladies in the gallery fainted. Allen proceeded to the reading-desk and read the prayers; and then, finding the pulpit unguarded, ascended to preach a sermon hostile to King, waved Tait's licence at the people amid applause and clapping, and read the articles of religion.[1] Under an act of George II the rector must afford the lecturer the use of the pulpit 'from time to time'. A fatal agreement was thereafter reached by which Allen's afternoon service preceded King's afternoon service; and meanwhile press reports of 22 May persuaded Protestants and hooligans and Sunday-bored that St. George's offered fun.

Between June 1859 and May 1860, except from 19 September to 5 November, when Bishop Tait closed the church, Sunday afternoons at St. George's were the zoo and horror and coconut-shy of London. The best days witnessed pew doors banging or feet scraping or hissing or coughing or syncopated responses. The worst days witnessed gleeful rows of boys shooting with peas from the gallery, fireworks, flaming speeches from tub-orators during service, bleating as of goats, spitting on choirboys, a pair of hounds howling gin-silly round the nave, cushions hurled at the altar, orange-peel and butter, kicking or hustling of clergy. One of the altar carpets was crammed into a stove and pew number 16 in the south aisle was used as privy.[2] Lowder once had to flee from the crowd; Mackonochie was assaulted and rescued by police; but the two mission-chapels were less troubled, for there it was legally possible to allow entry only to persons with tickets.

Some sixty to eighty gentlemen, including that amateur boxer and ex-socialist Tom Hughes, came after the early Sundays to act as bodyguard to the rector.[3] But though everyone agreed that brawling in church was a crime or misdemeanour, no one knew how to stop it. Brawling was an ecclesiastical offence which the police could not stop. The only act of Parliament giving policemen summary powers of arrest was an act of Philip and Mary, designed to protect Catholic churches from Protestant rioters. Nor were strenuous endeavours made to stop the riot. For several months London believed that Bryan King could stop it easily by yielding vestments and intoning. Even

---

[1] Best account in R, 1 June 1859: Allen was elected 31 March 1859, licensed 17 May. Cf. Crouch, Bryan King, 46, 47; Trench, Life of Lowder, 173; Davidson-Benham, Life of Tait, i, 236; Reynolds, Martyr to Ritualism, 60ff.

[2] PP, 1860, liii, 158.

[3] Robert Brett was one: Life of Brett, 92. List of thirty-three of the bodyguard in PP, 1860, liii, 139. G. J. Palmer is among them, and G. A. Skinner of Trinity College, Cambridge, and a schoolmaster G. Bond from Hurstpierpoint College.

high churchmen, even Dr. Pusey, blamed him for obstinacy and crotchet-martyrdom.[1] Even Bishop Tait contributed to public blindness by seeming to blame King more than the rioters. The police could not see why they should suffer broken heads to protect an illegal or fanatical clergyman. Tait ordered the churchwardens to keep order. One of the churchwardens was a Methodist and the other was the local publican, coryphaeus among pew-thumpers.

In November 1859, after Tait offered clumsily to arbitrate and King yielded the vestments and the time of service, it was suddenly seen that neither could King end the riot by yielding nor Allen by withdrawing. St. George's had become a Sunday fair-ground like Cremorne Gardens, a Sunday trip like Hampton Court. Fifty uniformed policemen appeared in church for six weeks of November and December. They were withdrawn on 1 January 1860, partly because the home office and police thought that they were protecting sin, partly because the police authorities alleged that their routine work elsewhere was suffering, and partly because no squad of truncheons can establish reverence. When they were withdrawn the rioters behaved worse than before. A local body calling itself the Anti-Puseyite League met at the Wesleyan schoolroom on Tuesday evenings to plan interruption and stimulate Protestant piety.[2] Fifty-one ratepayers sent a petition against policemen to the home secretary, stating, 'There has been no mob or rabble, in the understood sense of the words, in the parish church at any time.' The police said that the bodyguard of gentlemen provoked disturbance. King replied that so long as the police refused protection he needed a bodyguard.

Tait and Brougham and Dungannon hammered away in the House of Lords. The ancient Bishop Phillpotts appeared in the House of Lords to assert that the abandoned vestments were strictly legal[3] and shocked Tait into a reply that the Bishop of Exeter was misleading young clergy. In June 1860, more than a year after the riots began, seventy-three policemen were stationed in St. George's church every Sunday.[4] Bryan King consented to take a prolonged holiday, and left early in the morning to escape the brass band which opponents hired

---

[1] Keble is said by King's family to have been more sympathetic, cf. Crouch, *King*, 132; but see Keble's worried letter to Mackonochie of March 1860 in E. A. Towle, *Mackonochie*, 64.

[2] King to Mayne, 16 November 1859, PP, 1860, liii, 129.

[3] Hansard, clvi, 1860, 910-11.

[4] Hansard, clix, 1860, 1510-11; Crouch, 114-15.

to escort him to the station. He stayed away for three years, until Bishop Tait found him the quiet benefice of Avebury in Wiltshire.

The riots of St. George's-in-the-East raised Anglo-Catholic ceremonial into a flag. The curates of St. George's, Lowder and Mackonochie, were men of tough fibre, and round them in the next decade gathered those who had come to identify Protestantism with gross irreverence. Tractarian disciples henceforth looked not only to the cloisters of Christ Church and the rural peace of Hursley vicarage, but to the slum parishes of east London. The older Puseyite austerity and fear of ceremonial began to vanish; for restraint was now associated withcowardice and lack of principle. The riots ensured that in the long run, unless Parliament devised some form of high commission to maintain discipline, chasubles and incense and roods and tabernacles would establish themselves more widely in the Church of England than any early Victorian could have predicted. A bill was indeed introduced in 1860 to enforce a plain white surplice in conducting services and a black gown in preaching sermons, on penalty of £10 for the first offence, £50 for the second and £100 for all subsequent offences. But a half-Anglican Parliament blushed to interfere, and men tried to imagine a House of Commons deciding that Baptist ministers should wear white ties on Sundays.

Meanwhile high churchmen found it pious to be a bodyguard. Anglo-Catholics were now a party of fighters; their organisation, the English Church Union, formed in 1859–60 out of local unions. Ritual troubles in English church and state began in earnest. The party, believing Tractarian divinity and therefore valuing bishop in idea, was marked from the first by suspicion of bishops in flesh. For *bishops* meant Tait, and Lord Shaftesbury, and Lord Palmerston, and a bloody-handed secularised state poking amidst fenced and holy altars within the temple of Catholic truth.

The trials of Samuel Wilberforce

Wilberforce was no Tractarian. But by a strange providence the son of the evangelical slave-emancipator gathered to himself during the later fifties the leadership and the unpopularity of English high churchmen.

Samuel Wilberforce was another Blomfield; eager for work, impulsive, darting here and hurrying there, restoring or building churches, diligent in business and zealous in pastorate, no wide reader nor profound thinker but a man of strong character and practical energy. Like Blomfield he loved managing; and except when led astray by impulse managed effectively. But he possessed gifts which Blomfield could not rival; emotional and missionary enthusiasm derived from evangelical parents, eloquence and unction which touched summits beyond the reach of any other bishop, breadth of sympathy and fervent devotion, Victorian and romantic mind outrunning the dry witty classical grammarian behind Blomfield's mask. He was born to be a great ecclesiastic. He almost failed to attain this destiny because he saw it too clearly and pursued it too consciously.

He had the disadvantage over Blomfield that his manners were charming. His handshake was hearty, he gushed forth pleasure at meeting, and men suspected that the inward pleasure was less than the outward, that the gesture was kinder than the heart. His sympathies were so exuberant that he would go far to meet the man to whom he talked; and as with everyone who tries to be all things to all men, he sometimes said one thing to one man and the opposite to another man. The world was quick to tax him with insincerity, even with hypocrisy. His charm was not agreeable to rugged silent critics.[1]

His second important disadvantage was a reputation for worldliness, pose of piety concealing ambition. Benjamin Jowett said harshly that he never lost sight of the spiritual in pursuing the temporal.[2] About his ambitions he was perfectly naïve. He wanted to be bishop. He wanted to be Bishop of London. He wanted to be Archbishop of York. He thought he might be Archbishop of Canterbury. To intimates he was frank; and his frankness was bruited through the gossip-rooms of London, which followed with amusement or contempt his hopes and his as frequent disappointments.

The charges of hypocrisy and worldliness died slowly away during his later years; to be revived by hack journalists of the eighties. The warts were more of face than of soul. His chaplains, themselves of high quality, were driven hard and admired him. The nearer men came to Wilberforce the more they liked him. He was neither humbug nor (in Jowett's phrase) semi-humbug. And if he wanted to be archbishop and talked of higher spheres of usefulness, the wish diverted him not a point off his course of duty. Far from scheming to

[1] D. Newsome in *History Today*, September 1963, 624ff.; ER, 1883, April, 540; Golightly, *Letter to the Bishop of Ripon*, 1881.
[2] Abbott and Campbell, i, 152.

ascend eminence, he perpetually embarked on courses which disqualified him.

At one time Gladstone thought him suitable for the archbishopric of York. Gladstone was wrong. Wilberforce had a contentious streak which he could not control. Assailed in the House of Lords, he rose like a smoother Phillpotts and poured scorn or vituperation on his assailants; and unlike Phillpotts agonised afterwards into penitence. Indeed, there was little chance of preferment. For Palmerston and Wilberforce reciprocated dislike and distrust. Palmerston told Queen Victoria that if the bench were filled with men like the Bishops of Oxford and Exeter there would be no religious peace in the land.[1] Wilberforce abused Palmerston's nominations as insulting to the church, and despised his bishops as wild elephants.[2] If Gladstone really expected Palmerston to prefer Wilberforce, he was unusually sanguine.

In the last years of the fifties Wilberforce collected almost by accident the full hostility of low churchmen and thereby rose to lead high churchmen.

The Tractarians revived private confession. Keble and Pusey became noted confessors. An extended practice of confession spread with Tractarian ideas into Anglican parishes. In the history of Protestantism the practice of confession was less rare than was sometimes supposed. The prayer book made provision for it in agonies of conscience or of sickness. Its use had never quite died out among English Protestants, and was difficult to distinguish from private consultation of a godly pastor. But it was hardly fit for newspaper articles. And as represented in newspapers it suffered from all the suspicion which attached to popery and priestcraft and whatever was unEnglish. For years Shaftesbury assailed it as corrupting and indiscreet.

In the summer of 1858 profligate women in two parishes—one St. Barnabas in Pimlico, the other Boyn Hill at Maidenhead—were persuaded to complain that their curates asked them improper questions. The evidence was at first sight graver against Alfred Poole, curate of St. Barnabas; and there was evidence that a lady worker refused to give alms to the woman unless she would go to confession. Poole denied the charges. When the attack widened into a general onslaught upon the practice of confession Bishop Tait of London withdrew Poole's licence without giving his grounds, and on appeal

---

[1] *Letters of Queen Victoria*, I, iii, 416   [2] Ashwell-Wilberforce, ii, 376.

Archbishop Sumner confirmed the withdrawal. Though Poole and his backers chased Tait and Sumner into law courts, it was four and a half years before they achieved the result that no redress could be obtained, and by that time everyone had lost interest.

Meanwhile Wilberforce of Oxford acted differently. Instead of withdrawing his curate's licence without a formal hearing, he appointed a commission of enquiry, and made a public declaration that as a reserve remedy the Church of England authorised private confession. When the enquiry acquitted the curate of Boyn Hill, Wilberforce suffered a torrent of abuse from the national press. He was already suspect because he led the movement to restore Convocation or because his three brothers became Roman Catholics and it was inferred that he was dangerous. A meeting at Banbury ostentatiously refused to drink the health of its bishop. When he lectured at Bradford in October part of the audience of 4,000 tried to hoot him down and found that he was equipped to make hecklers ridiculous.[1]

Across the road from his palace at Cuddesdon he founded in 1854 a college to train ordinands discontented with the preparation provided by the degrees of Oxford and Cambridge. The desire to defend cathedrals from the Ecclesiastical Commission had produced colleges at Wells (1840) and Chichester (1839). The impetus of the fifties derived rather from a belief that royal commissions were slowly secularising the old universities. Cuddesdon was the first college with a common life. Wilberforce was rash enough or big enough to appoint as vice-principal a rigid young disciple of Pusey: H. P. Liddon. These two devout men admired, even revered each other; but nothing could make their physical juxtaposition other than uncomfortable.[2] When storms blew over confession Golightly seized Cuddesdon College and its vice-principal as sticks to beat the bishop for encouraging popery. Wilberforce sacrificed Liddon and saved his college.

In all these troubles Liddon was the only offering thrown to the wolves. High churchmen admired the bishop's stamina and gathered beneath his banner. He never quite satisfied all the aspirations of the heirs of the Tractarians. They found him liable to what Keble once called the most curious twirls and circumbendibuses. But he represented their reforming ideals of hard-working episcopate and devoted clergy, stood courageously for the independent life of the church, was

[1] G, 27 October 1858.
[2] *The Founding of Cuddesdon*, 1954.

known to think Russell unscrupulous and Palmerston calamitous, and behaved with a steady fairness to the Catholic minds of the Church of England. A new generation of Tractarians confused Wilberforce with Pusey and was surprised when their acts disagreed.[1] He became the first figurehead which high churchmen found since Archbishop Howley tottered to his grave. It is a sign of changed times, and of the Palmerston age, that this new leader had a quality totally absent from Howley's frame. He was a fighter.

7. REVIVAL OF SISTERHOODS

The Tractarians revived monasteries and nunneries. The feat was astonishing and almost unique among the Protestant churches. In the long run they thus changed the colour and complexion of Anglican devotion.

A law of Queen Elizabeth asserted that monasteries were contrary to the law of Christ. But nothing forbade monasteries and no Tractarian thought that an obsolete law of the state committed the Church of England. They held before their disciples the highest ideals of holiness and understood these ideals in a medieval or romantic spirit. Newman and Pusey and Hurrell Froude set a Catholic value upon celibate life and looked to Catholic models as guides to sanctity. In the history of Newman's spirit no act was more consistent than the flight to Littlemore.

Three strands of thought lived incongruously together: devotional, romantic, pastoral. Devotion was content with peace and simplicity, rows of cells knocked out of stables, hours of retirement which needed filling with modes of prayer or penitential discipline. Romance yearned to restore ruined arches, and could hardly imagine a convent except within Gothic windows and castellated draughts. Pastoral care saw urban deserts and believed that only a community could settle among them if nourished by private oases, pure amid public dust. This pastoral motive derived strength from the sight of Roman Catholic nuns in slums or hospitals or orphanages; not only nuns in French or Belgian parishes, but nuns who fled to England from the French Revolution, and nuns from a growing number of convents in resurgent English Catholicism. Unmarried women were necessary to

[1] *Life of J. D. Coleridge*, i, 116; Add. MSS. 43,222, 23–24; A. J. Butler, *Life of Dean Butler*, 191.

care for orphans, prostitutes, female prisoners, helpless old, and the sick. Beyond other ages early Victorians knew that gentle ladies could only work in Stepney or nurse cholera if sustained by grace beyond the common lot.

First to take a vow was Marian Hughes, daughter of a Gloucestershire rector. In 1840 she read Newman's desire for a sisterhood in the Church of England; and on 6 June (Trinity Sunday) 1841 at the age of 24 dedicated herself under Pusey's guidance to holy celibacy. But perforce she continued to look after her parents for another eight years. In 1844 Lord John Manners suggested that a sisterhood of mercy should be the memorial to the poet laureate, Robert Southey, who had expressed the opinion that sisterhoods should be revived. With the aid of Dodsworth, Pusey, Hook and Gladstone, Manners founded at Park Village West near Regent's Park the first community of sisters, starting with four ladies. The founders approached Bishop Blomfield, who said that the proposal was dangerous at the present time; but after consulting Howley he wrote a guarded letter which Manners took as warrant to proceed.[1] The sisters taught a school of pauper children and ran an orphanage and visited the hovels of labourers off the Euston Road. In 1848 W. J. Butler, the vicar of Wantage, put two ladies into two cottages to begin a teaching community, and two years later they founded a penitentiary or home to reclaim prostitutes or unmarried mothers. In the same year, with encouragement from Pusey and blessing from Bishop Phillpotts, Priscilla Lydia Sellon founded a community to work among the poor of Plymouth and Devonport. Within two years she established an orphanage, a home for delinquent boys, a refuge to train girls for domestic service, a home for old sailors, a school to teach seventy girls needlework, five ragged schools, six model lodging-houses for poor families with a school attached, and a soup kitchen serving over eighty meals daily to paupers too old to work. In 1851 she opened more institutions in Bristol and a convalescent home at Alverstoke. Child of a naval officer who supported her with money, she inherited a capacity and power of command unknown to any other of the lady founders of sisterhoods. In 1854-6 she took control of the remnants of the community at Park Village West. Pusey toyed with a dream of Miss Sellon as abbess-general of all religious communities in Britain.

[1] Anson, 226; Williams and Campbell, 7, 52ff.

She must be remembered among the indomitables of Victorian womanhood.[1]

These sisterhoods were started with such casual ease that contemporary enthusiasts overlooked the barriers to establishing them successfully within a Protestant church. The English people believed nuns and monks to be popish. They were justified this far, that many of the earliest men or women to practise this form of life ended as Roman Catholics. Newman's entire community at Littlemore joined the Church of Rome. F. W. Faber gathered a group of men at his rectory of Elton in Huntingdonshire and took them with him into the Church of Rome (17 November 1845). At St. Saviour's, Leeds, built by the secret almsgiving of Pusey and intended to be a community of celibate mission priests in a northern slum, the venture was destroyed by the most numerous secessions of priests in any parish of the country. The first superior of Park Village West, the first superior of the Wantage sisters (Elizabeth Lockhart, sister of the Lockhart whose secession caused Newman to resign St. Mary's, Oxford), and a few other early sisters departed from the Church of England and weakened the movement.

Most of the sisterhoods escaped unscathed from popular onslaughts. Miss Sellon at Devonport endured years of persecution. The nuns of St. Margaret's, founded (1855) at East Grinstead by John Mason Neale, were assaulted by a mob at the funeral of one of themselves, Miss Scobell, whose father accused Neale of forcing her to leave money to the sisterhood and then to nurse a patient with scarlet fever. But most Englishmen were more inclined to despise nunneries as medieval toys and fancy-dress than to fear them as cells of the kidnapped. These rabblings were exceptional; and their importance consisted in the furtive air which they imparted to the minds of those responsible for the foundations. Newman must act casuist and deny to Bishop Bagot that he was founding a monastery in the Roman Catholic sense of the word. Dodsworth and Pusey looked through the proposed rules of the Park Village sisterhood to strike out phrases which might offend the pious ears of Bishop Blomfield. Dodsworth vainly recommended that out of doors the sisters should wear coloured shawls to show that they were not nuns.[2] So long as they felt compelled

[1] Anson, 260ff.; T. J. Williams, *Priscilla Lydia Sellon*, 2nd ed., 1965.

[2] Liddon, iii, 22; Anson, 232. Likewise the Roman Catholic Bishop Walsh vainly advised Ambrose Phillipps to call his Trappists by another name than monks, to disguise them as an agricultural and philanthropic community, and above all to avoid the public wearing of habit and cowl. Purcell, *Life of Phillipps*, i, 74.

to secrecy, they could not feel at home in the Church of England; and until they felt at home, they would remain an eccentric fringe.

They could not take an experienced nun and make her head of a community, for no experience existed. Pusey approached Roman Catholic sisters of mercy for help, but they refused;[1] and it is not easy to see how they could have helped if they had consented. Pusey and Butler and Dodsworth and Neale and Lord John Manners secured Roman Catholic books, Marian Hughes visited France to study nunneries. But it was a hard way to learn. Until they ceased to be suspect they could attract few women of sense and capacity. And many of them looked to Pusey as a guide. Grim towards his body, ecstatic in mystical religion, humble beyond reason, most experienced of Anglican confessors, he exercised decisive influence on life and prayer among these early sisterhoods. But he was backward-looking, a man of hair-shirt and of such exalted standards that unwittingly he promoted excessive severity of rule. At Park Village the frail Miss Ogilvie refused all food in Lent 1850 except a dish of thick oatmeal at 9 p.m., consumed no drop even of water between Maundy Thursday and Easter Day, and died in June. Pusey knew too little of the world to judge women by the world's standards, bowed too low before the forcible judgment of Miss Sellon, who paced her bridge like an admiral, forgetful of money and prudence.

The best of the early superiors were the unromantic. Harriet Day at Wantage was a farmer's daughter with few gifts of presence or intelligence, but earthy good sense. Harriet Monsell, a parson's widow who was summoned by T. T. Carter to be head of the penitentiary founded in his parish at Clewer in 1851, was a woman of sterling judgment. The communities became stable as they filled gaps of social service, the needs of prostitutes or orphans or education or hospitals. Nearly all began as little groups of ladies helping a vicar to extend his parochial duty: W. J. Butler and the Wantage sisters, Marian Hughes and her little sisterhood in St. Thomas's parish at Oxford,[2] T. T. Carter and the Clewer penitentiary, Elizabeth Neale (sister of John Mason Neale) and her ladies who (1857) joined Charles Lowder at St. George's-in-the-East, a penitentiary at Horbury in 1858. The community of All Hallows at Ditchingham in Norfolk was founded in 1854 to be a diocesan penitentiary.

---

[1] Ornsby, i, 234.
[2] Now (1964) the Society of the Holy and Undivided Trinity at West Malvern.

The worst times were the years immediately after papal aggression, when *Maria Monk* was reprinted, Newman was accused of constructing dungeons beneath the Oratory at Birmingham, Pierce Connelly vainly sued his nun-wife for restitution of conjugal rights,[1] and in the House of Commons Spooner and Henry Drummond kept demanding enquiry into and legislation against nunneries, not without vile innuendo. This was improved by the Crimean War. Earl Nelson asked Anglican sisterhoods each to contribute two or more sisters as nurses in the east. Florence Nightingale took ten Roman Catholic and fourteen Anglican sisters. The hospitals of Scutari did not escape ecclesiastical criticism. But the reality and legend of Florence Nightingale changed English attitudes to the social service of women and brought with it, though slowly, respect for sisters of religion.

But this was not yet time for religious orders of men.[2]

In grafting sisterhoods into a church of the Reformation, no one did more than Bishop Wilberforce of Oxford. The relation of these communities to their bishops was delicate and doubtful. Bishop Blomfield was timid of Park Village West and at last refused his approval because it used Pusey's versions of Roman devotions and otherwise

---

[1] Pierce Connelly, though married with three children, persuaded his wife that he had a vocation to the priesthood and that she should become a nun. With Lord Shrewsbury's support and amid much publicity this was sanctioned by Rome. In 1848, aided by Henry Drummond of Albury, Connelly went to law to compel his wife to return to him. The dean of arches (Jenner Fust) held in May 1849 that papal decree could not effect a legal separation and that the husband must succeed. On appeal the judicial committee of the privy council held in 1851 that further evidence was admissible and sanctioned a re-hearing. Connelly had no money to press the suit. Meanwhile he sold numerous pamphlets on the issue and sent a petition to Parliament containing matter so prurient that the House of Commons decided not to print it for public inspection. Cf. Juliana Wadham, *The Case of Cornelia Connelly*, 1956.

In addition an impostor pretended to have been imprisoned by the monks of St. Bernard in Charnwood Forest and the miners and stockingers of Whitwick threatened to blow up the monastery (W. J. Jeffreys, *A Narrative of Six Years Captivity among the monks of St Bernard*; and *A full report of a most extraordinary investigation . . . on Tuesday June 26, 1849, at Mount St Bernard Monastery*—Jeffreys got three months hard labour at Handsworth petty sessions). A little perjured orphan called Mary Anne Burke sued vainly for forcible detention at the Convent of the Good Shepherd in Hammersmith, *Tablet*, 1 November 1851, 6 December 1851; Dessain, xv, 50. In August 1852 the nuns of a Norwood convent were accused of cruelty to Henrietta Griffiths whom they expelled for bad conduct; and were acquitted but forced to pay £450 costs, of which Newman found them £400 from the surplus of his Achilli fund, Dessain, xv, 390.

[2] After the collapse of Littlemore and Elton, there was only one significant male attempt before those of Ignatius Lyne and R. M. Benson in the sixties; the brotherhood of St James at Tamworth (1855), gathered by Edward Steere, later bishop in Central Africa. It had no social meaning, was grafted into no parish, and collapsed after a few months Steere complained of the romantic in some of his men. They 'dreamed with delight of singing out of illuminated breviaries', Anson, 51.

tended to Rome.[1] Bishop Phillpotts, after covering Miss Sellon with a giant buckler for three years, withdrew his patronage. Bishop Gilbert of Chichester took away all recognition of East Grinstead after the riot at the funeral of Miss Scobell.

Part of the difficulty was the religious practice of convents. They needed hours of prayer and could only use adaptations of the breviary. They needed devotional guidance which, as Pusey believed, could only be found in Roman Catholic manuals. Pusey scoured the continent for the literature of perfection,[2] published bowdlerised editions of Roman Catholic classics of devotion, and offended the bishops by encouraging aspirations beyond the normal ways of the Church of England. In their private chapels they wished to satisfy their worshipping instincts and could disregard the public traditions of parish churches. One of the first chasubles to be worn in modern Anglican history was worn by Neale in the chapel at East Grinstead in 1850. Marian Hughes is said to have sewn out of two Oxford M.A. hoods a red chasuble, used for the first time by Chamberlain, vicar of St. Thomas's, Oxford, on Whitsunday 1854, without complaint from his flock.[3]

Bishops were prickled by vows. Knowing that Bishop Blomfield would refuse his sanction, some of the Park Village sisters took vows privately to Dr. Pusey. When Blomfield helped to found a sisterhood of nurses at Fitzroy Square, London, in 1848[4] he assured the supporters that there would be no vows of poverty, obedience or celibacy. Bishop Phillpotts withdrew his protection from Miss Sellon because he doubted whether sisters were free to leave the community. Samuel Wilberforce refused to allow a clergyman to perform a ceremony of profession because it contained a public resolution of chastity and devotion. He said that vows not sanctioned by Christ were certainly dangerous and probably unlawful.[5] Bishop Tait argued that vows needed dispensing power which the Church of England had rightly abolished;[6] that vows partook of the nature of illegal oaths; that a clergyman receiving such an oath might perhaps be liable to prosecution and certainly acted with impropriety.

[1] Blomfield to Pusey (from Cuddesdon palace), 3 December 1850; Blomfield Papers, FP 384/186.
[2] Cf. Ornsby, ii, 46–47.
[3] Proby, ii, 103; Ollard, 125.
[4] Now (1964) the Community of St. John the Divine, Hastings.
[5] Ashwell-Wilberforce, iii, 331–2; Anson, 230–1; 300–1.
[6] Davidson-Benham, i, 457, 461; Anson, 301–2.

In the diocese of Oxford were three stable communities; Wantage, Clewer, Marian Hughes in Oxford. But they were new, and their stability unknown. At first Wilberforce fussed them. He disapproved regular confessions and regular direction of souls, drove all the crucifixes from the house at Clewer, tried to exclude Roman Catholic books of devotion. But as the sisterhoods grew and became familiar Wilberforce treated them with sympathy and defended them against critics. He began to be demanded as visitor to communities outside his diocese. They found in him that link with Anglican hierarchy which even in early years enabled them to feel at home in their church.

8. CHARITIES

Before 1853 no effective instrument could divert an obsolete charity to new uses. It slowly dawned upon Englishmen that large numbers of charities were not being used for the purposes which the testators intended; whether because all the trustees died and there was no provision for appointing new trustees, or because the value of money had changed, or because the objects were obsolete, or because the purposes were undesirable. In a Radnorshire village a trust gave over £3,000 a year to give meat drink and physic to the poor. Peasants flocked to the village, immorality was rife and drunkenness constant, yet no one had power to alter the terms of the trust.[1]

Brougham poked his nose into the papers in 1818, but public opinion only started to exert pressure in the reform epoch. A clerical schoolmaster of Berkhamsted, who sold up the school and went away to live on his stipend in Lincolnshire, was still respected as late as 1828-9. Five years later the citizens of Berkhamsted were holding protest meetings in Berkhamsted church and at the King's Arms.[2] The thirties called all charities to justify their existence. The reformed corporations represented a new local opinion. A commission investigated every county, produced massive volumes of evidence which few M.P.s could master, and drew the attention of the attorney-general to the behaviour of some 400 charities. Processes in the courts recovered a lot of money to the true purposes of the charity; and the threat of processes in the courts recovered more. Trustees of 1836 behaved more responsibly than trustees of 1826.

The reform must benefit the churches by securing more money to

---

[1] Hansard, cxxvi, 1016.   [2] PP, 1835, vii, 681-768.

educate and more money for alms in return for less money to the trustees of the education or the alms. The charity commissioners, after their constitution in 1853, compelled various headmasters to do the work or resign; and as a number of headmasters were also incumbents of neighbouring parishes, the separation might be expected to help both school and parish. Thus the headmaster of Spalding grammar school was forbidden to hold other preferments, the headmastership of Coventry high school was sundered from the rectory of St. John.[1] In securing the effective use of ancient funds the commissioners sometimes diminished the privileges of clergymen who were drawing comfortable stipends.

The glaring cases occurred when the charity contained a provision that the residue should go to the head or master. For as money declined in value over the centuries the residue might have risen till it was far the largest piece of the income. Under the will of Stephen Perse the master of the Perse school in Cambridge was to receive £40 and the master of Caius £3. In 1829 the master of the school indeed received £150, but the master of Caius £280. Summoned to the court the fellows pleaded that their attention had never seriously been drawn to the subject until the last few years.[2] Brougham himself said that far the most numerous troubles arose from negligence and not from intentional corruption.

A similar case was Sherburn hospital in Durham. The master till his death in 1854 was an evangelical divine, G. S. Faber, uncle of the Tractarian Frederick Faber. The hospital went back to King Henry II and was intended for thirty lepers. With Durham mines the income rose. The master was entitled to the residue, which in 1851-3 averaged £3,323. The charity commissioners of 1854-5 proposed to make it less of an almshouse and more of a hospital, to declare that the head must be no longer a preacher but a physician, to recover £3,000 as a gift to Durham county hospital, to provide schools in the neighbourhood and to increase the stipends of seven neighbouring incumbents.[3] Bishop Maltby was shocked, and the bill failed in Parliament. The commissioners carried part of their plan by a scheme in chancery, leaving the master still a clergyman and the bishop still retaining the right to appoint. At first sight the commissioners were seeking to abolish an ancient institution of the church and to create a modern

---

[1] PP, 1856, xxii, 263, 330.
[2] J. M. Gray, *History of the Perse School*, 106ff.   [3] PP, 1854-5, xv, 117 ff.

institution of the state. The Bishop of Durham would have lost a valuable way of rewarding a divine with a sufficient stipend. But church as well as state gained rather than lost by reform of the charity.

Far the most famous cases of this kind to reach the court were the St. Cross case at Winchester (1845–53) and the Whiston case at Rochester (1848–53). At Winchester the Earl of Guildford held the livings of St. Mary's, Southampton, and Alresford and was master of St. Cross hospital. At St. Cross he had no duties except to sign leases and was suspected of drawing a 'residue' of fabulous wealth, but which was in truth about £1,500 a year. A series of chancery suits persuaded or compelled him to resign the two livings (1850) and finally the hospital. At Rochester the headmaster of the cathedral school, Whiston, sued the dean and chapter for not using the increased funds of the endowment to benefit the school. As the press rollicked through the cases, the public interest little profited the Church of England[1] because they seemed to identify the clergy with good pay for no work. They were an incident in a general revaluing of old charities which helped the churches and English education. It must not be thought that the only notorious scandals were ecclesiastical. Some of them concerned corporations, others defaulting or negligent trustees, one the insertion of another 9 after 99 in the period of a lease. In the House of Lords the lord chancellor described the visit by the Mercers company to its charity in Greenwich, together with the menus which the visitors partook; and the description is one of the most amusing ever recorded by Hansard.[2]

At Dulwich the new charity commissioners (1854–6) suppressed an old-fashioned college of celibates. It had a master, a warden, four fellows, six poor brethren, six poor sisters, and twelve poor scholars. With the arrival of the Crystal Palace and the growth of suburbs the property rose in value, until the annual income was £8,600 and still rising. Local residents grumbled at the exiguous education offered by a school which for eighty years had sent no one to a university. The master received about £1,000 in pay and allowances, the fellows about £500. In return they ran the property, the school, the picture gallery, and the college chapel which was famous as a public church.

---

[1] For the St. Cross case, R. B. Martin, *Enter Rumour*, 1962; for Rochester, R. Arnold, *The Whiston Matter*, 1961; for Dulwich, PP, 1856, xxii, 291; for the general question, G. F. A. Best, 'The Road to Hiram's Hospital' in *Victorian Studies*, December 1961, 135–50.

[2] Hansard, lxxxvi, 746–7.

The commissioners suppressed the entire college, respected the vested interests of the occupants in stipend while allowing them to marry, and created a good school.

The charity commissioners achieved almost as much, and almost as slowly, as the Whig government to end the use or misuse of ecclesiastical money in sinecures or partial sinecures for leisured clergymen or laymen. Sometimes the money was not quite so ecclesiastical when they had finished.

9. PAROCHIAL WORSHIP

When Legh Richmond first visited the dairyman's daughter in the servants' parlour of the squire's mansion, she said, 'Sir, I take it very kind that you have condescended to leave the company of the rich and converse with the poor.' Even in 1836 Archbishop Howley defended the sale of the next presentation to a living on the plea that it enabled wealthy and respectable persons to secure livings and bring their talent into the service of the church.[1] Thirteen years later Bishop Blomfield ended the confirmation at the Chapel Royal which was restricted to the sons of the nobility,[2] and although the ordinances of Cambridge university continued until 1970 to provide special seats for noblemen at university sermons, no noblemen ever occupied them.

In the early thirties one devout layman, who went to church twice every Sunday, received the sacrament only twice during the first five years after his confirmation.[3] The growth in the habit of weekly communion was one big change in Anglican worship during the forties and fifties.

Confirmations were transformed by railways. Bishop Marsh of Peterborough, who died in 1839, found that the quickest way from one end of his diocese to the other was via London. For a short time bishops continued to allow the huge numbers of candidates familiar in the pre-railway age. In 1846 Bishop Monk of Gloucester confirmed 1,500 persons at Cheltenham.[4] But smaller confirmations were more reverent, and railways allowed the bishop to travel round his diocese as never before in Christian history. Younger and energetic bishops, led by Wilberforce, were willing to face the hard labour of this travelling. Few changes benefited parochial life so instantaneously. In

---

[1] Charge at Maidstone: JB, 36, 307.   [2] G, 49, 238.
[3] Goulburn, *Life of Burgon*, i, 20-21.   [4] G, 46, 458.

a novel of 1844 one character argued that railways now spread the gospel like the printing press at the Reformation.[1] Confirmations were usually held in the evening because factories often refused to allow their children a free afternoon to be confirmed. The change was rapid. In the diocese of Salisbury Bishop Burgess (died 1836) confirmed only in large towns; Bishop Denison (died 1854) confirmed in large towns and large villages; Bishop Hamilton (1854–69) in almost any church where the incumbent asked for him.[2]

Communion and week-day services grew slowly more frequent in these twenty years. The pace of change varied according to diocese, and was always slower in rural areas. As late as 1864 nearly a third of the parishes in the Lincoln diocese celebrated the sacrament four times a year or less. In 1854 many country pastors still issued tickets for communion.[3] The strangers and crowds in city churches broke the system of tickets. The number of confirmed increased rapidly, but this increase was not reflected in a corresponding increase in the rising numbers of Easter communicants.

Country people were still partly illiterate. Between 1842 and 1845 nearly half the women and a third of the men who were married signed their names in the register with marks. In remote districts witchcraft was still practised and strange superstition could be unearthed. In Cornwall there were even some incumbents who believed in witchcraft. Parish life in the country changed little because democracy and the press took longer to reach the people. Squire and parson still ruled the village. Old Roman Catholic families influenced their little societies, Whitefield in Lancashire was ruled by a Quaker squire, Allingham in Wiltshire by a Strict Baptist squire, Bavington by a Primitive Methodist squire. But most squires and farmers were Anglican and the countryside followed them. The parishioners of Huntspill in Somerset were shocked in 1858 to discover that their new incumbent was not a Tory.[4] The Duke of Wellington attended church once a Sunday, except when in London, because the law of England required it. 'I consider that the attendance at divine service in publick is a duty upon every individual in high station, who has a large house and many servants, and whose example might influence the conduct of others.'[5]

[1] *Mary Spencer*, by Anne Howard, 135.   [2] G, 46,403; 69,956.
[3] C. M. Yonge, *Patteson*, i, 64; G, 64, 984.
[4] *Memorials of Dean Lake*, 92.
[5] *Wellington and his Friends*, 1965, 279–80.

Into the sixties Anglican writers assumed that they held the country-side. Though parish minutes show the strains of church versus dissent in a tiny community, and though village churches suffered dilapidation like town churches, the Anglicans were agreed that despite exceptions the villages were Anglican. The country clergy might be old-fashioned, but they held a people who preferred old fashions. Robert Landor, brother of the poet, presented himself in 1829 to the living of Birlingham in Worcestershire. He died there forty years later, still the squarson of the little parish, having missed perhaps six Sundays from his church. The villagers liked him, respected him, were afraid of him, and came to church. A very few dissenters in the parish remained dissenters, but made no attempt to build a chapel, from affection or from reverence to the incumbent. His single excess or extravagance, apart from alms to his people, was the collection of old masters, which in vast frames crammed the walls of his house. He would have no innovation, desired no modern ritual, was not willing for intoning or chanting, instituted no candlesticks nor surpliced choir into the chancel, destroyed no pews. But he was the ancient feudal parson continuing far into the mid-Victorian age.[1]

Lest we leave too halcyon a mood, or attribute too white a cleansing to Whig reform, we must recall that even in 1860 survived ecclesiastical lumber more noisome than a nostalgic sentiment for box pews. The vested interests of the past settled on some clergymen who lived unconscionably long. At Doddington in the fens a regency buck continued to draw the largest stipend of an incumbent in England, £8,000 or more a year derived from reclaimed land. When he died he was drawing more pay than any bishops but the two archbishops, the Bishop of London, and Bishop Sumner of Winchester who also survived from some cloud-capped Georgian Eden. To the end of his days he endeavoured to appear in the character and clothes of a dandy. It must not be supposed that Doddington always suffered from his presence. The air of the fens was unhealthy. The parishioners were entrusted to curates, one of whom lost three children and a sister-in-law during a single pestilence. Yet the people respected him, and on his death all the principal inhabitants of the parish drew down the blinds of their rooms. As these survivors of endowed corruption died away one by one, the little remnant became always odder. In the fifties they were still common enough to give gloom and gaiety to

[1] DNB; G, 69,203; biography by E. Partridge, 1927.

Trollope's novels. In the sixties they were prodigies. When the rector of Doddington died at last in 1868 a sense of incongruity filled the public mind. Such relics seemed as remote as those ancient clergymen who still dressed in gaiters and kneebreeches, though gaiters were fast becoming the mark of dignity; wearing their antique black from no motive of pomp or ostentation, but solely because this was the way when the world was younger.

The relation of squire with parson sometimes ended in conflict. The squire of Helmingham in Suffolk would stand up, watch in hand, if he thought the sermon too long; and we have a full record of what could happen from a little Norfolk parish during these years.[1] At a village in Gloucestershire a squire, who quarrelled with his rector, opened a room in the parish for service and himself read the liturgy in a surplice and preached. But such troubles were rare.

It was still difficult to make old-fashioned country congregations join the responses, more difficult when a new reforming parson wanted them to sing psalms. They left responses to the clerk and sat passive until the hymns. But congregational worship slowly made its way. In the country a new service took root, the harvest festival. In the starving year of 1842 the abundant harvest saved lives, and public authority (as on occasion before) issued a form of thanksgiving.[2] Country parishes celebrated harvests with beer and drunkenness. More and more parsons diverted their parishioners with a special service in church followed by dinner of beef and plum pudding and beer. Several clergymen claimed to have been the first: Hawker of Morwenstow in Cornwall; Piers Claughton, rector of Elton in Huntingdonshire; G. A. Denison at East Brent.

By 1860 many churches, whether restored or not, were cleaner than they used to be. Many chancels had been built new, many old chancels had been incorporated into the worshipping area of the church; again with exceptions—as late as 1869 the chancel at Swingfield near Dover was criticised because there could be seen so many excellent specimens of ferns.

[1] Loane, Ryle, 25: cf. E. D. H. Tollemache, The Tollemaches of Helmingham and Ham, 1949, 170; Chadwick, Victorian Miniature, 1960; G, 61, 323. In 1836 the Bishop of Lincoln presented a petition to the House of Lords from the squire of Hulgrust, near Caistor (Lincs.), praying their lordships to abolish an indecent custom by which he held certain lands; on every Palm Sunday a person deputed by him must hold a whip over the head of the clergyman as he ascended the pulpit. Br. Mag., 9, 1836, 705–6.
[2] CO, 1842, 640. The Bishop of Hereford asked Melbourne for a harvest festival in 1838. Melbourne refused on the ground that one would then be obliged to have a thanksgiving for everything.

The pace varied from parish to parish and diocese to diocese. But the trend was always towards more frequent services, use of organs, choirs (though few yet in surplices) joining in responses, replacing pews with benches, decorating the chancel (often with altar rails and cross and candlesticks) and unlocking churches on weekdays. In 1830 it was matter for comment if a clergyman could be distinguished from a layman in ordinary life. In 1860 it was matter for comment if he could not be so distinguished.

Sermons were more frequent but shorter. The mean of quality in sermons is a statistic inaccessible; but observers agreed that the elevation of the altar lowered the pulpit. A pamphleteer of 1854 grumbled that a popular preacher was suspect of clap-trap and supposed to be neglecting his pastoral duties.[1] More prejudice existed in 1860 than in 1830 against preaching sermons written by other people. But publishers still did well from printing sermons.

A rare evangelical parish began to provide celebrations of holy communion in the evening. An afternoon celebration was known in parts of Wales during the early forties.[2] J. C. Miller, evangelical vicar of St. Martin's, Birmingham, is said to have been the first to institute a regular evening communion twice a month.[3] The change was disliked by most clergy. Miller also divided the morning service, so that the old unity of matins-litany-communion became three different services. Thus shortened service and shortened sermon reduced morning service from two and a half to one and a half hours.

Before 1860 hymnody, once the property of dissenters and evangelicals, was accepted into almost every church. An indescribable variety of hymnbooks were in use, for many vicars published hymnbooks for their congregations. This chaos had manifold inconveniences. In 1855 the five central churches of Nottingham each used a different hymnbook. The triumph of hymnody, and the marriage of old Catholic with modern evangelical or romantic hymn, was marked in 1861 by the publication of *Hymns Ancient and Modern*, a collection seeking to incorporate the treasure of the Christian centuries, and thenceforth slowly conquering the manifold local collections.

When the queen came to the throne, organs were not common outside large churches in towns. The country band still reigned in the

[1] *Preachers and Patrons: or Pulpit Reform*, 37.
[2] CO, 1843, 24.
[3] Proby, ii, 22–23: it was in 1851-2, cf. R. Seymour and J. F. Mackarness, *Eighteen years of a Clerical Meeting*, 153; the meeting much disliked the idea.

village gallery, or their special pew. Village congregations made no attempt to sing psalms, except the metrical psalms which were hymns. The normal band consisted of two clarionets, a bassoon, a violoncello, and sometimes a small flute. Puddletown in Dorset had eight players in the west gallery, Maiden Newton had nine, and both included serpents as well as clarionets. Bands entered into competition with each other, and retained the loyalty and interest of young men in the village. The novelist Thomas Hardy was descended from two generations of church players; and was drawing upon memory when in *The Mayor of Casterbridge* he described how church choir and clerk and forty male members of the congregation repaired after service to the *Three Mariners*, smoked a clay pipe, drank half a pint each (a point of honour not to have more) and discussed the sermon. In odd places these bands continued throughout the reign, but everywhere they declined. At Steepleton church in 1879 the orchestra consisted of a shoemaker who played the bass viol and his mother who sang the air. Their endeavours were not welcome to those who wanted the congregation to sing and who found strident wood-wind incompatible with reverence. Musically the organ was unquestionably an improvement if anyone could play it. Sir Frederick Gore Ouseley, who perhaps did more than any other person to raise the standards of Victorian church music, believed that the introduction of an organ or harmonium was necessary to the improvement because it enabled the band to be suppressed.[1] Those who regretted the fiddlers never regretted them for musical reasons, but for the loss of a strong church interest in the village.

The schoolmasters of the National Society probably did more than the clergy to create choirs. Their colleges, especially St. Mark's, Chelsea, offered a training, and the old unisons of the charity children were slowly turned into more sensitive and knowledgeable choirs. The age of choir practices began. The movement for better music was retarded because many villages, unable to provide an organist, bought a barrel-organ with a small repertory of tunes and a tone inferior to that of the clarionets which it replaced. Ouseley denounced the barrel-organ as praising God by machinery and compared it to an oriental prayer-wheel. During the fifties or sixties, if the vicar was a high churchman, the choir was put into the chancel and then or later clothed in surplices. Some objected to women appearing in surplices,

[1] *Church Congress Report*, 1874, 97.

and thereby lost the benefit of soprano voices. At Lichfield cathedral in October 1856, and again in 1857, gatherings of parish choirs assembled; and Southwell followed Lichfield in encouraging and educating the new musicians of the country parishes. The evidence of elevated standards is plentiful. And the evidence that the music of many village churches was as raucous or uncongregational as ever is also plentiful. Some parishes were too small for the necessary equipment or persons. The rector of Chilcombe in Dorset had twenty souls. In 1874 his music still consisted of his clerk who sang, and himself who played the harmonium. At his other village of Whitchurch Canonicorum he found a choir of four girls and an old man, replaced them with seventeen surpliced boys, and then began to lament that the boys never sang in tune.[1] Music in many country churches was still confessed to be execrable.[2]

In the parish churches pews gave rise to one of the legal and pastoral arguments of the age. According to the law of the Church of England pews were appropriated by the ordinary of the parish in accordance with the substance of the parishioners. Many churches in the cities were built under an act of Parliament which licensed the sale or lease of pews. Most parish churches of 1830 contained large box pews, lockable and controlled by a pew opener. Private seats for the middle class thus filled the main body of the church and left the poor on benches at the back, in side aisles, or in the gallery. The box pews occupied many chancels, and their occupants inevitably sat facing the pulpit and with backs towards the altar. In 1847 St. Mary's at Bridgwater contained 845 sittings, of which less than an eighth were open to the public. As late as 1846 it was proposed, when building the church of All Saints in St. John's Wood, to put pews in the chancel with their backs towards the altar.[3]

The great pews of the eighteenth century slowly disappeared in the wave of church restoration, though traces may still be seen in many churches. At Luton the vast pew of the Bute family, forming a gallery which hid the chancel from the nave, lasted till 1855. The great pew called Golgotha in Great St. Mary's at Cambridge, where the vice-chancellor and dignitaries sat for the university sermon, facing the preacher at the west end and dividing chancel from nave, lasted till 1863.

[1] *Church Congress Report*, 1874, 120.
[2] Cf. G, 46, 207: R. Druitt, *A Popular Tract on Church Music*, 1845.
[3] G, 47, 275; 46, 235.

In country churches the inconvenience was small. Country churches were usually large enough for the people. In underchurched London the system generated hard feeling. And even in the country occasional abuses of the system created litigation or some argument. It was odd to see the aisles crammed with people while areas of locked pews were untenanted. The courts ruled that the ordinary of the church controlled all seats in church, that no one possessed property in seats, that seats were private only by faculty or by such ancient usage that a faculty must be presumed. Yet at Horsham church (1852) pews were freely bought and sold, a book was kept to record prices. And everywhere pews might be attached by custom to important property in the parish. The most criticised pews were square, sometimes called 'company pews' because their occupants sat round in a square, in some country churches round a table, and must kneel face to face, some with backs to the east.

Parishes slowly altered their seating system, usually as part of a more general restoration. Professor Burton, restoring Ewelme church out of his pocket in 1834, persuaded the parishioners to remove the locked doors and high pews. But others were not content with slow change. The implacable enemy of pews was John Mason Neale. At an early date in the history of the Cambridge Camden society he committed its managers to a programme of abolition on principle. He produced twenty-four reasons for getting rid of pews; they were not primitive, were invented by people who thought themselves too good to pray by the side of their neighbours, shut out the poor who are driven away to meeting-houses, make it impossible to pay proper attention, cause quarrels in the parish, spoil the look of a church and endanger its safety, allow parishioners to go to sleep without fear, harbour dust and mildew, introduce the nuisance of pew openers, and were part of the wicked system of men who murdered Charles their anointed sovereign. Neale became fanatical on the subject.[1] When he went to Crawley in Sussex he took an axe and hacked the pews. Hawker of Morwenstow persuaded all the farmers but one to yield their curtains and locks. The last one could not be persuaded. Hawker arranged to meet him in church and hacked his pew before his eyes. Archdeacon Hare of Lewes conducted a more judicious campaign against pews.

Not everyone accepted these condemnations. As rates became more difficult to collect churches depended even more on pew rents.

[1] *History of Pues*, 3rd ed., v–viii.

Some evangelicals suspected the attack as another attempt to un-protestantise the church.[1] Defenders of pews like Blomfield or Samuel Wilberforce took higher ground. A family was helped to worship as a family. The village was right to worship as a village, each in due order. A Christian soul should be encouraged to become attached by custom and sentiment to his particular place in church. To abolish pews in crowded churches meant disorderly scramble.

The relentless process continued, of freeing more and more seats in the churches. But it was slow. The argument was as keen in the sixties as in the forties. In 1868 even Ripon cathedral was still full of rented pews.

The curate might expect, if he were lucky, £100 a year. But in twenty-two advertisements of 1858 only two offered £100, fourteen ranged from £70 to £20. A respectable butler or coachman would hardly accept £70 a year unless board and lodging were added. In one London slum a curate on £100 a year lived opposite a school-master with £150 a year plus lodging rent-free in the schoolhouse.[2]

Partly because the fleecy rewards of the church were now shorn; partly because other careers were now respectable; and perhaps in some small part by reason of the intellectual shifting of the day, the twenty years after 1840 saw a decline in the number of graduates taking orders, while the number of ordinands very slowly increased. In 1862 were ordained fewer than half as many men from the university of Oxford as in 1841. In 1841 270 Cambridge men, in 1862 178 Cambridge men, took orders. The number of non-graduates was only 48 in 1841, and in 1850 was 188. In 1862 something like one-third of all persons ordained were not graduates.[3] Unquestionably the chief reason for this change was social. Many gentlemen of 1830 looked upon holy orders as the most attractive of all professions. The work offered leisure, reasonable comfort, the chance of greatness in the national counsels, and fulfilment to pastoral ideals of the conscience. Few gentlemen of 1860 so viewed the calling. The ideals became more prominent while the social incentives declined. The mammonish Sydney Smith would simply remark that the clergyman of 1860 must work harder for less pay than the clergyman of thirty years before.

[1] CO, 1844, 86–87. A. J. C. Hare's tale (*Story of My Life*, i, 113) that Archdeacon Hare went about with saw and hammer, is almost certainly untrue, like so many of A. J. C. Hare's stories.

[2] CO, 58, 401.

[3] Statistics in E. Phillips, *The Church and the Ecclesiastical Commissioners*, 1863, 4.

Such a verdict is too crude. The change depended on social movements more profound than the raw figures of stipend and population.

Fewer clergymen of 1860 became magistrates. But this change is more to be attributed to a feeling against the work as unsuitable to the ministry, and to the experience of incumbents who saw a barrier rising between their parishioners and themselves. In the light of strong remarks, by dissenters and by clergymen, against clerical magistrates, the numbers were slow to fall. We have the figures for Oxfordshire. In 1816 36.8 per cent of the magistrates were clergymen; in 1837, 27 per cent; in 1857, 21 per cent.[1] In view of public opinion the number of clerical magistrates was still surprisingly high.

The northern parishes felt different to the southern. A clergyman who moved from south to north found himself missing the reverence of the peasantry and the respect of the middle class. Northerners judged him as a man. The strong dissenting communities bred a friendly but less respectful attitude of society even towards Anglican incumbents. The Oxford and Cambridge graduates who dominated the Anglican clergy were not tempted northward in sufficient numbers. After 1836 the West Riding lay in the diocese of Ripon; and for ten years its bishop, Longley, received not a single graduate curate into his diocese.[2]

The cathedral lost place as England became industrial; but still more because it was curtailed by the Ecclesiastical Commission. The act of 1840 allowed the cathedrals to continue in sunshine by respecting the vested interests. But by 1860 the full extent of the curtailment was becoming plain, and inside the close the dean and canons began to wonder how the cathedral should fulfil its duty. During the fifties even the minor canons of Barchester discussed, as their dean lay dying, how their deanery was cut down. A strong cathedral commission of 1852–4 made many useful recommendations on which no one acted. Meanwhile the separate cathedrals shared in the age of church restoration. Their roofs and monuments were cleaned, their interiors heated, their windows repaired. In many cathedrals the old tradition of sacred music was maintained in all its beauty. To others the choral service was translated as it was taken into the parish churches. When Bristol cathedral (1849) tried to abandon choral services it caused local controversy and national scandal. Five years later Llandaff was the only cathedral without choral services.

To render the loveliest forms of musical worship was not enough to

[1] McClatchey, 179. [2] CO, 59, 49.

justify the cathedral. A few (Wells, Chichester, Lichfield and later others) accepted the duty of training ordinands. But where a population surrounded the cathedral the chapter began to share in the ideals of the age by reaching out towards the people, by exercising a pastoral ministry. The railway did for the cathedral what it also did for the bishop. It made both cathedral and bishop more effective as capitals of the diocese. But this was slow to happen. In the fifties Peterborough was said to be the only cathedral into which you could achieve entry without tipping a verger.

In London stood two mighty cathedrals, St. Paul's and Westminster abbey. When Bishop Blomfield made his famous speech of 1840 to the House of Lords he evidently thought St. Paul's to be useless to the people. But he had endured ridicule from a canon of St. Paul's and was perhaps guilty of overstatement. As the railways helped country cathedrals, so they brought more and more visitors to London. The average congregation at a week-day afternoon service in St. Paul's about 1841 was fifteen or twenty,[1] and on Sundays the choir was crammed. The nave and space under the dome were used only for state occasions. The pence for admission were abolished in 1851. And though the music of the forties and fifties was notorious for its sloppiness, the cathedral of London was beginning to reach outward. In 1856 an evangelical writer even declared that it was beginning to radiate evangelical truth. The monuments continued filthy, the angels black, the heroes dusty. The feather-duster which Dean Buckland carried round Westminster abbey was not a mere sceptre of eccentricity.

The age of the evangelicals perceived the contrast between the teeming masses of east London and the vast empty spaces of St. Paul's. Bishop Tait professed this contrast to St. Paul's more courteously than his predecessor. And the example of Spurgeon at last compelled the two great cathedrals to attempt a feat of evangelism for which they were ill suited.

Spurgeon when he turned to morning services made no special attempt to reach the working classes. But the needs of the working men, and the example of Spurgeon, persuaded the evangelical leaders of the Church of England to imitate his methods.

It was illegal to assemble outside churches for the religious worship of the established church, if more than twenty persons assembled.

[1] Matthews-Atkins, 254.

During the summer of 1855, not without difficulty, Shaftesbury passed a bill through Parliament abolishing the proviso of twenty persons. He hoped thereby to legalise worship in the open air or in public halls, and so enable clergymen to imitate Spurgeon. Under this law leading evangelicals preached mission services in the cities. W. Carus Wilson preached to more than 2,000 people in Portsmouth circus on Sunday evenings.[1]

Accordingly the evangelical leaders planned a course of services in Exeter hall on Sunday evenings in May and June 1857. Bishop Villiers of Carlisle preached the first sermon on 25 May and drew great crowds, among them many working men. The organisers requested habitual worshippers not to come, but in vain. High churchmen much disliked these services, and accused them of introducing Spurgeonism into the church. The mode of worship was not Anglican. The preachers were partisan. The surroundings were not reverent. The atmosphere was like a conventicle. Why choose Exeter hall when two great consecrated buildings stood empty in London, Westminster Abbey and St. Paul's cathedral? In the House of Lords, Bishop Tait protected the experiment with his broad shield.

Encouraged by success, evangelicals arranged another course of sermons in November 1857. Two days before, A. G. Edouart, the incumbent of St. Michael's in Burleigh Street, in whose parish lay Exeter hall, prohibited the services. It was suspected that he had the legal right to do so. The dissenters took over the conduct of the services. Edouart's church was disturbed by the groanings of a large crowd which came out of Exeter hall. Shaftesbury introduced a religious worship amendment bill allowing any ordained minister to conduct services in any parish with a population of 2,000 unless the inhibition of the incumbent was countersigned by the bishop. Archbishop Sumner introduced a counter-bill, with right to appeal from bishop to archbishop. The House of Commons refused to pass any such bill.

Under the pressure of mounting demand the chapter of Westminster resolved to begin evening services in January 1858, the chapter of St. Paul's appealed for £11,000 to make the nave suitable for large popular services. Dean Trench of Westminster was afraid that no one would come in the icy weather. On the first Sunday (3 January) a multitude assembled and froze in the cold outside, until

[1] R, 26 October 1857; Hardman, 250ff.

the doors were unlocked and a screaming crowd rushed in to occupy the chairs which (as was too evident) had been hired from the Crystal Palace. And at once the difficulty of using these cathedrals as mission halls was obvious. The service must be solemn evensong. Few joined in. The organist exhibited his skill. Policemen stood ominous in the aisles. No one could kneel. The nave was so cold that worshippers huddled down into their greatcoats. Of necessity and precedence the preacher was Dean Trench, an admirable man, but heavy with a melancholy drawl. Though crowds continued, it was soon evident that Westminster abbey did not serve the function of Exeter hall.

Encouraged by the abbey, St. Paul's opened its evening services in December 1858. Ludgate Hill was crammed with thousands unable to enter. This time the cathedral was heated to fifty-five degrees before the service. But the acoustics and the preacher proved less suitable than those of the abbey. From a great tub-pulpit decked in green velvet Bishop Tait boomed upwards into the echoing dome for nearly an hour, and even the front rows could scarcely distinguish the words.

Thus the great cathedrals were not able to do what Spurgeon could do. And yet they were slowly finding a pastoral opportunity of a different kind, more suitable to their genius. They endeavoured to reach outward.

CHAPTER VIII

UNSETTLEMENT OF FAITH

FAITH would not be faith if it were knowledge. The act of religious assent was always known to be more certain than its probable grounds in reason. But English thinkers found it easy to be Christian because the grounds in reason looked probable enough. As they searched the realms of nature they traced the beauties of pattern and of purpose. In 1830 science sustained the head truths of religion.

Revolution discredited deism and the undevout reason. Outside the ranks of working Chartists or the little group of utilitarian philosophers, early Victorian Englishmen were sure that God existed and revealed himself. They believed the contrary doctrine untrue less because they could prove it false than because they could see it as immoral. The atheist or agnostic was not welcome in polite society. A man who said that he was irreligious lost public face. If a candidate for office was suspected of irreligion, his political opponents used the suspicion as top among their appeals to the electors. A fond parent would almost as soon have allied his daughter to a scandalous adulterer as to a notorious infidel.

The bases of Christianity—creator God, Christ divine, inspired Bible, future life—were as entrenched among the axioms of ordinary Englishmen in 1837 as fifty years before. Deist philosophers were more skilful than their predecessors and in young John Stuart Mill bred a prodigy whose questions England would one day need to answer. Town labourers sipped the red liquor of French Revolution and happily supposed the churches to be engines of oppression. Middle classes were more earnest in religion. The infidel was more disreputable, the public school a little less negligent of its spiritual duty, the average parson or minister lived better.

Within this earnestness was the haste of beleaguered men. Though Christians felt assured of their intellectual safety, they could hear wolves prowling in the undergrowth and built their protective hedge a little higher. It had happened, the incredible, the judgment, apostasy of a Catholic nation, ruin of an historic church of Europe. It must not happen here. Then haste to educate the children, haste to build churches for the poor, haste to practise the self-sacrifice which alone could bring Christian doctrine into real life, revere tradition, guard every precious drop of the orthodox stream. The haste was a sign of inner insecurity. The feeling helped to breed the attacks upon Hampden, and drove Newman into questing an assurance which should be infallible. Confident of Christian truth, they wanted to be more confident. Grateful for their treasure, they felt nervous enough to want it locked from prying hands. You will end a sceptic unless you believe all the doctrines of the ancient church. You will end a sceptic unless you become a Roman Catholic. You will end a sceptic unless you believe that the Holy Spirit penned every comma of Leviticus—the dire refrains were chanted too often to be preaching tricks. Beneath the certainty and expansive power the Christian doctrine of early Victorian England felt vulnerable. The divines did not question the axioms. They saw no need of apologies for belief. But they worried how their defence might fare in a world of shout and soap-box. Henceforth the purveyor of every opinion had a right to set his stall in the market-square. Voltaire and Hume had lived, and the earth could never be the same.

I. NEOLOGY

The subject which troubled minds quickest was the Old Testament. There lay the weakness in the Christian system of doctrine. At first the moral objection to the Old Testament was more important than the intellectual. A man who endured the nursery of an ignorant Calvinist nurse remembered how trivial misdemeanours of childhood were visited with threats of hell. From such memories Charles Dickens acquired a moral revulsion against the God of Israel or the doctrine of avenging wrath,[1] and attributed half the misery and hypocrisy of the Christian world to forcing the Old Testament into unnatural alliance with the New Testament. Men with the wide reading and historical sense of the romantics read the Bible no longer as a series of separated texts, but as books to be understood in their context, and revived the ancient gnostic battle between a god of anger and a God of love. These were not truculent heresiarchs. Sensible reverent laymen found their highest moral sense offended by Jehovah. William Makepeace

[1] *Letters of Charles Dickens*, ed. Dexter, i, 221; iii, 79; Pilgrim ed. i, 568.

Thackeray, who once was intimate with the best of the Cambridge evangelicals, privately raged at what God was supposed to have done in the Old Testament. He refused to believe that God commanded Israel to slaughter the Canaanites or Abraham to kill his son.[1] The proposition that God was the author of hell he found intolerable. He could not listen to the lesson about Jehu murdering the priests of Baal without disgust violent enough to make him commit to paper such savage cries as 'Murder them Jehu Smite smash run them through the body Kill 'em old and young.' Nor was it only the men of reading. About 1842 a couple of workmen met a clergyman in Fleet Street and instantly asked him whether he believed that God commanded Joshua to kill all the Canaanites. Yes, said the clergyman, he did believe, and saw nothing better to believe about it. 'What,' said the red-faced one, 'the women and children, too? What harm had they done?'[2]

The clergyman did believe, saw nothing better to believe. Conservatives, safeguarding their treasure of truth, were prickly if they met the least hint that every word of the Bible might not be inspired. They attacked Niebuhr, the great historian of Rome, because he suggested that the human race could not be descended from a single pair and that the Mosaic genealogies were erroneous descriptions of races; Milman, the historian of the Jews, because he called Joseph a vizier and offered a natural explanation of the miraculous quails; Buckland because he said that the world was much older than six thousand years; Thirlwall because he was interested in the literary problem of the Gospel narratives; Coleridge because he rested inspiration upon the Bible's effect in religious experience; Arnold because he thought the book of Daniel far later than the prophet Daniel. The latitude achieved by theologians half a century before was suspect to the religious reaction of the age. Conservative divines who once accepted an inspired Bible without thinking much about it now gripped total inspiration with a fiercer assent.

Howsoever bold minds demanded or practised occasional liberty in attributing error to the Bible, for eighteen centuries most men believed and taught that it was free from error in all its parts. By 1850 an important group of educated Englishmen, Christian as well as non-Christian, were persuaded that it was not true in all its parts; and some

---

[1] *Letters*, ed. Ray, i, 402–3, ii, 204–6, iii, 93–95.
[2] T. Mozley, *Reminiscences*, ii, 221: the date is fixed because he was on business connected with his editorship of the *British Critic*.

were persuaded that only if it were recognised to contain error could the truth about God continue to be seen. The discovery was bound to weaken the intellectual (and later therefore the social) influence of churches and preachers who were shown to have taught what was not true; to cause agony within the churches as they contemplated their articles of faith; and to demand an effort to restate the doctrine of Christianity in the light of new knowledge. The resulting argument governed the intellectual history of Victorian England.

The conservatives were afraid of Germany. In the late twenties a new word was invented, *neology*, to describe lax doctrines of inspiration, especially German laxity. For Germany entered this phase in the history of ideas nearly half a century earlier than England. On his arrival Prince Albert could not help regarding English clergymen as obscurantist. Conversely English travellers were surprised to discover that the Germans treated many narratives as allegory or parable or even fiction.[1] A hint of German influence lessened the authority of several leading English divines, Julius Hare, Connop Thirlwall, Thomas Arnold. Pusey repented that in his youth he commended German critics with mildness.

Strauss

Modern divinity dates from the *Life of Jesus* published in 1835 by David Friedrich Strauss of Tübingen. Old-fashioned attacks upon the New Testament rested on the axiom that the narratives were false and the narrators were lying. Older deism in England assumed that Christianity was an imposture. This short way of dismissing the New Testament descended to many working-class atheist pamphleteers of the thirties and forties. Utilitarian critics of religion shared it. Its defect was only that no educated man of sense could believe it. Jeremy Bentham wrote a fat unreadable book to prove that St. Paul always acted from self-interest; and his account of the vision on the Damascus road illustrated how the logical application of unfounded axioms ends in unconscious but delightful folly. German divines proposed a middle opinion between the beliefs that Christianity is true or fabricated. The narrators were telling the truth that they saw. But since they narrate miracles and miracles do not happen, they mistook natural causes for supernatural. To the eyewitness Jesus looked as though he walked across the water, but he walked along the shore.

[1] Cf. *Letters of Thackeray*, i, 140.

The witness did not notice when the five thousand took their baskets. The miracles of healing were skilled medicine. These proposals suffered from the defect that the natural explanations of the miracle were as speculative as the miracle which they were supposed to explain.

Strauss accepted the axiom that miracles do not happen. Confronted with the alternative between unmiraculous miracles and lying evangelists, he seized upon the romantic understanding of myth and applied it systematically. The myth-makers were the early Christian communities, their myth-making instrument was the expectation of a Messiah who must conform to Hebrew prophecies. Strauss did not doubt that Jesus existed. The texts proved him not only a man but enough of a moral genius to hit his community as Messiah. But the texts also proved that no biography could be written because the critic had no means of separating the kernel of reality from its engulfing husk of legend.

The methods or conclusions of Strauss soon faded into academic backwoods. Within a few years no reputable German critic accepted his strait-jacket for New Testament writers. What mattered was the impact upon European thought. Half a century earlier Lessing asked how historical events could be vehicles of eternal truths. Strauss snatched the question from the desks of philosophers and demanded an answer from divines. He declared that Christianity rose free and unchained when its historical shackles were jettisoned. The dogmas of the church were truths of the human species. Borrowing the language of Hegelian philosophy, he said that humanity is the union of God with man, infinite with finite; humanity the miracle-worker, the sinless, risen and ascended. Shall we interest ourselves more in the cure of sick people in Galilee than in the miracles of intellectual and moral progress? Strauss shocked Christendom because he claimed to be the authentic Christian divine.

Christendom was familiar with assailants of Christian orthodoxy. The first controversies were domestic among the German schools of divinity. Strauss was ejected from his lectureship at Tübingen a few weeks after he published his first volume. Nearly four years later he attained European celebrity by securing election through a casting vote to a chair of divinity at Zurich, source of the Swiss Protestant Reformation. The election was caught into a political whirlpool which cancelled the election, not without a pension of 1,000 francs to compensate

Strauss, and destroyed the government of the canton in a *coup d'état* (5 September 1839).

Professors of divinity who help a government to fall are not so common as to be overlooked by newspapers. English deists seized upon Strauss and used his name as a scourge. So few Englishmen could read the German language that not all the scholars knew what the *Life of Jesus* contained. The name of Strauss became a ghostly whip, a bogey, a talisman. The blasphemy laws prevented daring publishers from risking their reputations. Two half-educated translations were offered to London publishers and refused. They were nevertheless circulated sufficiently for bishops and cabinet ministers to argue gloomily about the inexpediency of prosecuting.

England was not so well equipped as Germany to examine Strauss with equanimity. Religious conservatism kept the critical study of the New Testament out of the curriculum. Milman confuted Strauss in a few pages.[1] The Cambridge polymath W. H. Mill, who had great repute as a Tractarian leader and would have been influential if he had not preached in a medley of stutter and bellow,[2] devoted four solid years of Hulsean lectures to refuting Strauss. Then came the legal judgments that blasphemy was not blasphemy unless it scoffed. No one could doubt that Strauss was a grave enquirer. From 1844 flowed a spate of translations, Strauss against German critics, German critics against Strauss. And in 1846 came a full translation of the *Life of Jesus*, completed by Marian Evans, the ex-evangelical Warwickshire girl of 27 years who is better known to posterity as the novelist George Eliot.

Christian liberal intellectuals were faced with a new and more perturbing doubt. Accustomed by slow degrees, by Coleridge or by Arnold, to think less rigidly about the inspiration of the Old Testament, they did not question the New. Dickens hated the Old Testament and loved the New as best of all books. Thackeray jettisoned the Old Testament and clung to the divine character among the pages of the New. But eternal certainties of faith could hardly hang upon the critical probabilities of historians. To a few souls sensitive about miracle and legend Strauss, or what Strauss represented, came as liberation. He seemed to free Christian truth from the shackles of history and so the mind from the torment of doubt. Among young

[1] *History of Christianity*, 1840, i, 115.
[2] Romilly's *Diary*, 18 June 1843.

graduates during the later forties the name of Strauss kept reappearing. What he stood for helped to change the mentality and the life of Matthew Arnold, Thomas Arnold the younger, John Sterling, Arthur Clough.

The ship of faith rocked gently at its moorings. Some accused Carlyle; some, Sterling and Hare and Maurice; some, Coleridge;[1] some, geologists who unsettled minds by demanding unimagined ages for the earth. But in the age of Gorham case and papal aggression many educated men favoured a simple explanation. Puseyites were the culprits. They demanded excess of authority and so drove men to repudiate all authority; crushed reason before creed and so inspired rationalism instead of faith; cried for belief in ridiculous miracles and so raised suspicion of authentic miracles; demolished middle quiet sober ways; offered the awful choice, popery or infidelity.

For several years the Puseyites laboured serenely under this imputation. In February 1849 James Anthony Froude published his second novel *The Nemesis of Faith*. No book could have been better suited to prove the charge. And that is not surprising, because Froude designed that end.

Froude

The youngest brother of Hurrell Froude, Anthony, was a sad, bullied schoolboy and extravagant, idle, debt-ridden undergraduate. His father, the strong archdeacon, could not fathom feebleness of character and believed in Sinai-menace and stick. Frightened of father and mismanaged by pedagogue, Froude grew a weak introspective recidivist, alternating lies or debts with heart-searing fruitless penitence, always falling, always self-disgusted, always resolving to do better, and bearing a demoniac yoke of guilt. He saw himself a liar, a coward, an incompetent. He knew that he must love home, and home was hateful.

Oxford helped him to stand upon his feet, separating him from home and giving self-confidence to his intelligence. Through the memory of his dead brother he came hesitantly into Newman's orbit. In still enchantment he sat under the sermons in St. Mary's, visited

---

[1] Coleridge's *Confessions of an Inquiring Spirit*, in which he showed how loosely he treated the conservative doctrine of biblical inspiration, was published posthumously in 1840.

the enclosure at Littlemore, and went once at least to private confession and momentarily dipped his sack of guilt in the river of absolution. Catholic devotion touched and moved his heart. He thought Newman a genius and was overwhelmed by his sympathy. But his fast-growing mind fell into sudden torments. He seemed so melancholy and so self-pitying that his adult friends knew him as Poor Froude. Newman saw the quality of the mind and tried to guide it by a Catholic employment. He persuaded Froude to write the Life of St. Neot in *The Lives of the Saints*. It is the best-written Life of the series.

Froude was never intimate with Newman.[1] For everything and everyone Tractarian he felt hate as well as love. The Oxford Movement meant Hurrell Froude and Hurrell meant father and home. He admired the memory of Hurrell and knew that he ought to have loved him. But what he remembered was Hurrell watching with approval while his father flogged him, Hurrell examining his lessons and finding them lamentable,[2] Hurrell holding his heels over a stream and his head under water. The memory of his dead brother was a cell in the family prison. To the Oxford Movement he knew that he owed the highest in his soul. And the Oxford Movement was a thrall whence he must flee for very life.

The young Froude is intelligible only in his love-hate. His attack upon orthodox Christianity was not crude like Holyoake, shallow like Paine, academic like Strauss, rhetorical like Carlyle. Its force consisted in this: that he understood the moral power of orthodox faith and devotion, knew it experimentally, and with half, but only half, his inmost being yearned to share it.

The books of Carlyle first tempted his mind out of the zareba-reason of Littlemore and led him to Goethe and German literature. By 1847 he was still the Reverend J. A. Froude, in deacon's orders in the Church of England and Fellow of Exeter College. But his intimates knew that his mind was troubled and that he would not take priest's orders. In May 1847 he published under the pseudonym *Zeta* a little autobiography passing as a novel entitled *The Spirit's Trials*.[3]

---

[1] Cf. Newman's evidence, Dessain, xiii, 86, xv, 399, that they were not in the same room above six times and then not for an hour at a time.

[2] W. H. Dunn, i, 18, 39.

[3] Published as the first of two parts of *The Shadows of the Clouds*. Hostile review, G, 47, 412; cf. *Athenaeum*, 19 June 1847. For an extraordinary bowdlerizing of the book, see *The Diaries of Lewis Carroll* (1953), i, 50.

The autobiography oscillates curiously between resentment and repentance. Part of its purpose is exomologesis, public confession, unloading guilt pseudonymously upon the world; portrait of an anti-hero, sneaking and craven. Another part of the purpose is to repudiate the past, to pillory the cigar-tortures of Westminster School and the solemn iciness of father. It was the image of a young man with religious doubts. These doubts were portrayed ostensibly as the off-spring of a morally deranged constitution.[1] It was conventional to believe that wickedness causes doubt. The autobiography is odd and interesting because only a fragment of the author believed the doctrine in a conventional form. The other fragment excused the doubt by excusing the wickedness which caused it.

The occupation of writing his history in bad novels was a disease which must take its course and a medicine for the soul; a confessional, fulfilling belly-need to sound the drums against his adolescence. 'What a beast one is,' he told Kingsley, 'to be fretting and bothering with one's little pitiful individuality. . . . One can't help it, but why can't one help it? It is this which makes me most hate it and crave to cut myself out of it. . . . It drives me mad to think it may stick to me for ever.'[2] He wandered away to Killarney, shut himself in a wood-ranger's lodge for the summer, and there wrote *The Nemesis of Faith*. It came as though he could not help it. 'I cut a hole in my heart and wrote with the blood.'[3] He felt extraordinary relief. 'I had thrown off the weight under which I had been staggering. I was free, able to en-counter the realities of life without vexing myself further over the unanswerable problems.' He decided to leave melancholia in England and escape to the colonies, perhaps to be a merchant's agent in South Australia, perhaps a schoolmaster in Tasmania, to go anywhere that an ex-clergyman would not be scandalous. He now hated the Thirty-nine Articles and hated attending college chapel. His father was enthusiastic that he should disappear across the ocean.[4]

The Nemesis of Faith was published on 21 February 1849, with Froude's name upon the title-page. As a novel it suffers from clumsy plot, melodramatic confrontations and sentimental sighs. To a world which knew Dickens and would soon know George Eliot it could not bear comparison. But it stands above the preaching-novels of the

[1] See J. A. Froude to William Long, 30 January 1848, in W. H. Dunn, i, 111.
[2] Froude to Kingsley, 19 March 1848, W. H. Dunn, i, 116.
[3] So he told Kingsley, 1 January 1848, Dunn, i, 131.
[4] Dunn, i, 126–8.

forties, the tales of Kingsley or Newman or Paget or Sewell or Gresley. For the author had a genius which not even lachrymose floods of emotion could quite conceal. The only character that matters is not a puppet for the pulpit but a tangled living person with real hopes and fears. He is Froude. When challenged, he publicly denied that it was either autobiography or credo. But he knew it to be a truthful picture of his mind.[1] And the strength of the book rested there; that no one could read the book without seeing that he peered far into the thickets of its author's tortured soul.

It was another portrait of the anti-hero; still cringing, falling, disgusted at falls; but an anti-hero who has grown stature, a force in writing incompatible with supposed anaemia of the soul. His melancholy history was used to prove a different lesson. The earlier book illustrated in unconventional mode the belief that Wickedness causes Doubt. *Nemesis* now illustrated in unconventional mode the belief that Doubt causes Wickedness. Or, no morality without religion.

Sutherland had Doubts. He disbelieved the literal truth of many narratives in the Bible. He conceived as immoral the substitutionary idea of atonement and the doctrine of torture in hell. These scruples filled him with guilt. He knew that he owed his ideals to the church of his childhood and saw that in casting aside the church he abandoned his better self. He would listen to the bells, watch the people walking in Sunday dress, go with them into service and hear the church full of voices whispering, Infidel, Infidel, Apostate; and shed tears that he could not regain the faith of childhood. His father found him a living and, unknowing, confronted him with a choice. Friends told him to eschew these morbid questionings, remember the mystery of the universe, and adhere to the old argument that if the Bible is difficult it has no more difficulties than the world. So he took the orders of deacon and priest during the winter of 1844. At a party in his parish he abused the Bible Society in extravagant terms and was denounced to the bishop. The ensuing strain revived the dormant scruples. He resigned his living, escaped abroad to Como, fell weakly in love with another man's wife, was rescued from physical suicide by Newman, and committed the intellectual suicide of entering an Italian monastery and pretending a Roman Catholic faith which he could never believe.

The plot was edifying. Doubt caused Wickedness. But the manner of its unfolding was so agonised and perceptive that the reader cannot

[1] Preface to 2nd ed., in 1904 ed., xlix, lvi; Dunn, i, 149.

avoid seeing the author in Sutherland. And why the title, *The Nemesis of Faith*? The book seemed to describe The Nemesis of Doubt. Incongruously woven amidst the story lay attacks upon Newman and Newman's doctrine of faith. To annihilate reason was not to settle Doubt. It ended in suicide.

All his life Froude admired Newman. He thought him a genius and remembered what he owed. But Newman was a friend of Hurrell and Hurrell was prison. Tom Mozley, who lived briefly on an Oriel staircase with Froude, guessed that he felt the same necessity for self-assertion against Newman as against his father and Hurrell.[1] Newman taught him that reason always ended in doubt, that on rational grounds the atheist philosophers were unanswerable, that religious truth was known through conscience, that reason must be surrendered. Froude put into Sutherland's mouth an overdrawn onslaught upon Newman's idea of faith. Faith, when so sceptical of reason that it turned into credulity, was Froude's target. He seemed to be defending his scruples by saying, 'If you do not choose honest doubt you must choose popery.' Two ways are set before you. One is Rome, the other Infidelity. Newman and Ward dared to use the dilemma to prove the Catholic faith. Froude used the same dilemma as a pit of waste and destruction. Either you credit the incredible or you end in moral ruin.

The fellows of Exeter College first made known their displeasure. They started cutting Froude. On Sunday evening the sermon in chapel denounced him. On Tuesday the sub-rector Sewell, giving a lecture in hall, spotted an undergraduate with a copy of *Nemesis* and threw it in the fire. Everyone, Tractarian or Unitarian, Kingsley or Frank Newman, disliked the book and thought it better unwritten. Carlyle detested its sentimentalism and growled that Froude ought to consume his own smoke and not trouble other people's nostrils. Anxious Roman Catholics wanted Newman to answer it from his retreat at Birmingham.[2] The orthodox press denounced it as a blaspheming poisonous manual of infidelity. Froude made the mistake of protesting to the *Standard* the injustice of attributing to the author the sentiments of a character in a novel, and the press gleefully enlarged upon the identity of author and character. Bishop Phillpotts of Exeter was attacked for ordaining Froude deacon and denied that he did any such thing. The rector of Exeter College was attacked for admitting

---

[1] *Reminiscences*, ii, 30.   [2] Dessain, xiii, 85–86; Dunn, i, 145.

Froude to a fellowship and disclosed that the election was in his absence and against his wish. Froude resigned his fellowship before being dismissed. In March he lost his promised appointment as head-master in Tasmania, and as his father would have nothing more to do with him he did not know where to go. Bunsen suggested two years at the university of Bonn, Kingsley generously invited him to stay at Ilfracombe and Frank Newman tried to make him editor of the *Manchester Guardian*.[1]

'Such', said the *Morning Herald*, 'are some of the fruits of Mr Newman's teaching.' Prophets of woe exulted at their vindication. Brother of a Tractarian leader, ex-inmate of Littlemore, contributor to *The Lives of the Saints*, candidate rejected by colleges as a suspect Puseyite, avowed admirer of Newman and of private confession, Froude ends in infidelity and attributes his fall to a credulous Tractarian doctrine of faith. John Henry Newman and Francis Newman were brothers and alike in mind, yet one was a Roman Catholic priest and the other a Unitarian professor. Bishop Hampden was disgusted with *Nemesis*, but valued it as evidence.[2] If only half of Froude wanted to knock the Oxford Movement the whole of him could have done no better. He was curiously happy. His mind felt honest, his wrists free from the manacles of home. In the autumn he married Kingsley's sister-in-law and settled to new life as historian. He had taken bitter medicine into his belly and was healed. He continued to practise daily prayers and consider himself a member of the Church of England.

Froude was not alone in swinging from Tractarian faith towards liberal divinity. Mark Pattison of Lincoln College was another subject of Newman who veered slowly away. Arthur Clough the poet, fellow of Oriel College, fell into a brooding tangle of doubt because Arnold and W. G. Ward fought for his mind. He was Arnold's leading pupil at Rugby School. At Balliol, Ward, who was emotionally attached to him, bombarded his mind with irrepressible logic. When Oxford saw Ward and Clough walking together it was remarked, 'There goes Ward, mystifying poor Clough and persuading him that he must either believe nothing or accept the whole of church doctrine.'[3] Ward battered Clough out of allegiance to Arnold, but could not

---

[1] Dunn, i, 158; 132ff.; MH 6–16 March 1849; S, 9 March 1849; G, 49, 176; *Athenaeum*, 17 March 1849; *Fraser's Mag.* (Ludlow writing), May 1849, 545ff. Froude was reconciled to his father again within a few years; cf. *Life of Milman*, 209–10, 222.
[2] *Memorials*, 177; cf. T. Mozley, *Rem.*, ii, 33; *Corr. of Clough*, i, 246ff.
[3] Ward, *W. G. Ward and the Oxf. M.*, 107, 110.

quite drive him into Catholicism. Carlyle and Strauss completed the glissade into melancholy troubled uncertainties which wasted the rest of his short external life but conditioned his poetic inspiration.

Provost Hawkins of Oriel treated his vacillation with respect and sympathy. The letters to Clough prove that Hawkins was a bigger and better man than Tractarian assailants represented. But his intellectual mode of treating Clough's difficulties came from a world of thought which had ceased to have meaning. To this unhappy chaos of Clough's mind, where Arnold and Ward and Carlyle and Strauss exchanged blows that brought neither victory nor vision, Hawkins recommended Paley's *Natural Theology* to prove the existence of God, Butler's *Analogy* for the correspondence between religion and nature, Lardner's *Supplement to the Credibility* to prove that the early Christian documents were authentic and true.[1] Clough simply answered that these books would not meet the difficulties of young men in the present day. Hawkins was puzzled, and asked to be told what difficulties most perplexed young men. Clough referred him to *The Nemesis of Faith*.

Clough was right. The old faithful books which proved Christianity true were becoming useless. Someone must restate Christian divinity so that readers of Carlyle and Strauss would find ideas to bite and convince, ideas which did not sound obsolete.

Sterling

Sterling lost his faith. He was a man of fervid romantic enthusiasms, passionate now for Coleridge, now for radical democracy, now for Maurice, now for Carlyle. In the revolutionary time of 1831 he helped to organise a futile raid upon the coast of southern Spain by fifty-five Spanish refugees under General Torrijos. It ended on the esplanade at Malaga in the shooting of all fifty-five and Sterling's cousin Robert Boyd. Sterling never forgave himself and would not afterwards speak of it. Encouraged by Julius Hare, who taught Maurice and himself at Cambridge, Sterling was ordained deacon and became Hare's curate at Hurstmonceux in Sussex. The curacy lasted nine months until ill health and doubt caused him to retire. Strauss completed the retirement. Fascinating to meet and pallid to read, Sterling went through his short life struggling for breath and causing others to talk and write intelligently. He died in 1844 and divided his papers between two literary executors, Archdeacon Julius Hare and Thomas Carlyle.

[1] Hawkins to Clough, 20 November 1848; *Corr. of Clough*, i, 226, 248.

Carlyle and Hare agreed that Hare should edit Sterling's *Remains* and write a memoir.

To place before the English public a memoir of a clergyman who became a disciple of Strauss was a delicate or dubious task for an archdeacon. As friend Hare could not denounce the curate whose tall slender form once crossed the fields of Hurstmonceux almost daily to enliven or comfort the rectory. As archdeacon he owed responsibility to church and flock and could not write without sounding a knell of warning. He hardly dared to write. Yet he must write to prevent his fellow executor Carlyle from writing. To refuse might mean a biography of Sterling baked in Scottish ovens by an unorthodox and unpredictable chef, a Sterling whose pliable weak frame would be transmogrified into a bludgeon by the foremost warrior of literature. When Sterling died Carlyle was wrestling paper-bound with Oliver Cromwell, a soul bigger and tougher than a pleasant second-rate essayist. But Hare wrote a biography of Sterling because he wanted to stop Carlyle writing a different biography of Sterling. He knew that an archdeacon telling of such a man would offend pious ears. He suffered agony from the duty. Even his friend Maurice would have prevented the book appearing if he could, even to walking many miles barefoot. Hare wrote it fearing that a life by Carlyle would be a worse evil than this offence against the canons of piety.[1]

Sterling's collected Essays and Tales appeared with a memoir by Hare in January 1848. The memoir is good and for the most part conventional: quiet little lights and shades without passion or thunder, decorous and sincere. Even when Sterling sailed with Torrijos to start a revolution in Spain, the conspirator is an unquenchable predestined curate disguised in stage-bandolier. Hare described with skill and honesty a developing religious mind. But he sounded the tocsin against Strauss. He warned the public that they could hardly read Strauss without suffering hurt, that they would be walking through a mire which must stink, that they are never to read from curiosity books written to undermine truths set before us as the lodestars of our moral nature.[2] The memoir suffered because the partial breach of communication, caused by Strauss, prevented Hare from seeing the later Sterling whose life was not religion but literature. He remem-

[1] See Hare's too candid admissions in *Thou shall not bear false witness*, 1849, 3–4. Cf. *Life of Maurice*, i, 548. Even if Carlyle did not write it, Mill would insist on doing so; cf. *Journals of Caroline Fox*, 1882, ii, 95.

[2] *Memoir*, cxxxiv.

bered always the lover of Coleridge and German theology, the curate, the devout soul struggling vainly for faith. The sin of Hare's book, said the angry Carlyle to himself in a letter which he foisted upon an imaginary correspondent, was taking up Sterling merely as a clergyman; a sickly shadow in torn surplice, weltering bewildered amid heaps of Hebrew Old Clothes and impotently wrestling to free itself from the baleful imbroglio as if that had been its one function in life.[1]

Hare was anxious what critics would say of the memoir. It fell cold and dead upon the reading public. Few knew about Sterling and few were interested in his unexciting life. The Tractarian *Guardian* reviewed it sympathetically, admiring Sterling's character or genius and seeing a useful lesson and warning in the fatal issue of his subservience to Strauss.[2] For ten months afterwards the memoir was forgotten.

Then in December 1848 Newman's former colleague and critic, driest of the stern unbending Oxford Tractarians, William Palmer of Worcester College, released a cry of agony. The article in the *English Review*[3] distresses the reader. By temperament Palmer was a cold prosaic analyst. Contemporary trends in English divinity so moved him that he lost balance and lobbed a row of unequal books into a single frying-pan. Hare found himself not only with Maurice but with Arthur Stanley and Thomas Arnold, Chevalier Bunsen and Neander, Richard Trench and Thomas Carlyle, Francis Newman and John Stuart Mill, even with Blanco White, who ended his life as a Unitarian of the left wing; and Sterling was pilloried as bishop among the priests of infidelity. Palmer accused Hare of proffering a villain to public admiration; of encouraging an avowed heretic to take holy orders; of fostering the taste now gratified by translations of Strauss and other mischief; of conspiring to undermine English Christianity by false ideas from Germany. He portrayed Maurice as accessory to the plot.[4]

[1] Carlyle, *Sterling*, 3; cf. what Henry Hallam heard, in *Journals of Caroline Fox*, 1882, ii, 138: it portrayed Sterling as a mere bookworm always occupied with some abstruse theological problem, rather than the man of genial buoyant feeling. But Hallam never met Sterling.

[2] G, 48, 60.   [3] x, 1848, 399.

[4] The article is said by *Life of Maurice*, i, 504, to be by William Palmer of Worcester College; and in Maurice's letter appended to Hare's *Thou shall not bear false witness* there is a curious reference to Palmer's *Treatise of the Church* which would be out of place unless Palmer were the author of the article. G, 49, 146, thinks that Hare may have been unjustly treated, but that his published letter (*Thou shall not bear false witness*) was a waste of time and words.

Hare wrote a long boiling letter to the editor of the *English Review* and published it as *Thou shall not bear false witness against thy neighbour*. Maurice rejoiced to place himself beneath any shower of bombs raining upon a friend and appended a short little vigorous letter. This joint publication drew the fire of a powerful organ which rarely read Tractarian journals but already distrusted Hare and Maurice: the *Record*, mouthpiece of partisan evangelicals. Even the *Record* at first thought the accusation of conspiracy to be unfair. It then discovered the *Sterling Club*: a club of popish Tractarians and Germanised Straussians—meeting at the Freemasons tavern at 7.15 p.m. to consume dinner at 15s. a head, with Wilberforce, Stanley, Archdeacon Allen, Maurice, Hare, Trench, Carlyle, John Stuart Mill, Thirlwall, Manning—founding its society in honour of an infidel—eating its meals unsanctified by grace—'we almost wonder that it was not called the *Strauss Club*'.[1] The members explained (9 March 1849) that the club was founded by Sterling and not in his honour; that Sterling asked them to change the name, but they refused; that Sterling hardly ever attended meetings; even that grace was said before and after dinner. What, asked the press, would be said of a Voltaire Club or a Rousseau Club populated by bishops, archdeacons, and two professors of divinity? By Maurice, responsible for teaching the Bible to young ordinands, uttering dark and unintelligible sentences, aiming at paradox, lax about the inspiration of the Bible, denying eternal punishment: was it not the duty of authority to dismiss the professor from King's College?[2] At an April dinner of the Sterling Club Archdeacon Allen of Salop moved that the name be changed and resigned when the motion failed. A few months later[3] the survivors voted the same motion to victory.

In November 1851 Carlyle published his rival life of Sterling. He half wanted to do it from the first; was looking round for something to write; almost resolved to write a corrective as soon as he saw Hare's memoir.[4] In the fight between *Record* and Hare the character of Sterling was tossed like a dud grenade from side to side. Sterling's brother pressed Carlyle to set matters right. He was strangely slow to act. He

[1] R, 8 and 15 March 1849.

[2] R, March and August 1849. Cf. 3 September, 29 November, 20 December 1849.

[3] Carlyle, *Sterling*, 165. According to Purcell, i, 276, quoting a conversation with Gladstone, Manning and Samuel Wilberforce also resigned. For correspondence over the Sterling Club cf. BL Wilberforce Papers, Dep. c. 201, 15.

[4] D. A. Wilson, *Carlyle*, iii, 409.

afterwards claimed that Hare's memoir and the heresy-hunt set him to work by standing the radiant Sterling in a *sanbenito* of Inquisition with ghastly spectralities prowling round him and inarticulately screeching and gibbering.[1] Three years elapsed between the appearance of Hare and Carlyle setting pen to paper, nearly four years before Carlyle's *Life* was published. By that interval Carlyle's inward furnace must have needed stoking. Carlyle wrote for his own sake as well as for Sterling's. Some of his friends believed that after *Oliver Cromwell* he was looking for a chance of telling the world that despite his sympathy he did not share Cromwell's creed. He wrote the Life in two months. At the end he grumbled uneasily whether it was too trivial to publish.[2]

The performance is unique in the annals of English literature: a biography where every atom of interest is contributed by the biographer and none by the subject. Carlyle did not make Sterling live, did not even give so fair a portrait as Hare, corrected the clerical bias at the expense of amputating quarter of Sterling. Hare's life was a smooth shining sea, Carlyle's a storm of breakers upon rocks. As Sterling was not a rugged person, the rocks were thrown round him in a circle. We read the biography not for Sterling but for everyone else, Torrijos, Sterling's whirlwind father, Carlyle himself, Coleridge; especially Coleridge.

That winter religious England disliked Carlyle's book. For fourteen years he had been the sage in English literature and history, admired for multi-storied style and severity which struggled past shams and cant and slogans to reality and truth. To souls longing for religion but troubled by orthodox religion he gave a sense of relief and power. Optimists said that however he abused ecclesiastics he was better able than most to make men feel the need of a church;[3] that, crashing through the traps of atheism and mammon and progress-worship, he came out upon his minaret and like a raucous muezzin gesticulated Britain to ideals and to God. Intimates knew how he passed as a youth through the turmoil of losing and finding faith, how his hatred of shams consumed ecclesiastical cant, how unorthodox were such dogmas as he professed. He had published little to disclose his mind to the general public; though the discriminating were perturbed by curious moral judgments in his book *On Hero-Worship*. *The Life of John Sterling* drew the veil from at least half his mind. He

---

[1] *Life of Sterling*, 2–3.   [2] D. A. Wilson, *Carlyle*, iv, 336.
[3] So Maurice in January 1840, *Life*, i, 278–9.

hinted at a tidy interpretation of Sterling's career. Sterling's life divided precisely. First he fell under the evil genius of Coleridge and crowned his folly by taking orders. Then he broke through superstition by submitting to the good genius of Carlyle and crowned his emancipation by vowing himself to literature.

Folly to take orders? Folly for Sterling or folly for anyone? It was a rampage of old churches dying, old dogmas dead, old arguments hollow, poor noble idealist misled by bottled moonshine of Coleridge, by nonsensical transcendental dreams, into conforming with the world's madness. The pantheist streak in Carlyle was plain to the reader; man and the universe eternally divine, song of morning stars, temple of immensity, nature-worshipper stooping to the little gems that glitter still amidst the rubble of ruined chapels.

2. ATTEMPTS AT RESTATEMENT

When Julius Hare was attacked for writing a memoir of the dangerous Sterling he made a noble retort. Rationalising and infidel theology has come. We cannot build a Chinese wall to shut it out. We cannot defend ourselves with clatter of anathemas. Either we must meet the challenge or we shall discover in a while that we dance round a dry mummy of orthodoxy, scaring the young by sightless eyes and shrivelled skin. We cannot fight guns with spear and crossbow. So far from repudiating the powers and subtleties of the intellect we must marshal them. So far from shrinking and skulking from perplexities of the mind we must grapple. We cannot garrison a fortress while the host of the human mind sweeps by. English infidel rises in the land to join German invader. We shall not beat this confederacy by donning the rusty battered armour of fathers or schoolmen. We need the weapons of Germans to defeat Germans.[1]

The principle was easier to assert than to practise. During the eighteen-fifties a small number of liberal Anglican divines made staccato efforts. Hare himself scattered his interests and energies too widely and died. But by 1853 a school of divinity was publicly hailed as the broad church school.[2] The group was believed to look back

---

[1] Julius Hare, *Thou shalt not bear false witness against thy neighbour*, 1849, 47–50.

[2] Conybeare, 'Church Parties' in *Edinburgh Review*, 1853, ii, 330. The name *broad church* was used by Stanley in one of his sermons about 1847, but W. C. Lake heard it used by A. H. Clough before that, Lake, 35.

to Arnold and Coleridge. Professor Maurice was seen as its eminent divine. Arthur Stanley, Arnold's biographer, was suspected of being a warrior for the cause. The *Record* told everyone that down in Brighton was a Germanised preacher of dangerous fascination, F. W. Robertson, but few contemporaries were acquainted with him. No one knew quite who was in the party, or what it was supposed to represent. Maurice hated the very notion that he might be a broad churchman.

The term is vague. The group was not a group but scattered individuals working towards similar ends. But the loose diagnosis contains this truth: Maurice and Stanley, and Stanley's friend Jowett, and Hampden's friend Baden Powell, were working separately and cautiously and in different modes towards restating certain Catholic doctrines.

Maurice's 'Theological Essays'

Maurice was first a preacher and produced his best writing out of the pulpit. From February to May 1853 he preached a course of sermons in Lincoln's Inn chapel upon the main doctrines of Christianity and afterwards converted each sermon into an essay. *Theological Essays* were dedicated to Tennyson[1] and published in June.

They are filled with literary head-scratching. Maurice engaged ghostly objectors in vehement dialogue. The tone was intense, the inspiration jerky. He waded along a stream of rhetorical questions and littered the banks with parentheses, dashes, inversions, notes of exclamation. The reader is battered and fatigued by the demand to feel indignation on subjects where he did not know himself to feel anything; unable to grasp the author's meaning while seeing that this meaning is life or death to the author.

Maurice addressed the book to Unitarians. His manner of controversy was characteristic; concede as much as possible to opponents. He let sympathy lead him to the brink and then tottered backwards gasping. Unitarians disliked Calvinists. Maurice joined in bitter assaults upon Calvinists. Unitarians disliked theories of atonement. Maurice denounced 'popular' theories of atonement, theories of satisfaction and substitution. Unitarians rejected hell and eternal punishment. Maurice agreed. The New Testament word *eternal* meant a quality of life, not an endless time. But when his head reappeared

---

[1] Maurice was godfather to Tennyson's son Hallam.

above the maze he was observed to be still teaching atonement in Christ and the possibility of endless death.

Readers, amused or distressed or bewildered at the antics, were not tempted to be scornful. Maurice threw his being into his books. From their pages his person stood out lovable and earnest, a person to whom God was all. Those who did not reject the book found its strength not in coherence nor in clarity, but in a posture of mind which approached divine mystery. During the next decades theology could not proceed by hurling squared rocks of dogma at Sterlings or geologists or Carlyles. It would approach God as the burning bush, with shoeless feet and the awe of supernatural numen. It would see through a glass darkly, probing and searching, eschewing pride and hesitant of assurance. From complexion of mind to indefinable air of countenance Maurice was reverent. He felt the heat of God flaming and knew it as indescribable in human language. Words tormented him because they could hardly unveil truth, yet truth must be unveiled, and by words. Dogmas were true; but in being true they pointed to realms of truth far beyond.

Away then from the hard literal force of the canonised sentence 'The Bible is inspired'. Shibboleth of complacent orthodoxy or floor of ice-marble palace of doctrine? It is the breath of divine afflatus; resounding woods of Dodona and springs of Parnassus, Sinai and Olympus, prophet and dervish, tongue of flame and book of Sibyl, wind of God among the forest branches of earth. Do not separate the Bible as inspired from all else uninspired. See the breath of God in common books, in nature and grace, in words spoken to dying men, crashing through human conflict and comforting human agony. They talk of *verbal* inspiration or plenary inspiration; pretty toys of speech for those with leisure to play; pallid definition, noise to the suffering soul.[1]

In Platonic moments and fragments of beauty and clouds of obscurity you hear echoes of Coleridge. But Maurice was no sage pontificating aloft. You listen to a mind engaged with the dust of back streets. Coleridge the half-philosopher puffed ideas like cigar-smoke, rich and scented. Despite the Platonic axioms, Maurice was no philosopher. The ground of his ideas was compassion for simple men. He could not play with concepts.

His doctrines were orthodox as they loomed out of the mist. And

---

[1] *Theological Essays*, 1st ed., 342.

Maurice was more orthodox than he sounded in these *Theological Essays*. But the sympathy shown to Unitarian objectors alarmed evangelicals, who since papal aggression exerted weight in the Church of England. The only doctrines for which Maurice showed no sympathy were the beliefs commonly labelled evangelical. He was notorious as friend of Sterling and Hare, as member of the Sterling Club, and as oracle of Christian Socialism. Under fire in the national press, and examined two years before by the authorities of King's College, already a professor on approval, he knew that his essay on hell risked the loss of his divinity chair and would be a crisis in his career. He gloomily exaggerated the shock of the book and wondered whether it might cause a schism. Kingsley blamed him for obscurity of style and told him that the book marked a new era of ecclesiastical history.[1]

The much-plagued Dr. Jelf, principal of King's College, courteously turned the wheels of investigation. He carried the book to the leisure of the long vacation at Oxford. He found the book confused; carried the book round to other divines in Oxford and discovered that they equally diagnosed muddle. But one point could be made clear. Did Maurice believe in everlasting punishment? If he did not, he was unsuitable to train clergymen. On 8 July 1853 Jelf wrote to ask Maurice the question. Throughout that summer a climbing mound of letters testified that the two divines used identical words in different meanings. In August Jelf decided that (so far as he could understand) Maurice was unfit to be a teacher at King's College. Maurice decided to fight for the liberty of English clergy. Hare and Stanley and Thirlwall backed him with advice or sympathy. Bishop Wilberforce of Oxford disliked the essays, but, perceiving that Maurice was more orthodox than his essays, tried to protect him.[2] The *Globe* and *Morning Chronicle* rallied Whiggish to his aid. Kingsley prodded the unlikely gladiator into armour. He reported that he preached to his Hampshire village a cruder version of the essay on eternal death and that the sermon was received with pleasure and delight by gentry and by clods.

Jelf said that the choice was resignation or dismissal. He begged Maurice to choose resignation for the sake of King's College. Maurice refused to resign. 'I must bear what testimony I can,' he told Ludlow, 'for the right of English divines to preach the gospel of God's love to

---

[1] *Life of Kingsley*, i, 372; *Life of Maurice*, ii, 165–9.
[2] *Life of Maurice*, ii, 179; S. Wilberforce to Jelf, 27 August 1853, Ashwell-Wilberforce, *Life of Wilberforce*, ii, 209; *Life of Kingsley*, i, 375.

mankind.'[1] He no longer wished to remain at King's College. He only wished to be dismissed as incompatible with Jelf, that the right of English clergy to deny endless punishment might not be questioned.

On 27 October 1853 the council of King's College was confronted with a motion by Bishop Blomfield to thank Maurice for his zealous and able discharge of his duties and to dismiss him as teaching a dangerous doctrine on the future punishment of the wicked. It was a fuller quorum than usual, but still not a full meeting. Dean Milman of St. Paul's failed to turn up; Dean and Professor Buckland of Westminster abbey had gone mad; Lord Harrowby was in Ireland; Anderson of Lincoln's Inn was bereaved; Bishop Lonsdale of Lichfield received no notice of the meeting; Sir Benjamin Brodie, seeing that Maurice had no chance, went away in the middle.[2] Gladstone moved an amendment that competent theologians examine the essays. The amendment collected two other votes and was lost. On 11 November a much smaller quorum of the council met again and declared Maurice's offices vacant.[3]

An inarticulate and devout public was led by this quarrel to contemplate the doctrine of hell. Leading laymen were sure that a majority of laymen disbelieved the doctrine of endless punishment. Clergymen who went into Parker's bookshop in London told the shopman that it was not a doctrine of the church—'If you take the Bible and common sense to judge by,' said the shopman to the Christian Socialist Furnivall, 'why, sir, it's the most abominable and horrid doctrine ever preached.'[4] Maurice had the advantage of standing for

[1] *Life of Maurice*, ii, 176.

[2] J. M. Ludlow, *King's College and Mr. Maurice*, 23.

[3] Maurice published his last letter of explanation to Jelf as *The Word 'Eternal' and the Punishment of the Wicked: a letter to the Reverend Dr. Jelf*, 3 November 1853. This went through 5,000 copies and two more editions, each with a new preface. At Maurice's demand Jelf published the correspondence of the summer as *Grounds for laying before the Council of King's College, London, certain statements contained in a recent publication entitled Theological Essays*. This also went through three editions, but only one new preface. In March 1854 J. M. Ludlow published a pamphlet called *King's College and Mr Maurice: no. 1 The Facts*. He intended to issue no. 2 the Doctrine and no. 3 the Man, but Maurice protested so vehemently against no. 3 that Ludlow also abandoned no. 2; cf. Christensen, 338.

The two who voted on 27 October for Gladstone were J. H. Green, an eminent physician of St. Thomas's Hospital, and the literary executor of Coleridge, and Sir John Patteson. Sir Benjamin Brodie, another eminent physician, would have voted the same way if he had stayed. The only clergymen present were Bishop Blomfield and Archdeacon Harrison. The leaders of the motion to dismiss Maurice were Lord Radstock, Lord Howe, Lord Cholmondeley and Sir Robert Inglis. Fifteen persons were present out of a possible forty-two.

[4] *Life of Maurice*, ii, 204.

the love of God. He had the disadvantage of appearing to play with words. The lay public was largely for Maurice, but had little patience with the idea that eternal could not mean endless. Jelf claimed fifty-seven passages of the New Testament where *eternal* needed time in its meaning.

Maurice's character was admired more than ever. His intellect began to be underestimated. While his stature grew his intellectual influence declined. He became more a symbol than a guide. But as a symbol he commanded wide loyalty among the young.[1]

In November Maurice resigned his connexion with Queen's College (a college of female education which he helped to found in 1846) and was unanimously re-elected to be principal. Lincoln's Inn sent him a testimonial and the benchers refused to consider his offer of resignation. His Christian Socialist Bible class in Castle Street—which consisted of two tailors, two pianoforte-makers, six barristers, three clergymen, one lithographer, two members of Parliament, one city missionary, two booksellers, one stationer, one printer's reader, one watchmaker, two law students, two Masters of Arts and one gentleman not otherwise described[2]—presented him with a quarto Bible. On 27 December 960 working men assembled at Castle Street to present him with an address. The chairman said that it was extremely creditable to the Reverend Mr Maurice that he had given a more liberal, merciful and genial interpretation to the Holy Scriptures than was usually given to them, and on this account the working classes were grateful to him.

Maurice suggested to this meeting that education like that at King's College should be offered to working men. Christian Socialists had for two years discussed the project of founding a people's college. Ludlow invented the scheme. The workers suggested that as Maurice was barred from being a professor in King's College he might become professor in a college for them. The Working Men's College opened on 31 October 1854 with 120 students.[3] Maurice was principal. All the leading Christian Socialists helped with teaching—Neale, Tom

---

[1] At the Lancashire independent college Mr. Kelly addressed the theological students on the mischief wrought by Maurice to introduce German neology. The students began volleys of hisses. Bubier rose to defend Maurice and was received with thunderous applause. Kelly rose to refute Bubier and was again hissed, G, 56, 960. The well-known neologist Davidson was a professor at the college.

[2] Ludlow, *King's College and Mr. Maurice*, 48.

[3] Christensen, 351; cf. J. F. C. Harrison, *A History of the Working Men's College 1854–1954*, 1954.

Hughes, who taught boxing, J. S. Brewer, the Tudor historian. John Ruskin and D. G. Rossetti joined the force of lecturers. The college was so linked to the Christian Socialists that it declined with their decline, and fifteen years later was in low water.[1]

Bishop Colenso

John William Colenso was a fellow of St. John's College in Cambridge and the rector of Forncett St. Mary in Norfolk. He was distinguished as the author of an arithmetic used in nearly every school in the country and even in the royal class-room. His algebra and his plane trigonometry were used in schools which advanced thus far. Interested in foreign missions, he was selected during 1853 to be first Bishop of Natal and was to be consecrated that autumn. His flock at Forncett St. Mary may not have been stirred by his village sermons, for his style was thought to be dismal in the pulpit and insufferable at the reading-desk.[2] Their printed version, which appeared in this autumn of 1853, is full of good feeling and betrays nothing of controversy. It is dedicated to the people of Forncett St. Mary. He now betrayed the unimaginative and splendid imprudence which later made him the sharpest prickle of the Anglican rose. To the dedication he added a letter extolling Maurice as master. He might as well have invited the parishioners to throw stones.

Even the *Record* admitted *Village Sermons* to be written with beauty and chasteness of style, however deficient in clear reasoning.[3] At the end of the third week in November the anti-Maurice party gathered a petition to stop the Archbishop of Canterbury from consecrating Colenso to be Bishop of Natal. If Maurice was not allowed to be a professor of divinity, they saw stronger reason to refuse a bishopric to his professed disciple. Bishop Blomfield was widely advertised as willing to participate in the consecration on 30 November. Blomfield had so established a repute for double-headedness that it was thought possible for him to dismiss Maurice and consecrate Colenso.

The campaign forced Colenso to clear himself. At Archbishop Sumner's suggestion he wrote an open *Letter to the Archbishop of Canterbury*. Reiterating that he loved and honoured Maurice as a great religious teacher, he published disagreement with Maurice. He affirmed his belief in endless punishment. The *Record* was silenced

---

[1] Masterman, *Ludlow*, 168-9.
[2] Romilly's *Diary*, 18 June 1843; 5 May 1844.   [3] R, 10 November 1853.

Colenso humiliated. Colenso of Natal and Armstrong of Grahamstown were consecrated by Archbishop Sumner, Bishop Blomfield,
Bishop Wilberforce of Oxford, and Bishop Hinds of Norwich. Two
of the four consecrators lived to regret the day.

Jowett

The dismissal of Maurice and humiliation of Colenso were the first
successes in a row of attacks on English liberal divines.

Liberal divinity or neology was suspected of importing German
philosophy and criticism into English thought. If its advocates read
not a word of German, they might still stink of 'Germanisms'.
Germanism consisted in anything from Straussian myth-theories to
lax attitudes towards Jonah's whale. It was at least held to include
recognition of legend in the Old Testament, and willingness to torture
scriptural truth into the ill-fitting jacket of idealist philosophy.

During the fifties the leading Oxford student of German philosophical divinity was Benjamin Jowett of Balliol College.

Silent, remote and feminine, Jowett began upon the fringe of
the Oxford liberals—W. G. Ward, A. H. Clough, Arthur Stanley,
A. C. Tait, Frederick Temple—and as they dropped away to Rome or
London university or headmasterships found himself the survivor. He
was a man for the few. Eliciting discipleship from his friends, he was
neglected or feared or despised by the many who knew him little. In
the early years his intimate was Arthur Stanley. He helped Stanley in
the battle to protect Ward. By an absurd error evangelicals therefore
labelled him an extreme high churchman,[1] another Froude, moving
from anti-rational Romanising towards scepticism. He was never
anti-rational. He read Strauss early, studied Kant and Hegel, visited
Germany to meet eminent critics, introduced lectures on Plato into
Oxford. He rarely said anything. But Oxford suspected that this most
taciturn of men would propagate Germanism if once he opened his
mouth.[2]

Three forces were driving Christianity to restate doctrine: natural
science, historical criticism, moral feeling. Natural science shattered
assumptions about Genesis and about miracles. Criticism questioned
whether all history in the Bible was true. Moral feeling found the love
of God hard to reconcile with hellfire or scapegoat-atonement.

[1] R, 11 July 1855.
[2] Suspicion, Abbott and Campbell, i, 210–11, as early as 1846.

These three forces were mirrored in English divinity of the fifties. Baden Powell derived his impetus from the uniform laws of nature believed to be dictated by science. Maurice knew nothing of science or criticism and derived his impetus solely from moral experience. Jowett knew nothing of science and despised Maurice's mind while he respected his person.[1] His impetus came from the historical criticism of the Germans, and his restatement was guided by German philosophy.

Dr. Arnold wanted to edit a Rugby edition of the epistles of St. Paul. After his death Arthur Stanley inherited the task. Stanley's commentary on Corinthians and Jowett's commentary on Thessalonians, Galatians and Romans were both published in June 1855. Jowett had spoken at last.

They do not compare in weight. Stanley's commentary is charming, readable, easy, superficial, the human St. Paul, everything about St. Paul except what mattered, Paul without ideas. Jowett's commentary was almost the reverse, ideas without Paul. If more of Paul had been allowed to come through it would have been a great commentary. Behind the barricade of reserve Jowett possessed a probing mind and a religious understanding. Baden Powell was so critical that he was hardly religious, Maurice so religious that he was hardly critical. Jowett succeeded in being both. Never so attractive nor so sincere, he stepped before the public eye and for a moment was himself. He came shyly out of his college rooms and let the inner flame be seen.

The best contents were the essays which he dispersed amidst the commentary, for he was better equipped to handle ideas than texts. These essays disclose a longing for a simple faith, freed from scholastic argument, at times almost freed from definition. Once the mind passed from utter simplicity it fell into mazes through which the reason could not lead it, and objectors soon charged Jowett with being destructive. In the eyes of every conservative the worst essay was that upon the atonement, where he revolted[2] from legalistic interpretations and rested upon the fact as symbol or figure, yet always with a feeling of mystery too great for the mind. This interpretation of the New Testament was very free, in the sense that he seemed sharply to distinguish the understanding of the apostles from the language of his own age, and would hardly confess any continuous tradition of Christianity as from childhood to manhood.

[1] Jowett on Maurice, cf. Abbott and Campbell, i, 212, 220, 262, ii, 45.
[2] 1st ed., ii, 471.

Three months later, by the unfortunate timing of Dean Gaisford's death, Lord Palmerston appointed Jowett to be regius professor of Greek.[1]

The appointment was not as disturbing to conservatives as if Jowett had suddenly been made a professor of divinity; which office Jowett would himself have preferred. The professor of Greek must teach the Greek Testament. But there was no prospect of a war like the Hampden war. If no war better no sniping. Pusey preached two sermons to prevent faith from being narrowed or mutilated by the intellect, and warned the university that throwing away one revealed truth must soon lead to throwing away others.[2] The notes to the published copy subjected Jowett to severity.

In Oxford appeared the sergeant-sniper of the established church, cackling jack-in-the-box Golightly. Bursting among tutors and heads of houses, he persuaded the evangelical and lay principal of Magdalen hall, Dr. Macbride, to join with him in delating Jowett to the vice-chancellor on a charge of heresy. The vice-chancellor was tiny and wizened Dr. R. L. Cotton, Provost of Worcester College and brother-in-law of Pusey. Cotton asked Jowett to subscribe again the Thirty-nine Articles. Jowett consented, loathing. One side reported that he faltered when he signed, the other that he coolly asked for a new pen. He knew himself humiliated before the world. He felt signing to be the meaner part, a schoolboy degradation. On returning to his room his first angry words were, 'They have done me harm. But I shall live it down.'[3]

Baden Powell

Baden Powell was the Savilian professor of geometry at Oxford. At first the only able representative in Oxford of mathematical physics, he investigated heat, light, radiation. But he was a philosopher who did not eschew the duty of entering theological lists. He delivered assaults impartially upon the enemies of Hampden, the Tractarian doctrines, the critics of science, the Mosaic cosmogonists. He delivered these assaults with so sedate a tone, so impassive an urbanity, so quiet a confidence, that for years readers failed to perceive that behind this neutral mask was the most radical mind of contem-

---

[1] H. G. Liddell was first offered the chair and refused it, but became Gaisford's successor as Dean of Christ Church. Stanley and Liddell both worked to secure Jowett's appointment; Abbott and Campbell, i, 236–7.

[2] Liddon, iv, 7–9. [3] *Life*, i, 239–40.

porary divinity. Yet he was one of the last of the Newtonian philosophers who married science to religion by their wonder at the
harmony of the universe. Supremely assured and highly organised,
he looked down upon persons distinguished more by zeal than knowledge. Upon intricate doctrinal points he could preach an extempore
sermon without meandering. He had three wives in succession and
thirteen children,[1] was a fair painter and enthusiastic singer, and
nevertheless betrays not a glow of fire or passion. Sermons, essays,
books, articles, all flow down the clear mountain stream of reason
exalted. Never was a more Olympian rebel. Other reforming divines
were warm with the warmth of defendants pleading in a dock. Baden
Powell sat impassive on a judge's throne and delivered verdicts.

First among English divines, six years before evolution became the
talk of society, Baden Powell blessed evolution and held some form of
it to be the only scientific solution of the problem.[2] Believing Genesis
to be irreconcilable with geology, he said so plainly. The Word is
incompatible with the Works of God and the Word must bow
because never intended to give scientific information. First of English
divines, he suggested (without asserting dogmatically) that Genesis
might embody ideas commonly received among the Jews and perhaps
borrowed from some epic cosmogony, a parable and not history, the
language of figure and poetry.

During the forties he was vocal as scientist and dumb as theologian.
In the fifties he began again to speak. As the Royal Society obituarist
reported doubtfully, he became a controversial theologian. The
important books were three related series of essays, of which the most
complete and most controversial appeared in 1859.[3] Nature obeys the
laws of God. The world is a cosmos of God's order. That order is
uniform, its causes inscrutable. Miracles do not happen. Man evolved
by natural laws. Science is a revelation of God and the truest aid to
theology. The miracles of the New Testament are received for the

---

[1] *Proc. R.S.*, 1860–2, XI, xxvi. There is a charming portrait of Powell in W.
Tuckwell, *Pre-Tractarian Oxford* (1909), 165ff.; see also E. E. Reynolds' life of Lord
Baden-Powell (2nd ed. 1957) who was one of Powell's sons.

[2] *The Connexion of Natural and Divine Truth*, 1838; dedicated to Bishop Edward
Stanley of Norwich.

[3] *Essays on the Spirit of the Inductive Philosophy, the unity of Worlds, and the philosophy of
Creation*, 1855: *Christianity without Judaism*, 1858: *The Order of Nature considered in
reference to the claims of Revelation*, 1859. There is an important and illuminating article
on Jowett and Baden Powell entitled 'Recent Latitudinarian Theology' in CR, 38,
1860, 388ff.

divine truths which they were designed to convey, without prejudice to the invariable laws of physiology, of matter, and of gravitation. The Old Testament may be abandoned without loss, and must be abandoned to free the gospel from Jewish trappings.

This radical theology was not avowed without complaint and criticism and anxiety. But no one tried to prosecute Baden Powell. The magisterial ice-cold air of mathematical reasoning which ringed Baden Powell made him too academic to be offensive outside the caucus of scholars. For his impact upon the world at large he might have been writing in Latin.

His immunity was not the only sign that a less traditional divinity was establishing a place within the churches. In July 1860 Maurice was appointed to the living of St. Peter's, Vere Street. Only a stalwart twenty of London clergymen petitioned Bishop Tait to refuse institution and so test the doctrine as Phillpotts tested the doctrine of regeneration. Tait received a big counter-petition headed by the names of Thirlwall, Gladstone and Tennyson. Provided that liberal divinity was reverent, it was evidently secure. In 1856 the vicar of Halstead protected his flock by burning a copy of lectures on Strauss and two years later the Bishop of London first defended the truth of Genesis in a sermon.[1] But to believe that fire might not be everlasting and to spiritualise the idea of atonement and to hold novel views about inspiration was becoming possible, though not common, among clergy as already among laity.

Provided that it was reverent. It would shortly appear before the public in a form chargeable with irreverence. The churches had still to endure their pain of belly.

Maurice and Jowett and Baden Powell represented three roads which Christian restatement could follow. Baden Powell stood in the old tradition of science-proving-religion; but the religion which science was alleged to prove contained neither Old Testament nor miracle. Jowett stood by that new Platonism with which German idealist philosophers wrapped and interpreted Christianity as an ethical parable of spiritual philosophy. Maurice was also a Platonist, but based his unsystematic divinity upon the direct experience of God. Of these three modes of liberal divinity—by the natural philosophy of science, by metaphysics, or by religious experience—the future lay with the third. There faith, seeing through a glass darkly, still possessed and was sure.

[1] G, 58, 279, 543.

Mansel

In the spring of 1858 Oxford University was excited by a course of lectures. They were the Bampton lectures delivered by Mansel of St. John's College. The Bampton lectures were (and are) always delivered in the university church. These lecture-sermons were not reckoned valuable by the instructed public. They had achieved the reputation of being wordy and men's consciences were sorely taxed by the duty of attending. Hampden made them more famous, but not more respected. Mansel changed this reputation.

Oxford was feeling uneasy as liberal divinity grew and modified the older Tractarian mind, uneasy as the young felt that Pusey was the sole bulwark of faith and yet that Pusey was obsolete. The young knew Mansel as a philosopher of religion who could make his philosophy intelligible and interesting. They searched for a defence of Christian faith in language which they would understand. No one could remember crowds at St. Mary's comparable with those which now flocked to hear the most instructive lectures of the century. Hearers of Newman could recall congregations hanging upon his words. But parochial sermons are not philosophical lectures. Mansel's delivery was superb. In the beginning he may have owed part of the crowd to a repute among undergraduates as the best of teachers, and a repute among dons as the first conversationalist in Oxford. But he played down to no one, allowed nothing to relief, took his audience austerely along the flowerless path of logic. A don in the church wondered whether one in a hundred could understand him.[1] Yet the audience could be felt breathless with excitement. The undergraduates might not know what they were hearing, but knew enough to know that they were hearing something important, and reached upwards. They watched fascinated, as though before their eyes the greenhouse of liberal divinity was battered and crumbled into dust by the hammer-blows of reason.

Part of the magnet was a juxtaposition of religious language in German philosophy and religious language in the gospels; complexity versus simplicity, speculation versus conscience, metaphysics versus parable, absolute—infinite—impersonal versus father of hopes and agonies. By the side of the cradle of Bethlehem Mansel set placards of portentous utterance from Strauss and Hegel, and exclaimed with contempt, 'These be thy gods, O Philosophy!'[2] So far from regarding it as a merit to abandon the anthropomorphic language of religion in

[1] Burgon[2], 339.   [2] *Limits of Religious Thought*, 161.

the effort to satisfy the intelligence, Mansel declared that religion must use this childlike language and that the philosophical language of metaphysics was no more satisfying to the intelligence.

For God is a mystery. We cannot know him as he is. We can only know him as we need to act in relation to him. In prayer and conscience we apprehend him as personal. When we try to frame what personality might be to God, intelligence fails. We form no conception of an infinite personality. But we need no such conception. We need only to find him as he speaks to us and to act upon what he speaks. Even when he speaks we must understand by our imperfect analogies from human life, understand his love by our love, his justice by our justice. Therefore the truths of religion are not speculative but regulative. Ideas and images which do not represent God as he is may nevertheless represent him as it is our duty to regard him. To say of faith that it is picture-language and parable is to say nothing against it. That is the only language upon which faith can act.

That philosophy cannot know God is no argument against God. It is an argument against the sufficiency of the human mind. We find philosophy incompetent not only when it is defining God but when it is trying to define free will or causation. Therefore the difficulty of philosophical theology is a difficulty of philosophy and not of theology. The contradictions of metaphysics are inherent to the constitution of the mind.

We must therefore separate the language of prayer from the language of philosophy. Since God is in himself unknowable, a philosophy of God is vanity and a striving after wind.

Mansel turned to the doctrines attacked: the idea of atonement, the moral nature of Jehovah in the Old Testament. Thinkers like Kant or Jowett say that God cannot act contrary to their highest standard of morality. Since we cannot frame conceptions of what goodness is in God as he is, we have no means of criticising an act of God revealed to us. The only question is whether it is revealed or not. And in determining whether it is revealed, reason and conscience are guides. Mansel was weakest when he came to this keystone—how we know revelation (which he has argued to be the only source of knowledge of God) to be revelation.[1]

When the Bampton lectures appeared in print they caused a prolonged and useful argument. Everyone that mattered joined in, from

[1] Cf. W. R. Matthews, *The Religious Philosophy of Dean Mansel*, 1956, 15–17.

John Stuart Mill and Herbert Spencer to James Mozley and Frederick
Denison Maurice. No one was happy with Mansel's destination of
philosophy. The defence looked like a gun which misfired. Mansel
was compared to the fool sitting on the inn-sign and sawing busily.
The spear of criticism pointed to the absolute difference between
human morality and divine morality; as though Mansel declared that
a deed criminal on earth might be virtuous in heaven and so justified
the hewing of Agag in pieces. An able critic[1] confessed the lecturer to
be a great thinker and the lectures to be the most useful publication to
have issued from Oxford in many years, by reason of their skill in
assailing rationalism with the weapons of rationalism. But even
this friend objected to the absolute doctrine of an unknowable God
and believed that Mansel gravely undervalued the internal evidence
for the divine.

The doctrine of an unknowable God roused Maurice to wrath, for
it challenged the reality of immediate experience of divinity. Maurice
never appeared more unpleasing before the public than in the
pamphlets which he now released against Mansel. To study the two
sides of the controversy embarrasses, as the reader watches the cool
philosopher strip clouds of incoherence from the infuriated divine.
Maurice was vanquished, demolished. There looked to be nothing
left of him. But however the philosopher of religion proved that
mortals cannot criticise God for ordering Joshua to murder women
and children, English mortals continued to criticise God; or rather,
they had ceased to be able to believe that God ordered any such thing.
The Christian conscience of England rose against Jehovah. On moral
grounds they must diminish the authority of the Old Testament. And
on other grounds than moral this was then becoming easy.

3. GENESIS AND GEOLOGY

Between 1820 and 1840 geology became the science of the day. It
captured popular imagination. In this age the names iguanodon,
pterodactyl, dinosaur, gigantosaurus, megatherium, plesiosaurus became part of the English language; all inferred from evidence collected
upon walks round countryside or sea-coasts, digging in caves,
exploring in quarries. The geologists studded their pages with drawings of beasts hitherto confined to children's story-books. A skilfully

---

[1] CR, 1859, i, 352ff.

produced survey of geology sold more copies than a novel by Sir
Walter Scott. They peered through a window into a fairyland with
real ogres.

The first step of their advance demanded time; time on a scale unknown; vistas of unimagined time while the strata of rocks were
formed and embraced their fossils. They met the calculation of Archbishop Usher, placed in the margins of the King James version, that
God created the world in 4004 B.C. Historical critics who examined
Chinese or Egyptian records extended this calculation largely to
6000 B.C. or even earlier. But geologists demanded millions of years of
time.

Genesis and geology went to war. Some said that as Genesis was
certain and geology uncertain, geology must yield. Some said that as
Genesis was intended to teach religious and spiritual truth, the science
was independent of interference from Mosaic evidence. Some said,
God is the author of both nature and revelation, and therefore
reconciling truth exists and may be discoverable.

No one who possessed faith lost it by learning geology. Relentless
inspirationists wrote a series of Mosaic geologies which are now the
dustiest corpses on library shelves. Infidels searching for weapons to
attack Christianity discovered new ammunition in arguments over
Genesis. But at first, anyway until 1844, the conflict troubled only
minds anxious for trouble. Geology can hardly be compared with
Strauss or Carlyle as a shifter of the Christian sub-soil. The most
eminent English geologists were not only Christian but clergymen,
not only clergymen but devout. The Reverend Adam Sedgwick held
the chair of geology at Cambridge, the Reverend William Buckland
the chair of geology at Oxford. Neither had anything but dislike and
regret for the cruder Mosaic geologists. Neither had difficulty in
reconciling their studies with the Bible. On the contrary. Both, and
especially Buckland, saw the discoveries as a marvellous new demonstration of the purpose and providence of an Almighty Creator.

First to go was Genesis-time: next to go, a universal flood.

Informed geologists taught that the world was much older than
man. Strata and fossils clamoured for millennia. In his inaugural
lecture to Oxford university (1820) Buckland freely declared that the
words of Genesis chapter 1 verse 1 'in the beginning' described an
immense period; that the six 'days' of creation were epochs of
unspecified length and not days of twenty-four hours. Fossils and

strata proved the action of catastrophic floods. Since we have a Genesis record of catastrophic flood, Buckland at first believed that the new evidence pointed to the truth of Noah. In the face of evidence he soon jettisoned this theory. The best chronologists calculated that Noah's rain began to fall on Sunday, 7 December 2347 B.C. Charles Lyell, the layman appointed professor of geology at King's College, London, for a short time in 1831, adduced much evidence to show that the length of time needed was far greater than the years available since Noah. He struggled cogently for the uniformitarian theory, which disputed catastrophic action in favour of the gradual, and so demanded more time yet. Even if the accepted date of Noah could be somewhat pushed back by lax calculation, Buckland conceded to Lyell that so recent an event could not be the catastrophe needed to explain his strata. In 1836 he gave offence by confessing Noah's flood to be a 'tranquil inundation' compared with the waters required for his catastrophe.[1] The flood became a local flood, sufficient only to drown all mankind who then lived (perhaps) in the Euphrates valley. The animals of the ark became domestic pets or food for Noah's use, not two of every species.

Geologists like Buckland and Sedgwick were authentic successors of the divinity of the eighteenth century. Newton proved the harmony of religion and science. The physico-theologists who succeeded him investigated the design of the universe and hymned the Designer whom they demonstrated. Each new investigation was applied to the same great end. Paley took comparative anatomy and adapted the argument from design to the beautiful mechanisms of eye or finger. Buckland and Whewell and Sedgwick adapted the same argument to rocks and mastodons.

In 1825 the Right Honourable the Earl of Bridgewater made a will which provided that these proofs of design and purpose should be collected. He was unique among eccentric clergymen. Prebendary of Durham, prince of the Holy Roman Empire, incumbent of two little parishes in Shropshire, he lived in the Rue St. Honoré at Paris, with countless pairs of boots, several illegitimate daughters, a garden full of rabbits and a house full of dogs, two of which were dressed in yellow coats and silver-gilt collars and fed by lackeys at his table.[2] He collected manuscripts which became the Egerton collection in the British

---

[1] *Bridgewater Treatise*, i, 94–95, note.
[2] Bernard Falk, *The Bridgewater Millions*, 185.

Museum. His will left £8,000 in trust to the president of the Royal Society, who should select and reward a person or persons to publish a work *On the Power, Wisdom and Goodness of God, as manifested in the Creation; illustrating such work by all reasonable arguments, as for instance the variety and formation of God's Creatures in the animal, vegetable, and mineral Kingdoms; the effect of digestion, and thereby of conversion; the construction of the hand of man, and an infinite variety of other arguments; as also by discoveries ancient and modern, in arts, sciences, and the whole extent of literature.* These terms suggest that the theologico-anatomists like Paley came first to his mind. When Bridgewater died in 1829 the president of the Royal Society summoned to his assistance Archbishop Howley and Bishop Blomfield. The committee divided the money between eight authors whose works became *The Bridgewater Treatises.* These are the late flowering of the physico-theology of the previous century. With such money the committee could command the best science of the day.

Four of the eight authors were Edinburgh-trained physicians who applied new anatomy and physiology to the proof of design, the anatomy of the hand and the physiology of the digestion of animals. (One of the four was Peter Mark Roget, who in old age gave the world a still more precious production; his *Thesaurus* of English words and phrases.) Of the non-medical four, William Kirby was pastor of the country church of Barham in Suffolk for sixty-eight years, collected 153 wild specimens of bees in his parish, and helped to found the modern study of entomology. The Scottish divine Thomas Chalmers manifested the adaptation of nature to the moral and intellectual condition of man. William Whewell, still a tutor at Trinity College in Cambridge, observed the application to theology of astronomy and physics. The remaining author was Buckland. In the Bridgewater treatises the reader roamed enchanted from barnacles to migrating swallows, from the habits of worms to the mouths of whales, from the duodenal tube to electrical galvanism, and marvelled at the beautiful machinery of God. The merits were unequal. Whewell and Buckland knew science and theology and produced a respectable amalgam. Prout's book is of little value in either science or theology. Kirby knew about bees, but where he ventured into geology the informed reader averted his eyes.

The attitude towards the geologists was perplexed and varied. Rigorous Biblicists wrote books of Mosaic geology to condemn these heretics. Six days must be six days. The flood must be universal. The best calculators reckoned the ark at 42,413 tons. By contrast the chief evangelical journal, *The Christian Observer* (1834), produced a series of friendly and balanced articles. In August 1836 the British Association held its annual meeting at Bristol. Buckland told the assembly that the world is thousands of years old and was received with applause. *John Bull*[1] said that the report was shameful, professed to believe it false, and denounced the quackery of modern geology and zoology. Pamphlets were published against him; and he was forced to issue a paper denying that he inculcated sceptical views and affirming that geology afforded new evidence for the being of God and was strictly consistent with the creation-narratives of Moses.[2]

The most absurd but most public of Buckland's assailants was William Cockburn, Dean of York. His first wife was the sister of Sir Robert Peel. Thus the world was not easily capable of perceiving that he knew nothing. In 1838 he issued a pamphlet against Buckland, and another pamphlet against the British Association.[3] Mercifully for the geologists he became entangled in curious litigation where the archbishop's court deprived him of the deanery for simony; and though he appealed to the court of queen's bench and so preserved his deanery, the queen's bench did not reverse the verdict. Thereafter he lost reputation and his assaults probably helped Buckland and Sedgwick to public esteem. In 1844 the rash British Association met in York and could not stop the dean reading a paper which described Buckland's theory of creation as a tissue of absurdities too palpable to escape the notice of a schoolboy. He lamented that Oxford university, so long the seat of learning and orthodoxy, should lead the people directly to infidelity and indirectly to atheism. Sedgwick, who rarely minced words, rose to reply. Never has a dean been exposed to such withering contempt. The dean's pamphlet describing the battle attained five editions.[4]

The opinions of leading Christian divines quickly changed during the late thirties or early forties. Dr. Pye Smith was the head of London

---

[1] JB, 36, 293, 302.

[2] Pamphlets against him, e.g. S. Best, *Afterthoughts on reading Dr. Buckland's Bridgewater Treatise*; J. Mellor Brown, *Reflections on Geology*. An incumbent in Durham pointed out that the water, declared by Buckland to be a comparatively tranquil inundation, must have risen by 700 inches a day in order to cover the Himalayan peaks. Mellor Brown, 32 note.

[3] *A Letter to Professor Buckland; The dangers of Peripatetic Philosophy*.

[4] *Athenaeum*, 1844, 903; *The Bible defended against the British Association*, 5th ed., 1845.

Congregational teachers. At the end of 1837 he still maintained a universal flood. The attacks upon science during 1838 caused him to study the subject. In 1839 he published a series of lectures[1] in which he jettisoned six traditional points: the recent creation of the world; an original chaos over the whole earth; the creation of heavenly bodies after the creation of the earth; the derivation of all animals and vegetables from one centre of creation; the belief that the animals were not subject to death until the fall of man; and a universal deluge—though he still believed that the flood drowned all human beings but eight. Most moderate divines went this way. By 1844 the gap between educated theology and popular theology was widening. Popular opinion conceived geology to be somehow dangerous to scripture. Educated divines had already abandoned the more vulnerable places of Mosaic story. By the fifties they were saying that for many years no man of sense had believed in a creation of the world during six days of twenty-four hours.

Scientists as yet received small credit for utility. They were remote theorists. They gained credit when they confirmed the Christian revelation. The image of an absent-minded professor was quick to form. The annual meetings of the British Association (founded 1831) were hailed as irresistibly funny. Their lavish entertainments and curious enquiries were pilloried as absurd; learned eccentrics meeting to eat dinners and report with pomp the results of laboured investigations. Charles Dickens wrote a skit upon them called *The Mudfog Papers*. When they met at Oxford Keble was cross that honorary degrees were bestowed upon the hodge-podge of philosophers.

The fun was not quite innocuous. It contained fear. The scientists were mocked partly because they were funny and partly because their influence ought to be diminished. Ridicule was more efficacious than abuse in deafening the people to the words of scientists.

The sufferers were not the Christians but the scientists *qua* scientists. Charles Lyell once grumbled about the public reading in church of the first chapter of Genesis without comment or explanation. The people accepted the recent origin of the world and man, and therefore regarded scientists with suspicion and prejudice. Yet by a paradox no educated clergyman could enter the field against the popular creed of the geologist or astronomer.[2] The sufferings of scientists

[1] *On the relation between Holy Scripture and some parts of Geological Science.*
[2] Lyell to George Ticknor, 1850: *Life of Lyell*, ii, 168.

amid popular fun or abuse had serious consequences for their future psychology.

Educated divines had no fear of scientists. Popular opinion suspected them. Popular opinion was wiser than educated divines. Buckland talked airily of a few little difficulties between Genesis and geology. The snarl was neither six days nor flood. Partly it was an expansion of created time without man and therefore without evident purpose. Partly it was the impetus which geological strata gave to theories of evolution. The strata seemed to show a slow succession of higher and higher animals. The biological evidence of more elaborate structures agreed with the record of the rocks. The strata clamoured for a theory of animal development—if any theory could be found less improbable than the theory of special creations.

Scientists were discontented with the national provision for science in schools and universities, and especially for lay scientists. In few posts could a scientist without private means earn sufficient bread. Scientists who were clergymen were well supplied. Kirby and Henslow were content with their Suffolk livings, Sedgwick flourished on a Norwich canonry, Buckland was fat with a Christ Church canonry and the deanery of Westminster. In 1855 the parliamentary committee of the British Association recommended that scientific (as well as literary) merit should be considered in selecting clergymen for preferment; on the ground that scientific clergymen would be useful in countering the scepticism of an age disturbed by misunderstanding science.[1] But lay scientists looked wistfully at Buckland's canonry. Lyell rumbled that England was more parson-ridden than any country in Europe except Spain.[2] Neither scientist nor churchman was quite pleased with this use of church preferment. The scientist observed how church duties removed clerical scientists from their enquiries. He saw Henslow becoming more of a pastor and less of a botanist, Sedgwick diverted to being canon-in-residence of his cathedral, Buckland unable to investigate anything after he became dean of Westminster.[3] Churchmen of that pastoral age were equally dubious about promoting parsons because they were scientists. Nearly everyone but Sir Robert Peel and Prince Albert thought Buckland an unwise choice for the deanery. Men asked whether the deanery of Westminster was intended to

[1] *Report of the British Association*, Glasgow 1855, lvi.
[2] *Life of Lyell*, ii, 169 (1848).
[3] *Life of Lyell*, ii, 208 (1856).

reward research in mineralogy. They said that Buckland knew all the ologies except theology.[1]

The year 1844 marked the change in this public atmosphere. A theorist brought forward a form of Lamarck's old theory of evolution. Geology, which to sensible men looked only awkward against Genesis, began suddenly to look menacing. Buckland affirmed in his Bridgewater treatise of 1836 that no reasonable man could doubt all the natural world to have originated from God. After 1844 the universal assertion became a little more doubtful.

Robert Chambers was a self-made Scottish journalist who built a publishing firm and a famous encyclopaedia.[2] He made himself a well-read amateur at many subjects, a popular author of recent Scottish history, and a fair practitioner of geology. *Vestiges of the Natural History of Creation* was published anonymously in October 1844. Chambers took elaborate precautions to keep the authorship secret. Even the proofs went to the printer through trusted intermediaries. He never admitted the authorship during his remaining twenty-eight years. After death twelve editions of his biography concealed that there was even suspicion. The repute of the publishing firm must be protected. The author may even have been ashamed of his profitable book. He was rumoured to be Prince Albert; or Byron's daughter Lady Lovelace; or Charles Darwin, whom the informed knew to be working at a theory of evolution; or Lyell or Thackeray or George Combe the phrenologist or Sir Richard Vyvyan.[3]

Vestiges of Creation was a gift to the critics.

All the species of the world descended by transmutation from lower to higher. The second highest species gave birth to man. Chambers dismissed Moses casually and exalted God in continuous creation. He asserted that on planets live beings of flesh and blood; gave an instance of a field sown with oats yielding a harvest of rye; illustrated spontaneous generation from a recent claim that two English gentlemen created a living acarus by passing electric current through inorganic matter; thought it possible to hatch a rat from a goose's egg. A seven-month child has the brain of a beast. Dogs can play an excellent game of dominoes. Clover will grow spontaneously without being sown or carried by wind. Wild pigs never have measles and therefore the

[1] R, 20 November 1845.

[2] Best book on Chambers is M. Millhauser, *Just before Darwin*, Middleton, Connecticut, 1959.

[3] Gillispie, 163.

measle germ was evolved after men began to eat bacon. A set of perfectly black children were born to Arab parents who lacked any drop of black blood. All the scholars found Chambers as slip-shod as a writer of popular novels. The reviewers revelled in vituperation. Professor Sedgwick drove a rollicking coach through the book for eighty-five pages of the *Edinburgh Review* (July 1845)—inaccurate superficial trash, mischievous antisocial nonsense, brain-heated visions, credulity, raving madness. Sedgwick jeered at girls learning chess from a spaniel and dowagers playing whist with a poodle. Even Charles Darwin, working away quietly at his notes at Downe, read this review by Sedgwick in fear and trembling,[1] and disliked its pulpit air.

Meanwhile *Vestiges* embarrassed serious students of evolution. It embarrassed literate Christian geologists because it encouraged illiterate Mosaic cosmogonists. From hollow caverns of the deanery at York echoed a stentorian voice warning the world that this bubble was no more empty than Sedgwick and Buckland. The book embarrassed the tiny handful of serious students working towards a tolerable and scientific theory of organic development. Huxley never forgave Chambers for making truth ridiculous.[2]

A book so scorned was a book to read. It sold 23,750 copies in eleven British editions alone; four of the editions in the first six months. Many readers enjoyed it as science fiction. Others read it with a wistful hope that evolution and transmutation of species might be true. The geologists had conjured a vacuum about the creation of the world. Intelligent orthodox who postulated aeons of time after the first verse of Genesis invited speculation about the course of those aeons. Chambers offered the public the first popular history of the prehistoric world. The history was suspect for romancing. But suspect or not, it crudely tried to fill a new and yawning gap in man's belief about the origins of the world and of himself. Even if no one had believed *Vestiges of Creation*, educated Englishmen could not afterwards treat the mystery as though the book was not published. Among books it was unique in being simultaneously discredited and powerful. Touch it with a little finger and it fell. And in falling it seemed the debris of a strange half-hidden magnetic synthesis of new knowledge.

Tennyson read *Vestiges* soon after it appeared.[3] He published *In Memoriam* in 1850, but had been writing the poem for seventeen

---

[1] *Life of Darwin*, i, 344.   [2] *Memoir*, i, 223.   [3] Millhauser, 133.

years. He brooded over popular science with vague uncritical reflectiveness. His son claimed that the evolution-stanzas of *In Memoriam* were written and read to friends several years before *Vestiges* was published.[1] Loving the dead Arthur Hallam with a pure affection beyond the wont of men, Tennyson rested upon faith that a being so noble could not be destined to extinction, that a love so profound must reach to eternity. Then science stepped in to criticise, with fossils and bones showing countless types extinguished, cast as rubbish to the void; dragons tearing each other in the slime, nature red in tooth and claw, shrieking against his creed. The poet represented his soul as coming through to faith in the purpose and design of the universe. But his faith, which once had firmly trod, now faltered—

> And falling with my weight of cares
> Upon the great world's altar-stairs
> That slope through darkness up to God
>
> I stretch lame hands of faith, and grope,
> And gather dust and chaff, and call
> To what I feel is Lord of all,
> And faintly trust the larger hope.

Whether or not these stanzas were complete before *Vestiges*, as Hallam Tennyson claimed, or altered afterwards as I suspect, the public admired *In Memoriam* partly because it is one of the loveliest of English poems and partly because they received the impact of *Vestiges*.

Tennyson's faith, stumbling up the altar-stairs in darkness, marks an epoch in English religious life.

Antagonism between religion and science had reached popular non-philosophical minds only in the sense that one or the other was instantly known to be wrong. Atheists or deists knew that Christianity was untrue and were not helped to that belief by science. Christians knew that Christianity was true and were not perturbed in their belief by science. Antagonism between science and religion was a ploy of atheist Holyoake or of anti-rational Cockburn. But Tennyson's mind mirrors a more sensitive and anxious predicament; a soul

---

[1] *The Princess* (1847) shows signs of it. *Memoir*, i, 223, shows that he bought a copy in November 1844 after seeing a laudatory review in the *Christian Examiner* for 9 November 1844.

seeking faith amid the rocks and waters, bruised and fearful but at last triumphant. Science thereby attained a new stature for the religious mind of England. Hume and deists, Strauss and Germans, Carlyle and pantheists, were like birds finding a cuckoo's egg in the nest; still a large mysterious egg, but one day destined to overshadow every fledgling in the nest. We shall believe where we cannot prove. Faith will be founded on feeling. The proof of design, which for a century and a half served to marry science and religion, slid into the dust of prehistoric rocks.

I have tracked the history of the English churches through thirty momentous years. The constitution of England was adjusted between 1828 and 1835. These changes lessened the unique public influence of the established Church of England, released the zeal of Roman Catholics, granted equality to Protestant dissenters and encouraged them to public life. The cardinal fact of those years was the frightening growth of the towns. There was bred a proletariat estranged from religious practice, by belief that religion was bourgeois, by shortage of churches and ministers, by immigrants from Ireland whom the Roman Catholic church was too small to gather, by immigrants from the countryside whom the Church of England was too inflexible to gather, by immigrants from Ireland or the countryside too poor for any church to gather, unless here and there Strict Baptist or Primitive Methodist touched the illiterate with wildfire. The bounding population gave to every denomination but the Friends a sense of well-being as they built churches and chapels to keep pace with the growth of worshippers; to the Roman Catholics an almost disastrous euphoria, as the crowd of Irish immigrants fostered dreams of triumph. But this boundless energy and expansive power, which was reflected overseas in a missionary drive without parallel in Christian history, was not complacent. Everyone saw how the cities ran away from churches and schools. The building of churches and chapels in England was a vast endeavour of generosity and hard work, accompanied by its troubles in debt-loaded dissenting chapels or almost bankrupt Roman Catholic bishops or impoverished Anglican curates, but sprinkling the cities with places of worship and Sunday schools and day schools. The early Victorians cannot be blamed because success proved far beyond their resources. The effort deserves a monument.

Churches cannot be understood in solitude. They are open to the movements of spirit and intelligence in the society which they share. While their call to love God and man gave Christian society its heart, they did not live behind a convent wall, but housed many citizens whose lungs breathed the economic or political or philosophical air of their age. If no one can understand a society without contemplating its religious forces, no one can understand a denomination without contemplating the secular society around. The gospel of liberty, equality, fraternity entered the world with issue unforeseeable. Coal and cotton and railways and steamships hurried the human race towards a different structure of society. Urban England demanded services which the churches could no longer provide as once they provided for rural England. The state must offer burial, marriage, registration, charity, and above all education, as of necessity it organised police or drains or roads. In acting benevolent mother of the poor the state could use and encourage the churches less than reason might require; for some churches were jealous of aid to other churches and some churches refused aid because they would allow no magistrate to interfere in their privacy. Only in education was the state able to work through churches and chapels; and the fears and rivalries of church versus dissent compelled England to delay in creating its national system of schools.

The Victorians moved towards a time of true competition in religion or irreligion. They moved in jerks, and took a futile step backwards when Russell tried to legislate against Roman Catholic bishops. The Church of England retained privileges in the levy of church rates, the government of the older universities, the laws of burial, the House of Lords. But though in 1859 atheists could not sit in Parliament and bequests to promote atheism were invalid, the movement towards true competition was relentless. The magnificent Gothic cathedrals of Catholics and the magnificent Gothic chapels of London dissenters were signs in stone of an equality which reached through the life of England.

Free competition harmed Christianity in villages. The minutebooks of Victorian churches and chapels reflect angry bickering at the parish pump. In the towns it probably helped Christianity more than it hindered. When we observe a Primitive Methodist chapel built across the street from a Wesleyan Methodist chapel we are inclined to heave an ecumenical sigh and to forget that at first they ministered to different layers of society. While the expanding cities sowed a heritage of irreligion or anti-religion for posterity, Victorian England remained extraordinarily Christian in its tone and habits; and the reason was the multicoloured fervour of religious endeavour. Those who repealed the test act and emancipated the Catholics were concerned with social justice or political expediency. But unwitting they released an energy which changed the Church of England as well as nonconformity and imparted its peculiar strength and flavour to Victorian religious practice.

Every denomination therefore worried over its reason for existence, its doctrine and authority and government. As they moved towards free churches in a free state, they needed to strengthen their internal government, to organise themselves as coherent societies. The instinct which persuaded Baptists or Congregationalists to struggle incongruously but not vainly for denominational union was similar to the instinct which led ultramontanes to elevate the authority of Rome or Bunting-Methodists to elevate the authority of Conference or Anglicans to battle for the rights of Convocation. In every church the need for authority conflicted with the heritage of freedom and generated tension or schism. In their different ways Wiseman the Roman Catholic and Phillpotts the Anglican bishop and Bunting the Wesleyan and Chalmers the Scottish Presbyterian and Campbell the Congregationalist stood for the independent authority of a religious society to rule its life and teaching; and each of those stout fighters faced enemies within as well as without his denomination. The early Victorians witnessed a schism or two among the Methodists, schism among the Quakers, schism on the grand scale among Scottish Presbyterians, secession from the Church of England so grave as to amount to schism, a Baptist body divided over open communion and Calvinism, a Roman Catholic body divided over everything but the necessity for not being divided. Because the armies not seldom wheeled into this battle under the generalship of bigots or fools, we may forget that in some form the battle was necessary to health, an unavoidable pace in the march towards free churches in a free state.

By law and history the established church retained its sense of call to the nation. The Anglicans, even in Ireland and Wales where they were minorities, were not willing to see themselves as a denomination; not so much because they wished to retain outmoded privilege as because their reason for existence was integrated into the political history of the English people. Their doctrine and authority and government were in one aspect a mission to those of the English who would listen, like the mission of Catholic or dissenter; but in another aspect they felt themselves to represent a national profession of faith and national aspiration to God. Therefore their inward turmoil was unique; between those who wanted the church to profess and teach truth, whatever people or Parliament professed, and those who wanted doctrine or organisation to be broad enough to reflect (within reason) the loose Christian mind of the nation. This stress marked a new phase in the historic debate between high churchman and low churchman, between Catholic mind and Protestant mind. The English nation was more anti-Catholic in ethos than the most thoughtful among Anglican leaders. As the national aspiration towards God the Church of England would be more Protestant than as teacher of dogmatic truth whether the nation hear or forbear. And with the power of dissent after the reform act this discrepancy made always more anguish. A church which stood for Catholic truth would not be recognised by the people as the Church of England. If conversely the Church of England was recognised by the people as national, what precise doctrines would it teach? The established church must slowly move towards breadth of thought and practice while seeking simultaneously to prevent this breadth from being Christianity-and-water.

This alternative was not seen before the Gorham case, nor clear until the sixties. Tractarian strength before 1850 lay in the conviction that no choice was needed and that the nation could be made Catholic. In that conviction Newman and his disciples raised the eyes of English divinity from its insular introspection, ransacked the devotional treasures of the Christian centuries, and so imparted new beauty and depth to the authentic traditions of English religion; influencing at last dissenting practice as well as the establishment. Though the Tractarians wanted authority, ultimately and by no paradox they made the Church of England more free.

In the land of free religion all churches sought to tighten their dogmatic authority. At the same time they met new ideas which threatened their dogmas and authority at source. The historical method could not leave the Bible a document exempt from its anatomising. Geology forced more educated people to jettison their axioms about the origin and age of the world. Utilitarian philosophers or German metaphysicians were foes better armed than the crude old-fashioned deists whom Christian apologists were accustomed to despise. The encounter drove some into the refuge of more and more authority, into the choice put starkly by James Anthony Froude in *The Nemesis of Faith*—either crucify your reason or end in scepticism. The perils of atheism did not begin the quest for authority. But they hurried it, unbalanced it, made it agitated or fanatical.

So Christianity entered another age of flowering divinity. The philosophers and scientists asked inescapable questions, which could not be answered without confession of error. To confess error is hard for any society and hardest for a church conscious of bearing divine truth within its mind and even upon its lips if it could but frame the words. The churches were destined not to escape without prolonged suffering. But before 1859 a reverent and hesitant and modest approach to the intellectual tangle was already formed in men like Frederick Denison Maurice or James Martineau. They went quietly and slowly, though they could not conceive the height of the mist-capped ranges ahead. By a merciful providence the inmost soul of Christianity knew that all truth is of God.

ABBREVIATIONS

Add. MSS.	Additional manuscripts in the British Museum
AR	*Annual Register*
BC	*British Critic*
BL	Bodleian Library
Br. Mag.	*British Magazine*
CM	*Congregational Magazine*
CO	*Christian Observer*[1]
CR	*Christian Remembrancer*
C Witness	*Christian Witness*
DNB	*Dictionary of National Biography*
DR	*Dublin Review* (later *Wiseman Review*)
EHR	*English Historical Review*
ER	*Edinburgh Review*
ET	*English Translation*
FP	*Fulham Papers*
G	*Guardian*[1]
H	*Hansard*
HP	*Howick Papers*
JB	*John Bull*[1]
JEH	*Journal of Ecclesiastical History*
JFHS	*Journal of the Friends' Historical Society*
JHSW	*Journal of the Historical Society of the Church in Wales*
LC	Newman, *Letters and Correspondence*, edited by Anne Mozley
LQR	*London Quarterly Review*
MC	*Morning Chronicle*
MH	*Morning Herald*
MP	*Melbourne Papers*
MS	*Millennial Star*
NLW	National Library of Wales
OM	Oratory Papers, Birmingham
PA	Archives of the Congregation of Propaganda
PP	*Parliamentary Papers*
PRO	Public Record Office
Proc. R.S.	*Proceedings of the Royal Society*

[1] If the date is not cited, the first figure after CO or G or JB is the year. Thus G, 59, 207 means *Guardian*, 1859, page 207.

PWHS	*Proceedings of the Wesley Historical Society*
QR	*Quarterly Review*
R	*Record*
RA	*Royal Archives*
S	*Standard*
T	*Times*
Unit. Mag.	*Unitarian Magazine*
VS	*Victorian Studies*
WMM	*Wesleyan Missionary Magazine*
WR	*Weekly Register*

BIBLIOGRAPHY

This is neither a comprehensive list of relevant books, nor even a list of those studies whereby knowledge upon the subject has lately been increased. It is intended only to make the use of the footnotes easy.

I UNPUBLISHED PAPERS

Aberdeen Papers	British Museum Add. MSS.
Archives of Archdiocese of Westminster	Westminster
Archives of the Congregation of Propaganda	Rome
Diary of John Peter Boileau	Norwich City Library
Diary of John Stephenson Rowntree	Friends House, London
Diary of Joseph Romilly	Cambridge University Library
Diary of Lord Shaftesbury	Broadlands Archives Trust
Hurrell Froude Papers	Oratory, Birmingham
Fulham Papers	Lambeth
Gladstone Papers	British Museum Add. MSS.
Golightly Papers	Lambeth
Gorham Papers	Queens' College, Cambridge
Howick Papers	Durham
Keble Papers	Keble College, Oxford
Liddon Papers	Keble College, Oxford
Longley Papers	Lambeth
Manning Papers	Bayswater
Melbourne Papers	Windsor
Newman Papers	Oratory, Birmingham
Oriel College Papers	Oxford
Peel Papers	British Museum Add. MSS.
Pusey Papers	Pusey House, Oxford
Royal Archives	Windsor
Rugby School Papers	Rugby
Russell Papers	Public Record Office
Selborne Papers	Lambeth
Tait Papers	Lambeth
Wadham College Papers	Oxford
Whewell Papers	Trinity College, Cambridge
Wilberforce Papers	Bodleian Library, Oxford

II PRINTED BOOKS

The place of publication is London except where otherwise stated.

Abbott, E., and Campbell, L. *The Life and Letters of B. Jowett*, 2 vols., 1897.

Adamson, J. W. *English Education 1789–1902*, Cambridge, 1930.

Alexander, E. *Primate Alexander, Archbishop of Armagh. A memoir*, 1913.

Alford, H. *Life, journals and letters*, ed. by his widow, 3rd ed., 1874.

Allen, William. *Life, with Selections from his Correspondence*, 3 vols., 1846.

Anson, P. F. *The Call of the Cloister*, rev. ed. by A. W. Campbell, 1964.

Arbuthnot, Charles. *Correspondence*, ed. A. Aspinall, 1941.

Armstrong, H. B. J. (ed.). *Armstrong's Norfolk Diary*, 1963.

Arnold, R. *The Whiston Matter*, 1961.

Ashley, Evelyn. *The Life and Correspondence of H. J. Temple, Viscount Palmerston*, 2 vols., 1879.

Ashwell, A. R., and Wilberforce, R. G. *Life of Samuel Wilberforce*, 3 vols., 1880–1882; 2nd ed. of Vol. 3, 1883.

Aspinall, A. (ed.). *Letters of King George IV*, 3 vols., Cambridge, 1938; *Three Early Nineteenth Century Diaries*, 1952.

Aspland, R. B. *Memoir of the Life, Works and Correspondence of R. Aspland, of Hackney*, 1850.

Bamford, T. W. *Thomas Arnold*, 1960.

Baring-Gould, S. *The Church Revival*, 1914.

Bateman, J. *Life of Henry Venn Elliott*, 1868.

Battiscombe, G. *John Keble; a study in limitations*, 1963.

Beaumont, Joseph. *Life of the Reverend Joseph Beaumont, M.D.*, 1856.

Beck, G. A. (ed.). *The English Catholics, 1850–1950*, 1950.

Belcher, T. W. *Robert Brett of Stoke Newington, his life and work*, 2nd ed., 1891.

Bellasis, E. *Memorials of Mr. Serjeant Bellasis*, 1893.

Bellot, H. Hale. *University College, London, 1826–1926*, 1929.

Bennett, F. *The Story of W. J. E. Bennett*, 1909.

Bennett, J. *The History of Dissenters during the last thirty years, 1808–1838*, 1839.

Best, G. F. A. *Temporal Pillars*, Cambridge, 1963; *Shaftesbury*, 1964.

Birks, T. R. *Memoir of the Rev. E. Bickersteth*, 3rd ed., 2 vols., 1852.

Birrell, C. M. *Life of William Brock*, 1878.

Blachford, Lord, Letters of, ed. G. E. Marindin, 1896.

Blackwood, S. A. *Some records of the life of Stevenson Arthur Blackwood*, compiled by a friend, and ed. by his widow, 1896.

Blomfield, A. *A Memoir of C. J. Blomfield*, 2nd ed., 1864.

Bogan, B. *The Great Link: a history of St George's, Southwark, 1786–1958*, 2nd ed., 1958.

Boyce, E. J. *A Memorial of the Cambridge Camden Society*, 1888.

Brady, W. Maziere. *Annals of the Catholic Hierarchy in England and Scotland, 1585–1876*, 1883.

J. Bevan Braithwaite. A Friend of the Nineteenth Century, by his children, 1909.

Bricknell, W. S. *The judgment of the bishops upon Tractarian Theology,* Oxford, 1845.

Broderick, J. F. *The Holy See and the Irish Movement for the repeal of the Union with England, 1829–47* (Analecta Gregoriana, 55), Rome, 1951.

Brodrick, G. C., and Fremantle, W. H. *A Collection of the judgments of the judicial Committee of the privy council, in ecclesiastical cases, relating to doctrine and discipline,* 1865.

Brown, Abner William. *Recollections of the conversation parties of the Reverend Charles Simeon,* 1863.

Buchanan, Robert, *The Ten Years' Conflict,* 2 vols., Glasgow, 1849.

Bunsen, F. Baroness. *Memoir of Bunsen,* 2 vols., 1868.

Bunting, T. P. *The Life of Jabez Bunting,* 2 vols., 1859, 1887.

Burgess, H. J. *Enterprise in education: the story of the work of the established church in the education of the people prior to 1870,* 1958.

Burgon, J. *Lives of Twelve Good Men,* 2nd ed., 1891.

Butler, A. J. *Life and Letters of Dean Butler,* 1897.

Campbell, John, Lord. *Life of John, Lord Campbell,* ed. by his daughter, the Hon. Mrs. Hardcastle, 2 vols., 1881.

Carlile, J. C. *C. H. Spurgeon,* 1933.

Carlyle, Jane Baillie Welsh. *Letters and Memorials of Jane Welsh Carlyle,* ed. T. Carlyle and J. A. Froude, 3 vols., 1883; *New Letters and Memorials of Jane Welsh Carlyle,* 2 vols., 1903.

Carlyle, Thomas. *The Life of John Sterling,* 1851.

Carpenter, J. E. *James Martineau, Theologian and Teacher,* 1905.

Carpenter, L. R. *Memoirs of the life of the Reverend Lant Carpenter,* Bristol, 1842.

Carus, W. *Memoirs of the Life of Charles Simeon,* 3rd ed., 1848.

Cassan, S. H. *Lives of the Bishops of Bath and Wells,* 2 parts, 1829–30.

Chadwick, W. O. *The Founding of Cuddesdon,* Oxford, 1954; *From Bossuet to Newman; the idea of doctrinal development,* Cambridge, 1957; *Victorian Miniature,* 1960.

Chapman, R. *Father Faber,* 1961.

Chew, R. *James Everett,* 1875; *William Griffith: memorials and letters,* 1885.

Christensen, T. *Origin and history of Christian Socialism 1848–54,* Aarhus, 1962.

Church, R. W. *The Oxford Movement 1833–45,* 1891.

Churton, E. *Memoir of Joshua Watson,* 2nd ed., 1863.

Clough, A. H. *Correspondence,* ed. F. L. Mulhauser, 2 vols., Oxford, 1957.

Coleridge, E. H. *Life and Correspondence of John Duke, Lord Coleridge, Lord Chief Justice of England,* 2 vols., 1904.

Coleridge, J. T. *A Memoir of John Keble,* 3rd ed., 1870.

Coley, Samuel. *The Life of Thomas Collins,* 2nd ed., 1869.

Conklin, R. J. *Thomas Cooper, the Chartist, 1805–92,* Manila, 1935.

Connell, B. *Regina v. Palmerston,* 1962.

Copleston, W. J. *Memoir of Edward Copleston,* 1851.

Crouch, W. *Bryan King and the riots at St George's-in-the-East,* 1904.

Dale, A. W. W. *The Life of R. W. Dale,* 1898.

Dale, R. W. *Life of John Angell James,* new ed., 1862.

Dallas, G. M. *Letters from London, 1856–1860*, ed. by his daughter, 2 vols., 1870.

Darwin, F. *The Life and Letters of Charles Darwin*, including an autobiographical chapter, 3rd ed., 3 vols., 1887.

Davidson, R. T., and Benham, W. *Life of Archibald Campbell Tait, Archbishop of Canterbury*, 2 vols., 1891.

Davies, G. C. B. *Henry Phillpotts, Bishop of Exeter*, 1954.

Davison, John. *The Life of the Venerable William Clowes*, 1854.

Dendy Marshall, C. F. *A History of the Southern Railway*, 1936.

Denison, E. B. (Lord Grimthorpe). *Life of Lonsdale*, 1868.

Denison, G. A. *Notes of My Life*, 3rd ed., Oxford, 1879; *Fifty Years at East Brent. The Letters of G. A. Denison*, ed. L. E. Denison, 1902.

Dessain, C. S. (ed.). *The Letters and diaries of J. H. Newman*, ed. at the Birmingham Oratory (in progress), vol. xi– , 1961– .

Doncaster, P. *John Stephenson Rowntree; his life and work*, 1908.

Drummond, A. L. *Edward Irving and his Circle*, 1938.

Drummond, J., and Upton, C. B. *The Life and Letters of James Martineau*, 2 vols., 1902.

Dunn, W. H. *James Anthony Froude*, 2 vols., Oxford, 1961–3.

Ellenborough, Earl of. *A political diary 1828–1830*, ed. Lord Colchester, 2 vols., 1881.

Faber, F. W. *Notes on Doctrinal and Spiritual Subjects*, 2 vols., 1866.

Facts and figures about the Church of England, 1959.

Fairweather, E. R. (ed.). *The Oxford Movement*, New York, 1964.

Faulkner, H. U. *Chartism and the Churches: a study in democracy*, New York, 1916.

Ferrey, B. *Recollections of A. N. Welby Pugin, and his father, Augustus Pugin*, 1861.

Finlason, W. F. *Report of the trial and preliminary proceedings in the case of the Queen on the prosecution of G. Achilli versus Dr. Newman*, 1852.

Fitzmaurice, E. G. P., Baron. *The Life of Granville George Leveson Gower, Second Earl Granville*, 2 vols., 1905.

Fletcher, J. *Life of the Rev. Joseph Fletcher*, 1846.

Fox, Caroline. *Memories of old friends, Extracts of journals and letters 1835–71*, ed. H. N. Pym, 2nd ed., 2 vols., 1882.

Frampton, Mary. *Journal from 1779 to 1846*, ed. with notes by H. G. Mundy, 1885.

Fulford, R. T. B. *The Prince Consort*, 1949; (ed.) *Dearest Child; letters between Queen Victoria and the Princess Royal*, 1964. (See also Greville.)

Fullerton, W. Y. *C. H. Spurgeon*, 1920.

Gash, N. *Mr. Secretary Peel*, 1961; *Reaction and Reconstruction in English Politics 1832–1852*. Oxford 1965.

Gilbert, J. A. *The Change; or the passage from death into life: a memoir of Lieutenant-Colonel Holcombe*, new ed., Bath, 1853.

Gillispie, C. C. *Genesis and geology*, Cambridge, Mass., 1951.

Gladstone, W. E. *Gleanings of Past Years*, 7 vols., 1879.

Godwin, Thomas. *Autobiography and letters*, 1878.

Gordon, Mrs. E. O. *The Life and Correspondence of William Buckland*, 1894.

Goulburn, E. M. *John William Burgon*, 2 vols., 1892.

Gray, J. M. *A History of the Perse School, Cambridge*, Cambridge, 1921.

Gregory, B. *Side lights on the conflicts of Methodism during the second quarter of the nineteenth century*, 1898; *Autobiographical Recollections*, ed., with memorials of his later life, by his eldest son, J. R. Gregory, 1903.

Greville, C. C. F. *The Greville Memoirs*, ed. L. Strachey and R. Fulford, 8 vols., 1938.

Grey, 2nd Earl. *The Correspondence with King William IV, and with Sir H. Taylor*, ed. Henry, Earl Grey, 2 vols., 1867.

Gurney, J. J. *Memoirs of Joseph John Gurney; with selections from his journal and correspondence*, ed. J. B. Braithwaite, 2 vols., 2nd ed., Norwich, 1855.

Gwynn, D. R. *Lord Shrewsbury, Pugin and the Catholic Revival*, 1946.

Härdelin, A. *The Tractarian Understanding of the Eucharist*, Uppsala, 1965.

Halévy, E. *A History of the English People*, E.T., 2nd ed., 6 vols. in 7, 1949–52.

Hall, J. V. *Autobiography*, ed. N. Hall, 1865.

Hall, Newman. *An Autobiography*, 1898.

Halsbury, 1st Earl of. *The Laws of England*, 3rd ed., by Lord Simonds, 1952–1965.

Hammond, J. L. le B., and Hammond, B. *The Age of the Chartists, 1832–54: a study of discontent*, 1930.

Hampden, H. (ed.). *Some Memorials of Renn Dickson Hampden, Bishop of Hereford*, 1871.

Hardy, F. E. *The Life of Thomas Hardy*, 1962.

Hare, A. J. C. *The Story of My Life*, 6 vols., 1896.

Hare, J. C. (ed.). *Essays and tales of John Sterling, with a memoir of his life*, 2 vols., 1848.

Henriques, H. S. Q. *The Jews and the English Law*, 1908.

Hill, T. *Letters and memoir of the late Walter Augustus Shirley, D.D.*, 2nd ed., 1850.

Historical Companion to Hymns Ancient and Modern, ed. M. Frost, 1962.

Hodder, E. *The Life and Work of the Seventh Earl of Shaftesbury, KG*, 3 vols., 1886.

Howitt, Mary. *An Autobiography*, ed. Margaret Howitt, 2nd ed., 1891.

Huth, A. H. *The Life and Writings of Henry Thomas Buckle*, 2 vols., 1880.

Hyamson, A. M. *David Salomons*, 1939.

Isichei, E. *Victorian Quakers*, Oxford 1970.

Jackson, T. *The Life of Robert Newton*, 1855; *Recollections of my own life and times*, ed. B. Frankland, 1873.

Jay, William. *Autobiography with reminiscences of some distinguished contemporaries*, ed. G. Redford and J. Angell James, 2nd ed., 1855.

Jenkins, H. *The Life of George Borrow*, 1912.

Jones, H. Festing. *Samuel Butler. A memoir*, 2 vols., 1919.

Jones, R. M. *The later periods of Quakerism*, 2 vols., 1921.

Julian, J. *A dictionary of Hymnology*, rev. ed., 1907.

Kaye, John. *Works*, 8 vols., 1888.

Kendall, H. B. *The Origin and History of the Primitive Methodist Church*, 2 vols., 1906; *History of the Primitive Methodist Church*, rev. ed., 1919.

Kent, J. H. S. *Jabez Bunting, the last Wesleyan*, 1955.

Kingsley, Charles. *His letters and memories of his life*, ed. by his wife, 2 vols., 1877.

Kitchin, G. W. *E. H. Browne*, 1895.

Knight, W. *Memoir of Henry Venn*, new ed., 1882.

Lake, William. *Memorials of William Charles Lake, Dean of Durham*, ed. Katharine Lake, 1901.

Laver, J. *Victorian Vista*, 1954.

Le Marchant, D. *Memoir of John Charles, Viscount Althorp, 3rd Earl Spencer*, 1876.

Levi, Leone. *Digest of the Actings and Proceedings of the Synod of the Presbyterian Church of England, 1836–1876*, 1877.

Liddon, H. P. *Walter Kerr Hamilton, Bishop of Salisbury*, 3rd ed., 1890; *Life of E. B. Pusey*, ed., J. O. Johnston and R. F. Wilson, 4 vols., 3rd ed., 1893–5.

Linforth, L. *Route from Liverpool to Great Salt Lake City*, Liverpool, 1855.

Loane, M. L. *John Charles Ryle, 1816–1900*, 1953.

London Yearly Meeting during 250 years, 1919.

Longford, E. *Victoria R.I.*, 1964.

Lovett, W. *The Life and Struggles of William Lovett in his pursuit of bread, knowledge, and freedom*, 1876.

Lyell, Sir Charles. *Life, letters and journals*, ed. by his sister-in-law, 2 vols., 1881.

Lyttelton, Sarah, Lady. *Correspondence 1787–1870*, ed. H. Wyndham, 1912.

McCabe, J. *Life and Letters of G. T. Holyoake*, 2 vols., 1908.

McClatchey, D. *Oxfordshire Clergy, 1777–1869*, Oxford, 1960.

McCrie, T. *Memoirs of Sir Andrew Agnew of Lochnaw, Bart.*, 1850.

McDowell, R. B. *Public opinion and government policy in Ireland, 1801–46*, 1952.

Marsh, William. *The Life of the Reverend William Marsh, D.D.*, ed. by his daughter, 1868.

Martin, R. B. *Enter Rumour*, 1962.

Martin, T. *The Life of the Prince Consort*, 5 vols., 1875–1880.

Martineau, Harriet. *Autobiography*, with memorials by M. W. Chapman, 3rd ed., 3 vols., 1877.

Masterman, N. C. *John Malcolm Ludlow*, Cambridge, 1963.

Mathieson, W. L. *English Church Reform, 1815–1840*, 1923.

Matthews, W. R. *The Religious Philosophy of Dean Mansel*, 1956.

Matthews, W. R., and Atkins, W. M. (ed.). *A history of St Paul's Cathedral and the men associated with it*, 1957.

Maurice, F. *Life of Frederick Denison Maurice*, 2nd ed., 2 vols., 1884.

May, Erskine. *The Constitutional History of England since the accession of George III*, Ed. and continued to 1911 by F. Holland, 3 vols., 1912.

Merivale, Charles. *Autobiography and Letters of Dean Merivale*, ed. J. A. Merivale, 1st ed., Oxford, 1898.

Miall, Arthur. *Life of Edward Miall*, 1884.

Millhauser, M. *Just before Darwin*, Middleton, Connecticut, 1959.

Milman, Arthur. *Henry Hart Milman, Dean of St Paul's*, 1900.

Morley, J. *The Life of William Ewart Gladstone*, 2 vols., 1908.

Moule, H. C. G. *Charles Simeon*, 1892.

Mozley, J. B. *Letters of the Rev. J. B. Mozley, D.D.*, ed. by his sister, 1885.

Mozley, T. *Reminiscences; chiefly of Oriel College and the Oxford Movement*, 2nd ed., 2 vols., 1882.

Newman, J. H. *Lectures on the Prophetical Office of the Church, viewed relatively to Romanism and popular Protestantism*, 1837; *Apologia pro vita sua*, Everyman ed.,

1912; *Correspondence with John Keble and others 1839–45*, ed. at the Birmingham Oratory, 1917. (See also Dessain.)

Newsome, D. H. *Godliness and Good Learning; four Studies on a Victorian ideal*, 1961.

Ornsby, R. *Memoirs of J. R. Hope-Scott of Abbotsford*, 2 vols., 1884.

Pagani, G. B. *The Life of the Rev. Aloysius Gentili*, 1851.

Palmer, W. *A narrative of events connected with the publication of the Tracts for the Times*, Oxford, 1843; *A Treatise on the Church of Christ*, 2 vols., 1838.

Parker, C. S. (ed). *Sir Robert Peel, from his private papers*, 3 vols., 1891–9.

Patterson, A. T. *Radical Leicester: a history of Leicester, 1780–1850*, Leicester, 1954.

Payne, E. A. *The Baptist Union: a short history*, 1959.

Pease, Edward. *The Diaries of Edward Pease, the father of English Railways*, ed. Sir A. E. Pease, 1907.

Peel, A. *These Hundred Years: a history of the Congregational Union of England and Wales, 1831–1931*, 1931.

Perceval, A. P. *A Collection of papers connected with the theological movement of 1833*, 1842.

Petty, John. *The History of the Primitive Methodist Connexion*, new ed., 1864.

Philpot, J. H. *The Seceders, 1829–1869: the story of a spiritual awakening as told in the letters of J. C. Philpot and W. Tiptaft*, ed. J. H. Philpot, 2 vols., 1930.

Pollard, A., and Hennell, M. M. (eds.). *Charles Simeon, 1759–1836; essays written in commemoration of his bi-centenary*, 1959.

Proby, W. H. B. *Annals of the Low-Church Party in England, down to the death of Archbishop Tait*, 2 vols., 1888.

Purcell, E. S. *Life of Cardinal Manning*, 2nd ed., 2 vols., 1896; *Life and Letters of Ambrose Phillipps de Lisle*, ed. E. de Lisle, 2 vols., 1900.

Reynolds, M. *Martyr to Ritualism; Father Mackonochie of St Alban's, Holborn*, 1965.

Richard, H. *Memoirs of Joseph Sturge*, 1864.

Roth, C. *A History of the Jews in England*, 2nd ed., 1949.

Rowntree, J. S. *Quakerism, past and present, being an inquiry into the causes of its decline in Great Britain and Ireland*, 1859.

Rule, W. H. *Recollections of my life and work at home and abroad*, 1886.

Russell, Bertrand and Patricia (eds.). *The Amberley Papers: the letters and diaries of Lord and Lady Amberley*, 2 vols., 1937.

Sanders, L. C. (ed.). *Lord Melbourne's Papers*, 1889.

Scholefield, H. *Memoir of the late Rev. James Scholefield*, 1855.

Selborne, Lord. *Memorials*, 4 vols., 1896–8.

Seymour, R., and Mackarness, J. F. (eds.). *Eighteen Years of a Clerical Meeting*, 1862.

Shelford, L. E. (ed.). *A Memorial of the Reverend William Cadman*, 1899.

Skeats, H. S. *History of the free Churches of England:* with a continuation to 1891 by C. S. Miall, 1894.

Smith, F. *The Life and work of Sir James Kay-Shuttleworth*, 1923.

Smith, G. *History of Wesleyan Methodism*, 2nd ed., 3 vols., 1859–62; *The Reverend John Rattenbury*, 1880.

Smith, H. *The Protestant bishopric of Jerusalem; its origin and progress.* 1847.

Smith, Nowell Charles (ed.). *Letters of Sydney Smith*, 2 vols. Oxford, 1953.

Smith, Sydney. *Works*, new ed., 1850.

Speck, E. J. *Church Pastoral-Aid Society: Sketch of its Origin and Progress*, 1881.

Stanley, A. P. *The life and correspondence of Dr Arnold*, 1st ed., 2 vols., 1844; *Memoirs of Edward and Catherine Stanley*, 2nd ed., 1880; *Letters and Verses*, ed. R. E. Prothero, 1895.

Stephens, W. R. W. *Life and Letters of W. F. Hook*, 2 vols., 1878; *Memoir of Lord Hatherley*, 2 vols., 1883.

Stoughton, J. *Religion in England from 1800 to 1850*, 2 vols., 1884.

Sweet, J. B. *Memoir of Henry Hoare, with a narrative of church movements*, 1869.

Tait, A. J. *Charles Simeon and his Trust*, 1936.

Tennyson, Alfred, 1st Baron. *A memoir by his son*, 2 vols., 1897.

Thackeray, W. M. *Letters and private papers*, ed. G. N. Ray, 4 vols., 1945–6.

Thirlwall, C. *Letters, Literary and Theological*, ed. J. J. S. Perowne and L. Stokes, 1881.

Thirlwall, J. C. *Connop Thirlwall, historian and theologian*, 1936.

Thompson, Joseph. *Lancashire Independent College, 1843–1893*, Manchester, 1893.

Tibawi, A.-L. *British Interests in Palestine, 1800–1901*, Oxford, 1961.

Tollemache, E. D. *The Tollemaches of Helmingham and Ham*, Ipswich, 1949.

Torrens, W. T. M. *Memoirs of William, second Viscount Melbourne*, 2 vols., 1878.

Towle, E. A. *Mackonochie, A. H. A memoir*, ed. E. F. Russell, 1890; *John Mason Neale. A memoir*, 1906.

Travis Mills, J. *John Bright and the Quakers*, 2 vols., 1935.

Trench, M. *Charles Lowder*, 1881.

Trevelyan, G. M. *The Life of John Bright*, new ed., 1925.

Trevor, M. *Newman, the pillar of the cloud*, 1962; *Newman, light in winter*, 1962.

Trollope, F. E. *A Memoir of Frances Trollope*, 2 vols., 1895.

Tudur Jones, R. *Congregationalism in England 1662–1962*, 1962.

Twiss, H. *The public and private life of Lord Chancellor Eldon, with selections from his correspondence*, 3 vols., 1844.

Tylor, C. *Samuel Tuke; his life, work, and thoughts*, 1900.

Ullathorne, W. B. *History of the restoration of the Catholic Hierarchy in England*, 1871.

Underwood, A. C. *A history of the English Baptists*, 1947.

Vernon, A. *A Quaker business man: the life of Joseph Rowntree, 1836–1925*, 1958.

Victoria, Queen. *The letters of Queen Victoria*, ed. A. C. Benson, Viscount Esher, and G. E. Buckle, 9 vols., 1907–32. (See also Fulford, R.)

Wadham, Juliana. *The Case of Cornelia Connelly*, 1956.

Walpole, Spencer. *A History of England from the conclusion of the great war in 1815*, new and rev. ed., 6 vols., 1890; *The Life of Lord John Russell*, 2 vols., 1891.

Ward, Bernard. *The sequel to Catholic Emancipation*, 2 vols., 1915.

Ward, Wilfrid. *William George Ward and the Oxford Movement*, 2nd ed., 1890; *The Life and Times of Cardinal Wiseman*, 2 vols., 1897.

Webb, S. J., and Webb, B. *English local government*, 9 vols., 1906–29.

Webster, A. B. *Joshua Watson*, 1954.

Wellington, 1st Duke of. *Despatches, Correspondence and Memoranda of F.M. Arthur Duke of Wellington*, ed. by his son, 8 vols., 1867–80; *Wellington and his friends; letters of the 1st Duke of Wellington*, selected and ed. by the seventh Duke of Wellington, 1965.

Wells, J. *Wadham College*, 1898.

Westcott, A. *Life and Letters of Brooke Foss Westcott*, 2 vols., 1903.

Whately, E. J. *Life and Remains of Archbishop Whately*, 1st ed., 2 vols., 1866.

Wheaton, N. S. *A Journal of a residence in London . . . in the years 1823 and 1824*, Hartford, U. S., 1830.

White, B. D. *Liverpool 1835-1904*, 1951.

White, J. F. *The Cambridge Movement: the Ecclesiologists and the Gothic Revival*, Cambridge, 1962.

White, W. *Memoir of T. T. Lynch*, 1874.

Whiting, C. E. *The University of Durham, 1832-1932*, 1932.

Wilberforce, Samuel. *Essays contributed to the Quarterly Review*, 2 vols., 1874.

Williams, Isaac. *Autobiography*, ed. G. Prevost, 1892.

Williams, T. J. *Priscilla Lydia Sellon*, 2nd ed., 1965.

Williams, T. J., and Campbell, A. W. *The Park Village Sisterhood*, 1965.

Wilson, D. A. *Life of Thomas Carlyle*, 6 vols., 1923-34.

Wilson, W. *Memorials of R. S. Candlish*, Edinburgh, 1880.

Winstanley, D. A. *Early Victorian Cambridge*, Cambridge, 1940.

Wiseman, N. *Recollections of the last four popes, and of Rome in their times*, new rev. ed., 1859.

Workman, H. B., and others (eds.). *A new history of Methodism*, 2 vols., 1909.

Yonge, C. M. *Life of John Coleridge Patteson*, 2 vols., 1874.

INDEX

Aberdeen, Bishop of (William Skinner), 479

Aberdeen, 4th Earl of (1784–1860: foreign secretary, 1841–6, prime minister, 1852–5) and Jerusalem bishopric, 191; on Gladstone's book, 478; as prime minister, 318–24; use of crown patronage, 468, 474; and Convocation, 318–24; carries Oxford university act (1854), 480

Abergavenny, 248

Accession service, 491

Achilli, Giacinto, 306–8

Ackworth school, 430, 432

Acton, Cardinal, 278–80, 286

Addams, Dr., ecclesiastical lawyer, 245

Additional Curates Society, 449

Agnew, Sir Andrew, 456–7

Ainslie, Dr. Gilbert, Master of Pembroke, 93

Airy, Professor G. B., 92

Albert, Prince, later prince consort, and coronation oath, 16; marriage, 162; religion, 162–6; baptism of infant prince, 193; suspected of writing *Vestiges*, 565; influence on Russell, 235; preferment of Buckland, 564; of Prince Lee, 236; wants liberal divines, 530; and moderate divines, 471; and Hampden's nomination, 241, 243–4; supports Sumner for Canterbury, 247; and Great Exhibition, 461–2; and ecclesiastical titles bill, 304; against Convocation, 319–20; on Palmerston's nominations, 476; receives memorandum from Wellesley, 474; is sent *Book of Mormon*, 437; cf 259

Alcock, Dr., rector of Graigue, 49

Alexander, Mrs. C. F., 347

Alexander, M. S., Bishop in Jerusalem, 190–2

Alexander, W., Bishop of Derry, 53

Alford, Henry, 218

Allen, Hugh, 498–9

Allen, John, librarian of Holland House, 55, 95, 107

Allen, Archdeacon John, 542

Allen, Joseph (Bishop of Bristol, 1834–6;

of Ely, 1836–45), 37, 93, 112, 442

Allies, T. W., 171, 270, 289

Altar, 221, 518; use of word *altar*, 496

Althorp, Viscount (from 1834 Earl Spencer), 37, 56–57, 59, 99; and church rates, 87–89, 146

Alton Locke, 357, 363

Alton Towers, 273

Ampleforth, prior of, 167

Anderson, Rev. Mr., preacher of Lincoln's Inn, 348, 548

Andover, Primitive Methodists at, 391

Andrews, William Eusebius, Catholic journalist, 22

Anglicanism, early use of word, 171

Anglesey, Marquess of, 51

Anson, secretary to Prince Albert, 165

Apocalyptic ideas, 35–36, 437, 451

Apostolic succession, 71ff.

Archdale, George, Master of Emmanuel College, 93

Archdeacons, 137

Armstrong, B. J., of East Dereham, 303

Armstrong, John, Bishop of Grahamstown, 551

Armstrong, Mary, 393

Arnold, Matthew, 533

Arnold, Thomas (1795–1842; headmaster of Rugby, 1828–42; regius professor of history at Oxford, 1841–2) as headmaster, 10, 38; sermons, nobility of, 43; sermons attacked, 43, 113; sermons admired by Melbourne, 113, 160; read by Queen Victoria, 160; and Catholic emancipation, 10; *Principles of Church Reform*, 42–46, 70; pessimism, 47; and Birmingham refusal of church rate, 86; expects revolution, 100; on Whately's elevation, 53; fierce against evangelicals, 451; prefers R.C.s to Tractarians, 296; *Oxford Malignants*, 119, 121, 240; view of Froude's *Remains*, 176; Tractarian fear of Arnold, 78; Arnold controverted by Palmer, 70; and Sunday travelling, 458; does not wish Jews in Parliament, 484; invited to preach Stanley's consecration sermon,